June 1940, Great Britain and the First Attempt to Build a European Union

June 1940,
Great Britain
and the First Attempt
to Build a European
Union

By

Andrea Bosco

**Cambridge
Scholars**
Publishing

June 1940, Great Britain and the First Attempt to Build
a European Union

By Andrea Bosco

This book first published 2016

Cambridge Scholars Publishing

Lady Stephenson Library, Newcastle upon Tyne, NE6 2PA, UK

British Library Cataloguing in Publication Data
A catalogue record for this book is available from the British Library

ISBN (10): 1-4438-9475-3
ISBN (13): 978-1-4438-9475-3

CONTENTS

Introduction 1

Chapter I 15
The Birth of the Federal Union Movement

Chapter II... 61
Federal Union becomes a Popular Movement

Chapter III 104
Federal Union, the Foreign Office and the Development of Federalism
on the Continent

Chapter IV 135
Federalism and the Debate on War Aims

Chapter V 203
Chatham House and the Federalist Project

Chapter VI 260
Federal Union and the May Crisis

Chapter VII... 289
Jean Monnet, Churchill's Proposal and the Downfall of France

Conclusion.. 321

Bibliography 328

Index 385

INTRODUCTION

June 2016 could represent a turning point in British history. The decision to leave the European Union at the most critical period since its existence could bring unpredictable and far reaching consequences both for the United Kingdom and the Union itself. Outside the European Union, the United Kingdom might face a renewed challenge of disintegration—by losing Scotland and Northern Ireland—and a dramatic loss of financial, economic and political influence in international relations. The fundamental basis for the so-called 'special relationship' with the United States, lies in fact with the specific and key role which the United Kingdom has played, since 1973, within the European construction. The marginalization of the City of London from capital flows, a reduction of economic growth, and a general retreat from world influence could almost be inevitable.

Without Great Britain, the European Union might drift towards collapse, bringing to an end the European experiment, and opening the way to the restoration of European political division into conflicting groups of States, with the reconstruction of rival blocks. The choice is therefore, as it has always been, between reaching a union through the pooling of sovereignty, or through its exercise and projection in terms of traditional power politics.

The fundamental reason for the existence of the European Union has not been, in fact, the defence of a specific cultural, racial or religious identity, but the creation of a definite method of resolving conflicts among States by peaceful and constitutional means. The first Community institutions were actually not imagined and created 65 years ago simply to establish a free-trade area and promote economic development among its members. They were conceived as the first step in a political process which, through the pooling of certain vital governmental functions such as economy and currency, aimed to achieve a federation, not a league of nations, establishing economic stability as a fundamental condition for political stability.

June 1940 was a turning point in British history. On the afternoon of 16 June, a few hours before the French Government opted for the capitulation, Churchill made, on behalf of the British Government, an offer of "indissoluble union." "There would have been great difficulties to surmount," commented Sir John Colville, Private Secretary to Churchill, "but we had before us the bridge to a new world, the first elements of European or even World Federation."[1]

When a sceptical Churchill put forward to the British Cabinet the text of the declaration drafted by Jean Monnet, Sir Arthur Salter, and Robert Vansittart, he was surprised at the amount of support it received. Clement Attlee, Ernest Bevin, and Sir Archibald Sinclair had already declared themselves in support of the idea of a European federation based on the Anglo-French nucleus. The Cabinet adopted the document with some minor amendments, and de Gaulle, who saw it as a means of keeping France in the war, telephoned Reynaud with the proposal for an "indissoluble union" with "joint organs of defence, foreign, financial and economic policies," a common citizenship and a single War Cabinet. The proposal, however, never reached the table of the French Government. The spirit of capitulation, embodied in Weygand and Pétain prevailed, and France submitted herself to the German will, for the second time in seventy years.

After the Munich crisis, Great Britain had to face the danger of another European war, with the inevitable loss of the Empire, and it was at this point that the country first began to favour the application of the federalist principle to Anglo-French relations. In this conversion to federalism, a fundamental role was played by the Federal Union, the first federalist movement organised on a popular basis, and created in the autumn of 1938 by three young men: Charles Kimber, Derek Rawnsley, and Patrick Ransome.

The contribution of the Federal Union to the development of the federal idea in Great Britain and Europe was to express and organise the beginning of a new political militancy: the aim of the political struggle was no longer the conquest of national power, but the building of a supranational institution, a federation (not a league) of nations. With Federal Union, the European federation was no longer an abstract "idea of reason", but the first step of a historical process: the overcoming of the nation-State, the modern political formula which institutionalises the political division of mankind. Federal Union represented a paradigmatic experience since it embodied the incarnation of the idea of European unification into a movement, and as such it also signified its first and decisive step in the history of that process. To write the history of Federal Union means to analyse the formation of ideas and decisions which dominated the first months of the Second World War, bringing the

---

[1] John Colville, *The Fringes of Power* (London: Hodder and Stoughton, 1985), 74.

federalist project to enter the threshold of the Foreign Office and Downing Street.[2]

Such an epic episode of the Second World War has been almost completely forgotten in Great Britain today, in spite of the fact that it deeply marked the future process of European integration. Not only the two major pioneers and architects of the European Union—Jean Monnet and Altiero Spinelli—owed much to the Federal Union for their federalist 'conversion', but the British political tradition—of which federalism is a major product— also provided the theoretical basis for the European construction. It is not an exaggeration to argue that the European Union is very much the creation of the British political tradition, as opposed to the Continental one.[3]

During the interval between the Munich Pact and the downfall of France, a large and powerful literature was actually produced in the United Kingdom by a number of distinguished representatives of Liberal and Socialist thought, such as Lord Lothian, Lionel Curtis, William Beveridge, Lord Lugard, Lionel Robbins, Arnold Toynbee, Henry Wickham Steed, Ivor Jennings, Kenneth Wheare, William Curry, Norman Angell, Norman Bentwich, James Meade, J. B. Priestley, Alan L. Rowse, Henry Noel Brailsford, Barbara Wootton, G. D. H. Cole, Julian Huxley, Ronald Gordon Mackay, Konni Zilliacus, Margaret Storm Jameson, Cyril Joad, and Olaf Stapledon. This literature, which had both a direct and indirect

---

[2] On the role played by Federal Union in the history of the federal idea, see: Andrea Bosco ed., *The Federal Idea. The History of Federalism from the Enlightenment to 1945* (London: Lothian Foundation Press, 1991), 3-17; id., *The Federal Idea. The History of Federalism since 1945* (London: Lothian Foundation Press, 1991), 1-19; id., Introduction to *Towards the United States of Europe. Studies in the Making of the European Constitution*, ed. Patrick Ransome (London: Lothian Foundation Press, 1991), 1-46.

[3] For an analysis of the British federalist tradition, see: Michael Burgess, *The British Tradition of Federalism* (Leicester: Leicester University Press, 1995); John Kendle, *Federal Britain* (London: Routledge, 1997); id., *The Round Table Movement and Imperial Union* (Toronto: University of Toronto Press, 1975); Andrea Bosco, *Lord Lothian. Un pioniere del federalismo, 1882-1940* (Milan: Jaca, 1989); John Pinder and Richard Maine, *Federal Union. The Pioneers* (London: Macmillan, 1990); Deborah Lavin, *From Empire to International Commonwealth: A Biography of Lionel Curtis* (Oxford: Clarendon, 1995); Andrea Bosco, *Federal Union e l'unione franco-britannica. Il dibattito federalista nel Regno Unito dal Patto di Monaco al crollo della Francia, 1938-1940* (Bologna: Il Mulino, 2009); id., *From Empire to Atlantic Order. The Round Table Movement and the Unwinding of the British Empire, 1909-1919* (Cambridge: Cambridge Scholars Publishing, 2016).

influence on British political thinking at the time, has been almost completely forgotten in Britain today. However, it is held in high regard by Continental scholars, where it is referred to as the "Anglo-Saxon Federalist School," and thought of as the most illuminating contribution to the evolution of the federal idea towards a mature theoretical articulation, and its application to the unification of Continental Europe.[4]

Between the winter and spring of 1940, not only intellectuals, but also a number of prominent politicians—such as Chamberlain, Halifax, Churchill, Eden, Attlee, Bevin, Sinclair, and Amery—and members of the Anglican Church—such as the Archbishops of York and Durham—openly supported the federalist project. The major national daily and weekly newspapers—*The Times, Daily Telegraph, Manchester Guardian, News Chronicle, Daily Express, Daily Herald, Daily Worker, Observer,* and *Sunday Times*—gave wide coverage to a lively debate on federalism.

It was this debate on federalism in general, and on Anglo-French wartime collaboration in particular, that brought the British Government to consider the application of the federal principle in order to transform Anglo-French war co-operation into a permanent and stable political union. Jean Monnet—then Chairman of the Anglo-French Coordination Committee, a body based in London and created on the initiative of Monnet himself in order to give greater effect to the war effort—had been

---

[4] Lionel Robbins, *Economic Planning and International Order* (London: Macmillan, 1937); id., *The Economic Causes of War Conflicts* (London: Jonathan Cape, 1939); id., *The Economic Basis of Class Conflict and Other Essays of Political Economy* (London: Macmillan, 1939); id., *Economic Aspects of Federation* (London: Federal Union Publishing, 1941); Barbara Wootton, *Socialism and Federation* (London: Federal Union Publishing, 1940); William Beveridge, *Peace by Federation?* (London: Federal Union Publishing, 1940); Lionel Curtis, *Civitas Dei. The Commonwealth of God* (London: Macmillan, 1939); id., *The Way to Peace* (London: Oxford University Press, 1944); id., *World Revolution in the Cause of Peace* (Oxford: Basil Blackwell, 1947); William Curry, *The Case for Federal Union* (London: Penguin, 1940); Ivor Jennings, *A Federation for Western Europe* (Cambridge: Cambridge University Press, 1940); Ronald Gordon Mackay, *Federal Europe* (London: Michael Joseph, 1940); Kenneth Wheare, *What Federal Government Is* (London: Federal Union Publishing, 1941); id., *Federal Government* (London: Oxford University Press, 1946); Philip Kerr (Lord Lothian), *The Ending of Armageddon* (London: Federal Union Publishing, 1939); id., *The American Speeches of Lord Lothian* (London: Oxford University Press, 1941); id., *Pacifism is not Enough. Collected Lectures and Speeches of Lord Lothian (Philip Kerr),* eds. Andrea Bosco and John Pinder (London: Lothian Foundation Press, 1990); Mario Albertini, *Il federalismo. Antologia e definizione* (Bologna: Il Mulino, 1979), 157-66.

strongly influenced by that lively debate. Monnet recalled that in this respect he became persuaded of the need for a federation between the two countries by just reading *The Times*, and that he took the initiative to discuss it with Chamberlain before the German offensive in May.[5]

From March 1940 the Foreign Office had very seriously examined an "Act of Perpetual Association between the United Kingdom and France," drafted by Arnold Toynbee and Alfred Zimmern at Chatham House, and set up an *ad hoc* inter-ministerial Committee chaired by Maurice Hankey in order to translate it into a Constitution. The fact that the Foreign Office paid serious attention to a federal scheme in order to outline a new basis for Anglo-French relations was certainly for the strategic role played by Chatham House and, within the organisation by its main architect, Lionel Curtis. However, it would not have happened without the popular support for federalism which Federal Union had generated within British society at large. It was Federal Union actually which acted as a catalyst for ideas and behaviours which had already been relatively widespread within British society for some decades.

In order to understand the cultural climate in which Federal Union operated, it is necessary to trace a general outline of British federalism during the first decades of our century. The propulsive centre of British federalism in the years between the two world wars had definitely been the Round Table Movement, created in 1909 on the initiative of Milner's "Kindergarten"—and particularly by Curtis, Philip Kerr (later Lord Lothian), Robert Brand, John Dove, Waldorf Astor, Lionel Hichens, Dougal Malcolm, Peter Perry, Sir Edward Grigg, Leo Amery, Frederick Oliver, Alfred Zimmern, William Marris, Robert Cecil, and Geoffrey Dawson—in order to promote the institutional reform of the Empire on federal lines.[6]

---

[5] PJM, AME 8/3/1.

[6] For an analysis, see: Walter Nimocks, *Milner's Young Men: The Kindergarten in Edwardian Imperial Affairs* (London: Hodder & Stoughton, 1970); William Palmer, *The Selborne Memorandum* (London: Humphrey Milford, 1925); Kendle, *The Round Table Movement*; Andrea Bosco and Alex May eds., *The Round Table Movement, the Empire/Commonwealth and British Foreign Policy* (London: Lothian Foundation Press, 1997). On Milner, see: Edward Crankshaw, *The Forsaken Idea: A Study of Viscount Milner* (Westport, CT: Greenwood Press, 1974); John Marlowe, *Milner, Apostle of Empire* (London: Hamish Hamilton Press, 1976); Terence Henry O'Brien, *Milner: Viscount Milner of St. James's and Cape Town, 1854-1925* (London: Constable & Robinson, 1979); J. Lee Thompson, *A Wider Patriotism: Alfred Milner and the British Empire* (London: Pickering & Chatto Publishers, 2007).

After the Second Anglo-Boer War, the problem of Imperial defence merged with the wider problem of European and world peace because of the German threat. The burden of Imperial defence was carried by Great Britain alone, and decisions for the Dominions were taken by the British Government only, responsible to a national parliament and electorate. The defence of the Empire was necessary to prevent Germany's penetration into Western Africa and her subsequent elevation to the rank of a Great Power, with the inevitable consequence of the break-up of the nineteenth-century political system which had given Europe and the world an era of relative peace.

The movement's principal aim was to promote the creation of a central authority to conduct the foreign policy and defence of the Empire, in which the self-governing Dominions would play the role of equal partners. The Round Table advocated a division of governmental power between two organs, each responsible to the people for the exercise of power in its own sphere, and neither having power over or being accountable to the other. In defining the demarcation line between the powers to be exercised by the body representing peoples in their capacity of citizens of the Empire and those exercised by the body representing them in their national capacity, the Round Table proposed an Imperial Government for foreign policy and defence, responsible for an Imperial Parliament, directly elected by the peoples of Britain and her Dominions. Matters of national competence would be handled by the respective national parliaments. In the long run, the inevitable alternative to unity, which the movement considered a guarantee of world peace, was the disintegration of the Empire.

Although the Round Table maintained that, in theory, the solution to the problem of Imperial defence coincided with the application to the Empire of the great American political experience, they were aware that this would not be a solution in the short term. It was agreed, therefore, that a quarterly journal dealing with foreign and imperial affairs would be published to educate the peoples of the Empire on federalism. The first issue of the *Round Table*, under the editorship of Philip Kerr, was published in November 1910. In the period between the two world wars the journal became the major vehicle for the debate of the federal idea, and its application to the Empire, Ireland, India, and Europe.[7]

---

[7] For a survey of the editorial policy of the Round Table during the inter-war period, see "The Lionel Curtis-Philip Kerr (Lord Lothian) Correspondence 1909-1940," *Annals of the Lothian Foundation*, 1, (1991): 239-415. Henry Philip Kerr, became Lord Lothian in 1930, was born in London on 18 April 1882, and died in Washington on 11 December 1940. For a critical analysis, see: James R. M.

The Round Table could be considered—in spite of its well-defined and precise character—a continuation into the twentieth century of a nineteenth-century political tradition which found in the Imperial Federation League an organisational form. With the creation of the League in 1884—and the production, at the suggestion of Prime Minister Lord Salisbury, of a "Federal Plan" in 1892, aiming to secure by federation the permanent unity of the Empire—for almost a decade federalism gained increasing support among the British public at large. The formation of 31 branches throughout the country and in Canada, Australia, South Africa, and New Zealand—totalling over 2,000 members—fostered closer Imperial union, and associated the colonies with bearing the burden— financial and military—of Imperial defence, at a time of rising nationalism and power politics in Europe.[8]

However, following the rejection by Gladstone in April 1893 both of the League's "Federal Plan", and the request for an Imperial *ad hoc* Conference to discuss reforms of Imperial relations, the League collapsed in December 1893, failing to agree upon an alternative policy for the

---

Butler, *Lord Lothian (Philip Kerr) 1882-1940* (London: Macmillan, 1960); Bosco *Lord Lothian;* id., "Lord Lothian e la nascita di Federal Union (1939-40)," *Il Politico*, 48, 2, (1983); id., "La dottrina politica di Lord Lothian," *Annali della Fondazione Luigi Einaudi*, 18, (1985); id., "Lord Lothian e la grande illusione (1928-30)," *Critica Storica*, 21, 4, 1985); id., "L'eredità kantiana e Lord Lothian," in *Coscienza civile ed esperienza religiosa nell'Europa moderna*, ed. Romeo Crippa (Brescia: Morcelliana, 1983); Giulio Guderzo ed., *Lord Lothian. Una vita per la pace. Atti del Lothian Colloquium. Londra, 23 novembre 1982* (Florence: La Nuova Italia, 1985); John Turner, *Lloyd George Secretariat*, (Cambridge: Cambridge University Press, 1980); David Reynolds, *The Creation of the Anglo-American Alliance, 1937-41: A Study in Competitive Co-operation* (London: Europa Publishing, 1981); id., "Lord Lothian and Anglo-American Relations, 1939-40," *The American Philosophical Society*, 93, (1983); id., "Lothian, Roosevelt, Churchill and the Origins of Lend-Lease," in *The Larger Idea. Lord Lothian and the Problem of National Sovereignty*, ed. John Turner (London: The Historians' Press, 1988); John Pinder, "Prophet not without Honour: Lothian and the Federal Idea," in *The Larger Idea*, 137-50; Kenneth Ingham, "Philip Kerr and the Unification of South Africa", in *The Larger Idea*, 20-32; Gerard Douds, "Lothian and the Indian Federation", in *The Larger Idea*, 62-75; Rhodri Jeffreys-Jones, "Lord Lothian: Ambassador 'To a People'," in *The Larger Idea*, 77-91; Ira Straus, "Lothian and the Anglo-American Problematic," in *The Larger Idea*, 124-135.
[8] Michael Burgess, "'Forgotten Centenary': The Formation of the Imperial Federation in the UK," *The Round Table*, 289 (1984): 76-85; id., "Imperial Federation: Continuity and Change in British Imperial Ideas, 1869-1871," *The New Zealand Journal of History*, 17, 2, (1983).

1890s, and to find a compromise among the conflicting schools which coexisted within it. Since it was the expression of heterogeneous currents of opinion, united by the common interest to promote a radical solution of the Imperial and Irish questions, the League was not able to express a well-defined political culture, in spite of the publication, from January 1886, of the monthly *Imperial Federation*, and the creation in 1888, of the Imperial Institute.[9]

The ambiguity in which the federal idea was proposed, in the guise of simple devolution, was a consequence of the contradiction in terms of the concept of "imperial federation", where imperial was just the opposite of federation. The federal principle seemed more applicable to England, Ireland, Scotland and Wales rather than the Empire, since their existence as former distinct States—which had opted for the unitarian principle—allowed them to amend the form of union. Nationalist sentiment would have, however, welcomed the application of the federal principle, with the creation of independent legislatures and executives, as an intermediate stage towards full independence.

The Round Table took up the League's goals not only on the question of the "organic unity" of the Empire, but also for the Irish question, advocating a federation of the four 'spontaneous' nationalities of the British Isles—England, Scotland, Wales and Ireland—as the only solution to the question of the Irish claim for independence. This plan dated back to the first half of the nineteenth century and had returned to the political limelight with Gladstone in the last twenty years of the nineteenth century, as well as in 1904-05 when the Unionist Party considered granting administrative autonomy to Ireland, and finally at the Constitutional Conference in 1910, when Curtis thought that the federation of the British Isles should precede that of the Empire.[10]

As soon as the Round Table members realised, during the First World War, that the Dominions needed to go all the way through the full exercise of national sovereignty before being ready to federate, they turned to the United States, and envisaged a period of time during which through Anglo-American co-operation and alliance it would be possible to restore the necessary international economic and political stability to give time for federal ideas to take root. The economic and political co-operation between Great Britain and her thirteen rebellious former colonies was then

---

[9] Michael Burgess, "The Federal Plan of the Imperial Federation League 1892: Milestone or Tombstone," in *The Federal Idea*, 1, 139-53.

[10] Frederick Oliver, *Federalism and Home Rule* (London: John Murray, 1910); id., *The Alternatives to Civil War* (London: John Murray, 1913); id., *What Federalism Is not* (London: John Murray, 1914).

regarded by the Round Table as the only practical solution to the problem of world instability, inherent in the political division of the world into sovereign States.

The entrance of the United States to the forefront of world power politics had permanently changed the world's balance of power, which now required the United States' direct and perpetual association with the maintenance of the world's economic and political stability. The Round Table thus envisaged the re-establishment in the twentieth century, with American support, of the political and economic conditions of the nineteenth, during which, after Trafalgar, Great Britain gained an unchallenged world hegemony on a military basis (with the Royal Navy), in the economic and financial system (with the sterling gold standard, and the centrality of the City of London), and at the political level (with the joint action of the Foreign Office and intelligence). This supremacy, which is known as *Pax Britannica*, lasted almost a century, and gave the world the longest period of truce in world history after the fall of the Roman Empire, a period which saw—according to the Round Table—the most spectacular jump of Western civilization in all its forms, particularly in the field of scientific and technological discoveries, but also for ever-growing standards of the quality of life.

Aware of the fact that the United States lacked a foreign policy élite able to carry out new American global responsibilities, the Round Table created in Paris, in May 1919, in collaboration with members of the "Inquiry"—a group of young academics and business leaders led by Walter Lippmann, which gathered in the winter of 1917-18 in New York and in Paris during the Peace Conference to advise President Wilson on the post-war settlement—the nucleus of two organisations which had to play, from then on, a central role in the process of formation of British and American foreign policies: the Royal Institute of International Affairs in London (better known as Chatham House), and the Council on Foreign Relations in New York.

On the initiative of Curtis, the Round Table achieved "the strategic object" of strengthening Anglo-American relations—in spite of the fact that they were strained—"with a necessary tactical change," namely with the creation of an "institutionalised" and coordinated élite, responsible for the process of formation of foreign policy on both sides of the Atlantic. That tactical change was necessitated by the fact that from 1917 the Round Table had been in irreversible crisis, and the leading figures of the movement had been involved, over and after the war, in professions that did not allow them more active engagement in the movement.[11]

The major exponent of British federalism during the inter-war years was certainly Lothian, whose writings on the theme of war and peace are considered among the classics of federalist thought. Lothian's contribution, for which federalists today consider him a pioneer, was to apply the Hamiltonian lesson to the situation of interdependence of the industrial age. Lothian pointed out that pacifism and patriotism were necessary but not sufficient virtues to build peace. The nucleus of Lothian's political doctrine is expounded in *The Prevention of War*, a text of three lectures delivered in August 1922 at the Institute of Politics of Williamstown, Massachusetts, and in *Pacifism is not Enough*, the text of a lecture given at Lincoln's Inn, London, in May 1935.[12]

The contribution of Lionel Curtis—"the Prophet" as he was called by his Round Table friends—the other great exponent of British federalism, was mainly connected with the activities of the Round Table and Chatham House. Even though he was the most dynamic leader of the movement, his name remained until recently relatively obscure in British historiography. The fruits of his political doctrine are offered in *The Commonwealth of Nations* and *Civitas Dei*, a philosophical work on the origin, development and end of history, in which he gave an ethical and teleological interpretation of history, identifying in federalism the final stage of historical development.[13]

The third main representative of the British federalist school is Lionel Robbins, whose writings on the economic causes of war and the economic aspects of federation are ranked among the classics of federalist thought. Robbins's fundamental contribution was to show that the working of the industrial system of production required, at both national and international levels, the existence of a government that created and implemented the rules of the system as a whole. He pointed out that the limits of the market system, if left to themselves, were bound to generate conflicts between classes at the national level, and between nations at the international level. Robbins defined, with extreme clarity, the functions and powers of the federal government in the planning of the world economy. Of fundamental importance also is Robbins's criticism of the Marxist-Leninist theory of imperialism, pointing out that they are not the interests of imperialists as a

---

[11] Curtis to Lothian, 6 Dec. 1936, quoted in Andrea Bosco ed., *Two Musketeers for the Empire. The Lionel Curtis-Philip Kerr (Lord Lothian) Correspondence 1909-1940* (London: Lothian Foundation Press, 1997), 150-1.

[12] Lothian, *Pacifism is not Enough*.

[13] Curtis, *Civitas Dei*; id., *The Way to Peace*; id., *World Revolution*.

class, but the interests of social groups historically determined to produce the economic causes of war. Private ownership of the means of production does not lead, in itself, according to Robbins, to international wars.[14]

Along with these three major exponents, one should also remember other members of the Kindergarten, such as Geoffrey Dawson (Editor of *The Times*), Leo Amery (prominent Unionist leader), Waldorf Astor (Chairman of Chatham House and owner of *The Times* and *The Observer*), Alfred Zimmern, and Arnold Toynbee (Directors of Research at Chatham House), all of whom directly or indirectly contributed to the development of the federalist debate from Munich to the downfall of France. Special mention should also be made of intellectuals such as H. G. Wells, Bertrand Russell, Harold Laski, Max Waetcher, Salvador de Madariaga, and Norman Angell. Even without a political programme to offer, their indictment of national sovereignty obtained widespread support, particularly as events increasingly revealed the shortcomings of the League of Nations.[15]

In the panorama of British federalism, a special role was also played by the New Commonwealth Society. Founded in 1923 by Lord Davies, its aim was to create an international police force and court. Thanks to the

---

[14] Robbins, *Economic Planning*; id., *The Economic Causes*; id., *The Economic Basis of Class Conflict*; id., *Economic Aspects*.

[15] Harold Laski, *The Foundation of Sovereignty and Other Essays* (London: Allen & Unwin, 1922); id., *Studies in the Problem of Sovereignty* (New Heaven: Yale University Press, 1917); id., *Nationalism and the Future of Civilization* (London: Watts, 1932); id., *A Grammar of Politics* (London: Allen & Unwin, 1925); Herbert George Wells, *The Shape of Things to Come* (London: Hutchinson, 1933); Max Waechter, *How to Abolish War: The United States of Europe* (London: 1924); Bertrand Russell, *Freedom and Organisation, 1814-1914* (London: Allen & Unwin, 1934); Norman Angell, *The Great Illusion* (London: William Heinemann, 1909); Luigi Einaudi, *La guerra e l'unità europea* (Florence: Le Monnier, 1984); Giovanni Agnelli and Andrea Cabiati, *Federazione europea o Società delle Nazioni* (Turin: 1919); Maurice Renoult, *La Fédération et la paix* (Paris: 1930); Bertrand de Jouvenel, *Vers les Etats-Unis d'Europe* (Paris: 1930); Roger Manuel, *L'union européenne* (Paris: 1932); Herman Kranold, *Vereinigte Staten von Europa* (Munich: 1924); Edo Fimmen, *Labour's Alternative: The United States of Europe or Europe Limited* (London: 1924). For a discussion, see: Jean-Pierre Gouzy, *Les pionniers de l'Europe communautaire* (Lausanne: Centre de Recherches Européennes, 1968); Henri Brugmans, *L'idée Européenne 1918-1965* (Bruges: De Tempel, 1965); id., *La pensée politique du fédéralisme* (Leyden: A. W. Sijthoff, 1969); Bernard Voyenne, *Histoire de l'idée européenne* (Paris: Payot Saint-Amand, 1964); id., *Histoire de l'idée fédéraliste* (Nice: Presses d'Europe, 1981); Alexandre Marc, "Histoires des mouvements fédéralistes depuis la première guerre mondiale," in *Le Fédéralisme* (Nice: Presses d'Europe, 1964); Olivier Dard, *Bertrand de Jouvenel* (Paris: Librairie Académique Perrin, 2008).

funds given by Davies himself, the Society founded the New Commonwealth Institute, and also published a monthly journal, the *New Commonwealth Quarterly*. The Society gained the nominal support, among politicians, of Winston Churchill and Anthony Eden, and among intellectuals, of William Rappard, George Scelle, George Keeton and Salvador de Madariaga. However, it was only after the publication in January 1940 of *A Federated Europe* by Davies, that the Society was converted to federalism, advocating the transformation of the Anglo-French Alliance into a federation.[16]

Count Richard Coudenhove-Kalergi had significant influence on British federalism. In 1923 he had founded in Vienna the Pan-Europa movement, which advocated the political union of the Old Continent on a federal basis. It had the support of Edouard Herriot—who, in a speech to the French National Assembly on 29 June 1925, launched the idea of a European Union—Aristide Briand and Gustav Stresemann. Coudenhove-Kalergi revised his initial opposition to British participation in a European federation, following the entry of Nazi troops into Vienna, having acknowledged the progressive decline of France in Central Europe, and the strong involvement of Great Britain in Continental affairs. Even though he did not succeed in establishing good relations with Federal Union, Coudenhove-Kalergi's efforts were effective in forming a federalist transversal group in the House of Commons.[17]

British historiography has studied with special interest the state of Anglo-French relations during the so-called *drôle de guerre*, without however giving much attention to the lively debate on the war and peace aims which had developed during those months in Great Britain. In addition, little interest has been shown in the role played by Chatham House, either towards the Foreign Office in promoting Anglo-French Union, or in the formation of an *élite* opinion favourable to the federal idea as a whole. Moreover, until the publication of a volume which analyses the alternative fortune of British federalism since 1939, British historiography has also ignored the Federal Union Movement. On the contrary, much has been written on Churchill's proposal.[18]

---

[16] David Davies, *A Federated Europe* (London: Victor Gollancz, 1940).

[17] Richard Coudenhove-Kalergi, *Pan Europe* (New York: A. A. Knopf, 1926).

[18] Pinder and Maine, *Federal Union*; Michael Newman, "British Socialists and the Question of European Unity, 1939-45," *European Studies Review*, 10, (1980): 75-100; R. A. Wildford, "The Federal Union Campaign," *European Studies Review*, 10, (1980): 101-14; Andrea Bosco, "Lothian, Curtis, Kimber and the Federal Union Movement (1938-1940)", *The Journal of Contemporary History*, 23, (1988): 465-502; Andrea Bosco and Cornelia Navari eds., *Chatham House and*

This study principally examines the first eighteen months of Federal Union, during which the movement, from its modest beginnings, was able to raise itself in the attention of the general public, and the political class, as the heir of the League of Nations Union, the organisation which during the First World War shaped the idea of "collective security". Although the main object of this study is Federal Union—its birth and development, the activities of the branches, the internal debate and conflicts—it also deals with the federalist debate in the British and French press, and its impact on political and religious élites.

Special attention has been given to the role played by Lothian in London, helping the three young founders of Federal Union to shape the movement; and in Washington, as British Ambassador, promoting the entry of the United States into the conflict, on the basis of the federalist project. Special relevance has also been given to the tenacious work of Curtis in trying to link Federal Union with the Round Table, and in the attempt to transform Chatham House—through Richard Coudenhove-Kalergi, Arnold Toynbee and Alfred Zimmern—into a bridge-head to get the federalist ideas accepted within the Foreign Office and the government. Finally, the analysis of the Foreign Office papers outlines the process which brought about the formation of the Hankey Committee for a "perpetual" Anglo-French Union, and the final failure of the enterprise. The research was based on very rich and unpublished archival material, found mainly in London, but also in Oxford, Brighton, Edinburgh, Washington, Paris, and Geneva.

My debt of gratitude goes first to Professor Giulio Guderzo, founder of the "Pavia school", which studied the historical-social aspect of the federal idea—the bipolarity between the sense of belonging to a local and world community—and promoted the systematic investigation of the movements for European unification, placing at the centre of historiographic research the study of the subjective factor in the building of the European supranational institutions, thus reversing the dominant paradigm which, on the contrary, places on governments absolute primacy for the creation of the European Union.[19]

British Foreign Policy. The Royal Institute of International Affairs During the Inter-War Period 1919-1945 (London: Lothian Foundation Press, 1994).

[19] See the proceedings of a number of conferences on the theme: Sergio Pistone, *I movimenti per l'unità europea, 1945-1954* (Milan: Jaca Book, 1992); id., *I movimenti per l'unità europea, 1954-1969* (Pavia: Pime, 1996); Ariane Landuyt and Daniela Preda, *I movimenti per l'unità europea, 1970-1986* (Bologna: Il Mulino, 2000); Paolo Caraffini, *Costruire l'Europa dal basso. Il ruolo del*

Let me express profound gratitude to Luigi Vittorio Majocchi, for having introduced me to the thoughts of Mario Albertini, who laid the theoretical foundations for the socio-historical paradigm developed in this work.[20]

A particular mention should be made to the memory of John Pinder and the Hon. David Astor, whose teachings, encouragement and, last but not least, financial assistance, had been of vital importance in the establishment of the Lothian Foundation, and the development of historical research on the British federalist tradition. Particularly dear to me is also the memory of Sir Charles Kimber, the founder with two other young men in early 1939 of the Federal Union Movement, archetype of all subsequent federalist movements for European and Atlantic unification. Our long conversations, over the years, at his cottage on the bank of the Thames in Oxfordshire, offered me an invaluable opportunity to attain a more definite insight into Curtis's multiform, magnetic, and complex personality.

The research would not have been carried out without the generous patronage of the Accademia Nazionale dei Lincei, and the Consiglio Nazionale delle Ricerche, which have offered fellowships several times over. Among my friends in England, Scotland and the United States who have aided me in my research and allowed me to collect valuable accounts, I should like to thank especially: Max Guderzo, Lubor Jilek, Henry Usborne, Enrica Malcovati, Alex May, Gregory Jones, and Julian Bavetta.

Last but not least, this work is dedicated to the memory of my beloved grandmother, who always helped me to overcome the considerable difficulties along the way.

Ios, Cyclades, spring 2016.

Consiglio italiano del movimento europeo, 1948-1985 (Bologna: Il Mulino, 2005); Bosco, *Federal Union e l'unione franco-britannica.*
[20] Luigi Vittorio Majocchi, *La difficile costruzione dell'unità europea* (Milan: Jaca Book, 1996); Mario Albertini, *Tutti gli scritti*, 9 vols. (Bologna: Il Mulino, 2006-10).

CHAPTER I

THE BIRTH OF THE FEDERAL UNION MOVEMENT

I. *Lionel Curtis, Lord Lothian and "Union Now"*

Just when Hitler was about to realise, even for a short time, the economic and political union of the Old Continent, an American journalist, Clarence Streit—for nearly two decades correspondent in Geneva of the *New York Times*—decided to launch to the democracies a dramatic appeal: unite or perish. In the volume *Union Now*—privately printed by Streit himself in Geneva in 1937, and made known to the general public in March 1939, at the same time in New York and London—Streit outlined the features of a highly ambitious project, the federal union of the fifteen democracies then in existence: Great Britain, France, the United States, Ireland, Canada, Sweden, Norway, Denmark, Belgium, Holland, Finland, Switzerland, Australia, New Zealand and South Africa.[1]

---

[1] Clarence Streit, *Union Now. A Proposal for a Federal Union of the Democracies of the North Atlantic* (London: Jonathan Cape, 1939). Clarence Kirshmann Streit (1896-1986) was a reporter on the *New York Times* at the League of Nations, from 1929 to 1939. In 1949 he created the "Atlantic Union Committee", and in 1962 the "Association to Unite the Democracies". On Streit's contribution to the formation of Atlantic politics, see Tiziana Stella, "Euro-Atlantismo. L'eredità del federalismo americano nel secondo conflitto mondiale," in *Storie e percorsi del federalismo. L'eredità di Carlo Cattaneo*, eds. Daniela Preda and Cinzia Rognoni Vercelli (Bologna: Il Mulino, 2005), 1043-1090. More generally, on Streit see: Joseph Preston Baratta, "Clarence Streit e l'idea dell'unione delle democrazie," *Il Federalista*, 30, 2, (1988): 129-40; Tiziana Stella, *Federalismo e Atlantismo nella politica estera degli Stati Uniti*, PhD Diss., University of Pavia, 1998-99. For a background of the debate on Atlantic unification in the context of Streit's writings and action, see: Owen J. Roberts, *Background for Atlantic Union. A Study of International Federalism: Its Implications and Possibilities in Our Times* (Washington, DC: American Association of G.P.O., 1950); Joseph Schwartz, *Atlantic Federal Union* (Milwaukee: Marquette University Press, 1950); Estes Kefauver, *Atlantic Union: The Way to Peace* (Washington, DC: United States

The categorical imperative seemed to Streit to give life to democracy at the international level, overcoming therefore the contradictions which had reduced it to a pure simulacrum: first of all, national sovereignty. The goal that Nazism aimed to reach by war, democracy could have reached through an institutional revolution. The result would have been quite different: to an empire held together by German militarism, the democracies would have opposed a federation based on popular consent. Streit proposed for the fifteen democracies a common citizenship, defence, customs system, currency and postal organisation.

He observed that one could not find a more homogeneous group than these fifteen democracies. No two of them had been at war with each other for more than a century. Each bought most of its goods from and sold the majority of its products to the others; they owned almost half the countries of the world, and ruled all its oceans; they governed half the world's population and handled two-thirds of world trade.

Lionel Curtis had met Streit in early January at a Conference held at the Council on Foreign Relations in New York to present his volume *Civitas Dei*—published in Great Britain in June 1938, and re-released in the United States in October 1939—with a foreword by Lawrence Lowell—President of Harvard University—under the title *World Order.* In the debate which followed the Conference, Streit criticised Curtis for having supported the view that the advent of the federation was God's project, which would sooner or later be realised. If the federation had not been made within six months, Streit argued, Western civilization would have been destroyed. Curtis replied that it certainly could not be realised in such a short space of time, "everything" depending on "the movement of opinion in the United States." It would take, Curtis thought, "perhaps not years, but generations."[2]

Curtis then read the proofs of *Union Now* on his return trip to England, and he had been so impressed to think that Streit had triggered a movement of even greater importance for the world than that of the American founding fathers, and similar to that for the abolition of slavery. Streit had moved, according to Curtis, "the assault" to "an almost

---

Press, 1953); Barbara Ward, *Britain's Interest in Atlantic Union* (Washington, DC: Friends of Atlantic Union, 1954); Georg Schwarzenberger, *Atlantic Union: A Practical Utopia?* (Washington, DC: Federal Educational and Research Trust, 1957); Istvan Szent-Miklosy, *The Atlantic Union Movement, Its Significance in World Politics* (Southlake, TX: Fountainhead Press, 1965); Ellen Gould Harmon White, *Atlantic Union Gleaner Articles* (Payson, AZ: Leaves-of-Autumn Press, 1981).
[2] Curtis to Streit, 9 Feb. 1939, CP, 13/115-7.

universal obsession," namely the myth of unlimited national sovereignty. Governments, Curtis thought, would take the initiative to set some limits, indispensable to the maintenance of world order, only when that movement had succeeded to "disintegrate" that obsession in the minds of people. Like John Woolman, the initiator of the movement for the abolition of slavery, Streit had "lit a candle" which, by God's grace, would never be extinguished. The final victory might have taken decades, "perhaps a century," but it was one of those things which "had to happen." As soon as people realised that the nation-State was not the final stage on the road of political progress, and that it was not possible to create any stable social system on the basis of agreements between sovereign States, they would also understand that federation was the only alternative. Mankind "will achieve world government," Curtis concluded, but on the corpses of politicians, and professors of political science.[3]

Curtis guaranteed the appearance in *The Times* of February 24, of a press release by Reuter, which announced the publication of *Union Now* in New York, and its imminent release in London, stating that Streit's plan contemplated the creation of a common citizenship, defence, customs and financial system among those democracies—monarchies or republics— which were willing to join. He also took the initiative to send copies of

---

[3] *Ibidem;* Curtis to G.V. Ferguson, n.d., CP, 13/172-3; Curtis to Streit's wife, 25 Feb. 1939, CP, 13/228-9; Streit to Barrington-Ward, 23 Feb. 1939, CP, 13/240; Curtis to G. W. Howard, 1 Feb. 1939, CP, 14/2. Lionel Curtis (1872-1955) was a member of Milner's "Kindergarten" in South Africa, from 1904 to 1908, and in 1909 took part in the creation of the Round Table Movement, becoming its leader. In 1919 he was co-founder of the Royal Institute of International Affairs, and from 1921 he was a *fellow* of All Souls. On Curtis see: M. S. Donelly, "J. W. Dafoe and Lionel Curtis: Two Concepts of Commonwealth," *Political Studies*, 7, 2, (1960): 170-85; Deborah Lavin, "Lionel Curtis and Indian Dyarchy," in *The Federal Idea*, 1, 193-209; Andrea Bosco, "Lord Lothian, Lionel Curtis and the Making of the Indian Federation," *Annals of the Lothian Foundation*, 1, (1991): 123-55; Gerard Studdert-Kennedy, "Political Science and Political Theology: Lionel Curtis, Round Tablers and India," *Annals of the Lothian Foundation*, 4, (1994): 299-319; Deborah Lavin, *From Empire to*; Gerard Studdert-Kennedy, "Lionel Curtis: Federalism and India," *Journal of Imperial and Commonwealth History*, 24, 2, (1996): 200-7; id., "Curtis, Lionel George: Intense Beliefs of," in *The Round Table, the Empire/Commonwealth*, 251-65; David Meredith, "Lionel Curtis, the Round Table Movement and the Montagu-Chelmsford Reforms (1919)," in *The Round Table, the Empire/Commonwealth*, 381-405; Bosco, *Two Musketeers for*; Daniel Gorman, "Lionel Curtis, Imperial Citizenship, and Quest for Unity," *The Historian*, 68, (2005): 67-96. Of special interest is Curtis's portrait by Streit: Clarence Streit, "Lionel Curtis: The Federalist," *Freedom and Union*, 9, 4, (1949): 8-20.

Union Now—and the text of one of his lectures delivered in support of the
Streitian project at the Royal Institute of International Affairs, on February
21—to seventy-one leading figures of the international political and
cultural community, including the Lords Davies and Cecil, Sir Arthur
Salter, Harold Nicolson, Wickham Steed, Anthony Eden, Herbert
Morrison, Winston Churchill, the Counts Sforza and Titulescu, Henry
Rollin, Alexis Leger, Paul Van Zeeland, and Arthur Henderson.[4]

In the letter which accompanied Streit's volume Curtis returned to a
theme often expounded, observing that agreements between sovereign
States are founded "on sand," and the reign of law, if based on those
agreements, tended inevitably to create "conflicts of loyalty." The
interdependence of the industrial age produced the need, according to
Curtis, for the creation of a "world government," responsible not in front
of the States, but "of all citizens." Streit had elaborated a project which for
the first time in history immediately gained broad popular support, and the
study of details for its realization had become imperative. That had to be
the task of the four major institutions in the English-speaking world
dealing with international affairs: the Council on Foreign Relations in New

---

[4] Curtis to Streit, 25 Feb. 1939 CP, 13/275, 139; 13/154-5. David Davies, Baron
Davies of Llandinam (1880-1944) was a businessman, politician, and
philanthropist. Liberal MP for Montgomeryshire (1906-29), he became Baron in
1932, and played a prominent role within the League of Nations Union. Sir Arthur
James Salter, Baron Salter of Kidlington (1881-1975), was a member of the
Commission for the Reparations of the League of Nations (1922-30). From 1934 to
1944 he was Gladstone Professor of Political Theory and Institutions at Oxford
University, and, from 1937 to 1950 Independent MP for Oxford University. He
was then Conservative MP for Ormskirk, from 1951 to 1953, and became Baron in
1953. Sir Harold George Nicholson (1886-1968), diplomat, author and politician,
was an officer at the Foreign Office from 1909 to 1929. He was Labour MP for
Leicester West from 1935 to 1945. Wickham Henry Steed (1871-1956), journalist
at *The Times* since 1896, was foreign Editor, from 1914 to 1919, then Editor, from
1919 to 1922. He was Editor of the *Review of Reviews*, from 1923 to 1930, and
Professor of History of Central Europe at London King's College, from 1925 to
1938. Herbert Morrison (1888-1965), was among the founders of the Labour Party,
and became its President, from 1928 to 1929. He was Major of Hackney, from
1920 to 1921; a member of the London County Council, from 1922 to 1934;
Labour MP for South Hackney, from 1923 to 1945; Home Minister and Deputy
Prime Minister, from 1945 to 1951; Foreign Minister, from 1951 to 1955, and
Deputy General Secretary of the Labour Party, from 1951 to 1955. He was
elevated to the peerage in 1959. Arthur Henderson (1863-1935) was President of
the Labour Party, from 1908 to 1910, from 1914 to 1917, from 1931 to 1932. He
was Home Minister in 1924, Foreign Minister, from 1929 to 1931, and Chairman
of the International Conference for the Disarmament in 1932.

York, the World Peace Foundation of Boston, the Institute of Pacific Relations, and Chatham House, which was based in London, and had branches in all of the Commonwealth's capitals.[5]

Curtis also tried to align the League of Nations Union—which still had more than one hundred thousand members—in support of *Union Now*, even though Gilbert Murray—leader of the organisation—while recognising in national sovereignty the "fatal obstacle" to the achievement

---

[5] CP, 128/191-201. On Chatham House, the Council on Foreign Relations, the World Peace Foundation, and the Institute of Pacific Relations, see: Stephen King-Hall, *Chatham House: A Brief Account of the Origins, Purposes and Methods of the Royal Institute of International Affairs* (Oxford: Oxford University Press, 1937); Laurence H. Shoup, "Shaping the Postwar World: The Council on Foreign Relations and the United States War Aims During World War Two," *Insurgent Sociologist*, 5, 3, (1975): 9-21; Laurence H. Shoup and William Minter, *Imperial Brain Trust: The Council on Foreign Relations and United States Foreign Policy* (New York: Authors Choice Press, 1977); Elisabeth Jakab, "The Council on Foreign Relations," *Book Forum*, 4, 3, (1978): 418-31; John K. Fairbank, "William Holland and the IPR in Historical Perspective," *Pacific Affairs*, 52, 4, (1979): 587-90; Robert D. Schulzinger, *The Wise Men of Foreign Affairs* (New York: Columbia University Press, 1984); William L. Holland, "Source Materials on the Institute of Pacific Relations," *Pacific Affairs*, 58, 1, (1985): 91-7; Paul Hooper, "The Institute of Pacific Relations and the Origins of Asian and Pacific Studies," *Pacific Affairs*, 61, 1, (1988): 98-121; James Perloff, *The Shadows of Power: The Council on Foreign Relations and the American Decline* (Appleton, WI: Western Islands Publishers, 1988); Gerald Studdert-Kennedy, "Christianity, Statecraft and Chatham House: Lionel Curtis and Word Order," *Diplomacy and Statecraft*, 6, 2, (1995): 470-89; Inderjeet Parmar, "The Issue of State Power: The Council on Foreign Relations as a Case Study," *Journal of American Studies*, 29, 1, (1995): 73-98; Peter Grose, *Continuing the Inquiry: The Council on Foreign Relations from 1921 to 1996* (New York: Council on Foreign Relations Press, 1996); Hiroaki Shiozaki, *Seeking International Order: The Lineage of the RIIA, CFR, and the IPR and their Interconnections to the Two World Wars* (Fukuoka: 1998); Tomoko Akami, *Internationalizing the Pacific: The United States, Japan and the Institute of Pacific Relations in War and Peace, 1919-1945* (London: Routledge, 2001); Andrew Williams, "Before the Special Relationship: The Council on Foreign Relations, The Carnegie Foundation and the Rumour of an Anglo-American War," *Journal of Transatlantic Studies*, 1, 2, (2003): 233-51; Laurence H. Shoup and William Minter, *Imperial Brain Trust: The Council on Foreign Relations and United States Foreign Policy* (New York: Authors Choice Press, 2004); Inderjeet Parmar, "Anglo-American Elites in the Inter-war Years: Idealism and Power in the Intellectual Roots of Chatham House and the Council on Foreign Relations," *International Relations*, 16, (2002): 53-75; Christian Haase, "In Search of a European Settlement: Chatham House and British-German Relations, 1920-55," *European History Quarterly*, 37, 3, (2007): 371-97.

of a world order, and in the federation the only guarantee for peace, on 11 February 1939 claimed in *Time and Tide* that "all we want" was to re-read the Covenant, to understand it, to strengthen it a little, and "above all to keep it." According to Murray, member-States should be represented within the League by their governments, not by members elected in a supranational Parliament. Also, its decisions had to be taken with unanimity which, according to Murray, had "never paralysed" the actions of the League. Discouraged by this statement, which in fact did not take into account the evidence of twenty bitter years of experience of the League, Curtis asked Wickham Steed, Lord Webster, Arnold Toynbee, and Lord Lytton for their help to induce the leaders of the Union to take the side of Streit, and to invite the members of the organisation to read *Union Now*.[6]

Curtis also tried to propagate *Union Now* in South Africa, where he had influential friends, including Sir Abe Bailey, whose generous

---

[6] Murray a Curtis, 10 Feb. 1939, CP, 13/267; Curtis to Murray, not sent, 24 Feb. 1939; Curtis to Wickham Steed, 24 Feb. 1939, CP, 13/265-6; Curtis to Lytton, 1 March 1939, CP, 13/258. Arnold Joseph Toynbee (1889-1975), was an officer at the Foreign Office from 1915 to 1919; Professor of Greek at the University of London from 1919 to 1924; Director of studies at the Royal Institute of International Affairs, and Professor of International History at the University of London, from 1925 to 1955. Lord Victor Alexander George Robert Lytton (1876-1947) was Under-secretary of State for India from 1920 to 1922; Governor of Bengala, from 1922 to 1927; and Viceroy for India in 1925. Lord James Brabazon Forrester (1910-1960) was a businessman. On the League of Nations Union see: Robert Cecil, *A Great Experiment. An Autobiography by Viscount Cecil* (Oxford: Oxford University Press, 1941); id., *Letters from Sir Robert Cecil to Sir George Carew*, ed. John Maclean (Whitefish, MT: Kessinger Publishing, 2007); Henry R. Winkler, *The League of Nations Movement in Great Britain* (New Brunswich, NJ: Rutgers University Press, 1952); Donald S. Birn, *The League of Nations Union, 1918-1945* (Oxford: Oxford University Press, 1981). On the central role played by the League in British foreign policy, see: George W. Egerton, *Great Britain and the Creation of the League of Nations: Strategy, Policy and International Organisation, 1914-1919* (Chapel Hill, NC: University of North Carolina Press, 1978); id., "Collective Security as Political Myth: Liberal Internationalism and the League of Nations in Politics and History," *International History Review*, 5, (1983): 497-522. On American public opinion and the League, see: Michael J. Hogan, *Woodrow Wilson's Western Tour: Rhetoric, Public Opinion and the League of Nations* (Tamu, TX: Texas A&M University Press, 2006); Francis Anthony Boyle, *Foundations of World Order: The Legalist Approach to International Relations, 1898-1922* (Durham, NC: Duke University Press, 1999); Lloyd E. Ambrosius, *Wilsonianism: Woodrow Wilson and His Legacy in American Foreign Relations* (New York: Palgrave Macmillan, 2002).

patronage had played a decisive role in supporting the activities of the Milnerian Kindergarten, the Round Table, and Chatham House itself. On February 12, Curtis sadly remarked that Great Britain was spending ten per cent of her national wealth in the effort to save civilization, while the Germans were spending double the amount in order to destroy it. And he concluded that the only way he could see to prevent that rapid lean towards chaos, was the one illustrated in Streit's book.[7]

Writing to his friend Alexander McLeod, Editor of the *Rand Daily Mail* of Johannesburg, Curtis urged him to review *Union Now*, being "absolutely sure" that Streit's idea would "sooner or later" be realised "in one form or another." The question of time would depend on the speed with which ordinary people, like the ones who read the *Rand Daily Mail*, would be induced to understand that it was not "simply an academic proposal," but a project which "can and must be achieved."[8]

Curtis managed to secure review articles of *Union Now* for *The Times*, *The Observer*, *The Times Literary Supplement*, *Reynold's Weekly*, and *The Express and Star*.[9]

Curtis also tried to convince the Primate of St. Paul's Cathedral, Walter Matthews, to read *Union Now*, where he would find the theoretical and factual reasons for the failure of the League of Nations, to which the Anglican Church had hitherto granted an unconditional trust. Streit was according to Curtis one of those rare men who could read facts, and during his stay in Geneva had understood that the League was unable to guarantee peace, "but only to jeopardise it." Had the churches, Curtis wondered, had the courage to say that they too had read the experience of the last two decades, and come to see the need for "a world authority responsible in front of men and not the sovereign States?" Streit's volume, he concluded, was already gaining support within the Anglican Church.

It was wrong, according to Curtis, to argue about the immediate applications of Streit's plan. It rather appeared necessary to wonder whether or not they were based on sound reasoning and "on truth" and, if so, to act in order to make them less remote. If the "transition from national sovereignty to the international one" was a process in theory that was irrefutable, but appeared in practice and was immediately unachievable, because people were unreasonable, then the Christian faith in reason was "a mere illusion," and a world based on force "was the only reality." The fact that the federation was not immediately achievable was not essential, according to Curtis. "Our Lord," Curtis observed, did not ask

---

[7] Curtis to Bailey, 12 Feb. 1939, CP, 13/150-1.
[8] Curtis to McLeod, CP, 13/64-5.
[9] Curtis to W. R. Howard, 9 March 1939, CP, 13/57-8.

that the Kingdom was realised before he was put on the cross. The task of each man of good will was to gain proselytism, and in so doing to shorten the "painful road that humanity has to travel before reaching the day of his resurrection."[10]

Young people who more than adults seemed ready to recognise the truth, were organising themselves in a movement, and multiplying their followers until they were numerous enough "to attract the attention of political leaders." The church, Curtis was wondering, would it just watch? The Sermon on the Mount had to be "translated into political terms," and as long as mankind was divided into national sovereignties, although democratic, that translation could not be complete. The only possible way to maintain and extend freedom, with all its spiritual implications, was to realise a transition from the national to the supranational level. It was not enough that religious authorities exhorted people to pray to God to avert war, since God had given man "the power to abolish war." The "special mission" of Christianity was to overcome the cult of nationalism, and participate in the creation of those political institutions that would realise peace on earth.[11]

On his return to London from the United States in late February 1939, he did not fail to send the draft of *Union Now* to his friend Lothian, who had been particularly impressed by the clarity of the Streitian project. Lothian then engaged himself in a campaign to support Streit's book, using it as a lever to favour the birth of a federalist movement in Great Britain. In a letter of 28 February 1939 to Jonathan Cape, he observed that "the importance" of *Union Now* was that it

> penetrated through the jungle of political confusion and economic compromise which have befogged the world since 1920 to the only principle which can solve the problem of war and prosperity in the modern world. Only when the democracies grasp the profound nature of that principle and begin to give effect to it will they resume their leadership of mankind.[12]

Lothian regarded Streit's book as standing "in the direct succession from Washington and the Fathers of the American Constitution, the writers of *The Federalist* and Abraham Lincoln." On 6 March, Lothian

---

[10] CP, 16/39-42, 49-54.

[11] *Ibidem.* See also a letter by Curtis to the Archbishop of Canterbury, 8 June 1939, CP, 17/36-43. Walter Robert Matthews (1881-1973), theologian, was Professor of Philosophy of Religions at London King's College from 1918 to 1932, Primate of Exeter from 1932 to 1934, and of St. Paul from 1934 to 1967.

[12] LP, 369/42.

wrote to Frank Aydelotte—President of the Swartmore College in Pennsylvania, and in charge of the Rhodes Trust in the United States—advocating the creation of an organisation in the United States:

> I have no doubt that *Union Now* will have an immense press welcome, but unless my judgement of American public opinion is wrong, within a week or two it will be pushed out of people's minds by some new sensations unless there is a pretty solid piece of organisation possessed of some funds to keep the idea in front of the public mind and to build up support for it. I hope you will see your way to taking an active hand in the game.[13]

Writing to Henry Hodson, young Editor of the *Round Table,* who sent Lothian a draft review article of the book for publication in the journal, Lothian made it clear that the "essence" of Streit's volume was not the draft Constitution "but the argument that the democracies have no choice between war, possible defeat and the loss of liberty and union." Streit told Lothian

> that he put in the draft scheme simply because so many people had told him that it was impossible to formulate a scheme so he had produced the best he could as something to be shot at....I have never thought that Federal Union of Nations would take the same form as the American constitution. Nationality is too vigorous and valuable a plant to allow itself to be treated like statehood in the USA or Australia or a province in Canada. What matters is making it clear that co-operation between sovereign nations cannot be made to work and that they must find some system for organic union which will pool the sovereignty of all their people for certain purposes without losing the national individuality of the parts. Your article in its present form will strike the reader as being a theoretical approval and then a blasting criticism of Streit's plan, as if that plan was really the essence of this proposal.[14]

---

[13] LP, 369/42.

[14] LP, 386. On the Round Table, see: Dewitt Clinton Ellinwood, "The Round Table Movement in India," *Journal of Commonwealth Political Studies,* 9, 1, (1971): 183-209; Leonie Foster, *The Men and Motives of the Australian Round Table* (Melbourne: Melbourne University Press, 1986); Bosco and May, *The Round Table*; Henry Hodson, "The Round Table: Until the Early 1930s," *The Round Table,* 352, (1999): 677-94. For an analysis of the Imperial ideology supported by the Round Table, see: Andrew Thompson, *Imperial Britain: The Politics, Economics, and Ideology of Empire, 1880-1932* (Harlow: Longman, 2000); John Wolffe, *God and Greater Britain: Religion and National Life in Britan and Ireland 1843-1945* (Harlow: Longman, 2007): 215-25; Daniel Gorman, *Imperial*

Lothian sent copies of *Union Now* to influential friends, in order to test the ground for the creation of a popular movement in support of Streit's ideas in Great Britain and the United States. At the end of February the Round Table discussed at Blickling Hall—Lothian's county house—ways of implementing Streit's project.

In support of Streit's project, Lothian intervened publicly with three editorials in *The Observer* in early March, just when the first reports about the German violation of the Treaty of Munich were dispatched to the Foreign Office from the British Ambassador to Berlin. Taking up a central theme of his political thought, Lothian proposed the creation of an Atlantic bloc of the democracies for the control of naval power which, in his opinion, was the only effective instrument of international policing able to deter dictators from resorting to further acts of strength. Democracies should have come together, in international relations, to play the stabilising role that British sea power had performed by itself in the course of the nineteenth century after Trafalgar. This alliance, dictated by the emergency, could open the way for negotiations, contributing to the reduction in trade barriers, the main cause of unemployment, and restoring trust in democratic institutions, so gravely threatened by the apparent success of the totalitarian regimes. The North Atlantic would have then become the centre of gravity of Western civilization, and the federal system would offer the democracies the legal instrument for transforming a temporary and precarious alliance into a permanent and organic union. *The New York Times* of March 6 recorded this pronouncement by Lothian—whose nomination as Ambassador in Washington was not yet official—presenting him as the most active and prominent British politician in the campaign for closer Anglo-American cooperation.[15]

Citizenship: Empire and the Question of Belonging (Manchester: Manchester University Press, 2007).

[15] On Lothian's political doctrine, see: Bosco, *Lord Lothian*, 267-287; id., "Lord Lothian's Political Doctrine," *Annals of the Lothian Foundation*, 4, (1994): 321-42. On isolationist and internationalist currents within American public opinion, see: Walter Johnson, *The Battle Against Isolation. FDR and the Era of the New Deal* (Cambridge, MA: Da Capo, 1973); Ronald E. Powaski, *Towards an Entangling Alliance: American Isolationism, Internationalism, and Europe, 1901-1950* (Westport, CT: Greenwood Press, 1991); Thomas J. Knock, *To End All Wars: Woodrow Wilson and the Quest for a New World Order* (Princeton, NJ: Princeton University Press, 1995); Daniela Rossini, *From Theodore Roosevelt to FDR: Internationalism and Isolationism in American Foreign Policy* (Keele: Keele University Press, 1995); Robert David Johnson, *The Peace Progressives and American Foreign Relations* (Boston, MA: Harvard University Press, 1995); Walter Isaacson and Evan Thomas, *The Wise Men: Six Friends and the World*

During a dinner in May at the Overseas League in London, Lothian acted in concert with Curtis to present *Union Now* to a very qualified audience. Introducing the discussion, Lothian presented another of his themes, arguing that the problem of international anarchy would be resolved by events, not by propaganda. History had shown a slow and linear process from the birth of the State at the city level to the creation of large sub-continental federations. Mankind had always solved the problems which had arisen from time to time. It was therefore necessary to discover on the one hand a political mechanism able to consent to the worldwide extension of the principle of the State, and on the other hand, to develop a "prevailing feeling of unity" which would favour the process of sovranational unification. The growth of world patriotism should not have destroyed the national one, while the events were forcing nations to march in a direction which a short time before would have seemed impractical or undesirable. Lothian thought that the world was being forced in the direction of a federal union more rapidly than people thought both by the impending tragedy, and wisdom.[16]

Wickham Steed, former Editor of *The Times*, and then Professor at London King's College, intervened in the debate claiming that democracies were confronted with no less urgent problems than those faced by the thirteen North American States in 1787. They controlled sixty per cent of the world's resources, and their political union, not just a military and economic alliance, would have constituted an "effective deterrent" against dictators.

Less absolute were the speeches by other personalities. Sir Arthur Salter, while identifying in international anarchy the main cause of war, and in the federal principle the only way out, believed that the immediate creation of the federation would be impracticable, and that the enemy to beat was primarily the cult of "unlimited sovereignty." Frank Pakenham, Oxonian Professor, declared himself against the Streitian project, since it implied the domination of the world by the English-speaking peoples suggesting, conversely, a customs union among the democracies.

They Made (New York: Simon & Schuster, 1997); Lise Namikas, "The Committee to Defend America and the Debate between Internationalists and Interventionists, 1939-1941," *The Historian*, 61, 4, (1999): 843-63; Steven Casey, *Cautious Crusade: Franklin D. Roosevelt, American Public Opinion, and the War against Nazi Germany* (New York: Oxford University Press, 2001).
[16] CP, 17/178-86. For an analysis of Lothian's views, see: Prishilla Roberts, "Lord Lothian and the Atlantic World," *The Historian*, 67, (2004): 97-127; David P. Billington, *Lothian: Philip Kerr and the Quest for World Order* (Westport, CT: Praeger, 2006).

Frank Darvall, Director of the English-Speaking Union, considered the
Streitian project unrealistic, since it had proven impractical even among
the member-States of the Commonwealth, which had in common not just
language and culture, but also material interests. Its realisation seemed
very unlikely between States which had little more in common than just
democratic ideology. Moreover, Britain and the United States were world
powers, and could not merge without losing their national identities, and
their roles in the world. The creation of a European federation based on the
convergence of common interests by States of different ideologies and
institutions seemed more realistic. R. B. Gillet, Mayor of Oxford, while
siding in favour of the federal principle, believed that it was necessary to
start with the creation of a customs and monetary union.

The philosopher Cyril Joad pointed out that the realisation of Streit's
project entailed human beings having an enormous capacity to control
their own destinies, while experience showed how men had often been
overwhelmed by events. It was therefore necessary to "take history by the
throat," and deliberately alter its course. The creation of a political
mechanism was not enough, and Lothian was right when he said that it
was necessary to create "the spirit which rouses the mechanism," namely
world patriotism.

W. Horsfall Carter, Editor of *Fortnightly Review*, observed that there
was no point continuing to accuse Hitler and Mussolini of undermining the
international order, because the responsibility for the anarchy which the
world was experiencing fell on democracies, since they failed to transform
the League of Nations as the appropriate instrument to establish a
European union. The plan for European unification by the French Foreign
Minister Aristide Briand was a great lost occasion as Great Britain had
dashed it for the sake of national sovereignty. In the early 1930s, Great
Britain had not the slightest intention of "speaking European". At that
moment the British people were forced to speak European, offering
guarantees to Poland, Greece and so on. The creation of a supreme
European federal authority for certain limited functions had become
imperative.[17]

---

[17] CSP, Federal Union Inc., Lionel Curtis 1938-1942. On the Foreign Office's
responsibilities about the failure of the Briand Plan, see Andrea Bosco, "The
British Foreign Office and the Briand Plan," in *Le Plan Briand d'Union fédérale
européenne,* eds. Antoine Fleury and Lubor Jilek (Geneve: Peter Lang, 1997): 347-
58. Cyril Edwin Mitchison Joad (1891-1953) was Director of the Department of
Philosophy at Birkbeck College, London (1930-41), collaborator of the BBC, and
author.

Particularly significant was the intervention by John Strachey, well known writer and founder of the Left Book Club, who later contributed to the debate on the meaning of the federalist project, with the volume *Federalism or Socialism?* While acknowledging the validity of Lothian's thesis that the only possible cure for international anarchy required the merging of national sovereignty, Strachey declared that the fundamental cause of that anarchy lay in the capitalist mode of production, and in the social system that it entailed. The abolition of capitalism had therefore to precede the creation of the federation, since the material causes of social and international conflicts had to be eradicated first. Great Britain had very specific historical responsibilities for obstructing the process of world and European organic unification. If Streit's book was collecting such an immediate and enormous success, it was because the British people, much more than the Americans, felt themselves in danger, and therefore they seemed willing to do anything, after having produced the disunion the world, to save their Empire.[18]

These brief accounts of the debate that the publication of Streit's volume raised among some leading figures of British politics and culture give us the measure of the kind of support which Streit was gaining in those crucial months. The British people began to understand the full intrinsic value of the federalist alternative, albeit in general terms, and that was the starting point of a conversion that, in the space of fifteen months, would entangle the great majority of the vital forces of the country. It is true that this large portion of British public opinion was persuaded to adopt a federal policy only because they felt threatened by the impending outbreak of a new war, but it is also true that without that project the British people would have slipped into war without a specific plan for post-war order, and therefore without positive motivation for facing that desperate struggle.

Federalism was certainly not everybody's ideal horizon, but it offered to most open minds a coherent interpretation of the root causes of international anarchy and war, by advancing, in principle, a permanent remedy. It was this need for radicalism to attract the attention of many young people, who were psychologically preparing themselves for a moral rearmament unprecedented in the history of the country. Streit's book acted therefore as a catalyst for a current of opinion that had repeatedly

---

[18] CP, 17/178-86. John Strachey (1901-63), Labour MP for Aston from 1929 to 1931, and for Dundee from 1945 to 1963, Minister for War from 1950 to 1951, and author of a number of publications on European social and political questions.

appeared and disappeared in British cultural and political history. It opened a new horizon for political action.[19]

A letter by Streit to Lothian of May 1939 gives us a clear idea of the political significance that his action was meanwhile having in the United States, in juxtaposition with a still prevalent pacifist and isolationist movement:

> The Union will come about with miraculous speed when it does come...My reasoned belief is that we shall none of us be able to stay out of war for two years more unless we make this Union, and that if war does come without it, the USA will not enter it except on the Union basis. As I said in my talks, if we do let the war come on we shall be faced by the same problem: how we organise our relations with the democracies and what shall we fight or organise for? For our own Union system? or the Old World system of leagues and alliances?...This issue rouses the deepest feeling in the American people, it is no ephemeral matter as is so often the case with you, and those who are not already astonished at the way this idea has spread and roused enthusiasm in this country will be before six months are gone...The union has been rolling on for the past few months as a snowball—and you know what that means for the coming weeks and months. Believe me, to work for a Union within five years is no longer a dream, and to think it may come in the next two years is no longer a forlorn hope...Even if we didn't have Hitler to help us, once we get a good many leaders shaken from their natural first assumption that of course this can't be done now and afraid to express belief in its remoteness, for fear of being ridiculous through all future ages, why, the battle is half won.[20]

---

[19] On the immense historiographic debate on the origins of the Second World War, see: Peter M. H. Bell, *The Origins of the Second World War in Europe* (Harlow: Longman, 1986); R. Rosencrance and Zara Steiner, "British Grand Strategy and the Origins of World War II," in *The Domestic Bases of Grand Strategy*, eds. R. Rosencrance and A. A. Stein (Ithaca, NY: Cornell University Press, 1993); Justus D. Doenecke, "U.S. Historiography and the European War, 1939-1941," *Diplomatic History*, 19, (1995); Andrew J. Crozier, *The Causes of the Second World War* (Oxford: Blackwell, 1997); Richard J. Overy, *The Origins of the Second World War* (Harlow: Longman, 1998); Gordon Martel, *The Origins of the Second World War Reconsidered: A. J. P. Taylor and the Historians* (London: Routledge, 1999); Robert Boyce, *The Origins of World War Two: The Debate Continues* (New York: Palgrave Macmillan, 2003); David Reynolds, "The Origins of the Two 'World Wars': Historical Discourse and International Politics," *Journal of Contemporary History*, 38, 1, (2003): 29-44.

[20] LP, 386. On American peace movement in the inter-war period, see: Charles DeBenedetti, *Origins of the Modern American Peace Movement, 1915-1929* (New York: Kto Press, 1978); Patricia F. McNeal, *The American Catholic Peace*

The battle for federation of the democracies was still far from being "half won," since the initial enthusiasm with which Streit had been greeted by a section of the American public, was soon to come up against the reality of the situation: that new ideas are not accepted if they do not fit into a practical political pattern. The federalist revolution, born in North America a century and a half earlier, was to find its real *raison d'être* in Europe, the historic seat of the first affirmation and diffusion of the national principle. By exporting the principle of the nation-State worldwide, Europe had also spread what Lothian had to define in 1938 as the "demonic influence of national sovereignty."[21]

World federation, or as Streit believed, a federation of fifteen existing democracies had to begin in Europe: the United States could only give support from outside. The division of Europe into two armed camps, the first led by Nazi Germany, and the second by a declining Imperial Power,

---

Movement, 1928-1972 (Boston, MA: Ayer Publications, 1980); George Peter Marabell, *Frederick Libby and the American Peace Movement, 1921-1941* (New York: Arno Press, 1982); Charles F. Howlett, *The American Peace Movement: History and Historiography* (Washington, DC: American Historical Association, 1985); Twayne Chatfield, *The American Peace Movement: Ideals and Activism* (Boston, MA: Twayne Publications, 1992); Harriet Hyman Alonso, *Peace as a Women's Issue: A History of the U.S. Movement for World Peace and Women's Rights* (Syracuse: Syracuse University Press, 1993); Anne Klejment and Nancy L. Roberts, *American Catholic Pacifism: The Influence of Dorothy Day and the Catholic Worker Movement* (Westport, CT: Praeger, 1996); Ted Gottfried, *The Fight for Peace: A History of Anti-War Movements in America* (New York: 21st Century, 2004); Charles F. Howlett, *History of the American Peace Movement 1890-2000: The Emergence of a New Scholarly Discipline* (Lewiston: Edwin Mellen Press, 2005); Marian Mollin, *Radical Pacifism in Modern America: Egalitarianism and Protest* (Philadelphia, PA: University of Pensylvania Press, 2006); Julius Moritzen, *The Peace Movement of America* (Whitefish, MT: Kessinger Publishing, 2007).

[21] Philip Kerr, "The Demonic Influence of National Sovereignty," in *The Universal Church and the World of Nations* (London: Jonathan Cape, 1938). On Anglo-French relations and the United States during the inter-war period, see: Alan Sharp, *Anglo-French Relations in the Twentieth Century* (London: Routedge, 2000); Greg Kennedy, "Neville Chamberlain and Strategic Relations with the U.S. During His Chancellorship," *Diplomacy and Statecraft*, 13, (2002); Michael Dockrill and Brian J. C. McKercher, *Diplomacy and World Power: Studies in British Foreign Policy, 1890-1951* (Cambridge: Cambridge University Press, 2002); Marvin R. Zahniser, *Then Came Disaster: France and the United States, 1918-1940* (Westport, CT: Praeger, 2002); Patrick O. Cohrs, *The Unfinished Peace after World War I: America, Britain and the Stabilisation of Europe, 1919-1932* (Cambridge: Cambridge University Press, 2006).

created the conditions that were needed for the birth of a popular movement to organise the federalist battle. The time was now ripe to start a federalist revolution, and Lothian's prediction of four years earlier— "Mankind will be driven to constitutional federalism by its own sufferings"—was about to come true.[22]

II. *Charles Kimber, Derek Rawnsley and Patrick Ransome*

The publication of *Union Now* gave, in fact, momentum to an initiative which had significantly preceded it by a few months.

In the summer of 1938, when war appeared inevitable, two young men, Charles Kimber and Derek Rawnsley, decided to start a movement in Great Britain to gain popular support for the idea of a federation of the European democracies, as an alternative to the League of Nations. "We realised," Kimber recollected,

> that short of a miracle we were too late. But at least it was a positive reaction at a time when most people could only hope and could not bring themselves to believe that anything so insane could actually come about and who, instead, persuaded themselves that appeasement would bring the reasonable settlement which the Peace of Versailles had failed to do.

The story of their friendship, as well as their decision to attempt the impossible—namely to stop Hitler—deals perhaps more with the personal than the public side of their undertaking. It is however worthwhile to describe it at some length, because it contains the key to understanding the

---

[22] On the United States and the internatonal situation towards the end of the 1930s, see: Ronald E. Powaski, *Towards an Entaingling Alliance: American Isolationism, Internationalism and Europe, 1901-1950* (Westport: CT: Greenwood Press, 1991); Robert Dallek, *Franklin D. Roosevelt and American Foreign Policy, 1932-1945* (New York: Oxford University Press, 1995); Kenneth S. Davis, *FDR: Into the Storm 1937-1940* (New York: Random House, 1995); Benjamin Welles, *Sumner Welles: FDR's Global Strategist. A Biography* (New York: Palgrave Macmillan, 1997); Brian McAllister Linn, *Guardians of Empire: The U.S. Army and the Pacific, 1902-1940* (Chapel Hill, NC: University of North Carolina Press, 1999); Benjamin D. Rhodes, *United States Foreign Policy in the Interwar Period, 1918-1941: The Golden Age of American Diplomatic and Military Complacency* (Westport, CT: Praeger Publishers, 2001); Greg Kennedy, *Anglo-American Strategic Relations and the Far East, 1933-1939: Imperial Crossroads* (London: Routledge, 2002).

atmosphere in which British people were living during a crucial and decisive period of their history.[23]

The story of these two young men illustrates the extraordinary capacity of the British not just to believe in universal values, but also to employ all available means to achieve them. The fact that the federal project encompassed the ideals and fears of an entire generation which did not identify with the policy of Chamberlain or any others, made possible their amazing success. The great merit of Kimber, a pioneer of European unification, was to give verbal expression to the dreams and anger of that generation.

Rawnsley, the nephew of an Anglican priest who had founded the National Trust, was an exuberant twenty-six year-old young man, with a strong sense of adventure. Keen on skiing, sailing, and especially flying, he loved those enterprises which were generally considered impossible just for having never been attempted. After his tragic death in Kenya in 1942, Lionel Curtis remarked:

> It is natural for those who spend their minds in studying the past to assume that where men have always failed they will always fail, and that as things have been they will remain...The essential evil of mechanized 'totalitarian' war is not the immeasurable suffering it imposes on countless people; for that will pass as the sufferers pass away by the process of nature. What will not pass is a rapid lowering in the spiritual quality of human material. The youths of vision, the spiritual leaders of their own generation, such as Rawnsley the founder of Federal Union, always too few in number, seek the post of danger especially in air-war, and perish out of all proportion to those who need such leaders and are left without them.[24]

---

[23] From a letter to the author of 15 Sept. 1983. See also the letter by Kimber to John Pinder of 29 Feb. 1980: "Curtis himself saw federation as God's will and as a vehicle for extending the Pax Britannica by way of an Imperial federation to which, I suspect under Lothian's influence, he was prepared to admit lesser breeds if they conformed to Anglo-Saxon good manners. He was tremendously valuable in the early days in giving the movement respectability—or, as he would have said, weight—particularly at Chatham House," Pinder and Mayne, *Federal Union*, 10-11. For a background discussion, see: András D. Bán, *Pax Britannica* (New York: Columbia University Press, 1997); Jan Morris, *Pax Britannica: Climax of an Empire* (Fort Washington, PA: Harvest Books, 2002); Kenneth Weisbrode, *The Atlantic Century. Four Generations of Extraordinary Diplomats Who Forged America's Vital Alliance with Europe* (Philadelphia, PA: Da Capo Press, 2009).
[24] Lionel Curtis, *World War. Its Cause and Cure* (Oxford: Oxford University Press, 1945), 123-4.

Kimber, like Rawnsley, was twenty-six years old, and a pilot as well, but he was a conscientious objector, and a supporter of the wing of the Conservative Party led by Harold Macmillan. He was working in the Press Relations Department of Shell Oil. He had been at school and university with Rawnsley, who was doing a similar job with B.P. From 1937 onwards they used to meet regularly for lunch with friends at a London pub. By the time of the Munich crisis, they had come to the conclusion that the League was incapable of reaching agreement among the member-States, and even if it did, would be unable to enforce such an agreement. They were of the opinion that a new League, with a supranational parliament, law enforcement capability, and common army was necessary, without mentioning the word federation. Kimber left his job at Rawnsley's suggestion and started to draft a pamphlet under the title of *Pax Union*, outlining their ideas. It was then that Patrick Ransome, a barrister ten years older than Kimber and Rawnsley, was introduced to them.[25]

---

[25] Charles Kimber, Introduction to *Studies in Federal Planning*, ed. Patrick Ransome (London: Lothian Foundation Press, 1990), viii-ix. Macmillan, author of *The Middle Way* (London: Macmillan, 1938), opposed Chamberlain's policy. Patrick Ransome (1902-54), studied law at Cambridge under Sir Hersch Lauterpacht, and was called to the Bar in 1938. In 1936 he worked at the Geneva International Labour Office. From 1937-39 he was a member of the editorial Committee of *Night and Day*, and a journalist at the BBC, from 1941 to 1952. On the Munich crisis and the relations among Great Powers, see: R. J. Young, "The Aftermath of Munich: The Course of French Diplomacy, October 1938 to March 1939," *French Historical Studies*, 8, (1973): 305-22; Donald C. Watt, *How War Came: The Immediate Origins of the Second World War* (London: Pantheon, 1989); Nicholas J. Cull, "The Munich Crisis and British Propaganda Policy in the United States," *Diplomacy & Statecraft*, 10, 3, (1999): 216-35; A. W. Purdue, *The Second World War* (London: Macmillan, 1999); Michael Jabara Carley, *1939. The Alliance That Never Was and the Coming of the Second World War* (Chicago: Ivan R. Dee, 1999); Hugh Ragsdale, *The Soviets, the Munich Crisis, and the Coming of World War II* (Cambridge: Cambridge University Press, 2004); Ben Vessey, "Anglo-German Relations 1918-1939," *Modern History Review*, 15, 2, (2003): 25-28; Benjamin F. Martin, *France in 1938* (Baton Rouge, LA: Louisiana State University Press, 2006); Alexander Werth, *France and Munich Before and After the Surrender* (London: Brousson Press, 2007). On Chamberlain and appeasement see: Donald C. Watt, "Roosevelt and Neville Chamberlain: Two Appeasers," *International Journal*, 28, 2, (1973): 185-9; Peter Ludlow, "The Unwinding of Appeasement," in *Das "Andere Deutschland" im Zweiten Weltkrieg* (Stuttgard: Klett, 1977): 46; C. A. MacDonald, *The United States, Britain and Appeasement, 1936-1939* (London: Macmillan, 1981); Larry W. Fuchser, *Neville Chamberlain and Appeasement: A Study in Political History* (New York: W.W. Norton, 1982);

Ransome had worked at the Geneva International Labour Office, and wrote occasionally for the *Morning Post*. Once he had become part of the group, his enthusiasm for the undertaking was as great as that of its two original founders:

> I had only just started work in an office provided by Derek—Kimber recollects—when we were introduced to Patrick Ransome and he agreed to throw in his lot with us. Neither Derek nor I laid any claim to being academics; Patrick, although not technically one, in the sense of being attached to any educational institution, had got a first at Cambridge under Professor Lauterpacht in International Law and then studied under Harold Laski at the London School of Economics. He gave us academic respectability. He was a person of great charm and wholly exceptional. Below the unruly black hair, long hollowed sallow face and sunken eyes, was a body pathetically crippled with legs which had never developed from birth. Yet the need to live permanently in a chair and to be carried up and down stairs were handicaps which he had succeeded in dismissing from notice. His delight in good conversation and wide ranging talk and quickness of response deflected all attention from his physical disabilities and even overcame the fascination of watching the lengthening ash which seemed perpetually to droop from unending cigarettes before dropping away into the creases of a permanently crumpled waistcoat.[26]

The project of the immediate union of the European democracies was discussed on 14th September 1938, right in the middle of the Munich crisis, at a meeting in Rawnsley's office, at 44 Gordon Square, London. The meeting was called "the barrel of beer", for the barrel of a hundred pints around which eighty friends met. As they saw it, a union, not a league of nations, was the only practical solution to the problem of European peace. Their friends were enthusiastic about the idea and gave Kimber and Rawnsley financial support to immediately print and distribute a pamphlet presenting the idea and for setting up an organisation. It was the first printed statement of the views of the movement's founders, and was circularised with a personal handwritten letter to over 500 distinguished personalities selected from *Who's Who*. The response was very encouraging, and Kimber was able to build a

---

R. A. C. Parker, *Chamberlain and Appeasement: British Policy and the Coming of the Second World War* (New York: Palgrave Macmillan, 1993).

[26] Charles Kimber, Introduction to *Studies in Federal Planning*, ix. On British attitudes towards the Geneva International Labour Office in the 1920s, see Henry R. Winkler, *Paths Not Taken: British Labour and International Policy in the 1920s* (Chapel Hill: University of North Carolina Press, 1994).

nucleus of an organisation, with a number of volunteers willing to help. Among them were the names of Lothian and Curtis.[27]

III. *Lothian, Lionel Curtis and Federal Union*

Lothian and Curtis had been informed of the activities of Kimber, Rawnsley and Ransome on 7 December 1938 by Gerald Bailey, Secretary of the National Peace Council, before the three young men asked for their assistance:

> I have had some discussion with a small group of people led by a Mr. Ransome, a barrister, who are concerned about the future of the international organisation for peace on the political side, and have done a certain amount of useful thinking and have produced a tentative scheme along federal lines. They are mostly young people and their work is not very experienced, but they are anxious to submit their ideas to one or two people of knowledge and authority and I gather that Mr. Ransome would very much like to have the opportunity of a few minutes talk with you at a convenient time.[28]

At that time Lothian was about to leave for two months in the United States in order to make preliminary contacts for his diplomatic mission—in August 1938 he had been chosen by Halifax as the successor to Sir Ronald Lindsay as British Ambassador in Washington—and Curtis, who was in an analogous situation, asked his friend W. K. Hancock—constitutional law scholar and Professor of history at the University of Birmingham—to meet the three young men to verify their seriousness. On the basis of a positive impression received by Hancock, once he had returned from Australia—where he participated with Lothian in the Commonwealth Conference—Curtis decided to take an interest in that group. Writing to Kimber on January 31, he invited him to get in touch

---

[27] See Charles Kimber, "Federal Union," in *Lord Lothian. Una vita*, 145-50; id., Introduction to *Towards the United States of Europe. Studies in the Making of the European Constitution* (London: Lothian Foundation Press, 1990), 1-11

[28] LP, 369/43. The National Peace Council was established in 1908 by the seventeenth Congress for Universal Peace held in London in July-August of that year. From 1923 to 1930 the organisation changed its appellation to the National Council for the Prevention of War. On Bailey and the National Peace Council, see: *H. G. Wells, S. De Madariaga, G. Middleton Murry, C. E. M. Joad on the New World Order* (London: National Peace Council, 1940); Gerald Bailey, *The Politics of Peace* (Earlham: Earlham College Press, 1963); id., *Problems of Peace* (London: Ginn, 1970).

with Professor Vincent Harlow of London University in order to get a
copy of the proofs of *Union Now*, warning him that a large amount of
spade work had already been done by Streit.[29]

Kimber had already learned of the existence of *Union Now* when in
December 1938 he met with Harold Butler—Secretary of the International
Labour Office of Geneva—in the round of consultations with the heads of
British organisations generally involved with the question of peace, but he
only read Streit's volume in February 1939, when the movement, while
not yet having an official capacity, had however already been formed and
acquired a specific character. It was therefore Curtis who transmitted to
the three young men a copy of the proofs of *Union Now*, since the book
had only been published by Jonathan Cape in March.

After having read *Union Now*, Kimber and Rawnsley arranged with
Jonathan Cape that a card should be inserted in each copy giving the
address of the newly-formed organisation, Federal Union, suggesting that
readers might subscribe to it. This produced a massive response but it was
also a source of great difficulties, since the volume supported the case to
federate the United States with the European democracies and the
Dominions. Europeanists and Atlanticists had then to find a compromise
advocating a union of democracies open to any country willing to join.
This compromise was however later to be one of the main causes for the
movement's eventual disintegration.[30]

Lothian also exhorted the three young men to read *Union Now*, in
order to attain a deeper grasp of the ideas illustrated in their pamphlet *Pax
Union*: "It is much the most interesting proposal which has yet been made
on the general lines of your pamphlet, but it goes into a great deal more
detail." Having identified in unlimited national sovereignty, "the
fundamental cause for the failure of the League of Nations," which was
nothing but a "simple alliance" between States, more concerned to defend
the *status quo* than to promote "peaceful changes" according to
transformations of power relations among States, the document of the three
young men proposed the creation of a federation with a Parliament directly
elected by the citizens, an Executive responsible in front of the Parliament,
and a Court "with compulsory jurisdiction in matters under its jurisdiction,
and a police force." The future movement should have promoted "the idea
of federation," highlighting the devastating consequences of national
sovereignty, and the need for international cooperation, by demonstrating
that the federation was the only institution capable of "limiting national

---

[29] CP, 13/80-1.
[30] Kimber, Foreword, 4-7.

sovereignty" enough "to allow international cooperation to become creative and not repressive."

As a propaganda device, the movement would elaborate and publish a draft Constitution, on the basis of which they would, in due course, ask "politically mature and geographically suitable" States to join, and to hold a popular referendum. If the referendum had a positive outcome, it was "probable" that "one of the governments involved" would be "induced to convene an Institutional Conference to adopt the Constitution." The federation would initially include a nucleus of like-minded States, open for membership by others, until the formation of a world federation. The movement would not have constituted itself as a political party, nor would it have supported a specific party, but it would have supported or opposed the various candidates at the General Elections, on the basis of their declared adherence, or aversion, to the project.

This would pave the way to the recognition of the referendum, which was "the final step." Meanwhile, the movement would organise study-groups and employ every means of propaganda to demonstrate that the federation should not "be considered a remote and idealistic enterprise." The federalist project had been realised in the United States "after a very brief campaign," and also in India, Switzerland, Canada and Australia where federation had been successfully established.

The three young men considered themselves committed to play the same role as those who had formulated the idea of the League of Nations during the First World War. Within five years their idea had in fact been "translated into reality," and they believed that the goal of the federation was not farther off then "than….that of the League of Nations in 1914." They hoped that it could be realised before another war had to be waged, but if war came, they had to make sure that the federation was "its outcome."[31]

In order to help the three young men to acquire a better grasp of the theoretical concepts of federalism, Lothian sent them on March 17, just the day after the entry of Nazi troops into Prague, his article "Federal Union Now," with which he intended to openly support Streit's plan, and induce Kimber, Ransome and Rawnsley to spread it in Great Britain. Revisiting a familiar theme, Lothian identified in international anarchy "the most fatal and destructive of all social diseases." In an anarchic system, international cooperation was made difficult, and imperialism was the only way in which it was possible "to put an end to anarchy and the risk of war." Cooperation or alliances could serve to temporarily unite sovereign States

---

[31] LP, 367.

in facing a common threat, but "the anarchy inherent in sovereignty" would have inexorably divided them, and brought them to resume power politics as soon as the pressure produced by the crisis had disappeared.[32]

The fatal weakness of any system based on cooperation, Lothian observed, lay in the fact that it was a league of governments, while the foundation of democracy was not in the government, but in the citizens. Leagues of governments were necessarily concerned "to perpetuate national sovereignty and not to make the world safe for democracy and for the people." The only way "to realise in practice the pacifist ideal" was in the creation of a federal government, competent in the fields of defence, currency, commerce and communications, and with the power to directly levy taxation.

Entering into the merits of the Streitian project, Lothian noted that it was not possible to find a more homogeneous group than the suggested fifteen democracies, since it incorporated, without taking into account the colonies, a quarter of a billion people, appeared invincible from attack by any aggressor, and constituted an integrated economic unit, within which the standard of life could be improved. Lothian was aware of the difficulties inherent in the project, such as the challenges "to the tradition of national sovereignty," national practices, ethnic feelings, and national pride. Also, the question of the Constitution remained unsolved as it could not be modelled on that of the United States, Canada and Australia, with two Houses directly elected, and an Executive based on a compromise between the parliamentary and presidential systems. Linguistic differences and the existence of monarchies constituted further difficulties, however surmountable. As for the time, Lothian had no doubts: it had to be done immediately.[33]

Ransome was particularly struck by the lucidity of the article and suggested publishing it in the Rotary quarterly. Ransome answered on 30 March—two days after Chamberlain's speech in the House of Commons in which he announced the British guarantee to Poland— sending Lothian a memorandum, intended to be "a short and popular exposition of a complicated idea," and an elaboration of the programmatic document of January, in the light of Streit's book and Lothian's article. Ransome, who had been "much impressed" by Streit's "detailed argument," thought that the current international crisis could give rise only to a pact or war. A pact with dictatorships would however only have been possible if the

---

[32] *Ibidem*. On the annexation of Bohemia and Moravia by Hitler, see E. L. Butler, R. Orde and A. Woodward, *Documents on British Foreign Policy, 1919-1939*, 4, (London: Her Majesty's Stationery Office, 1952), doc. n. 282, 288: 275, 278.
[33] LP, 367.

democracies had been united. It would, moreover, have been respected only if the union of the democracies had been permanent. The federation therefore appeared necessary. If they had to fight, it was necessary to know what they were fighting for, namely for the federation. "This is the time," Ransome stressed, to think in clear and courageous terms and "to act effectively."[34]

The alternative to a constitutional union of democracies was the domination of dictatorships. It was no longer possible for States to be independent, Ransome noted, because the policy of each depended on that of the others. Also, it seemed futile, in international relations, to try to "isolate the problems," since the world had become an interdependent reality. The League of Nations had failed because, as an Assembly of sovereign States, it had neither the power nor the authority to formulate a common policy. In order to induce the leaders of the democracies to take those courageous actions which the world needed, it was necessary to alert democratic public opinion. For this purpose the movement had been organised in three sections: a Research Institute directed by Ransome himself; a Public Relations Department run by Rawnsley; and a Central Office "as the nucleus of the popular movement for a supranational authority on a federal basis," with Kimber as General Secretary.[35]

Lothian and Curtis, unquestionably the two most prominent British federalists at the time, appreciated the document and decided to help the three young men to found a solid federalist movement. In a letter to Lothian on 2 April, Curtis revealed his plans:

> I have received the enclosed from Ransome which strikes me as really first-rate. I suggest that we should model our attitude towards these young men on the way in which Lord Milner treated us when we were founding the Round Table. One of our difficulties at the present moment is that everyone connected with the Round Table, especially those who see eye to eye with you and me, are up to their necks and over with war work, besides I have so preached to Ransome and his friends the importance of not starting separate organisations that I should hate not to carry them along with us. I dare say you will be able to improve this draft a lot, especially the three points on the last page but one; but they seem to have got the root of the matter in them.[36]

---

[34] LP, 367, 386. Ransome's memorandum has been published in Bosco, *Lord Lothian e la nascita*, 298-300. On the British guarantee to Poland, see Butler, Orde and Woodward, *Documents on British*, 4, doc. n. 509-609: 492-586.
[35] LP, 386.
[36] CP, 13/232; LP, 386.

"I have read Ransome's paper," Lothian answered on 4 April,

and think it is very good, though not adequate as a basic statement of principles. He rang me up this morning and I told him that I thought that the next step was to agree upon a few basic principles which could be printed out on a half sheet of notepaper to which we could ask adherents to subscribe, and to publish behind it a series of pamphlets written by different people from different points of view in support of the general thesis but to which nobody would be asked to agree in all their details. I am going to see him tomorrow afternoon. One of the things we shall have to do is to convince people that the problem is not solved merely by creating a new alliance for defence, even if we avoid war.[37]

Curtis's assumption that Rawnsley, Kimber and Ransome and by then many others who had independently given them their support—including such well-known public figures as Barbara Wootton, Kingsley Martin, Harold Butler, C. E. M. Joad, and Lancelot Hogben—could be manipulated as he wished, reveals to us the tactics he tried to employ. If over a short period he was in some ways successful, in the long run he failed. Lothian on the other hand kept the three young men at a more respectful distance, certainly trying to link them with Streit, but accepting their youthful spirit of independence, and their Europeanist vocation, which had little in common with his Atlanticist outlook.

IV. *Federal Union and the World Peace Foundation*

Lothian and Curtis had been approached in late February by Robert Holland-Martin—Director of the Bank of England and founder of the Round Table movement—asking them to join a group of intellectuals who had launched a campaign for world government. Standing out among them were the names of Salvador de Madariaga, H. G. Wells, Olaf Stapledon and Vivian Carter. On 29 October 1938, in a letter to *The Times*, they had argued for the need to create in Great Britain a movement for world federation, linked to the World Peace Foundation of Boston. In December they had decided—with a view precisely to founding an organisation able to bring them together and thus give more strength to the movement—to ask Caradog Jones, Professor of political science at the University of Liverpool, to carry out a survey on organisations then working in Britain to promote world unity.

The study by Caradog Jones documented the existence of a hundred organisations, for the most part engaged in research and educational

---

[37] *Ibidem.*

activities, such as Chatham House, the Workers' Educational Association, the British Association for Intellectual Cooperation, the English-Speaking Union, and various peace organisations. Among organisations interested in the political aspect of the issue of peace, some stood out, such as the New Commonwealth Society, the International Arbitration League, the League of Nations Union, the International Peace Campaign, the International Law Association, and the Women's Peace Union; but only the Pan-Europa Union, the Federation of Progressive Individuals and Societies, the World State Volunteers, and Federal Union were federalist organisations. In particular, the purposes and instruments of propaganda of Federal Union seemed, according to Caradog Jones, the "most similar" to those of the group of intellectuals for whom he had done the survey.[38]

The report clearly showed that the majority of those organisations aimed for a "better understanding" among States, "by promoting friendly relations between men and women from different countries," and that some favoured the importance of an "individual moral life and the value of personal service in the search for a solution to social and international problems," while others were mainly aimed for the application of "ethical principles" to the political questions which emerged between States. All organisations promoted world unity, on roads that "not often" ran parallel, or even met, but only a very few of them had assumed as a starting point the fact that in some respects the world already constituted a union, pledging themselves to study how to achieve world order in the light of that fact.[39]

---

[38] LP, 394. On the Women's Peace Union see Harriet Hyman Alonso, *The Women's Peace Union and the Outlawry of War, 1921-1942* (Knoxville, TN: University of Tennessee Press, 1997).

[39] LP, 394. Robert Martin Holland-Martin (1872-1944), banker, Director of Martin's Bank Ltd, Honorary Secretary of the Bankers' Clearing House, from 1905 to 1935, was Director of the Bank of England, from 1935 to 1941. Salvador de Madariaga (1886-1978), Spanish Diplomat and historian, was Spanish Ambassador to the United States, from 1931 to 1932, and to France, from 1932 to 1934. A political refugee in Great Britain from 1936, he returned to Spain in 1976. Herbert George Wells (1866-1946) was the author of several novels and political essays, including *The Time Machine* (1895), *War of the Worlds* (1898), *Tono Bungay* (1909), and *The Shape of Things to Come* (1933). He was active in the Fabian Society and the League of Nations Union. Olaf Stapledon (1886-1950), author of essays of political philosophy, was Professor at the University of Liverpool. Vivian Carter (1878-1956), Editor of *The Bystander*, from 1908 to 1916, was General Secretary of the British section of the Rotary Club, from 1921 to 1928, and Special Commissioner of the International Rotary Club, from 1928 to 1931. On the pacifist organisations in the inter-war period, see: Cecelia Lynch,

A Conference held at Ovebury Court on 10-13 March should have defined the programme of action of the group, and Holland-Martin, who acted as convener, invited a number of personalities, including Curtis, Lothian, Kimber, Rawnsley and Ransome. During the debate two clearly different approaches emerged: the first, headed by de Madariaga, supported the need to spread among public opinion knowledge of the principles of world citizenship, by highlighting the interdependence of interests among nations, which had transformed the world into "a single community," and therefore showing the need for a proper planning of world affairs on that basis.

According to de Madariaga, a federal government could be realised only through a process of slow fermentation of public opinion, or by a single major dramatic initiative, capable of producing a rapid and broad revolution in the way of thinking. Since that act was unthinkable, and even unlikely, he suggested following the educational option. The second group, headed by Kimber, conversely claimed the need for immediate action on the principles advocated by Federal Union. They should awaken and bring together the enthusiasm of ordinary people on a specific federalist project, on the model produced by the fathers of the American Constitution of 1787, and force politicians to act: this appeared to Kimber "the only radical solution to the problem of sovereignty."

Most of those present, about thirty in all, supported de Madariaga's case, and decided therefore to create an "association for world unity," with purely pedagogical purposes, aiming to influence intellectuals, churches, universities, schools, political parties, and professional, financial, commercial and industrial organisations. The association would seek to promote the birth of sister organisations in other countries, and to coordinate the activities of existing organisations; it would establish, at Curtis's suggestion, a *comité d'étude*, in order to analyse events, and see how far all the different organisations could be routed through a single channel. The newly-established organisation would address, at Murray's suggestion, those who had recently deserted the League of Nations Union due to disillusionment. It would organise seminars, conferences and summer schools, employing the volume *World's Design* by de Madariaga as a text book, and it would resort to every means of propaganda,

---

Beyond Appeasement: Interpreting Interwar Peace Movements in World Politics (Ithaca, NY: Cornell University Press, 1999); Martin Caedel, "Supranationalism in the British Peace Movement During the Early Twentieth Century," in *The Federal Idea*, 1, 169-91; id., *Thinking About Peace and War* (Oxford: Oxford University Press, 1987); David J. Dunn, *The First Fifty Years of Peace Research. A Survey and Interpretation* (London: Ashgate Publishing, 2005).

including the press, radio, and cinema. Then it was decided to hold an inaugural conference in London, during which the association would be officially launched, inviting participants to underwrite its Constitution.[40]

The Association was officially formed in April, as the British branch of the American World Peace Foundation. However its activities had a marginal influence on the federalist debate that was then developing in the country. It is significant that neither Curtis nor Lothian joined it, because the programme of action was too generic, and the Association too strongly influenced by de Madariaga, whose federalism was, according to Curtis, academic and "autocratic." By sending to Lothian on April 20—a week after the announcement of the extension of the British guarantee to Romania—a copy of the letter he sent to Ransome, Curtis assured his friend that he would soon let their mutual friend Martin-Holland know their thoughts. "We," Curtis remarked, "who know what we want as a result of years of work," cannot, in these critical times, in "hesitating like them," simply "drag with us people who are not ready to support an international federation until it has included the whole world." That would have meant to indefinitely delay everything.[41]

V. *Federal Union and the New Commonwealth Society*

Once Curtis's project to affiliate Federal Union to the Round Table—whose leaders, during the weekend of 5-6 March at Blickling had decided to support Streit—failed, Lothian proposed to associate Federal Union to the Research Institute of the New Commonwealth Society, created by Lord Davies in 1937. Lothian thought that it was the way to make available to Kimber, Ransome and Rawnsley the financial means to start a difficult and absorbent campaign.[42]

---

[40] LP, 394/687-92; CP, 13/286, 14/180-3, 130-6; CSP, Federal Union Inc., Lionel Curtis 1938-1942.
[41] Curtis to Lothian, 20 April 1939, CP, 15/58. Writing to Caradog Jones on 6 May 1939, Curtis observed, referring to de Madariaga, that he understood why "poor Spain" was hanging "between despotism and anarchy." Curtis's problem, "in meeting this group of people" was that he had "to constantly reiterate arguments" he had already argued in the press, "as a result of fourteen years of specific research," CP, 16/31-3. On the extension to Romania of the British guarantee, see Butler, Orde and Woodward, *Documents on British*, 5, doc. n. 53, 59, 61: 101-9.
[42] LP 379/81-2. Among the publications of the New Commonwealth Institute in the 1930s, see: Hans Kelsen, *The Legal Process and International Order* (London: New Commonwealth Institute, 1934); Georg Schwarzenberger, *William Ladd: An Examination of an American Proposal for an International Equity Tribunal*

The initiative to associate Federal Union to the Research Institute of the New Commonwealth Society was originated by its secretary, Professor George Keeton, with whom Kimber had held talks over the winter. Since the Institute was independent from the Society, and its political program, Keeton thought that on the research side their activities were "identical" and if they were pursued in separation there was "a good deal of wastage of effort, time and money." The Institute was "fully aware of the character and activities of Federal Union," and had undertaken a series of activities which were directly in line with those of Federal Union.[43]

The Director of the Institute, Harold Temperley, and Keeton had already scheduled a series of conferences on federalism, and its application to the problem of peace. Moreover, the whole of the September issue of the *New Commonwealth Quarterly* was in fact devoted to a critical analysis of Streit's book, and in the winter and spring of 1939 the Institute investigated the question of regional federalism, publishing a monograph on the subject. The Institute was a suitable place in which to hold periodic conferences and formed an ideal centre for University extension lectures. It possessed an extensive Information Department which could be developed in association with Federal Union. The growth of literature connected with international organisation tended to reduce its effectiveness—according to Keeton—and puzzle the public. The *New Commonwealth Quarterly* could be a vehicle for educating the public on federalism and broader issues of international organisation. Keeton suggested that the publication of further literature on the problem of European and world peace could be promoted from a common platform. Keeton also pointed out the danger of confusing British public opinion,

---

(London: Constable & Robinson, 1935); Karl Strupp, *Legal Machinery for Peaceful Change* (London: Constable & Robinson, 1937).

[43] LP, 379/54-9. Lothian discussed with Keeton the conditions for the affiliation on 18 May 1939, CP, 16/134. Harold William Temperley (1879-1939), Editor of *British Documents on the Origins of the War* (1928-38), had been Professor of History at Cambridge University from 1930 to 1939, and Rector of Peterhouse College, Cambridge, from 1938 to 1939. George William Keeton (1902-1989) had been Professor of Law at University College, London, from 1937 to 1969, Director of the London Institute of World Affairs from 1938 to 1952, and author of *National Sovereignty and International Order: An Essay upon the International Community and International Order* (London: Peace Book Company, 1939); *The Case for an International University* (London: Watts & Co., 1941); *China, the Far East and the Future* (London: Jonathan Cape, 1943); *Making International Law Work* (London: Garland Publications, 1972); *Keeping the Peace* (London: Rose, 1975).

with the presence of two federalist organisations in conflict or in competition.[44]

This in-depth proposal failed. Kimber and Rawnsley did not want to identify Federal Union with the anaemic political programme of the New Commonwealth Institute: there was no common political basis for co-operation. Its membership was very small, and consisted of subscribers to a quarterly journal. Lothian, on the other hand, thought that, provided Federal Union did not abandon its own character, co-operation with the Institute for purposes of research

> might put some very definite problems to them to investigate. They have a good house and David Davies supplies them with funds. I spoke to Ransome about this and he agrees. Next time you come to London we must have a talk about raising money for Federal Union.[45]

However, the aim of the association—the creation of an international police force—seemed frail in Lothian's eyes, as he wrote to E. Abraham in March 1939:

> Your proposal for an international police force does not really tackle the difficulty. You admit that an international police force built up of national contingents from the League of Nations will not work in practice, but your remedy is to create an independent air force which, if it existed, would admittedly be an immense deterrent to aggression, and entrust the control of it entirely to a Commander-in-Chief with instructions that he is to use it against an aggressor as defined in your Statute. In point of fact, no national State is going to entrust so terrific a power to a single man or group of officers. Unless they felt sure that he was going to use it to benefit them, they would immediately default on their payments.[46]

Writing to David Davies on 6 June, Lothian discussed the problem of the differences between "Federalists" and "Leaguers":

> Generally speaking, I agree with the view expressed by Sir Arthur Salter to the effect that it would be a mistake if Federalists and Leaguers began to get antagonistic to one another. I think it may be said that we both have the same ultimate goal, though we differ as to the practical road by which it is to be approached.[47]

---

[44] LP, 379/54-9.

[45] LP, 395, 389/140.

[46] LP 379/81-2.

[47] LP, 395, 389/141.

Lothian had no objection to the equity tribunal or the international police force advocated by the New Commonwealth Institute as immediate political stages, provided they made it clear in their propaganda that "the ultimate goal and the only one which can finally do the job is some form of federal union which substituted law and government for co-operation between sovereignties as a foundation for peace."[48]

The New Commonwealth Society recommended a gradualist approach to the creation of "international or inter-state institutions," contemplating the admission of even totalitarian States to the two proposed institutions, namely a Court of Justice and an international police force. They regarded the League of Nations "as a foundation on which to build," what Tennyson had described as "the Parliament of Man," and the world federation. If the Streitian project proved feasible, and the American President expressed his support, the Society would back it unconditionally, as—Keeton argued— the Kantian design of a universal peace would be realised without going through the intermediate steps. The decisive factor was the pressure exerted by the dictators, and the support which Streit was able to gain in the United States, since everything seemed to depend on the determination by "the greatest exponents of federalism" in extending "the benefits of that system to Europe." The initiative had therefore to start from the United States, and all that could be done in Great Britain was preparing public opinion to accept the American proposal, once it had become official.[49]

Intervening in the debate in December 1939, Keeton asserted however the necessity of an Anglo-French federation that was open to the inclusion of other European democracies: "It can be done, and if it is done, others will join." The United States even if not yet "prepared as yet to exchange her own security for the untried hazards of federal union," would however look with "active and unembarrassed sympathy" to the European union. The fact that such a union was "in process of formation under the strain of war-condition," was undeniable. The great challenge of the future was then to guarantee "its permanence."[50]

Keeton was right in thinking that Anglo-French co-operation was the fruit of the war, and that it was necessary to create an institutional framework to make it stable and permanent. With the signature in November 1939 of economic, financial and commercial agreements, Great Britain and France in fact reached their closest unity in the war effort, and the *New York Times* could identify in that close co-operation the rough

---

[48] CP, 16/199-209.
[49] *Ibidem.*
[50] George Williams Keeton, "Anglo-French Union. A Suggestion," *New Commonwealth Quarterly*, 5, 3, (1939): 234-5.

sketch "of a peace-time federation, which could be used as the starting point of a European federation."[51]

VI. *Federal Union takes shape*

The months of April and May 1939 were decisive. In that period, the small group of founding fathers worked hard to give a definite shape to the movement, and gain the support of public figures. Evidence of this is to be found in a letter from Lothian to Robert Barrington-Ward of 19 April:

> The Federal Union Now movement is gradually taking shape. We have got about 800 people already committed to it and are beginning to prepare the literature which will be available as soon as we are ready to form a definite society with the necessary public names to give it standing. All this, however, takes a little time.[52]

Lothian discussed with Curtis the problem of written material:

> It is also important to get a number of short pamphlets written from socialist and academic points of view—all of them setting out the basic creed but in terms which represent an individual view to which we do not expect all to subscribe. They talked about having a public meeting fairly soon. I said that I thought that it would be a mistake to hold any sort of public meeting until we had our creed agreed and could hold a meeting with the object of launching Federal Union Now and inviting people to subscribe to it. I am strongly of the opinion that the title of the movement should be 'Federal Union Now'. Streit in a recent letter said the title 'Now' was what aroused most interest in the public and I am sure he is right. Of course a number of highbrows and others will object, but that does not matter. If you want a movement containing a right idea to go, you must launch it in a challenging form and resist the suggestion of whittling it down to something so inoffensive that nobody will object to it and therefore take any interest in it.[53]

Despite all his efforts, Lothian failed to persuade Kimber, Rawnsley and Ransome to add "Now" to the name of the movement. They remained firm in maintaining the name with which the movement was launched, but they delegated Curtis to act as an arbiter. Although Curtis was sympathetic to Lothian's proposal, he supported Kimber, Ransome and Rawnsley: they

---

[51] *Ibidem*, 236.
[52] LP, 380. See Donald McLachlan, *In the Chair: Barrington-Ward of 'The Times', 1927-1948* (London: Weidenfeld and Nicolson, 1971).
[53] LP, 386.

were the backbone of the new-born movement. It fell to Lothian, however, to write the first pamphlet, the *Ending of Armageddon*, and it is significant, given the movement's lack of funds, that Lothian, handing over the script to Ransome on 13 June, offered the sum of £100 to defray the publication costs.[54]

Besides Lothian's initiative, the Astors and Bevin signed the statement outlining the movement's guiding principles, which was drafted by Kimber as a result of a meeting in April 1939 at Gordon Square, attended by Curtis, Kingsley Martin, Lothian, Barbara Wootton, Wickham Steed, Rawnsley and Ransome. At this meeting, it was agreed that they should act as a "Panel of Advisers" to canvass signatures for the statement of principles. Anthony Eden, Sir Archibald Sinclair, Herbert Morrison, Lord Cranbourne, Sir Drummond Shiels—Labour leader—Hamilton Fyfe—Vice-Chancellor of the University of Aberdeen—John Scott Lidgett—Wesleyan Methodist minister—Richard Gregory—Editor of *Nature*—and General Sir Ernest Swinton—developer of the tank and Chichele, Professor of Military History at Oxford—while not officially adhering, expressed themselves in favour of the federalist project. Lothian also tried to obtain the adhesion of C. E. Raven, prominent pacifist leader of Christian inspiration, who in a letter to Lothian on 5 May declared his interest, although was not willing to commit himself. Lothian also tried to gain the support of the Archbishop of Canterbury who, in a letter of 5 May, proved to be favourable to the federal idea:

> During my cruise on the Mediterranean I have been reading parts of Lionel Curtis's treatise on the *Commonwealth of God* and Streit's book on *Union Now*. I am quite sure that things must move or rather be moved in that direction and that the dominance of national sovereignty must be abated, but I cannot as yet persuade myself that the steps can be anything more than tentative, and that responsible statesmen must think out these steps before people like me can advocate the constitutional change which would be involved.[55]

Although the Archbishop of Canterbury did not sign, the Archbishop of York, William Temple, who was a much more influential personality,

---

[54] LP, 395; *The Ending of Armageddon* also became well-known on the Continent: "The contents of your booklet *The Ending of Armageddon* is the very voice which should be shouted all over Europe increasingly. The Europa Union, a Swiss Movement for the Federation of Europe, has been working for the past seven years to help to direct Europe into a new order" (from a letter from L. Klaesi to Lothian, 14 Feb. 1940, LP, 402/145).

[55] LP, 380.

did. Lothian was fully aware that Curtis's ideas, stated in *Civitas Dei*, were "quite unworkable," but he regarded his old friend as a very dynamic spirit whose creative ideas had at least the merit of forcing people to take a position regarding them.[56]

However, Lothian's attempt to involve Keynes in the movement failed. Writing to him on 18 May 1939, Lothian stated:

> I commit the unpardonable crime of enclosing a reprint of my farewell address to the Scottish Liberal Federation. I do not suppose you will agree with it but you may care to read it. Fundamentally, Streit's view is sound and the League thesis unsound, in the sense that while the construction may be more remote, Streit provides a foundation upon which you can build, while the Covenant does not.[57]

On the other hand, Curtis's approach to the other distinguished economist, Lionel Robbins, was successful. However, it was Robbins who first got in touch with Curtis on 24 May 1939:

> I have just been reading your interesting paper in the current number of *International Affairs*, and it has occurred to me that you might care to read chapters 9 and 11 of the enclosed essay, in which, some years before the publication of Mr. Clarence Streit's book, working on similar problems from a rather different point of view, I struck a somewhat parallel line of thought. There is something reassuring in the discovery that so many people, working quite independently, are finding themselves led more and more to the adoption of the federal idea.[58]

"I must confess," Curtis replied on 6 June,

---

[56] LP, 380/182.

[57] LP, 383/401. For a critical analysis of Keynes's conception of international relations, see Donald John Markwell, *John Maynard Keynes and International Relations: Economic Paths to War and Peace* (New York: Oxford University Press, 2006).

[58] CP, 16/173, 174-5. Lionel Charles Robbins (1898-1984) was Professor of Economics at the London School of Economics from 1929 to 1961; Director of the Foreign Office Economic Relations Section from 1941 to 1945; President of the Royal Economic Society from 1954 to 1955, and President of the *Financial Times* from 1961 to 1970. For an analysis of Robbins's doctrine, see: Denis Patrick O'Brien, *Lionel Robbins* (New York: Palgrave Macmillan, 1988); id., *Lionel Robbins and the Austrian Connection* (Durham, NC: Duke University Press, 1989). On the creation of the Foreign Office Economic Relations Section, see Donald Graeme Boadle, "The Formation of the Foreign Office Economic Relations Section, 1930-1937," *Historical Journal*, 20, 4, (1977): 919-36.

that I was simply astounded when I read the last three chapters of your book to find how you, approaching the subject from the economic angle, arrived at conclusions which are practically identical with those reached by Clarence Streit. He, of course, approached the subject primarily from the political point of view. I was at the same time approaching it mainly from the moral and religious point of view, but I never reached the clear and specific conclusions as to Free Trade, Migration and Common Currency, at which you and Streit arrived.[59]

Curtis suggested that Robbins contact Ransome, Kimber and Rawnsley, and offered a report of the progress of the movement in the United States:

Streit is going ahead like steam in America. He seems to me a man of the type of Lloyd Garrison who started the abolition movement in New England. My only fear is that he may wreck his health by the stupendous energy with which he is devoting himself and indeed most of his earnings to convert his countrymen to the truth that nothing short of an International Federation can avail to prevent war. He is one of those men who combine with drive and enthusiasm the faculty for keeping his feet on the ground. He clearly sees that the initiative has got to come from the United States and is devoting himself primarily to the Middle West from which he comes. Our job over here is to start now preparing public opinion for making the necessary response to the American initiative whenever it comes...I have long felt that the human race is approaching the greatest and most difficult crisis in its history—the transition from the national to the international State. Streit is absolutely sound in insisting that what we need is 'Union Now'. It has got to come. It will come. But when it will come is merely a question of how much suffering human beings are to go on inflicting on one another before enough of them recognise the necessity of an International Union. It is no use bothering about statesmen at present. We have got to make every ordinary John Citizen see that the root of the trouble is his own obsession of nationalism, until we have enough of them in the leading democracies to sit up and make political leaders take notice. On this point Streit is absolutely sound.[60]

Curtis shared Lothian's view that Federal Union had to back the American initiative and adopt Streit's plan, assuming that mankind will be driven to constitutional federalism, he foresaw, by its own sufferings. Robbins followed Curtis's advice and later became associated with the movement's Research Department. His writings on the economic aspect of European federation rank among the classics of federalist literature. It is

---

[59] CP, 16/174.
[60] CP, 16/175.

interesting to note, however, that Robbins was driven to the federalist approach on economic matters through reading some of Lothian's writings, notably *Liberalism in the Modern World* and *Pacifism Is Not Enough*. Through Robbins, Federal Union gained the support of another eminent economist, Friedrich von Hayek.[61]

Federal Union had the patronage of a further distinguished British economist, who was the architect of reform administered in the United Kingdom as well as in many other countries. Rawnsley, who studied at the Oxford college of which William Beveridge was Master, in spring 1939 obtained the promise from Beveridge that he would join the organisation and put his whole weight behind it if war broke out. He kept his promise and supervised in Oxford the activities of the Research Department of the organisation, with the significant production of "Federal Tracts" by distinguished authors.[62]

Lothian tried to convince Gerald Bailey, Secretary of the National Peace Council—an umbrella organisation appointed to keep a certain degree of unity among the various British peace organisations—to give his and his institution's support to Federal Union:

---

[61] Lionel Robbins, *Autobiography of an Economist* (London: Macmillam, 1971). Friedrich August von Hayek (1899-1991) had been Director of the Austrian Institute for Economic Research, from 1927 to 1931; Tooke Professor of Economics and Statistics at the London School of Economics, from 1931 to 1950; Professor of Social and Moral Science at the University of Chicago, from 1950 to 1962; and Professor of Economics at the University of Freiburg, from 1962 to 1969. He was awarded the Nobel Prize for Economics in 1974. On von Hayek, see: C. E. Cubitt, *A Life of Friedrick August von Hayek* (Gamlingay: Authors onLine, 2006); Edward Freser, *The Cambridge Companion to Hayek*, (Cambridge: Cambridge University Press, 2006); John Wood, *Friedrich von Hayek* (London: Routledge, 2004); Peter J. Boettke, *The Legacy of Friedrich von Hayek* (London: Edward Elgar Publications, 2000).

[62] William Beveridge, *Power and Influence* (London: Hodder & Stoughton, 1953), 266. Sir William Henry Beveridge (1879-1963) had been a researcher for the Permanent Secretary of the Ministry of Food, from 1918 to 1919; Director of the London School of Economics, from 1919 to 1937; Vice-Chancellor of the University of London, from 1926 to 1928; and Rector of University College, Oxford, from 1937 to 1945. He was a Liberal MP, from 1944 to 1945, and author of the *Beveridge Report on Social Security* (1942), and *Full Employment in a Free Society* (1944). On Beveridge, see: Jose Harris, *William Beveridge: A Biography* (New York: Oxford University Press, 1997); John Hills, John Ditch and Howard Glennester, *Beveridge and Social Security: An International Retrospective* (New York: Oxford University Press, 1994.

The League is dead partly no doubt through the feebleness of its member governments, but far more because it attempted the impossible, namely to combine a peace organisation with national sovereignty, which inexorably destroys peace, prosperity and freedom. The federalist principle is, in point of fact, the only way in which the pacifist ideal can be realised.

If Bailey agreed personally with the view that a federal union was the only way of giving practical effect to the pacifist creed, he could not do much to help the case for the Federal Union inside the National Peace Council. Pacifists and Leaguers held the overwhelming majority of its seats. Pacifists were convinced that they would never fight for "King and Country" and Leaguers did not accept the reality of the failure of the League: they were still convinced that the nations had failed the League.[63]

Writing to Eden on 3 May, Lothian recommended him to read *Union Now*:

I write to you because I hope that if you read the book and are impressed by its general case, you could see your way to saying something friendly about it, partly to get people here to consider it and partly to give encouragement in the United States, for while the United States will never take an idea from this country, they are always extremely anxious to know whether the more experienced English think well of the idea which has been started in the United States.

Eden did not sign the statement of aims of Federal Union so as not to commit himself at that early stage, but he showed himself "extremely sympathetic" to the movement, almost until the downfall of France in June 1940.[64]

Lothian kept Streit informed of the progress they were making in Britain:

I believe that Curtis has kept you in touch with what we are doing here. *Union Now* is selling well and the number of people who are reading the book is steadily increasing. The first step is clearly to let the argument of the book spread. Meanwhile, however, we have tried to form the nucleus of what we shall call the Federal Union Now Society. We have added the word 'Federal' because people in this country take union to mean

---

[63] LP, 387/809-10.

[64] LP, 386. On Eden, see: David Dutton, *Anthony Eden. A Life and Reputation* (New York: Hodder Arnold, 1998); D. R. Thorpe, *Eden: The Life and Times of Anthony Eden, First Earl of Avon, 1897-1977* (New York: Random House, 2004); Alan Campbell, *Anthony Eden* (London: Hesperides, 2006).

something different from federation...*Union Now* of course will be the main source book to which we direct our members' attention.[65]

The drafting of the statement of principles reveals the deep commitment of Lothian and Curtis to contribute in the shaping of the organisation of the movement, but also shows that the first conflict of opinions was about to arise among the founders. Regarding this last problem, it is worth considering the following passage taken from a letter Lothian wrote to Curtis on 29 May:

> I think that Ransome has sent you a copy of his revised statement of basic principles. I am afraid it won't do. Like all these people who have no practical experience, they begin to degenerate into woolliness. He has an incurable aversion to using the words sovereignty or constitution because, being a lawyer, he realises how different they are to our existing unwritten system, but unless we use these words we shall eventually breed incurable differences in our own ranks. I therefore enclose a revision of his text which I am also sending him and which, if you think well, you might discuss at your lunch on Wednesday.[66]

Writing to Drummond Shiels about the revised statement of basic principles, Curtis noted that its drafting took weeks and months of work. The fundamental question which confronted the democracies was not Stalin, Mussolini, or Hitler, but "the obsession of nationalism in ordinary people's minds." Therefore, Federal Union first had to approach ordinary people.[67]

Sharing Streit's view in which the priority in the struggle was to persuade the Americans to take up the leadership of the federation, Curtis believed that the first move in the creation of the Atlantic federation should be made by the United States, and attributed to Federal Union—to which he gave "in the strongest terms" his "blessing"—the task of preparing the British public to respond readily to that initiative. Curtis therefore tried to play, in the months of the foundation of the movement, the role of intermediary between the two federalist organisations which arose almost simultaneously on both sides of the Atlantic. The Federal Union leaders did not agree, however, to be led by Curtis in supporting the Atlantic Federation. Eventually they reached a compromise that

---

[65] LP, 386.
[66] LP, 395. On the drafting of the statement of principles, see CP, 15/38-9, 69-70, 74-7; Curtis to Lothian, 20 April 1939, CP, 15/59; Curtis to Ransome, CP, 15/73; Curtis to Ransome, 19 May 1939, CP, 16/149-50; Ransome to Curtis, 23 May 1939, CP, 16/151; Lothian to Curtis, 18 May 1939, CP, 16/135.
[67] CP, 15/73.

represented together the strength and the weakness of the movement in the following months.

The compromise, which left undefined the geographic dimension of the federation of democracies, certainly contributed to the extraordinary success of the movement until the downfall of France, but it was also, as it has already been mentioned, one of the main reasons for its political failure soon after, when Federal Union was organised in 227 local branches, with the support of 12,000 subscribers. The clash of ideas implied the closure of many local branches, and the abandonment of the movement by a large number of members, with a substantial reduction of its influence in the political debate on the war aims. The crisis can be explained, on the other hand, also as a result of the dispersion of energies caused by the defeat at Dunkirk and the subsequent mobilization. The majority of members and activists of the movement were in fact made up of young people who, once called up to the army, ceased to take an active part in the movement.[68]

The difficulties between Kimber and Curtis were not just due to ideological factors but, also to character. Then there was the generational issue. Curtis was sixty-eight, and Kimber twenty-six. The relative solitude in which Curtis had fought all his life for the federation of the Empire, the fact that the danger of war was threatening what still remained of Imperial unity, and his religious fervour, led him to behave as a "prophet" in the biblical sense of the term. Kimber was agnostic, and could not accept being covered by Curtis's mystic mantle. He was a conscientious objector and could not also share Curtis' patriotic zeal. Finally, he was, by temperament, rather absent-minded and inattentive—despite being an Etonian and belonging to the lower nobility—to those formalities of which Curtis was respectful.

Meanwhile the collaboration was however intense. In a long letter to Curtis of May 16, Kimber was referring to having met Gerald Bailey— Secretary of the National Peace Council—now "extremely favourable to the idea of the federation," and determined to deploy the organisation at the Annual General Meeting of July, in support of the Streitian project.

---

[68] Streit to Curtis, 13 May 1939, CP, 16/104-5; Curtis to Streit, 15 May 1939, CP, 16/110-1. On Atlantic federalism, see: Clark M. Eichelberger, *Organizing for Peace: A Personal History of the Founding of the United Nations* (New York: Harper & Row, 1977); Ira Straus, "Lothian and the Anglo-American Problematic," in *The Larger Idea*, 124-35; Wyne S. Cole, *Roosevelt and the Isolationists, 1932-1945* (Lincoln: University of Nebraska Press, 1983); Andrew Johnstone, "Private Interest Groups and the Lend-Leas Debate, 1940-1942," *49th Parallel. An interdisciplinary Journal of North American Studies*, 7, (2001).

Kimber seemed to agree—perhaps more to please the old federalist rather than being persuaded—on the necessity of closer relations with Streit. Eager to engage himself in the creation of local branches across the country, he realised, though, that they should wait until they were able to give them "something to do," and had in mind to twin the new sections with others existing in other countries, particularly in the United States.

Kimber planned to convene towards the end of June a large inaugural conference, in which participants would appoint local leaders, around whom sections would be created. They were "giving birth to a crusade," and they had to "work hard for it." Kimber invited Curtis to figure as one of the speakers of the inaugural conference, and regarding the relationships with the League of Nations Union, Kimber recorded Gilbert Murray's more favourable attitude towards Federal Union, yet thinking was premature for starting an official collaboration, because of the divergent policies of the two organisations. The movement had rather to approach the Union's branches at the local level, and build the support "from the bottom."[69]

By the beginning of June 1939, Federal Union had acquired a definite shape. The movement availed itself of the support of prominent political figures, and of a distinguished panel of speakers willing to spread the federal idea throughout the country. The statement of principles had been published by *The Times* at the end of May, and the pamphlet *The Ending of Armageddon* was in print, and several others were being prepared; there were more than 800 people interested in the movement even before its public launch.

VII. *Federal Union on the eve of the debut*

The month of June was spent in organising the first public meeting, which was to be the culmination of the work developed up until then. Kimber was anxious to bring forward the date of the meeting, and asked Lothian to take an active part in it, involving the greatest possible number of people, before leaving for Washington:

> If we wait longer we shall have to postpone the whole thing until after the summer holidays—the beginning of October: but by that time the publicity for *Union Now* will have come to an end and we shall have to work it up all over again. Moreover, our members are getting very impatient for results, so that there is a real danger of losing their enthusiasm...I am proposing, therefore, to make an announcement to the Press between the

---

[69] CP, 16/122-4, 67.

19th and 30th of June: to follow this by a conference of members on July 1st and 2nd, from which perhaps a little additional publicity might be obtained, and at which instructions should be given to speakers and to organisers of local groups. The conference is badly needed as we have a number of members who are very keen but lack direction.[70]

Kimber enclosed with the letter the following draft resolution:

1. The Anti-Aggression League is a purely military arrangement differing fundamentally from the League of Nations since there is no machinery to obtain peaceful change. Its value depends on its power to produce a deadlock during which a settlement may be reached. 2. No settlement is possible on the basis of national sovereignty, since nations remain judges in their own cause. 3. The only way to cure power politics is to pool power: therefore a federal solution is the only one possible. 4. There is no need to wait for the dictators: the democracies can give evidence of their own good faith and can obtain all the benefits of federation by uniting now and leaving it open to attract people in totalitarian countries.[71]

"I think," Lothian answered in mid-June, "it is too strong to say that no settlement is possible on the basis of national sovereignty." If there was a balance or a preponderance of force, a settlement may be reached, "it will be a temporary settlement leaving all the underlying causes of war intact." The real point, Lothian stressed, was "that national sovereignty implies that peace treaties or settlements simply record temporary agreements between recurrent wars." Similarly, Lothian thought that the point to stress with regard to the third paragraph was "not power but unity." "Thus the only way to cure power politics is that the nations should unite to form a common constitution in which power is used to enforce laws designated to promote the interest not of the parts but of all people."[72]

The policy adopted by the Federal Union was aimed, according to Kimber, to bring the British Government to a historic decision: to call a Conference of the European democracies to discuss the immediate creation of a federal government. The British Government should:

(1) state the principles of government on which it is based and by which it stands; (2) state its readiness to discuss now with any government the creation of a federal union similarly based and having the power to legislate at least in those fields enumerated by Streit and set out in our

---

[70] CP, 16/125-6.

[71] LP, 395. Federal Union had already held a meeting gathering the militants at the end of May, at the Friends' Meeting House, headquarter of the Quakers, with Joad and Barbara Wootton as speakers.

[72] LP, 395.

statement of aims, and to guarantee responsible self-government to each of
the federated States, and therefore certain minimum liberties to their
citizens; (3) invite Hitler and Mussolini to a conference to discuss this
suggestion with the leaders of the democratic States and simultaneously to
use every means to get news of the proposal to the German and Italian
peoples; (4) announce its determination at once to set up this federal
government, essentially based on these principles, with any which are
prepared to do so, even if all who attend the conference will not agree.[73]

The author of this ambitious project was Charles Kimber, who
outlined it in a long letter to Lothian on 23th July 1939, only a few weeks
before his departure for Washington. The advantages of such action were
that:

(1) all people are offered freedom, equality and security; (2) Hitler's and
Mussolini's governments are given the responsibility of refusing their
benefits to their people; (3) American and neutral and indeed progressive
opinion throughout the world is relieved of the suspicion that Britain is not
so much concerned with moral principles and international order as with
the preservation of her own possessions and material interest at the
expense of the interests of the other peoples and of all moral values; (4) if
the initiative fails and we fight, at least it is known for what we are
fighting and federal union is assured as the basis of peace terms ...; (5)
opposition opinion in Germany and Italy is given something to which it
can rally. No secure settlement is possible with the present governments of
these countries and they can only be overthrown by war or by revolution.[74]

Apparently aware of the difficulties inherent in such an undertaking, as
well as the increasingly tenuous possibility of stopping the military
machine mounted by Hitler, Kimber proposed that Lothian should
approach the Cabinet. In his reply on 25th July, Lothian, however sceptical
about the possibility of the British Government adopting such an initiative,
promised to take the necessary steps with some leading members of the
Cabinet:

I am quite sure that it is not possible for the British government to take the
initiative you suggest at this moment. On the one hand, the Axis powers
are not yet willing to consider anything except their own triumph. On the
other hand, British public opinion has not been prepared to consider
federation. In my view, you will not get any serious consideration of the
settlement until it has been proved either with or without war that neither
side can overthrow the other. That may happen as early as this winter. In

---

[73] *Ibidem.*
[74] *Ibidem.*

the meantime, however, there is everything to be said for private people putting forward the kind of solution you discuss. It is far more likely to have an effect in Germany and Italy than if it came from the British government, and far more public discussion is needed here and among the democracies before any politicians or statesmen can take up the theme as a practical proposition.[75]

When Lothian was appointed by the British Government to be spokesman of the leading European democracy in the country upon which the fate of the war was to depend, he let his younger friend continue the federalist battle on the European front, while he fought the federalist and patriotic battle on the American one, for as long as his physical strength permitted. Despite being a leading exponent of the Atlantic school, Lothian was well aware—as he later emphasised several times in his speeches to the Americans—of the need to secure in federalism the institutional framework of military and political cooperation between his country and France, which since the Anglo-French talks of 21 and 22 March constituted the backbone of British foreign policy.[76]

The results were different from those they had envisaged, but were nonetheless significant. On the one hand, although European federation did not come about, the foundations were laid down for the birth and development of a political federalist force in Europe. On the other hand, while Atlantic federation did not take place, the United States came to aid Great Britain, entering into a kind of undeclared war against Germany and Italy. Moreover, when the possibility of a federal union between Great Britain and France disappeared, the British and the Americans, by signing the Atlantic Charter, adopted the policy advocated by Lothian throughout the inter-war period. If the policy of closer Anglo-American co-operation had been adopted five or ten years earlier, it would probably have prevented the outbreak of the Second World War, and made possible a peaceful revision of the Versailles settlement.

Yet the original idea of an Anglo-French union as a nucleus of a European federation—even if contemplating the inclusion of the Soviet Union!—had been by Konni Zilliacus, a well-known left-wing writer, and member of the Council of Federal Union. In writing to Kimber on the 21st April—while British diplomacy had already begun negotiations with the Soviets to guarantee the neutrality of the Soviet Union in the Polish

[75] LP, 395.
[76] On the talks between the foreign ministers Lord Halifax and Georges Bonnet of 21-22 March 1939, see Butler, Orde and Woodward, *Documents on British*, 4, doc. n. 446, 458, 469, 471, 484: 400, 422-7, 434, 457-63.

question—Zilliacus outlined his vision of the strategy, which was quite different from both that of Federal Union, and that of Streit. He was convinced that a world federation was possible only on the basis of "social justice and democracy," and therefore thought that the destruction of fascism as a system of government was a priority, and that it would happen both through an internal revolution, or a war.[77]

He proposed a military alliance between Great Britain, France and the Soviet Union, as a deterrent to persuade the dictators not to resort to force, and to come to an agreement. In a less tense international situation, this defensive alliance could have developed into a true union, open to the adhesion of the other European democracies, and of the United States. Once the constituent process began, the union had to deal with Nazi-Fascism, first encouraging the forces of internal resistance, and finally destroying it with a war. This plan was, according to Zilliacus, more realistic than that of Streit, and it would have had the support of the Labour and Liberal Parties, as well as of most of the Conservatives who opposed Chamberlain's policy.[78]

In order to achieve the goal of building the consensus of public opinion for the project of an Anglo-French federation, Federal Union's leaders

---

[77] CP, 1561-7. Konni Zilliacus (1894-1967) was an officer of the League of Nations from 1919 to 1939; Labour MP for Gateshead from 1945 to 1949; Independent MP for Gateshead, following his expulsion from the Labour Party, because of his opposition to the party's foreign policy line, from 1949 to 1950; and Labour MP for Manchester Gorton from 1955 to 1967. On the Left and the international crisis, see: Mark Minion, "Left, Right or European? Labour and Europe in the 1940s: The Case of the Socialist Vanguard Group," *European Review of History*, 7, 2. (2000): 229-48; Talbot Imlay, "From Villain to Partner: British Labour Party Leaders, France and International Policy during the Phoney War, 1939-40," *Journal of Contemporary History*, 38, 4, (2003): 579-96; Gidon Cohen, *The Failure of a Dream: The Independent Labour Party from Disaffiliation to World War II* (New York: Tauris Academic Studies, 2007). On the Anglo-Soviet Union relations during the inter-war years, see: Louise Shaw, *The British Political Elite and the Soviet Union, 1937-1939* (London: Frank Cass, 2003); Keith Neilson, *Britain, Soviet Russia and the Collapse of the Versailles Order, 1919-1939* (Cambridge: Cambridge University Press, 2006). On the internal Resistance to Hitler's regime, see: David Clay Large, *Contending with Hitler: Varieties of German Resistance in the Third Reich* (Cambridge: Cambridge University Press, 1994); Michael Geyer and John W. Boyer, *Resistance Against the Third Reich: 1933-1945* (Chicago, IL: University of Chicago Press, 1995). On Franco-Soviet relations, see Michael Jabara Carley, "Prelude to Defeat: Franco-Soviet Relations, 1919-1939," in *French Defeat of 1940: Reassessments*, ed. Joel Blatt (Oxford: Berghahn Books, 2000), 171-202.
[78] CP, 1561-7.

were well aware that they should establish an organisational structure that would allow the movement to be present in the political debate. In this regard it turned out to be decisive due to the publication in the national press, on June 24, of the declaration of the guiding principles, signed by personalities like Waldorf Astor, Ernest Bevin, C. E. Raven, Drummond Shiels, C. E. M. Joad, Barbara Wootton, Wickham Steed, Lionel Curtis, George Catlin, C. J. N. Fleming, G. M. Paterson, Lady Rhondda, B. Seebohm Rowntree, Ramsay Muir, E. F. M. Durbin, Richard Law, J. Scott Lidgett, Edith Summerskill, Sir Ernest Swinton, Hamilton Fyfe, Sir Richard Gregory, Drury Lowe, John Orr, Arnold Toynbee and Eustace M. W. Tillyard.[79]

An immediate consequence of the publication of the aims of Federal Union was a Parliamentary interpellation on 26 June, by D. Leach MP, who asked the Prime Minister if he would take the initiative to propose to other governments the creation of a European federation "on the lines of the United States of America." Under-Secretary R. A. Butler replied on behalf of the Government that such a policy was certainly "in the interests of the entire world," but at the moment was not yet favourable. A similar question had been presented on 19 June by the Labour MP Reginald

---

[79] The text delivered to the press was the following: "We believe that: I) National sovereignty leads to competition in armaments, economic self-sufficiency and internal regimentation, and thus inevitably to war, imperialism, poverty and loss of individual liberty, because where sovereign states fail to agree there is no remedy save resort to violence in the form of power politics or war. II) No international order based on co-operation between sovereign states will prove either efficient or durable since all sovereign states in the last resort seek their own national self-interest. Nothing less than a union of the peoples can end this anarchy and give peace, justice and freedom to all. Accordingly we advocate: I) A Federal Union of those nations which hold that the state exists for the freedom and responsibility of man, and that government must be conducted with the consent of the governed. II) That this constitutional Union will assure national self-government to all units within the Union in those affairs which are solely of national interest, and will establish legislative, executive and judicial organs representative of and responsible to all citizens of the Union for such common affairs as defence and order, currency, trade, communications, and migration, and will possess the taxation and borrowing powers necessary to finance its own activities. III) As a first step a Federal Union of the established democracies to form a nucleus of the future world federation; such a nucleus to be open to accession by other nations which accept its basic principles; and to act as a loyal member of any larger organisations designed to promote international co-operation," Melville Channing-Pearce ed., *Federal Union. A Symposium* (London: Jonathan Cape, 1940), 12-13.

Sorensen, and Butler replied that the present circumstances did not seem "favourable for any initiative."[80]

A leader in the *Christian Science Monitor* of 20th June recalled how Lothian, the designated British Ambassador to the United States, had intervened several times in support of the federal idea. In the meantime in Britain, a political movement had been formed with the aim to spread the federal idea, which in turn represented a "leading force in the building of a more effective successor of the League of Nations." The aims and activities of the Federal Union were presented on the same line of succession as the ideas by Tennyson, Wells, Lord Davies, Lothian, and Streit.[81]

Also, the South African *Rand Daily Mail* recorded on the 22nd June, the Parliamentary debate raised by Sorensen, reporting that even though he expressed some doubts on the practicality of the federal idea, he reached the conclusion that "in the end...world union in some form or other is bound to come." The *Sidney Herald* of 3rd June recorded the speech by Bevin at the Annual Conference of the Labour Party in support of the federation of the democracies, and related it with the stands made by Streit and Curtis. It was a sign of the times that the "stubborn" Secretary of the British Transport Workers' Union shared the same opinion as the "British philosopher and the American journalist." All three were ahead of their generation, but neither the cynic nor the realist could deny the necessity "of courageous thinking in the crisis which threatens the world."[82]

By now, the movement was formed. In the space of nine months Federal Union had acquired an ideological identity which distinguished it clearly from other federalist organisations, and an independent organisational structure. Britain was about to go to war, and the first popular battle for the European federation had just begun.

---

[80] CP, 17/151, 46-7, 144-5; 18/37-8; FOP, FO371/24024. Sorensen put forward a similar Parliamentary interpellation on 23 March, following the publication of *Union Now*, FO371/23083. On Butler and the Foreign Office during WWII, see: Solomon Wank, *Doves and Diplomats: Foreign Offices and Peace Movements in Europe and America in the Twentieth Century* (Westport, CT: Greenwood Press, 1978); Edward Hertslet, *Recollections of the Old Foreign Office* (London: Adamant Media Corporation, 2002); Gaynor Johnson, *The Foreign Office and British Diplomacy in the Twentieth Century* (London: Routledge, 2005).

[81] *Christian Science Monitor,* 20 June 1939.

[82] *Rand Daily Mail*, 22 June 1939; *Sidney Herald*, 3 June 1939. On Bevin, see: Mark Stephens, *Ernest Bevin: Unskilled Labourer and World Statesman 1881-1951* (London: Spa Books, 1989); Peter Weiler, *Ernest Bevin* (Manchester: Manchester University Press, 1993); Alan Bullock and Brian Brivati, *Ernest Bevin: A Biography* (London: Politico's Publishing, 2002).

CHAPTER II

FEDERAL UNION
BECOMES A POPULAR MOVEMENT

I. *The Inaugural Meeting*

Federal Union entered the political debate in Great Britain after the meeting which took place at the Besant Hall, Baker Street, on 1st July 1939. The speakers were Curtis, Barbara Wootton, Joad, Wickham Steed, and Kingsley Martin, Editor of the *New Statesman*. More than three hundred people attended. Funds were raised to a total of £26, which was added to the £90 raised the previous week. The increase in membership was up to one hundred per week.[1]

Curtis gave the inaugural speech—published by the *Calcutta Statesman* on 22nd July—reminding the audience, with a Biblical quotation, that when one loses sight of the final goal, one also loses the road to follow. The principal task confronting mankind, was "to translate freedom into political terms," namely in institutions, since institutions formed the character and judgement of citizens. That institution was the State. However, the ever closer identification between State and nation, fed by nationalism and national sovereignty, generated international anarchy, in which war between nation-States became a recurrent and inevitable instrument to solve their conflicts:

> so long as the world was in water-tight compartments, the creation of national sovereignties was a necessary means to the growth of freedom. But now, mechanisation has broken down all the compartments, socially and economically. It has made every people dependent on every other. What one does, or leaves undone immediately affects all the others. Human society is now one closely integrated whole. The political fragmentation of human society into sixty or seventy sovereign States, is

---

[1] CP, 18/4. Kingsley Martin (1897-1969) had been Assistant Professor at the London School of Economics from 1923 to 1927; journalist at the *Manchester Guardian* from 1927 to 1930; and Editor of the *New Statesman and Nation* from 1930 to 1960.

now utterly obsolete. The maintenance of national sovereignty is to-day fatal to the very existence of that freedom, to that rule of law which it once helped to establish on the national scale.

There was a need for a federalist vanguard to accomplish a world revolution in the cause of freedom and peace. Mankind was approaching "the last and most difficult stage in the history of freedom—the transition from the national to the international commonwealth." In spite of the relatively small number of people gathered in Baker Street, where there was "hardly a man or woman whose name is known to the world outside," Curtis exhorted all not to despise "the day of small things," since movements "which count in the world's history are begun in upper chambers" like that. "Look at Russia today", Curtis observed:

> The movement which made Russia what she now is, began in Euston Road hard by this place, in a room meaner perhaps, than this, in a gathering of fifty souls...Don't think of yourselves, how few you are or how unimportant. Don't think of yourselves at all. Think and think only to the truth with which you are charged, of its transcendent importance. That truth is the infinite duty of every man to his fellow men, a duty which cannot be limited to a British fragment, a German fragment, an American fragment, or to any other fragment of the human race.

The task of the militants of the new organisation was "to root the obsession of nationalism out of the minds of ordinary men," and "to see that this vital truth is expressed in institutions." The "tremendous factor" which was on their side, was that the truth they held was "the only one which offers a genuine ray of hope to a world dark with despair." "So, and not otherwise," Curtis remarked, "can this world be delivered from the scourge of war." Truth was "the ace that wins the game for the hand that holds it." They held "that ace" in their hands:

> Don't start off by lecturing Governments and telling them how to do their jobs. In this matter be warned by the record of the League of Nations Union. Above all avoid premature publicity. Don't waste your time trying to convert important people whose names carry weight. Your business is with ordinary people like yourselves.

They had "got to get ordinary people to see that we ourselves are to blame, that nothing can bring peace to the world until we create a government for the world, in the real sense of that word." The people who saw that truth at that moment were "not perhaps more than a few hundred in number," but those few hundreds had "to convert millions to think like themselves, and then and not till then, the important people, whose names are known to the world, the politicians and statesmen, will sit up and take notice." "Begin now," Curtis urged them:

> You are wasting time when you talk or think of the time it will take. It must be done, it will be done. It is merely a question of how much suffering human beings are to inflict on each other before it is done. Every single man you convert to this truth will help to reduce that suffering, and to bring the hour of deliverance nearer.[2]

The meeting roused the enthusiasm of the three hundred participants. There were by then 37 branches all over the country, including 1,300 subscribers. Volunteers offered to help at the headquarters in Gordon Square. However, differences of opinion soon began to emerge, as Federal Union brought together leaders and followers of different federalist schools: Europeanists, Atlanticists, and worldists. It was certainly not easy for Kimber to keep the various souls together, and to bring the convergence of the forces into a single project.[3]

Thanking Curtis for his speech which had "set the tone for the whole Conference," Kimber asked for a meeting to discuss the programme of action:

> the one word which everyone is using...is 'inspiring'. Offers of help are pouring in, and we shall very soon have groups all over the country. We have found a first-rate man to do the whole of Scotland for us, complete with offices and secretarial staff offered him free.[4]

II. *The first internal conflicts*

The Conference however failed to define a specific policy to fight for. Federal Union had not yet acquired a distinct political and organisational character. The growing consensus which the three young founders were meeting was still the result of a generic and spontaneous adherence to federalist ideals, rooted within British political culture for at least a quarter of a century. The most difficult task that was before Federal Union's leaders was to elaborate, on the basis of that consensus, an innovative strategy able to introduce into the political scene a force completely new and anomalous for the insular tradition, whose political directives were

---

[2] CP, 18/44.
[3] For an assessment of Federal Union from Streit's perspective, see: "The Birth of Federal Union," *Freedom and Union*, 3, 3, (1948): 16-25; id. "The Birth of Federal Union, 1939," *Ibidem,* 4, 3, (1949): 16-21.
[4] CP, 18/45.

mostly to be invented. In the British tradition of federalism an adequate culture did not exist, as federalism generally identified with the theory of the federal State.

The theoretical basis for the elaboration of such a strategy existed in the thoughts of the two leading exponents of British federalism, Curtis and Lothian. Kimber, Rawnsley and Ransome had come to federalism following an empirical approach, directed at Europe, whereas Lothian and Curtis had moved from the universalistic experience of the Empire, finding in the Atlanticist policy the conclusive and coherent landing of their political itinerary. The fundamental contradiction which hindered the movement in the aftermath of its onset was the fact of being led by a group of young people without strong theoretical gear and a consequent political strategy, at the same time as having to face within the organisation the strong influence of a substantial number of subscribers who identified with Atlanticism.

This contradiction is well expressed in the memorandum of 9 July sent to Kimber and Curtis by Herbert Brewer, who remarked on how the interest and support which Federal Union had gained in such a brief space of time, were not due to the theoretical federalism of the inter-war years, but to the publication of *Union Now*. What made the volume by Streit "the greatest book of the century" was not its argument but the fact that it combined "a comprehensive grasp of fundamental truths and principles," with a "definite, detailed and practical" plan, "capable of being realised now."[5]

Federal Union should declare how it stood "in relation to the only clear plan and policy" which then existed "for uniting the world on federal lines." The July meeting had been a wonderful school of federalist faith and theory, but it had failed to define a programme of action. Yet the declaration of the guiding-principles was in perfect accord with the Streitian project, and Federal Union published in the form of a pamphlet the first chapter of *Union Now*, being unable to publish an economic edition of the entire volume. The growing success showed that Federal Union had "passed out of the stage of poetic aspiration and philosophical speculation into that of political action." In order to convert public opinion to federalism it was not enough to discuss principles. The movement had to study their "detailed application," and sooner or later express a clear judgement on the Streitian project.[6]

---

[5] CP, 18/70-4.
[6] *Ibidem.*

Kimber did not wait to meet Curtis before replying to Brewer, and on 20 July he sent him a letter—sending Curtis a copy—in which he distanced himself from the Streitian project as it had been formulated. Federal Union was for the immediate creation of a federation of all the democracies ready to join, including the United States, but it could not demand as a condition the simultaneous adhesion of all fifteen democracies. It was necessary to create, as soon as possible, a federal nucleus of willing democracies. Moreover, Streit's draft Constitution was according to Kimber too closely modelled on that of the United States. The Constitution of the union should be drafted by a Constituent Assembly, composed of the representatives of the federal peoples.[7]

Curtis realised then that it was no longer possible to keep the three young founders of the movement under control, and turned to Lothian, who was leaving for the United States, asking him to take the three young men for lunch in order to "strengthen" his hand, and to make them overcome their "latent jealousy of Streit as an American," since it could be "very dangerous." Writing to Brewer on 22 July, after having met Kimber, Curtis tried to reassure him, although with some embarrassment:

> The task which Federal Union has set before itself, is I believe the greatest and most important in the world. It is like a mountain which has to be climbed. A mountain has many aspects, and the people who join in the movement all see the task before them from slightly different angles; you from one perhaps, Kimber from another. If all climb as best they can, you will meet at the top. I see a somewhat different aspect from Kimber, but it is no more than a question of emphasis. We can all work for the same object, even though we work in slightly different ways. The task is so great that it admits of some difference in approach.[8]

Kimber was then expending a lot of energy for the movement, and according to Curtis it was important "to prevent fissures starting in a young organisation." Curtis failed however to persuade Kimber to invite Streit to Great Britain to give some talks on *Union Now*. The visit would have been "a good investment for Federal Union," as shown by a cheque of £1,000 from a keen Atlanticist, which had just come to strengthen the poor finances of the movement. Curtis, however, did succeed in dissuading Kimber from presenting candidates who represented Federal Union to the General Elections at University constituencies. Kimber, however, continued to think that the movement's participation in elections

---

[7] CP, 18/85, 84, 118-20, 116.

[8] Curtis to Kimber, 22 July, and Kimber to Curtis, 25 July 1939, CP, 18/117, 121; CP, 18/77-8.

would increase its impact on public opinion. It would then be able to rely, in the House of Commons, on a nucleus of members "dedicated to the cause of Federal Union, and to that alone." Federal Union was "essentially a young men's movement," and Curtis preferred not to figure as its representative, continuing to work from a rear-guard position, and concentrating his energies on Chatham House.[9]

The tension between Curtis and Kimber grew at the end of August, as the Molotov-Ribbentrop Pact consumed the fate of Poland, in spite of the signing on 25 August of the Anglo-French Treaty of Guarantee, and Chamberlain seemed determined not to face a new Munich. In fact, the British Government had already sent Hitler signals of firmness, reintroducing conscription—for the first time during peacetime in British history—and accelerating rearmament which, since the publication of the 1936 White Paper—used by Hitler as a pretext for the remilitarization of the Rhineland—had indeed never met setbacks. It seems appropriate to mention here that despite the strong opposition of the Labour Party, it was precisely Chamberlain, Chancellor of the Exchequer from 1931 to 1937, who advocated the need to allocate for this purpose three hundred and ninety-four million pounds for five years, part of which would be covered by public loans, thus deeply reviewing a pre-Keynesian conception of financial policy, according to which a budget's deficit represented "the high road that leads to destruction." Great Britain would have achieved, according to Chamberlain, a position of relative military strength only from the winter of 1938-1939, and only then could she hold a more firm line against Hitler. It was only in February 1939 that the British Government approved the creation of a Continental Expeditionary Force, and Great Britain found itself at war with just two infantry divisions and one armoured division which were badly equipped.[10]

---

[9] Curtis to Kimber, 18 Aug. 1939, CP, 18/207; 14 Aug. 1939, CP, 18/179, 212; 21 Aug. 1939, CP, 18/179, 212.
[10] See the letter of 11 Sept. 1938 by Chamberlain to his sister Ida, Keith Feiling, *Life of Neville Chamberlain* (London: Macmillan, 1947), 324. On the question of military strategy and British rearmament during the second half of the 1930s, see: John Dunbabin, "British Rearmament in the 1930s: A Chronology and Review," *Historical Journal*, 18, 3, (1975): 587-605; Francesco D'Ovidio, "Politica e strategia britannica nel Mediterraneo, 1936-1939," *Storia e Politica*, 15, 3, (1976); G. C. Peden, "Sir Warren Fisher and British Rearmament Against Germany," *English Historical Review*, 94, (1979): 29-47; Uri Bialer, "Elite Opinion and Defence Policy: Air Power Advocacy and British Rearmament During the 1930s," *British Journal of International Studies*, 6, 1, (1980): 32-54; R. A. C. Parker,

War seemed in fact only a matter of days, being by then manifest from the failure of the Anglo-Franco-Soviet military talks of late August, and the Bristol branch of Federal Union sent Chamberlain, and members of the Government—without asking Kimber for authorization—a telegram published by the *Bristol Evening Post* of 25 August, asking "to sponsor Lord Lothian's policy, 'Ending Armageddon', outlined in Streit's remarkable book, 'Union Now'." The Bristol branch sent members of the Cabinet a copy of Lothian's article, and to Lothian himself a message of good wishes for his mission via radio.[11]

As a consequence of this bold action, Curtis went off the deep end, reminding Kimber that such an irresponsible action would not have facilitated the difficult task which Lothian was going to undertake in the United States. On the result of Lothian's mission could depend "the very existence of the British Commonwealth." The leaders of Federal Union should not embarrass an ambassador at the most difficult and critical moment of his career. Kimber replied, on 4 September, that he was not responsible for the decisions of just one out of the 45 branches of what had already become a lively popular movement. Kimber enclosed the draft of a resolution by the Council, according to which mankind had a common destiny, and a common government had to be created to solve the common questions. The Federal government should be democratic and, once the Nazi regime was overthrown, Germans should become members of it. On

---

"British Rearmament 1936-1939: Treasury, Trade Unions and Skilled Labour," *English Historical Review*, 96, (1981): 306-39.

[11] CP, 19. On the British guarantee to Poland, see Butler, Orde and Woodward, *Documents on British*, 12, doc. n. 309: 249-50; Robert C. Self, *Neville Chamberlain: A Biography* (London: Ashgate Publishing, 2006). On the British, French, and Polish reactions to the Ribbentrop-Molotov Pact, see Butler, Orde and Woodward, *Documents on British*, 12, doc. n. 99-211: 96-177. On the failure of the Anglo-French-Soviet military talks, see FOP, C 11776/3356/18, and Butler, Orde and Woodward, *Documents on British*, 12, doc. n. 1-98: 1-95. On Chamberlain and British rearmament, see: B. E. V. Sabine, "The Six Budgets of Neville Chamberlain, 1932-1937," *British Tax Review*, 4, (1981): 223-42; A. J. Robertson, "British Rearmament and Industrial Growth, 1935-1939," *Research in Economic History*, 8, (1982): 279-91; Gaines Post, "Mad Dogs and Englishmen: British Rearmament, Deterrence and Appeasement, 1934-35," *Armed Forces*, 14, 3, (1988): 329-44; J. P. Harris, "British Armour and Rearmament in the 1939s," *Journal of Strategic Studies*, 11, 2, (1988): 220-45; David G. Anderson, "British Rearmament and the 'Merchants of Death': 1935-1936," *Journal of Contemporary History*, 29, 1, (1994): 5-38; N. J. Crowson, "Conservative Parliamentary Dissent Over Foreign Policy During the Premiership of Neville Chamberlain: Myth or Reality?," *Parliamentary History*, 14, 3, (1995): 315-29.

the basis of this document, which contained the first declaration of war
aims by any British political organisation, Federal Union would begin the
campaign to widen popular consent to the federal plan. Curtis endorsed the
document, thus giving his imprimatur to the policy of the movement, but
was already looking for an alternative leadership to that of Kimber,
intensifying contacts with Melville Channing-Pearce—Secretary of the
Oxford branch, and Principal of South Leigh College, who had openly
supported Streit's scheme—in order replace Kimber at the first occasion.[12]

III. *The Organising Conference and first struggle for the Secretaryship*

Kimber should have been replaced during the Organising Conference of
23-24 September. Channing-Pearce had the idea of the conference after
visiting the headquarters of the movement at 44 Gordon Square.

---

[12] CP, 19/1, 5. Melville Channing-Pearce (1886-1969) studied at Canterbury and
Worcester College, Oxford. During the First World War he had been captain in the
Fourth Regiment Dorset; Private Secretary of the British High Commissioner in
Iraq until 1924, and then founded and directed the Swiss Alpine College and the
Oxonian College, both being high schools for young Swiss students. He published
Chiron or the Education of a Citizen of the World (London: 1931); *The Religion of
Youth* (London: 1934); *Religion and Reality* (London: 1937); *Federal Union. A
Symposium* (Oxford: Oxford University Press, 1943). The secretaries of the
branches of the Federal Union up to August, were: C. T. Chambers (Bedfordshire),
Basil Sutton (West Berkshire and North Wiltshire), D. L. Graham (East Berkshire
and Buckinghamshire), E. M. W. Tillyard (Cambridgeshire), Olaf Stapledon
(Merseyside), Valentine Davis (Cheshire), Russel V. Uren (Cornwall), M. Piper
(Derbyshire), R. E. Hope Simpson (Dorset), D. Neylan (Devon), H. Brewer (East
Essex), E. A. Berthond (West Essex, East Hertfordshire), J. R. M. Morrice
(Gloucestershire), R. Lloyd (Hampshire), James Agers (Herefordshire), J. E.
Williams (West Hertfordshire and Central Buckinghamshire), B. Lorsignol (Kent),
A. H. Wallace (Lancashire), F. Sikes (Lincolnshire), L. A. Howlett (Middlesex), J.
M. Hastings (Norfolk), M. Walker (Northamptonshire), N. Goodson (West
Oxfordshire), R. Channing-Pearce (South Oxfordshire), H. B. Huntley, N. Lowe
and R. W. Trowbridge (Somerset), L. Parry Griffiths (Staffordshire), H. R. Morris
(Suffolk), D. W. Tweddle (West Surrey), L. G. Ashworth (East Surrey), Rathbone
(North Surrey), H. MacMaster (Sussex), Henry C. Usborne (Warwickshire), L. G.
Harris (Worcestershire), F. Akroyl, J. H. Dufty, A. Hayese and P. Hendy (West
Riding), D. J. I. West (North Riding), R. A. Allan (Glasgow), C. R. Dunford
(Edinburgh), R. V. Williams (Wales), E. Washbrook (London N.1), S. Wilson
(London N.6), S. Fox (London N.W. 2, 3, 6, 8) and C. Dowson (London N.W. 4, 9,
11), CP, 18/144-5; CP, 162; CP, 19/15-7, 35-6.

Channing-Pearce reported to Curtis that he found it in "total chaos." In order to avoid the movement becoming "another vague and ineffectual" organisation, a new galvanizing leadership was necessary. Kimber accepted Channing-Pearce's offer to organise the conference in his college, unaware that with Curtis he would launch an attack on his role as secretary. Curtis's help would be decisive and would light "another candle in England," which would never be extinguished, because it was going to generate "a dynamic drive of released faith," with "the latent power to change history and that within a year." Everything depended "on what we do over this week-end."[13]

Channing-Pearce was ready "to take hold" of Federal Union: "I know that this is my work, and I know that I (or, rather, some force latent and only now rising in me) could do it." Kimber was not fit for the job and there was "no-one on the field," because Ransome was a "heroic cripple," and Rawnsley was "for practical purposes, out of the picture." Channing-Pearce thought that Kimber and his staff would accept the changing of the guard: "The thing needs a leader; I believe that the fate of the world—no less—depends upon that leadership being found; I know that I ought to lead it and can lead it." It was necessary to give him a wage of £1,000 to £1,500 per year, however, because he had to support five sons, and if the college closed because of the war, the Government would have allocated it to other functions. The "blessing" by Curtis was necessary to let his spirit rise to the historic task: "If this thing is to happen it will happen and I shall know my way; I shall not shirk it. Then I shall not forget what you have done and said or your vision."[14]

Even though Curtis did not guarantee his support, he agreed to intervene on the 23 September with a speech at the inaugural meeting of the Oxford branch of Federal Union, in which two hundred people took part. Speaking as an Old Testament prophet, Curtis opened by saying that he was going to present the conclusions he had reached in thirty years of research and thinking. In political matters, it was dangerous to decide which steps to follow before deciding the goal to reach: "I have done this so often that people put me down as a dreamer with eyes fixed on a distant future remote from immediate interests."[15]

The aim of human history was the full achievement of freedom— the "reign of law"—with which the "rule of force"—the "power of the strongest to decide disputes in his own interest"—would be replaced. This revolution had been accomplished at the national level, and the time had

---

[13] Channing-Pearce to Curtis, 18, 19 and 20 Sept. 1939, CP, 19/37, 46-8.
[14] CP, 128/229-30.
[15] CP, 128/19/74.

come to extend it to the international one. The profound significance of the
war was to create "a bridge towards the ultimate goal"—not a new
Covenant, "which opened an abyss of Anarchy"—but the creation of the
nucleus of the world federation.[16]

Also held on 23-24 September in Oxford was the Organising
Conference of the movement, which *The Times* of 25 September widely
reported. It was attended by Robert Byron, Curtis, Lancelot Hogben, C. E.
M. Joad, Wickham Steed and Barbara Wootton; six members of the
Oxford branch, including Sir William Beveridge; nineteen representatives
of the local branches; as well as Kimber and Ransome. In opening the
proceedings, on the evening of Saturday 23 September, Kimber recalled
the genesis of the movement, remarking that the outbreak of war had
overturned the strategy, making the federation no longer a preventive
factor, but a consequence of the war. The object of the movement should
be to include federalism in the peace aims for which Great Britain was
fighting. The movement should focus its objective on getting the
Government to propose an immediate Anglo-French federation as the
nucleus of a European federation at the end of the war. The creation of the
union would rationalise the allied war effort and favour the growth of
internal opposition to the Nazi regime. On the basis of such a union, the
war would be shortened by years, and the neutral countries would be
encouraged to join the union, as they would be convinced of the honesty of
the Allies.[17]

---

[16] *Ibidem.*

[17] Barbara Frances Wootton (1897-1988) had been a researcher at the headquarters
of the Labour Party, from 1922 to 1925, Director of Morley College, London, from
1926 to 1927, and Professor of Social Studies and Director of Studies at the
University of London, from 1927 to 1944. From 1967 to 1988 she had been Vice-
Chairman of the House of Lords. Robert Byron (1905-1941) was a correspondent
of various papers from India, China, and the Soviet Union; author of *The Road to
Oxiana* (1937), public relations officer at the Petroleum Information Bureau, from
1936 to 1939, and at the BBC, from 1939 to 1941. Lancelot Hogben (1895-1975),
was Professor of Zoology at the University of Cape Town, from 1927 to 1930;
Professor of Biology at the University of London, from 1930 to 1937; Professor of
Natural History at the University of Aberdeen, from 1937 to 1941; Professor of
Zoology at the University of Birmingham, from 1941 to 1947; and Professor of
Medical Statistics at the University of Birmingham, from 1947 to 1961. On the
debate in those months on the development of the Anglo-French Union, see: O.
Gollancz, "Practical Steps Towards Anglo-French Union," *New Commonwealth
Quarterly*, 5, (1939): 286-95; J. T. Delos, "L'Union Franco-Britannique," *New
Commonwealth Quarterly*, 5, (1939): 296-304; A. B. Keith, "Constitutional
Aspects of Anglo-French Union," *New Commonwealth Quarterly*, 5, (1939): 263-

The debate recorded two conflicting political lines. The first, advocated by Beveridge and Tillyard, supported the urgency of a declaration by the Government of war aims. The second, advocated by Brewer, Hogben, Neylan, Henry Usborne and T. G. Usborne, supported the necessity of creating, during the war, a union either with France, the Scandinavian countries, or the United States. Channing-Pearce criticised both these positions, and observed that the force of the movement was proportional to its coherence, and therefore it was imperative to operate an "evangelization of the federalist faith." Declarations of war aims seemed completely useless, and the only practical achievement attainable during the war was the immediate federation of Great Britain, Australia and New Zealand. Sanders, secretary of the notorious Bristol branch, supported Channing-Pearce's view, and observed that the reason for the existence of the movement transcended the war. The movement had to investigate the specific features of the federation.[18]

Beveridge at last was asked to draft a document which expressed the political line of the movement in unequivocal terms. Approved with minor formal amendments, the document stated that the standing objective of Federal Union was

> directly and by co-operation with similar organisations in other countries, to secure acceptance of the principles of federal union in any democratic

75; George Keeton, "Anglo-French Union: A Suggestion," *New Commonwealth Quarterly*, 5, (1939): 230-41.

[18] CP, 162/26-62. Henry Charles Usborne (1909-1996) was Labour MP for Acock's Green, Birmingham, from 1945 to 1950; for Birmingham Yardley, from 1950 to 1959; and in 1946 he created the British Parliamentary Group for World Government (1946). Of Henry Usborne, who played a major role in the inter-war British federalist movement, see: *A Warning and a Way Round: The Case for a Minimal Federation of Nations* (Birmingham: Minifed Publications, 1980); id., "A History of the British Parliamentary Group for World Government," in *The Federal Idea*, 2: 113-30. For a critical analysis, see: Joseph Baratta, "Henry Usborne and the Creation of the World Movement for World Federal Government," in *The Federal Idea*, 2: 81-110; John C. de V. Roberts, *World Citizenship and Mundialism: A Guide to the Building of a World Community* (Westport, CT: Praeger, 1999): 76-8; April Carter, *Political Theory of Global Citizenship* (London: Routledge, 2001), 144-5. On Australia at war, see: Michael McKernan, *The Strength of a Nation: Six Years of Australians Fighting For the Nation and Defending the Homefront in World War II* (London: Allen & Unwin, 2007). On the impact of Streit's plan in Australia, see A. H. Charteris, "An Australian Comment on Streit's Union," *New Commonwealth Quarterly*, 5, (1939): 314-28.

countries with a view to the union of such democracies in accord with
these principles at any time.

The movement would continue "to pursue this objective by all
appropriate means." Federal Union had to promote the inclusion, in the
official declarations on the war aims, of both Great Britain and other
countries, of the federal idea and the "readiness" to create with "any
country now belligerent or neutral" a federal union, "including Britain."
This document took for granted the knowledge of the working of the
federal government.[19]

As for moving the headquarters from London to Oxford,
Channing-Pearce suggested contacting the warden of Manchester College,
while Curtis offered Rhodes House, where ten rooms were available.
Kimber rejected both offers, since the headquarters needed at least
fourteen rooms. A provisional Council of fourteen members was elected,
and included Wootton, Wickham Steed, Lancelot Hogben, Robert Byron,
Joad, Kimber, Ransome, Rawnsley, Hamilton Fyfe, Henry Usborne,
Channing-Pearce, Sir John Orr, and Julian Huxley. An Executive
Committee including Wootton, Kimber, Richard Law, Ransome and
Hogben, was also set up. The first task of the Council was to draft the
Constitution of the movement, and to revise the statement of the guiding-
principles. Kimber was elected provisional Secretary of the Council and
the Executive Committee.[20]

The debate on the relation between the centre and the branches clearly
revealed the heterogeneity of the movement, due to its spontaneous and
tumultuous growth all over the country. The objectives followed by local

---

[19] CP, 162/26-62.

[20] *Ibidem.* Henry Hamilton Fyfe (1869-1951) was a journalist at *The Times*, from
1889 to 1902; Editor of the *Morning Advertiser*, from 1902 to 1903; the *Daily
Mirror*, from 1903 to 1907; special correspondent of the *Daily Mail*, from 1907 to
1918; Editor of the *Daily Herald*, from 1922 to 1926; and columnist of *Reynolds
News*, from 1930 to 1942. Lord John Boyd Orr (1880-1971) was Director of the
Rowett Research Institute, and Professor of Agriculture at the University of
Aberdeen, from 1942 to 1945; he was the first Director of the United Nations Food
and Agriculture Organisation, from 1945 to 1948. He was awarded the Nobel
Peace Prize in 1949, and was raised to the House of Lords in the same year. Sir
Julian Huxley (1887-1975) was Professor of Biology at Oxford, from 1919 to
1925; and at King's College, London, from 1925 to 1935. He was Secretary of the
Zoological Society, from 1935 to 1942. Richard Kidston Law, Baron Coleraine of
Haltemprice (1901-1980), was Conservative MP for Hull, from 1931 to 1945; for
South Kensington, from 1945 to 1950; and for Hull Haltemprice, from 1950 to
1954.

leaders had been inhomogeneous, and they had developed relations with the headquarters for organisational reasons only. In fact, the branches developed their activities independently and sometimes—as in the case of the Bristol branch—in conflict with the centre. The absence of guidelines, the vast success of Streit's volume, the publication of *The Ending of Armageddon*—in support of the Streitian plan—the absence of a "popular" version of the statement of the guiding-principles, and the lack of a subscription fee, favoured the birth and development of federalist groups which barely co-ordinated among themselves. They continued to consider federalism as a simple remedy to an emergency situation. It was a 'spontaneous' federalism, which had to be organised in a movement. The aim of the Conference was, according to Curtis, to transform Federal Union from a shapeless and irregular organisation into a "definite and regular" one.[21]

It was Channing-Pearce—at the suggestion of Curtis, drawing on the experience of the Round Table—who pointed out the nature of the choice. On the one hand, they could follow the orthodox federal doctrine with activities of research and dissemination, a decentralised structure, small headquarters, and strong autonomous local groups. On the other hand, they could create a mass movement with an aggressive propagandistic action, building a centralised structure, a strong leadership, and several branches with limited autonomy. The questions of strategy and procedure were closely connected.

The debate confirmed however the differences of opinion. On the one hand, there were the supporters—headed by Curtis—of an *élite* movement, and on the other, those—headed by Kimber—of a mass movement. At the end a compromise was found, but it left the positions unchanged, and in the following months, they were bound to clash. Kimber, who had come out of the Conference as a winner, and greatly strengthened within the Council, proposed that the branches should remain fully autonomous. The Executive Committee accepted the proposal, and was charged with the responsibility of raising comments, and circulating them among the Council members, and the branch secretaries. The branches had to be small, grouped by geographical areas, and in direct contact with the centre. War did not allow the creation of an organisational system which allowed the branches total autonomy. If concrete results had to be achieved, Federal Union had to become a mass movement, in spite of the small financial resources, and the amateurism of its local leaders. The conference accepted Kimber's proposal not to determine a fixed subscription fee, but to

---

[21] CP, 162/26-62.

continue the self-financing practice at the local level, leaving the branches to send the excess of their income over expenditure to the centre each month.[22]

In spite of the defeat, Curtis wrote to Channing-Pearce on the 26th September, that he left the conference "most hopeful":

> Thanks heaven you were elected at the Council. The next step should be to get some people who really count co-opted to support you...If people in the branches are to do their work the Central Office must send them out proper munitions, and not merely arm them with leaflets suitable for the kind of people who read the *Daily Mail*.

Channing-Pearce, however, did not seem to share Curtis's satisfaction with the outcome of the Conference, and asked for Curtis's support in order to be elected onto the Executive Committee, in the event promising he would work full-time for the movement starting in January.[23]

The first meeting of the Council elected by the Conference was held in London on 4 October, with Curtis, Hogben, Kimber, Joad, Channing-Pearce, Ransome, Wickham Steed, H. Usborne, Richard Lawe, and Wootton present. A statement of aims was approved. Curtis proposed that the Executive Committee should elect a treasurer, and Channing-Pearce offered his candidature. The Committee also proposed to elect a public relations officer, with a wage of £600 a year. All the propagandist material published by the branches had to obtain authorisation from the centre.[24]

---

[22] *Ibidem*. The income of Federal Union, from 28 July to 30 September, was £1,469, of which £1,258 came from subscriptions, £73 from the sales of literature, £125 from the balance till 28 July, and £11 from various other incomes. Of the £776 spent, £16 went to the rent of the headquarters, £232 to wages, £118 to stationery, £37 to post and telephone, £54 to the purchasing of furniture for the office, £10 to the assistance of employers, £16 to travel expenses, £119 to advertising, £25 to Rawnsley's mission to Geneva, and £54 to various other expenditures. The excess of income over expenditure—£693—had been provisionally transferred, for security and convenience purposes, to the United States (CP 19/53-9).

[23] CP, 19/76, 80.

[24] CP 19/145-8. On the role played by Curtis within Federal Union, see: Clarence Streit, "Lionel Curtis: The Federalist," *Freedom and Union*, 9, 4, (1949): 8-9; id., "Lionel Curtis: Prophet of Federal Union," *Freedom and Union*, 16, 1, (1956): 10-11.

IV. *The development of the movement's activities*

The newsletter of the movement, *Federal Union News*, under the provisional editorship of John Usborne—brother of Henry, who played a leading role in the activities of the Birmingham branch, and in the post-war development of the world dimension of British federalism—just appeared at the beginning of September, a few days after the outbreak of the war. Although it was printed with an apparent poverty of means, it aimed to stimulate and focus the action of militants, and make its readers feel part of a growing organisation. The magazine hosted leaders and articles by prominent exponents of the movement, offered information on significative facts and book reviews, and a large section was devoted to the activities of the branches. The first issue, dated 5 September, was only four pages long, but was full of messages and news. "NOW," the slogan on the front page ran "we say, is the time for Union, because the world is sick and Union is the only efficient purge for its poisoned system."

The readers were informed that a "Comité d'Action Pour l'Union Fédérale des Peuples Libres" had been created in Paris, and the situation seemed favourable also in Holland, Belgium, Switzerland, and the Dominions for the creation of federalist organisations. The summer school of the Liberal Party and the Peace Pledge Union included the federalist project in their discussion on war aims, producing the effect of increasing the membership of Federal Union. Distinguished politicians, intellectuals, and churchmen had signed the document of the guiding-principles. The BBC was to broadcast, on 12 September, a programme to debate the federalist project, including Streit from the United States, Robert Byron from London, and Alfred Zimmern from Geneva. Members had doubled during the last two months, reaching 2,500.[25]

---

[25] *Federal Union News*, 1. The most distinguished members of the Federal Union at the outbreak of the war were: Lord Astor, Sir Herbert Baker, Norman Bentwich, Ernest Bevin, Sir Montague Burton, the Bishop of Chichester, E. F. M. Durbin, George Emorfopoulos, H. Hamilton Fyfe, Sir Richard Gregory, Lynda Grier, J. L. Hammond, Lancelot Hogben, Julian Huxley, Storm Jameson, Cyril E. M. Joad, E. McKnight Kauffer, Richard Law, B. H. Liddel-Hart, Scott Lidgett, Lord Marley, R. M. Holland-Martin, B. Kingsley Martin, Ramsay Muir, Sir Walter Napier, Sir John Orr, J. B. Priestley, C. E. Raven, Lady Rhondda, Lionel Robbins, Sir Charles Grant Robertson, Seebohm Rowntree, Sir Thomas Drummond Shiels, Wickham Steed, Sir Ernest Swinton, Arnold Toynbee, C. V. Usborne, Sir John Fischer Williams, Vaughan Williams, Barbara Wootton, and the Archbishop of York, *CP*, 18/194. On the Peace Pledge Union, see: Roy Walker, *The Organisation of Peace Pledge Union Meetings* (London: Peace Pledge Union, 1939); William Over, *World Peace, Mass Culture and National Policies* (Westport, CT: Praeger

The second issue, published on 18 September, outlined for the militants the strategy which the movement would follow during the war: it was not enough to oppose force with force, it was necessary "to supplement armed force with the most disruptive and revolutionary of all weapons: the truth." "Though peace is dead," ran the headline, "Federal Union most certainly is not." It was up to militants "to see that all men knew it." The RAF was doing a wonderful job in reminding the Germans, with the dropping of leaflets, "why the British people cannot trust Hitler." They had to do more: to ask Germans "to get rid of Hitler," and to show them how only federation could guarantee equality of rights and security. Federal Union had however the historic task of convincing "the British government that the Germans should be offered Federal Union as the alternative to Hitler." Federal Union's voice would become louder "as our membership grows." It was imperative to enhance their efforts in order to gain public opinion of the federalist cause. They might seem like idle dreams. But there were many, north of the English Channel, to not consider them as such.[26]

The period of the "phoney war" allowed further progress to be made, and for Federal Union to return to Gordon Square from Dorset where the office had been evacuated on government advice to organisations not essential to the war effort. There was great activity in October. Reports from the branches give us a picture of what was going on in the country. The Edinburgh branch multiplied its membership tenfold, thereby bringing their number up to 100. Various personalities, including Sir Robert Grieg—Vice-Chancellor of Edinburgh University—Sir Herbert Grierson, Charles Warr, J. G. Jameson, and D. S. Cairns, gave their support. The *Scotsman* published fourteen letters on Federal Union, including one from a German student who had recently returned from the United States. The student was very enthusiastic about the idea of a European federation, and thought that it should be made known to Germans as part of British war

Publishers, 2004); David P. Barash and Charles P. Wabel, *Peace and Conflict Studies* (London: Sage Publications, 2002); David L. Clough and Brian Stiltner, *Faith and Force: A Christian Debate about War* (Washington, DC: Georgetown University Press, 2007). On the BBC during WWII, see: Richard Havers, *Here Is the News: The BBC and the Second World War* (London: Sutton Publishing, 2007).
[26] On the RAF at war, see: Michael Eliot Howard, *Strategic Deception in the Second World War* (New York: W.W. Norton & Company, 1995); Denis Richards, *RAF Bomber Command in the Second World War: The Hardest Victory* (London: Penguins Books, 2002); Martin Bowman, *Scramble: Memoirs of the RAF in the Second World War* (London: Tempus, 2006).

aims. He was convinced that with serious backing from the British Government, it would have tremendous support from his people.[27]

A branch had just been formed thanks to the initiative of Olaf Stapledon in Manchester. In Norwich, leaflets had been distributed at the railway station. At Melbourne, Derbyshire, the militants tried "to make two converts a day," resorting to all methods, principally the Socratic one, "on a bus, for example." At Oxford, a conference by Curtis—a "prophet not without honour in his own country"—was so well attended that Wickham Steed had to sit on the floor. At Beaminster, in Dorset, the initiative of another University teacher, Dr. Hope-Simpson, generated a press campaign on the *Bridport News*.[28]

The Birmingham branch, which "attained an almost mythical reputation for furious energy" with which it developed its activities, under the inspiring leadership of Henry Usborne, was organising a vast membership campaign by circulating Federal Union literature to "2,000 influential Midlanders." The Rotary Club, which was doing such great propaganda work for Federal Union all over the country, was devoting three successive lunches to a debate on federalism. In Bedfordshire, a new branch was created on 22 October, on the occasion of a speech by Professor Eustace M. W. Tillyard from Jesus College, Cambridge, and in co-operation with the pacifist organisations Peace Pledge Union, and Fellowship of Reconciliation. In South Devon, at Reading and at Winchester, memberships increased due to the enthusiasm of local militants such as Canon Lloyd, Lawrence Waddy and Mr. Sutton. A University branch had been created in Sheffield and at Cambridge some student groups were in the process of being formed.[29]

In London, even though it was not possible to organise many public meetings—"no black-out can darken the enthusiasm of a fast-growing membership for gathering at one another's flats and houses"—T. G. Usborne gave a lecture in German at the Friends Hall of Hampstead to a group of refugees. In the house of C. E. M. Joad, a meeting was held on 14 October, where forty members, including Kimber, were present. "A speakers' class" was started for those who wished to address small

---

[27] On Scotland at war, see: Andrew Jeffrey, *This Time of Crisis: Glasgow, the West of Scotland and the Northwestern Approaches in the Second World War* (Edinburgh: Mainstream Publishing, 1994); Simon Wood, *Scotland and the Second World War* (London: Hodder Gibson, 1997); Derek Young, *Scottish Voices from the Second World War* (London: Tempus, 2006).

[28] *Federal Union News*, 2.

[29] *Ibidem.*

meetings and "make themselves *au fait* with all the arguments for and against federal Union."[30]

The technique of the "snowball," and the most intense "word-of-the-mouth-cum-pamphlet propaganda" was being rewarded with astonishing success. The Hampstead group was particularly active, but the palm of the month went to the newly-formed Peckham group "conducted on communal lines," which produced thousands of little typed slips of paper bearing the sentence: "*Have you heard of* Federal Union?" They were left everywhere, from seats in public vehicles, and in library books, to the counters of shops.[31]

The Harrow branch decided to ask members to write a personal letter to the Prime Minister asking him to include the federal project in the peace aims. "Notes for speakers" were available at the headquarters, and anybody who wanted to discuss any issue with the national leaders, could meet them from 6.00 to 8.00 pm at the "The Marlborough" pub in Torrington Place, near Goodge Street station. Federal Union branches had also been formed in France, Switzerland, New Zealand, Tasmania, the United States and the Scandinavian countries.[32]

An economists' Conference was held on 21-22 October at University College, Oxford. Beveridge, Robbins, Wootton, F. A. von Hayek, E. F. M. Durbin, J. M. Fleming, R. F. Harrod, and the future Prime Minister James Harold Wilson discussed "the economic aspects of a federal solution to the problem of peace and world order." The conference was to elaborate on a scheme to apply the federal idea to concrete problems, and to pave the way, on a theoretical basis, to the creation of the federation.[33]

---

[30] *Ibidem.*

[31] *Federal Union News*, 3, 4.

[32] *Federal Union News*, 5.

[33] *Federal Union News*, 6. See the proceedings of the Conference in Ransome, *Towards the United States.* On New Zealand at war, see: John Crawford, *Kia Kaka: New Zealand in the Second World War* (New York: Oxford University Press, 2002); Ian McGibbon, *New Zealand and the Second World War: The People, the Battles and the Legacy* (Auckland: Hodder Moa Beckett, 2004). On Harold Wilson, see: Austen Morgan, *Harold Wilson: A Life* (London: LPC Group, 1992); Ben Pimlott, *Harold Wilson* (London: Harper Collins Publishers, 1993). On the impact of federalist ideas on Wilson's post-war European policy, see: Helen Parr, *British Policy Towards the European Community: Harold Wilson and Britain's World Role, 1964-1967* (London: Routledge, 2005); Oliver Daddow, *Harold Wilson and European Integration: Britain's Second Application to Join the EEC* (London: Routledge, 2002); Melissa Pine, *Harold Wilson and Europe: Pursuing Britain's Membership of the European Community* (New York: Tauris

In November, thirty-two new branches were formed, thus increasing the number to one hundred and thirty four, with an increase of five hundred members per week. *The Case for Federal Union*, by W. B. Curry was published as a Penguin Special. More than six volumes were available: *Union Now*; *Civitas Dei* by Curtis; *The Federalist* by Hamilton, Jay and Madison; *Modern Democracies* by James Brice; *National Sovereignty and International Order* by G. W. Keeton; and *The Economic Planning and International Order* by Lionel Robbins. *Federal Union News*, now edited by Kimber, assisted by Dorothy Mears went from bi-monthly to weekly, and increased from four to eight pages. Thousands of Christmas cards wishing "a Federal Union year" were printed. Every day some thirty letters favourable to the federal project appeared in the national and local press all around the country. During the last week of November one hundred and fifty newspapers gave wide coverage to the activities of the movement. It was not an exaggeration to say—as did H. G. Wells—that the word federation had become "a magic catchword," and there was the danger that politicians and political parties "will use it in a different sense to which we in 'Federal Union' use it."[34]

In November university branches were formed at Oxford, Cambridge, London, Bristol, and Aberdeen. In Edinburgh, during a public meeting, Alec Douglas Home, Conservative MP and future Prime Minister, declared, in front of an audience of two hundred and fifty people that "to argue now whether one should be socialist, conservative or liberal is like arguing on the relative merits of facing towards or away from the engine in a train that is travelling at 70 m.p.h. to destruction." The playwright Richard Wessel wrote a fairy-story with a federalist moral, which was to appear on the screen of the Everyman Cinema, Hampstead, where the

Academic Studies, 2007); Jane Toomey, *Harold Wilson's Second EEC Application* (Dublin:, University College Dublin Press, 2007).

[34] *Federal Union News*, 7. William Burnley Curry (1900-62) was Director of the Dartington School (1931-57). *The Case of Federal Union* sold 100,000 copies. On the Women's International League, see: Catherine Foster, *Women for All Seasons: The Story of the Women's International League for Peace and Freedom* (Athens, GA: University of Georgia Press, 1989); Joyce Blackwell, *No Peace Without Freedom: Race and the Women's International League for Peace and Freedom, 1915-1975* (Carbondale, IL: Southern Illinois University Press, 2004). On the United Free Church Youth Movement see: Kenda Creasy Dean, *Practicing Passion: Youth and the Quest for a Passionate Church* (New York: Harper Collins, 2006). On the Industrial Christian Fellowship, see: Gerald Studdert-Kennedy, *Dog-Collar Democracy: The Industial Christian Fellowship, 1919-1929* (New York: Palgrave Macmillan, 1982); R. B. Y. Scott and Gregory Vlastos, *Towards the Christian Revolution* (Whitefish, MT: Kessinger Publishing, 2006).

public meetings of the local branch (with the London primacy of 112 members) were held.[35]

Since the movement was taking on an increasingly European identity, the branches frequently debated "the differences between Federal Union and *Union Now*." Joint activities with other organisations such as the League of Nations Union, the Women's International League for Peace and Freedom, the New Commonwealth Society, the United Free Church Youth Movement, the Peace Pledge Union, and the Industrial Christian Fellowship, were organised. A national competition for the best slogan for Federal Union, led them to choose between the following three: "The Allies may win the war. Only Federal Union can win the peace"; "Federated we flourish, separated we perish"; "We must federate or perish."[36]

The Birmingham branch printed and circulated a leaflet in German which outlined the federal project, identifying in the United States of Europe the aim which Allies were fighting for. Contacts with political refugees, particularly Germans, were intended to involve them in the activities of the movement. A federal hymn had been composed.[37]

V. *The second struggle for the Secretaryship*

With the increased size and influence of the movement, the internal struggle also became fiercer. Within the Council, a clear cut break had been created between Curtis and Channing-Pearce on one side, and Kimber, Wootton, Hogben, and Byron on the other. Writing to Kimber on the 5 October, Channing-Pearce portrayed the movement's situation as very critical, as an increasingly fast growing membership had "very little confidence" in the group of leaders. There were those who considered the movement "inefficient," or "too "secular"—without a defined religious impulse—and almost completely in the hands of people to whom religion "meant little or nothing." There were also those who criticised the leaders

---

[35] *Federal Union News*, 7. Alec Douglas-Home, *Our European Destiny* (London: Conservative Group for Europe, 1971); id., *The Way the Wind Blows: An Autobiography* (London: Times Book, 1977). On Douglas-Home, see: Richard Thorpe, *Alec Douglas-Home* (London: Sinclair-Stevenson, 1996); David Dutton, *Douglas Home* (London: Haus Publishers, 2006).
[36] *Federal Union News*, 7.
[37] *Ibidem.*

because they managed the enterprise not as a "crusade" but as "a business concern."[38]

Channing-Pearce therefore thought it necessary to permeate the Executive Committee with the "crusading' spirit," and for somebody who had organisational experience to aid Kimber. Since the members of the Executive Committee could not give Kimber more than advice, it appeared necessary to Channing-Pearce to propose a split in the responsibilities of the management of the movement, leading to a proper dyarchy. Channing-Pearce was persuaded he could control the majority of Council members, and decided to put up his own candidature to the Secretaryship. The success of the Oxford branch, of which he was Secretary, would be the best test to show his skills, with a view to transforming it as the new headquarters of the movement.[39]

In spite of a negative answer from Kimber, who did not accept the idea of the dyarchy, Channing-Pearce returned to the attack on 28 October, proposing the transfer of the headquarters to his college, and offering himself as Organising Secretary, with an annual wage of £600. He would occupy the vacant post of public relations officer, and his wife could take care of the office, for a total sum of £1,000. Channing-Pearce would control the selection and management of the staff of the headquarters; while Kimber would become treasurer, devoting himself full-time to fund-raising. The movement "would automatically fall into sound hands"—Channing-Pearce wrote to Curtis—he would prevent "wild local action" as the telegram stated from the Bristol branch, and also turned away the suspicion that Federal Union was "a mere nest of pacifists and hotheads." The situation made necessary "a considerable measure of wise autocracy," and for a charismatic personality "to lead and focus the faith." Channing-Pearce felt himself up to "the magnitude of the task," having "absolute certainty" that the time was "ripe for a Crusade." Having failed

---

[38] *Federal Union News*, 7, 8, 9, 10. CP, 19/109-13. On the diplomatic and war situation of autumn 1939, see: François Fonvieille-Alquier, *The French and the Phoney War, 1939-40* (London: T. Stacey, 1973); David Dilks, "Great Britain and Scandinavia in the Phoney War," *Scandinavian Journal of History*, 2, 1-2, (1987): 29-32; Thomas Munch-Petersen, *The Strategy of Phoney War, Britain Sweden and the Iron Ore Question, 1939-1940* (Stockholm: Militarhistoriska Forlaget, 1981); Murray Williamson, "The Strategy of the Phoney War: A Re-evaluation," *Military Affairs*, 4, 1, (1981): 13-21; Brian Bond, "The Calm Before the Storm: Britain and the Phoney War, 1939-1940," *Journal of the United Service Institution*, 135, 1, (1990): 61-75; Jean-Jacques Becker, "L'Europe dans la 'drôle de guerre'," *Histoire*, 129, (1990): 10-7.
[39] CP, 19/99-100.

to get support from other members of the Council—Law, Wickham Steed, Henry Usborne, and Ransome—he asked for intervention from Curtis.[40]

In order to gain the sympathy and support of Curtis, Channing-Pearce made the Oxford branch one of the best organised and most active in the Country. His propaganda campaign with the local press, the University, the Morris car factory, and the Pressed Steel Works, had been exemplary. In writing to members through weekly circular letters, Channing-Pearce asked them to put their "missionary" zeal into "the propagation of the federalist faith and the increase of active supporters." It was the moral duty of everybody to recruit "at least ten new members a month," from their own circles of friends and colleagues. The president of the branch was the city Mayor, J. H. Gillett. Curtis often spoke at public meetings, where some outstanding speakers included Richard Law, Wickham Steed, Beveridge, Sir Arthur Salter, and Sir Henry Lawrence. The literature produced by the branch also became available for the movement. Ransome had been recruited by Curtis in Oxford as an officer at the Foreign Press and Research Service.[41]

The strong link with the League of Nations Union—created by Kimber at the national level, in the ambitious attempt to make Federal Union the heir of the Union—gave some problems to Channing-Pearce, who on 15 October wrote a letter to the Editor of the *Oxford Times* to deny that Federal Union had "fallen into the hands of ex-League of Nations pacifists," with a reminder that he had fought in the First World War, and that in spite of being fifty-three years old, he was ready to leave for the front. Not only was he in charge of the organisation of the branch, but thanks to the intervention of Curtis, the publisher Cape offered him the editing of a volume on Federal Union, presenting to the reader the various aspects of federalist thought and action. In writing to Curtis on 10 October, he presented the volume as "the charter of federalism." He would accept the offer however only if the publisher paid him a fee, because the time necessary to complete the volume would take him away from his responsibility as Principal of the college. He still imagined that the Oxford branch would "become the Headquarters of the movement."[42]

Even though Curtis continued to oppose Kimber, he recognised in the twenty-six-year-old young man the same missionary spirit of his early

---

[40] CP, 19/164-7, 133-4, 151, 162-3.
[41] CP, 19/130, 116, 189-90, 135. Sir Henry Staveley Lawrence (1870-1949) was a member of the Indian *civil service*, from 1890 to 1921, and a member of the Council of India, from 1921 to 1926. On the League of Nations Union in those months, see Birn, *League of Nations*, 81-98.
[42] CP, 19/120, 124-5, 129-30.

days, and backed the offer from Beveridge to act as Chairman of the Executive Committee. Curtis then dropped his support for Channing-Pearce, who with some understandable resentment towards Curtis himself, threatened to resign.[43]

The extreme attempt by Curtis to gain Beveridge on his side also failed. In this circumstance, he resorted to Waldorf Astor, who in a letter to Beveridge of 20 November outlined the plan which he had in mind in order to re-organise the movement:

> I invited Lady Ravensdale and Hulton to lunch. I told her of my talk with you and Lionel Curtis and that I know considerable dissatisfaction existed with the running of Federal Union, an important body, as it is the main national organisation advocating the principles of Federalism. I further told her that you were prepared to give personal help and advice to a rejuvenated executive which possessed a Chairman of adequate status, that I had gathered that Kimber understood that the cause which he had genuinely at heart was likely to suffer if he continued to be its chief organiser and that consequently he was prepared to facilitate the appointment of a salaried secretary who should do a great deal of the work which has hitherto fallen to him. I told her that if a new executive with some person like herself in the Chair, with yourself and Kimber and two or three others, were set up a considerable number of people like myself would be prepared to lend our names as patrons and that then the movement could go forward with increased and increasing support. I told her I also thought it was desirable that somebody representing the Federal Union Movement should meet some representative of the League of Nations Union, and either arrange for a basis of cooperation, or at all events agree not to attack each other in public, but that it was essential to clear up the fundamental difference between Federalism and the existing Covenant...Lady Ravensdale has agreed to run down to Oxford and to meet you (and possibly Lionel Curtis should you think it is desirable) to talk over the whole situation.[44]

In a long letter to Curtis on 30 November, when the battle over the Secretaryship had by then concluded with his full victory, Kimber explained the reasons for his conduct, clarifying that Federal Union "can and should win the support of so many different interests and sections of opinion that I think it is extremely unlikely that one man can keep them

---

[43] CP, 20/17, 6, 18-9.

[44] CP, 20/33, 89-90. Waldorf Astor, Viscount Astor (1879-1952) was Conservative MP for Plymouth, from 1910 to 1919; President of the Royal Institute of International Affairs, 1921-1941; and proprietor of the *Observer*, from 1914 to 1950.

together." The activities of the movement were "so varied that no one man would have the knowledge or the time to direct them all unaided by a Committee." He needed

> a directing committee which meets frequently in order to keep him straight, and he will also have to have a departmental staff of experts to work out the details of the different schemes which it will be his job to set on foot.

A directorate rather than a single man could guarantee the movement that pluralism. Kimber intended to co-ordinate that directorate, without exercising any kind of personal control over the entire movement.[45]

Regarding Curtis's criticism of Kimber's alleged questionable judgement, for having moved the headquarters to Dorset, he replied with firmness against Curtis's "unjustified criticism" that "presumably therefore in any crisis" he was likely to lose his head again. Moreover, the evidence produced, that Kimber had "sent a telegram to prominent supporters asking if they would subscribe to a telegram to the Prime Minister," was "hardly sufficient for such a sweeping condemnation":

> The telegram may have been futile but I cannot see that it could discredit the movement...The evacuation...turned out to be a mistake, I do not deny, but to say more is, to say the very least, unjust...The second reason you gave was that I could not make use of older and more experienced men, and you based this on my treatment of...Mr. Channing-Pearce...I gave you reasons for certain doubts which had arisen in my mind but you were not disposed to consider them. In the light of events which have occurred since, I suggest that those doubts were well founded.[46]

Kimber resentfully wrote to Curtis:

> I would remind you that when I saw you about a week after the war began, in the course of a long talk you gave no suggestion of a loss of confidence, in fact the very opposite; yet when I met you a bare month later you told me that in the course of the previous six months your experiences of my activities had caused you to lose all confidence in me, that you were inclined to think I was not dishonest but you did consider me jealous and totally lacking in political judgement. I have given you my comments on these opinions, I hope reasonably and without bitterness, though I must confess that the memory of our last meeting is extremely sour. I know that it is your habit and your strength to paint things black and white, but I do ask you before you take a final and unalterable stand to consider the record

---

[45] CP, 20/78.
[46] CP, 20/79.

of Rawnsley, Ransome and myself. A record in which I claim my share. I do not think you recognise the amount of sound, solid and unbiased work which has been done, and I think you have made up your mind on very partial and slender evidence, without making any very great effort to get the full evidence or to verify facts.[47]

Due to the fact that he was a conscientious objector, Kimber was ready to leave the Secretaryship—as in fact he did in July 1940—in case a court decision should attract the attention of the press, and therefore damage the movement. Nobody could support the case, however, that Kimber had tried to transform Federal Union into a pacifist movement, and only the members who knew him intimately were aware of the fact that he was a conscientious objector. Kimber did not intend to keep the Secretaryship from everybody, but he was determined "to fight to the very last ditch to preserve Federal Union from sectionalism and from any distortion of the purposes" for which it had been founded:

In the early days, Rawnsley, Ransome and myself were faced with the difficulty of not being ever influenced by the partial views of the one or two more experienced people whom we succeeded in interesting. I think we can claim to have been moderately successful. Right and Left, Christians and humanists, militarists and pacifists, can still meet at 44 Gordon Square. The difficulties now are those connected with setting up a balanced directorate.[48]

Kimber was trying "to preserve Federal Union both from the direction of eminent men and women who, though experienced, influential and ready to pay lip service to Federal Union are not wholehearted Federalists," and therefore may "be prepared to compromise." But also "from those who though wholehearted Federalists, wish to attain it through some particular medium whether it be Socialism, Christianity or pacifism."[49]

In contrast the argument used by Curtis was that most success had been achieved because of the publication of *Union Now*, and Kimber acknowledged "the very great debt we owe" to Streit for the publicity which the book gained for the idea, but he did not believe Curtis could "at all appreciate how few people have succeeded in finishing the book or the intense suspicion which it has aroused in left wing and League of Nations Union circles and the very great difficulties which it has consequently made for us." Curtis had also "so little idea of what we were doing that it

---

[47] CP, 20/80.
[48] CP, 20/81.
[49] CP, 20/82.

was still possible for you in the late summer to ask if any of us were working full time":

> For the six previous months Rawnsley and Ransome had put in a good deal more than half time and Joan Becher (my secretary) and myself had been working seldom less than ten hours a day, often sixteen hours and once or twice the full twenty-four hours. I do not say this to put forward any claim to continuing in this job, but I think it is important evidence to show firstly that the fact that Federal Union is talked about so generally and in terms which antagonise only a tiny section of opinion does reflect creditably upon our energy and common sense, on our ability to put the case in sane language and on our versatility of approach, and secondly, that it is not possible to run Federal Union (as I think you propose that it should be run) as the spare time activity of a few voluntary enthusiasts.[50]

Because Kimber was a pacifist Curtis may have considered him "unbalanced and a crank." In fact it was Kimber himself

> who has insisted from the start that the focus of Federal Union propaganda should be on the right wing, that we should try to get the right before the left, and that we should put forward the proposal in simple commonplace language and in terms which would make it comprehensible to simple common sense people. I can only hope that the reading of this letter is not as distasteful as the writing of it.[51]

The answer from Curtis to this sorrowful letter was never written, but it is plausible that the old "prophet" recognised in the young Kimber the same missionary zeal which marked his own existence, and that made him make many mistakes during the early years of the Round Table experience, when the world, or more exactly the British Empire, seemed within his hand's grasp. Differing views, but also personality conflicts, led Curtis to progressively distance himself from Federal Union, and to continue to support in almost complete solitude, at the end of the war, the plan for an Atlantic federation. It was only in 1947 when he understood the bitter reality of the uselessness of his efforts, and that the United States, with the Marshall Plan, seemed determined to favour European unification, that he came to support the necessity of a European federation. However, Federal Union was by then almost non-existent, and his sermons had few listeners in Great Britain.

---

[50] CP, 20/83.
[51] *Ibidem.*

VI. *The development of the branches*

The issue of *Federal Union News* in the first week of December was entirely dedicated to the story of some of the most representative branches, showing how the movement had in fact sprung from the local level out of a sense of despair, with spontaneous growth, and was only later organised at the national level. The story of the Edinburgh, Peckham, Birmingham and Hampstead branches has, to this concern, a paradigmatic value.

D. Dunford wrote from Edinburgh:

> Like many another branch ours had its beginnings in Clarence Streit's book. Five or six Edinburgh people who had read it learned of the London organisation. They were put in touch with each other by that organisation, and unanimously agreed that the first item on the agenda should be to call a meeting of those interested. Fifty people came. Mr. C. R. Dunford was appointed secretary and Mr. J. W. Taylor press secretary. The month of August was devoted largely to setting machinery in motion—sending out dozens of circulars asking for support, meeting people likely to be especially helpful in propagating F.U. and discussing ways of doing so, asking secretaries of societies to accept F.U. speakers. In September the secretary went to the Oxford conference and returned determined to treble his efforts...By September 30th it was possible to issue invitations to over 70 members to attend a meeting in order to set going a really live organisation...This month also saw the start of a correspondence on F.U. in the *Scotsman*. It has been kept going ever since. October was a month of consolidation. Contacts with local newsagents resulted in twelve of them consenting to sell our booklets. There were more and more requests for speakers, and happily more and more members coming forward to answer them. An Edinburgh leaflet setting out very briefly the aims and objects of F.U., side by side with details of the Edinburgh organisation, was compiled and three thousand copies printed. Two thousand of these have already been issued. The highlight of all the foregoing work came on November 4th, when 250 people attended a public meeting. It was an unqualified success, and the membership that week-end soared past the 100 mark. The same week five discussion groups were set going. They meet every fortnight in the houses of the various members. Their membership ranges from seven to ten. Each member can take a friend.[52]

Howard Fox began his militancy at Peckham, after reading something on the necessity of limiting national sovereignty and building a supranational authority to guarantee peace:

---

[52] *Federal Union News*, 15.

The days passed. The German-Polish crisis swung into the finale...I hurried back to London a week before the outbreak of war, determined to round up my friends and found a new Party. I heard of Federal Union two days after my return. I signed up. In due course I received the name and address of my nearest group secretary. It was an impossible way away...could I start a group in the Peckham area?...The formation of the nucleus was easy. I knew many students of the Goldsmith College, and it was merely a matter of revealing to them the aims of Federal Union for them to join in at once. We held our first meeting on September 30th...and there were 10 of us...We are now about 50 in number. Not more than one-third are regularly to be found at the Saturday meetings, however, because of the black-out nuisance and the vile weather to be endured on this Island—but all, without exception, are carrying on propaganda work of one form or another. Soon we shall, like the amoeba, reproduce by fission—it will be a painful, but very necessary step for a growing organism.[53]

Henry Usborne from Birmingham was no less surprising:

One evening towards the end of August I called on Leyton Richards to discuss Federal Union. We decided there and then to try and start the movement in Birmingham. On August 28th I went to London to see Mr. Kimber and returned with as many pamphlets as I could carry away. From a list of about 20 people which Mr. Richards had made I called our first general meeting, which was held in my office at 5.30 on September 15th. Fifteen people turned up. I opened the meeting by explaining our intentions and then called on Mr. Richards to take the chair. At the end of the meeting each person took away a supply of pamphlets which they afterwards distributed among their friends, and undertook to send me a list of names of others who would be interested. In September we held our first committee meeting also in my office. It was resolved that the most influential person in the Midlands be approached with a view to getting a President and Vice-Presidents, that 5,000 pamphlets should be ordered from London and that 2,000 of these should be posted with a suitable covering letter to prominent people in the Midlands. On October 10th the second general meeting was held, but this time 46 people arrived and my little drawing office, in which we assembled, was in grave danger of collapse...At the conclusion of the meeting I circulated our official membership forms, which had just arrived hot from the press, and I think practically everyone signed up. After this meeting it was clearly impossible to hold another general meeting in the same office; it wasn't large enough. Instead we have arranged little group meetings organised by our district secretaries which are going on almost every day. Our next monster meeting is arranged for December 13th in the Digbeth Institute in

---

[53] *Ibidem.*

Birmingham at 7.30 p.m. We hope to fill the hall to its capacity of 1,400 people.[54]

The Hampstead branch held the primacy of the London ones. Thus Stephenson Fox wrote:

> The history of the Hampstead branch started with the calling of the first meeting on July 27th, 1939, when Mr. Derek Rawnsley addressed a meeting on the aims of Federal Union. Although only 19 were present, so great was their enthusiasm that we were able to form a fully-fledged branch. The propaganda committee immediately decided to obtain the support of the local newspapers. So effectively have they worked that at least twenty letters, articles and reports have appeared in the local press. When the war clouds began to gather a committee was called to discuss the position and decided to distribute a leaflet outlining the aims of the movement and calling for subscriptions and members. Within four days of the calling of this committee, 12,000 leaflets had been distributed in Hampstead and other districts. Besides gaining a number of new members, the famous Hampstead technique of leaflet distribution evolved, resulting in a traffic hold-up in one of Hampstead's main streets. With the outbreak of war the prospects of the survival of the branch seemed remote, as a number of members evacuated to the country, but Professor Joad came to our rescue by inviting the members to a meeting in his home. Despite the 'black-out' on the *blackest* of nights, during which the chairman and I spent ten minutes outside the front gate looking for the entrance, about thirty members attended a most enthusiastic meeting. Fortunately Mr. Kimber was able to attend the second meeting, which was held in Professor Joad's home. These two meetings not only consolidated the position of the branch, but produced a frenzy of activity resulting in a rapid increase of membership in the branch...Mr. R. B. Gillet and his shop committee are building up a mail order business with Federal Union members throughout the country.[55]

The magazine became the principal channel of internal discussion, hosting a debate on the war aims in December, and on the strategy and nature of the movement itself, which from many corners was considered to be pacifist. Federal Union was not, according to the 30 December issue of the magazine, a "peace society," but a "militant force," the "spearhead of civilization's war against Nazism." The movement could destroy Nazism "more quickly and more utterly than the bombs and bullets of the Allied armies." Federal Union was "the key to the war," a key that militants held "on trust for humanity." Time and money which went for the benefit of the

---

[54] *Ibidem.*
[55] *Ibidem.*

movement meant "not only a more certain and lasting peace but a quicker victory and a shorter period of waste and misery."[56]

Joad declared about this that the aim which the Allies were fighting for was the "the supersession of the Nation-State and the transference of at least some of its functions to a common government." The process, which at the end of the First World War had brought about the Balkanization of Europe, had been based on the principle of self-determination, which ended with the destruction of democracy itself. Only federation would let minorities obtain self-determination and peaceful cohabitation with other nationalities.[57]

The immediate aim was to defeat Nazism, however without precluding the possibility of the German people redeeming themselves, and contributing to the building of the new Europe. Germany was the heart of Europe, the largest and most populated State, and it was not possible to ignore it, as at Versailles, but it was also impossible to impose upon unwilling Germans, a federal solution at the end of the war. T. G. Usborne suggested involving German political refugees living in Great Britain within the Federal Union, either to use them as propaganda channels towards the Continent—many refugees were in direct and constant contact with the press of neutral countries—or to use their intelligence and their competence to study all the implications of the federal project. "When the day comes," Usborne argued, "this will be the indispensable ammunition for our propaganda campaign through Europe."[58]

VII. *The last act of the struggle for the Secretaryship*

In December Federal Union had completed the organisation of its headquarters. In seven rooms in Gordon Square, eighteen people worked full-time, with a weekly salary that ranged from two to three pounds. The improvement in the organisational situation of their headquarters was not enough to shelter Kimber from the attacks by the dissident fringe. On 4 December, an important Council meeting took place, presenting the last act of the struggle for the Secretaryship. Kimber's report clearly outlined the picture of a movement in reckless quantitative and organisational expansion, with the creation of five co-ordinated departments. The Research Department was based in Oxford under the direction of Ransome, who organised conferences of economists, constitutionalists and

---

[56] *Ibidem*, 17.
[57] *Ibidem*, 16.
[58] *Ibidem*.

experts of colonial problems at University College, of which Beveridge was Principal. The Education Department, directed by Beveridge with the help of Ransome and Channing-Pearce, was producing "the necessary material in the form of booklets, study notes, bibliographies, etc., to establish contact with the various educational organisations," since "the field it covers is so large, and the general ignorance in this country of even the principles of Federalism is so great."[59]

The Information Department was also under the responsibility of Ransome, and was working in strong co-operation with the other departments, in order to give information, stimulate research, and make contact with other centres of research, in order to multiply propaganda efforts. The Public Relations Department managed relations with the press, and needed a full-time director. Finally, the Foreign Relations Department under the responsibility of Rawnsley, was trying to create a bridge over the Channel, so as to bring the political experience of Federal Union to the Continent. The project was, in particular, to create in Great Britain some "professional Federal Union groups," as those of journalists, scientists, trade union leaders and churchmen, who, in their turn, had to establish contact with colleagues abroad. In turn, they would hopefully create, in their own countries, other federalist professional groups, which could be fed with Federal Union literature. The advantages of this plan were that:

(1) Federal Unionism is spread through responsible channels, (2) that if movements are started abroad, they will start with a full and accurate knowledge of what is happening here, (3) they could be started by natives of each particular country, and (4) by a triangular process, using neutral countries, it might be possible to get information of Federal Union into dictator countries. It seems probable that the best arrangement would be to have a supervising Committee of foreigners resident in this country, who could advise for their own particular nation, and that a contact with the Foreign Office should be obtained. Names for this supervising Committee are being collected.[60]

During the meeting, Kimber reported on a talk that he had had with the Executive Committee of the League of Nations Union—at which Lord Lytton, Lord Cecil and Gilbert Murray were present—to discuss possible joint activities, because it would be "very unfortunate" if the two organisations were to compete against each other. The Committee accepted Kimber's proposal for the creation of a European federation

---

[59] CP, 20/117-20.
[60] *Ibidem.*

within a "wider League," since—Cecil observed—without a "revived
League" the creation of a Continental or regional federation would lead to
"the creation of a rival bloc." Following the meeting, *Headway*, the organ
of the organisation, dedicated the December issue to presenting to the
reader the case of Federal Union, with very favourable articles by Gilbert
Murray and K. D. Courtney, significantly contributing to widen the
popularity of the movement within the disillusioned membership of the
organisation.[61]

Contacts had been taken from Sir Archibald Sinclair, leader of the
Liberal Party, and Clement Attlee, head of the Labour Party, and both of
them encouraged Kimber to continue his work. Finally, the Associated
British Picture Corporation decided to produce a film with a federalist
moral, to be transmitted during those public meetings that were held in a
cinema. Accepting the advice of H. G. Wells in a letter to *The Times*, it
was also decided to draft a new "charter" of human rights with a "short
description of the kind of federal machinery necessary to guarantee these
rights."[62]

Only Hamilton Fyfe and Sir John Orr did not take part in the Council
on 4 December. Beveridge chaired the works which were almost entirely
dedicated to the approval of the Constitution and the by-laws drafted by
the Executive Committee. With some formal amendments, the Council
approved the Constitution. Channing-Pearce then presented, with the
support of Henry Usborne, a motion which called for the convocation,
within six weeks, of a Conference of forty delegates—the Council
members and the representatives of the most active branches—in order to
elect the Chairman, the organisational Secretary, the National Council and
an Executive Committee. The Conference would also ratify the
Constitution, adopt a logo, approve a propaganda strategy, and check the
financial situation of the movement.[63]

---

[61] *Ibidem*. On the League of Nations Union in those months, see Birn, *League of
Nations*, 109-33. On Cecil and Murray, see: Winkler, *The League of Nations
Movement*, 45-70, 120-35.

[62] CP, 20/120-21. On Sinclair and Attlee, see: Gerard de Groot, *Liberal Crusader:
The Life of Sir Archibald Sinclair* (New York: New York University Press, 1993);
Jonathan Swift, *Labour in Crisis: Clement Attlee and the Labour Party in
Opposition, 1931-1940* (New York: Palgrave Macmillan, 2001); David Howell,
Attlee (London: Haus Publishers, 2006); Linne Olson, *Troublesome Young Men:
The Rebels Who Brought Churchill to Power and Helped Save England* (New
York: Farrar, Straus & Giroux, 2007).

[63] CP, 20/102-6.

Federal Union becomes a Popular Movement

In approving a motion presented by Wootton, the Council decided to summon "at the earliest possible moment" a Conference of the delegates elected on the basis of the bye-laws—with all branches having the right, and not only the most active—to be represented. Since the first attack came to nothing, Channing-Pearce then planned to extend the attendance of the conference to delegates who would support his candidature to the Secretaryship. He therefore launched his final attack, and made Henry Usborne ask for the immediate resignation of Kimber, and the election of a new General Secretary. After some anxiety from other Council members, Byron and Wootton intervened proposing a vote of confidence in support of Kimber. Joad, Hogben, Law, Rawnsley and Ransome also voted for Kimber. Usborne was then forced to express "the deepest appreciation of the work Mr. Kimber has done in building up the Federal Union movement almost single-handed in the course of one year." Finally, a motion was approved which asked Beveridge "to make a full enquiry into the organisation of the movement and to report to the Executive at the earliest possible date." The meeting was adjourned to the 7 December, in an atmosphere of general bitterness, which led to the resignation of Wickham Steed from the Council.[64]

At the resumption of the proceedings only seven council members were present, those being the supporters of Kimber. McAllister was appointed responsible for the Public Relations Department with a salary of £600 a year; some worries were expressed for the precarious financial situation, because since November the movement had had a deficit of fifty pounds a week; the bye-laws were approved, and on Kimber's proposal—seconded by Wootton—Rawnsley was elected to the Executive Committee.[65]

In spite of the burning defeat and the fact that Curtis did not support him any longer, Channing-Pearce wrote to him on 5 December, giving his version of the facts:

> The movement is obviously at the cross-roads...The meeting was plainly 'packed'. Rawnsley had been summoned and Byron had been brought in. The attack on me was launched immediately Wickham Steed had to leave. It had obviously been planned.[66]

If the January Conference had not produced a change in "this clique," he would have resigned with Usborne. Curtis could only "save the

---

[64] *Ibidem.*
[65] *Ibidem.*
[66] CP, 20/143, 149-53, 165.

movement" from an inevitable split or ruin. Even Beveridge, in spite of
"his great qualities," was not the leader that Federal Union needed. Curtis
did not have any intention of renouncing his detached and influential role
in Chatham House, and therefore replied to Channing-Pearce on the 8th
December: "our best course is to leave the thing to liquidate itself in this
way and then construct something fresh. I don't think they are likely to be
able to go on long if they have now alienated a realist like Wickham
Steed." Channing-Pearce consoled his wounded pride by accepting the
offer from Cape to edit a volume of federalist essays by various authors,
Federal Union. A symposium.[67]

Before giving in and leaving Federal Union at the beginning of April,
Channing-Pearce grouped together some of the "disappointed" people of
Kimber's management, and also some exponents of the New
Commonwealth Society, in order to create "a single mass movement"—
the Federal Commonwealth—intended to unify the British federalist
forces. At No. 30 Bedford Square—the office of Jonathan Cape, publisher
of *Union Now*—almost next door to Gordon Square, in the heart of
Bloomsbury, on 16-17 March, a meeting was held for that purpose,
including Channing-Pearce, Wickham Steed, J. H. Oldham, Margaret
Storm Jameson, H. G. Wells, Canon Raven, Olaf Stapledon, Karl
Mannheim, Duncan Wilson, Eustace Tillyard, Gilbert Murray and
Keeton.[68]

The formation of a "united front" of the forces which worked for
federalism remained a noble intention, because the "spiritual impulse"
which animated the militants of different organisations was different. The
members of the New Commonwealth Society did not accept the radical

---

[67] *Ibidem.* On Cape see Michael S. Howard, *Jonathan Cape, Publisher* (London:
Penguin, 1977).
[68] CP, 21/159-61. Joseph Houldsworth Oldham (1874-1969), theologist and
missionary, was Secretary of the World Missionary Conference, from 1908 to
1910 and the International Missionary Council, from 1921 to 1938; and Editor of
the *Christian News-letter*, from 1939 to 1945. Margaret Ethel Storm Jameson
(1891-1986), author of some fifty novels, was an activist of the New
Commonwealth Society and the English PEN. Charles Earle Raven (1885-1964)
was Canon of Liverpool, from 1924 to 1932 and Canon of Ely, from 1932 to 1940;
Professor of Theology at Cambridge, from 1932 to 1950; and Rector of Christ's
College, Cambridge, from 1939 to 1950. Sir Archibald Duncan Wilson (1911-83),
was an Officer at the Ministry of Economic Warfare, from 1939 to 1941 and an
Officer of the Foreign Office, from 1941 to 1964; British Ambassador in
Yugoslavia, from 1964 to 1968; and in the Soviet Union, from 1968 to 1971. He
was Rector of Corpus Christi, Cambridge, from 1971 to 1980. With Elizabeth
Wilson he was author of *Federation and World Order* (London: Nelson, 1939).

stances of Federal Union, and the mundialist followers of Wells were unable to produce a practical scheme, or form a popular movement. The final decision was to create a "common home" using what was left of the League of Nations Union, but nothing came of it.[69]

Curtis had the good sense to keep himself out of this enterprise from the beginning, but the obstinate Channing-Pearce played the last card before leaving the game for good, in writing to him on 27th March:

> Meanwhile 'F.U' goes, I am afraid, from bad to worse. It is now in the hands of Dr. Joad and his entourage. People of weight (e.g. Beveridge, the Archbishop of York, Stapledon) are either hesitating in their allegiance or contemplating open repudiation. A month after the London Conference there is still no indication of either internal or external policy. I am resigning from the Secretaryship of the Oxford Branch since the position has become too equivocal and I feel that I can do better work independently. It is still, I think, not too late, to make F.U. into the mass movement for which all the country is looking. But only a drastic reconstruction can bring that to pass...If you want to see me on your return please let me know.

Curtis replied that he no longer wished to be involved in Federal Union, nor in the games of Channing-Pearce. In fact, he was following an alternative road to replace Kimber.[70]

VIII. *Federal Union and the "drôle de guerre"*

At the beginning of February, there were 204 branches of the movement and more than 8,000 members, while in February of the previous year there had only been 37 branches and 150 members. Every week some 190 national and local newspapers reported comments, accounts, and letters on the aims and activities of the movement. Curry and Kimber were engaged from the outbreak of the war in a series of lectures all around the country. Beveridge, Tillyard, Robbins, Brailsford, Wootton, Joad and Norman Bentwich helped Kimber to spread the federal doctrine within Oxford and Cambridge Universities, particularly among the students, but also to the teachers. Ransome put forward his candidature—following a decision of the Executive Committee which was strongly criticised by Curtis—to the Cambridge by-elections, but as soon as the independent-progressive

---

[69] CP, 21/159-61.
[70] CP, 66/185-72.

candidate, Professor Ryle, declared himself a supporter of Federal Union, Ransome withdrew his candidature.[71]

Publishing the reports of five sections at a time, the newsletter launched, coordinated, and recorded the results of a monthly discussion among the branches on various themes: in December on "Federal Union and the colonies," in January on "Federalism and Socialism," and in February on "The federation and Germany's membership." The Federal Union Club had been inaugurated in Piccadilly by Robert Byron, and had become a major venue—with the magazine *World Review*—for the spread of the federal idea in conservative circles.

On 24-25 February, a public meeting took place—with some 2,500 people present—at the Queen's Hall—just before it was bombed—with Kimber, Wootton and Curry as speakers and Sir Drummond Shiels in the Chair. During the meeting the first National Conference of the delegates was also held. All sections created before 20 January were represented, and after a lively debate, with the presentation of two hundred amendments, the Statute was ratified. Under the Chairmanship of Joad and Curry the strategy of the movement was also extensively discussed, with the unanimous acceptance of Kimber's proposal to infiltrate the German Federal Union's propaganda instruments, the launching of an appeal to the German people to overthrow Hitler, and the federation as the basis of peace. The new Council was composed of thirty members, including academics and political and media figures, as well as representatives of the branches, thus forming "one of the best and most representative executives of any organisation in this country."[72]

---

[71] *Federal Union News*, 16, 17, 19, 20, 21. See the letter of 16 Febr. from Channing-Pearce to Beveridge, CP, 21/108-12. In 1897 Henry Noel Brailsford (1873-1958), left the position of assistant Professor of Logics at the University of Glasgow, and joined the Greek Foreign Legion in order to take part in the war against the Turks (1897); he was Editor of the weekly Labour Party journal *The New Leader*, from 1922 to 1926, and collaborator to a number of papers, including the *Manchester Guardian,* and the *Daily Herald.* He was the author of *The Federal Idea* (London: Federal Union Publishing, 1939). Norman Bentwich (1883-1971), was Attorney General of the Government of Palestine, from 1920 to 1931; Professor of International Relations at the University of Jerusalem, from 1932 to 1951; Director of the High Commission for Refugees in Germany, from 1933 to 1935; President of the National Peace Council, from 1944 to 1946; and of the Foreign Office Committee on Restitutions of the British Zone in Germany in 1951. He was author of *The Colonial Problem and the Federal Solution* (London: Macmillan, 1941).

[72] *Federal Union News*, 22. Members of the National Council were: W. Atherton, N. V. Bailey, Norman Bentwich, Robert Byron, Ritchie Calder, F. A. Campbell,

Federal Union News thus commented on the first mass meeting: "It was indeed a great moment in the story of the movement, and there have been very few of the 2,500-odd who did not only feel that history was in the making but were proud to be there to witness it." The evidence for that success without precedents had been the raising of £552 in just fifteen minutes, with a net profit of £398 for the cash-poor movement.[73]

Every week *Federal Union News* announced from fifteen to twenty public meetings, organised by the 225 branches, and animated by well-known speakers such as Beveridge, Robbins, Laski, Lauterpacht, Wootton, Curry, Wells, De Madariaga, Joad, Brailsford, Jennings, Kingsley Martin, and the Lords Lytton and Forrester. The themes were most diverse: the problem of unemployment; federalism and the political engagement of the Christian churches; the workings of the Federal Government in Switzerland, in the United States, in Canada and in Australia; the future of the British Empire and the question of colonies within the federation; the financial, economic, commercial, educational, judicial, social and electoral problems of the federation; Federal Union and the political refugees in Great Britain; the Anglo-French federation as a first step towards a European federation; nationalism, imperialism and the future of western civilization; the German question and European post-war order; federalism *vs.* socialism and liberalism; the relations between

---

William Curry, C. Dowson, C. R. Dunford, Howard Fox, Stephenson Fox, R. B. Gillet, L. T. M. Gray, I. Hastilow, Ivor Jennings, Cyril E. M. Joad, M. Borwn, W. S. Mitchell, D. Neylan, M. J. Richards, C. Rowland, D. W. Sanders, Sir Drummond Shiels, H. G. Southcombe, Olaf Stapledon, E. M. W. Tillyard, Henry Usborne, R. Vallance, J. Weiner, W. W. Wood, Barbara Wootton, G. McAllister, F. Heppenstall, Edwards, Ransome, Rawnsley and Kimber. Sir Drummond Shiels (1881-1953), was Labour MP for Edinburgh from 1924 to 1931; Parliamentary Under-secretary at the India Office in 1929 and in charge of the Colonial Office from 1929 to 1931.

[73] *Federal Union News*, 24. The deficit was, in fact, worrying. Each week the expenditure was £120, and the income was only £50, with an annual deficit of £3,640. Out of the expenditure of £6,768, allocations were: £400 to pay for the rent of the headquarters, and £150 to electricity, heating, and cleaning. Other expenditure included: £500 to travel refunds, £400 to stationery, £100 to the telephone, £300 for the mail, £25 for bank interests, £4,723 to wages, and £45 to insurance. If the salaries had been paid at the average tariff, the deficit would have increased by £2,500. This was the reason why the newly appointed public relations officer, Gilbert McAllister, proposed that the Council—in a report that was rather critical of Kimber's management—should authorise a national campaign to recruit 1,500 members willing to donate £10 a year to the movement. Federal Union would only continue to expand on a self-financing basis (JP).

Federal Union and the League of Nations Union; the question of
sovereignty and federation in international law; Federal Union and the
aims and conduct of war; and Federal Union and human rights.[74]

One of the themes that mostly embroiled the militants was the question
of the movement's relationship with organised pacifism, which despite an
obvious crisis, continued to command passionate opinions. Relations were
excellent between the Federal Union and the League of Nations Union,
whose members had found in the federalist doctrine the explanation for the
failure of the League system, and in the federal system an effective
remedy for those shortcomings. Many members of the Union had

---

[74] *Federal Union News*, 25. From Oct. 1939 to May 1940 the speakers of the
movement were: Beveridge, Barbara Wootton, Maude Royden, William Curry, C.
R. Dunford, Herbert G. Wells, Salvador de Madariaga, Cyril E. M. Joad, J.
Middleton Murray, Vernon H. Porter, Noel Wallace, Ronald Mackay, Philip
Edwards, Gilbert McAllister, C. M. Young., A. C. Rankin, H.G. Green, R. D. C.
Graham, Stephenson Fox, Arthur Duxbury, J. Middleton Murray, Kenneth
Bowden, Lady Duckham, George Padmore, Leslie Aldous, A. T. Wells, H. R.
Morris, G. P. Pittock-Buss, Duchess of Atholl, James Avery Joice, C. A Radice, T.
G. Usborne, Noel Brailsford, Cecil Willson, Howard Fox, Ivor Jennings, E. H.
Tabraham, Harold Laski, R. W. Orme, H. Lauterpacht, W. Platt, Charles Vereker,
Lionel Robbins, Marshall Brown, Andrew Campbell, Vandeleur Robinson, E. M.
Wilson, Stephenson Fox, R. H. Tawney, Barbara Escombe, Ernest Raymond, J. D.
Chambers, R. B. Gillett, Sir Felix Brunner, J. Fletcher Key, V. de S. Pinto, L. A.
Howlett, C. D. Eades, Robert W. Orme, E. M. W. Tillyard, John Hoyland, Ronald
Plant, Ronald Hindle, K. Kitchin, D. Graham, A. Lynch, Cyril Moore, Lord
Lytton, J. Crawley, Ritchie Calder, K. B. Glasier, John Usborne, John Humphreys,
W. M. Dawson, Paul Bowman, Phillis Wallance, Norman Wall, W. R. McIntosh,
N. Richards, Kingsley Martin, F. J. Adler, Paul Groeber, C. H. G. Ross, A.
Godfrey, Freda Gurling, Terence Lancaster, Hugo Glaser, Vernon Porter, J. S.
Titley, G. G. Thomson, Vernon Bailey, A. J. Macdonald, R. H. Gill, L. T. M. Gray,
Jack Jones, L. G. Harris, Lord Forrester, R. Wetherby, L. Barnes, Louis Mares,
William Platt, George House, Ralph Vaughan Williams (*Ibidem*). Harold Joseph
Laski, (1893-1950), was Professor of Political Sciences at the McGill, Harvard,
and Yale universities from 1926 to 1950. He was a leading member of the Fabian
Society, and the Labour Party. Sir Hersch Lauterpacht (1897-1960) was Professor
of International Law at the London School of Economics, at the University of The
Hague and Cambridge from 1938 to 1955, and Judge at The Hague International
Court from 1954 to 1960. Sir William Ivor Jennings (1903-65), was Professor of
English Law at the London School of Economics from 1930 to 1940; Professor of
Political Sciences at the University of British Columbia from 1938 to 1939; Rector
of the University of Ceylon from 1942 to 1955; Vice-Chancellor of Cambridge
from 1962 to 1963; and Downing Professor at Cambridge from 1962 to 1965. He
was author of *A Federation for Western Europe* (Cambridge: Cambridge
University Press, 1940).

subscribed to the movement, undoubtedly acting as moderator elements, compared to the advocates of a more strongly centralised federal government.

Among the militants there were therefore a number of pacifists and conscientious objectors, who in federalism had found the rational expression of the pacifist ideal and in the movement the possibility of giving positive content to their actions. The adhesion of numerous pacifists, however, had given rise to some tensions within Federal Union, because with the increase of popularity, and therefore of the influence of the movement, opponents had a good play of charging Federal Union with defeatism.

In order to clear this misgiving, the magazine hosted a debate on March 16, with a letter by a soldier engaged in Aldershot for a training course. The soldier had decided to spread the federalist case among comrades, having found in Federal Union the organisation which expressed "in more depth" the same ideas on which he had been pondering for some time, namely "the problem to conceive and organise a new system to govern and order" international relations. It was not for Hitler, or the dictatorships, or any other system of government, to produce wars, but their causes rather lay in a "disease" inherent in "the world's political structure," which it was not possible to cure by "merely suppressing Hitler and Hitlerism."

"We successfully solved the problem within each State," the soldier remarked, and asked: "why the Constitutional method will not work if applied internationally." Federal Union would, however, be able to realise this "further stage of social evolution of man" only when a fairly extensive critical mass of opinion was persuaded that war could not be ended by simply fighting a war, "but only with a positive world reconstruction in peacetime." Federal Union should have immediately asked for the guarantee that if and when the Allies won the war, they would engage themselves with all their energies, with the same determination, and the same common effort, to lay down the foundations of a world order based on the federation. And he concluded:

> I...have already put myself in trouble for 'spreading revolutionary propaganda', but I thank God for giving me this golden opportunity to work for the Federal Union among my friends in the army, many of whom I have already converted. I am committed to not grant me a moment's rest and to never cease to strive until the cause is won.[75]

---

[75] *Federal Union News*, 26.

Margaret Bradish, as soon as she learned of the existence of the movement, intervened in the debate on March 23, asking if, in order to meet the needs of those pacifists who, while sharing the aims of Federal Union rejected military service being conscientious objectors, it was possible to create, within the movement, a "pacifist group," which would subscribe to Federal Union, working for all its aims, except for the creation of Federal Armed Forces. The movement would thus have attracted sympathisers of pacifist organisations—such as the Peace Pledge Union, of which Bradish was a member—which had fallen into irreversible crisis.[76]

There was one however who, as a conscientious objector, was deeply engaged for several months in the activities of the movement. D. M. Hastilow wrote on March 30 that in Birmingham there were men whose names were well-known all over England, who were inflicted, during WWI for their pacifist beliefs, with "deprivation, abuse and imprisonment." At the time they were working "in all possible ways and with irresistible enthusiasm" for Federal Union. At every single meeting there was always somebody asking them: "you were pacifists, well, what do you think about the federal army?" They had enough courage, humility, and nobility to answer: "Yes, my friend, we believe in compromise, because without compromise I can save my soul, but the cause that I love will be lost."[77]

The magazine gave special attention to the debate because Kimber himself was a conscientious objector. The leadership then took the opportunity to reiterate their determination to fight the Nazis to the end.[78]

Federal Union was often a target of attacks both from left and right, accused of being an organisation of renouncers and cowards, which even threatened national security. The *Hull Daily Mail* wrote that Federal Union was "the latest intellectual abortion that our half-baked semi-pacifist and pale pink would-be communists are desirous of fathering upon society." The *Huddersfield Daily Examiner* reported that the movement was

---

[76] *Ibidem,* 27.

[77] *Ibidem,* 28.

[78] Regarding the debate on the *drôle de guerre,* see: Willard Germaine, *La drôle de guerre et la trahison de Vichy* (Paris: Editions Sociales, 1960); id., *De Munich à Vichy: La drôle de guerre* (Paris: Editions Sociales, 1975); Haim Shamir, "The 'drôle de guerre' and French Public Opinion," *Journal of Contemporary History,* 11, 1, (1976): 129-45; P. Bauden, "Finances publiques et Économie pendant la drôle de guerre," *Revue Historique,* 561, (1987): 83-97; V. P. Smirnov, "Le Komintern et le Parti Communiste français pendant la 'drole de guerre'," *Revue des Études Slaves,* 65, 4, (1993): 671-89.

a desperate attempt to patch up the fast-decaying system of international finance and trade that the Labour Party, when it was a revolutionary party, called 'capitalism'. We are passing through one of the greatest revolutions in history, and Federal Union is just a note in the swan-song of the old gang.

For the *Portsmouth Evening News*

all we need worry about at the moment is the presence in our country of such vocally powerful people as those who talk about 'union of peoples rather than governments', 'new order of mankind', 'European Federalism' and similar political dope.

Again, Raymond Burns wrote in the same newspaper:

one has become so sceptical and suspicious of these Bloomsbury panaceas and world settlements. I have met so many supporters of Federal Union who, elated by the approximate federal nature of the Anglo-French financial agreement for this war, speak in broad and glowing terms of a 'federated democratic world' without knowing what they are talking about.[79]

In order to face the targeted attacks since the press had noticed its existence, Federal Union approved the document of the official policy on 30-31 March, and delegated Kimber, Wootton and Joad to prepare a pamphlet which outlined and deepened the strategy of the movement: "It is our duty to show the world," wrote Kimber in the *Federal Union News* of 6 April, "that we have indeed made a revolutionary invention of quadruple significance." Federal Union had first discovered "a war-weapon which to be effective must be the exact opposite of secret." This "war-weapon" was intended "to win the war for three sides"—the Allies, the neutrals and Germany—"and lose it for only one": Nazism. It was a weapon which would not shed blood and finally it would make the armistice "really permanent."[80]

The aim of the movement as originally drafted remained. It was to gain support for a federation "of free peoples under a common Government, directly or indirectly elected by and responsible to the peoples for their common affairs, with national self-government for national affairs." The Federal Government would deal with the foreign, military, commercial, financial, and migratory policies and guaranteed "that colonies and dependencies were administered in the interests of the inhabitants and not

---

[79] *Federal Union News*, 27.
[80] *JP*.

for the benefit of any particular country." The federation would be based on "economic security and civil rights for all," and considered it "as the first step towards ultimate world Federation." Federal Union was fighting to induce Allied governments to define war aims on the basis of a declaration of human rights, as an alternative to the doctrine of the superiority of race and "of readiness to federate with any people whose Government is prepared to recognise these rights." Entry into the first federal nucleus would be granted to all democratic countries, Germany included, when democracy had been re-established.[81]

Under the Chairmanship of L. T. M. Gray, the Council—with its 37 members all present— decided to recognise the activities of the Foreign Relations Department, under the direction of Rawnsley, and the Research Department, which since November 1939 had begun activities in Oxford under the direction of Ransome. Beveridge had offered hospitality at University College for the meetings of the various research committees. Three committees had been created to study the economic, constitutional and colonial aspects of the federation. The economists' Committee produced a document on which basis had been organised an economists' Conference in Paris on 13-14 March, while the works of the constitutionalists' Committee had been the basis of the drafting of *A Federation for Western Europe* by Ivor Jennings.[82]

The Council also decided to co-opt four new members—Sir Richard Acland, Beveridge, E. Acworth, and E. M. F. Durbin—R. B. Gillett was unanimously elected Honorary Financial Secretary, and an Executive Committee of nine members was appointed—Joad, Gray, Curry, S. Fox, F. A. Campbell, Wootton, Jennings, Shiels and Robbins—with the exclusion of leading figures such as Norman Bentwich, Robert Byron, and Sir Robert Greig. Kimber was reconfirmed as Political Secretary, Heppenstall as Co-ordinator of their headquarters, Q. Lumsden as Assistant Public Relations Manager, John Usborne as Deputy Editor of *Federal Union News*, and Ransome as Secretary of the Research Institute.[83]

---

[81] *Federal Union News*, 29.

[82] *Ibidem*.

[83] *Ibidem*. Sir Richard Thomas Acland (1906-1990), was Liberal MP for Barnstaple 1935-1945; and Labour MP for Gravesend from 1947 to 1955. Evan Frank Mottram Durbin (1906-1948), was Professor of Economics at the London School of Economics, an official of the War Cabinet Office from 1940 to 1945; and finally, Labour MP for Edmonton from 1945 to 1948. Sir Robert Blyth Greig (1874-1947), was Permanent Secretary of the Department of Agriculture for Scotland from 1928 to 1934, and Director of the railways for London, the Midlands and Scotland.

The fourth session, chaired by Joad, in the late afternoon of 31 March, was particularly agitated. Kimber opened the discussion with the request for the resignation of McAllister—responsible for the Public Relations Department—who he charged with disloyal behaviour towards the movement and his colleagues, offering his own resignation if the Council would not endorse his request. Rawnsley and Wootton defended Kimber's position, by offering their own resignations as well, but their efforts to overcome the resistance of members of the Council to dismiss a colleague were in vain. After a discussion which lasted until late in the evening, they reached a compromise, however unsatisfactory for Kimber and his closest supporters.

A motion presented by Gillet, backed by Sanders, and approved by fourteen votes to two, declared that no staff member could ask for the resignation of a colleague; that officials could only express personal opinions about the performance of their departments; that the appointment and dismissal of officials belonged to the Executive Committee, not to the Council. The Council therefore refused to endorse Kimber's request, and at the same time invited the General Secretary, the Secretary of the Foreign Relations Department, and Wootton to withdraw their resignations. The Council finally appointed Campbell as Administrative Secretary, in order to assist Kimber in the increasingly burdensome management of the headquarters, and Gillett as Honorary Secretary. The process which within four months would bring Kimber's abandonment of the leadership of the movement had thus began, and also the decline of the movement itself. By losing one of its three founding fathers—of the three the one who undoubtedly contributed most to the success of the organisation—the movement would lose that youthful strength of expansion and even strike force that until then had been a key factor in the extraordinary success of federalism in Great Britain.[84]

---

[84] *Federal Union News*, 29.

CHAPTER III

FEDERAL UNION, THE FOREIGN OFFICE AND THE DEVELOPMENT OF FEDERALISM ON THE CONTINENT

I. *Rawnsley's mission in Switzerland*

The *Federal Union News* of 13 January 1940 stated that the movement had to strengthen its international connections. Federalism abroad was still elitist and, therefore, unable to influence the great political choices. The development of the movement was compared "to the movements of a fleet at sea. Our maximum speed towards our objective is the speed of the slowest ship." After the success achieved in Great Britain, the priority was no longer to strengthen the movement in Great Britain, but abroad. Federation could not be realised without the Dominions and those Continental countries necessary to form the first federal nucleus, and it would depend upon the strength of the movement in those countries:

> Luck had it that the first Federalist organisation should start in England; political circumstances have made its development here more rapid than in other countries. This does not mean that we should mark time in England until the other countries are level—such passive tactics are not in the Movement's character—what it does mean is that we must devote special energy to helping the Movement forward in other countries. And here many members can help by sending the names and addresses of every single friend or acquaintance they may have in any Dominion or foreign country.[1]

---

[1] *Federal Union News*, 17, 18. For an analysis of British war strategy during the first months of 1940, see: Llewellyn Woodward, *British Foreign Policy in the Second World War* (London: Her Majesty's Stationery Office, 1962), 72-9, 100-10; Nick Smart, *British Strategy and Politics During the Phony War: Before the Balloon Went Up* (Westport, CT: Praeger, 2003).

The Federal Union did not wait however until the winter of 1940 to grasp the strategic importance of the development of federalism on the Continent. In fact, it was just after the July 1939 Conference that Kimber went to France to make the first contacts with French federalist forces. On the basis of names given by Curtis, he established a bridge-head with the Union Economique et Douanière Européenne, in the hopes of establishing a branch of Federal Union in Paris.[2]

Of the three founders, Rawnsley was definitely the most gifted with the pioneering spirit, and once the headquarters of the movement had been fixed under the control of Kimber, on 23 August he crossed the Channel in search of federalists in France, Switzerland, Belgium and Holland, in order to establish contacts where he could found embryo organisations. Rawnsley followed Kimber's pattern by asking Curtis for letters of introduction to influential friends, as it was "essential" to start "indigenous movements" in those countries before the winter, and it was not "less essential" that they were "in the right hands from the start." Curtis gave only a couple of letters to the young Rawnsley—not without certain embarrassment, because as he never thought in terms of a European federation he did not have contacts with Continental federalists—for André Siegfried in Paris and William Rappard in Geneva. However, he gave his most sincere "blessing" to the brave young man, who reminded him of his own missionary zeal of thirty years before.[3]

Arriving in Geneva just after the outbreak of the war, Rawnsley went to the British Consulate, where he met H. B. Livingston, who, writing on 16 November to C. J. W. Torr, officer of the British Embassy in Berne, commented:

> Federal Union...is, I understand, an association formed to propagate the idea of federation, in fact, Pan-Europe in another guise. The headquarters are at 44, Gordon Square, London, and I believe that Richard Law is the Secretary...Derek Rawnsley who is about 25, wears an O.E. tie and says

---

[2] CP, 18/28-9.

[3] CP, 18/174, 176-7. William Rappard, *The Geneva Experiment* (Oxford: Oxford University Press, 1931); id., *Pacifism is not Enough. Lectures Delivered at the Geneva Institute of International Relations, August 1934* (London: Allen & Unwin, 1935); id., *The Crisis of Democracy* (Chicago, IL: University of Chicago Press, 1938); id., *The Quest for Peace since the World War* (Boston, MA: Harvard University Press, 1940). On Rappard see: Ania Peter, *William E. Rappard und der Völkerbund: Ein Schweizer Pionier der internationalen Verständigung* (Frankfurt am Main: Peter Lang, 1973); Victor Monnier, *William E. Rappard: Défenseur des libertés, serviteurs de son pays et de la communauté internationale* (Basel: Helbing et Lichtenhahn, 1995).

that Federal Union was founded at Oxford by himself and a few friends. Rawnsley came to see me shortly after the outbreak of war. He explained that he was not returning to England because, although not an out and out pacifist, he does not believe in war and thinks that he can do better work spreading the F.U. gospel in neutral countries. On my replying that our main business now was to win the war, he agreed that this might be so, but he considered that the sooner we prepared the foundations of a new equitable order in Europe, the easier it would be to convince Germans of the advantages of peace over war. I asked how this good news was to be conveyed to the Germans, and he said through the neutrals! Before leaving the consulate Rawnsley asked us to recommend a cheap pension. About two weeks later we were told that he had left Geneva unexpectedly without paying his hotel bill; he also had other debts. I heard by chance that he had gone to Italy with the avowed intention of interesting Mussolini in Federal Union. The weeks passed, and we had almost forgotten Rawnsley, when the pension rang up to say that he had returned and paid his bill.[4]

During his second stay in Geneva—and after having visited his parents in Capri, and refueling with money—Rawnsley created a Federal Union branch, and convinced S. G. Rendel, the brother of a British diplomat in Sofia, to accept the Chairmanship. During a preliminary meeting at the Palais Wilson, at the beginning of November, the organisational structure of the branch was devised. The first public meeting took place on the 11th, with one hundred people present, including Leopold Boissier—General Secretary of the Union Interparlementaire—and Émile Borel, President of the radical youth of Geneva.

Rawnsley was aided by Edgeworth Leslie. Twenty-six years old, Leslie was a writer who lived in Austria till the outbreak of the war. He had been put in touch with Rawnsley by the Consul himself, who reported to Torr about the meeting as follows:

He came to see me in the early days of September and asked if I thought it might be possible for him to find work in one of the international

---

[4] FOP, FO371/22947, 176-7. For an analysis of Swiss federalism during the war, see Francesca Pozzoli, "Svizzera e federalismo europeo durante la seconda guerra mondiale," in *Storia e percorsi del federalismo. L'eredità di Carlo Cattaneo*, eds. Daniela Preda e Cinzia Rognoni (Bologna: Il Mulino, 2004), 465-517. On the Anglo-Swiss relations during the war, see: Neville Wylie, "'Keeping The Swiss Sweet': Intelligence as a Factor in British Policy Towards Switzerland During the Second World War," *Intelligence and National Security*, 11, 3, (1996): 442-67; id., *Britain, Switzerland, and the Second World War* (New York: Oxford University Press, 2004); Denis MacShane, "Britain, Switzerland and the Second World War," *International Affairs*, 82, 3, (2006): 567-73.

organisations in Geneva, such as the Red Cross, to which I replied in the negative. He then confessed to being one hundred per cent pacifist and a conscientious objector and said that he refused to work for England in any capacity whatever as long as the war lasted. He went to Rawnsley's pension and thus their collaboration started. The activities of these young men are giving rise to considerable comment in various Geneva and foreign (including League) circles, and some people feel that consciously or unconsciously the two of them are helping enemy propaganda. I strongly question Rawnsley's claim to represent *the* Federal Union (whose notepaper he uses) and I think it would be a good thing if enquiries could be made in London, for if his story is untrue, it would not be difficult to discredit the movement locally. In certain circles, it was thought that, because of the increasing federalist debate in Great Britain, the two young men were emissaries from the British government, hence the surprise that we should put out such odd propaganda!. According to certain rumours, the Geneva branch of the Federal Union was making rapid headway, and...they would soon have sufficient money to send propaganda material into Germany![5]

Replying to Torr on 29 November, I. Kirkpatrick, senior official at the Foreign Office, confirmed that Rawnsley was one of the founders of Federal Union, and observed that nothing could be done "to prevent an Englishman proclaiming pacifist sympathies, whether at Hyde Park Corner or at the Hotel des Bergues, so long as they are not seditious." He suggested that Consul Livingston made it clear in Geneva circles that the two young men had "nothing whatever to do with HMG." Torr's duty was "to do his best to see that they aren't taken too seriously by his French colleague." Finally, with an English sense of humour, he observed: "but if one can't say at Geneva that 'it is necessary for the peoples of the world to renounce, in a future organisation, part of their sovereignty', I don't know where one can." Kirkpatrick's view was, however, not shared by other officers such as F. K. Roberts, who suggested intervening with the London Federal Union's leaders to convince Rawnsley to suspend his Geneva

---

[5] FOP, FO371/22947, 178-9. On the British peace movement, see: Martin Caedel, *Pacifism in Britain, 1914-45: The Defining of a Faith*, (Oxford: Oxford University Press, 1980); James Hinton, *Protests and Visions: Peace Politics in Twentieth Century Britain* (Oxford: Oxford University Press, 1989); Cecelia Lynch, *Beyond Appeasement: Interpreting Interwar Peace Movements in World Politics* (Ithaca, NY: Cornell University Press, 1999).

activities, in order not to further upset the French, and another officer recorded: "Quite useless. These people are unteachable."[6]

II. *Rawnsley and the Association Suisse pour la Société des Nations*

Rawnsley was in Geneva while the Association Suisse pour la Société des Nations—the Swiss equivalent of the British League of Nations Union—was going through a deep investigation on the causes for the failure of the League. War had put an end to its very reason for existing, forcing its supporters to seriously review their outlook. In a circular letter to members of the Central Committee and to the presidents of the Association's branches, E. Spühler, Secretary General, noted that only a federation with a "geographical basis (a European federal union)," or an "ideological union (a federation of democratic peoples)" could "organise and ensure peace." The function of the Association was, in particular, that of "persuading the Swiss people that our country has to be ready when the time comes, to assume their responsibility in the reconstruction of a new order." Addressing, on November 23, William Rappard, President of the Association and well-known publicist, Spühler presented Rawnsley and his recruit, Leslie, as representatives of an organisation which deserved "special interest," that was going to influence "the future direction of our Association." The two emissaries of the organisation had settled "for a more or less prolonged time" in Geneva, in order "to fully disseminate their ideas" in international circles, and Swiss public opinion. Spühler had already met Rawnsley a week before, and was going to have dinner with Leslie, who was in charge of raising interest particularly in German-speaking Switzerland.

Before the Central Committee of the Association formulated an official view about Federal Union, Spühler expressed privately to Rappard a broad positive judgement on Federal Union's ideas, particularly on the need for a "considerable strengthening of international solidarity and the creation of a supranational authority." He expressed however reservations about the movement's rejection of the "structure" of the League, and on the question of the method, Spühler "strongly recommended" Rawnsley "not to create a

---

[6] FOP, FO371/22947, 187-8, 174. On the Foreign Office's views on British organised pacifism, see Martin Caedel, *Thinking about Peace and War* (New York: Oxford University Press, 1987).

separate and rival organisation in the small Swiss territory," but, on the contrary, to try to involve "all those who are working for peace."[7]

Rappard—who through Alfred Zimmern was well aware of the ideas of Lothian, Curtis and other exponents of the Round Table and Chatham House—had in the meantime been approached by a group of Swiss friends of Rawnsley—Léopold Boissier, Georges Thudichum, and Henri Revilliod—who, from that moment, came to play leading roles in the creation of the Geneva Federal Union's branch. The major scholar of Swiss federalism had "a dual state of mind" on the issue, and shared Spühler's impression that "on one hand these young people are very nice," and thought that their idea "of strengthening international solidarity at the expense of national sovereignty," was "necessary and useful." The Association should, therefore, "do everything possible to encourage the dissemination of their ideas among our members." However, they had "no reason to give priority to that specific idea of international federalism that they support," more than to those of Streit, Coudenhove-Kalergi, Davies, or "any other journalist who supports them." Rappard believed that without hindering them, they had to be "careful not to encourage the formation of new groups devoted to the exclusive propaganda of the ideas of these young Englishmen." Rappard then suggested to Spühler to ask Leslie to write "a short article" on Federal Union's aims, to be published in the bulletin of the Association, and to prepare "a comparative study of the various federal projects currently under discussion."[8]

Leslie happily accepted Spühler's offer, but evidently dissatisfied with only the partial willingness of the Association to underwrite Federal Union's programme, decided, in early December, to act independently,

---

[7] ASSDN, newsletter 1939/2; RP, J.I. 149/59. On Rappard and the Association, see Daniel Bourgeois, "Entre l'engagement et le réalisme: William E. Rappard et l'Association suisse pour la SdN face à la crise de 1940," in *L'historien st les relations internationales* (Geneva: Institut Universitaire de Hautes Études Internationales, 1981), 215-36.

[8] ASSDN, letter wrongly dated "January 1939," since it was December 1939. Sir Alfred Zimmern (1879-1957), was lecturer in Ancient History at Oxford from 1903 to 1909; Professor of International Relations at the University of Aberystwyth from 1919 to 1921; at Cornell University from 1922 to 1923; at the Institute of Intellectual Cooperation, Paris, from 1926 to 1930; and finally at the University of Oxford from 1930 to 1944. By Zimmern's works, see: *Nationality & Government* (London: Chatto & Windus, 1919); id., *The Prospects of Democracy and Other Essays* (London: Chatto & Windus, 1929); id., *Spiritual Values and World Affairs* (Oxford: Oxford University Press, 1938); id., *The League of Nations and the Rule of Law, 1918-1935* (London: Macmillan, 1939); id., *Modern Political Doctrines* (Oxford: Oxford University Press, 1939).

and formed a "Comité Genevois d'Initiative," composed of two Professors—George Thudichum and J. Pisteur—a medical doctor—Henri Revilliod—and a lawyer—A. Borel—for the creation of a "Mouvement populaire Suisse en faveur de l'Union Fédérale des Peuples." In the first circular letter, the four signatories expounded upon the aims and the programme of action of the new movement, on the lines of the official Federal Union policy:

> The Union Fédérale des Peuples... appeals to hundreds of thousands of people, including a good number of statesman, men of culture and churchmen, as the only solution able to put an end once and for all to the wild and stupid war between nations, which incessantly threatens our civilization...The Swiss people feel strongly committed to contribute to the realisation of this project. We do not have then any doubt about the fact that you will want to join our popular movement, created to promote the principles of a federal union of peoples. From this moment it is necessary to prepare public opinion to construct the foundations of the Union, so that at the end of the war we can begin to work to ensure that from this terrible chaos arises the Federal Union of Peoples, being the only solid foundation for peace. Whether you like or not to join our movement, please return to us the enclosed form as soon as possible, in order to enable us to assess whether the Swiss public opinion is more or less favourable to this project.

The appeal, which asked subscribers to also contribute with financial support to No. 12 Avenue Léon Gaud, Geneva, did not have immediate success. Only in early May could Rawnsley count on the support of a handful of Genevans—41 in all—mostly academics, medical doctors and lawyers. The difficulty met by Rawnsley in starting a federalist movement in the capital of institutional internationalism—suffice here to remember the fact that H. Golay, Secretary General of the Bureau International de la Paix, refused to join the movement—shows how neither the failure of the League's experiment, nor the bleak picture of Europe once again at war, were enough to form a consensus for a federalist solution, where a supportive political culture was already well rooted.[9]

---

[9] ASSDN. Members of the organisation, on 15 May, were: A. Auber, hotel manager; A. Babel, Dean of the Faculty of Social Sciences at the University of Geneva; P. Balavoine, chemical; Charles Beguin and Georges Berger, professors; Frédéric Boissonnas, photographer; Pierre Bordier, banker; Pierre Bovet, professor; Gaston Bridel, journalist; Jacques Brun, pharmacist; Edouard Claparède, professor; Edouard Dantan, pastor; Théodore de Félice, publicist; Adolphe Ferrier, sociologist; Henri Flournoy, doctor; Gagnebin, Director of the Music Conservatory of Geneva; John Galliard, professor; Leopold Gautier, College Director; Rodolphe

The most comforting success of Rawnsley's mission was to have "converted" some prominent leaders of the Association—such as Professor Paul Meyhoffer, Secretary and Treasurer—to Federal Union's thesis. A tangible sign of how the Association dealt with Federal Union was, for example, Rappard's Conference of 12 February, "Some Reflections on International Federalism."

The fundamental nucleus of Rappard's reasoning was that—discarding the idea of absolute domination by one State on the rest of the world, and also the hypothesis of a world within which States were living in absolute isolation without any relationship to each other—at the end of the war humanity would have to choose between a new anarchy and a "federative system" which, on the basis of the renunciation of absolute national sovereignty, would guarantee a just and stable peace. The condition to the creation of a federal system lay however in the defeat of the forces which had resisted international collaboration. The fact that within all free countries was revealed the growth, in depth and amplitude, of a current of opinion in favour of creating a "federal union"—on an ideological basis, as in Streit's project of the union of democracies, or by geography, as in Federal Union's scheme for a European Union—it testified that the time was ripe. "In fact," Rappard concluded, "the federalist movement is the ideal of free peoples."[10]

A few days later, on February 18, the session of the Central Committee of the Association discussed the various federalist projects and the organisation of future peace, inviting for the occasion Hans Bauer, President of Europa-Union—a federalist organisation active in Berne since

---

Grimm, hotel manager; F. Grosselin; Robert Hercod, Director of the International Bureau Against Alcoholism in Lausanne; René Jaccard; Auguste Lemaitre, professor; Paul Meyhoffer, professor; Martin Naef, former Councillor of State; André Oltramare, professor; Henri Petit, prelate; Paul Pictet, lawyer and journalist; J. Pisteur, Edmond Privat and Marcel Raymond, professors; F. Rellstab, bookseller; Henri Revilliod, doctor; F. Roquette, Director of the Geneva International School; M. Schenker; Albert and George Sechehaye Thudichum, professors; M. Veillard, lawyer and judge in Lausanne; Rolin Wavre, professor; Marcel Wiegandt, optician and former president of the Rotary Club. See *La Société des Nation*, 17, 5: 30. On the Bureau International de la Paix, see Armand Mattelart, *Histoire de l'utopie planétaire* (Geneve: La Decouvérte, 2000).

[10] ASSDN. The President of the Pietermaritzburg section of the League of Nations Union had even gone so far as to write to Halifax, inviting the Foreign Minister to take a position in relation to the Streitian project: "Do you agree that the idea of an unlimited, autonomous, State sovereignty should be abolished and a voluntary limitation of absolute sovereignty guaranteed within a federation, under the ultimate authority of God?", FOP, FO 371/24363, 128554.

1934—and Leslie himself. The presentation of the Continental and insular
views, converging in several aspects, increased the credibility of the
federalist approach among the leaders of an association manifestly in
crisis, and also its capacity to win converts among its members. The
presentation of the federalist thesis in the newsletter of the Association on
1 March, including the report of the debate at the Central Committee,
witnessed the openness to the British initiative.

Entering into the merits of the role played by the League of Nations in
contemporary history, Leslie observed that it represented—like all the
leagues which in the past had developed into an organic union of States—a
necessary stage in the process of European unification. Since not all
European or world States would enter at the same time to become
members of the federation, and it was not possible to create the federation
on the basis of the hegemony of one State over others, Leslie suggested the
creation of a "confederation" including all the countries of the world,
together with the "federation" of those European Countries which were
ready to pool part of their national sovereignty in order to conduct their
common affairs.

Members of the "confederation" would be, according to Leslie,
"progressively attracted by the federation." The "confederation" would
certainly have "the advantage of universality," by promoting the growth of
the cosmopolitarian spirit in the world, but since member-States remained
the holders of their national sovereignty, in practice there was not much to
hope for. The leadership of the historical process towards world federation
could not therefore be taken by the "confederation," but by the
"federation," which in order to effectively influence its development, had
necessarily to be limited to a number of "like-minded" and "motivated"
States. It had however to be strong enough to ensure its survival in a world
of sovereign States, and above all had to be based on the "popular will,"
without which "nothing can be done to really start a federation after the
war."[11]

---

[11] *La Société des Nations*, 2/3, (1940): 12-3. On Hans Bauer and Europa-Union,
see Pozzoli, *Svizzera e federalism*, 465-74; Walter Lipgens, *A History of European
Integration, 1945-1947. The Formation of the European Unity Movement* (Oxford:
Clarendon Press, 1982), 117-24; Hans Bauer, *Le 50 ans de l'Union européenne de
Suisse, 1934-1984* (Bern: Europa Union, 1984); Lubor Jilek, *L'esprit européen en
Suisse da 1860 à 1940* (Geneva: Cahiers d'Histoire Contemporaine, 1990); id.,
*L'Union européenne à Bâle entre 1938 et 1946: pôle helvétique et versant mondial
dans les projets d'une association européaniste*, in *Plans des temps de guerre pour
l'Europe d'après-guerre, 1940-1947* (Bruxelles: Bruylant, 1995): 275-96; Thomas
Staffelbach, "Die Europa-Union 1945 bis 1949," *Studi e fonti*, 18, (1992): 159-

Also, the April issue of the newsletter gave ample space to the federalist perspective, with the article "Conceptions Fédératives" by the Belgian jurist Jean Hostie, former General Secretary of the Central Commission for Navigation on the Rhine, and former Director General of the Belgian Ministry of Foreign Affairs. The crisis of European civilization coincided for the author with the crisis of the nation-State. International society, being the result of the interdependences of the modern age, was based on legal bodies—such as The Hague Court—and legislative bodies—such as the Assembly of the League of Nations—however as it was just advisory, it was lacking an executive body. The fundamental limitation of the international community was that of being a society of sovereign nations. The principle of international cooperation, in a world that was shrinking and developing at once, had become insufficient. Only a federal system could guarantee the governability of the world community. However, the United States, Japan, the Soviet Union, and China would hardly become its members. From the point of view of Continental Europe, the federal system suggested by Hostie was therefore made up of three concentric circles:

> A Union, universal by vocation, built around a Court of Justice; a Federation including the British Empire and Continental Europe for defence and internal order; and at the centre of this federation, an economic union of Continental Europe, and perhaps other economic unions to be gradually realised.[12]

In the article "The Federal Idea: Towards a Lasting Peace," Leslie claimed that the reality of war left no room for optimism, but reason should not remain a prisoner of that reality, and should look forward to an evolutionary solution of the ongoing conflict. Federal Union represented the moral tension for the preparation of the future, trying to win popular consent to the federalist idea not just in Great Britain. The initiative for a radical reform of the European system could not have come from governments unless it had found substantial support among public opinion. At the end of World War I federalism was discussed, but since it was then not "rooted in the popular will," it could not "have a real effect."

Over the next twenty years, public opinion was carried away by an "illusory optimism" for the capacity of the League to maintain peace.

230; Walter Lipgens ed., "Swiss Plans for the Postwar Order in Europe," in *Documents on the History of European Integration*, 1 (Berlin-New York: Walter De Gruyter, 1985), 750-72.

[12] Jan Hostie, "Conceptions Fédératives," *La Société des Nations*, 18, 4, (1940): 18-22.

Federal Union had been created just to promote public reflection on the causes of the failure of the League, and to suggest new principles on which to build peace. The initial composition of the federation would depend on the developments of the international situation, but its original nucleus should have been gradually extended to include the whole world. If France and Great Britain had been able to overcome the limits of cooperation, intended to meet the Nazi danger, thus constituting a real federation, and if the neutral countries had joined it, Europe would have become "the founding nucleus of a larger world federation." It was a priority, according to Leslie, not so much to discuss which countries would become founding members of the federation, but to "convert public opinion to federalism."[13]

In an interview published in the late December issue of *Federal Union News,* Rawnsley commented upon the success achieved in Geneva, observing that to the Swiss people, the Streitian project seemed just another "Anglo-Saxon recipe," and that they would never accept becoming "the frontier state of an ideological block directed against Germany and Italy." Switzerland would join the federation only if Germany and Italy also joined it on a parity basis with France and Great Britain. Switzerland provided a strategic location to reach Germany and Italy with federalist propaganda, and Federal Union had by then consolidated a bridge-head.[14]

Undoubtedly Switzerland was then the most dynamic centre for the dissemination of federalist ideas on the Continent, not only and not so much for obvious historical and institutional reasons, but because it housed many political refugees who, having weakened loyalties to their countries of origin, were more open and ready to transfer them to a political order which overcame national States.

III. *The Foreign Office and the activities of Federal Union in Geneva*

The zeal of British censorship, charged by the Foreign Office to check the correspondence coming from abroad to Federal Union, saved from oblivion a series of documents of extraordinary importance in reconstructing the framework of the activities of Federal Union in Geneva.

---

[13] ASSDN; Edgworth Leslie, "Die bündische Idee: der Wegweiser zu einem dauernden Frieden," *La Société des Nations*, 1, 20 (1940): 3-4. For an analysis of the role played by the League in the promotion of a universalistic spirit, see *The League of Nations in Retrospect* (New York-Berlin: Walter De Gruyter, 1983).
[14] ASSDN, newsletter 1939/2; RP, J.I. 149/59.

Referring to the activities of the Federal Research and Information Centre established in Geneva at the Hotel Balmoral, Leslie wrote to Rawnsley on March 18:

> it is supplying the need for an international, neutral and impartial centre to the federal movement. Immediately the plan and programme were circulated, all sorts of enquiries came along, Governments included. Most important of all it established an official contact with those people we were discussing during our last afternoon together in Paris.[15]

The Rockefeller Foundation promised the necessary financial aid to make the Centre the point of reference of federalism at world level, and Leslie stressed the importance of keeping the Centre completely independent from the Research Department of Oxford. Even if it was only in Great Britain that federalism was experiencing a much greater development compared with other European countries, it should not allow Federal Union to control the Centre in Geneva. The Centre had been created for federalists of all schools to build a common home and express their own specific contribution to the development of political thought still in formation. The British school should influence the others on the basis of its intrinsic strength. The suspicion by neutral countries that Great Britain was not really willing to enter into a federation on an equal basis with other European countries had to be overcome: "to them this talk of a possible federal solution is merely a trick to win the neutrals' support." They were afraid that behind the apparent enthusiasm for federalism the British were in fact hiding their old imperialistic spirit.[16]

The Centre was intended to co-ordinate the studies and research on federalism, world order, and post-war problems, which were being carried out by well-established institutes of research across the world. The Centre would also try to promote, with its own resources, studies of those aspects of federalist thought which had not yet been studied, and would publish the results in the main languages. The Centre would also undertake to strengthen the links among the different federalist movements "working toward the realisation of a new international order," thus building a bridge on which people, ideas, and resources could meet and unite to achieve

---

[15] FOP, FO 371/24363, 128554, 232-40.

[16] *Ibidem.* On the Rockefeller Foundation, see: Robert Shaplen, *Towards the Well-Being of the Mankind: Fifty Years of the Rockefeller Foundation* (New York: Doubleday & Co., 1964); Raymond D. Fosdick, *The Story of the Rockefeller Foundaton* (Piscataway, NJ: Transaction Publishers, 1988); Joel Fleishman, *The Foundation: A Great American Secret. How Private Wealth Is Changing the World* (New York: Public Affairs, 2007).

their common goals. Governments would turn to it as soon as the inevitability of the federal solution, both for Europe and the world, became manifest. The Centre had, according to Leslie, to unite the efforts of those who were producing the culture which the world needed. [17]

The Foreign Office showed great interest in the documents that had fallen into the hands of the censor, and began to modify its initial opinion in which Federal Union was a "fifth column", whose success was threatening the solidity of the internal front. After examining these documents, Warr wrote:

> there seem to be two tendencies in the movement itself; one represented by the London office which seems rather naturally to be in favour of making it an English affair, and the other represented by Mr. Edgeworth Leslie, the Geneva representative, whose idea seems to be that the movement is too much tarred already by the British brush and that the movement should be handed over to neutral control...It is a little difficult to estimate the significance of the movement in England. I do not myself think that its effect has yet become deleterious, and insofar as its supporters propagate the view that Federal Union must start on the basis of Anglo-French co-operation they may be performing a useful service. Now that the Norwegians have become belligerent and a footing thus obtained in Scandinavia, there is more of a nucleus from which to develop post-war international organisation. I think myself that organisation, presuming an Allies' victory will have to be built up experimentally through the extension of Inter-Allied Committees and Boards in the military, economic and political spheres. Insofar as Federal Union develops an interest in this type of idea, I do not think that it need be officially discouraged, though I fear that it is bound to attract a great many cranks and idealists who will no doubt do their best to develop the movement on hopelessly impractical lines. [18]

IV. *The Foreign Office, Federal Union and the activities of Federal Union in France*

From Switzerland Rawnsley went to France where, after a first failure, his efforts began to produce concrete results.

During his second stay in Paris, at the beginning of March 1940, Rawnsley met Champetier de Ribes, Foreign Under-secretary, the Socialist leader Charles Spinasse—Economics Minister in the First Government of the Popular Front—the industrialists Louis Marlio and Claude Mercier, the

---

[17] FOP, FO 371/24363, 128554, 232-40.
[18] FOP, FO 371/24364, 128554, 356.

banker Roger J. Truptil, and the former Private Secretary of Colonel
François de La Rocque, Jean de Souches.[19]

The first step towards the creation of a movement had to be the
convening of a Conference in Paris at the Institut de Co-operation
Intellectuelle, with the participation of some prominent exponents of the
Federal Union—such as Beveridge, Robbins, Frederick von Hayek, B. F.
Wright, E. Kahane, and Ransome—the American Walter Lippmann, the
Swede Bertil G. Ohlin, and the French industrialists Marlio, Truptil and
André Detoeuf. The British Embassy in Paris was immediately alarmed
because most people seen by Rawnsley belonged to the Abbaye de
Pontighy International Group, which was "of very doubtful determination as
regards the prosecution of the present war." According to the Ambassador,
Sir Ronald Campbell, there was "the danger that these people and those
who share their views in France will find encouragement in Federal Union
and the activities of its representatives, and that they will exploit it for the
development of a movement out of harmony with the resolve of His
Majesty's Government and the French Government to win the war." On 12
March the Ambassador asked Halifax for instructions, and in particular
what the official position of the British Government was towards Federal
Union.[20]

The answer from the Foreign Office was awaited until 2 April, and it
reflected the embarrassment and bewilderment of the senior officials, who
recorded that "an opportunity may well be taken by some member of the
Government to indicate the utopian character of its ideas." Federal Union
had "not been encouraged nor discouraged." It was therefore necessary "to
refute any suggestion that Federal Union is recognised or supported by His
Majesty's Government." It was desirable "to counteract any suggestion to
this effect, and, if the occasion arises, to warn Federal Union representatives
of the desirability of avoiding a misunderstanding on this point." That
however was not valid for the "advocacy of the idea of closer union
between France and the United Kingdom."[21]

---

[19] On the role played by Colonel de La Rocque and de Ribes in those months, see:
Jacques Nobécourt, *Le colonel de La Rocque, 1885-1946: Ou Les pièges du
nationalisme chrétien* (Paris: Fayard, 1996); Frank Dazet-Brun, *Champetier de
Ribes 1882-1947* (Paris: Seguier, 2008).
[20] CSP, Federal Union Inc., Subject File, France (1939-1940); FOP, FO
371/24363, 128554, 186-7. On the predecessor of Campbell, Sir Eric Phipps, see
John Herman, *The Paris Embassy of Sir Eric Phipps: Anglo-French Relations and
the Foreign Office, 1937-1939* (Eastbourne: Sussex Academic Press, 1998).
[21] FOP, FO 371/24363, 128554, 186-7.

This contradictory answer was based on minutes taken by Rex Leeper on March 24:

I do not think we need bother about Mr. Lionel Curtis's admonitions...
H.M. Govt. has taken up no attitude to the Federal Union movement; in
the United Kingdom it enjoys complete freedom to propagate its ideas;
and it is rather encouraged not discouraged. When it comes to the question
of the representatives of Federal Union abroad, we have to discourage any
suggestion that Federal Union is recognised or encouraged by H.M. Govt.,
and Paris should do what they can to counteract any suggestion to this
effect and to warn F.U. representatives against the danger of any
misunderstanding on this point—except insofar as the closest
Anglo-French co-operation is concerned.[22]

The reports by Warr of 20 and 21 March, on which basis Leeper
drafted his minutes, had been, however, rather evasive:

my object was to discover more about Federal Union...I have not however
been able to find out the exact size of the membership of the Federal
Union society in England. The society which has been established at 44
Gordon Square is most reticent on the subject. But there are about 200
groups scattered around the country and I would be surprised if the total
membership exceeded 200,000.[23]

At the foot of the memorandum he however stated:

I have since discovered that this estimated membership is wildly out. The
F.U. say that they have 10,000 members registered at their head office:
and 10,000 registered in the provinces. Mr. Lionel Curtis when he was
consulted about the foundation of the society by Mr. Rawnsley and others
said that on no account should an approach be made to Prime Ministers,
Foreign Secretaries or government officials until the membership had
reached at least one million; to raise their members to that figure should be
the first and exclusive object. In ignoring this sage advice Mr. Rawnsley
has been guilty of the utmost folly. I suggest that the line to be taken with
him when he next calls at the Embassy should be one of the greatest
reserve. At the same time it might be possible to repeat in an unofficial
form the substance of Mr. Curtis's advice. People like Mr. Rawnsley and
his muddle-headed associates can only obscure any good which the
principles of Federal Union may have.[24]

---

[22] FOP, FO 371/24363, 128554,182-3.
[23] *Ibidem.*
[24] *Ibidem.*

Thus Warr summarised on April 5 the trends of opinions within
Federal Union:

> Mr. Streit, in his book *Union Now*, and his disciple Mr. Curry, in his book
> *The Case for Federal Union*, are against bringing in Germany. Sir John
> Fischer Williams, Mr. N. L. Brailsford and Sir William Beveridge take the
> opposite view, but emphasise that the Germany in question must be
> democratic. For without some form of democracy in all its components
> parts, Federal Union would not in any case work. On the whole I should
> guess that the majority of the more intelligent Federal Union opinion in
> this country takes the view that Germany should be excluded, at any rate
> in the initial stage. But this is a doubtful point, whatever the Federal Union
> Society may say. In view of this doubt and in view of the extremely small
> section of the public (not more than twenty thousand) who are so far even
> interested in Federal Union, I submit that we should not give an
> encouraging answer to the question.[25]

Not happy with the brief and inaccurate information collected by Warr,
at the request of Under-Secretary Butler, Leeper asked Warr himself to
start his job again. The memorandum which followed—"The Aims and
Literature of Federal Union and the Various Currents of Opinions in the
Movement"—is certainly the most accurate and comprehensive document
produced by the Foreign Office on British organised federalism. Dealing
with the origin of the movement, Warr presented Curtis—"probably the
most important single convert to Federal Union"—as the champion of
federalism since the South African years, trying to conjugate American
federalism with English colonialism, but only after having read *Union
Now*, had Curtis decided "to devote the remainder of his life to the
propagation of a Federal Union gospel."[26]

Curtis had the tendency, common to most British federalist writers, "to
invest with the rubber stamp of God the purely political theories which
they expound." With his "ridiculous eschatological theories," Curtis was
"by far the worst offender":

---

[25] *Ibidem*. In a minute of 7 April Leeper did not, however, seem happy with the
research by Warr: "We clearly cannot be drawn by this rather naive attempt to
extract an opinion on Federal Union. I think the position is that we neither
encourage nor discourage the activities of various organisations, such as 'Political
and Economic Planning', 'Federal Union' and others which are trying to work out
proposals for international co-operation. I therefore tentatively suggest a possible
supplementary if Sir J. Leech presses his question," PRO, FO371/24362,
C5392/7/62.

[26] FOP, FO 371/24364, 128554, 359-71. For a critical analysis, see V. de Payen-
Payne, "Anglo-French Union," *Journal of Education*, 72, (1940): 282-97.

nobody ever has read or ever will read *The Commonwealth of God* because the author's absorbed anxiety to translate into political terms the special revelation which the Almighty has vouchsafed him, is hardly interesting for one who is not so favoured.[27]

The federalist writers pretended "to be inspired," but in fact they were simply "distended with their own conceits." That made most of their books "infinitely tedious to read." The practical consequence of their "empty conceit" was that for those who pretended to be "divinely guided," the "verdict of history" had not been "kind in the long run and sometimes in the short run." If Federal Union did not purify itself "of this element it will not easily catch the popular imagination, nor having done so will it be able for long to put its theories into practice." If this did not happen it would be "a pity...because the theory in itself has many attractions and it seems probable that, at least insofar as Anglo-French union is concerned, it has possibilities which are of immediate interest."[28]

The idea to apply the federalist principle to Anglo-French political integration had been "strangely neglected by the enthusiasts of the movement," although it had been "very clearly realised by Mr. H. A. L. Fisher, who believes in a limited form of Federalism, by Mr. Brailsford and by Mr. Wilson Harris, who has recently been writing articles in the *Spectator* which are sceptical about the wider forms of Federalism." The major objection to Anglo-French unification "as a nucleus of Federation" came only from Curtis, who believed that federation could not "be initiated as a military alliance." The public consent to Anglo-French unification was at that historical turning point that was "powerful in both England and in France," and could "further be consolidated here, and an amorphous but growing body of opinion won over to enthusiastic co-operation, if the magic word 'Federal' were included in any further agreement with the French which may be made."[29]

---

[27] FOP, FO 371/24364, 128554, 359-71.

[28] FOP, FO 371/24364, 128554, 359-71. See de Payen-Payne, "Anglo-French Union", 282-97.

[29] FOP, FO 371/24364, 128554, 359-71. Herbert Alfred Laurens Fisher (1865-1940) was Vice-Chancellor of the University of Sheffield, from 1912 to 1916; Liberal MP for Sheffield Hallam, from 1916 to 1918; and for the English universities, from 1918 to 1926; President of the Board of Education, from 1916 to 1922; and Warden of New College, Oxford, from 1925 to 1940. John Boynton Priestley (1894-1984), well-known novelist, play-writer and radio commentator, was author of the essay "Federalism and Culture", in Channing-Pearce, *Federal Union*, 93-100. Lord Godfrey Elton (1892-1973) was Professor of History at Oxford, from 1919 to 1939; Secretary of the National Labour Committee in 1932;

That would have implied—Warr continued, demonstrating having properly understood the meaning of the process taking shape in those troubled days—the creation of "a common parliament, of two Houses, directly elected by the citizens of the two countries and a common executive body." Federal Union was "certainly 'in the air'":

> it has sprung up simultaneously and according to the enthusiasts independently, in the United States of America, in the United Kingdom and possibly on the Continent. It is a popular movement for which I suggest some satisfaction must ultimately be found, and Anglo-French union seems the most obvious first step.[30]

Among the distinguished supporters of Federal Union, Warr recalled the journalist J. B. Priestley, the Socialist MP Sir Archibald Sinclair, Lord Elton, the Conservative MP Richard Law—son of the former Prime Minister Andrew Bonar Law—Arnold Toynbee, Lionel Robbins, J. L. Hammond, Captain Liddell Hart, Wickham Steed, the Archbishops of York and Durham, William Beveridge and the left-wing publicist Noel Brailsford. It was not however possible to identify with clarity the different trends of opinion within the movement, which resembled "not so much a sheet of water, with clearly discernible drifts and currents, as a marsh, over which hangs an opaque miasma of belief in the perfectibility of man."[31]

The fear that Federal Union could be associated in France with "pacifist or defeatist elements" was very strong within the Foreign Office, even though on 18 April W. Mack from the British Embassy in Paris, assured R. M. Markins of the Foreign Office that Federal Union was not doing anything in France which could "give the impression that His Majesty's Government approves its activities." Rawnsley turned to the Embassy for advice regarding the choice of representative figures to contact in order to gain popular support in France for the idea of federation, suggesting the names of the Minister Anatole de Monzie—

---

and Editor of the *News-Letter*, from 1932 to 1938. Sir Archibald Sinclair (1890-1970) was Liberal MP for Caithness and Sutherland, from 1922 to 1945; Minister for Scotland, from 1931 to 1932; Air Minister, from 1940 to 1945; and Leader of the Liberal Party, from 1935 to 1945. John Lawrence Hammond (1872-1949), journalist and historian, was author of essays on social history. Sir Basil Henry Liddell Hart (1900-1976) was war correspondent of the *Daily Telegraph*, from 1925 to 1935; of *The Times*, from 1935 to 1939; the author of essays of military history and a theorist of mechanized warfare.

[30] FOP, FO 371/24364, 128554, 359-65.
[31] FOP, FO 371/24364, 128554, 366-71.

suspected by the British Embassy of not being "a very firm believer in the necessity of the present war"—André Detoeuf, Jules Romains, Georges Duhamel and Charles Spinasse. All these political exponents seemed "tinged one way or another with defeatism or pacifism." The Foreign Office thought that Rawnsley did "not seem to have thought of a very suitable selection of candidates (particularly Mr. Jules Romains)."[32]

V. *The federalist debate in France*

Rawnsley's efforts in France aimed at creating a branch of Federal Union, were not, in the end, crowned by the same success known in Switzerland. This was due first of all to the fact that Rawnsley had found there was competition in Paris with the "Comité d'Action pour l'Union Fédérale des Peuples Libres," created by Streit in June, with their headquarters at No.

---

[32] FOP, FO 371/24364, 134921, 335-7. On the French pacifist movement, see: J. B. Barbier, *Le Pacifisme dans l'histoire de France* (Paris: La librairie française, 1966); Nicolas Faucier, *Pacifisme et antimilitarisme dans l'entre-deux-guerres* (Paris: Editions Syndicalistes, 1983); Michel Auvray, *Objecteurs, insoumis, déserteurs: Histoire des réfractaires en France* (Paris: Stock 2, 1983); Jean-Louis Crémieux-Brilhac, *Les Français de l'an 40. La Guerre, Oui ou Non?*, 1 (Paris: Gallimard, 1990). On pacifism of Socialist orientation, see: Richard Gombin, "Socialisme et pacifisme," in *La France et les Français en 1938-1939*, eds. René Rémond and Janine Bourdin (Paris: Les Presses de Sciences Po, 1978); Michel Bilis, *Socialistes et pacifists 1933-1939: Ou l'intenable dilemma des socialistes français* (Paris: Editions Syndicalistes, 1979); Guy Rossi-Landi, "Le pacifisme en France (1930-1940)," in *Français et Britanniques dans la drôle de guerre: Actes du colloque franco-britannique tenu à Paris du 8 au 12 décembre 1975* (Paris: Editions du Centre Nationale de la Recherche Scientifique, 1979); Emmanuel Naquet, "Eléments d'étude d'une génération pacifiste dans l'entre-deux-guerres. La laures et le rapprochement franco-allemand. 1924-1933", in *Matériaux pour l'Histoire de Notre Temps*, 18, (1990): 50-8; Norman Ingram, *The Politics of Dissent* (Oxford: Oxford University Press, 1991); id., "Romain Rolland, Interwar Pacifism and the Problem of Peace," in *Peace Movements and Political Cultures*, eds. Charles Chatfield and Peter van den Dungen (Knoxville: University of Tennessee Press, 1988); Mona L. Siegel, *The Moral Disarmament of France: Education, Pacifism, and Patriotism, 1914-1940* (Cambridge: Cambridge University Press, 2005). On Jules Romains see: André Cuisenier, *Jules Romains, l'onanisme et les hommes de bonne* (Paris: Flammarion, 1992); Dominique Memmi, *Jules Ronains ou la passion de parvenir* (Paris: La Dispute, 1998). On the political climate which existed in France in those months, see: Jacques Nobécourt, *Le colonel de La Rocque, 1885-1946: Ou Les pièges du nationalisme chrétien* (Paris: Fayard, 1996); Frank Dazet-Brun, *Champetier de Ribes 1882-1947* (Paris: Seguier, 2008).

76 rue Réamur. It was a follow-up of the publication of *Union ou Chaos,* the French version of *Union Now* which had been translated by his wife Joanne. Streit recruited the industrialist Achille Lafage as General Secretary, the merchant Jacques Mougin as Director, Simon Vincent as Treasurer, and Robert Artmann, Jean Chauvigne and Louis Corniere, with University Professor Maurice Ponthiere as Council Members. The text of the appeal asked the French people to adhere to the principles of the movement which had been organised in Great Britain and the United States: "a life-giving breath is going through the world, and from our joint efforts will spring the Federalist Union of Free Peoples."[33]

Rawnsley's failure is attributable also to the fact that there had been, in French culture since the Revolution, and especially in Proudhon, a current of federalist thought that was profoundly different from the British one. Proudhon, in fact, focusing on the study of an abstract model of federal society, which had to exist before the creation of a federal government, privileged the study of the communitarian aspect of federalism— subsequently developed by Raymond Aron, Arnaud Dandieu, Denis de Rougemont, Henry Brugmans and Alexandre Marc, exponents of the personalist movement—rather than the constitutional approach favoured by the Anglo-Saxon school, and then developed by the Italian one, which tended to identify federalism with the theory of the federal constitutional process, and with the struggle for the creation of a federal government.[34]

---

[33] CP, 18/28-9, 41-3. CSP, Federal Union Inc., Subject file, France (1939-1940). The appeal was: "à quelque milieu que nous appartenions, une même opinion nous unit tous aujourd'hui: nous en avons assez des vieilles formules impuissantes à nous assurer la paix et la prospérité. Or, quelle que soit notre situation personnelle, nous n'avons pas le droit de nous désintéresser de notre propre sort, car l'abstention, quand a sonné l'heure de l'action, cela s'appelle la trahison, et nos enfants nous en demanderaient compte. Que seuls donc, les timorés, les incapables et les lâches demeurent par leur passivité les complices aveugles des fauteurs de guerre! Pour notre part nous avons choisi l'action. Sachons d'ailleurs que nous ne sommes pas seuls, et que spontanément des mouvements parallèles au notre ont pris naissance aux Etats-Unis, en Angleterre et dans d'autres pays susceptibles de se fédérer avec nous. Un souffle vivifiant parcourra le monde et de nos efforts conjugués sortira l'Union Fédérale des Peuples Libres" (*ibidem*).

[34] Pierre-Joseph Proudhon, "Du principe Fédératif," in *Œuvres complètes* (Paris: Romillat, 2004); Mario Albertini, *Proudhon* (Milan: Giuffrè, 1974); Bernard Voyenne, *Le Fédéralisme de Pierre-Joseph Proudhon* (Paris: Presses d'Europe, 1973); Raymond Aron, *Paix et guerre entre les nations* (Paris: Calmann-Lévy, 2004); Raymond Aron and Alexandre Marc, *Principes du fédéralisme* (Paris: Le Portulan, 1948); Alexandre Marc, *Proudhon* (Paris: Egloff, 1945); id., *L'Europe dans le monde* (Paris: Presses d'Europe, 1965); id., *L'Europe pour quoi faire?*

There had also been a vain attempt, in March of 1940, by the MP Jean Hennessy—who had been French Ambassador in Berne, and Minister of Agriculture—and of Jean-Charles Brun—"ardent regionalist apostle" and professor at the University of Leurs—to establish in Paris a "Comité d'Etudes et d'Action fédéraliste," which not by chance favoured the internal aspect of the federalist doctrine—the construction of a federal society—rather than the external one, namely the construction of a supranational political system.[35]

The only sign of the existence of this Committee was a Conference on "Fédéralisme de la Grande France," held on April 10 in collaboration with the "Société de Géographie Commerciale et d'Etudes Coloniales." Among the speakers, Coudenhove-Kalergi had identified in the Anglo-French Alliance the beginnings of a federal nucleus, capable of progressively enlarging, and including the whole of Europe, excluding Russia.[36]

Hennessy, referring to Proudhon as "the one who has best studied the problem," observed that Proudhon thought that the only alternative to what he defined purgatory—a time of suffering and pain—was represented by the principle of federalism. Referring to the "Comité," Brun echoed the slogan launched in London by Attlee on 8 November of the previous year:

we believe in the federalist principle and in its application we see the future salvation of Europe...We do not cease to repeat that if Europe does not federate, it will perish. There is no way out from the dilemma between federate or perish.

(Paris: Presses d'Europe, 1962); id., *La révolution fédéraliste* (Paris: Presses d'Europe, 1969); id., *De la méthodologie à la dialectique* (Paris: Presses d'Europe, 1970); Brugmans, *La pensée politique*; id., *L'idée européenne*. The personalist movement developed through the joirnals *L'Ordre Nouveau* and *Esprit*. See in this respect: Ferdinand Kinsky, *Fédéralisme et personalisme* (Paris: Presses d'Europe, 1976); Tony Judt, *The Burden of Responsibility: Blum, Camus, Aron, and the French Twentieth Century* (Chicago, IL: University of Chicago Press, 1998); Alain Boyer, Georges Canguilhem, François Furet, Jean Gatty and Jean-Claude Chamboredon, *Raymond Aron, la philosophie de l'histoire et les sciences sociales* (Paris: Rue d'Ulm, 2005); Emilie Courtin, *Droit et politique dans l'ouvre d'Alexandre Marc: L'inventeur du fédéralisme intégral* (Paris: L'Harmattan, 2007).

[35] Julian Wright, *The Regionalist Movement in France 1890-1914: Jean-Charles Brun and French Political Thought* (New York: Oxford University Press, 2003).

[36] John Lukacs, *The Last European War, September 1939-December 1941* (New Haven: Yale University Press, 2001): 489-91. On Coudenhove-Kalergi see Hanne Dezsy, *Gentleman Europas. Erinnerungen an Richard Coudenhove- Kalergi* (Wien: Czerning Verlag, 2001).

The European federation might not yet have achieved perpetual peace, only reachable through a world federation, but it certainly would have made "wars less frequent." As for the stages of European unification, Brun believed that "the creation of a whole federated Europe in one fell swoop" was not possible, and that they should begin with a "primary federation" which other nations would join.[37]

During the crucial months of spring 1940 other representatives of French culture intervened in favour of the federalist project, without however producing the embryo of a federalist organisation. Georges Scelle, renowned jurist and Professor at the Sorbonne, for example, intervened on 19 March in *Dépêche*, observing that peace would actually have rebuilt the Continent on a new basis only if the Anglo-French Alliance had been transformed, during the war, in an "organic union of unlimited duration." It was necessary for this purpose to establish permanent bodies, such as an inter-governmental Council, inter-parliamentary delegations, and a unified military command. There was also the need to implement a common policy in the areas of industry, commerce, agriculture and finance. The free movement of peoples, goods and capital would also be necessary. A centre of gravity for more extensive European unification would then have been created among those States which shared the same ideals and values. "The organisation of Europe," he vaguely concluded, "requires a certain homogeneity and you can realise it only by degrees and with prudence."[38]

Jean de Pange, in the article "How to make indissoluble the Franco-British Union" published on 25 March in the *Petit Parisien*, replied to Scelle noting ironically that Marianna was preparing herself for marriage with John Bull with excessive shyness. A certain inferiority complex was perhaps understandable for a husband who had always won, but in order to avoid friction which could later lead to divorce, the "marriage contract"

---

[37] P40, 104, 125-33. At a Conference at the Martigny Theatre in Paris, the Greek Ambassador to France, M. Politis, advocated, on March 13, "the creation of the United States of Europe...The new organisation of Europe will be born essentially in a function of the Anglo-French strength of cohesion and expansion", around which it "will unite, under certain conditions to be determined, all European peoples of good will", (see *Le Temps* of 14 March 1940). Mr Politis returned to the theme of the European federation at a Conference in Paris on 15 April, and in Marseille on 28 April, (see *Le Temps* of 16 and 29 April). Wright, *The regionalist Movement*, 18; Hans Kelsen, Kurt Ringhofer and Robert Walter, *Auseinandersetzungen zur reinen Rechtslehre: Kritische Bemerkungen zu Georges Scelle und Michel Virally* (Berlin: Springer, 1987).[38] P40, 104, 125-33.
[38] P40, 104, 125-33.

should ensure "full equality of rights." It was necessary to take measures to adapt to peacetime those "essential federal structures" that already existed, and to place them under the control of the two parliaments, which would have to establish a Commission to deal with issues of common interest. Composed of forty MPs and twenty Senators of the two countries, the Commission would meet twice a year in London and Paris; it would not have legislative powers but only control, and would grant the executive for war credits. The Committee could also exercise a positive influence on the activities of the Supreme War Council, which would continue its activities, becoming the Government of the Union.[39]

Bernard Lavergne argued in *Epoque* on April 24, that the common economic policy and the new constitutional bodies would create

> day after day, a network of interests and common values between our two countries. The organic union between France and England...will thus assume towards the European Continent, that political and economic leadership, which alone is able to guarantee the rule of law among States.[40]

Gaston Jeze observed on 26 April in *Ere Nouvelle* that "the foundation stone of the new European house" had to be "the organisation of a permanent Franco-British co-operation," without which peace would be precarious. The co-operation of other States would be "a consequence of the intimate and permanent Franco-British Union."[41]

From these timid and isolated stances emerges all the backwardness of the political debate in France on war aims and post-war order. The federalist idea in France, despite having been on the agenda in the late 1920s at the time of the Briand Plan, was still far from having assumed an organised political form, and therefore capable of expressing a shockwave comparable to that achieved in Britain. Aware of this gap, the French Ambassador in London expressed to the Foreign Office, on 10 November, his worry that "persistence of rather idealist views on the lines of a Federation of Europe" in Great Britain,

> might give a handle to some people in France and elsewhere to seize any opportunity, however really insufficient, provided by some development in

---

[39] P40, 104, 125-33. See also Jean de Pange, "A Plea for Anglo-French Union," *Contemporary Review*, 171, (1940): 267-79.
[40] P40, 104, 125-33.
[41] *Ibidem.*

the situation to suggest that the moment had come to attempt a settlement
on the basis of some such theory of a future adjustment of Europe.[42]

The speed with which federalism had rooted in Great Britain was not
just the fruit of preliminary work done by Lothian, Curtis and the Round
Table over the inter-war years. Much of its success owes to Federal Union,
a movement composed principally of young people who had however been
able to involve in the development of their political program some of the
most influential figures of British culture of the time. That did not happen
vice versa in France, where federalism was supported by isolated and
marginal figures, or by foreigners such as Streit, Coudenhove-Kalergi and
the same Rawnsley, who had failed to persuade the French to support the
federalist project with an organised political action.

The activities of Coudenhove-Kalergi had already attracted the
attention of the British Consul in Berne, Christopher Warner, who in a
memorandum to Halifax of the 14 September 1939 reported the results of
a conversation with the Bohemian Count. According to the Consul,
Coudenhove-Kalergi thought that the war would last only a few months if
France and Great Britain stipulated an anti-Soviet Alliance with Japan, and
showed their determination to create a United States of Europe. The
federation would have guaranteed "European solidarity in foreign,
military, economic and monetary policy," independence, security, equality
of rights, and respect for the national traditions of all member-States;
respect for human rights, and ethnic and religious minorities; the transition
from war to a peace economy; it would have also promoted the creation of
an international organisation, including the extra-European countries, able
to promote peaceful relations among its member-States.[43]

A measure of the difficulty for "foreign" federalism to root in France,
and the delay of the *Quai d'Orsai*—compared with the Foreign Office—to
consider the application of the federal project, is given for instance by the
suspicion with which French officials saw the activities of Rawnsley in
Switzerland, by judging them as "pacifist propaganda" at the service of the
enemy. In writing on 13 November to the French Ambassador, the French
General Consul of Berne censored Rawnsley's attempt to form Federal
Union branches in Geneva and Bergues, advocating the necessity for the

---

[42] FOP, FO371/22947, 104-6, 293-4, 238-42. On Briand Plan, see: Antoine Fleury
and Lubor Jilek eds., *The Briand Plan of a European Federal Union* (Oxford:
Peter Lang Publishing, 1998); Achille Elisha, *Aristide Briand: La paix mondiale et
l'union européenne* (Louvain-la Neuve: Bruylant, 2000).
[43] FAE, *Fonds AP 2*, Correspondence, 1939-40.

European peoples "to renounce, in a future organisation, part of their sovereignty!!!"[44]

The same British diplomats in Paris were well aware of this gap, and in a report to the Foreign Office emphasised that the idea of a European or world federation was "certainly much less discussed in France than in Britain and much of the debate that has developed has been provoked by comments to British plans for a new world order on federal lines."[45]

Once the project of Anglo-French Union had become the official policy of the British Government, the Embassy in Paris began to be identified, from spring 1940, as the propulsive centre of federalist propaganda: "we have not been idle here," Oliver Harvey wrote to Orme Sargent on April 27, "and have done a good deal of spade work on the subject with officials, politicians and journalists we meet. In fact we rub it in to everyone we see."[46]

VI. *The French Press and the Anglo-French Union*

In the spring of 1940, French political culture appeared to be almost completely paralysed by the danger of Nazi invasion, and just saw the military aspect of the Alliance with Great Britain. The debate on the war and peace aims undoubtedly also had a relevant space in the French press, but it was apparently a reaction to what was happening in Great Britain. Moreover, the positions were very dissimilar. In France, for example, they did not accept the distinction, almost universally acknowledged in Britain, between the German people and Hitlerism, considering the latter in France a "manifestation of the eternal Germany," an evil connected with the very nature of the German people.[47]

---

[44] FOP, FO371/22947, 181-6. On the political and psychological climate which permeated the *Quai d'Orsai* in those months see: Raymond de Sainte-Suzanne, *Une politique étrangère: Le Quai d'Orsay et Saint-John Perse à l'épreuve d'un regard Novembre 1938-Juin 1940* (Paris: Viviane Hamy, 2000); Pierre-Jean Rémy, *Diplomates en guerre: La Seconde Guerre mondiale racontée à travers les archives du Quai d'Orsay* (Paris: Jean-Claude Lattès, 2007).

[45] FO371/24299, 134921.

[46] *Ibidem*. On the special attention given by the Foreign Office to the debate in France on the possible development of the Anglo-French collaboration, see Wank, *Doves and Diplomats*.

[47] For a survey of the psychological climate in France during the first months of the war, see Crémieux-Brilhac, *Les Français*. For a discussion of French public opinion on Great Britain, see "L'opinion publique française, l'Angleterre et la guerre," in *Français et Britanniques*.

On the right, *Action Française* of 2 October 1939 welcomed Chamberlain's statement of 25 September, according to which it was necessary to "redeem Europe from the constant and recurring fear of German aggression," recognising the need for a radical solution for the German problem. Georges Bidault wrote on October 7 in *L'Europe Nouvelle* that despite its cruelty, the militarism of 1914 "did not fail to express its own contradictions," while the one which "had trampled Poland and which now seeks to seduce ourselves in order to overwhelm us more effectively," became an instrument of the "empire of terror, in disregard of the values that even in its worst hours had not completely ignored."[48]

The Minister for Armaments, Raoul Dautry, with an astoundingly geographical determinism believed, according to *Paris Soir* of 7 November, that German despotism was the "product of the great plains of the north." France, like Switzerland was, on the other hand, "anchored to its mountains, in the same way that England was to its coasts." The peoples of the great plains, in not being able to bind themselves to the steppes, lacked therefore "a set of moral and spiritual values," and invented the concept of the "vital space," which "no people anchored to its own soil would ever devise." The "problem of the future" was therefore, to anchor to the soil the German-Russian peoples: this was the "historic mission of France."[49]

There were several proposed remedies. Always on the right, *Action Française* of December 2, advocated the dismemberment of Germany on the basis of the 1648 Treaty of Westphalia. *Dépêche de Toulouse* of 17 November endorsed *The Times*'s suggestion of 3 December for the

---

[48] Georges Bidault, *Resistance: The Political Autobiography of Georges Bidault* (Westport, CT: Praeger, 1967). On Bidault see: Reinhard Schreiner, *Bidault, der MRP und die französische Deutschlandpolitik 1944-1948* (Frankfurt am Main: Peter Lang, 1945); Jean-Claude Demory, *Georges Bidault, 1899-1983: Biographie* (Paris: Julliard, 1995). On French right during the inter-war period, see: Robert Soucy, *Le Fascisme français 1924-1933* (Paris: Presses Universitaires de France, 1989); Brian Jenkins, *France in the Era of Fascism: Essays on the French Authoritarian Right* (Oxford: Berghahn Books, 2007).
[49] See the memorandum "The Public Controversy on War and Peace Aims in France up to 31st December, 1939," CP, 111/161-5. On Dautry see: Remi Baudoui, *Raoul Dautry, 1880-1951: le technocrate de la République* (Paris: Balland, 1992), 183-217; Michel Avril, *Raoul Dautry: la passion de servir, 1880-1951* (Paris: France-Empire, 1993), 111-45; Crémieux-Brilhac, *Les Français de l'An 40*, 2: 106-9, 113-4; Vladimir Haplerin, *Raoul Dautry: Du rail a l'atome: L'aventure sociale et technologique de la France dans la première moitié du XXe siècle* (Paris: Fayard, 1997).

creation of an international police force under the control of an "international authority." Georges Duhamel argued in *Figaro* of 12 December that it was necessary to "bring back Germany with force in the community of European States," a thesis also shared by *Oeuvre* of November 27, which considered what was under way as "a war to build Europe," in order to "win with force the secession of Germany from the European Continent."[50]

The French, however, would not accept the "mystification" of another League of Nations. The Allies had to offer to France, Pierre Bernus claimed in *Journal des Debats* of November 5, "effective guarantees," to give "teeth" to a new League of Nations, as requested by *Ordre* of November 22, reintroducing an expression by Attlee. There were those who argued, as Vladimir d'Ormesson in *Figaro* of 14 September, and Léon Bailly in *Jour* of 27 September, for the need of a Danubian federation, including Austria, Hungary and Czechoslovakia, as a counterweight to Germany. Since the crisis of the Austrian Empire, Europe had lived in a permanent state of war. Julien Benda, intervening in *Ordre* of October 5, argued that there would be no real peace in Europe as long as the States "renounced the right" to unlimited national sovereignty. The union of the three major democracies, France, Great Britain, and the United States, would create the "moral superior body" capable of organising the social order.[51]

On the left, Léon Blum observed in *Populaire* of October 30, that it was not possible to establish a lasting peace in Europe until the democratic

---

[50] On Action Française see: Oscar L. Arnal, *Ambivalent Alliance: The Catholic Church and Action Française 1899-1939* (Pittsburgh: University of Pittsburgh Press, 1985); Eugen Weber, *L'Action Française* (Paris: Hachette, 1990); Hugues Petit, *L'église, le Sillon et l'Action Française* (Paris: Nouvelles Editions Latines, 1998). On Duhamel see: Arlette Lafay, *La sagesse de Georges Duhamel* (Paris: Minard, 1984); *Georges Duhamel et l'idee de civilisation* (Paris: Biblioteque Nationale de France, 1994); François Mauriac, *Le croyant et l'humaniste inquiet: Correspondance, François Mauriac-Georges Duhamel, 1919-1966* (Paris: Klincksieck, 1997).
[51] CP, 111/161-5. On Bernus see Martin Cornick, *French Intellectuals and History: The "Nouvelle Revue Française" under Jean Paulhan, 1925-1940* (Amsterdam: Rodopi Bv Editions, 1995), 110-5. On d'Ormesson see Volfram Kaiser, *Political Catholicism in Europe, 1918-1945* (London: Routledge, 2004), 147, 182-7, 258-61. On Benda see: Ray L. Nichols, *Treason, Tradition and the Intellectual: Julien Benda* (Lawrence, KS: University Press of Kansas, 1979); Louis Albert Revah, *Julien Benda: Un misanthrope juif dans la France de Maurras* (Paris: Plon, 1991); Sandra Teroni, *La passione della democrazia: Julien Benda* (Rome: Bulzoni, 1993).

principle coexisted with the totalitarian one. However, it was also vital to reach a new equilibrium in the international sphere, between individual freedom and collective discipline. States, like individuals, had to sacrifice part of their freedom, namely their national sovereignty in order to perform a joint action, without which it was impossible to cope with the problems of the industrial age. Intervening again in *Populaire* of November 28, Blum pushed his political analysis to the extreme consequences, stating clearly that "the mass of the French people" saw "in a federated and disarmed Europe the guarantee to lasting peace," the one which the Allies were fighting for. If Aristide Briand was still alive, Blum concluded, he would "look beyond the victory, to the prospect of the United States of Europe."[52]

With the development of an increasingly close cooperation between the two countries, the press began indeed to find in this new course the beginning of an irreversible historical process. While the *Temps* of 12 February gave ample space to an intervention of Firmin Roz in favour of an Anglo-French Union as the nucleus of a European federation, the magazine *Nouveaux Cahiers* devoted the February issue to the British debate on the war aims, with articles by Harold Nicolson, Wells, J. H. Oldham, Horsfall Carter, Jules Castier, de Madariaga, Pierre Combret de

---

[52] Pierre Côt, intervening in *Oeuvre* of December 3, firmly supported the project of an Anglo-French federation as the nucleus of a world federation. See Pierre Côt, *Triumph of Treason: Contre Nous de la tyrannie* (London: Ziff-Davis, 1944). On Côt see Sabine Jansen, *Pierre Côt: Les pièges de l'antifascisme, 1895-1977* (Paris: Fayard, 2002). John Efremoff, former Vice-president of the 1917 Provisional Government and a Russian refugee in France, heartily embraced the federalist proposals which came from across the Channel, and on November 19 he sent to Chamberlain a call by suggesting concrete steps to initiate the establishment of a federation of free peoples (*Oeuvre*, 19 Nov. 1939). On Blum see: Jean Lacouture, *Léon Blum* (Paris: Seuil, 1979); Joel Colton, *Léon Blum: Humanist in Politics* (Durham, NC: Duke University Press, 1987); Alain Greilsamer, *Blum* (Paris: Flammarion, 1996); Richard L. Stokes, *Léon Blum: From Poet to Premier* (Whitefish, MT: Kessinger Publishing, 2007). On the popular front, see: Guy Bourdé, *La Défaite du Front Populaire* (Paris: La Découverte, 1977); Nicole Jordan, *The Popular Front and Central Europe: The Dilemmas of Impotence, 1918-1940* (Cambridge: Cambridge University Press, 1992); Jean-Michel Gaillard, *Les 40 jours de Blum* (Paris: Perrin, 2001); Martin S. Alexander and Helen Graham, *The French and Spanish Popular Fronts: Comparative Perspectives*, (Cambridge: Cambridge University Press, 2002); Jacques Kergoat, *La France du Front Populaire* (Paris: La Découverte, 2003).

Lanux, Nicolas Halasz, and an article by Robert Byron, member of the
Council of Federal Union, on the activities of the movement.[53]

Speaking of the possible differences between France and England
concerning war aims, and convinced that the French would not accept
from the British just "moral" guarantees for their future security, but only
"material" undertakings, Nicolson accepted however in principle the thesis
by Georges Scelle, according to which "a world order based on the
coexistence of national sovereignty" would have made "inevitable a new
war against Germany," and also the need to "adopt some form of
economic federalism," from which a "federal idea" would be born that
would force the present national States "to surrender some of their
sovereign rights to an international government."[54]

In *Towards Tomorrow's Europe*, W. Horsfall Carter argued that
European unity was the only alternative to the hegemony of the strongest
European State that in the last seventy years had been Germany. If the
immediate creation, at the end of the war, of a European federation was
impracticable, the twenty-five Continental States could form some
"groupings on a federal basis." Great Britain would not, however,
participate in any Continental grouping, since its role was to manage, in
close cooperation with the United States, the world order as a whole.[55]

---

[53] See the Foreign Office's reaction to the relevance given by the French press to
the views expressed by British intellectuals: FOP, FO371/24299, 134921, 347-52.
By Firmin Roz see *La Lumière de Paris* (Paris: La Renaissance du Livre, 1933).
By Pierre de Lanux see: *Young France and New America* (London: Macmillan,
1917); id., *European Manifesto* (London: Creative Age Press, 1945). On the inter-
war Paris political and literary *milieu* see Noel Riley Fitch, *Sylvia Beach and the
Lost Generation: A History of the Literary Paris in the Twenties and Thirties* (New
York: W.W. Norton & Company, 1985).

[54] Harold Nicolson, "Divergence possible entre les buts de guerre de la France et
de l'Angleterre," *Nouveaux Cahiers*, 54, (1940): 2-4. On Nicolson see: James Lee
Milne, *Harold Nicolson: A Biography, 1886-1929* (London: Trafalgar Square
Publishing, 1988); Nigel Nicolson ed., *The Harold Nicolson Diaries, 1907-1963*
(London: Orion Publishing, 2005); Derek Drinkwater, *Sir Harold Nicolson and
International Relations: The Practitioner as Theorist* (New York: Oxford
University Press, 2005); Norman Rose, *Harold Nicolson* (New York: Random
House, 2006).

[55] Horsfall Carter, "Vers l'Europe de Demain," *Nouveaux Cahiers*, 54, (1940): 7-
10. William Horsfall Carter (1900-76), was Editor of *The New Commonwealth
Quarterly* from 1932 to 1936; of the *Fortnightly Review* from 1937 to 1939;
collaborator of the *Manchester Guardian,* and the BBC; was official of the Foreign
Office Research Department from 1943 to 1951. He became a member of the
Council of Europe from 1951 to 1963. By Horsfall Carter see also *Speaking*

In *The Movement 'Federal Union' in Britain*, Robert Byron defended the view that the European Federation was the only final solution to the German problem, because it would allow European countries to defend themselves against the most powerful State, and Germany "to take her place among the other nations." The new European order should have been based on law, not just on a peace treaty which recorded a precarious power situation. Regarding the success that the federalist idea was gaining in Great Britain, Byron pointed out that Federal Union aimed not just to create the instruments to establish a European federation, but also "to persuade the British people that, once the war ended, the noblest form of patriotism will be to support the only system which will allow nations to live in peace and in prosperity."[56]

The journal also recorded other positions by representatives of British political culture, such as, for example, the testimony of the writer A. A. Milne—"I am a partisan of a world federation of democratic States"—and of Sir Christopher Robinson—General Secretary of the Kipling Society—who declared that he was a supporter of the federation, and thought that England "will join it."[57]

The interest in the post-war order which was growing in France was seen by Federal Union as a consequence of the fact that Great Britain was radically changing the traditional lines of its foreign policy. As long as Britain was seeking the balance of power in Europe, the Europeans could not realistically expect to achieve a European federation, despite the fact that the federal idea was for them "more familiar and more readily acceptable." The dream of a United States of Europe had been envisioned by philosophers such as Immanuel Kant, and politicians such as Aristide Briand, Richard Coudenhove-Kalergi, and Hans Bauer, who had certainly paved the way for its acceptance, "but it was not until six months ago"—Kimber remarked in *Federal Union News*—"that this dream suddenly lost its utopian air and stepped out of the cloud into the harsh reality of practical Continental politics." As soon as "the proud isolationist" began

---

European: The Anglo-Continental Cleavage (London: George Allen & Unwin, 1966).
[56] Robert Byron, "Le Mouvement de l'Union Fédérale en Grand Bretagne," *Nouveaux Cahiers*, 54, (1940): 10-3. By Robert Byron see *The Road to Oxiana* (New York: Oxford University Press, 2007). For a critical analysis, see James Knox, *Robert Byron* (London: John Murray, 2004).
[57] *Nouveaux Cahiers*, 54, (1940): 10-3. Alan Alexander Milne (1882-1956), became well-known for the volumes *Peace with Honour* (1934) and *War with Honour* (1940). On Milne see Ann Thwaite, *A. A. Milne: His Life* (London: Tempus, 2007).

to speak "of consolidating a union of peoples to embrace not only Europe but almost half the world as well," it was understood immediately on the Continent that a European federation was a dream no longer. "This organisation," concluded Kimber,

> which started hardly eighteen months ago, has achieved such tremendous support, not from pure numbers alone, but from serious and influential people in all walks of English life, and has proved to them that behind the statesmen's words stands the reality of public opinion, which no one can afford to misread.[58]

Federalism was gradually losing that utopian character which hitherto had marked it, and was beginning to inspire projects for the post-war order. The leadership of the process of transition from the national to the sovranational State was—Kimber sustained— naturally up to the British people. The French and gradually the other peoples of the Continent would follow them.[59]

Federal Union was by then a political reality whose existence nobody could deny to acknowledge. The struggle for the European federation had begun, and the federalist troops were ready.

---

[58] *Federal Union News*, 28.
[59] *Ibidem.*

CHAPTER IV

FEDERALISM AND THE DEBATE ON WAR AIMS

In the months before the outbreak of the war, the British did not generally have a precise idea of the profound reasons they were prepared to fight for. The questions, to which they were looking for answers, were related to the causes of the impending conflict, and how to prevent its recurrence. In particular, the debate tended to emphasise the limits of the Peace of Versailles, and of an international system that survived only for two decades. The mobilization was developing to keep faith with an international pledge—the defence of the independence of Poland—whose contents had not yet been clearly defined. The proponents of appeasement did not yet disappear, and the old Prime Minister Lloyd George was identified as the most likely successor to Chamberlain, if the man of "peace in our time" had not softened his hard line against Hitler. Historiography has not failed to point out that the unwinding of the appeasement party did not conclude in the summer of 1939, but in the summer of 1940, during the first months of the Battle of Britain, when policy had by then to give up every manoeuvring space to military action. In those summer months of 1940, the British people knew very well what they were fighting for: for their very survival.[1]

---

[1] On the debate on appeasement see: Neville Thompson, *The Anti-Appeasers: Conservative Opposition to Appeasement in the 30s* (Oxford: Clarendon Press 1971); Ritchie Ovendale, *'Appeasement' and the English-Speaking World: Britain, the United States, the Dominions, and the Policy of Appeasement, 1937-1939* (Cardiff: University of Wales Press, 1975); Stephen Walker, "Solving the Appeasement Puzzle: Contending Historical Interpretations of British Diplomacy During the 1930s," *British Journal of International Studies*, 6, 3, (1980): 219-25; Paul Kennedy, "The Study of Appeasement: Methological Crossroads or Meeting-Place?," *British Journal of International Studies*, 6, 3, (1980): 181-95; Scott Newton, *Profits of Peace: The Political Economy of Anglo-German Appeasement* (New York: Oxford University Press, 1996); Martin Thomas, *Britain, France and Appeasement: Anglo-French Relations in the Popular Front Era* (Oxford: Clarendon Press, 1996); Peijian Shen, *The Age of Appeasement. The Evolution of British Foreign Policy in the 1930s* (Stroud: Sutton Publishing, 1999); Peter

During the first ten months of the war the objectives for which the British were fighting were not, on the contrary, so clear and the Government found itself even forced to appoint a Select Committee to define them. If the defeat of Nazism was the objective generally shared by all those who believed in the war and then in progress, on the strategy to achieve this end, and on the characteristics of the post-war international order, wide divergences were recorded. There were essentially three currents of opinion which divided the British, and were running within political parties themselves.[2]

The current which, until June of 1940, seemed to gain most acclaim advocated the construction, at the end of hostilities, of a European centre of gravity, on the basis of a permanent Anglo-French Alliance. The ongoing war was not so much against the German people, but against Nazi ideology, that had to be militarily destroyed, before it was possible to re-create in Europe the conditions for an economic and orderly civil life. By choosing France as a permanent ally, the British knew the ties which bound them to the Empire would have to be renounced to place this at the top of their political agenda. Privileging Europe meant keeping in the Channel the traditional centre of gravity of British politics.[3]

Neville, *Appeasing Hitler: The Diplomacy of Sir Neville Henderson, 1937-9* (London: Macmillan, 1999); Neil Forbes, *Doing Business with the Nazis: Britain's Economic and Financial Relations with Germany, 1931-1939* (London: Frank Cass, 2000); R. A. C. Parker, *Churchill and Appeasement* (London: Macmillan, 2000); Norman Rose, *The Cliveden Set: Portrait of an Exclusive Fraternity* (New York: Random House, 2000); Richard Davis, *Anglo-French Relations before the Second World War: Appeasement and Crisis* (New York: Palgrave Macmillan, 2001); Richard S. Grayson, *Liberals, International Relations, and Appeasement: The Liberal Party, 1919-1939* (London: Frank Cass, 2001); Ian Kershaw, *Making Friends with Hitler: Lord Londonderry, the Nazis, and the Road to War* (London: Penguin Press, 2004); Peter Neville, "The Foreign Office and Britain's Ambassadors to Berlin, 1933-39," *Contemporary British History*, 18, 3, (2004): 110-5, 125-29; id., *Hitler and Appeasement: The British Attempt to Prevent the Second World War* (London: Hambledon Continuum, 2006). On the possibility of a return of Lloyd George to Downing Street see Paul Addison, "Lloyd George and Compromise Peace in the Second World War," in *Lloyd George: Twelve Essays*, ed. A. J. P. Taylor (London: Atheneum, 1971).

[2] On the works of this Committee, see Christopher Hill, *Cabinet Decisions on Foreign Policy: The British Experience, October 1938-June 1941* (Cambridge: Cambridge University Press, 2002), 188-23, 230.

[3] Union of Democratic Control, *Report of the U.D.C. Conference on War Aims and Peace Terms, on December 9th and 10th 1939* (London: Union of Democratic Control, 1939); Clement Attlee, *Labour's Peace Aims* (London: Labour Party, 1940); Edward Hallet, *The Future of International Government* (London: National

A minority current of opinion, which however was supported by the most markedly conservative circles—which were then closest to the centre of power—called for the reorganisation of Europe in a number of regional units of equal weight, held together by a new League of Nations, where Great Britain could exercise, precisely because of her Empire, the traditional role of the needle on the scales. To these ultra conservative circles it appeared therefore necessary, on the one hand to strengthen the ties with the Dominions, that in times of greatest difficulty had never turned their backs to the motherland, and on the other hand, to create at the heart of Europe political counterweights—such as a Balkan federation and a Danubian one—to a weakened Germany.[4]

A third current of opinion—which had its headquarters in Chatham House and in the English-Speaking Union—looked, *vice versa*, across the Atlantic, and called for the creation of a world system of States dominated by the two leading democracies of the English-speaking world: Great Britain and the United States. The convergence of interests of Nazi Germany and the Soviet Union seemed purely temporary, and bound to be replaced, in the turning of time, by conflict, inherent in the geo-political situation of Central-Eastern Europe. If Europe could be kept under their control thanks to this rivalry, in which the Latin peoples could play some role, in the Far East the two Anglo-Saxon powers should have to try to

---

Peace Council, 1941); Harold Joseph Laski, *The Economic Revolution* (London: Stanhope Press, 1941); John MacMurray, *The Foundations of Economic Reconstruction* (London: National Peace Council, 1942); Amy Hewes, *Labour's Aim in War and Peace* (London: Commission to Study the Organisation of Peace, 1944). Within this current of opinion, a post-war order vision founded on the dominance of the moral factor gained strength in Anglican circles. See in this respect: Richard Martin Fagley, *The Study of Peace Aims in the Local Church: Why? What? How? Suggestions for Groups Concerned with Principles of World Order* (London: Church Peace Union, 1941); Herbert George Wood, *The Spiritual Basis of Peace* (London: National Peace Council, 1941); Carl Heath, *The Present Crisis and the Spirit of Man* (London: National Peace Council, 1941); Powell Spring, *The Peace Aims of Humanity* (London: Orange Press, 1944).

[4] G. D. H. Cole, *War Aims* (London: The New Statesman and Nation, 1939); G. O. G. Luetzens, *A New Order for Germany* (London: National Peace Council, 1941); Rita Hinden, *Freedom for Colonial People* (London: National Peace Council, 1942); G. D. H. Cole, *When the Fighting Stops* (London: National Peace Council, 1943); National Peace Council, *Peace by Compulsion?* (London: National Peace Council, 1944); Adam Pragier, *Polish Peace Aims* (London: Maxlove, 1944); John Boyd Orr and G. D. H. Cole, *Welfare and Peace* (London: National Peace Council, 1945); J. Middleton Murray, *The Third Challenge* (London: National Peace Council, 1945).

maintain the balance of power, taking advantage of the rivalry between China and Japan. In a sort of theoretical division of tasks and responsibilities, Great Britain would have managed the control of the Eastern Hemisphere, and the United States the Western one. From this close Anglo-American cooperation would be born a new geo-political system able to give the world a new era of stability, just like the one known during the nineteenth century: the *Pax Britannica* would have been followed by the *Pax Atlantica*.[5]

It is possible to convey the stands that prominent exponents of the world of culture, politics, churches, and economy took on these three currents of opinion over the so-called *drôle de guerre*. Although differing so much on the aims to be achieved, they did however adopt, regarding the

---

[5] For a debate on Allied war aims, see: *Peace and War Aims: A Correspondence from The Times* (London: Peace Book Company, 1939); *British War Aims. A Collection of Extracts from Speeches Delivered by H.M. Ministers in the United Kingdom between 3rd September, 1939, and 31st March, 1940* (London: HMSO, 1940); William Teeling, *After the War: A Symposium of Peace Aims* (London: Sidgwick & Jackson, 1940); Laszlo Ledermann, *Official Statements of War and Peace Aims. European Belligerents, September 1, 1939 to August 31, 1940* (Geneva: Geneva Research Centre, 1940); Percy Ellwood Corbett, *War Aims and Post-War Plans* (New York: American Committee of International Studies, 1941); Frawn McKay Brodie, *Peace Aims and Postwar Planning: A Bibliography* (Boston, MA: World Peace Foundation, 1942); Paul Tillich, *War Aims. The Real Meaning of this War. Who Can, and Who Can't Carry Out these War Aims* (New York: Protestant Press, 1942); Julia E. Johnsen, *The Eight Points of Post War World Reorganization* (New York: The H. W. Wilson Company, 1942; reprinted by Johnsen Press, 2007); Harold Albert Hansen, *Issues and Aims of the War* (Pasadena, CA: Pasadena Junion College Press, 1943); *War and Peace Aims of the United Nations, September 1, 1939-December 31, 1942* (Boston: World Peace Foundation, 1943); Charles M. Meredith, *Peace? A Critical Study of America's Peace Aims* (Washington, DC: The Universal Press, 1944); Walter Lippmann, *U.S. War Aims* (London: Hamish Hamilton, 1944), 64-77; B. G. Bell, *Route to Potsdam: The Story of the Peace Aims, 1939-1945* (London: Allan Wingate, 1945). For an historiographic analysis, see: Peter Ludlow, "Le débat sur le buts de la paix," in *Français et britannique*, 93-122; Michael Howard, *War and the Liberal Conscience* (London: Maurice Temple Smith, 1981); Fréderic Seager, "Les buts de guerre allies devant l'opinion (1939-1940)," *Revue d'histoire moderne et contemporaine*, 32, (1985): 617-38; Bosco, *Lord Lothian*, 113-149; David Stevenson, *French War Aims and Peace Planning* (Berkeley, CA: University of California Press, 1994); Bosco and Navari, *Chatham House and British*; Bosco and May, *The Round Table*; Theron F. Schlabach and Richard T. Hughes, *Proclaim Peace: Christian Pacifism from Unexpected Quarters* (Champaign, IL: University of Illinois Press, 1997); Rothwell, *War Aims;* Toledano, *War Aims*.

instruments to be employed—at least for their overwhelming majority—a common element. It was federalism, meant as a form to be filled with concrete historical contents: Europe, the Commonwealth, and the United States. A review of the positions taken by the federalists, within these three groupings, offers us a measure of the interest, unprecedented not just in Great Britain, which British civil society showed for a political doctrine which was based on the criticism of unlimited national sovereignty.

Referring to the theoretical concepts and the practical experience of federalism, British society was able to anchor the debate on the war aims—in itself abstract—to coherent and achievable political projects. This debate was to show the limits of traditional ideologies—liberalism, democracy, and socialism—and to interpret the deep crisis into which Europe was plunging, and to point out concrete remedies. Since traditional ideologies did not have the adequate conceptual instruments for understanding the historical process in its specific manifestations—power politics and war—and as a whole—the economic and political integration of mankind—federalism appeared as the revelation of an absolute truth. It was used not only as the main criterion to interpret and understand the past, but also as the fundamental principle of action to build the future. Stripped from ideologically distorting connotations—namely no longer seen as an instrument of capitalism—federalism was almost universally adopted as a necessary condition to realise other ideals, such as peace, freedom, democracy and socialism.

During the first ten months of the war, the federalist option became then the confluence point of different political, religious, and cultural experiences. In that extraordinary period of British history that goes from the invasion of Poland to the downfall of France, it can be said that almost all roads led to Federal Union. It was definitely in Great Britain, more clearly than anywhere else that all the novelty of thought arose that had played until then a rather marginal role in the development of Western political culture. It is precisely for this extraordinary value, and in order to disclose all the richness of the themes and nuances that a chronological report will be offered here, which seems to be best suited to show the parable of an idea that eventually came to conquer a very substantial section of British public opinion.

I. *The British press and federalism*

The *Manchester Guardian* was the first great newspaper to pay any attention to the federalist debate. On 7 September, Lancelot Hogben, a member of the Federal Union's Council, supported the necessity of an immediate peace offensive on the basis of the offer of the federation:

> It is neither too late nor too early to invoke the good offices of President Roosevelt to explore the willingness of neutral States to cooperate in building a new international order. The propaganda machine of the Nazi Government would be paralysed by the spectacle of the United States of Europe with both hands of welcome extended to the peoples of Germany.[6]

"A half-hearted attempt," Hogben again stated on 18 September regarding the Treaty of Versailles,

> to patch up a loose federation under the hegemony of the victors was foredoomed to failure by the lack of any central Government with authority to keep the peace. It is now clear that the only basis of lasting peace is a federal union of constituents who validate their peaceful professions by relinquishing their powers of defence and Imperial ambitions to international administration.[7]

In a letter to the *Manchester Guardian* of 13 September, J. McLellan observed that the war was a consequence of the "deification of the sovereign State," and that it was not possible to have a "lasting peace" if not "based on some form of federal or world government, on democracy, and on social justice." The "only alternative to pooling armaments for social purposes is the anarchic use of them in support of conflicting, self-judged national rights." The world had to be "planned...economically and politically," in order to defy once and for all "nationalist anarchy that has sacrificed international peace on the altar of the sovereign State."[8]

Julian Huxley also shared that view in a letter to *The Times* of 21 September, the very day that the leading British opinion-making newspaper began to provide a platform for the federalist debate. Huxley observed that the breaking up of Germany would not have resolved the problem of European peace, but would simply have postponed "the emergence of a new anarchic crisis," and that the only solution was "some move in the direction of federalism." The "incipient federalization of Western Europe" would have implied a better distribution of raw materials, a more efficient system of public transport, wider horizons to

---

[6] Lancelot Hogben, *Manchester Guardian*, 7 Sept. 1939.
[7] *Ibidem*, 18 Sept. 1939.
[8] J. McLellan, *Manchester Guardian*, 13 Sept. 1939.

research and education, an integrated fiscal system, and national disarmament through the creation of a European army.[9]

The *Manchester Guardian* of 23 September published for the first time the views of two representatives of Federal Union, C. E. M. Joad and R. G. Mackay, thus acknowledging the existence of the movement. Joad stated that the best guarantee to prevent a repetition of the mistakes of Versailles was

> to announce here and now, before the bombs begin to drop and to let loose a wave of hatred and a lust for vengeance which will make the passions of the last war look like the tantrums of children, the terms upon which we should be prepared to make peace.[10]

The British Government had to declare its intention of offering to the Germans "a common Government to take over the administration of those spheres of interests which States have in common, if only because what one State does in any one of these spheres necessarily affects the peoples of other States." The offer of union would be extended to other European democracies, including Italy, providing the restoration of free institutions. The European Government would be responsible for foreign, military, commercial, colonial and monetary policies.

"The time has come," Joad remarked, "to supersede the absolute sovereignty of the nation-State and to transfer some part of its functions to a Federal Government." The war would otherwise have been fought in vain: "if only because by leaving the existing European anarchy uncontrolled with each nation-State as arbiter of its own interests and judge and jury in its own cause, it will pave the way for a series of future

---

[9] Julian Huxley, *The Times*, 21 Sept. 1939. By Julian Huxley, see: *Religion Without Revelation* (London: Harper & Brothers Publishers, 1957); id., *Evolutionary Humanism* (London: Prometheus Books, 1992). For a critical analysis, see: J. R. Baker, *Julian Huxley, Scientist and World Citizen, 1887-1975* (London: Unipub, 1978); Kenneth C. Waters and Albert Van Helden, *Julian Huxley: Biologist and Statesman of Science: Proceedings of a Conference Held at Rice University 25-27 September 1987* (Houston, TX: Rice Univesity Press, 1992).

[10] Cyril E. M. Joad, *Manchester Guardian*, 23 Sept. 1939. See the National Peace Council's pamphlet on war aims: *H. G. Wells, S. De Madariaga, J. Middleton Murry, C. E. M. Joad on the New World Order* (London: National Peace Council, 1940). By Joad see also: *The Story of Civilization* (London: A. & C. Black, 1931); id., *Manifesto: Being the Book of the Federation of Progressive Societies and Individuals* (London: George Allen & Unwin, 1934); id., *Why War?* (London: Penguin Book, 1939); id., *The Philosophy of Federal Union* (London: Macmillan, 1942); id., *Philosophy for Our Times* (Pomona, CA: Pomona Press, 2007).

wars." The federal union had by then become "the supreme political need of our time."[11]

Ronald Mackay—an Australian lawyer who would take over the Secretaryship of Federal Union from Kimber—also included financial policy and the minorities issue among the competencies of the federal government. The Allies were not just fighting to "resist aggression," but "to create a world in which aggression will not be used as a method of change and where aggression will not be necessary, as adequate machinery for peaceful change will exist." The European federation was the first step towards world federation, without which "ultimate peace cannot be established." "With a United States of Europe established at the end of this war," he concluded, "the world would be in a position to consider a world union with other units, such as the United States of America, the United States of Europe, the British Commonwealth, the United States of Russia, and the Asiatic States."[12]

H. G. Wells also took part in the debate with a letter to *The Times* on 26 September. Wells' argument became widely utilised by the left against constitutional federalism. Federalism in itself, without social values, Wells remarked, was no more than a magic formula, which would have seduced and mislead public opinion, diverting it from the real goal, which was the triumph of socialism for a better world. The leader of the same day, *The End and the Means*, was entirely devoted to the discussion of Wells' view, and criticised his "materialistic" conception of history and observed: "the 'simulacrum' of Geneva is shattered, but Federal Union has sprung up to thwart the 'inevitable' logic...of the only *homo sapiens*, the economic man."[13]

---

[11] Cyril E. M. Joad, *Manchester Guardian*, 23 Sept. 1939.

[12] Ronald Gordon Mackay, *Manchester Guardian*, 23 Sept. 1939. By Ronald Gordon Mackay, see also: *Peace Aims and the New Order: Being a Revised and Popular Edition of 'Federal Europe', Outlining the Case for European Federation, Together with a Draft Constitution of a United States of Europe* (London: M. Joseph, 1941); id., *Towards a United States of Europe: An Analysis of Britain's Role in a European Union* (Westport, CT: Greenwood Press, 1976).

[13] Herbert George Wells, *The Times*, 26 Sept. 1939. By Wells see also: *The Outline of History* (London: Garden City Publisher, 1925); id., *The Open Conspiracy* (New York: Doubleday, 1928); id., *The Shape of Things to Come* (London: Penguin Classics, 2006); id., *The New World Order* (London: FQ Classics, 2007); id., *A Modern Utopia* (New York: 1st World Library, 2007). For a critical analysis, see: Anthony West, *H. G. Wells: Aspects of a Life* (New York: Random House, 1984); David C. Smith, *H. G. Wells: Desperately Mortal: A Biography* (New Haven: Yale University Press, 1988); Harold Bloom, *H. G. Wells* (London: Chelsea House

John Bouverie, in the article "War Aims" in *News Chronicle* of 27 September, criticised the negative attitude of Wells towards the "popular idea of 'Federation' as a cure for Europe's recurrent troubles," and observed that Wells failed to realise that "federalism in a true sense is essential to the realisation of his ideal of the World State":

> The whole development of the modern civilised world—Bouverie observed—increasingly emphasises the obsoleteness of complete national sovereignty. Almost every intervention, every new social and commercial institution, makes a mockery of it. The aeroplane, radio, international shipping and postal codes...emphasise the inter-dependence of one people with another and the crazy anachronism of rigid national frontiers on the old, mutually antagonistic lines. The world is ripe, in its technical organisation, for the breakdown of these barriers; only the political ideas and the will to reform lag behind.[14]

Norman Angell, author of *The Great Illusion*, in *For What Do We Fight?* observed that in order to persuade the world of the sincerity of the profession of faith in a new international system, the British people had to pass from words to facts: "to begin now to build a real federal union with France." France and Great Britain had to form an "organic political union...not merely for war purposes, but as the beginning of the permanent reconstruction of Europe and the world along new lines." "Concurrently" —Angell observed—"a persistent drive should be made towards a real Federal Union of the Commonwealth." The transformation of the Commonwealth into a federation would have accelerated the process of the perception of France and Great Britain not as two States, each of forty million inhabitants, but "as a single country of eighty millions, the pivot of a union of an additional five hundred millions, girdling the world."[15] The beginning of "some sort of Franco-British federalism" could initially be based on the Supreme War Council, strengthened by a "Franco-British Inter-parliamentary Conference, first of all between like-minded parties of both parliaments, going on to conferences of representatives of all British and all French parties." The mechanism thus constituted in war-time had to continue to exist, even with some modifications in peace-time for the management of foreign, military,

---

Publications, 2005); John S. Partington, *H. G. Wells's Fin-de-Siecle: Twenty-First Century Reflections on the Early H. G. Wells* (Oxford: Peter Lang, 2007).

[14] John Bouverie, "War Aims," *News Chronicle*, 27 Sept. 1939.

[15] Norman Angell, *For What Do We Fight?* (London: 1939), 264-9; id., *The Great Illusion* (London: William Heinemann, 1909). Sir Norman Angell (1872-1967), had been Labour MP from 1929 to 1931.

economic and financial common policies. Federation would also silence
the supporters of a "Carthaginian peace" towards Germany, because at the
end of the war it was not necessary to break up Germany into a number of
States: "The Federal principle, imaginatively and consistently applied,
might make even the policy of 'breaking up Germany' a step to peace
instead of another war in the next generation."[16]

John Gardner acknowledged on the 26 September in the *Manchester
Guardian* that "there has been lately much talk of the importance of
instituting a European Federation at the end of the war." The following
day, G. B. Valentine, Professor at the University College of Wales,
Cardiff, wrote:

> The first step towards the creation of an effective League must be the
> formation of a European Parliament. Such an Assembly once formed and
> allowed to get into working order would eventually become the nucleus of
> a larger League, and finally of a League of which every State in the world
> would be a satisfied member.[17]

On the 28 September, in a letter to *The Times*, Wickham Steed
emphasised the necessity of a "more positive and sustaining" ideal rather
than the destruction of Nazism. Once the war was overcome the
democracies had to face the German question, having to integrate as
equals a people of eighty million into

> a union of nations democratically self-governed and banded together not
> only against lawless violence but for the mutual helpfulness which is
> peace...To frame and to proclaim such a policy would be the most
> powerful propaganda.[18]

---

[16] Angell, *For What Do*, 269.
[17] *Manchester Guardian*, 26 Sept. 1939. Lawrence Holt observed in the
Manchester Guardian of 15 September that Great Britain and France had "only to
make a public offer of a Europe federated for purposes of international trade into
one common fiscal system." Speaking in Manchester on 26 September on the
invitation of the International League, Olaf Stapledon, dismissed the Streitian
project as "naive", and supported the need for the transformation of the Anglo-
French Alliance on federal lines. See the article "Possible Developments after the
War" in *The Times*, 27 September.
[18] Henry Wickham Steed, *The Times*, 28 Sept. 1939. On the following day, C. A.
Alington asked the Editor of *The Times* "if a definition of our war aims is
desirable...might it not be enough to say that we are fighting for the ideal of a
United States of Europe." On the question of pacifism and international order by
Wickham Steed, see: *Vital Peace: A Story of Risks* (London: Macmillan, 1936);

Wickham Steed returned to support the case for a European federation in early October, with the articles *Foreground and Background* and *Our War Aims*, where he expounded the Federal Union's version of the war aims. It was not enough to defeat Nazism and bring back Germany within the 1919 frontiers, but it appeared vital to promote "the formation, if possible during the war, of the beginnings of a federation or federal union between all the peoples allied or associated with the present enemies of Hitlerism." At the end of the war, this federal nucleus would have accepted the adhesion of a democratic Germany, of any other European democracy, and also of the colonial territories, once they were developed into individual nationhood. The war would then have become "a struggle for the right of entry into a new and higher phase of human existence."[19]

The war marked one of the "decisive moments in human history," which required "bold thinking and high aims." The federal idea was by then gaining wide and growing consent "in many countries," but the practical and still unsolved problem was "how to begin." If a solution could not be found before the end of the war, it was likely to fall "into errors similar to those that were destined to ruin much of the work done by the architects of the League of Nations Covenant." There would have come into existence an "elaborate written Constitution, another League or federation of sovereign States, each jealous of its own sovereignty." It was instead preferable to follow the "rule of thumb" and work "with the tools and the materials that lie ready at hand," namely the union of France, Great Britain and the Dominions:

> France and Great Britain are now united, far more than allied, in this war...This union should be broadened and deepened until the principle of a Supreme Council...would be embodied in a permanent institution. From it might evolve something in the nature of a federal Government for the British and French democracies, with one proviso of ultimately decisive importance...that whatever federal institutions may be set up, or federal government that may be formed, should be responsible not to the Governments but directly to the peoples of the countries belonging to the federation...One of the authors of the Constitution of the United States, Madison learned from the study of confederacies, ancient and modern, that only those federations which were founded upon the assent of individual citizens, not on that of States, had endured or could endure...Each member of a workable federal system must retain control of its own internal affairs

---

reprinted by Baker Press, 2007); id., *Our War Aims* (London: Secker & Warburg, 1939).

[19] Henry Wickham Steed, "Foreground and Background," *Fortnightly Review*, 146, (1939): 369-70; id., *Our War Aims* (London: 1939), 207-9.

while surrendering to a federal government, drawing authority from the peoples not from the States of the federation, sovereignty over affairs that are common to all.[20]

The leader of the *Manchester Guardian* of the 29 September stated that a great war was certainly "the greatest of all revolutions," with immense consequences for the way of thinking and living. Europe was facing the same choice which Proudhon saw a century before, when "Europe left by the Treaties of Vienna was breaking up into a complex of sovereign national States." The choice was "between Caesarism and Federalism." Only a revolution would have won over inertia and the conservative tendency of the old structures of the nation-State: "If a definition of our war aims is desirable...might it not be enough to say that we are fighting for the ideal of a United States of Europe?"[21]

On one side there was the Streitian project, based on "a certain community of ideas and interests," while on the other there was the project of Coudenhove-Kalergi for a European federation. The merit of these opposing projects, which were based on two different conceptions of the historical course, was to begin a debate on the "problems that have to be met by any system of union, whatever the powers it bestows on the Federal Government." It was a necessary debate because it equipped people's minds for that revision of values which was necessary for the creation of the supranational course of history. The British people had, in particular, to consider closely "the special problems of the British Commonwealth as a federation whose members include a great variety of political forms and as a Power that is both inside and outside Europe."[22]

The letters of the same day from Raymond O'Malley, on the 3rd October from Maude Royden and Lord Davies, and on 4th October from Sydney Havelock, confirmed the interest with which the paper was considering the federalist project. "What impresses me first," Rennie Smith, Secretary of the Friends of Europe, wrote on 13th October, "in your correspondence columns to date, is the atmosphere of unreality which it reveals." Great Britain could certainly contribute to the reconstruction of Europe on a federalist basis, but she could do little without the consent of the other European States: "If a federal solution is to be reached...many sub-groupings, along federal lines, of the smaller States of Europe are an

---

[20] Steed, "Foreground and Background", 370.

[21] *Manchester Guardian*, 2 Oct. 1939. Also the leader of 5 October returned on the theme, observing how the Allies were fighting for a Europe based "on some form of Federal Union."

[22] *Ibidem.*

indispensable part of this process of organic growth and voluntary consent." The British contribution has to limit itself to stimulating and encouraging "European citizens of various nations to work out these ideas." A discussion on war aims, which did not take into consideration the involvement of Allies and neutral public opinion, seemed "highly academic," and, besides, "success in war" was "the indispensable preliminary to this end."[23]

According to the leader of the *Manchester Guardian* of the 7th October the federalist project was still just supported by isolated voices, and the major impulse towards the debate on war aims tended to present federalism as a seductive alternative to the potential opponents of Hitler, rather than as an immediate solution to the problems of Anglo-French co-operation. The *Guardian* was not completely wrong. Only after the November economic agreements between Great Britain and France did the federalist project begin to be in fact considered for application in the short term.[24]

The *Guardian* of 13th October also published the manifesto signed by fifty-seven scientists, all members of the Royal Society of Science. Remarking how scientific discoveries "greatly increased man's power of destruction," while the "continued progress of science and its application to human well-being" were "threatened by the prevailing anarchy of international relations," they declared "a special responsibility to their fellow citizens at this time," and their commitment to building "a stable international order" based on the federalist principle.

> The undersigned—the manifesto declared—believe that the safeguards of this new international order must go far beyond the provisions of the League Covenant, which permitted rival powers to retain their separate armed forces, left the control of backward communities and access to raw materials to individual nations, and established no central authority to legislate for the common needs of the constituent States.

"The necessary condition for a new peaceful world order was", they declared, "the union of *all* nations...under a federal Government with a supreme and *single* authority".[25]

---

[23] *Manchester Guardian,* 29 Sept., 3, 4 Oct. 1939; Rennie Smith, *Manchester Guardian,* 13 Oct. 1939.

[24] *Manchester Guardian*, 7 Oct. 1939.

[25] *Manchester Guardian*, 23 Oct. 1939. The signatories were: A. C. Aitken, H. Stanley Allen, E. B. Bailey, W. Lawrence Balls, J. H. Browning, Harold Carpenter, Sidney Chapman, A. J. Clark, G. R. Clemo, A. M. Dirac, C. A. Edwards, J. Evershed, A. Mostyn Field, H. J. Fleure, H. Munro Fox, Percy Frankland, Ruggles

The implications of the firm stand taken by the scientists were even felt in Rome, where the *Messaggero* of the 14th October reproduced their ideas under the title "Si parla di federalismo europeo," specifying that in Great Britain it was not only the scientists who were calling for a "federal government for Europe."[26]

"The war of ideas," Lord Davies wrote in the *Manchester Guardian* of 19th October, "must be waged with the same courage, energy and determination as the war of trenches." Davies asserted the necessity of an ideological counter-offensive, based on the establishment of a confederation which a few years before had been described as the United States of Europe by the French Prime Minister Aristide Briand:

> Its membership would be open to all European States who were willing to abandon war as an instrument of policy. The functions of such a confederation should include the settlement of all disputes by a Federal Parliament, assisted by an Equity Tribunal; the control of a common defence or police force; concerted measures of economic cooperation; and for the joint administration of non-self-governing colonial territories.[27]

On 2nd November the *News Chronicle* devoted two whole pages to an analysis of the war and peace aims for which the Allies were fighting. According to Sir Walter Layton, in *A Plan for European Peace,* it was possible to guarantee "absolute security against military aggression" in only two ways: through total disarmament, or with the creation of a European federation. Since they were at that time unattainable ideals, Layton proposed the creation of a "European Association of Nations,"

Gates, C. S. Gibson, Major Greenwood, Richard Gregory, H. Hartridge, H. L. Hawkins, G. G. Henderson, H. G. A. Hickling, Arthur Hill, Lancelot Hogben, Harold Jeffreys, A. D. Imms, Karl Joardan, Stanley Kemp, J. Kenyon, E. A. Milne, Peter Chalmers Mitchell, C. S. Myers, John Orr, John Parsons, Slater Price, H. S. Raper, John Read, Lewis Richardson, H. N. Ridley, Alexander Russell, F. S. Russell, Redcliffe Salaman, J. L. Simonsen, George Simpson, J. W. W. Stephens, J. S. B. Stopford, A. G. Tansley, Jocelyn Thorpe, Miles Walker, F. E. Weiss, J. T. Wilson, F. Wood Jones.

[26] *Messaggero*, 14 Oct. 1939, (quoted in *Federal Union News*, 4).

[27] See also David Davies, *The Way to Peace: A Brief Exposition of the New Commonwealth Programme* (London: New Commonwealth Press, 1937). For a discussion, see: Daniel Laqua, *Internationalism Reconfigured: Transnational Ideas and Movements Between the World Wars* (New York: I.B. Tauris, 2011); M. Pugh, *Liberal Internationalism: The Interwar Movement for Peace in Britain*, (New York: Palgrave Macmillan, 2012).

based on the principles which had to be realised on a world scale: disarmament, political guarantees, and economic cooperation.[28]

The limitation of armaments would create a sense of security without which justice and the creation of an international police force were not possible. Political and economic co-operation as a pre-condition for the creation of a free-trade area and to prevent aggression would have followed accordingly, and Germany would be admitted to the Association on an equal footing, on condition that she returned to democracy. Thus the road towards the European federation would be opened, because without Germany's co-operation it would never be possible. This new European system could work successfully with the creation of two "federal groups," that of Scandinavian countries, which were already united in many respects, and that of the former Austro-Hungarian Empire, with the addition of Poland. Austria would have chosen to be annexed to Germany, or to the Central European federation.[29]

On 3rd November, *The Times* took part in the debate with a view expressed in its leader "The Foundations of Federalism":

> One of the outstanding features of this war—a "special correspondent" wrote—is the widespread eagerness to discuss not merely how it will end in terms of victory and defeat, but how a new order can be built after it when the moment comes, simply to make peace first and to organise it later, when elementary salvage has been performed and the first bitterness has subsided.[30]

The task of Great Britain and France was to give a "fresh and dynamic expression" to the "tested values of Western Civilization, and to give new life to its cultural inheritance from Greece and Rome, from Christianity

---

[28] Sir Walter Layton, "A Plan for European Peace," *News Chronicle*, 2 Nov. 1939. The impact in France of Layton's article were partuculary favourable, especially among radical and socialist circles, (see "Allied War Aims: What Europe Thinks," *News Chronicle*, 3 Nov. 1939). Sir Walter Thomas Layton (1884-1966) was Professor of Economics at the Universities of London and Cambridge, and Editor of *The Economist*, from 1922 to 1938. He was created Baron in 1947. On British public opinion and the question of the limitation of armaments in the early 1930s, see: G. C. Peden, *British Rearmament and the Treasury, 1932-1939* (Edinburgh: Scottish Academic Press, 1979); Catherine Krull and B. J. C. McKercher, "The Press, Public Opinion, Arms Limitation, and Government Policy in Britain, 1932-34: Some Preliminary Observations," *Diplomacy & Statecraft*, 13, 3, (2002): 103-36; Carolyn J. Kitching, *Britain and the Geneva Disarmament Conference: A Study in International History* (New York: Palgrave Macmillan, 2003).
[29] Layton, "A Plan for European."
[30] "The Foundations of Federalism," *The Times*, 3 Nov. 1939.

and from modern science." Democracies had been "slow to grasp that in the congested, highly organised modern European community it is no longer realistic to think in terms of a sharp division between domestic and foreign affairs or between politics and economics." The attempt by the totalitarian regimes to solve the problem of the interdependence of the modern age through autarky, was just a transitory phase and "an ever-expanding *Lebensraum* for a few giant States emerges as the only practical alternative to more and more comprehensive co-operation between neighbouring countries large and small."[31]

The principle of the nation-State adopted at the end of the First World War was demonstrated as "patently unworkable," in view of the fact that, in order to survive, nations needed to enjoy prosperity and autonomy. The only alternative was to "unite them in larger groupings, the beginnings of which may be seen in the Oslo Group and the Balkan Entente." The war, which was showing itself increasingly to be a civil war among Europeans, "brought to a head the question of giving effective political and economic expression to the unity of the European community of nations, already clearly expressed in their civilization." Only a "limitation of sovereign rights" could offer a decisive contribution to its concrete realisation:

> We have in being today, in the Supreme Council and the inter-Allied High Command, a standing organ of government with a powerful influence over two distinct sovereign States, and a combination of armed forces under unified control. If by common consent these arrangements could be kept functioning after the war it would only be necessary to add to the Supreme Council representatives of other States, and to add to the armed forces contingents from ex-neutral and ex-enemy countries in order to have an international organ of government with an international police force at its disposal...It may well be that eventually the solution of European or even world problems is some form of federalism, but at the present stage it seems impracticable to attempt more than to create favourable conditions for federalism to develop...The difficulties are formidable, but they must be measured against the existing alternative, which is to fight a major European war every 25 years.[32]

Colonies would be brought together and benefit from the union of resources of the British and French Empires "through the creation of international technical and economic services backed by an international grant-in-aid system." This Anglo-French international authority would be able to exercise control over the world economy and protect the

---

[31] *Ibidem.*
[32] *Ibidem.*

"international community" from "harmful economic policies" unilaterally undertaken. The definition of British war aims, according to *The Times*, coincided only partly with the Federal Union scheme, while Streit's project was ranked as "rough."[33]

In the leader of 3rd November, *The Times* also reviewed the speech given by Lothian to the Pilgrims, presenting it as "an eloquent interpretation of the cause for which Great Britain and France are at war." "Some form of federation...at any rate for part of Europe," *The Times* observed, "is a necessary condition of any stable world order":

> At present even the first step to such a revolution is hard to see. Some thinkers in this country hold that a starting point may be found within the British Empire, by way of the voluntary transfer by two or more of its self-governing communities of some of their powers over their own subjects to an authority transcending them. Lord Lothian suggested to his American audience that they might find a model for the world commonwealth of the future in their own federation of States. However they approach their goal, those idealists must look far beyond the conclusion of the present war who believe with Victor Hugo that a day will come when those two immense groups, the Unites States of America and the United States of Europe, shall be seen placed in the presence of each other, extending the hand of fellowship across the ocean, exchanging their produce, their commerce, their industry, their arts, their genius...ameliorating creation under the eyes of the Creator, and uniting, for the good of all, these two irresistible and infinite powers—the fraternity of men and the power of God.[34]

Even the *Daily Telegraph* and the "popular press"—*Reynold News*, *Picture Post*, *John Bull* and *Everybody's Weekly*—had taken a special interest in the federalist debate ever since early November, giving wide coverage to their presentation of Federal Union. The federalist project, being installed in that great debate, could in that way reach almost five million readers.[35]

In *The Times* of 7th November, Maxwell Garnett, Secretary of the League of Nations Union, intervened on a letter by Ernest Barker published on the 3rd, and on Lothian's speech:

> The issue that threatens is federalism versus inter-State cooperation. Lord Lothian and the federalists would find in the American Commonwealth 'a model for the world commonwealth of the future'. The inter-State party

---

[33] *Ibidem.*
[34] *Ibidem.* See Bosco, *Lord Lothian*, 311-7.
[35] *Federal Union News*, 7.

takes the British Commonwealth as their model: they argue that a system capable of preserving peace and promoting cooperation among the governments of a quarter of the world has a good chance of meeting the needs of the world as a whole; and that if, as Mr. Joseph Chamberlain discovered, federation on the American model proved impracticable for the British Commonwealth, it is *a fortiori* impracticable for the world commonwealth they wish to see.[36]

Since both schools asserted the necessity of a "supreme authority, whether directly representative of the people (as the federalists would prefer) or representative of their Governments (like the Franco-British Supreme Council)," Garnett proposed a compromise solution in the creation of a double political system:

Why then should not both parties accept what might be called a 'commonwealth' solution and agree that, while the federal union of as many democracies as possible is to be desired and encouraged, federation is hardly likely to unite a sufficient number of States for it alone to form the basis of a settlement in the 1940s; and that therefore we must also hope and work for an inter-State system that will include many other States besides the Federation? From this inter-State nut with its federal kernel might spring a tree so tall and strong as to give shelter and security to all nations.[37]

In "The Tradition of British Policy," an essay published in the October issue of *Political Quarterly,* and reviewed by *The Times* of 7th November, A. L. Rowse expressed the view that Great Britain was abandoning because of necessity her traditional policy of the balance of power, which enabled her to lead the coalition of European States against the strongest Continental State with hegemonic aspirations. The lesson of modern European history has shown how "no single great power is strong enough to dominate all the rest, and it really is not worth its trying." Even if it was "successful for a time, the lesser powers that have been subjugated will

---

[36] Maxwell Garnett, *The Times,* 7 Nov. 1939. Ernest Barker wrote in *The Times* of 3 November: "a new and united Europe, beginning its first essays in the building of a federal system, would then treat, and seek to administer, these territories in the same general way in which the United States has sought to treat and administer its territories. There would be no rival imperialisms: there would be a single federal imperialism, which would not be imperialism at all, because it offered the eventual status of a federal partner to its territories." Maxwell Garnett (1880-1958), was Rector of the Manchester College of Technology from 1912 to 1920, and Secretary of the League of Nations Union from 1920 to 1938.
[37] Maxwell Garnett, *The Times,* 7 Nov. 1939.

only seize the first opportunity of revolting." It was no longer tolerable to continue to fight in European wars at intervals of a quarter of a century. The only remedy was identified by Rowse in the creation of the United States of Europe: "The traditional policy of this country is in no sense an obstacle to its achievement, in fact it points directly towards it; that end is its logical conclusion."[38]

The *News Chronicle* of the same day observed that the "greatest step towards human progress taken as a result of the last war was the drafting of the League of Nations Covenant." The historical significance of the League went beyond its capability to prevent the outbreak of war, and assumed an educational meaning, witnessed by the fact that "there are millions today—where there were only a few hundred in 1914—who realise that war is a poor method of settling international disputes." The experience of the League at least showed that "collective security is impossible without the surrender of national sovereignty." The war could have helped mankind to advance towards a peaceful society, if it brought into being a "new machine...very different from the old League. It may call itself Federal Union."[39]

The federalist debate in the *Manchester Guardian* continued to be lively throughout November. On the 15th the paper published the "Manifesto of Educationalists":

> Once before—the twenty educationalists declared—the young men of this country laid down their lives in the hope that a lasting peace would be the outcome. As educationalists, it is our special responsibility to see that the hopes of another generation are not betrayed because the terms of the peace settlement are left till vision is blinded by hatred and moral resolution is sapped by the strain of war.

The appeal was for all educationalists in the world to ask their governments to stand for a limitation of national sovereignty in the building of a "lasting peace," a necessary condition for the progress of mankind, and particularly of the "backward countries" that were paying a high price for the war without being responsible for it.[40]

---

[38] *The Times*, 7 Nov. 1939. Alfred Leslie Rowse (1903-1997) was a *fellow* of the Oxonian All Souls College from 1925 to 1997.

[39] *News Chronicle*, 7 Nov. 1939.

[40] *Manchester Guardian*, 15 Nov. 1939. The signatories were: Cyril Burt, George Catlin, V. Gordon Childe, W. B. Curry, J. C. Flugel, A. G. Fraser, Lindley Fraser, W. H. Fyfe, Lynda Grier, Eileen Power, I. A. Richards, Lionel Robbins, Charles Grant Robertson, E. G. R. Taylor, E. W. A. Walker, Herbert G. Wells, Ralph Vaughan Williams, Helen Wodehouse, and Barbara Wootton.

On the same day Beatrice E. Morton observed:

> Now that federal union for European countries is being widely discussed
> as a basis for peace...it may be well to remind ourselves that this plan is
> not merely an adventitious expedient for procuring law and order nor a
> bright new idea to be foisted on a doubting public by unpractical
> enthusiasts. It is an advance in our political life for which the tracks have
> already been well laid, and an integral and orderly development of all our
> past.[41]

A. Cecil Edwards wrote on the following day how the division of the
British federalist movement into three groups—the Atlanticists following
Streit, the Europeanists of Federal Union, and the supporters of a new
League—was limiting its strength, and proposed convergence on a single
common aim: the rebuilding of a new League:

> Let us use this idea of federalism to infuse a new vigour into the
> League...and let us expand it, slowly and cautiously, in the direction of a
> United States of Europe, and perhaps of the six great federal unions of the
> world.[42]

Henry Noel Brailsford intervened in the debate with the pamphlet *The
Federal Idea*, mounting an attack on the League—"The main stream of
history flowed past Geneva and ignored the League"—and reaching the
conclusion that what was needed, not only for the maintenance of peace,
but also "the orderly development of all the resources of civilization," was
not a League of sovereign States, but "some form of International
Government." It was possible to end war in fact only "by widening
patriotism":

> Our Federation will organise the democratic discussion and decision of our
> common affairs. It will respect the rich variety of a Continent, that has
> preserved many stocks, many cultures, many tongues, through the
> vicissitudes of its history. It will end the anarchy of our economic life by
> orderly planning for the common good.[43]

---

[41] *Manchester Guardian*, 15 Nov. 1939.

[42] *Manchester Guardian*, 16 Nov. 1939.

[43] Brailsford, *The Federal Idea*: 7-8. See also: H. N. Brailsford, *Our Settlement
with Germany* (New York: The John Day Company, 1945; reprinted by Roberts
Press, 2007); id., *The Levellers and the English Revolution* (Standford: Standford
University Press, 1961). On Brailsford see: F. M. Leventhal, *The Last Dissenter:
H. N. Brailsford and His World*, (Oxford: Oxford University Press, 2000).

C. B. Fawcett, Professor at University College, London, expressed the view on 17th November that the creation of the European federation did not represent a "real advance," because even if it reduced the number of sovereign States, it would have created a "new 'European' patriotism over an American patriotism and a Russian patriotism." According to J. F. Price, in a letter of 18th November, the project of a European federation was even "the most dangerous notion" which could be presented to the public, for it was not able to include all European States from the beginning, and would deepen the divisions with the countries left out— Italy, Spain, Portugal, and Russia—and lead to a new and dangerous form of European nationalism.[44]

Julian S. Huxley, writing on 21st November, observed that the federalist principle could represent "a possible interim solution" of the colonial question, through "some limitation of sovereignty at the periphery, coupled with a certain degree of international control at the centre." The creation of a European Government would have limited the control by the member-States on their own colonies, and promoted from the centre the process towards their self-government, and subsequently their adhesion to the federation on an equal footing.[45]

The *Daily Worker* of 8th November confronted with the opinion favourable to the formation of a federation of "European capitalist States which in effect would be ruled by Britain and France":

> The pressure of public feeling against the war—the *Daily Worker* commented—has already, perhaps prematurely, forced into the open plans for an Anglo-French super-Empire, dominating all western and central Europe, after the war, when the great imperialist rival across the Atlantic will be pressing US claims even more aggressively than after the war of 1914-18, and when at the same time the rebellious peoples of Europe will be turning more and more for light and leadership to the immense Socialist Great Power in the east of Europe.[46]

Federal Union replied on 24th November to this attack with an article in the *Daily Worker* by Quentin Lumsden, responsible for the public relations of the movement:

> The Federal Union organisation...has a cut and dried programme for a new Europe that is neither imperialist nor capitalist, nor Communist. Europe's new constitution must, in our opinion, be free from all the 'isms' that have

---

[44] *Manchester Guardian*, 17, 18, Nov. 1939.
[45] *Manchester Guardian*, 21 Nov. 1939.
[46] *Daily Worker*, 8 Nov. 1939.

to date proved such a baneful influence on European affairs. It means to achieve, if it is not too late, a government of the people, by the people, for the people. Not by one people, or one group of people, but all the people.[47]

The *Daily Worker* replied on the very same day:

Federation is impossible until Socialism. Without Socialism, every project for 'European Federation' is simply a project for bringing the resources of small countries more effectively under control and exploitation by the big capitalist monopolies of the States that supply the biggest battalions of the international police.[48]

The debate continued in the left wing papers with the *Daily Herald,* which on 22nd November published replies by Barbara Wootton and H. G. Wells to the question "Should the nations federate?" The view of Wootton was the official one of the movement and represented its left wing grouping, according to which the fundamental mistake till then committed by all progressive forces had been "struggling to promote international ends through national institutions." The day had come—Wootton stated—to create "a democratic federal union," extending the principle of the State: "Federation is a word. It would be disastrous if it became a magic word. It is our business to make it a thing."[49]

Wells, even if accepting the federal idea as a matter of principle, did not share the growing enthusiasm which the idea was generating in Great Britain, because he feared that the British people did not understand all its implications as, for example, the abolition of the monarchy, the creation of a single currency, and a capitalist bloc. If, on the other hand, the forces of the left in France, Great Britain, and the United States understood all the potentialities of the federal idea, integrating it into socialism and assuming "the leadership for world revolution and reconstruction that Russia has abandoned," the federalist struggle would have become a stage of the progress of mankind towards a socialist civilization:

Now that the Russian Revolution has rotted and lost its soul because it has been unable to combine collectivism with personal freedom, it rests with the liberal thought of the Atlantic world to take over the task. If Federation means that...I am for it.[50]

---

[47] Quentin Lumsden, *Daily Worker*, 24 Nov. 1939.
[48] *Ibidem.*
[49] *Daily Herald*, 22 Nov. 1939.
[50] *Ibidem.*

From the left, the historian G. D. H. Cole supported in *New Statesman and Nation* the view that in the struggle against Hitler, the British and French were not "defenders of the old Europe," but the "protagonist of the new," in which all European peoples were free "to manage their own internal affairs on condition that they were ready to play their parts in a wider Federal system." Since "the day of wholly independent small nations" was "over," the only choice was between the creation of a "Federal Europe in which national autonomy will be reconciled with common responsibility and acceptance of a general rule," and the division of Europe into "'spheres of influence' dominated by the major powers, which will promptly proceed to reorganise their forces in preparation for the next great war." A federal Europe should not be built on the rubble of the old League, but on the principle of the limitation of national sovereignty within a federation able to command the loyalty of the citizens.[51]

Regarding the colonial problem, Cole noted that it was not possible to solve it "simply by turning all the colonies into virtually independent States," because many colonies were not capable "of standing alone," and were not "any more hopeful of a solution of the world's problems to balkanise Africa than to balkanise Europe." The colonial question could therefore find a solution only at the international level:

> the only possible answer to the demands of the 'Have-nots' for colonial Empires is that we are prepared to throw our conquests together into a common pool, and to do our best to work out an international solution of the entire African problem...In effect, in Africa as well as in Europe, we have to work towards a *federal* solution on a democratic basis, even if the

---

[51] George Douglas Howard Cole, "War Aims," *New Statesman and Nation*, Nov. 1939: 13-5, 41-2. George Douglas Howard Cole (1889-1959) was Professor of Econimics at Oxford and a fellow of Nuffield College from 1925 to 1944, then of Social and Political Theory from 1944 to 1957; and President of the Fabian Society from 1939 to 1946. By Coole, see: G. D. H. Cole, *Great Britain in the Post War World* (London: Victor Gollancz, 1945); id., *Communism and Social Democracy, 1914-1931* (London: Macmillan, 1958); id., *Socialism and Fascism, 1931-1939* (New York: St. Martin's Press, 1960); id., *Fabian Socialism* (London: Routledge, 1971); Paul Q. Hirst, *The Pluralist Theory of the State: Selected Writings of G. H. Cole, J. N. Figgis and H. J. Laski* (London: Taylor & Francis, 2007). On Cole, See: A. W. Wright, *G. D. H. Cole and Socialist Democracy*, (Oxford: Oxford University Press, 1979); Gerald L. Houseman, *G. D. H. Cole* (London: Twayne Publications, 1979); Gary Taylor, *G. D. H. Cole and the National Guilds League* (London: Ihs Press, 2004).

advance has to be made more gradually and requires a period of international tutelage.[52]

In a memorandum of 22nd November "War Aims, federation and *The Times*" addressed to the Editor Geoffrey Dawson, the journalist Dermot Norrah observed that the paper had to define its policy towards the increasingly pressing request by the readers to define the war aims and the system able to prevent the repetition of the war:

> At present the outstanding claim to propound such a system is made by the movement calling itself 'Federal Union'. This movement seems to be gaining adherents very rapidly, and we are likely to hear so much about it before the war is over that I suggest we ought to define our attitude to it as soon as possible. I urge this because, as it grows and becomes extensively organised, it may harden into dogmatic system, and it may then be too late to attempt to modify it on the lines I am shortly going to suggest...We have published one turnover article setting out the skeleton of the scheme, with not unfriendly comment in the leading article. It may not be irrelevant that one of the leading advocates of federation represents his plan as the legacy of Lord Milner, who we need not forget was at one time a member of our staff, and to whose ideas we have seldom been opposed...I think...that *The Times*, like myself, is attracted by the underlying principle of federation, but would not accept Streit's application of it without very considerable modification. If that is the attitude of the paper, then I think our most effective course is to try and assume the leadership of the federal movement, in order to gain power to guide it in the direction we think desirable.[53]

First, Norrah remarked, it was necessary to dissociate the federal from the democratic idea, because it was dangerous "to attempt to base peace, which is a primary need of all peoples at all times, upon democracy, which is a political device that some nations at some times find convenient." The fact that "the father of American federalism, Alexander Hamilton," had been "throughout his life a whole-hearted opponent of democracy," gave weight to the idea that the adhesion to democratic principles had not to condition the adhesion to the federation. The American federation failed "to preserve the peace between its members" when the federal government tried "to compel some of its member States to change their social structure."[54]

---

[52] Cole, "War Aims," 43.

[53] CP, 24/23-5. On *The Times*'s editorial policy see Evelyn Wrench, *Geoffrey Dawson and Our Times* (London: Hutchinson, 1955).

[54] CP, 24/25-8.

Portugal and Turkey, for example, could have been included in the federation even if they were autocracies. The Allies were fighting Nazism not because it was totalitarian, but because it was aggressive, and aid from totalitarian States should have been accepted in the common fight against Nazism. War aims—the defeat of the Hitlerian hegemonic design and the restoration of the independence of Poland and Czechoslovakia—should have been detached from peace aims: the creation of a federation open to membership by all peoples. Following these guidelines *The Times* would have performed "very useful work in helping on the federal movement during, but not in direct relation to, the war."[55]

These observations were partially included in the leader of *The Times* of 30th November, which referring to the speech given by Lothian at the Library of Congress on the occasion of the provisional depositing of the best existing copy of the *Magna Carta*, underlined the links between the most significant document of modern democracy and the American Constitution, which "enabled thirteen petty and mutually jealous sovereignties to be transcended in a single nation reaching from ocean to ocean, the most prosperous in the modern world."[56]

Its success in keeping the peace among States brought "some American political theorists, as it were in payment for the debt of Magna Carta," to export their Constitution "as a remedy for the ills of war-distracted Europe." Two great historical facts allowed for that attempt: "The unchallenged success of federal union in America and the corresponding failure of Europe to solve the problem of peace by means of the League of Nations":

> Most Europeans—*The Times* stated—are now ready to acknowledge that the major reason for that failure was the refusal of the members of the League to compromise their separate sovereignties in order that the organ of their association might have authority to execute its judgements. In any crisis the individual subject of every member-State felt that it owed an absolute allegiance to its own country, with which the appeal of the League to the general conscience could not compete. We are now invited to contemplate the success of the American system, where the federal authority, appealing direct to the individual conscience without need for the mediation of the government of a State, commands the ultimate allegiance of all Americans. It is indeed an impressive contrast and many minds are already convinced that the ultimate salvation of Europe depends

---

[55] *Ibidem.*
[56] *The Times*, 30 Nov. 1939.

upon the development of an international patriotism, which, like the American, shall some day swallow up all competing nationalisms.[57]

The implications of the vast debate on the war aims also reached the United States, and in the *New York Times* of 5th November Raymond Daniell could be ironical:

> The European war is only two months old and its end is not yet in sight. Some blood-thirstier souls might scoffingly remark that its beginning is not either. Yet discussions of the kind of peace that Britain and France could accept occupy more space in the newspapers than accounts of military and naval action.[58]

The debate, Daniell noted, did not limit itself to the pages of *The Times*, where Wells, Huxley and Shaw argued on "the shape of things to come," but "talk goes on endlessly in restaurants, clubs and even the pubs where common folk gather to wonder what sort of daffy peace will follow this insane war":

> In the minds of leading British statesmen—Daniell concluded—there is a growing idea that permanent peace can be realised only through some form of federation in which economic cooperation would be fostered and national sovereignties curbed...Franco-British unity is one of the constants in this modern, inconstant world.[59]

"Probably never before in the history of the world"—the leader of the *New York Times* opened on 26th November—"has the idea of a world federation of States, or at least of a United States of Europe, been discussed as frequently and as seriously in responsible quarters as in the last month or more." In spite of the many obstacles "the dream of a federated Europe" did not seem unattainable:

> Our thirteen original States achieved a lasting union. Germany and Italy are themselves unions of once separate States. Perhaps in this direction, under pressure for common defence, we may eventually see further regional unions, as in Scandinavia and the Balkans. Or perhaps, out of the

---

[57] Raymond Daniell, *New York Times*, 5 Nov. 1939. On the representation of the European war offered by the newspaper, see Robert J. Young, "In the Eye of the Beholder: The Cultural Representation of France and Germany by *The New York Times*, 1939-1940," in *The French Defeat of 1940. Reassessments*, ed. Joel Blatt (Oxford: Berghahn, 1997), 245-67.
[58] Raymond Daniell, *New York Times*, 5 Nov. 1939.
[59] *Ibidem.*

terror and destruction of the present war, the idea of European union may be realised sooner than men now dare to hope.[60]

"Towards Federalism"—being the leading article of the *Manchester Guardian* of 31st January—summarised the different views on federalism and grouped them into three clearly distinct schools, noting that

> there is a real danger...as Mr Harold Nicolson has pointed out, in the ardour which the idea or the phrase 'Federal Union' has excited. Those two words have for many the magic that Marxian terms have for the faithful Communist, the magic, that is, which seems to absolve intelligent persons from the duty of responsible thinking...in the saving virtues of phrases.[61]

The refusal "to face hard facts" was the main failure of the League experiment, and that mistake should not be repeated by using "federalism now as we used self-determination then." In federalism there was "a truth of deep importance," but it should be considered as "a problem and not as a splendid battle-cry which by itself will solve our difficulties." Discussing the various federalist projects, the *Guardian* pointed out that "the best-known of the federal plans that have been proposed" was that described by *Union Now*:

> Mr Streit wanted to make community of ideas the basis of federation. By his scheme sixteen democracies would be linked in a federal Constitution, with common defence, common citizenship, and common Parliament.[62]

An alternative scheme was suggested by Coudenhove-Kalergi, who argued "that the world is moving towards a large group system of life and politics," advocating a Pan-European Union:

> For Europe, he is sure, will follow this general law, and the only question is by whom and on what principles it will be organised; if the democracies do not undertake it, the initiative will fall to those who would organise it in a very different spirit.[63]

William Beveridge—"almost equally distinguished as an economist and as an administrator"—submitted another plan, arguing that

---

[60] *New York Times,* 26 Nov. 1939.
[61] "Towards Federalism," *Manchester Guardian*, 31 Jan. 1940.
[62] *Ibidem.*
[63] *Ibidem.*

the Federal Government must be strong, a real supranational force, and that a federation must be a partnership of compatibles, that is, of Governments having sufficient experience of democratic machinery to be able to work together...For though he would exclude Italy and Russia from his democratic federation, he thought that if federation was to be a real contribution to the solution of the world's problems after the war it must be extended to Germany. His choice of States for a federal organisation is thus the same as Mr Streit's with the important difference that Germany is substituted for the United States.[64]

Beveridge's scheme was "no doubt, a most attractive idea," but it appeared "too precipitate." It was appropriate to adopt a gradual approach to the problem:

To many, the most hopeful way would seem to be to build on the new relationship between Britain and France, a relationship which may be extended before the war is over. If the statesmen of the two countries can make a success of the relationship they will acquire invaluable experience, provide a striking example, and help to educate all Europe, as well as their own peoples, in the federal spirit.[65]

Beveridge in fact intervened supporting the case for a European federation—including Great Britain, France, Germany, the four Scandinavian countries, the two Low Countries, Switzerland and the Dominions—on 25th January 1940 at the British Institute of Philosophy. Former attempts to face the German threat through unilateral disarmament, or even its own dismemberment had, according to Beveridge, failed and, because of the Soviet menace, it was no longer justified. France rightly demanded some guarantee for her security, and the only positive guarantee would be the "integration of Germany in a European system."[66]

Speaking at the Manchester Reform Club on 30th January, Beveridge, referring to a "federation across old-established national boundaries," noted that there were two fundamental needs for the citizen to have a

---

[64] *Ibidem.*

[65] *Ibidem.*

[66] See *The Times*, 26 Jan. 1940. On the role played by Great Britain and France in the negotiations for disarmament in the inter-war period, see: Ruth Henig, "Britain, France and the League of Nations in the 1920s," in *Anglo-French Relations 1898-1998: From Fashoda to Jospin*, eds. Michael Dockrill and Philippe Chassaigne (New York: Palgrave Macmillan, 2002), 139-55; Carolyn Kitching, "The Search for Disarmament: Anglo-French Relations, 1935-1939," in Dockrill and Chassaigne, *Anglo-French Relations*, 158-78; Carolyn J. Kitching, *Britain and the Geneva Disarmament Conference* (New York: Palgrave Macmillan, 2003).

happy and ordered life: "Internal order with security and external order with security." The external order could come "from the same place from which war came," therefore from the outward, from a "second Government." Federal government was based on three conditions. First, both governments—that which dealt with the internal order and that which administered the external one—had to be "real Governments," namely directly elected. Secondly, the member-States had to be democratic; thirdly, "if federation were to be a real contribution to the solution of the world's problems after the war it had to be extended to Germany." Federalism, Beveridge concluded, was

> an idea whose time has come...Federation came when people of different communities recognised a common interest which was so vitally important that they were prepared, for the sake of it, to give up something of their separatism.[67]

In January 1940 Margaret Storm Jameson intervened in the debate, stating in *Fortnightly Review* that "the choice between anarchy and some measure of federalism cannot wait." If European States did not sacrifice "as much of their sovereign independence as will allow them to establish the framework of an economic order," they would perpetuate "a Europe strangled by traffic barriers and crushed by the burden of defending its right to choke to death":

> If it were—Jameson noted with sarcasm—merely a question of slaughtering every twenty years an unstated number of men, women, children, our statesmen would doubtless resign themselves to the disagreeable necessity; they would either set up a Ministry of Cenotaphs or the Lord Privy Seal would get the job; and our religious leaders would accommodate themselves. But it has become a question of the survival of States, that is, of statesmen. If we do not organise Europe it will fall to pieces. The process, even for statesmen, will be damnably unpleasant.[68]

A "federal European Council, or Parliament" would have powers in the fields of foreign, military, financial, economic, commercial, and colonial

---

[67] See the *Manchester Guardian*, 31 Jan. 1940. The *Manchester Guardian* of 3rd February published a letter by Gertrude Lieben and Edward Foulkes supporting Beveridge's scheme.

[68] Margaret Storm Jameson, "The New Europe," *Fortnightly Review*, 147, (1940): 75-7. See also Margaret Storm Jameson, *The Decline of Merry England* (London: Jameson Press, 2007). For a critical analysis, see Jennifer Birkett and Chiara Briganti eds., *Margaret Storm Jameson: Writing in Dialogue* (Cambridge: Cambridge Scholars Publishing, 2007).

policies. It was necessary to be prepared "to achieve federal union in
Europe by stages," because it would not be easy "to replace uncontrolled
State sovereignty by some form of economic and social federation," but
without "the hope of such a new departure," the irony of the current war,
which followed "the war to end war," would be "unbearable":

> The ideals of social justice, tolerance, freedom, are being ground to dust
> between fragments of a disordered Europe. A mad and destructive
> nationalism has done this. Nothing matters but to get rid of it...To say that
> the obstacles to inducing States to limit their sovereignty are too great is to
> say that we cannot save Europe. If the war were to end this week, some
> measure of federation would still be an instant practical necessity. This
> war, in effect a civil war, will decide the issue between civilization and
> anarchy.[69]

In the debate the functionalist's view was also heard inspired by David
Mitrany. In the memorandum "European Order and World Order"—
written in the United States in early January after various meetings with
"Lord Lothian as well as with a large number of groups and individuals
working on these problems"—and sent to Foreign Minister Halifax on the
9th from Max Nicolson, General Secretary of Political and Economic
Planning, Julian Huxley observed that

> once the process of canalising and organising economic power has been
> carried to a certain point, the purely political aspect ceases to be, as it
> inevitably was in the case of the League, the kernel of the whole problem.

With the redistribution of economic power "along functional rather
than territorial lines," the territorial sovereign State was "ceasing to be the
sole repository of power." "The political problem" remained however "the
most intractable," since there was "the greatest temptation to elaborate
Utopian schemes," Utopianism being the "most dangerous."[70]

---

[69] Storm Jameson, "The New Europe," 78-9.

[70] FOP, FO371/24362, C582/7/62. David Mitrany (1888-1975) was a collaborator
of the *Manchester Guardian*, from 1919 to 1922; a researcher of the Carnegie
Endowment for International Peace from 1922 to 1929; Professor of Politics at
Harvard University from 1931 to 1933, and at Princeton from 1933 to 1975.
Among his writings: David Mitrany, *Progress of International Government*
(London: Elliots Books, 1933); id., *American Interpretations. Four Political
Essays* (London: Contact Publications, 1946); id., *World Unity and the Nations*
(London: National Peace Council, 1950); id., *Marx Against the Peasant: A Study
in Social Dogmatism* (London: George Weidenfeld & Nicolson, 1952); id., *The
Functional Theory of Politics* (London: M. Robertson, 1975). On Mitrany and

"Far-reaching schemes for the federalisation of Europe, or of even wider areas...pressed," Huxley argued, "as immediate possibilities," ignoring however "the essential condition for the creation of a closely-bound federal structure," which was the existence "of a socio-economic system...either homogeneous or which varies only within relatively narrow limits, so far as its dominant elements are concerned":

> Even in North America it required a civil war to complete the elementary process of federal unification, and to this day the federal government is powerless to enforce civil liberties in certain States. Experience of federalism in South America and in some of the Dominions has also shown that however necessary federalism may be it brings great difficulties of its own.[71]

"*Potentially*," Huxley observed, "the necessary conditions for the federalization of Europe undoubtedly" existed. Europe was "a convenient geographical unity," and it possessed "a long and powerful cultural tradition which, if rightly used, will be invaluable as a basis for achieving the conditions of unity." However, "in terms of existing fact, these potentialities" were "still undeveloped":

> Our aim must be to create political forms out of which a fully developed federal system can easily emerge when, as a result of the working of the economic and other mechanisms...the necessary degree of economic and cultural homogeneity in Europe has been attained...The principal agency

---

functionalism, see: Ernst B. Haas, *Beyond the Nation-State: Functionalism and International Organization* (Standford, CA: Stanford University Press, 1968); Kenneth W. Thompson, *Ethics, Functionalism, and Power in International Politics: The Crisis in Values* (Baton Rouge, LA: Louisiana State University Press, 1979); John Eastby, *Functionalism and Interdependence* (Washington, DC: University Press of America, 1985); Cornelia Navari, "David Mitrany and International Functionalism," in *Thinkers of the Twenty Year's Crisis*, eds. David Long and Peter Wilson (Oxford: Clarendon Press, 1995), 214-44; Lucian M. Ashworth and David Long, *New Perspectives on International Functionalism* (New York: Palgrave Macmillan, 1998); John R. Shook and Andrew Backe, *The Chicago School of Functionalism* (Bristol: Thoemmes Continuum, 2000); A. Hammarlund, *Liberal Internationalism and the Decline of the State: The Thought of Richard Cobden, David Mitrany, and Kenichi Ohmae* (New York: Palgrave Macmillan, 2005).

[71] FOP, FO371/24362, C582/7/62. Huxley supported the creation of a European federation after the war intervening at the American Association for the Advancement of Science of New York on 26 Jan. 1940, (see the *New York Times* of 28 January).

required would be a representative and co-ordinating body to form a nucleus for the development of European government.[72]

The beginnings of such a nucleus already existed in the Supreme Council established by the British and French governments, and according to Huxley it was "desirable to constitute a general European assembly, not nominated solely by governments, but directly representative of the peoples concerned, either on a functional or geographical basis." This would have provided "an embryo Parliament of Europe":

> We purposely refrain from attempting too specifically to define a formal constitution and powers, because for us the essence of the problem is to secure broad agreement on what has to be done. If this is achieved the necessary mechanism will not be hard to design...Europe, like South Africa after the Boer War, needs healing and organising by degrees before unity of feeling and therefore of government can have a chance of success.[73]

On 5th February R. W. Urie argued in the *Manchester Guardian* that "the now much-mouthed slogan of 'Federation' is already in grave danger of rapidly degenerating into a catchword." Those who advocated European federation "as the only solution for constantly recurring wars in Europe" were apt, "in their enthusiasm, to dismiss too lightly as small issues the many serious practical difficulties in the way of its successful accomplishment and functioning." "Slogans, platitudes and generalities as a contribution towards federalism" were, according to Urie, worthless: "They but succeed in laying the whole scheme open to cynical criticism and contempt."[74]

It should be remembered that *Union Now* and Curry's *The Case for Federal Union* had been written before the outbreak of the war, and that at that time federalism had not yet become a war aim, but just a possible way of preventing war itself. The Streitian project was just "a democratic federal front against totalitarian aggression." "It would appear," Urie observed, "that Federal Union, being born on the eve of war, had not yet had the opportunity of redrafting its peace aims. What it holds now as peace aims would have been more practical as peace aims before the outbreak of war."[75]

---

[72] FOP, FO371/24362, C582/7/62.

[73] *Ibidem.*

[74] *Manchester Guardian*, 5 Feb. 1940.

[75] *Ibidem.*

It appeared necessary for the leaders of the various federalist organisations active in the country—Federal Union, The New Commonwealth Society, Pan-Europa, and "those groups which sprang up on the lines advocated by Mr. H. G. Wells in the *Open Conspiracy*—to begin "to cooperate in securing a wider degree of support for their aims." "If those who preach cooperation amongst European States cannot cooperate among themselves," Urie urged, "because of wider differences of opinion over comparatively small issues, they are but defeating their common aim of setting up a federal system in Europe." Urie proposed a Conference among the leaders of the federalist organisations, with the aim of creating "a central coordinating committee" which would reduce the differences of approach and prepare "a manifesto of common aims." The "world-wide interest" provoked by the manifesto, and the debate which it would generate, certainly had "tremendous potentialities."[76]

Gerald Bailey, Secretary of the National Peace Council, writing to the *Manchester Guardian* on 8th February, remembered that the manifesto adopted by the organisation during the Annual General Meeting of July 1939 "reflected the commitment of the wider peace movement to the principle of federation." This commitment had been recently renewed in an appeal for a declaration of the conditions of peace, and the Council distributed it to the organisation's members. The Council was, moreover, organising all around the country a series of "consultative conferences...intended to give leading representatives of all the peace organisations an opportunity for a closer consideration of the problems involved in the making of a desirable peace settlement." The third Conference, with the participation of Wootton, Angell, and Joad, would take place in London in the space of a few weeks, discussing the constitutional aspects of future international co-operation, "with a particular relation to the federal proposal."[77]

On the same day, the *Guardian* also published a letter from George W. Keeton, in which the Director of the New Commonwealth Society agreed to co-operate with other federalist organisations, since there was an "urgent need" for serious research "before any proposals for the adoption of the federal machinery can be accepted." The following day, Munroe observed that "the popularity of the idea of federalism" was due to the preparatory work by the League of Nations Union and the New Commonwealth Society, "which has appealed to a smaller, but important section of the community, a section which has not lost both heart and head

---

[76] *Ibidem.*
[77] *Manchester Guardian,* 8 Feb. 1940.

to Federalism," because it envisaged a "scientific and realistic" approach to the problem.[78]

"That blessed word 'Federation'"—George Young wrote in the *Manchester Guardian* of 8th February—"is playing the same part in this war as the word, which we have now forgotten to speak, 'League', played in the last."

> It soothes our sorrow, heals our wounds, and gives us hopes of heaven...The ebullience of poetic visions of a time when the battle-flags are furled in a Parliament of man and a Federation of the world' is being boiled down to the practical exchange of views as to whether the League could be substituted or supplemented by some form of European Confederation.[79]

Surprisingly enough, "English intellectuals" were "all talking Federation." However, only the application of the federal system within the States themselves could guarantee peace: "Decentralisation is the road which we must seek, not only for better international security, but also the betterment of national society." If Great Britain had been divided into four nationalities, England, Wales, Scotland and Northern Ireland, then France and Germany would have "followed the same system." "Federation by democracy might save Europe from another international war and England from another internecine war.[80]

---

[78] *Ibidem.*

[79] *Ibidem.* The *Manchester Guardian* on 23 March published a joint letter by Kimber and N. B. Foot, General Secretary of the New Commonwealth, regarding the creation of a Committee to elaborate a common statement of policy: "the suggestion which emerged from the recent correspondence has not been disregarded". Ernest Barker and Ramsay Muir, Liberal leader, intervened in favour of the federal idea. Sir Norman Angell, speaking at the Manchester Reform Club on 28 February argued that "the key to the situation would be a strong federal unity between ourselves and France, and the opening up of the British Commonwealth to all who would accept its conditions", (*Manchester Guardian*, 9 and 16 Feb. 1940). Sir Norman Angell (1872-1967) was Editor of *Foreign Affairs*, from 1928 to 1931; Labour MP for Bradford North, from 1929 to 1931; and winner of the Nobel Peace Prize in 1933.

[80] *Manchester Guardian,* 8 Feb. 1940. On the history of attempts to transform the United Kingdom into a federation, see: John Kendle, *Federal Britain: A History* (London: Routledge, 1997). On the question of Irish neutrality, see: George Boyce, "From War to Neutrality: Anglo-Irish Relations, 1921-1950," *British Journal of International Studies*, 5, 5, (1979): 15-36; Raymond J. Raymond, "Irish Neutrality and Anglo-Irish Relations: 1921-1941," *International History Review*, 9, 3, (1987): 456-64; Andrew Baker, "Anglo-Irish Relations, 1939-1941: A Study in

Douglas Young, Professor at King's College in Aberdeen, proposed on 16th February in the *Manchester Guardian* the immediate creation of a federation among the six Allied countries: France, Great Britain, Australia, South Africa, New Zealand and Canada. On the representative basis of a deputy for every half million citizens, Young proposed the creation of a Federal Parliament of 221 members, of which 84 were French, 80 English, 21 Canadians, 13 Australians, 10 Scottish, 4 South Africans, 4 Welsh, 3 New Zealanders and 2 Northern Irish. The Anglo-French federation would offer security to Central Europe:

> In a strong federation on a democratic national basis, with pooled military sovereignty, it would be possible to solve minority problems by making those territorial and other concessions which, in the anarchy and insecurity of sovereign States, the Romanians and Serbs, for example, are at present afraid to make to the Magyars and Bulgars.

"A start must be made somewhere some time." Young concluded, "Why not now?"[81]

On 8th March, at a Conference at the London School of Economics, Lord Cecil criticised the project of an Anglo-French federation which would provoke the creation of rival blocks, and supported, on the contrary, the idea of a European "confederation" within a new League, including all "civilised" nations. By "confederation" Cecil intended a "constitutional union of independent States" in order to maintain European order, through monetary, commercial and military union.[82]

Multilateral Diplomacy and Military Restraint," *Twentieth Century British History*, 15, 4, (2005): 359-381. On Hitler's hegemonic ambitions, see Ian Kershaw, *Hitler: 1936-1945: Nemesis* (New York: W. W. Norton & Company, 2001).

[81] *Manchester Guardian*, 16 Feb. 1940. George Malcom Young (1882-1959) was an officer at the Foreign Office, from 1917 to 1932. As a historian of the Victorian age and Cromwell, Young published in 1952 a controversial biography on Stanley Baldwin. Douglas Young (1913-73), Scottish poet, scholar, and playwright, was Professor of Greek at the University of Aberdeen until 1941, when he was imprisoned for having refused to serve in the army, being a strong advocate of Scottish independence. In 1942 he was elected President of the Scottish National Party, and returned to academic life, teaching at the Universities of Dundee, St. Andrews, McMaster, and North Carolina.

[82] *Manchester Guardian*, 9 March 1940. On Anglo-French monetary relations in the inter-war period, see Robert Boyce, "'Breaking the Banque': The Great Crisis in Franco-British Central Bank Relations between the Wars," in *Anglo-French Relations 1898-1998: From Fashoda to Jospin*, eds. Michael Dockrill and Philippe Chassaigne (New York: Palgrave Macmillan, 2002): 80-91.

The leading article of the following day in the *Manchester Guardian* observed that "the most important part" of Cecil's speech was its treatment of Federal Union:

> He puts a strong case against the optimism of some of the advocates of the 'Round Table' who drew up a federal scheme for the British Empire. It was dropped because the Dominions were hostile. When the project was mooted in the Dominions it was so decisively rejected that its promoters regretfully abandoned it. They found that there was an insurmountable conviction among all the Dominion statesmen that their countries would never agree to accept the rule of any Imperial Legislature or Executive in which each of them would only have a minority vote.[83]

Cecil asked "pertinently whether, if that is the feeling in the British Commonwealth, with all its unifying influences and sympathies, this feeling would not much more animate States separated by language, literature, general culture, and historical tradition." In accepting "the fundamental doctrine of the advocates of Federal Union," according to which national sovereignty "is the great enemy of international co-operation," Cecil launched a plan "for a European Confederation... built on the foundation of the Anglo-French partnership," and "would hope to see similar confederations elsewhere of geographically related Powers":

> the closer union to which Federalists look, the union in a single Government and single Parliament, can only come after long and intimate association in common tasks. To-day we have a much clearer view of the nature of those common tasks than we had in 1919, and the main purpose of any new federation should be economic.[84]

An echo of the Federalist debate in Great Britain and, albeit to a lesser extent, in France, reached Germany and Romania, where on 31 January the director of *Le Moment*, a French-language daily, judged very favourably the project of an Anglo-French federation, leaving glimpses of the Romanian Government's intention to join it.

The *Münchener neueste Nachrichten* of 21 January, under the title "The World State as a screen of world domination," attacked the federalist project, which was nothing more than a cover for the intention to dismember Germany, and impose on her a "super Versailles." The paternity of the British federalist project was attributed to Curtis, Chatham House's "intellectual leader," employed by the Foreign Office for defining the

---

[83] *Manchester Guardian*, 9 March 1940. FOP, FO 371/2300, 134992, 27-41.

[84] *Manchester Guardian*, 9 March 1940.

official war and peace aims. In *Civitas Dei* Curtis had supported the view that "the whole world must be redesigned on the British Commonwealth's model." As soon as the first tensions emerged in Europe and Asia, the program, continued the German paper, has been "reformulated in different terms," on the basis of Streit's design. The support that these ideas were gaining without exception in the British press showed that it was "just the right kind of musical accompaniment to the encirclement policy of the Foreign Office against the Reich." This "ridiculous utopia" was looking for a practical way for an immediate realisation of the project of an Anglo-French federation. And it continued:

> France was rather uncertain about the real meaning of war. The British propaganda is working for a constitutional agreement with France. Foreign Policy and the colonial administration of both countries should be managed on a common basis. The weight of the war has already been, in large measure, transferred to the shoulders of France. According to the agents of British propaganda a customs union will follow. The idea of a 'dual empire' is about to be injected in France by means of a gradual infiltration process: the French colonial empire—although it is not said in these terms—will become part of the 'sphere of English power'. France is thus bound to become a subsection of the Commonwealth.[85]

These ideas, while they were discussed "extensively" in Great Britain, according to the well informed German paper, had not been welcomed with "great enthusiasm" in France, even if there was a group of very influential politicians—such as the ministers of finance and the colonies, Paul Reynaud and Ernest Mandel, "and a group of powerful Jewish financiers"—for some time at work "in support of British politics." Edouard Daladier, who "originally did not belong to this group of intrigants," was now "under its influence." The war was "just the latest chapter of three centuries of British imperialism." Bismarck had been "the only conqueror of modern times" who had "used his victories with moderation." "*Pax Germanica*" was substantially different from "*Pax Britannica*" because it aimed "to create a real order" in which it was

---

[85] *Münchener neueste Nachrichten*, 21 Jan 1940. For a discussion of Nazi war aims, see: Norman Rich, *Hitler's War Aims: Ideology, the Nazi State, and the Course of Expansion* (New York: W.W. Norton & Company, 1973); Christian Leitz, *Nazi Foreign Policy 1933-1941. The Road to Global War* (London: Routledge, 2003). About the perception of the decline of France as a consequence of German dominance in Continental Europe, see: Jean-Baptiste Duroselle, *La décadence 1932-1939* (Paris: Imprimerie Nationale, 1979); P. Jackson, *France and the German Menace, 1933-1939* (Oxford: Oxford University Press, 2000).

possible for all peoples "to live together on the basis of equal rights, not on that of an unconditional claim to supremacy over larger territories, even if disguised in the form of a super-State."[86]

II. *The Clergy and the federal idea*

In the wake of growing popular support the Anglican Church also took a clear stand supporting the federal project. Federal Union had established a "Committee of the Churches," and nominated as Secretary for the Anglican Church Christine Dowson, who had already won the confidence of the Student Christian Movement, and was trying to convince the Dean of St. Paul's to write a pamphlet on federalism and the Christian faith.

Speaking on 23rd October at the annual General Meeting of the League of Nations Union at Scarborough, William Temple, the Archbishop of York, attributed the failure of the League of Nations to the attempt to try to reconcile two principles—national sovereignty and collective security—which were in fact irreconcilable, and between which a choice should have been made. Even if "the journey must be a slow one," Temple did not have any doubt that, "the road that leads towards federal union" had to be chosen.[87]

In a letter to the *Daily Telegraph* of 4th December, Temple had proclaimed the necessity of renouncing "complete national sovereignty." This would open "the way to that Federal Union whose view I am expressing I would wish to make our ultimate goal, so that no step should be taken which would render it more difficult for attainment." The federation was "a Christian solution," because it was based "on recognition that we are fellow-members one of another in the one family of God."[88]

---

[86] FOP, FO/371/24985, 100-2; CP, 111/34-7.

[87] See the article by William Temple, "The Flaw Within the League," *Manchester Guardian,* 24 Oct. 1939. See also *The Times* of the same day. *The Guardian* of 9 Oct. 1939 reported a sermon by C. A. Alington, *Dean* of Durham, in which he expressed the wish to be included among "those dreamers who advocate a federation of the democratic countries of the world", a project which aimed for the political unity of mankind, and placed itself at a higher level rather than a mere European federation. William Temple (1881-1944) was Bishop of Manchester, from 1921 to 1929; Archbishop of York, from 1929 to 1942; and Archbishop of Canterbury, from 1942 to 1944.

[88] *Daily Telegraph,* 4 Dec. 1939. On the British Clergy and the war, see A. J. Hoover, *God, Britain and Hitler in World War II: The View of the British Clergy, 1939-1945* (Westport, CT: Praeger, 1999).

Kimber followed the Archbishop's letter on 14th December, pointing out that in order to preserve Western civilization, it was necessary to announce "its principles," namely "to declare the rights of man," and show "how these rights are to be preserved and extended." Federal Union held the view that

> in a context of power politics, human liberty is nowadays forfeit...unless we can provide some means of planning for the common good of men and women in different nations, we shall all be obliged to tread the path which Hitler has already trodden.[89]

Federal Union was fighting for the creation of a government "elected by the peoples of different nations to manage five matters which are of common concern to them all: trade, money, administration of colonies, foreign policy and armaments." All other political issues would be administered by national governments. The creation of a federal European order required liberation from the "crudities and perversions of present-day nationalism." It was necessary to declare the aims for which the Allies were fighting, and "the federal means by which these principles can be preserved":

> We are opposed—Kimber concluded—by the religion of blood and nationalism. It is not possible to fight a religion with force alone. We have to oppose it with a better idea. In the words of Victor Hugo 'there is one thing stronger than armies: an idea whose time has come'.[90]

Not all British clergy were however aligned with Temple. The Bishop of Gloucester intervened in the debate on 17th December, observing how it was dangerous to have the church supporting a "particular political scheme whether by 'idealists' or 'realists'," and considered impractical and groundless "any solution along federal lines." Another churchman, W. F. Geikie-Cobb observed on 21st December that federation was essentially "a mode of machinery," that "devoid of a living spirit behind it" had "no promise of permanence": "It is just possible that France and Great Britain, after having twice fought side by side, might enter into a Federation, and others might in time join them, but of these there is not any sign at present."[91]

Intervening again with a Christmas message in *Federal Union News*, the Archbishop of York noted with satisfaction that the federalist project

---

[89] *Daily Telegraph*, 14 Dec. 1940.
[90] *Ibidem.*
[91] *Daily Telegraph*, 17, 21 Dec. 1940.

"has made a staggeringly effective appeal to British minds," but he also added a cautious note:

> There are multitudes to whom the outbreak of war brought dismay, and who look to Federal Union as the one way of hope. Those who, like me, believe it to be the only real solution are bound to welcome this. But I confess that the initial success of the movement fills me with anxiety lest disillusionment may be in store.[92]

Believers of Federal Union had to do "a great deal of thinking and exercise a great deal of sympathetic imagination." What they had in mind was "a revolution in political feeling of the most gigantic magnitude." It was "not very difficult to draw up a constitution which, if cordially adopted and loyally worked, would deliver the world from war." Any system, Temple warned, "will have to fight one war for its own establishment, as the Union had in America." If the member-States of the League "had really worked the League, this war might have that historic place." The obstacles of tradition, sentiment and prejudice were however "mountainous," and it took "faith to remove such mountains." The creation of the political mechanism was not enough to solve the problem, which, "like all great problems," was essentially spiritual. Federalism was "the political counterpart of universal love," which man alone could not generate, because it was "God's gift."[93]

III. *Lothian in Washington*

A pioneering role in giving political expression to the current of opinion that was generally favourable to federalist ideals was played by Lothian, who arrived in Washington as British Ambassador a few days before the outbreak of war, and had then to face public opinion strongly opposed to any involvement of the United States in the European conflict. Speaking to

---

[92] *Federal Union News*, 13.

[93] *Federal Union News*, 13. The Archbishop of York renewed his public support to Federal Union on 5 February in Rugby at a meeting of the local branch of the League of Nations Union, advocating the creation of an Anglo-French federation as a nucleus of a larger federation, within a renewed League of Nations, including all of the world's nations. The Federal Government would be "sovereign within its own sphere of competence", and the right of secession would not have been recognized, (*Manchester Guardian*, 6 Feb. 1940). On the attitude of the Methodist, Baptist, Congregational, Quaker and Unitarian clergy towards the international crisis of the 1930s, see K. G. Robbins, "Free Churchmen and the Twenty Years' Crisis," *Baptist Quarterly*, 27, 8, (1978): 346-57.

the Pilgrims of the United States on 25th October, Lothian in fact attacked the principle of national sovereignty, supporting the case for a European federation at the end of the war. Lothian observed that "the establishment of a true reign of law" was "incompatible with universal national sovereignty," and that "some form of economic federation, perhaps even of political federation, at any rate for part of Europe" was "a necessary condition of any stable world order." The greatest mistake made in Paris in 1919 was not of an economic, rather than political nature:

> Few seemed to realise the inevitable consequence of dividing Europe, or for that matter the world, into a vast number of almost water-tight economic compartments, and then of imposing on these States fantastic reparations and other forms of intergovernmental indebtedness which it was quite impossible to pay across these economic frontiers without disaster for all.[94]

Another mistake was to assume that peace could be attainable through disarmament, which was certainly essential to peace, if realised on a vast scale, but it was not enough because peace depended on "overwhelming power behind law." The war was not a conflict among rival imperialisms, but between two conceptions of the world, the totalitarian principle, in its versions of Nazism, Fascism and Communism and the democratic one:

> The real question is whether power is to be behind a liberal and democratic kind of world or a totalitarian kind of world...The real issue in this war is whether there is going to be power behind the kind of world in which France and the British Commonwealth and the democracies of Scandinavia and you yourselves believe, or far more relentless power behind the kind of world in which National Socialism and Communism believe.[95]

---

[94] Kerr, *The American Speeches*, 27. For a critical analysis, see: Bosco, *Lord Lothian*, 311-35; Butler, *Lord Lothian*, 257-78. On the attitude of the American press against the intervention, see Garet Garrett, *Defend America First: The Antiwar Editorials of the Saturday Evening Post, 1939-1942* (London: Caxton Press, 2003).
[95] Kerr, *The American Speeches*: 28. On the role played by Lothian as interpreter of the Allied war-aims to American public opinion, see: Rhodri Jeffreys-Jones, "The Inestimable Advantage of Not Being English: Lord Lothian's American Ambassadorship, 1939-1940," *Scottish Historical Review*, 63, 1, (1984): 105-10; id., "Lord Lothian and American Democracy: An Illusion in Pursuit of an Illusion," *Canadian Review of American Studies*, 17, 4, (1986): 411-22; John Cull, *Selling War: The British Propaganda Campaign against American 'Neutrality' in World War* (New York: Oxford University Press, 1996); Susan A. Brewer, *To Win*

As in all the great crises in history, the outcome could be one of great advancement or of great regression:

> World crises mean that the old order is perishing and that something new must be born. That is the position to-day. The old world is perishing and a new world is seeking to be born. Though we do not see the way clearly, yet all of us, I believe—Frenchmen, Canadians, Australians, New Zealanders, and South Africans, and peoples of many other lands—believe that something brutal and vile, must be born out of the sacrifices of this time. That is the hope and the faith in which they all, old as well as young, now are prepared to lay down their lives.[96]

That was the first declaration of a European statesman, performing his official duties, attacking unlimited national sovereignty, and supporting the idea of a European federation.

This pronouncement by Lothian did not remain unnoticed in the United States, where the *Boston Transcript* commented on 29th November that Lothian's view raised many hopes because it acknowledged the limitation of national sovereignty as the priority in the shaping of a "stable world order." The idealism of Lothian and other politicians like Attlee, would certainly have rendered more noble an image of Great Britain in world public opinion. It was no longer possible, therefore, to affirm that the British people were fighting to enlarge their Empire, or to break up Germany, but that they were striving for a new world order, based on the American political experience.[97]

In spite of all the notes of caution which came from London, Lothian reconfirmed the validity of his former statement in the space of a couple of weeks, on 11th November, during the celebration of the founding of Swartmore College, Pennsylvania. The fundamental cause of the crisis of the European democracies was, according to Lothian, not in capitalism but in the "passion for national sovereignty," which made the working of capitalism impossible:

> Europe, though the smallest, has also been the most vital of the Continents. It has produced almost all the finest elements in modern civilization, and its most vigorous creative and talented peoples. You over here are, in the main, an extension of European civilization. But it has also been the most constant fountain of war—and wars which have constantly developed into world wars. If Europe could only conquer war and find a

---

the Peace: British Propaganda in the United States during World War II (Ithaca, NY: Cornell University Press, 1997): 98, 190-1.
[96] Kerr, *The American Speeches*, 28.
[97] *Boston Transcript*, 29 Nov. 1939.

basis for unity within itself, the whole world would have taken an immense step forward.[98]

In Great Britain, Lothian continued, there was increasingly wide support for the view that unlimited national sovereignty was "the primary reason for the political and economic breakdown of liberal and democratic civilization and for the reappearance of world war." Europe would find a "lasting peace" only through "the application of the federal principle, in some form, to its inter-state problems." It appeared obvious that "the division of Europe into twenty-six sovereignties, each with an army and air force, a foreign policy, sky-high tariffs, and insurmountable restrictions on migration of its own" was "incompatible either with peace or liberty or prosperity, and that this anarchy" had been "the main cause of the constant wars and revolutions which have been the bane of Europe in the past."[99]

Nobody was able to present a practical plan for the federation because it was impossible to include communist, fascist and democratic States. Since federation was rooted in democratic values, being "the result of voluntary agreement and not of compulsion," the necessary pre-condition for its establishment was "the defeat of totalitarian imperialism." The crucial fact was however that "the leaders of democracies in Europe" had "for the first time come publicly to recognise that national sovereignty is the real root of Europe's persistent troubles," and that "federalism" was "the basic remedy if Europe is ever to be united and prosperous, and to enjoy both individual freedom and national freedom for its varied races and peoples."[100]

Speaking of "the leaders of democracies," Lothian was referring to the speeches by Halifax and Attlee, which will be discussed later, favourable to the limitation of national sovereignty and the creation of a European federation. The Foreign Office did not appreciate however the repeated federalist stances of the Ambassador, and exerted pressure on Halifax himself to invite him to show prudence.[101]

---

[98] Kerr, *The American Speeches*, 27.
[99] *Ibidem*, 27-8.
[100] *Ibidem*, 28.
[101] One of Lothian's tasks during his American mission was also to counterbalance Chamberlain's suspicious and generally negative attitude towards Roosevelt, for which some senior officials at the Foreign Office were partially responsible. See, in this regard: William R. Rock, *Chamberlain and Roosevelt: British Foreign Policy and the United States, 1937-1940* (Columbus, OH: Ohio State University Press, 1988); Kennedy, "Neville Chamberlain and", 95-120; Michael Hughes, *British Foreign Secretaries in an Uncertain World, 1919-1939* (London: Routledge, 2005). For a study of the relations between Roosevelt and Churchill,

Commenting on the speeches in support of the federalist project delivered by Lothian during the first three months of his diplomatic mission, Kilpatrick, senior Foreign Office official, noted ironically on 7th November: "'federation' is the new religion. Mr Barrington Ward tells me that it is clear from the correspondence received by the 'Times' that many people are embracing it. But few have any idea what it means."[102]

Since Lothian's views were considered authoritative in the United States, the Foreign Office feared that they could be assumed to be the official stance of the British Government. In a note to Alexander Cadogan, W. Strang observed on 18th November:

> I am very doubtful whether it is wise for Lord Lothian to commit himself to sentiments of this kind. Is it really true to say that the leaders of democracy in Europe have publicly recognised federalism as the basic remedy for Europe's troubles? So far as I know, neither H.M.G. nor the French Government has done so, though it is true that the question has been the subject of a good deal of rather utopian speculation, especially in this country. Further, do we, from the point of view of foreign policy, want one of H.M. Ambassadors to preach a crusade not only against National Socialism, but also against Fascism and Communism? We might perhaps introduce a word of caution into the next review of the situation which the Secretary of State sends to Lord Lothian.[103]

Ignoring the irritation of the Foreign Office, Lothian intervened again, on 4th January at the Chicago Council on Foreign Relations, examining the mistakes made in Paris in 1919 and observed:

---

see Joseph P. Lash, *Roosevelt and Churchill, 1939-1940. The Partnership That Saved the West* (London: André Deutsch, 1976).

[102] FOP, FO371/22842, 116-7. On the attitude of the British establishment towards the United States, see: Eric Goldstein, "The British Official Mind and the United States, 1919-1942," in *Personalities, War and Diplomacy: Essays in International History*, eds. T. G. Otte and C. A. Pagedas (London: Routledge, 1997). On the difficult relations between Lothian and the Foreign Office see: David Reynolds, "Competitive Co-Operation: Anglo-American Relations in World War Two," *Historical Journal*, 23, 1, (1980): 233-45; id., *Lord Lothian and Anglo-American Relations*, 1-9. On the Foreign Office of the Cadogan's years, see Alexander Cadogan, *The Diaries of Sir Alexander Cadogan, O. M., 1938-1945*, ed. David Dilks (London: G. P. Putnam's Sons, 1972); Gaynor Johnson, *The Foreign Office and British Diplomacy in the Twentieth Century* (London: Routledge, 2005). On the relations between the Foreign Office and the British Embassy in Washington, see Cull, *Selling War*.

[103] FOP, FO371/22842, 116-7.

The idea of universal national self-determination was incompatible with the unity recently given to the world by the mechanical invention and economic progress and made both peace and prosperity impossible. The idea of federation, applied no doubt in some new ways, is, in the end, the only way out of that dilemma.[104]

However, "if any form of world organisation for peace is to work, the European problem must be separated from the world problem and Europe must be equipped to manage its own internal affairs, probably also by some application of the federal idea." The greatest of the mistakes made in Paris was economic, according to Lothian:

What did more to wreck civilization than anything else was the belief that a war-stricken world could recover by a system which combined immense international indebtedness with unrestrained tariff protectionism. That was probably the major cause of the world depression of 1929.[105]

The world problem was, according to Lothian, linked with the joint control of the seas by the democracies, "on the basis of common principles." In the control of the seas lay "the real key to world power," and it should not have been managed "by a single power," but "collectively" by democracies. The salvation of Western civilization depended, in those dramatic days, on the fact that Britain controlled the Atlantic, and the United States the Pacific. This had to be the fundamental basis of world power upon which to build the post-war order, if "the remainder of this century" had to lapse "without another world war."[106]

Referring to a classic theme of his political doctrine—a theme also often used by Curtis—Lothian asserted that it was necessary to re-establish in the twentieth century the political conditions of the nineteenth century, which gave Europe and the world an era of relative peace. That would be possible only through the union of the democracies, which had to perform collectively the historic role played by Great Britain alone. The world would experience economic prosperity and peace in the military sense,

---

[104] Kerr, *The American Speeches*: 58. On the impact of Lothian's speech in the United States and in Great Britain, see: Reynolds, *Lord Lothian and Anglo-American*, 18-35; Bosco, *Lord Lothian*, 325-30. On the question of American intervention within the Chicago foreign policy élite, see James C. Schneider, *Should America Go To War? The Debate over Foreign Policy in Chicago, 1939-1941* (Chapel Hill, NC: University of North Carolina Press, 1989).

[105] Kerr, *The American Speeches*, 60-1.

[106] *Ibidem.*

during which the process of transition from the national to the sovranational stage of historical development could be completed.[107]

Lothian's views raised tremendous enthusiasm in the United States, where twenty-six major newspapers reported favourable comments over the following four days, and the *New York Times* and the *Washington Post* printed the full text of the speech. The leader of the *New York Times* commented:

> No British Ambassador ever spoke more frankly to an American audience...In the light of this speech Britain is, in fact, ready to abdicate Empire in the interests of world-wide security for the democratic civilizations.[108]

The *New York Herald Tribune* described it "masterly":

> It is a skilful speech; but it is also both honest and thoughtful and is not to be dismissed with the label 'propaganda'. For though it is a statement of a case, it is a statement of a case on which Americans may well ponder and which they cannot disregard unless they can prove it to be unfounded.[109]

Dorothy Thompson, the most popular American columnist, wrote on 8th January in the *New York Herald Tribune* that Lothian's speech was "the clearest statement of British war and peace aims which has yet been made anywhere." The idea that the era of the nation-State was over, and that a new era was at that time wide open, was "a statement of faith in the future," which Americans would have taken seriously:

---

[107] *Ibidem,* 61.

[108] *New York Times*, 5 Jan. 1940.

[109] *New York Herald Tribune*, 5 Jan. 1940. On British propaganda in the United States during the war, see: K. R. M. Short, "The White Cliffs of Dover: Promoting the Anglo-American Alliance in World War II," *Historical Journal of Film, Radio and Television*, 2, 1, (1982): 3-25; Cull, *Selling War*; id., "Overture to an Alliance: British Propaganda at the New York World's Fair, 1939-1940," *Journal of British Studies*, 36, 3, (1997): 325-54; James Chapman, *The British at War: Cinema, State and Propaganda, 1939-1945* (New York: Tauris Academic Studies, 1998); Philip M. Taylor, *British Propaganda in the Twentieth Century* (Edinburgh, Edinburgh University Press, 2001); Todd Bennett, "The Celluloid War: State and Studio in Anglo-American Propaganda Film-Making, 1939-1941," *International History Review*, 24, 1, (2002): 64-102; Philip M. Taylor, *The Projection of Britain: British Overseas Publicity and Propaganda 1919-1939* (Cambridge: Cambridge University Press, 2007). On the presentation of the United States to British public opinion towards the end of the 1930s, see Peter M. H. Bell, "Uncle Sam Prepares: The Presentation of the United States in British Newsreels before the Second World War," *Film & History*, 30, 2, (2000): 50-9.

Lord Lothian's speech will be classed as British propaganda. Nevertheless, it must be judged wholly by its logic and truthfulness. We must ask ourselves whether this is a statement of the issue, not only the issue of this war, but the issue in this world.[110]

The *Springfield Republican* reaffirmed Thompson's judgement, observing: "No abler statement of the cause for the Allies has been presented in this country." The *Washington Post* considered it "an honest, straightforward and illuminating statement of the British point of view," and approved in principle the character of the new world order, even if expressing some doubt regarding its realisation. The *Chicago Daily Times* observed: "Since President Roosevelt's famous 'quarantine address'... Chicago has heard no public utterance as important as this speech."[111]

If the *Kansas City Star* thought of Lothian as "a liberal and enlightened spirit," the *Cincinnati Enquirer* commented that Lothian's world, even if being "somewhat tinged with the fanciful idealism of 'Union Now'," was much more realistic and sober than the Streitian plan. Even though it expressed some doubt about the capacity of Great Britain and the United States to assume the historical responsibility given to them by Lothian, it concluded: "it is not clear that Britain can so far abandon a selfish imperialism as to fit the larger role of co-arbiter in world affairs."[112]

Finally, the *Cleveland Plain Dealer* commented:

It is refreshing to be reminded by a man considered one of the outstanding thinkers of the age that the fight for democracy has been continuous since the dawn of recorded history. Persons who have been shouting for a declaration of war aims have it here. There is no escaping the fact that the destinies of all democratic peoples is bound up in the European conflict. Lothian did a commendable service in underlining the fact. He is not afraid to face facts, unpleasant though they may be.[113]

---

[110] Dorothy Thompson, "British War Aims," *New York Herald Tribune*, 8 Jan. 1940. On Thompson see: Marion K. Sanders, *Dorothy Thompson: A legend in Her Time* (New York: Avon Books, 1974); Peter Kurth, *American Cassandra: The Life of Dorothy Thompson* (London: Little, Brown & Co., 1991). On the tricky relationship between the Roosevelt Administration and the press, see Richard W. Steele, *Propaganda in an Open Society: The Roosevelt Administration and the Media* (Westport, CT: Greenwood Press, 1985).

[111] *Springfield Republican*, 5 Jan. 1940; *Washington Post*, 6 Jan. 1940; *Chicago Daily Times*, 7 Jan. 1940.

[112] *Kansas City Star*, 7 Jan. 1940; *Cincinnati Enquirer*, 8 Jan. 1940.

[113] *Cleveland Plain Dealer*, 8 Jan. 1940. FOP, FO371/24246,49-53. T. Whitehead, of the American Department of the Foreign Office wrote of Dorothy Thompson:

In London, on the other hand, the comments of the Foreign Office were rather critical. J. V. Perowne observed in a memorandum of 20th January that the enthusiasm for federalism led Lothian to forget that he was not "an apostle with an inspirational message to deliver directly from on high, but merely the servant of an earthly if distant Government." It was "very unwise and even dangerous" to speak to the Americans of European federation and the democratic control of the seas. They would certainly have taken Lothian as the spokesman of the British Government, and the undeniable "charm and sincerity of the apostle," would have added strength to his words. J. Balfour noted: "I agree that the time has come when we should warn Lord Lothian" against further federalist pronouncements.[114]

Interpreting the nervousness of the Foreign Office, Halifax sent Lothian his warmest congratulations for the extraordinary press coverage received by his speech, accompanied by a note of criticism:

> I regard this success as a great tribute to you. I doubt if even a Cabinet Minister has to be more careful than you, even though, as Winston said a day or two ago, to ask a Cabinet Minister to make a speech without causing offence in some quarter is like telling a centipede to go for a walk and not to put his foot in it!

Halifax asked Lothian not to present federalism as a "remedy for our present-day discontents," because the Government would disown his Ambassador, if forced to answer in Parliament.[115]

Lothian replied on 11th March, pointing out that "one of the difficulties of a British Ambassador in the United States is that he has to talk at the same time to two democratic audiences 3,000 miles away from one another and each with different backgrounds":

> I can imagine what my speeches would have been like if they had first been minuted by all veterans of the Foreign Office at home!...I don't think that my very guarded references to federation have done any harm.[116]

"Miss Dorothy Thompson is one of the most widely read article writers in the States. She is more English than the English in her defence of our cause," FOP, FO371/24246, 56.

[114] FOP, FO371/24246, 36-7. On Halifax at the head of the Foreign Office, see Andrew Roberts, *The Holy Fox. A Biography of Lord Halifax* (London: Weidenfeld & Nicolson, 1991).

[115] FOP, FO371/24246, 36-7.

[116] FOP, FO371/24246, 64-5. For a critical analysis, see: Butler, *Lord Lothian*, 280-303; Bosco, *Lord Lothian*, 325-335. On the state of Anglo-American relations

The greatest difficulty in the United States was, according to Lothian, "the cynicism of the public mind which has been taught to justify their own abandonment of international cooperation in 1920 by discrediting Wilson and all his works," by regretting their intervention in the European war, and "by crediting all other governments and peoples with the basest motives." Americans were however "hungering...for idealism and for sacrifice for a constructive cause." It was this hunger which, Lothian foresaw may "precipitate America into vigorous cooperation." At that moment it was paralysed "by fear of being drawn into war and by doubt about what the war is going to achieve in the way of lasting betterment and peace."[117]

Lothian "used 'federalism' to suggest two ideas." The first was that "so far as America is concerned a distinction must be recognised between the internal problems of Europe and World problems." The United States would "never undertake any responsibility for the internal affairs of Europe, which it regards as Europe's own business." But the Americans were "gradually becoming reconciled to the necessity of playing a hand in some form of world organisation not for war but to prevent world war." Lothian mentioned "'federalism' in the sense that a mere European anarchy cannot bring peace and that Europe must have some 'organisation' of its own." It was "a necessary condition if the United States of America is to take part in world organisation."[118]

The second idea implicit in the use of the word "federalism" was the democratic control of the seas. Since Great Britain could not alone perform that control, which was fundamental to prevent the spread of a local war into a world conflict, it was necessary to use a system—"the necessary power basis for the 20th Century"—in which the United States, with the assistance of the Dominions would control the Pacific, while the Royal Navy with the aid of France would control the Atlantic and the Indian Oceans. Americans did not yet acknowledge the fact that the Royal Navy had historically been their "best line of defence," because they were convinced that the British would never have accepted sharing naval power with them. That was, in fact, "the very case your die-hard friends put forward." That appeared to Lothian "in the long run...the only solution...the only real foundation for lasting peace in the future": it was "what 'parity' really means."[119]

---

from the outbreak of war to the fall of France, see Woodward, *British Foreign Policy*, 1: 155-72.

[117] FOP, FO371/24246, 65-6.

[118] FOP, FO371/24246, 66-7.

[119] FOP, FO371/24246, 67.

Lothian did not then let slip the opportunity that Halifax's speech of April 10 offered him—having the Foreign Minister explicitly speak of the need to create a federal order in the post-war world—and on 19 April, in a speech to the Chamber of Commerce at St. Louis, he returned to the attack, issuing a statement of great political importance. It reflected the favourable climate for federalism which had meanwhile flourished in Great Britain, but he also sought, as it was in Lothian's style, to induce his Government to consider more precise and advanced positions. The Allies, Lothian declared, "want to see a Europe organised…as a company of free nations united by some form of federal organisation." Not only did the Ambassador declare that the aim of the policy of his Government was the creation of a European federation, but he also took it for granted that it was the official policy of the Allies, and thus also of the French Government.[120]

The Allies were fighting a war of liberation, for the second time in the space of a quarter of a century. Lothian noted:

> There is no doubt that the war of 1914 was in fact a war of liberation. The real reason for the breakdown of the peace settlement was not the defects in the peace itself, though they were many, but the fact that the democracies, while they were right about national freedom, had not yet thought out how the new order of national freedom was to be effectively maintained. They did not realise what your ancestors learned between 1781 and 1789, that the condition of freedom is unity under the reign of law and freedom for trade and that without them both freedom and prosperity rapidly disappear. It was not enough that the thirteen original States in America cast off the authority of George III. They did not make their freedom and prosperity secure until, after great difficulties, they established their unity in your wonderful constitution, a constitution which created the largest free-trade area in the world. So in 1918, it was not enough to multiply the number of free nations…That had to be balanced by some form of unity, if it was not to degenerate into anarchy, imperialism, unemployment and war. It is the real explanation of the tragedy of the last twenty years.[121]

The Allies were not fighting for "the break-up and destruction of the unity of the German people." Their aim was to guarantee "security for everybody against aggression and war, poverty and unemployment;

---

[120] Lothian, *The American Speeches*: 81. FOP, FO371/24246, 128645, 68-9. On Halifax's declarations on post-war order, see: Frederick Winston Birkenhead, *Halifax: The Life of Lord Halifax* (London: Houghton Mifflin, 1966), 245-59; Roberts, *The Holy Fox*, 324-32.
[121] Lothian, *The American Speeches*, 73.

security for Germany no less than for her neighbours and ourselves." In
order to achieve these goals it was necessary to fight to the bitter end:

> A peace at present would only play into the hands of despotism. It would
> be no more than a truce—a short interval between two world wars. Now
> that the battle has been joined, it must be fought out until one system or
> the other...has definitely and permanently a preponderance of power
> behind it.[122]

An "indecisive peace" would certainly have meant the victory of the
dictatorships, because "the essence" of the Nazi system was that "it is
organised for instant war," while the democracies "genuinely demobilise"
in peacetime, and they needed some time to mobilise again. The war in
itself would not bring any benefits, but if fought "to resist aggression and
clear the foundations on which the free spirit of man can build
constructively," then it could be necessary. Once the war ended with the
total defeat of Nazism, they should not, however, repeat the mistakes of
1919, under the illusion that peace could grow out of "freedom carried to
the point of international anarchy" and from disarmament. Peace only
comes from "superior power behind law." The dictators "saw their
opportunity, created power for themselves, and began to remake the world
in their own image." What mattered most was that "at the end of this war
the superiority of power should rest unmistakably in the hands...of the
free peoples."[123]

It was, therefore, Lothian reiterated, "the question of power" not that of
intentions, that would decide the future world order. Lothian concluded:

> I doubt whether the end of this war will see another great Peace
> Conference like the last. The basic conditions of the post-war world will
> be settled by the terms of the armistice, by the question of power, by the
> fact of where the preponderant power will lie at the time when the 'Cease-
> Fire' sounds.[124]

The "question of power" to which Lothian referred, was that of sea
power which had "determined the kind of world in which we live."
Germany's "central objective" was "the capture of sea power...for it is the
key to world power." British naval supremacy had constituted the base of
the power which guaranteed the stability of the international system of the
nineteenth century, characterized by the convertibility of the pound into

---

[122] *Ibidem*, 79.
[123] *Ibidem*, 80.
[124] *Ibidem*.

gold, the freedom of trade and emigration, and by the existence of an international police force—the Royal Navy—which, while failing to prevent all wars, was however able to prevent the spread of a local conflict into a general war. While admitting that the British had in some ways "abused our power," Lothian observed that the so-called control of the seas had given "unity and an essential order to the world."[125]

Lothian's St. Louis speech provoked, on 1 May, a Parliamentary interpellation by Somerset de Chair, asking if the Government endorsed the declarations of the Ambassador and, in particular, if the creation of the United States of Europe was an official "thoughtful policy." In drafting the answer, however very evasive, R. M. Makins, Foreign Office official, noted that although these references to federalism were "undoubtedly well received" in the United States, federalism was by no means British Government policy. However, it was not possible to "categorically refute Lord Lothian," and therefore it seemed necessary to reiterate the willingness of the two Governments to collaborate in war and in peace.[126]

The Foreign Office was greatly irritated for being, once again, caught by surprise by Lothian, just when the Western front seemed threatened by enemy attack, which put an end to the so-called *drôle de guerre*, and also to the war fought by words. The role of the Americans in supporting the Allies, and probably to intervene directly in the conflict, seemed to gain weight increasingly. In trying to convince Halifax to send a firmer admonition to the relapsed Ambassador, J. V. Perowne confessed to believing it "very dangerous" of the Ambassador to mislead American public opinion in that way, since a European federation was not, in fact, a British peace aim.[127]

Lothian's attitude seen from London seemed even more dangerous in the perspective that the Americans would take part in the peace negotiations and find out that "after all the speeches delivered by Lord

---

[125] *Ibidem,* 80-1.

[126] FOP, FO371/24362, 128554: 157-62.

[127] FOP, FO371/24362, 128554: 78-9. See, on the *drôle de guerre* the masterly work by Marc Bloch, *L'étrange défaite* (Paris: Gallimard, 1990), and the essay by Carole Fink, "Marc Bloch and the drôle de guerre: Prelude to the Strange Defeat," in Blatt, *The French Defeat*, 39-54. See also François Bédarida and Denis Peschanski eds., "Marc Bloch à Etienne Bloch: Lettres de la drôle de guerre," in *Cahiers de l'Institut d'Histoire du Temps Présent*, 19, (1991). On Bloc see Carole Fink, *Marc Bloch: A Life in History* (Cambridge: Cambridge University Press, 1989), 79-204. See also: Dominique Lormier, *La drôle de guerre* (Paris: Les Chemins de la Mémoire, 1999); W. B. R. Neave Hill, *Franco-British Strategic Policy, 1939*, in *Relations franco-britanniques, 1935-1939* (Paris: CNRS, 1975); Pierre Rocolle, *La Guerre de 1940* (Paris: Armand Colin, 1990).

Lothian," the project of a European federation not only was not part of the Allied agenda, but it was "even rejected by ourselves and by the French." Writing to Lothian on April 30, Halifax confirmed the suspicions by Federal Union, and also by the French press, that the recent conversion of the British Government to a policy of "indissoluble union" with the Continent—which will be discussed later—was not sincere, and therefore that the English could still not be trusted. While welcoming the utility of bringing the Americans to accept the idea of international co-operation, in referring to federalism for Europe Halifax also reiterated "the disadvantage of being too categorical or trying to go beyond cautious statements," and without specific commitments already made by the Foreign Office "on these complex questions." Referring to his own speech of April 10, Halifax noted, not without some embarrassment, that the federal solution was mentioned "in rather vague terms, and with many reservations," and it was not therefore "prudent" to go further at least for the time being.[128]

Entering, as it has been discussed, at the heart of the political debate on the conduct of the war and the post-war order, the federalist project—supported by prominent figures of British culture, by the Anglican Church, by the most prominent British Ambassador at that time, and by a solid popular organisation—placed the British Government in the condition to choose between the traditional policy of the great defensive alliance, and the innovative policy of the European federation. The broad consensus created by Federal Union in the country in support of the federalist project, would eventually lead British statesmen to adopt, as a framework of European relations at the end of the war, a revolutionary perspective.

IV. *The political world*

The strategy followed by Lothian—on one hand to convince Americans to join in the conflict on the basis of a federal post-war order, and on the other hand to urge the British Government to enunciate clearly the principles and objectives for which they were fighting—had begun in fact to bear fruit since the beginning of the conflict. Lothian played, in this regard, a pioneering role on both sides of the Atlantic.

On September 11, Eden, in a radio broadcast to the Dominions and the United States, wondered:

> Will we eventually manage to liberate Europe from the caste barriers of creeds and prejudices? Will borders, faiths, languages and commerce

---

[128] FOP, FO371/24362, 128554, 78-9.

succeed to unite the States and not to divide them? Will we manage to create a true European unity?[129]

Following early public statements in favour of the federal idea, on 20th and 27th September, the MPs Geoffrey Mander and D. Leach—members of the federalist inter-group in the House of Commons, created by Richard Coudenhove-Kalergi—asked the Government if they were "prepared to make it known to the people of Germany that His Majesty's Government was willing to explore the possibility of joining a United States of Europe as part of the peace terms."[130]

The answer given by Under-Secretary Butler was that the Government welcomed the formation "of a stable international system having as its object the prevention of war and the just settlement of international disputes by pacific means," but it did not consider it "desirable" to commit "to any particular procedure for achieving this aim."[131]

On 25th October, Leach renewed the interpellation, again without success, and a similar appeal had been addressed to Chamberlain on 28th September by the Norwegian John Schiotz. The Society of Friends, a pacifist organisation, also asked the Government on 23rd September if it would become (together with other European States) a member of a Congress advancing the federal idea, receiving again a negative answer.[132]

The debate in Parliament on the possibility of a European federation was re-launched on 12th October by Leo Amery, who stressed its immediate necessity. Amery's speech was followed by those of Mander, Philip Noel-Baker, and Colonel Josiah C. Wedgwood, who identified in the Supreme War Council "the beginning of the federal system." Amery could conclude: "It is interesting to see how what I have been talking

---

[129] On Eden's Francophile policy as head of the Foreign Office, see: Glyn Stone, "Yvon Delbos and Anthony Eden: Anglo-French Cooperation, 1936-1938," *Diplomacy & Statecraft*, 17, 4, (2006): 799-820. On Eden, see: David Carlton, *Anthony Eden: A Biography* (New York: Harper Collins, 1986); A. R. Peters, *Anthony Eden at the Foreign Office, 1931-38* (New York: Dartmouth Publishing, 1986); James Rhodes, *Anthony Eden* (New York: McGraw-Hill, 1986); Alan Campbell Johnson, *Anthony Eden: A Biography* (Whitefish, MT: Kessinger Publishing, 2007).

[130] *The Times*, 12 Sept. 1939; FOP, FO371/22946, 332.

[131] FOP, FO371/22946, 227-9.

[132] FO371/24030, 310-3; FO371/22946, 232-3. On the Society of Friends, see: William Whiting, *The Society of Friends and What It Stands For* (Whitefish, MT: Kessinger Publishing, 2005); John S. Rowntree, *The Society of Friends: Its Faith and Practice* (Whitefish, MT: Kessinger Publishing, 2006).

about for fifteen years and more should now at last begin to be regarded as obvious."[133]

The Foreign Office also took a special interest in the question, showing how Chatham House, "where Mr. Curtiss [sic] is drafting the largest and perhaps the last of his constitutional projects," had been dealing with the matter for some time. It was desirable to "let Chatham House work in peace, exempt from the attentions of Mr. Mander and others." The federalist principle could perhaps be "a solution to the world's ills" and the limitation of national sovereignty "the only sure guarantee of a stable international system," but the practical difficulties were "enormous," and federalism could not be "forced on unwilling peoples."[134]

It was premature to draft "paper constitutions," because the federal principle had first to be accepted "far more widely" than it was at that moment, "and not only in Anglo-Saxon countries," where, however, it had not yet struck "deep root." Certainly it was "attractive" to proclaim federalism "in general terms as a war aim," but it was premature, and it would raise "false hopes." They should not discourage the discussion and a serious study of federalism, but it was absolutely necessary to avoid favourable official declarations.[135]

However, the Government continued to maintain a negative attitude towards federalist leaders. The Foreign Office delayed, for example, the concession of a visa to Lord Davies, who wished to go to France and Switzerland to strengthen the links between the New Commonwealth Society and the organisations of the two countries engaged to support the federal idea. In France Lord Davies planned to meet Pierre Comert, Pierre Côt, Paul Reynaud, Hermann Raushning, Georges Scelle, and Georges Berlia; and in Switzerland, Hans Bauer, William Rappard, Hans Kelsen, Hans Wehberg and Fritz Thyssen, the German industrialist whom he wanted to involve in the activities of the New Commonwealth.[136]

---

[133] *Hansard*, 5th Series, 352, col. 608n. Leopold Stennett Amery (1873-1955) was a journalist on *The Times* from 1899 to 1909; Conservative MP for Birmingham Sparkbrook from 1911 to 1945; First Lord of the Admiralty from 1922 to 1924; Minister for the Colonies from 1924 to 1929; and Minister for India from 1940 to 1945. On Amery see: David Faber, *Speaking for England: Leo, Julian and John Amery, the Tragedy of a Political Family* (Washington, DC: Free Press, 2005). On Wedgwood, see E. M Johnston-Liik, *Managing an Inheritance: Colonel J. C. Wedgwood, the History of Parliament and the Lost History of the Irish Parliament* (Dublin: Royal Irish Academy, 1989).

[134] FOP, FO371/22946, 337-42.

[135] *Ibidem.*

[136] FOP, FO371/22949. 90-8. The *News Chronicle* of 13 October reported of a memorandum which Davies dispatched to the branches of the organisation,

Davies advised the officials in Whitehall that he would act "merely as a scout," without any official capacity, in the attempt to pave the way for a British proposal of "European confederation" as the basis for peace, and for the solution of the German question. Orme Sargent, Permanent Foreign Office Under-Secretary, tried to persuade Halifax to negate Davies' visa request, since he seemed the least suitable person for that kind of "scouting mission," and that the moment was not right for those initiatives. Halifax was not persuaded by Sargent, but writing to Davies on October 16th, acknowledged the good intentions of that "mission" and invited him to be prudent, suggesting that he use his Swiss friends to arrange the meeting with Thyssen, in order to avoid the interference of the press.[137]

The beginning of November also saw one of the Government's most authoritative members become directly involved in the debate. On the 7th, Lord Halifax openly advocated a limitation of national sovereignty at the end of the war. Referring to Federal Union and reaffirming a view expressed at a conference at Chatham House on 29th June, Halifax observed: "A new order must be established on the basis of some surrender of sovereign rights by individual States in favour of a common authority."[138]

The following day *The Times* thus commented on Halifax's speech: "As Lord Halifax emphasised, federation must be the result of natural growth. There are, indeed, already signs in the willing grouping together of many of the smaller nations that the movement in this direction has

---

supporting the creation of the United States of Europe as an Allied war aim. For a discussion on international security and defence in France, see: Hermann Raushning, *The Revolution of Nihilism* (London: Alliance Book Corporation, 1940); Georges Berlia, *Problèmes de sécurité internationale et de défense* (Paris: Les Cours de droit, 1975); id., *Le maintien de la paix: Doctrines et problèmes: 1919-1976* (Paris: Les Cours de droit, 1976). On Kelsen, see: Carlos-Miguel Herrera, *Théorie juridique et politique chez Hans Kelsen* (Paris: Kime, 1997); Lars Vinx, *Hans Kelsen's Pure Theory of Law: Legality and Legitimacy* (New York: Oxford University Press, 2007); Hans Wehberg, *The Outlawry of War* (New York: Carnegie Endowment for International Peace, 1931); id., *Civil War and International Law* (Harlow: Longman, 1938). For a critical analysis of international law, see Martti Koskenniemi, *From Apology to Utopia: The Structure of International Legal Argument* (Cambridge: Cambridge University Press, 2006). On the Thyssen family, see: Peter Eikemeier, *Sammlung Fritz Thyssen: Ausgewählte Meisterwerke* (Munich: Hirmer Verlag, 1986); Jeffrey Fear, *Organizing Control: August Thyssen and the Construction of German Corporate Management* (Boston, MA: Harvard University Press, 2005).
[137] FOP, FO371/22949, 90-8.
[138] *Federal Union News*, 9.

begun and will continue." In the *London Letter* Reuter expounded in an article the aims of Federal Union, thus contributing to making the movement well known throughout the world.[139]

In the space of a few hours following Halifax's position, the leader of the opposition also declared his support for the idea of a European federation. In a speech at Caxton Hall at Westminster on 8th November 1939, in front of Labour MPs, Attlee—head of the party since 1935—condensed in a few, essential principles what he thought ought to be the basis of the post-war settlement. The first was a decisive "no" to a peace dictated by the winners; the others stated the right of all nations to self-determination, the renunciation of the use of force in international conflicts, the recognition of the rights of minorities, and the rejection of imperialism. The last and conclusive principle was significantly formulated as follows:

> There must be acceptance of the principle that international anarchy is incompatible with peace, and that in the common interest there must be recognition of an international authority superior to the individual States and endowed not only with rights over them, but with powers to make them effective, operating not only in the political, but in the economic sphere. Europe must federate or perish.[140]

Again, a memorandum on the peace aims signed by twenty Labour MPs on 10th November, asked for the creation of a system in which every nation was ready to sacrifice a part of national sovereignty in the interest of general security. The conservative MP Harold Nicolson also intervened in favour of the federalist project in his Armistice Day speech at the Albert Hall in Nottingham.[141]

The speech by Attlee was analysed in great detail by the national press. The leader of *The Times* of 9th November commented:

> Mr Attlee's pronouncement yesterday on Labour's peace aims was clear and decided. It matches well, though it was the speech of the Leader of the

---

[139] *The Times*, 8 Nov. 1939.

[140] *The Times*, 9 Nov. 1939. On Attlee as Labour leader, see: Francis Williams, *Twilight of Empire: Memoirs of Prime Minister Clement Attlee* (Westport, CT: Greenwood Press, 1978); Robert D. Pearce, *Attlee* (London: Addison Wesley, 1997); John Swift, *Labour in Crisis: Clement Attlee and the Labour Party Opposition, 1931-1940* (New York: Palgrave Macmillan, 2001).

[141] Attlee, *Labour's Peace*: 12; reprinted in *Labour's Aims in War and Peace* (London: Labour Party Publications, 1940). Clement Richard Attlee (1883-1967) was a minister in the Churchill Administration from 1940 to 1945, and Prime Minister from 1945 to 1950. On Nicolson see Milne, *Harold Nicolson*.

Opposition, with the declaration of the Foreign Secretary the day before. In no essential particular is there any divergence of opinion, and once again it is proclaimed to all the world that this country is of one mind and purpose in choosing the terrible resort to war.[142]

Even in France, as a direct consequence of the growth of interest in federalism which was occurring in Great Britain, there began to emerge— albeit more sporadically and timidly than in Britain—net stances inspired by federalist ideals. Daladier's speech to the Senate—agreed with Chamberlain himself—on 29th December was fundamental— wherein he declared:

> The Franco British union is open to all, but I state categorically that, without material and positive guarantees, France will not lay down her arms...Just as I distrust grand theoretical conceptions, so I prefer material guarantees against the return of events such as those which we are suffering from today, and so, too, I conceive that a new Europe should have a far wider organisation than that which now exists. It will be necessary to multiply exchanges and perhaps to envisage federal ties between the various States of Europe.

The comments of the French press on statements by Daladier were generally very positive. The leading article of the *Petit Parisien* of January 3, noted: "Anglo-French relations are becoming more and more the prototype of those which in times of peace should unite the various States in order to participate in a European federation."[143]

Commenting on Daladier's speech, the *News Chronicle* of 9th January hoped that the British Government was "*more suo* only lagging behind a little and will presently express their agreement with M. Daladier's words." Examining the paper prepared by Sir John Fisher-Williams for the Chatham House "World Order" study-group, the *News Chronicle* defined the constitutional conditions for the establishment of a European federation:

> in its foreign relations such a union must, *ex hypothesi*, be a single international person. Its foreign policy and armed forces, and the finance

---

[142] *The Times*, 9 Nov. 1939.

[143] On the collaboration between Daladier and Chamberlain see: Elisabeth du Réau, *Edouard Daladier, 1884-1970* (Paris: Fayard, 1993); David Dilks, *Neville Chamberlain*, (Cambridge: Cambridge University Press, 2002); Robert C. Self, *Neville Chamberlain: A Biography* (London: Ashgate Publishing, 2006); Stanton B. Leeds, *These Rule France: The Story of Edouard Daladier and the Men Around Daladier* (Whitefish, MT: Kessinger Publishing 2007).

applicable to these two departments of State, must therefore be under federal control. That is the irreducible minimum of federality.[144]

The areas of competence of the federal government would also be extended to the spheres of currency, customs, and trade, since they were "matters of common interest." In defining the point reached by France and Great Britain in the process of unification, the *News Chronicle* observed:

> We have got somewhere near to joint control of foreign policy and armed forces 'for the duration and six months after'. Substantially, what is now required in these departments is the further elaboration of the joint machinery of control—closer collaboration between the two Foreign Offices, for example—plus a decision and an announcement that the time limitation, the duration of six months, is withdrawn. The two countries must determine that they will permanently regard themselves as a 'single international person' in their foreign relations, and the sooner that is done the better. But towards community of action in the other 'affairs of common interest', we have not yet got very far. We have produced nothing very attractive to offer the others to whom the union 'is open'...But let us adopt complete custom union as a definite end of policy.[145]

It was also agreed that for the duration of the conflict a pound would be equivalent to 176 francs and a half, and in order to ensure the equivalence, the two governments created the rudiments of a specific organisation. Some differences emerged between the two central trade unions—the TUC and the French CGT—on the levels of salaries in time of war, and the two countries were still far from being able to guarantee that "parallelism in the economic policy which is essential for the permanent maintenance of stable monetary relations." The next step would be the creation of a complete customs union, and since the economic structures of Great Britain and France were already largely complementary, it would bring "good business to both." "It was commonplace in the twenties," the *News Chronicle* argued, to look with envy to American prosperity, as the United States was the largest trading area in the world. The population of Great Britain and France was two-thirds that of the United States and with their colonies they could create an area of free trade much larger in population than that of the United States. "So why not?" concluded the article.[146]

---

[144] *News Chronicle,* 9 Jan. 1940. On Chamberlain's policy towards France and the United States, see Kennedy, "Neville Chamberlain and".
[145] *News Chronicle,* 9 Jan. 1940.
[146] *Ibidem.*

Chamberlain seized the challenge of the *News Chronicle*, and intervened on the subject with a speech at the Mansion House on the same day, 9 January 1940, reaffirming the British determination to strengthen ties with France in the building of a new European order. The war-time Anglo-French co-operation represented "just another example of that close...even intimate association that exists between us": an association which will prove so valuable that when the war is over, neither the British nor the French would give it up. It may develop into something "broader and deeper" when the war was over, and extend to "other European States and perhaps the whole world."[147]

On 10th January, *The Times* commented ironically that Chamberlain's Mansion House speech was a sort of cuckoo egg in Federal Union's nest. The British Empire was, according to *The Times*, "the first organisation in history when distinct States, with the power to act independently at all times, have voluntarily decided to remain united." The Anglo-French Alliance was "the first association of great powers" which started the process of construction of "a common administration on questions of common interest." Chamberlain's willingness to extend the Anglo-French Union to include other States "and perhaps ultimately the whole world" was coherent with the British conception of the course of history that a "permanent sovranational system" should develop from limited beginnings.[148]

Chamberlain's speech also obtained very positive comments "from right to left" in France. *Temps* of 11 January noted that Anglo-French solidarity had to materialise in the everyday lives of the two peoples, coming to include their respective empires, and expand after the war, to include other countries, in the construction of a more stable world order.[149]

In a letter to *The Times* of 18th January, L. P. Jacks observed that the possibility of creating, at the end of the war a "new and better" Europe, was very remote, for the defeat of Germany would have brought "political disorder and economic ruin" in Central Europe, the end of the economic resources of the Allies, and "grave domestic problems arising in the

---

[147] *News Chronicle*, 10 Jan. 1940. On Chamberlain and the debate on war aims, see: Neville Chamberlain, *Britain's Peace Aims* (London: His Majesty's Stationery Office, 1940); Neville Chamberlain, *The Neville Chamberlain Diary Letters: The Downing Street Years, 1934-1940*, ed. Robert Self (London: Ashgate Publishing, 2005); Graham Macklin, *Chamberlain* (London: Haus Publisher, 2006).

[148] *The Times*, 10 Jan. 1940; Denis Nowell Pritt, *Federal illusion?* (London: Muller, 1940), 133. On Chamberlain's policy towards France, see John Charmley, *Chamberlain and the Lost Peace* (London: Hodder & Stoughton, 1989).

[149] *Temps*, 11 Jan. 1940.

change-over from a war to a peace economy." The beginning of the building of a new Europe had already been marked by the declarations of Daladier and Chamberlain, "the most important event since the conflict began." The Anglo-French union in the vital sectors of economy, finance, and war strategy had to speed up and become "the nucleus" of a "larger" union.[150]

The Mansion House speech had not been an isolated episode. Chamberlain had already intervened several times to emphasise the British intention to forge closer links with France in the construction of a new European order. In a radio broadcast on the previous 25 November, reported by *The Times* on the following day as "Victory before Utopia," Chamberlain sustained that the peace aims for which Great Britain was fighting were the building of a Europe without frontiers, in which armaments were no longer needed, apart from those necessary for the maintenance of internal order. In such a unified market, goods, capital and peoples could freely circulate, and every nation could have the "unconditional right" to choose their own form of government. A new political mechanism able to guarantee the continuity of a process which would progressively unify Europe was needed, and Chamberlain hoped that a democratic Germany could participate in that task.[151]

Intervening in the House of Commons on January 16, Chamberlain confirmed that, following the financial agreements of December 1939, "the unity of action of our two countries in the continuation of the war" had "become total." Chamberlain expected that the experience of Anglo-French co-operation could "lead to closer relations in the economic and financial sphere between the countries of Europe and the world." Speaking in his hometown of Birmingham on February 24, he observed that during the six months of war the Anglo-French Alliance had become so strong that the two governments were in fact thinking and acting as one. That "intimate entente" would provide the basis to "realise the authority and stability which are necessary to European security," contributing to solving the problems of the "new Europe which must emerge from the war." However powerful, Chamberlain continued, Great Britain and France could not, and did not want, at the end of the war, to "create the new Europe by themselves." Other nations should join it on the basis of shared values.[152]

---

[150] *The Times*, 18 Jan. 1940.

[151] "Victory Before Utopia", *The Times*, 25 Nov. 1839. On Chamberlain's declarations on war-aims, see: Chamberlain, *Britain's Peace Aims*; id., *The Neville Chamberlain Diary*; Self, *Neville Chamberlain*, 323-41.

[152] *News Chronicle*, 10 Jan. 1940.

V. The "Solemn" Declaration of 28th March

The public utterances of leading exponents of the political world were not without followed-up actions. At the sixth meeting, on 28th March, of the War Supreme Council, including Chamberlain, Halifax, Churchill, Oliver Stainley, and Sir Kingsley Wood—assisted by Sir Alexander Cadogan, Sir Cyril Newall, Sir Dudley Pound and Sir Edmund Ironside—Paul Reynaud—who recently replaced Eduoard Daladier as Prime Minister— César Campinchi and Laurent Eynac—assisted by Charles Corbin, Alexis Leger, Maurice Gamelin, Francois Darlan, Joseph Vuillemin and Louis Koeltz—the two Governments offered, for the first time since the beginning of the conflict, an official version of the war aims. In the final declaration the French and British Governments undertook not to negotiate, and at least to conclude a separate armistice or peace treaty which did not guarantee for both countries "an effective and lasting guarantee to their security," and about which both governments were not in total agreement. The two governments committed themselves

> to maintain after the conclusion of peace a community of action in all
> spheres for so long as may be necessary to safeguard their security and to
> effect the reconstruction, with the assistance of other nations, of an
> international order which will ensure the liberty of peoples, respect for law
> and the maintenance of peace in Europe.[153]

---

[153] CPA, WM(40)76, C4621/9/17. See the report of the Supreme War Council of 28 March 1940, CAB 99/3. On this meeting of the Supreme War Council, see: Paul Baudouin, *The Private Diaries (March 1940 to January 1941) of Paul Baudouin* (London: Eyrie & Spottiswoode, 1948); François Bédarida, *La stratégie secrète de la drôle de guerre: la Conseil Suprême Interallié, septembre 1939-avril 1940* (Paris: Presses de la Fondation Nationale des Sciences Politiques, 1979); Basil Henry Liddell Hart, *History of the Second World War* (Cambridge, MA: Da Capo Press, 1999), 55-8; Neville Wylie, *European Neutrals and Non-Belligerents during the Second World War* (Cambridge: Cambridge University Press, 2002), 45-8; Spencer Tucker, *The Second World War* (New York: Palgrave Macmillan, 2003), 47-9. On the reinforcement of the Anglo-French Alliance, see: Bédarida, *La stratégie secrète*; Michael Dockrill, "The Foreign Office and France During the Phoney War, September 1939-May 1940," in *Diplomacy and World Power: Studies in British Foreign Policy, 1890-1950*, eds. Michael Dockrill and B. J. C. Mckercher (Cambridge: Cambridge University Press, 1996); Martin S. Alexander, "'Fighting to the Last Frenchman?' Reflection on the BEF Deployment to France and the Strains in the Franco-British Alliance, 1939-1940," in Blatt, *The French Defeat*, 269-94; Nick Smart, *British Strategy and Politics During the Phony War: Before the Balloon Went Up* (Westport, CT: Praeger, 2003).

It was Reynaud who pressed for the inclusion of that commitment in what became well known as the "solemn declaration" of 28th March. The draft, approved the day before by the British War Cabinet, stated:

> The two Governments being equally determined to carry on the war with the utmost vigour until the purposes for which it was undertaken are attained, mutually undertake that during the present war they will neither negotiate nor conclude an armistice or treaty of peace except by mutual agreement. The two Governments further declare their intention to continue the closest co-operation in their financial, economic and defence policy after the conclusion of peace.[154]

Chamberlain and Halifax accepted Reynaud's amendment—thus satisfying the French claim for security at the end of the war— showing the identification of the framework of the problem in a project easily equivalent to the federalist one. The British Government had just recently abandoned all hopes of a negotiated peace with German leaders who would succeed in overthrowing Hitler. The attempts of Joseph Wirth and the Vatican to promote a change of government in Germany, had in fact failed. For the first time in the history of the Empire it was therefore believed plausible to ignore the point of view of the Dominions—which were certainly not favourable to Great Britain's permanent involvement in European affairs—and for the first time since the outbreak of the war the British Government closed the doors to any attempt for negotiated peace. Chamberlain, who in October had hoped to be able to persuade the Germans of the impossibility of them winning, on the 28 March declared his faith in "total victory."[155]

---

[154] CAB 99/3. Bédarida, *La stratégie secrete*, 70-3; William Philpott, "The Supreme War Council and the Allied War Effort, 1939-1940," in Dockrill and Chassaigne, *Anglo-French Relations*, 118-9. On the role played by Reynaud to strengthen Anglo-French co-operation, see: Christian Delporte, *La troisième République, 1919-1940. De Poincaré à Paul Reynaud* (Paris: Pygmalion, 1998); Krakovitch Raymond, *Paul Reynaud* (Paris: Tallandier, 2002); Thibault Tellier, *Paul Reynaud (1878-1966): Un indépendant en politique* (Paris: Fayard, 2005).

[155] *Actes et Documents du Saint-Siège relatifs a la Seconde Guerre Mondiale* (City of Vatican: Libreria Ed. Vaticane, 1965-81). On the Vatican's diplomatic action towards Hitler, see: Peter Ludlow, "Papst Pius XII, die britische Regierung und die deutsche Opposition im Winter 1939/40," *Vierteljahrs Hefte für Zeitgeschichte*, 22, (1974); Georg Herbstritt, *Ein Weg der Verständigung?: Die umstrittene Deutschland und Ostpolitik des Reichskanzlers a. D. Dr. Joseph Wirth in der Zeit des Kalten Krieges* (Frankfurt am Main: Peter Lang, 1993); Ulrike Horster-Philipps, *Joseph Wirth 1879-1956: Eine politische Biographie* (Paderborn: F. Schoningh, 1998); Pierre Blet, *Pius XII and the Second World War: According to*

Speaking in the House of Commons on 2nd April, a few days after the signing of the "solemn declaration," Chamberlain commented:

> If this declaration had dealt only with the conduct of the war, it might have been criticised as unnecessary in view of the complete unity of purpose already existing between the two countries. But it goes far beyond the expression of British and French determination to fight together for a common victory, and provides for continuous Anglo-French co-operation in the establishment of peace and in the reconstruction of an international order designed to ensure the liberty of peoples, respect for law, and the maintenance of peace in Europe.

The political significance of the "solemn declaration" was that

> after the conclusion of peace, while the assistance of other nations will be welcomed in the reconstruction of Europe, Anglo-French community of action will be maintained in all spheres so long as may be necessary to effect and consolidate the reconstruction.[156]

The declarations of 28th March were in fact the result of close Anglo-French co-operation, which from the sectors of the war-economy—

---

the Archives of the Vatican (New York: Paulist Press, 1999); Michael F. Feldkamp, *Pius XII. und Deutschland* (Göttingen: Vandenhoeck & Ruprecht, 2000); John Cornwell, *Hitler's Pope: The Secret History of Pius XII* (London: Penguin, 2000), 120; Owen Chadwick, *Gran Bretagna e Vaticano durante la Seconda guerra mondiale* (Rome: San Paolo Edizioni, 2007). On Allied strategy, see: Pierre Le Goyet, *Le Mystère Gamelin* (Paris: 1976); Bradford A. Lee, "Strategy, Arms and the Collapse of France, 1930-1940," in *Diplomacy and Intelligence During the Second World War: Essays in Honour of F. H. Hinsley*, ed. Richard Langhorne (Cambridge: Cambridge University Press, 2004), 43-66; Martin S. Alexander, *The Republic in Danger: General Maurice Gamelin and the Politics of French Defence, 1933-1940* (Cambridge: Cambridge University Press, 1992); id., *The Republic at War: Franco-British Strategy, Politics and Defeat, 1939-1940* (Cambridge: Cambridge University Press, 1998); Nick Smart, *British Strategy and Politics During the Phony War: Before the Balloon Went Up* (Westport, CT: Praeger Publishers, 2003).
[156] FOP, FO 371/24299, 134921, 118-9. On Anglo-French economic integration, see: M. Gowing, "Anglo-French Economic Collaboration Up to the Outbreak of the Second World War," in *Les relations franco-britanniques de 1935 à 1939* (Paris: Editions du CNRS, 1975), 179-88; P. Le Goyet, "Les relations économiques franco-britanniques à la veille de la 2e guerre mondiale," in *ibidem*, 189-200; L. S. Pressnell, "Les finances de guerre britannique et la coopération économique franco-britannique en 1939 et en 1940," in *Français et Britanniques*, 489-516; R. Frank, *La Hantise du déclin. La France, 1920-60: finances, défense et identité nationale* (Paris: 1994).

an agreement on a custom union between the two countries had been signed on 16 February—was steadily increasing to include the military and political ones. In a radio interview on 30th March, Churchill went so far as to declare: "the British Empire and French Republic are now joined together in an indissoluble union."[157]

VI. *The reactions in France and The Spectator*

The reactions of the French press to the "solemn declaration" were generally favourable. The only criticism came from the right-wing press— *Journal des Débats*, *Petit Journal*, *Action Française* and *Gringoire*— which pointed out the lack of an explicit reference to the Rhine frontier as being the only acceptable "effective and lasting guarantee" to French security. The special relationship with Great Britain would have detached France from her "Latin sisters," and the new sense of security thus achieved would have favoured an indulgent treatment of Germany in the terms of peace. Writing in *Jour-Echo de Paris*, Jean Fernand-Laurent advanced some doubt that the British had learned the lesson of 1919, namely that the European peace depended on "safeguarding the security of France."[158]

Among the enthusiasts, Vladimir D'Ormesson wrote in *Ouest-Eclair* on 29th March that, "never in history was an alliance more stable." The *Populaire* announced: "England and France proclaim their absolute union for peace as well as war." The *Temps* of March 30 noted: "A turning point

---

[157] FOP, FO 371/24299, 134921, 118-9. On Churchill as war leader, see: Martin Gilbert, *Churchill: A Life* (New York: Holt Paperbacks, 1992); id., *Winston Churchill's War Leadership* (London: Vintage, 2004); Winston Churchill, *Blood, Toil, Tears and Sweat: The Great Speeches*, ed. David Cannadine (London: Penguin Classics, 2007). On the military aspects of the Anglo-French Union, see J. E. Tyler, "Military Aspects of Anglo-French Union," *New Commonwealth Quarterly*, 6, (1940): 50-61.

[158] See the reports of *Journal des Débats*, *Petit Journal*, *Action Française* and *Gringoire* on 29 March 1940. For a discussion of the psychological attitude of the French people towards the war, see: Jean Fernand-Laurent, *Un Peuple Ressuscite* (New York: Brentano's, 1943); id., *Gallic Charter: Foundations of Tomorrow's France* (London: Little, Brown & Co., 1944); id., *Activities for the Advancement of Women: Equality, Development, and Peace* (New York: United Nations Publications, 1986). For a representation of the debate in France on war-aims, see: René Bouvier, *Quels sont les buts de guerre franco-anglais?* (Paris: La vie, 1940). On the attitude of the French Right towards Hitler, see Charles A. Micaud, *The French Right and Nazi Germany, 1933-1943: A Study of Public Opinion* (London: Octagon Books, 1964).

in the history of Europe." The *Petit Gironde* proclaimed: "A fundamental date in the history of the world." Henri De Kerillis declared in *Petit Dauphinois* that the moral value of the declaration was inestimable, because the two countries constituted "in very truth, through their ensemble, a beginning for the United States of Europe." It was then necessary to create "the magnetic field capable of attracting other States." Herve wrote in *Victoire* that "Today's clarion-call proclaims to all the peoples that after victory France and Britain have mutually sworn to remain united and armed until they have set up the Republic of the United States of Europe." *Paris Midi, Paris Soir, Figaro* and *Temps* pointed out that Great Britain had abandoned for good her "splendid isolation," and accomplished "a veritable revolution in her foreign policy." Great Britain was at last "in Europe!"[159]

Temps, on 29th March, presented the declaration in its leading article as an "act of the greatest importance," which marked "the beginning of a new phase of the European war," because it showed the determination of France and Great Britain to fight until the final victory "of the right cause for which they took up arms." For the first time in European history Great Britain had "abandoned her traditional policy in order to unite herself effectively with France in peace and war."[160]

On the left, Léon Blum, in the editorial of 29th March in *Populaire*, judged the declaration as the "logical conclusion of the unity of action already achieved during the past seven months." France and Great Britain had been challenged together, together they were fighting, and still together they would impose conditions of peace on Germany.[161]

---

[159] FOP, FO371/24298, 214-6. On d'Ormesson, see Kaiser *Political Catholicism*, 258-61

[160] FOP, FO371/24298: 214-5.

[161] FOP, FO371/24298: 215-6. For an analysis of the Socialist movement in France during the 1930s, see: Georges Lefranc, *Le Mouvement socialiste sous la Troisième République* (Paris: 1963); Joseph Frank, "French Intellectuals Between Wars," *Dissent* 31, 1, (1984): 103-8; Herbert R. Lottman, *The Left Bank Writers, Artists and Politics from the Popular Front to the Cold War* (Chicago, IL: Chicago University Press, 1988); B. D. Graham, *Choice and Democratic Order: The French Socialist Party, 1937-1950* (Cambridge: Cambridge University Press, 1994); P. Buffotot, *Le socialisme français et la guerre. Du soldat citoyen à l'armée professionnelle, 1871-1998* (Paris: Bruylant, 1998). On the French Communist Party and the question of national defence, see: Stéphane Courtois, *Le PCF dans la guerre* (Paris: 1980); Michel Dreyfus, "Le Parti communiste français et la lutte pour la paix du Front populaire à la Seconde Guerre Mondiale," *Communisme*, 18-9, (1988): 98-106; Georges Vidal, "Le PCF et la défense nationale à l'époque du Front Populaire (1934-1939)," *Guerres Mondiales at conflits contemporains*, 215,

From the right, General Raymond Duval noted in *Journal* that France had to be grateful to the British people for having ensured their co-operation at the end of the war, the lack of which would have had such disastrous consequences in 1919: this time victory would have a "greater meaning and a more lasting effect."[162]

At the centre, *Ordre* also noted that the discussions on the conditions of peace were certainly important, but for the time being it was more important to "take the lead in the conduct of war." G. Debu, intervening on 11 April in the open debate on the practical consequences of the declaration, supported the idea of a common parliamentary body that would meet every three months, alternately in the Palais Bourbon and Westminster, or halfway at the Castel of Dieppe, "which is on the cliffs and watches the sea that unites us." Emile Borel, a former Navy Minister and President of the French section of the League of Nations Union, suggested in *Dépêche* the creation of an Anglo-French Committee, composed of representatives of all political forces, to discuss the features of the post-war order, which was to be federal in its substance. Bernard Lavergne proposed, on 23 April from the columns of *Epoque* the creation of a customs union at regional level: among the Franco-British block, and the Danubian and Czech-Polish ones.[163]

The enthusiasm of the French, was echoed in the satisfaction of Federal Union's leaders, who judging positively the spirit that permeated these statements, commenting that France and Britain had created a Supreme War Cabinet which had quasi-federalist features. Its arrangements differed from Federal Union's scheme only because they lacked a common Parliament. In time of war it was perhaps necessary to accept without protest "these anti-democratic methods." However, in peacetime the fact that the Cabinet's decisions had to be ratified by two separate parliaments would bring its downfall. It was essential to establish

---

(2004): 47-73. For a panorama of the French internal situation towards the end of the 1930s, see: Serge Berstein, *La France des années 30* (Paris: 1993); William D. Irvine, "Domestic Politics and the Fall of France in 1940" in Blatt, *The French Defeat*, 85-98.

[162] FOP, FO371/24298, 214-6.

[163] FOP, FO371/24298, 254-6, 261-3. On Duval, Borel, the condition of the French armed forces, and the decline of the Third Republic, see Philippe Bernard and Henri Dubief, *The Decline of the Third Republic, 1914-1938* (Cambridge: Cambridge University Press, 1988), 95-8.

a common Parliament, "elected for that purpose and only responsible for these common affairs."[164]

The fact that Federal Union, founded just eighteen months earlier, had gained such a vast consensus, "not only among ordinary citizens, but among serious and influential people in all fields of British life," had shown "that behind the words of statesmen" there was "the reality of public opinion, which nobody can permit to misunderstand."[165]

In fact, political leaders could push themselves forward, at least on the level of intentions, because such a radical perspective would have met general public acceptance, at a time of grave national crisis, especially for the British people who were aware of having to give up the Empire, in one way or another, which until then had been the pivot of their foreign policy. Without the patient preparatory work of Federal Union in the country, and Lothian's Socratic skills across the Atlantic—where he could dare to do more than in London because he knew he was irreplaceable at that historical moment—the British Government would consider, with the French, the creation of a federal solution for the post-war order. In translating the statements of intent in the creation of the first rudiments of a common government, there was however very little that the young leaders of Federal Union could do. A very special role would be played, in this regard, by Chatham House, and by its main operator behind the scenes, Lionel Curtis.

---

[164] *Federal Union News*, 31, (1940). On the dominant role of the Executive on other organs of the State during WWII, see Christopher Hill, *Cabinet Decisions on Foreign Policy: The British Experience, October 1938-June 1941* (Cambridge: Cambridge University Press, 2002).

[165] *Federal Union News*, 30, (1940). On British public opinion towards the war and the Anglo-French Union, see Peter M. H. Bell, "L'évolution de l'opinion publique anglaise à propos de la guerre et de l'alliance avec la France" in *Français et Britanniques*, 45-61.

CHAPTER V

CHATHAM HOUSE
AND THE FEDERALIST PROJECT

I. *Curtis, Lothian and the creation of Chatham House*

It appears difficult to define with certainty the role played by Chatham House within British society as a whole, and in particular in the process of formation of its foreign policy. If one accepts the view expressed by Donald C. Watt—who was for a long time involved in Chatham House after World War II as director of the *Survey of International Affairs*—that the British are essentially an "oligocratic society...one in which power is exercised by a minority of its citizens grouped together in a cluster of smaller groups," it is plausible to identify in Chatham House one of these groups, and a very influential one indeed. According to Watt, these groups must be

> consistent enough in their membership over time...to be treated not only as a political, but also social phenomenon, and for the characteristics of their social organisation to be an essential element in the manner in which they perform their political function.

The number of members of Chatham House was tied, over the years, to the succession of political actors, but for the inter-war period, it appears to be framed in that social political reality known as "liberal imperialism."[1]

---

[1] Donald Cameron Watt, *Personalities and Policies. Studies in the Formulation of British Foreign Policy in the Twentieth Century* (Harlow: Longmans, 1965), 1. On Chatham House see: Wilfrid Knapp, "Fifty Years of Chatham House Books," in *International Affairs*, 46, 5, (1970): 138-52; Inderjeet Parmar, "Chatham House and the Anglo-American Alliance," *Diplomacy & Statecraft*, 3, 1, (1992): 23-47; id., *Think Tanks and Power in Foreign Policy: A Comparative Study of the Role and Influence of the Council on Foreign Relations and the Royal Institute of International Affairs, 1939-1945* (New York: Palgrave Macmillan, 2004); Elie Kedourie, *The Chatham House Version and Other Middle Eastern Studies* (London: Ivan Dee, 2004); Paul Williams, "A Commonwealth of Knowledge:

Chatham House's "political function" was discussed and decided by its
members from time to time, in relation to the foreign policy choices which
came up, but for the period between the wars it appears essentially aimed
at creating a consensus in the country for an Atlantic policy. According to
Curtis—the major architect of the Institute of International Affairs, and for
many years the great wire-puller, the persistent operator behind the
scenes—"the foundation of Chatham House was a necessary tactical
change to effect the same strategic object." When in 1919 Curtis realised
"the unforeseen limits of the Round Table organisation which represented
our tactics," he put forward a scheme to achieve the revised objectives of
the Round Table: the strengthening of Imperial and Anglo-American
relations, through the creation of an "institutionalized" foreign policy élite,
in spite of the fact that Anglo-American relations in 1919-20 were
characterized by "strain and tension."[2]

With the foundation of the Institute of International Affairs, the Round
Tablers tried to accomplish that "strategic object...with a necessary tactical
change." That change was necessary not only because the Dominions
groups of the Round Table organisation had reduced their activity to the
preparation of quarterly articles for the magazine, or because the members
of the London group had, during and after the war, become involved in or
taken up professions which could not give them enough free time to run
the organisation.

Empire, Intellectuals and the Chatham House Project, 1919-1939," *International
Relations*, 17, 1, (2003): 35-58.
[2] Brian J. C. Kercher, "'The Deep and Latent Distrust': The British Official Mind
and the United States, 1919-1929," in *Anglo-American Relations in the 1920s: The
Struggle for Supremacy,* ed. Brian J. C. Kercher (London: 1991), 1. On the
precarious state of Anglo-American relations in the inter-war period, see: Brian J.
C. McKercher, "'Our Most Dangerous Enemy': Great Britain Pre-Eminent in the
1930s," *International History Review*, 13, 4, (1991): 751-83; id., "No Eternal
Friends or Enemies: British Defense Policy and the Problem of the United States,
1919-1939," *Canadian Journal of History*, 28, 2, (1993): 257-93; Robert Self,
*Britain, America and the War Debt Controversy: The Economic Diplomacy of an
Unspecial Relationship, 1917-1941* (London: Routledge, 2006); id., "Perception
and Posture in Anglo-American Relations: The War Debt Controversy in the
'Official Mind', 1919-1940," *International History Review*, 29, (2007): 282-312;
Keith Neilson, "Perception and Posture in Anglo-American Relations: The Legacy
of the Simon-Stimson Affair, 1932-41," *ibidem,* 313-37. For a study of the
pioneering role played by the British establishment in promoting the association of
the United States in the management of the post-war order, see Nicholas J. Cull,
"Selling Peace: The Origins, Promotion and Fate of the Anglo-American New
Order During the Second World War," *Diplomacy & Statecraft*, 7, 1, (1996): 1-28.

The Empire, even a reformed Empire, was no longer able to guarantee, by itself, international stability. The centre of gravity of world power had already shifted from the Channel to the Atlantic—reflecting on the political scale, a process which on the economic and financial scales had already manifested since the beginning of the century—but the United States did not present the subjective conditions for their association with the direction of world politics. Kerr and Curtis felt that they had to prepare for the transition from an Anglo-French to an Anglo-American dyarchy in the management of world power. The Anglo-French dyarchy, which constituted the centre of gravity of international relations since the Italian and German unifications, appeared no longer able to guarantee a peaceful revision of the *status-quo* established by the Treaties, and thus prevent a regional conflict to spread worldwide.

Apart from the changed international situation, which rendered obsolete the original *raison d'être* of the organisation, another cause for its crisis has to be found in the changed role of Curtis within it. In 1918 it became apparent that the majority of its members would not endorse Curtis's plea for a federal structure of the Empire, as set forth in *The Commonwealth of Nations*. As a consequence, Curtis suspended his salary as General Secretary of the organisation. He returned to draw a salary from the Round Table funds after he married in 1920, but a few months later he was appointed acting Under-Secretary for Irish Affairs at the Colonial Office, once more serving the movement from a detached position. He worked as a civil servant till 1924, and it was in this period that he expended the most energy in the establishment of the Institute.[3]

The difficulties faced by the London group were not just temporary. The war had given the Dominions a fundamental and strategic role in the achievement of victory, and the Peace Conference had disrupted the diplomatic unity of the Empire, by giving each Dominion an independent representation at the negotiations table. During the war the Dominions were divided by conscription controversies, and on the battlefield they developed a sense of national identity. At the end of the war, the main argument for Imperial cohesion—the German threat—had disappeared,

---

[3] Kendle, *The Round Table*, 274. Kendle offers a clear picture of the situation of the movement in 1921: "The New Zealanders prepared a statement for the press each year on current problems, but this was never a very stimulating document. In Canada and South Africa the organisations lapsed completely into editorial committees for the preparation of articles, and in May 1921 at a meeting in Toronto it was decided not to revive the local groups," *ibidem,* 272.

and a sense of international détente—centred on the League of Nations—
strengthened centrifugal forces.[4]

Anglo-Dominion relationships had changed forever with the
recognition of the principle of equal partnership between the Dominions
and Great Britain, the development of independent military and diplomatic
apparatuses, and the questions of Irish and Indian independence. Even
Curtis recognised that federalism was no longer on the agenda, in spite of
the fact that Coupland recorded that "most if not all" of the members of
the Round Table "are convinced that the case for organic union has been
strengthened by the war and its sequel." The Round Table reversed to a
policy of "marking time."[5]

Kerr was the first Round Tabler to realise that the war had both
revealed and accelerated the historic decline of the Empire everywhere, as
well as the emergence of a new and more dynamic insular power, one
which would inevitably oust the old. The peace of Versailles undoubtedly
signalled the transition from a European to a world system of States, with
Germany at the centre of the international power struggle.[6]

---

[4] On the role played by the Dominions at the Paris Peace Conference, and the
process of decolonization, see: Erik Goldstein, *Winning the Peace: British
Diplomatic Strategy, Peace Planning, and the Paris Peace Conference, 1916-1920*
(New York: Oxford University Press, 1991); Manfred F. Boemeke, Gerald D.
Feldman and Elisabeth Glaser, *The Treaty of Versailles: A Reassessment after 75
Years* (Cambridge: Cambridge University Press, 1998); David George Boyce,
Decolonisation and the British Empire, 1775-1997 (New York: Palgrave
Macmillan, 1999); Michael Dockrill and John Fisher ed., *The Paris Peace
Conference, 1919: Peace Without Victory?* (New York: Palgrave Macmillan,
2001); Margaret Macmillan, *Paris 1919: Six Months That Changed the World*
(New York: Random House, 2003); Patrick O. Cohrs, *The Unfinished Peace after
World War I: America, Britain and the Stabilisation of Europe, 1919-1932*,
(Cambridge: Cambridge University Press, 2006); Ronald Hyam, *Britain's
Declining Empire: The Road to Decolonisation, 1918-1968* (Cambridge:
Cambridge University Press, 2007).
[5] Curtis to Murray Wrong, 3 Nov. 1920, RTP, c811, 10-11; Coupland to Australian
Groups, 22 March 1919, RTP, c802, 183-84; Coupland to Dove, 28 Feb. [1923],
RTP, c804, 197; Minutes of Round Table meeting, 4 May 1917, LP, 474, 4-8.
[6] Ludwig Dehio is the historian who has most clearly defined the characteristics of
the insular powers and their role in the history of the international relations system,
Ludwig Dehio, *The Precarious Balance. The Politics of Power in Europe, 1495-
1945* (London: Chatto & Windus, 1965). For a critical analysis, see: Graham Ross,
The Great Powers and the Decline of the European States System, 1914-1945
(Harlow: Longman, 1983); Williamson Murray, *The Change in the European
Balance of Power, 1938-1939: The Path to Ruin* (New Haven: Princeton
University Press, 1984).

During the Peace Conference, Kerr, as Private Secretary to Lloyd George, contributed to drawing up a framework for peace which reflected the factors which had most contributed to victory. "The underlying idea at Paris in 1919," Kerr was to say in his Burge Memorial Lecture sixteen years later, "was that the United States, France, and the British Empire should collectively discharge through the League of Nations, which gave representation to all peoples, the ultimate stabilising function which Great Britain alone had performed in the preceding century and in an even more liberal way," since "what preserved the peace of the world during the nineteenth century and ended the long series of world wars of the seventeenth and eighteenth centuries was the complete naval supremacy of Britain after Trafalgar." In an era of air navigation and technological and scientific discoveries which had tended to increasingly reduce the size of the world, Great Britain would be able to continue with her historic role of maintaining the balance of world power only in close collaboration with the United States.[7]

"Much the most important work that lies in front of the Round Table group or anybody else dealing with world politics," Kerr observed writing to Curtis in March 1927, "is to find the positive basis for co-operation between the English-speaking nations." Again, on 2nd September 1927, Kerr wrote to Curtis:

the English-speaking nations have either got to bring themselves under one sovereignty or they will drift into antagonism. The problem is fundamentally exactly that which confronted you in South Africa after the Boer War and which confronted the thirteen colonies after the Revolutionary War…America…is now by far the richest and most powerful nation in the world. It is being sorely tempted to succumb to the lure of imperialism in a bad sense of the word, to buy up the rest of the world, to mobilise the irresistible force in its own hands, and yet to refuse co-operation with other nations or to submit itself to the reign of law. Personally I am convinced that the forces for righteousness are so strong in

---

[7] Lothian, *Pacifism is not enough,* 255-6. On the role played by Lothian at the Paris Peace Conference, see: Michael Dockrill and Douglas Goold, *Peace Without Promise: The Peace Conferences 1919-23* (London: Batsford, 1981); id., "Philip Kerr at 10 Downing Street, 1916-1921", in *The Larger Idea.* On Lloyd George during WWI and at Versailles see: Inbal Rose, *Conservatism and Foreign Policy During the Lloyd George Coalition 1918-1922* (London: Routledge, 1999); Antony Lentin, *Lloyd George and the Lost Peace: From Versailles to Hitler, 1919-1940* (New York: Palgrave Macmillan, 2001); John Grigg, *Lloyd George: War Leader, 1916-1918* (London: Penguin Books, 2003); David Woodward, *Lloyd George and the Generals* (London: Routledge, 2004); Hugh Purcell, *Lloyd George* (London: Haus Publishers, 2006).

the United States that when they awake to the question they will bring the
United States into line for the world commonwealth.[8]

It was in Paris during the most critical period of the peace negotiations
that the members of the Round Table who were present decided to reverse
the order of their priorities. A letter from Curtis to Kerr of 1936, offers us
an extremely valuable insight into this fundamental turning point in the
history of the Round Table organisation:

> When Union [in South Africa] was achieved, more rapidly than even we
> had hoped, we felt that it was up to us to apply the same process to
> Imperial relations, especially in view of the German menace. The Round
> Table Groups and the magazine were the result...In the course of the war,
> the Dominions as well as the British Government seized on men trained in
> the Round Table Groups to help them with Imperial relations and Foreign
> Affairs, with the result that a large number of us found ourselves together
> at the Conference at Paris in 1919. Our years of Round Table experience
> had taught us the supreme importance of genuine research; but it had also
> taught us that genuine research is hampered insofar as it was connected
> with any element of propaganda. The Round Table, founded by people
> who believed intensely in the British Empire, necessarily suffered from
> this limitation. We, therefore, set out to establish a separate organ of
> research in which people of all differences of opinion, however great,
> could unite; an organ debarred from all propaganda. All this was settled in
> Paris in 1919. When in 1920 the work of creating and organising the
> projected institute was taken in hand it was Abe [Bailey] who stepped
> forward with a cheque which enabled a room to be hired, and stationery
> and stamps to be paid for, so that invitations could be sent out to some

---

[8] LP, 227. On the strengthening of Anglo-American relations and the creation of
the Atlantic Alliance, see: Inderjeet Parmar, *Special Interests, the State and the
Anglo-American Alliance, 1939-1945* (London: Routledge, 1995); Thomas J.
Knock, *To End All Wars: Woodrow Wilson and the Quest for a New World Order*
(New Haven: Princeton University Press, 1995); Michael Lind, "Pax Atlantica:
The Case for Euramerica," *World Policy Journal*, 13, 1, (1996): 1-7; Timothy E.
Smith, *Opposition Beyond the Water's Edge: Liberal Internationalists, Pacifists
and Containment, 1945-1953* (Westport, CT: Greenwood Press, 1999); Barry
Buzan and Richard Little, *International Systems in World History: Remaking the
Study of International Relations* (New York: Oxford University Press, 2000);
Valeria Gennaro Lerda ed., *Which 'Global Village'?: Societies, Cultures, and
Political-Economic Systems in a Euro-Atlantic Perspective* (Westport, CT:
Praeger, 2002); Carl C. Hodge, *NATO for a New Century: Atlanticism and
European Security* (Westport, CT: Praeger, 2002); Simon Serfaty, *Visions of the
Atlantic Alliance: The United States, the European Union, and NATO*
(Washington, DC: Center for Strategic & International Studies, 2005).

hundreds of people representing all parties to join the new institute. It was later on that Abe gave the institute permanence by giving it a perpetual endowment of £5000 a year. Apropos of the above, the time is gone when we need to be afraid of admitting...that Chatham House was the outcome of Round Table work. I have always lived in hope that a day would come when my Round Table colleagues would acknowledge their child and drop the habit of imputing its sole parentage to me.[9]

The achievement of the original "strategic objective" could not be implemented simply by creating a London-based centre of studies and debates on international relations. It was necessary to establish an adequate network that would extend overseas. If the ultimate goal was the creation of an Anglo-American Alliance so strong as to prevent the outbreak of a world war, and capable of creating the political conditions for a more stable world order, it appeared necessary to prepare American and Commonwealth public opinion to accept those aims. One of the first tasks of Curtis was therefore to reproduce the same Round Table network of local groups, establishing independent institutions in the capitals of the Commonwealth, and adding New York to the system, with the creation in 1925 of the Council on Foreign Relations.[10]

A special relationship with the so-called "quality press"—particularly *The Times* and the *Observer*, owned and controlled by the Astors—gave Chatham House the possibility to convey its voice worldwide, through speakers carefully selected, without appearing too closely associated with their views.[11]

---

[9] Curtis to Lothian, 6 Dec. 1936, (quoted in Bosco, *Two Musketeers for the Empire*, 150-1).

[10] *Ibidem*. On the role played by Curtis in the creation of Chatham House see the chapters by Deborah Lavin and Michael Dockrill in Bosco and Navari, *Chatham House.*

[11] On the Astors, see: Virginia Cowles, *The Astors: The Story of a Transatlantic Family* (London: Weidenfeld & Nicolson, 1979); John Grigg, *Nancy Astor: A Lady Unshamed* (London: Little, Brown & Co., 1983); Derek Wilson, *The Astors: 1763-1992: Landscape with Millionaires* (London: St Martins Press, 1993); Nancy Astor, *Nancy Astor's Canadian Correspondence, 1912-1962*, ed. Martin Thornton (Lewiston: Edwin Mellen Press, 1997); Karen J. Musolf, *From Plymouth To Parliament: A Rhetorical History of Nancy Astor's 1919 Campaign* (New York: Palgrave Macmillan, 1998); J. P. Wearing ed., *Bernard Shaw and Nancy Astor* (Toronto: University of Toronto Press, 2005). On *The Times* and *The Observer*, see: Henry Wickham Steed, *The Press* (London: Penguin Books, 1938); A. M. Gollin, *The Observer and J. L. Garvin, 1908-1914: A Study in a Great Editorship* (Oxford: Oxford University Press, 1960); David Ayerst, *Garvin of the Observer: A Life* (London: Croom Helm, 1984); Richard Cockett, *David Astor and the*

The study groups were an important additional feature of the method followed by Chatham House, which gave the opportunity to gather some of the most distinguished British, Commonwealth and American scholars for the study of contemporary history's issues from a specific point of view, however without this it appeared a corporate official view. Chatham House's studies, collected in volumes, imposed themselves on the general attention of the public as an indispensable source of information, and also an inspiration to political action. Chatham House's most impressive and influential publication was the *Survey of International Affairs*, which gave its first Editor, Arnold Toynbee, probably the highest degree of influence that a single historian has ever exercised on the process of formation of foreign policy in his own country. These publications, along with the quarterly magazine *International Affairs*, and a number of monographs, played a pioneering role in the worldwide recognition of contemporary history as an independent scientific discipline, with its own methods of investigation.[12]

Despite the fact that the two main founders of Chatham House were also the leading exponents of British federalism in the period between the wars, the federal project could not be openly supported by Chatham House as a concrete policy before the end of the 1930s. For Anglo-American relations the occasion was presented by the publication of *Union Now*, while for the relations between Great Britain and the rest of Europe, it was the decision by Richard Coudenhove-Kalergi to review his strategy to realise the European federation, which offered Chatham House the

Observer (London: Andre Deutsch, 1992); Simon J. Potter, *News and the British World: The Emergence of an Imperial Press System 1876-1922* (New York: Oxford University Press, 2003); Angela V. John, *War, Journalism and the Shaping of the Twentieth Century: The Life and Times of Henry W. Nevinson* (New York: I.B. Tauris, 2006); Linda Fritzinger, *Diplomat without Portfolio: Valentine Chirol, His Life and 'The Times'* (New York: I.B. Tauris, 2006).
[12] Bosco and Navari, *Chatham House*, 1-12; Roger Morgan, "'To Advance the Study of Political Sciences...': Chatham House's Early Research," in *ibidem*, 121-36. On Toynbee see: Roland N. Stromberg, *Arnold J. Toynbee: Historian for an Age in Crisis* (Carbondale, IL: Southern Illinois University Press, 1972); Richard Clogg, *Politics and the Academy: Arnold Toynbee and the Koraes Chair* (London: Routledge, 1986); Alon Kadish, *Apostle Arnold: The Life and Death of Arnold Toynbee, 1852-1883* (Durham, NC: Duke University Press, 1986); Kenneth Winetrout, *After One Is Dead: Arnold Toynbee as Prophet* (London: Hillside Press, 1989); William H. McNeill, *Arnold J. Toynbee: A Life* (New York: Oxford University Press, 1990); Elie Kedourie, "Arnold Toynbee," *New Criterion*, 7, 7, (1990): 18-29; Christopher Brewin, "Research in a Global Context: A Discussion of Toynbee's Legacy," *Review of International Studies*, 18, 2, (1992).

opportunity to directly influence the Foreign Office in shaping the future of Anglo-French relations.

II. *Count Richard Coudenhove-Kalergi*

Chatham House openly showed the first signs of interest in federalist questions in June 1938, when Leo Amery—Minister for the Colonies, one of the founding-fathers of the Institute, and a member of Milner's Kindergarten since the South African days—organised a Conference for Coudenhove-Kalergi on the historical and political reasons for a European federation, and the need to organise a federalist movement in Britain. From that moment on, Coudenhove-Kalergi came to assume a prominent role in the federalist debate in Great Britain, and also in the federalist conversion of many Conservative leaders. Also within Chatham House was thus ushered a "European trend".[13]

In supporting Coudenhove-Kalergi, Amery—who in a few months would play a prominent role within the Government in paving the way to the acceptance of Churchill's proposal of Anglo-French Union—actually intended to show to his countrymen the road that seemed more in line with the tradition of British foreign policy over the past two centuries: helping the Europeans to defeat a new hegemonic attempt, and to stake everything on the Empire for post-war reorganisation.

Coudenhove-Kalergi's idea to also organise Pan-Europa in Great Britain—thus deeply changing his political strategy contrary to British participation in a European federation—originated in January 1938. Writing on 1st February to Amery, Coudenhove-Kalergi observed that "the evolution of the last years" changed "entirely" the question of British

---

[13] On the involvement of Amery in Chatham House see his diaries: John Barnes and David Nicholson eds., *The Empire at Bay. The Leo Amery Diaries, 1929-1945* (London: Hutchinson, 1988). On Amery, see: Max Beloff, "Leo Amery: The Last Imperialist," *History Today*, 39, 1, (1989): 13-26; W. R. Louis, "'In the Name of God, Go!': Leo Amery and the British Empire in the Age of Churchill," *Neue Politische Literatur*, 37, 3, (1992): 412-29. On Coudenhove-Kalergi, see: Morinosuke Launay and Jacques de Kajima, *Coudenhove-Kalergi: Le pionnier de l'Europe unie* (Lausanne: Fondation Jean Monnet, 1971); Vanessa Conze, *Richard Coudenhove-Kalergi* (Zurig: Muster-Schmidt Verlag, 1998); Alain Larcan, *Richard Coudenhove-Kalergi et Charles de Gaulle* (Paris: Fondation Charles de Gaulle, 1999).

participation, and he thought it "necessary to found a Pan-European Union in London."[14]

Asking Amery to organise a conference at Chatham House, he observed:

> I am afraid that if things are going on as they do actually, war in Europe is inevitable and that Great Britain will be involved in it. The only way to get out of it is a Pan-European initiative coming from Great Britain that could play in the pacification of Europe an analogous role as the United States in Pan-America. You see that I have entirely changed my former conception, but I think that a new situation demands a new programme.[15]

Inviting Churchill on the 2nd February to become Chairman of the British branch of Pan-Europa, he underlined: "Actually it seems impossible to organise any kind of European union without the participation and even the leadership of Great Britain."[16]

Moving from the assumption that the world's tendency, as a result of scientific and technological innovations, was towards the creation of larger political units, Coudenhove-Kalergi outlined at Chatham House on 2nd June—while the Sudetenland crisis was taking up British diplomacy—the profound change in his strategy. "A purely Continental European federation," he argued, "would have been possible before the foundation of Greater Germany, as long as Germany was not the strongest Power in Europe." Since the Germans would soon become the "masters and rulers of Europe," "British participation in pan-Europe" became "necessary for the sake of a European balance of Powers and for the sake of the liberty of

---

[14] See the letter of 31 Jan. 1938 to Sir Andrew McFadyean, CKP, Correspondence, 554/7-96. Coudenhove-Kalergi wrote also to Cadogan, Eden, Vansittart, and Harold Nicolson, *ibidem*. Of the works by Coudenhove-Kalergi, see: *Crusade for Pan-Europa* (New York: A. A. Knopf, 1943); id., *Europe Seeks Unity* (New York: A. A. Knopf, 1948); id., *An Idea Conquers the World* (London: Hutchinson, 1953). For a critical analysis, see: Jerzy Lukaszewski, *Coudenhove-Kalergi* (Lausanne: 1977); Arthur Schlesinger, *Federalism in Central and Eastern Europe* (New York: K. Paul, 1945); Frank Vereechten, *La lutte pour les Etats-Unis d'Europe. Richard Coudenhove-Kalergi en exil, 1938-1947* (London: Lothian Foundation Press, 1996); Wilfred Loth, *Der Weg nach Europa: Geschichte der europäischen Integration 1939-1957* (Göttingen: Vandenhoech & Ruprecht, 1990), 10-25; Lipgens, *Documents on European*, 203-7. Gilbert Martin, *Winston S. Churchill: The Prophet of Truth 1922-1939* (London: Houghton Mifflin, 1977).

[15] CKP, Correspondence, 554/7-96.

[16] *Ibidem*.

all European nations." Great Britain should therefore assume "the leadership of the Continent."[17]

"By the solidarity of the English-speaking world through the cooperation of Great Britain and United States," Coudenhove-Kalergi pointed out, "pan-America and pan-Europe could form together stronger co-operation, and Atlantic co-operation whose aim would be to save the peace...which would save an Atlantic civilization for at least a century." With the elimination of the French, Italian, and Russian influences in Central Europe, the initiative successfully passed into the hands of Germany, which would also incorporate Czechoslovakia and extend her control over the rest of the Danubian and Balkan regions.

This process would stop only if Great Britain took the initiative:

> Great Britain can, if she wants, find a huge Dominion in Eastern Europe, a Dominion of a hundred and twenty million people, very gifted people, who will one day be the most important element of Europe. They are ready to follow Great Britain.[18]

Coudenhove-Kalergi thought that "any of the States between Estonia and Greece would choose any other leadership, if they could choose between British leadership and the leadership of any other nation." That was a "central problem for Great Britain and for Eastern Europe," and in that respect the relations between Great Britain and Poland were "especially important":

> Poland is the centre of this Eastern European world...On the force and influence of Poland depends the security and independence of all this region in Eastern Europe. Poland is linked with the Baltic nations and linked by its Alliance to Rumania with the Balkan nations. And there is the

---

[17] CKP, Correspondence, 554/7-96. On Anglo-French policy in Central Europe, see: R. A. C. Parker, *The Anglo-French Conversations April and September 1938*, in *Les relations franco-allemandes, 1933-1939* (Paris: 1976); David E. Kaiser, *Economic Diplomacy and the Origins of the Second World War: Germany, Britain, France and Eastern Europe, 1930-1939* (New Haven: Yale University Press, 1980); Henryk Batowski, "Les relations diplomatiques franco-polonaises pendant la 'drôle de guerre'," *Guerres Mondiales et Conflits Contemporains*, 42, (1992): 33-45; Traian Sandu, "La présence française en Europe centrale dans entre-deux-guerres," *Revue d'Europe Centrale*, 3, 2, (1995): 147-60; Anita J. Prazmowska, *Britain and Poland 1939-1943: The Betrayed Ally*, (Cambridge: Cambridge University Press, 1995); P. M. H. Bell, *France and Britain, 1900-40: Entente and Estrangement* (Harlow: Longman, 1996); Robert Young, *France and the Origins of the Second World War* (London: Macmillan, 1996).
[18] CKP, Correspondence, 554/7-96.

centre of the whole Eastern European world, and if it is possible to attach Poland to the entente between Great Britain and France...then peace in this region of the world can be maintained. And if it is possible to bring together the Balkan union with the Baltic States and with Poland then the great idea of Masaryk, Venizelos and Take Jonescu can be realised, then the United States of Eastern Europe can become the beginning of the United States of Europe.[19]

In the perspective of a Danubian or Balkan federation controlled by Great Britain, the Czechoslovakia question lost its importance and also its danger. The Sudeten could not be incorporated into Germany without overturning the existing strategic situation:

Only the fact that Europe is disunited, that there is always the danger of war, economic and political war between the European States, makes this situation impossible because if the German part of Czechoslovakia were to join Germany the rest would be a torso that could not live, neither strategically nor economically, it would be a State that could not live and would forcibly become a province of Germany.

The beginning of the United States of Europe, Coudenhove-Kalergi concluded—could be realised "not in Western Europe but in Eastern Europe."[20]

---

[19] *Ibidem.*

[20] *Ibidem.* On the French decline in Eastern Europe, see: Stephen A. Schuker, *The End of French Predominance in Europe* (Chapel Hill, NC: North Carolina University Press, 1976); Anthony Adamthwaite, *France and the Coming of the Second World War, 1936-1939* (London: Frank Cass, 1977); Alan Alexandroff and Richard Rosecrance, "Deterrence in 1939," *World Politics*, 29, 3, (1977): 404-24; Piotr S. Wandycz, *The Twilight of French Eastern Alliances, 1926-1936* (Princeton: Princeton University Press, 1988); Stephen A. Schuker, *The End of French Predominance in Europe* (Chapel Hill, NC: North Carolina University Press, 1989); Henryk Batowski, "Les relations diplomatiques franco-polonaises pendant la 'drôle de guerre'," *Guerres Mondiales et Conflits Contemporains*, 42, (1992): 33-41; Anthony Adamthwaite, *Grandeur and Misery: France's Bid for Power in Europe, 1914-1940* (London: E. Arnold, 1995); Christophe Laforest, "La stratégie française et la Pologne (1919-1939): Aspects économiques et implications politiques," *Histoire, Economie et Société*, 22, 3, (2003): 395-411. On Franco-Soviet relations, see: François Leveque, "Des diplomaties dans l'impasse: Les relations franco-soviétiques de Septembre 1939 à juin 1941," *Guerres Mondiales et Conflits Contemporains*, 43, (1993): 111-23; id., "Les relations franco-soviétiques pendant la seconde guerre mondiale: De la défaite à l'alliance (1939-1945)," *Revue des Etudes Slaves*, 69, 3, (1997): 439-46.

To the debate which followed, Geoffrey Gathorne-Hardy, a member of Chatham House, intervened taking the view that the direct interference of Great Britain into the affairs of Eastern Europe was not only contrary to the tradition of British foreign policy, but seemed impracticable. Gathorne-Hardy pictured Great Britain as the amphibian of the European zoo, plunging into her pond and at the same time being deeply interested in the general well-being of the zoo, keen to prevent the other animals from gaining too much freedom, or being unjustly treated, or having too little food, and throwing the greedy looking to the other side of the pond. No British statesman would have taken the initiative to intervene in Eastern Europe along the lines suggested by Coudenhove-Kalergi.[21]

On the other hand, Rennie Smith, former Secretary of the National Peace Council, strongly supported the views of Coudenhove-Kalergi, reminding the audience not only of the long Europeanist engagement of the speaker, but also his quite recent Anglophile conversion:

> Evidently, up till about 1933, he had conceived the possibility of a federal Europe under the conditions obtained with what might be called a Weimar Germany and a Briand France, and throughout the whole of this period he never hesitated in putting France in the role of leader of this federation. He had not been thinking of a quantitative Europe but of a qualitative Europe with free men in it, and therefore, he had appealed to the great tradition of France which since the 18th century had found a worthy embodiment in the late M. Briand.

The fact that "in this new revolutionary situation" Great Britain could assume "a role of leadership," was not "idealism but practical politics."[22]

In his brief reply, Coudenhove-Kalergi admitted his recent conversion, due entirely to the courage with which Great Britain during the previous weeks had intervened in the defence of the freedom of Eastern European peoples, and also after recognising the minor role represented by France in the international arena. Therefore, it was up to British public opinion to decide if it was better to run the risk of another European war, or to assume definite responsibilities in Eastern Europe, and to bring about the

---

[21] CKP, Correspondence, 554/7-96. For an insight, see Geoffrey Gathorne-Hardy, *A Short History of International Affairs, 1920 to 1934* (Oxford: Oxford University Press, 1934).

[22] CKP, Correspondence, 554/7-96. Rennie Smith (1888-1962) was Labour MP for Penistone from 1924 to 1931; Secretary of the Friends of Europe from 1933 to 1940; and Director of the Central European Observer from 1940 to 1946. By Rennie Smith, see *General Disarmament or War?* (London: George Allen & Unwin, 1927).

federation. In the course of history, federations came about because of the existence of a common danger, and in confronting the Nazi menace Great Britain should assume "moral leadership," not for her own national interest, but for that of Europe.[23]

Speaking a second time at Chatham House on 15 June 1939—after the British Government had brought the defence line from the Rhine to the Vistula—Coudenhove-Kalergi observed that "the most important thing that has happened in Europe during the past year is the fact that Great Britain has become a European State." This new fact was going to change the fate of Europe, since Great Britain had been strongly opposed to any design aiming to unify the Continent. The efforts by Briand had in fact been "frustrated by the attitude of Great Britain," opposed to a united Europe without British participation, but also "to link her fate to the fate of the Continent."[24]

Great Britain however could no longer, as in the Napoleonic age, intervene in European affairs during a crisis, and withdraw into an isolated position at the end of the crisis. The scientific and technological discoveries forced Great Britain to revise her foreign policy:

> The invention of the aeroplane is of the same significance to Great Britain as was the invention of the cannon to Venice. Just as the possibility of Venice being an island ceased with the invention of the cannon, so by the invention of the aeroplane England ceased to be an island from the strategic point of view; and if Venice had understood her destiny after the invention of the cannon, she would have taken the initiative in creating a union of the Italian States and would now be at the head of Italy.[25]

The two strongest nations of the Continent, Germany and the Soviet Union, were trying to annex the countries of Eastern-Central Europe in order to create a Continental union of an Imperial nature. The Second World War, the umpteenth war for hegemony, had already begun. It began

---

[23] CKP, Correspondence, 554/7-96. Amery thought that Great Britain could not "form an effective part of a pan-European system in the long run". The problem was that "you cannot get the public here interested in the idea. The kinds of people who should take an interest are mostly obsessed by Geneva". See the letter from Amery to Coudenhove-Kalergi on 5 Febr. 1938, *ibidem*. Coudenhove-Kalergi's speech had not been published by *International Affairs*, Chatham House's journal, (see the letter by Margaret Cleeve to Coudenhove-Kalergi of 16 Sept. 1938, *ibidem*).
[24] CKP, Correspondence, 554.
[25] *Ibidem*. For an analysis of the contribution offered by Coudenhove-Kalergi to the development of the idea of European unification, see Elizabeth du Réau, *L'idée d'Europe au XXe siècle. Des mythes aux réalités* (Paris: Complexe, 2001).

on the very same day that German troops violated the Austrian border, and went on "to destroy one of the oldest and most beautiful centres of European civilization." If Great Britain had decided "to take the leadership of the European union," the war would have become the clashing terrain of the federalist and Imperial projects: democracy against autocracy.[26]

France was ready to join, but was waiting for British leadership in order to participate in the "great task of uniting Europe":

> Since the days of Pierre Dubois in the fourteenth century, since Sully, since the Abbé St. Pierre, until our own day and Briand, the idea of European federation has always been the great objective of French policy, but it can only be achieved if Great Britain takes part in this effort and, jointly with France, undertakes to act as the trustees of the European idea.[27]

The moment was of enormous importance, because "the great historic events could only be accomplished in dangerous times," and if Europe lost such a favourable occasion, the question of European union would not reappear on the political agenda for a long time:

> All great things in history were difficult and are difficult...Only if we see the things that are coming can we change history, and only if we have the courage to fight for them can we do so. The Continent is ready to march; if you would make a plebiscite in Europe in any State, even in Germany and Italy, you would find a majority for European federation. France is ready to go ahead. Everything depends on Great Britain. If Great Britain has the European vision and the courage to fight for it, our generation will see the United States of Europe.[28]

Intervening in the debate, Amery, even though admitting the importance of the British role in the creation of a European federation, observed how, once unity had been achieved, and the hegemonic threat overcome, Great Britain would be inevitably attracted by her own worldwide interests. Her position would be of "absolutely friendly co-operation," but "not of complete participation." Vandeleur Robinson hoped, on the contrary, for a compromise between the European idea of Coudenhove-Kalergi and the Atlantic project by Streit, which seemed more practical.[29]

[26] CKP, Correspondence, 554.
[27] Ibidem.
[28] Ibidem.
[29] Ibidem.

Taking Austria as an example—which for two centuries controlled both the Danube area and the German States at the same time—, Coudenhove-Kalergi replied that the British people could drive the Commonwealth with the right hand and Europe—which "to a certain extent" could be "considered as the *Lebensraum* of England"—with the left. Great Britain would "lead Europe to prevent Germany from doing so." Regarding the Streitian project, Coudenhove-Kalergi affirmed that "all crimes against geography had always been punished by history and it would be a crime against geography to leave Central and Eastern Europe outside federation."

Any attempt aimed to involve the United States in a European federation would have had the consequence of strengthening American isolationism, and weakening the American determination to help the Europeans to defeat the Nazis. A federation of the democracies without Germany and Eastern-Central Europe would have created an "anti-democratic bloc consisting of Germany, Eastern Europe, Russia and the Far East." The United States could give a fundamental contribution to the building of a stable world order if they supported the British leadership in the creation of the European federation. It was up to the British and French governments to announce "a European programme," based on the creation of "common federal institutions open to all European States."[30]

On 22 June, a week after the second Chatham House Conference, Coudenhove-Kalergi established a transversal group for Pan-Europa at Westminster, with Alfred Duff Cooper as President, Victor Cazalet as Secretary, and Amery, Sir Edward Grigg—former Governor of Kenya— the Labour politician Leslie Haden Guest, the Foreign Under-secretary Geoffrey Mander, Harold Nicolson and Sir Arthur Salter as members. The group also had the support of Sir George Clark, former British Ambassador to Paris, Stephen King-Hall, Director of *News-Letter*, Sir Walter Layton, Rennie Smith—Secretary of the organisation Friends of Europe—and Sir Evelyn Wrench, President of the Overseas League.[31]

---

[30] *Ibidem.*

[31] On the members of the group, see: Robert Rhodes James, *Victor Cazalet: A Portrait* (London: Hamilton, 1976); John Charmley, *Duff Cooper: The Authorised Biography* (London: Orion Publishing, 1987); William V. Griffin, *Sir Evelyn Wrench and His Continuing Vision of International Relations During 40 Years* (Whitefish, MT: Kessinger, 2006); John Julius Norwich, *The Duff Cooper Diaries* (London: Orion Publishing, 2007). At the end of the war Coudenhove-Kalergi created the European Parliamentary Union, which played a crucial role in the early stages of the process of European unification. On this regard, see: Walter Lipgens, *Documents on the History of European Integration: The Struggle for European*

The aim of the group was to gain Parliamentarian support for a ten points programme:

1. European solidarity in foreign, military, economic, and currency policies; 2. An effective guarantee to all the federated States of their independence, integrity, security, and equality, and of the maintenance of their national character; 3. An obligation on all European States, regardless of differences in their constitutions, to respect the rights of human personality and the equality of their citizens belonging to ethnic or religious minorities; 4. The peaceful settlement of all disputes between European States by a court of justice having at its disposal the material and moral means necessary to make its decisions respected; 5. The establishment of a European institution designed to help member-States of the federation to meet their monetary and financial difficulties; 6. The progressive suppression of inter-European economic restrictions which are wrecking and ruining the European market; 7. A constructive plan for the necessary transition from war production to peace production designed to avoid the risk of unemployment; 8. The systematic organisation of collaboration in colonial matters with a view to fitting colonial raw materials and market into the economic complex of Europe; 9. The maintenance of and respect for the political, economic, and cultural links uniting various States of Europe with other parts of the world; 10. The promotion of international peace by collaboration with the British dominions, the American Continent, the Soviet Union, and the nations of Asia and Africa in a world-wide organisation.[32]

Union by Political Parties and Pressure Groups in Western European Countries, ed. Wilfried Loth (New York-Berlin: Walter de Gruyter, 1988), 54-9.

[32] Coudenhove-Kalergi discussed this programme of action after the Chatham House Conference at the house of Duff Cooper, in the presence of Anthony Eden and Sir Archibald Sinclair. Cooper—who had already resigned from the Government in disagreement with the signature of the Munich Pact—remembered the meeting with Coudenhove-Kalergi: "it was about this time that I again met Count Coudenhove-Kalergi, whom I had seen only once personally some fifteen years before. I had known then that he was working on plans for the federation of European nations which was known as the Pan-European Movement, and that he had gained the support of no less a person than Aristide Briand, who was then at the height of his power. I had vaguely classed this movement in my mind with the various idealistic and impractical schemes for ensuring international peace, all of which seemed to be now consigned to limbo as a result of the advent and the repeated success of...politicians. Almost my first words, therefore, at our second meeting were to suggest that I supposed he retained little hope now of carrying out his scheme for a united Europe. 'On the contrary', he replied quietly, 'Pan-Europe was never so certain as it is today. Europe will certainly be united in a near future. The only question now is whether the union is brought about by force or whether it

By hosting Coudenhove-Kalergi, Chatham House took into serious
consideration not only the Streitian project, supported in Great Britain by
the two leading figures of Milner's Kindergarten, and founders of
Chatham House itself—Lothian and Curtis—but also the project of a
European federation, supported by Amery, another member of the
Kindergarten and founder of Chatham House. European and Atlantic
federalists also had to co-exist within Chatham House, and it was the
diplomatic art of Waldorf Astor—its President, and another leading figure
of the Round Table—which kept Chatham House united in one of the most
difficult moments of its existence.

Despite having chosen Geneva as the base from which to conduct his
European battle, Coudenhove-Kalergi had decided to stake everything on
the United Kingdom, where, at the beginning of October 1939 following
his Chatham House conferences, he published with Mayflower Press the
volume *Europe must Unite*, which outlined his political project for the
public at large. "There is a great and glorious country which does not
know of its own existence," Coudenhove-Kalergi argued: "This country
lies between the Atlantic, the Soviet Union and the Mediterranean. Its
name is Europe." Europe was, like India and China, one of the three
"greatest cultural centres and cultural communities of our planet." It was
not a "natural," but an "artificial" Continent. Nature created the European
peninsula from the Asiatic Continent, and its culture, politics, and history
"converted this peninsula into a Continent." Even though Russia was not
an Asiatic country, it did not belong to Europe, but "groped" between Asia
and Europe, looking for "a new form of life."[33]

It would be impossible for Russia to join a European federation until
she either returned "to Western civilization or the whole of Europe had
become Bolshevik." Africa, "the garden of Europe," could become the
principal source of raw materials for the European peoples, and their most
important market. Since Europe needed the "African world for its

---

comes about by agreement and good-will under the moral leadership of England
and France. All the smaller nations would prefer the latter solution, which would
allow them to retain their freedom and independence, but since Munich they have
begun to doubt whether England and France have the power or the will to protect
them and therefore they are inclined to make the best bargain they can with
Germany before it is too late'. I was much impressed by the views he expressed,
by his grasp of the European situation, and by the practical character of his
program", Duff Cooper, *The Second World War* (London: 1949), 125; Richard
Coudenhove-Kalergi, *Crusade for Pan-Europe*, (New York: 1943), 202-3.
[33] Richard Coudenhove-Kalergi, *Europe Must Unite* (Plymouth: Mayflower Press,
1938), 17-8.

completion," the role of Egypt, South Africa, and therefore of Great Britain—a "bridge to both of them"—was fundamental to establishing a permanent link with the African Continent.[34]

Great Britain had a privileged role to play in the process of European unification. The process of "Europeanization" of her foreign policy speeded up following the reshaping of the Empire which, with the Westminster Statute, became a Commonwealth of sovereign States. Great Britain could then take part in European affairs with more freedom, and could perform, more than any other European country, the role of federator, like that played by Piedmont during the Italian *Risorgimento*. After the failure of Briand in 1930-31—"the first governmental initiative designed to create the United States of Europe"—France progressively lost her international prestige, and was forced to follow the British initiative:

> In the smaller European States in particular, the prestige of Great Britain is so great that they would find it easier to follow Great Britain's moral leadership than that of any Continental power, because among other things Great Britain has no territorial aims to pursue on the Continent and its leadership can never be transformed into domination or hegemony.[35]

Germany and Italy would also follow British leadership, once the totalitarian interlude had ended. Italy, in particular, which lacked raw materials, needed access to world markets, and since it was exposed to external attack, needed "a European system of security." "There can...be no question...that Italy," Coudenhove-Kalergi foretold, "will one day play a leading part in the unification and reconstruction of Europe":

> Piedmont, a little Italian State, stood against the great Empire of the Habsburg, against the Empire of the Pope, but it won the struggle because it was allied with the future...It was allied with all Italians who desired liberty and union, in Venice, in Milan, in Florence, in Naples, and so, by this alliance with the future, Piedmont became stronger than Austria, stronger than the Pope, and united and conquered Italy. If Great Britain and France follow this example they will have the whole of Europe behind them.[36]

The process towards federation was, according to Coudenhove-Kalergi inevitable because of technological innovations. The transport revolution

[34] *Ibidem*, 104-5, 97-101.
[35] *Ibidem,* 109-25. On the decline of the Third Republic, see Philippe Bernard and Henri Dubief, *The Decline of the Third Republic, 1914–1938* (Cambridge: Cambridge University Press, 1988).
[36] *International Affairs*, 18, 5, (1939): 628.

had drawn peoples closer, making political unity necessary. It was the development of the railway network which convinced Friedrick List and Cavour that it was necessary to unite their own countries to face the challenge of the times. "The aeroplane," Coudenhove-Kalergi observed, "in European unification plays the same part as the railways did in German and Italian unification." In spite of initial setbacks—the movements for Italian and German unification "suffered defeats before they triumphed"— the development towards larger political communities was written in the course of history:

> Only the Continental States of Europe have hitherto believed that they could withdraw themselves from its influence and remain in the national stage of development, while the hands of the clock show already the hour of history destined for Continents and large political unities.[37]

The European federation was, according to Coudenhove-Kalergi, the "third Europe," namely the result of a historic process which initiated from the breaking up of the unity of the Christian world, in the same succession line of the Roman Empire and Medieval Europe. Pan-Europa was "the first attempt to realise the unity of Europe in the spirit of the twentieth century," after the failure of those of the previous century: the Napoleonic Imperial design, the conservative plan of the Holy Alliance, and the "revolutionary" strategy of Mazzini's "Giovane Europa." The Napoleonic dream of unifying Europe had been partially realised by the Holy Alliance, "a united front against war, imperialism and revolution," but since it was a league of "rulers," and not of peoples, it had been defeated by nationalistic movements. The most advanced of these movements, "Giovane Europa," in spite of launching the slogan "the United States of Europe", in fact put national liberation first.[38]

Nationalism, Coudenhove-Kalergi pointed out, "became thus divorced from the European idea, and entered into conflict with neighbouring nationalisms," pursuing "the path of chauvinism," and ending in the World War. Pan-Europa was the heir, in the twentieth century, of the Mazzinian movement, and it was aimed towards the realisation of a new humanism based on Christian values:

> Our common European culture is today rooted in a humanist education, in a Christian morality, and in the spirit of chivalry now incorporated in the civic ideals of the English gentleman. This common European culture has grown out of a series of Pan-European events, beginning with the reform

---

[37] Coudenhove-Kalergi, *Europe Must*, 42-4, 65.
[38] *Ibidem*, 78, 81-84.

of Cluny and continuing with humanism and the Renaissance, the Reformation and the counter-Reformation, the age of Enlightenment and the Romantic age, ending with liberalism, nationalism, and socialism.[39]

Even though Amery thought that the British Commonwealth could not become a member of "another commonwealth," and that the British people were not willing to go further than "the kind of loose union based on mutual economic preference and consultation in policy and defence, such as we have raised in the British Commonwealth," he helped Coudenhove-Kalergi to popularise *Europe must Unite,* and opened a bank account to which the sympathisers could contribute, becoming members of the British section of Pan-Europe.

Amery also supported the candidature of Coudenhove-Kalergi to the Commission for the Nobel Price, declaring that the Count, "almost ever since the last War...with remarkable ability and unwearied persistence pleaded for a united Europe as the greatest immediate contribution which might be made to the peace of the world." Coudenhove-Kalergi combined "selfless devotion to an ideal with a real sense of the actual political situation in any given moment," and for that extraordinary capacity "many leading Statesmen in Europe were converted to his ideas," as was Briand in 1930, when he "put forward his project for European union." Harold Nicolson also supported his candidature for the Nobel Prize: "I said that you who are the pioneer of Federalism are about the only man who can become its pilot."[40]

III. *Curtis and the Atlantic school*

The interest by Chatham House in European federalism would have appeared totally astonishing to Curtis, because since its foundation he never managed to persuade his colleagues to give due consideration to federalist issues. Curtis was certainly not idle during those crucial months, and tried to channel that general interest for federalism into the only desirable outlet: the Atlantic Federation.

The publication of Streit's volume gave Curtis the long-awaited occasion, but he had to go as far as Scotland in order to be able to speak of *Union Now* within Chatham House. On 24, 25 and 26 May 1939, Curtis was addressing the Scottish branches of Chatham House at Edinburgh, Aberdeen and Glasgow, defining the boundary between strategy and tactics, in relation to the struggle for federation. Quoting Admiral Alfred

---

[39] *Ibidem*, 94, 131
[40] CKP, Fonds AP 2, Correspondence, 1939-40.

Mahan—when the strategy is correct one can afford to make tactical errors—Curtis noted that the true strategist had a clear understanding of the ultimate objective to attain, and kept it constantly fixed before him. With that goal in his head, he devised the means to achieve it, and these means were his tactics.

It was rare that a good strategist was also an able tactician. On the other hand, the pure tactician tended to consider tactical tools as ends in themselves, making him blind "to the ultimate goals for which they were devised." It was the case of politicians who, concerned about daily issues, mistook the means for the ends. They were inclined to think of themselves as realists, and consider strategists "as visionaries," becoming then "blind towards fundamental realities."[41]

Streit's volume had the merit of distinctly showing the inadequacy of the means hitherto employed for the purpose of maintaining peace. National sovereignty which had been "a necessary step towards freedom," ended up destroying freedom itself, if it was not overcome. The creation of national States had been a milestone in the development of democracy and the rule of law, but those which had to be mere means had become, with the triumph of economic and political nationalism, ends by themselves, and obstacles to progress. In order to face the threat of Nazism, seen as a byproduct of international anarchy, democracies were forced "to give up the benefits for which the democratic system works."[42]

The funds allocated to social reforms had been diverted to armaments, civil life was increasingly militarised, and individual freedoms were gradually limited in order to cope with the external threat. The reason why the nation-State had become self-contradictory, no longer "a necessary instrument for freedom," but a machine that worked "to destroy the freedoms that it created," was that "in the twentieth century the mechanization had melted human society into an integrated whole." The problem of how to overcome national sovereignty was therefore the major one which mankind had to face, and Streit had offered a rational solution. The strategists and not the tacticians therefore had the task of elaborating a political project of sovranational dimensions. Chatham House had been created precisely to provide politicians and diplomats—otherwise absorbed by the tactical aspects of international affairs—with that overview of international problems without which they would have lost sight of the ultimate goals.[43]

---

[41] CP, 17/108-17.

[42] *Ibidem.*

[43] *Ibidem.* For a discussion of Curtis's role supporting the Atlantic project, see Lavin, *From Empire to*, 202-19.

In London, Curtis tenaciously strove to raise funds and human resources to create a sounding board to Streit's volume. On 17 July 1939 he finally succeeded in creating at Chatham House the "World Order" study-group. It had not been easy for Curtis to overcome the resistance from colleagues, but eventually was able to involve in the works Sir John Fisher-Williams, Gathorne-Hardy, Max Nicolson, C. G. Vickers, and Hugh Wyndham—members of the Council of Chatham House—overcoming the opposition of Lord Healey, Sir Alfred Zimmern, and the fact that the Council on Foreign Relations did not agree to participate directly in the project—considered "too general and theoretical"—while promising to provide London's colleagues with comments on the studies produced.[44]

A few days later, on July 26, Toynbee, Director of research, distributed among his Chatham House colleagues a memorandum in which he strongly supported the immediate creation of a "permanent and complete federation, not a mere partial and temporary" Anglo-French alliance. The British war aim should be the "creation of a federal and democratic State able to dominate the world," and therefore it appeared necessary to "develop our Anglo-French nucleus into a federal State including all Western European and overseas democracies."[45]

Toynbee's federalist conversion was based on the argument that the great civilizations of the past had entered into decadence for failing to resolve the contradiction between the process of universalization of production and trade, on the one hand, and the limits, on the other, represented by historically established political systems that prevented the growth of the productive forces. A world State was certainly necessary, but "the line of least resistance," Toynbee observed, to achieve this end had been the method of military conquest—led to its triumph by Rome and at that time threatened by Hitler—with the inevitable consequence of the "end of civilization." The federalist project ensured the only real alternative to the catastrophe, and in order to speed up its practical realisation, Toynbee proposed that Chatham House should study the possibility of creating as soon as possible "a nucleus of a world State."[46]

---

[44] CP, 128/198-9; 13/192; 13/282; 13/150-1; 110/2-6. On Curtis's role in the creation and the activities of this study-group, see Studdert-Kennedy, *Christianity, Statecraft and Chatham House*, 475-81

[45] CP, 110/55-6.

[46] CHP, 9/18f, 7. There is evidence of this conversion in *Civilization on Trial* (Oxford: Oxford University Press, 1948). See, on Toynbee: Marvin Perry, *Arnold Toynbee and the Crisis of the West* (Washington, DC: University Press of America,

Atlanticists and Europeanists had therefore to cohabit not only at the lowest level of organised federalism, but also at the level closest to the centre of power, and consequently be more influential, destined to play a crucial role in the course of events which led to Churchill's proposal to the French of June 16, 1940.

In order to take advantage of the recent interest within Chatham House which was consolidating for European federalism, Curtis realized that a conflict between world and European federalists would be counterproductive, and therefore decided to promote another study-group, devoted to the problems of a "European Settlement," examining the mistakes of Versailles in the light of the two decades between the wars, and drawing up the main features of a new Europe. While the "World Order" study-group had to deal with, according to Curtis, "long term" problems, the "European Settlement" study-group would have to study the "medium-term" problems, namely the lines on which to progress towards some "settlement without conflicting with the largest and ultimate purpose...to achieve an effective world order." For the activities of both study-groups Curtis obtained, from "certain people who wish to remain anonymous" a cheque for £4,000.[47]

Curtis's activities were certainly instrumentally centred on Chatham House, but the "strategic objective" was to insert, through this tactical coverage, the federalist project in the official statements on war and peace aims. In order to obtain the greatest possible support for his ambitions, Curtis had also created, in October, in collaboration with the Labour dissident Richard Stokes, a "Peace Aims" study-group which, thanks to £6,000 made available by the York Trust, intended to reach out to the media with a well-defined political proposal, supported by prominent figures such as Harold Butler, Sir Arthur Salter, Tom Jones, Bevin, and Beveridge.[48]

1982); Marvin Perry, *Arnold Toynbee and the Western Tradition* (London: Grove/Atlantic, 1996).

[47] CP, 110/89-93.

[48] On the Peace Aims study-group, see the Stokes Papers (Files 73-6) at the Bodleian Library, Oxford, and more generally: Cameron Hazlehurst, *Sally Whitehead and Christine Woodland. A Guide to the Papers of British Cabinet Ministers 1900-1964* (Cambridge: Cambridge University Press, 1997), 348-9; Robert J. C. Young, *Postcolonialism: An Historical Introduction* (Oxford: Wiley, 2001), 180-2; Elisabeth Sifton, *The Serenity Prayer: Faith and Politics in Times of Peace and War* (New York: W. W. Norton & Company, 2003), 274-6; Julian Jackson, *The Fall of France: The Nazi Invasion of 1940* (New York: Oxford University Press, 2004), 203-4; Langhorne, *Diplomacy and Intelligence*, 298; Andrew Williams, *Liberalism and War: The Victors and the Vanquished* (London:

Curtis was also in close touch with the Post War Bureau, affiliated to Chatham House, and with the aim of coordinating the policies and public interventions of the various organisations concerned with the issues of the war aims and reconstruction. It included Sir Norman Angell, David Astor, Gerald Barry, Lord Ivor Spencer Churchill, Lord Davies, H. J. Harvey, Edward Hulton, J. A. Hutton, Sir Walter Layton, E. M. Nicholson and Beveridge, as members of the Political and Economic Planning, Chatham House, the League of Nations Union, the New Commonwealth Society, the Peace Aims Group and Federal Union. The activities of the Bureau—which established a sister organisation in Paris in January 1940—consisted mainly of the internal circulation of documents and publications related to those themes, but also in the preparation of articles and materials for the press. Just to underline the paradox of such fervent speculation in the post-war order, barely two months after Great Britain's entry into the war, on 9 November the MP David Adams presented a Parliamentary interrogation, asking the Government to appoint a minister for peace aims.[49]

Confirmation of the true intentions of Curtis, in aiming to distribute the Streitian project, is in the fact that he had secured from the Rockefeller Foundation £8,000 towards the publication costs of the papers resulting from the activities of the World Order study-group, which would subsequently be translated and published in French, German, Italian, Dutch, Spanish, Portuguese, and in the Scandinavian and Balkan languages. Curtis aimed to launch and coordinate "reflection at a truly international level," and to prepare public opinion to accept a "reasonable peace settlement," and it would also have reached Germany through the press of the neutral countries.[50]

Routledge, 2006), 110-3; Norman J. W. Goda, *Tales from Spandau: Nazi Criminals and the Cold War* (Cambridge: Cambridge University Press, 2006), 79-80; Mark S. Brocker, *Dietrich Bonhoeffer: Conspiracy and Imprisonment, 1940-1945* (Minneapolis: Fortress Press, 2006), 172-3; David Reynolds, *From World War to Cold War: Churchill, Roosevelt, and the International History of the 1940s* (New York: Oxford University Press, 2006), 79-81; John Jenks, *British Propaganda and News Media in the Cold War* (Edimburgh: Edinburgh University Press, 2006), 123-4.

[49] CP, 19/187, 168; BP, 2B III; FOP, FO371/22947: 280-2; FO371/ 22946: 29-30; FO371/22946: 87. See Stuart Ball, *Parliament and Politics in the Age of Churchill and Attlee: The Headlam Diaries 1935-1951* (Cambridge: Cambridge University Press, 2000), 244. On David Astor's involvement in the Bureau, see Jeremy Lewis, *David Astor* (London: Vintage, 2016).

[50] CP, 21/6-9. On the role of the Rockefeller Foundation in the process of formation of British foreign policy, see Joel Fleishman, *The Foundation: A Great*

However, Curtis's grand design met with criticism from the more cautious members of Chatham House's Council, who feared—given the recent official collaboration established between Chatham House and the Foreign Office, with the creation at Balliol College, Oxford, of the Foreign Research and Press Service (FRPS), which will be discussed later—the papers could be considered abroad as "*ballons d'essai* sent up by the Institute on behalf of the Government." Curtis's arguments that, in the perspective of the building of a new world order, the circulation abroad of these papers was indispensable, were rejected. Not only should the papers not circulate abroad, but for the time being, they should not be published even in Great Britain. They should be seen only by Chatham House members and associated institutes in the Commonwealth, the United States and France.[51]

Writing on the 1st December to Waldorf Astor, Chairman of Chatham House, Curtis did not accept that decision as final, reminding his friend that the aim for which Chatham House had been founded twenty years before was "to apply scientific methods of thought to international problems so far as they can be applied to international data." If the principal task of Chatham House was to "ascertain facts and see them with eyes unclouded by wishful thinking, propaganda and, above all, Government influence," it was no less important to give its members the possibility "to read the meaning of the facts ascertained," and to reach an independent decision regarding the action to take.[52]

The unquestionable prestige earned by Chatham House all over the world was "largely due to the fact that all responsible people in public affairs" recognised that Chatham House worked "free from all Government influence." If Chatham House's Council was to give way to pressure from the Foreign Office's officials to limit the internal and external circulation of new ideas, this would be tantamount to suspending "the most vital of its normal functions," and the reputation for independence "laboriously established since the last war will be shattered

---

American Secret. How Private Wealth Is Changing the World (New York: PublicAffairs, 2007).

[51] CP, 20/21. Keyserlingk, *Arnold Toynbee's Foreign*, 539-58.

[52] CP, 111/149; 20/28-30. Astor wrote to Curtis on 30 November 1939 that federalism was "little understood on the Continent." He therefore suggested: "Would it not be well to try and get a summary both of Streit's book and also of *The Federalist?*" Hugh Seton-Watson wrote to Curtis on 30 November, observing that "the Continental mind, even the French" was "quite unprepared for the federal idea." Streit's book made "its appeal to the Anglo-Saxon, not to the European," *ibidem*.

once and for all." With the loss of its own independence, Curtis warned Astor, Chatham House would also lose the financial contribution from the Rockefeller Foundation.[53]

Writing again to Waldorf Astor on 6 January, Curtis stressed the need for a wider and deeper debate by "influential people who do not hold Government positions," on "constructive federal arrangements as the result of the war." That would have balanced the inclination of a section of British and French public opinion to think "that Germany must be broken up and kept impotent, and indeed controlled from outside for a generation or more by the victorious democracies." Toynbee also shared Curtis's view that Daladier's speech referring to a federal post-war order "radically changed the whole situation." Beveridge—who according to Curtis "usually is a pretty well informed person"—told him that Daladier, before making his statement at the French Senate on Anglo-French closer union, "rang up Chamberlain and got his concurrence on the telephone."

With the decision of "withdrawing from publication the intellectual materials which the public most needs for the development of a constructive public opinion," Chatham House would renounce the "most important function it could possible discharge during war time." If the Council did not lift the veto on publication, nothing would prevent the various authors from publishing their own contributions, as indeed did Beveridge. If Chatham House—Curtis wrote to Margaret Cleeve on 9 January 1940—had betrayed the fundamental mission for which it has been established, namely the formation of consensus on issues of international politics, public opinion would not be ready "in time for those changes that may prove to be essential in order to create conditions of stability in Europe."[54]

Astor's reply came with a memorandum on 31st January, reaffirming the principle that Chatham House was "a scientific research organisation," not a propagandistic body. It was independent "but at the same time it has a delicate relationship with the Government, which can be easily

---

[53] CP, 111/149; 20/28-30.

[54] CP, 21/23. William Beveridge, "Peace by Federation?," in *World Order Papers*, (Oxford: Oxford University Press, 1940). Beveridge's essay was published as a pamphlet in February 1940, and in September in the volume *World Order Papers*. Beveridge sent a copy of *Peace by Federation?* to Halifax on 4 March 1940, and noted: "Until we can get peace aims announced, which are convincing to our young people and to the Americans and other neutrals, we shall not be using the strongest weapon we have…The Ministry of Information in some ways is our most important fighting Department, but it can only get effective munitions from the Foreign Office and the Government as a whole," BP, 2B, iv.

misunderstood and misrepresented." Chatham House was engaged, in the perspective of the "coming Peace Conference...to produce a team of expert advisers for the Government," and "to build up groups of instructed students not in Government service, in Britain, and in Allied and Neutrals countries." In order to realise these aims, Chatham House had established an official link with the Foreign Office, had branches in all the principal centres of the Dominions, had begun close co-operation with institutes in the United States and France, was making contacts with research institutes in Norway, Sweden, Belgium, Holland and Switzerland, and finally had a substantial publication programme for books and journals. Astor rejected the idea of sending the World Order papers to Chatham House's branches and foreign research institutes, because "any attempt to shower memos or Papers on most of Groups will merely produce congestion and indigestion." Chatham House should allow the authors to publish their own papers and could buy some copies for internal circulation.[55]

In a letter to Curtis of 9 February, Astor dealt with the more personal aspects of the controversy:

> All that has happened has convinced me that we should return to our well-tried Chatham House machinery. Such misunderstandings as exist are largely due to our having departed therefrom. Perhaps this was inevitable in the first disorganisation of war. Our improvisations have produced both delays and misgivings.[56]

As chairman, Astor was "jealous" for Chatham House's "welfare and reputation." "As a supporter of the Federalist Principles," Astor had "to be doubly careful to hold the balance and see that Chatham House does not appear to push or identify itself more with this controversial policy than with any other." "As a friend of yours," Astor wanted "to protect you from misunderstanding." In normal times Chatham House invited experts "to put forward their views on controversial topics by an address at our meetings and subsequently publishes these views," supplementing them with a report of the discussion on the address "so that the arguments against and criticism of, the views of the lecturer are published simultaneously and within the same cover." Curtis's original proposal would have resulted, according to Astor, "in the publication of views by experts on controversial policies without these being accompanied by criticisms of their views." The publication and distribution in the United Kingdom and foreign countries of single copies of the World Order

---

[55] CP, 111/55-60.
[56] CP, 111/169-73.

Papers, and not of the whole series, would have discontinued Chatham House's "normal practice," and some members "would not have desired to misrepresent us and would not have hesitated to do this unscrupulously if given the slightest opportunity."[57]

Astor reproached Curtis for having sent to the printer the paper by Fisher-Williams "several weeks earlier" before the Council could take a decision, thus producing "trepidation in the minds" of some Council members. Regarding the publication by Federal Union of Beveridge's paper *Peace by Federation?* Astor condemned the fact that Ransome tried "to use it in a by-election," as a Chatham House document. Beveridge's paper "appeared to link us up in a manner that could be misunderstood." Astor suggested the publication of the World Order papers in a form which did not harm Chatham House, and asked Curtis not to push himself "to record a Minority Vote of one on the *real issue*":

> I suggest to you confidently," Astor concluded, "that no one should go to the stake either for or against the wording of contradictory resolutions (even if such exist) passed by the Council in these troublous times. It is even possible for Chatham House to reverse one of two contradictory resolutions![58]

Curtis's position became particularly difficult because of a letter of 31 January by Geoffrey Gathorne-Hardy, in which he asked Curtis to resign as Secretary of the Committee for the publication of the papers. Gathorne-Hardy thought that Curtis was too "temperamentally impossible" to be impartial. "You are a passionate advocate of one solution of the problem," and Gathorne-Hardy did not "feel that the broad study of the question of world-order" was "safe" in his hands. Curtis should have found in Oxford "some suitably objective person" able to co-ordinate the works of the Committee, with an "open mind...less likely to exercise a dominating influence."[59]

Curtis had wrongly interpreted the declarations by Daladier, Chamberlain, and many other statesmen favourable to a post-war federal order:

> Since federalism was in the air, it was used by these speakers, or most of them, to popularise, and particularly perhaps to commend to American opinion, a quite different policy to which they attached importance.

---

[57] *Ibidem.*
[58] *Ibidem.*
[59] CP, 111/190-2.

Politicians naturally try to collect support from as many camps as possible, and to cloak realistic policies in idealistic language.[60]

Briand's plan for European union "obviously envisaged a Europe in which French influence would be dominant," Gathorne-Hardy observed. French politicians saw "advantages in paying lip-service to current British idealism," and federalism could "be a useful card to play in some parts of Europe, where there are too many small States." The idea was "kept alive and toyed with," but there was no serious intention, Gathorne-Hardy concluded, "to adopt it generally."[61]

Curtis's reply on 8 February was very resentful and gives us a singular portrait of the man:

We are at war, and ought to get on with our war jobs, which include winning the peace as well as the war. The organisation which Chatham House has built up during twenty years of so-called peace is magnificent, but the attempt to operate that organisation under war conditions must lead to an unconscionable waste of time unless the Council is prepared to delegate a great measure of responsibility to the people who are willing to serve it. In the last few months more than half my time has been consumed in trying to cope with the difficulties created by your intervention.[62]

Curtis felt that he could not "continue to carry on under these conditions, and if they are to persist" he was "impelled to turn to other work" which will allow him to devote his "whole energies...in helping to win the war and the peace." The peace-time procedures of Chatham House should be modified, according to Curtis, "to meet war conditions," and concluded:

In my view, I ought not to have to spend my time this morning writing a letter like this; nor ought you to have had to spend your time in writing the letters to which it is in answer."[63]

So Curtis's last attempt to bring Chatham House to openly support a federal Atlantic policy failed. The results of the study group were

[60] *Ibidem.*
[61] *Ibidem.*
[62] CP, 21/81. Members of Chatham House's Publications Committee were: Lord Meston, J. L. Brierly, G. N. Clark, C. A. W. Manning, Sir John Hope Simpson, C. K. Webster, Sir Alfred Zimmern, H. Harvey and M. Cleeve, CP, 111/30.
[63] CP, 21/81.

published in September 1940, as the "first series" of an ambitious project which never came about.[64]

If Chatham House never went so far as to advocate a real political union between the two leading Anglo-Saxon democracies, it did however play a fundamental role in creating the cultural and political basis on which would be born, during the war, the so-called "special relationship", harbinger of the Atlantic Alliance. Curtis's federalist design failed, but its geo-political content could be differently conjugated in the reality of twentieth-century politics. Chatham House undoubtedly played, in this regard, a pioneering role, which hitherto has still to be fully investigated.[65]

IV. *Arnold Toynbee, Alfred Zimmern and Anglo-French Union*

The Chatham House figure who mostly endeavoured to bring the British Government to adopt the federalist project on the basis of an Anglo-French Union, was certainly Toynbee, followed a short time later by Alfred Zimmern.

---

[64] The volume was at last published in September 1940 as *World Order Papers*, and intended as a "first series". It contained a foreword by Waldorf Astor, an introduction by Lord Samuel, and contributions by Sir John Fisher Williams ("World Order: An Attempt at an Outline"), Gilbert Murray ("Federation and the League"), Sir William Beveridge ("Peace by Federation?"), J. A. Spender ("Comments on the Papers by Professor Murray and Sir William Beveridge"), Horsfall Carter ("Some Doubts as to the Imminence of the Millennium"), Lionel Robbins ("Economic Factors and International Disunity"), and Geoffrey Vickers ("Purpose and Force—The Bases of Order"). The Committee also planned to publish in successive series—which never materialized—contributions by J. H. Clapham ("Franco-British Cooperation in the Present War"), L. Penson and C. K. Webster ("Historical Background of World Order"), J. H. Oldham, Archbishop of York, ("Christianity as a Possible Basis of World Order"), Wilson Harris ("The United States of Europe"), Leo Amery ("Pan-Europe"), Darrel Ford ("Geographical Elements in World Order"), R. T. E. Latham ("Federalism"), Leonard Woolf ("Towards International Government"), H. N. Brailsford ("Socialism and World Order"), Edwyn Bevan ("Cultural Aspects of World Order"), and E. A. Walker ("The British Empire and Federal Union").
[65] For an analysis, see Reynolds, *The Creation of the*; Randall Bennett Woods, *A Changing of the Guard: Anglo-American Relations, 1941-1946* (Chapel Hill, NC: University of North Carolina Press, 1990); Robert Dallek, *Franklin D. Roosevelt and American Foreign Policy, 1932-1945* (Oxford: Oxford University Press, 1995); David Reynolds, *From World War to Cold War: Churchill, Roosevelt and the International History of the 1940s* (Oxford: Oxford University Press, 2006).

At the beginning of the war the British Government turned to Chatham House for ideas to define the shape of the post-war settlement. In Chatham House was created a formidable group of academics, businessmen, and intellectuals who gave life to one of the "longest historical seminars on record, studying the past in order to draw up blueprint for the future." During the First World War, the Foreign Office had created for this purpose the Political Intelligence Department under the direction of the historian Sir James Headlam-Morley, with the collaboration of Arnold Toynbee, Lewis Namier, Allen and Rex Leeper. It was Rex Leeper, in the meantime appointed head of the News Department of the Foreign Office, who turned to Toynbee in May 1939 in order to provide the Foreign Office with a new Department of research, able to provide information on the historical aspects of war and peace questions.[66]

The Foreign Office initially equipped Chatham House with £80,000 a year, but after harsh parliamentary scrutiny, the Government was forced to halve the budget. However, the funds allocated allowed Toynbee to employ a staff of 131, consisting of 11 Oxford professors—whose wages were paid by the University—23 researchers—paid by the Foreign Office—24 volunteer researchers and 74 Foreign Office officials. With the denomination of the Foreign Research and Press Service—since 1943 directly incorporated into the Foreign Office as the Foreign Office Research Department—the new organism, housed at Balliol College, Oxford, began work in September 1939, with Toynbee as Director and Curtis as Chairman on the designation of Chatham House.[67]

---

[66] For a critical analysis, see Robert H. Keyserlingk, "Arnold Toynbee's Foreign Research and Press Service and Its Post-war Plans for South-East Europe 1939-1945," *Journal of Contemporary History*, 21, (1986): 539-58.

[67] FOP, FO371/2300, 134992, 320-37. See the letter by Curtis to Waldorf Astor, CP, 22, 6-7. On the Foreign Research and Press Service, see: Alison Smith, *Margery Perham and British Rule in Africa* (London: Routledge, 1992), 112-3; Cristopher Hill, *Two Worlds of International Relations* (London: Routledge, 1994), 42-3; E. Gates, *Race and U.S. Foreign Policy During the Cold War* (London: Routledge, 1998), 28-9; Charles Jones, *E. H. Carr and International Relations: A Duty to Lie* (Cambridge: Cambridge University Press, 1998), 71-2; Mark Aarons and John Loftus, *Unholy Trinity: The Vatican, The Nazis, and The Swiss Banks* (New York: St. Martin's Griffin, 1998), 308; Julian Lewis, *Changing Direction: British Military Planning for Post-war Strategic Defence, 1942-1947* (London: Routledge, 2002), 10-11; Lynn Picknett, Clive Prince, Stephen Prior and Robert Brydon, *Double Standards: The Rudolf Hess Cover-Up* (London: Little, Brown & Co., 2002), 66-7; Kedourie, *The Chatham House Version*, 352-3; A. Brocker, *Dietrich Bonhoeffer*, 337-8.

In the FRPS, Curtis saw an additional tool for instilling the guiding ideas of a federalist post-war reorganisation within Chatham House and the Foreign Office. The passage of a letter to Waldorf Astor is enlightening in this respect, where Curtis recollected a meeting in September 1912 on board the HMS *Enchantress* with officers of the General Staff of the Ministry of War, when Churchill told him and other members of the Round Table that officers were excellent at manoeuvring ships, but they had no idea about strategic issues. This was also true for civil servants absorbed by routine, particularly in times of war, and inevitably losing sight of the long-term problems, or the need to study them. Downing Street needed, according to Curtis, an institution in order to take these problems into account, in the same way that the Ministry of War and the Admiralty needed an institution which dealt with strategic issues, making sure that officials were not overwhelmed by tactical details. When the time comes to discuss how to make peace, the Government needs "a group of men who have long predicted that time," to consider the demands that arise, and the information that the Government will need to take care of those requests. At that moment the newly-established FRPS would, Curtis hoped, come into play throughout, helping the Government not to lose the peace once more.[68]

Curtis's vocation for grand designs certainly infected Toynbee, who in the memorandum "Second Thoughts on a Peace Settlement," written "seven weeks after the outbreak of war," addressed to Halifax, and put into circulation among the members of Chatham House, observed that "the capital problem that has been brought to a head by the war remains unchanged but the choice between possible alternative ways of trying to solve it has come into clearer focus." The problem was Germany, a country with a population almost double that of France, which because of her central position in Europe could "insulate the small nations lying to the east of her from France and Great Britain." The German people repeatedly showed themselves apt "to allow [themselves] to fall into the hands of despotic and aggressive rulers," who first deprived the German people of their own freedom, "in order then to use this pliant mass of beings as an immensely powerful instrument for attacking and subjugating the peoples round about."[69]

If at the end of the war Germany was to be left intact at the centre of a disunited Europe, "still amounting politically to nothing more than an unorganised cluster of separate sovereign independent States" it would

---

[68] CP, 100.
[69] FOP, FO371/24246, 64-5.

certainly become once again the "mistress of the rest of Europe." In a politically divided Europe, "not only the re-liberated Poles, Czechs and Slovaks, but also all the other surviving small nations" would rapidly fall "into a relation of helpless subjection to Germany in which a nominally sovereign and independent Slovakia finds herself today."[70]

Great Britain and France would therefore be "isolated 'States on the fringe'," and the result would, after another "armistice of perhaps twenty years' duration," be another European war, with the inevitable defeat of France and Great Britain, and their annexation to a German Empire. If France and Great Britain wanted to "continue to exercise the principal influence in the development of our common civilization," it was not enough to win the war, but it was necessary to "seize the opportunity" of the peace and organise "Europe politically on lines which would promise to rule out, permanently, the prospect of Germany being able to establish her domination over Europe at some future time."[71]

There were only two ways to prevent Germany from playing a hegemonic role once more. On one side, there was the dismemberment of Germany, with the consequence of leaving Europe "parcelled out into a patchwork of separate sovereign States, without making any serious effort either to revive the League of Nations or to bring about a European Federal Union." This policy would meet a "line of least resistance," because it required "the minimum of construction," since it was based "almost entirely upon the easier option of destruction." Toynbee however felt strong doubts about its practicability and opportunity, because it was not possible "to deny to the Germans that right to national unity which we French and British claim for ourselves."[72]

On the other side, there was the option of a European federation. According to Toynbee, there was no other way to conciliate the "necessity of doing justice to Germany, by allowing her to keep her national unity, with the necessity of doing justice to Europe, by making her secure against the danger of falling under German domination." There seemed to be three indispensable political conditions for the creation of the latter:

> (a) in lieu of Greater Germany, some other nucleus must be found round which Europe can unite, and this alternative nucleus must be one which will be at least as powerful as Greater Germany and at the same time more attractive, as a rallying-point, to other European peoples. (b) The European neutrals must be convinced that, in voluntarily rallying round this

---

[70] *Ibidem.*
[71] FOP, FO371/24246, 66.
[72] *Ibidem.*

alternative centre of union, they would be likely to preserve more of our common Christian tradition than if they were to be united forcibly through a common subjection to Germany; and at the same time they must be convinced that they can take this alternative path to union without exposing themselves to any really grave risk of reprisals on Germany's part. (c) The Germans themselves must, if possible, be induced voluntarily to enter this European Union that is to be constructed round a non-German nucleus.[73]

The heart of the European federation could be constituted by the Anglo-French Union which was equal in population to Greater Germany, and with a more favourable world strategic position than that of Germany, which was essentially still a Continental power. The Anglo-French Union should not, however, limit itself to the war-time emergency. During the First World War the two countries had become "practically one single State in respect of some of the public services that were most vital for winning the war and for carrying on the life of the French and British people in the meantime." If in 1919, when "this unified Anglo-French organisation was deliberately scrapped," they had understood that "the armistice had not really been converted into a peace and that the war was destined to break out again within twenty years, we would assuredly have retained our war-time organisation and have improved upon it." The emergency had forced the British and French peoples to rebuild that military, financial and economic unity. This time it should, "from the start," place the Anglo-French Union "under a united parliamentary control," and "on a permanent basis." "The very act of union between Great Britain and France would in itself operate as a powerful encouragement to neutrals to unite, in their turn, with the Anglo-French Union and thus to take the first step towards building an European Union round this Anglo-French nucleus."[74]

In fact, Chatham House played a fundamental role in persuading the Foreign Office of the reasonableness of the Anglo-French Union. The initiative started with Arnold Toynbee and Alfred Zimmern, who, after a brief visit to Paris—where, with Sir Walter Layton, they attended an economists' Conference, from 9 to 12 March, at the Centre d'Etudes de Politique Etrangère, the French associate of Chatham House, and had private talks with L. F. Aubert, Chef de Cabinet of Deladier, Jean Giraudoux, Commissaire de l'Information, and senator Vincent Honnart—understood that time was not on the side of the Allies and that it was

---

[73] *Ibidem.*
[74] FOP, FO371/24246, 67.

necessary to take extreme action to revert the balance of power. It was envisaged as a Treaty of "Perpetual Association between France and Great Britain."[75]

In a memorandum of 12 March, addressed to Hubert M. Jebb—later to become Lord Gladwyn—Toynbee suggested that the text of the treaty should be "brief and simple," contemplating the pooling of the military, foreign and economic policies of the two countries. The idea had already being discussed within a study-group established by the Centre d'Etudes de Politique Etrangère which aimed to draft a joint Anglo-French declaration on war-aims. On March 10, during a special session of the Conference, a declaration had been issued and enthusiastically welcomed by a heterogeneous public, "corresponding in character to the usual audience at a meeting of Chatham House."[76]

The Anglo-French Union would, according to Toynbee, have galvanised French morale, and persuaded the French people once and for all of the total reliability of the British, both in the joint war-effort, and in the organisation of peace. It would also have offered "an alternative centre of crystallization for a new Europe," acting towards the weak and confused neutrals as "a gravitational pull which might have some chance of counteracting and overcoming the pull of the Third Reich." The Anglo-French Union would be seen as a concrete sign of the determination to fight to the bitter end, and would dissuade the major neutral powers "from pushing too far their attempts to drive us into acquiescing in an inconclusive peace." Toynbee concluded, by pointing out that many French people "whose reaction to the idea of 'federal union' in the abstract was sceptical and hostile, were not only favourable to the idea of Anglo-French Union, but were prepared to think of this, with approval, as a nucleus to which other European countries might attach themselves at a later stage."[77]

Toynbee did not limit himself to transmitting the memorandum to the Foreign Office, but on the following day, March 13, he had a meeting with Permanent Under-secretary R. A. Butler, who in a letter of the same day to Halifax reported on the visit:

> in short, Professor Toynbee and Professor Zimmern's suggestion is that the creative energies of the French and ourselves should be turned not into a discussion of peace aims, but into building up, with a view to the future

---

[75] FOP, FO371/24294, 289-303. On Zimmern see D. J. Markwell, "Sir Alfred Zimmern Revisited", *Review of International Studies*, 12, 4, (1986): 279-91.
[76] FOP, FO371/24298, 134921.
[77] *Ibidem.*

of Europe, a strong and still stronger Anglo-French alliance, or Federation, or whatever you like to call it. I am at the moment studying a minute from these two learned gentlemen on this subject, which I have asked them to develop in their leisure hours at Chatham House. Just such a study may be the way to interest the French in the future after the war...The French feel that we should be more active in building up the Europe we want within the fortress of civilization, that is, this side of the Maginot line. I will report further on this when there are developments, but it may help to meet your desire that youth should have something to bite on.[78]

Butler entrusted Toynbee to draft the Treaty of Union, but also used the visit as a chance to rebuke Toynbee about the *imprimatur* of Chatham House on Beveridge's essay *Peace by Federation?* From January 1940 Chatham House was in fact officially at the service of the Foreign Office with the FPRS. Toynbee conceded to Butler, and in the space of ten days drafted, with the assistance of Zimmern, the "Act of Perpetual Association between the United Kingdom and France," and its commentary, being the first draft Constitutional Treaty establishing the nucleus of a European Union.[79]

---

[78] Thus Toynbee summarised the contents of the memorandum: "i) The only alternative to the domination of Europe by a Nazi German Reich is a union of democratic States on a scale which will make the union so decisively and manifestly stronger than Germany that the Germans will never venture to attack it. ii) The essential first step towards building up such a democratic union is for Great Britain and France to form it with one another. iii) To be effective and durable, a political union must be organic, in the sense that there must be a genuine common Government exercising direct authority over all citizens, in all the component States, for those purposes for which the union has been formed. iv) In a union of democratic States, common Government includes a common representative body to which the common Government must be responsible. v) Therefore our first step must be to establish, as between Great Britain and France, a common Government, responsible to a common representative body, with a competence restricted to defence, foreign affairs and the minimum amount of other powers and services that may prove to be inseparable from defence and foreign policy under present social and economic conditions. As far as may prove compatible with the effective pooling of foreign policy and defence, the aim should be to leave each of the component States in control of its own domestic social and economic life," (CP, 100, 19-31).
[79] *Ibidem*; FOP, FO371/24299, 134921, 57-68. On Anglo-French military and colonial collaboration, see: Brian J. Bond, *British Military Policy between the Two World Wars* (Oxford: Clarendon Press, 1980); Nicholas Rostow, *Anglo-French Relations, 1934-1936* (New York: St. Martin's, 1984); P. Dennis, *The Territorial Army, 1906-1940* (Woodbridge: Royal Historical Society, 1987); John Kent, "Anglo-French Colonial Co-Operation, 1939-49," *Journal of Imperial and*

The Act provided the creation of a common body responsible for the military, foreign and economic policies of the Union, in the framework of a common citizenship. They proposed the term "Act," and not "Pact" or "Treaty," in order to indicate "a solemn term of domestic politics." They preferred the term "Association" to "Union," because the gravity of the hour did not allow them to summon Constituent Assemblies in both countries. The close collaboration already existing between the two governments was to be recognised and incorporated "in permanent institutions".[80]

Toynbee referred to the origins of the Swiss Confederation, which began with a simple "defensive association" among three neighbouring cantons, and only later became "a political unit, inspiring an intense patriotism transcending differences of language, culture and tradition." The draft Constitutional Treaty suggested that the common body would be the "Supreme Council"—which would meet regularly, under the chairmanship of the two Prime Ministers—supported by a "permanent secretariat" to implement decisions. Regarding defence, the Anglo-French equivalent of the Committee of Imperial Defence would be set up, as well as an Anglo-French Defence College for the training of staff, and an Anglo-French general staff. An "economic general staff" would deal with the transition from war to peace economy, providing "the necessary European basis of confidence for eliciting effective American assistance in the economic rehabilitation of Europe."[81]

This lucid and valuable document, which was more forward-looking, if not in form, then certainly in substance, than Churchill's famous proposal of "indissoluble union" with France, has so far been neglected by historians. Similarly, the whole process of "conversion" to federalism by a significant portion of the British political class, which developed particularly during the spring of 1940, has also been neglected.

Evidence of this process is given by the minutes of Foreign Office senior officials, who were suddenly forced, not without some embarrassment and difficulty, to abandon the categories of traditional politics and to think in opposite terms according to the principles of federalism. If J. G. Ward continued to think of the Anglo-French Union as "too big an objective for immediate purposes," in a minute to Sargent of 26 March, Leeper wrote:

Commonwealth History, 17, 1, (1988): 55-82; Peter M. H. Bell, *France and Britain, 1900-1940: Entente and Estrangement* (Harlow: Longman, 1996).
[80] FOP, FO371/24299, 134921, 57-68.
[81] *Ibidem*.

I attach a paper on Anglo-French relations which was drawn up by Sir Alfred Zimmern as a result of several discussions which I have had with him and Professor Toynbee. Both he and Professor Toynbee are working at Balliol and I put this problem to them as one of several which the Secretary of State wished them to get to work on. In a recent minute you suggested that an inter-departmental committee should be set up under Lord Hankey. It occurred to me that a document such as this might be useful to such a committee to work on, though I do not know whether you contemplate the two governments issuing anything of this kind when agreement has been reached. What we here had in mind in our discussions was a short and simple document preceded by a preamble and accompanied by explanatory details...We felt that a short and striking document summing up a scheme for Anglo-French co-operation might be the best answer to Hitler's claim that he is establishing a new order in Central and Eastern Europe. Our new order, if it embraced the British and French Empires, would have a far wider scope, would strike the imagination of America and would provide a real peace aim for the youth of England and France.[82]

"As it is quite probable," Sargent wrote to Cadogan the following day, "that M. Reynaud may, in connection with the proposed Anglo-French declaration, raise the question of future co-operation between our two countries," the Secretary of State might "run his eye" over the scheme produced by Chatham House "as the basis on which Lord Hankey's inter-departmental Committee might start its work." It contained "a number of very useful ideas which clearly ought to be studied further," even if Sargent did "not for a moment suggest that it should be shown to M. Reynaud, or even that the ideas which it contains should be put to him." If Reynaud on his side volunteered "any proposals," then "it would be interesting to see how far they coincide with the ideas contained in this paper." Sargent reported that the French press was "already full of these ideas, whereas our press still remains completely silent on the subject."[83]

---

[82] FOP, FO371/24299, 134921, 80. For a background discussion, see: Max Beloff, "The Anglo-French Union Project of June 1940," in *The Intellectual in Politics and Other Essays*, ed. Max Beloff (London: The Library Press, 1970); Avi Shlaim, "Prelude to Downfall: The British Offer of Union to France, June 1940," *Journal of Contemporary History*, 9, 3, (1974); Richard Davis, *Anglo-French Relations Before the Second World War: Appeasement and Crisis* (New York: Palgrave Macmillan, 2001).
[83] FOP, FO371/24299, 134921, 57-9. Chamberlain was surprised to acknowledge the sudden rejection of the policy of appeasement by Halifax and Cadogan, since they had been two leading advocates of it. See, on this regard: Alexander Cadogan, *The Diaries of Sir Alexander Cadogan*, David Dilks ed. (London: Cassell, 1971);

On the same day, writing to Halifax, Cadogan commented: "at first sight it seems to contain much that is useful and suggestive and even, I think, practical." The following day Halifax remarked: "interesting—and a valuable start in the business of translating general aspirations into more concrete forms." For the first time in British history a Foreign Minister expressed a favourable opinion about a federalist project embracing Continental Europe, and British participation, thus initiating that swift process of revision of the aims for which the British people were fighting, which led, as it is known, to Churchill's proposal.[84]

V. *Toynbee, Curtis and the Foreign Office*

Zimmern continued meanwhile to inform Curtis of the involvement of Chatham House in the study of forms of Anglo-French Union. While not wishing to appear in person as the author of a specific project, Curtis exercised, always behind the scenes, that magnetic influence which left his victims with the impression of having come to certain conclusions quite freely and at the price of a hard-won conquest. In a note of April 18 to Toynbee, Curtis expressed some considerations on the memorandum of his friend, treating him almost as a negligent pupil. Reminding him that by then the French and the British had been "encouraged by their responsible leaders to expect after this war a system in Europe which has in its nature the seeds of stability," which would have been founded upon a "close and permanent association of France with Great Britain, as the nucleus of a stable system," Curtis observed that there were only two kinds of political systems: "organic and inorganic."[85]

Organic systems were represented by the model of sovereign States, which demanded of their citizens an exclusive and unlimited loyalism. Inorganic systems were exemplified by leagues and confederations, formed upon a "compact" among sovereign States, which could be bilateral as alliances, or multilateral as the League of Nations. The interests on which it is based, Curtis observed, "shift and change like a bed of sand under moving water." It was impossible to create a stable political system through unions of sovereign States, since the loyalty of citizens

---

Peter Neville, "Sir Alexander Cadogan and Lord Halifax's 'Damascus Road' Conversion Over the Godesberg Terms 1938", *Diplomacy & Statecraft*, 11, 3, (2000): 81-90.

[84] FOP, FO371/24299, 134921, 57-9.

[85] CP,100, 19-22. On Curtis's political doctrine, see: Lavin, *From Empire to International*; Studdert-Kennedy, "Curtis, Lionel George: Intense Beliefs of," in Bosco and May, *The Round Table*.

was for the State to which they belonged, and not to the union. A political system became organic when its authority was based upon the loyalty of the citizens who formed it, and it was able to exercise that authority directly upon its citizens.[86]

Analysing the conditions to guarantee the Anglo-French Union with "that stability which French and English statesmen are leading their peoples to accept," Curtis observed:

> so long as allied States are fighting for their very existence, alliances are relatively stable...the real test comes in peace when the allied States try to stand together and be jointly so strong as to render hopeless a renewed attack from their enemies.[87]

In fact, it was very difficult in peace-time to reach an agreement among sovereign States regarding vital strategic interests. "Estrangement develops first between Governments," Curtis observed, "and then between the peoples behind them." The Anglo-French Union could not "prevent the growth of German aggression" without the existence of an Anglo-French army, navy, and air force. The appointment of the commanders-in-chief of the three armed forces was a decision which involved vital interests, and it would have been done by a Supreme Allied Council. This was, during war-time, the executive organ of the Union, which had the duty to direct foreign, military and financial policies, and also to decide about the distribution of the costs among the French and British tax-payers.[88]

It was however within the competence of the two parliaments to ratify the decisions of the executive body which, according to Curtis, could hardly "stand for five years," since it had to "obtain its supplies from two or more separate legislatures elected by different nations, and therefore largely on their own domestic issues."[89]

The common executive had therefore to be directly responsible, according to Curtis, before a common Parliament, directly elected by French and British citizens, distinct from the National Assembly or the House of Commons. The common Parliament could not be composed of delegates of the two States, because they would have been subject to the control of national parliaments. "The decisive discussion will take place in two or more national legislatures," Curtis argued, "to which the members of the executive body responsible for security have no personal access."

---

[86] CP,100, 19-22.
[87] CP, 100, 22-25.
[88] CP, 100, 25-27.
[89] CP, 100, 27-9.

Only a Parliament with full powers in the fields of competence—including that of direct taxation—would have created an organic union. An inorganic union was, on the contrary, as a "reed which will always break when you lean on it but is yet strong enough to pierce your hand with the broken end." Regarding the powers to be allocated to the common bodies, Curtis did not agree with Streit, Beveridge, and Jennings, who thought that those powers should not be limited to the security sphere, and he included trade, industry and the colonies.[90]

It was possible, according to Curtis, to create a stable international order only by introducing the principle of the State "little by little" into the "chaotic structure" of the world, namely "by bringing two or more States into organic union." Curtis did not think, however, that "the day of the national State" was yet over. National States continued to perform "a permanent and all-important function in human affairs," by preserving and developing the differentiation of the structure and composition of "human society." The main obstacle to performing this fundamental role was just the "insecurity caused by the state of anarchy between them." Curtis's "guiding principle" in the division of competences between the national and sovranational spheres was thus formulated:

> the control of social affairs in the widest aspect must be left to national Governments, yet cannot be so left unless they continue to control the distribution of taxation and therefore tariffs within their several jurisdictions. The international Government must be restricted to security and matters absolutely inseparable therefrom, for which purpose it must have effective power to make security a first charge on all the resources of the nations included.[91]

Discussing the method and the timetable for the realisation of the union, Curtis thought that it was not realistic to expect "any real constitutional reconstruction whilst war is in progress." It was true that for any alliance it was "far harder...to stand the test of peace, than to stand the test of war, and survive it," but the emergency of the war prevented that deep constitutional reform which was the only way to give stability to the union. If the unitary mechanism created by the war could have proved effective in facing the problems of reconstruction—namely if it could have been supported by the determination of the two governments to maintain the promises—it would have spread a "sense of security" all over Europe. This would have induced the other European democracies, "whose

---

[90] *Ibidem.*
[91] *Ibidem.* Italics in the original.

sovereign independence this war is now revealing as a sheer illusion," to "rapidly" take part in the union, and strengthen it "greatly."[92]

European peace would not have been stable until a democratic Germany took part in the Union, and that would have depended on the "success or failure of her western neighbours in establishing responsible government on a footing too strong to invite destruction." "The conclusion," noted Curtis, "is that you must be content to begin with a union of England and France, which has, in the principle of its structure, the element of permanence."[93]

Curtis did not just limit himself to intervene with his friend Toynbee, but on April 22 sent to Halifax, at the suggestion of Leeper and Christopher Warner—responsible for maintaining contacts between the Foreign Office and the FRPS—a new version of the memorandum addressed to Toynbee, "Note on the Allied Peace Aims. The Stabilisation of Peace on the Basis of a Permanent Franco-British Alliance," with which he tried to directly affect the works of the *ad hoc* Committee chaired by Hankey to draw up the Constitution of the Anglo-French Union, which will be discussed later.

Halifax's comment was unequivocal: "It is a rather ambitious idea and I have some difficulties to believe that it is practical politics. But perhaps I am too timid." The Foreign Minister nevertheless allowed the document to be placed in front of the Hankey Committee, which however was dissolved before it could examine it. Curtis hoped that Halifax used the memo to tear up comments by French ministers "on the opinions of an obscure individual to whom Her Majesty's Government is not in any way responsible." The destinies of the war would be decided in the summer, and it was therefore necessary to "think now with detachment to what you should do when the fighting will be ended."[94]

Curtis was recidivist. From the outbreak of war, Curtis was engaged, at various levels, in incorporating the federalist project within the official declarations on war and peace aims. On 9 November 1939 he dispatched to Halifax a memorandum "On the Demand that the Allies Should Announce Their Peace Aims." Curtis requested the Foreign Minister to approach Herriot—since Daladier was apparently too involved into the war effort—and to dispatch a joint Anglo-French declaration on the war and peace aims. Halifax had however to circulate his memorandum within

---

[92] CP, 100, 29-31.
[93] *Ibidem.*
[94] FOP, FO371/2300, 134992, 320-37; CP, 22/67; 22/6-7. On Halifax's relations with Chatham House see: Birkenhead, *Halifax: The Life*, 331-49; Roberts, *The Holy Fox,* 225-40.

the Foreign Office "as a paper prepared by one who wishes to remain anonymous," and noted:

> I don't suppose for a moment that Hitler would accept such proposals if published. The really important factor is that they would commit the Allies to facing the question how the democratic system can be made strong to be attacked again after another 25 years.[95]

Curtis suggested keeping the war aims separated from the peace aims. If the war was directed to the defeat of Nazism, the peace could not be based on "the policy of weakening, crushing and disintegrating Germany." Peace should create a "world order," of which the European federation was just an aspect. Great Britain and the other English-speaking peoples should assume a leading role in establishing a world-wide political system able to prevent the outbreak of another global conflict. With the particular assistance of the United States, Great Britain had to re-establish, in the course of the twentieth century, the general political conditions of the nineteenth, when the naval power of Great Britain alone prevented the outbreak of a world war.[96]

VI. *Chatham House and the Foreign Office*

Curtis, Toynbee and Zimmern's efforts aimed at bringing the Foreign Office to apply federalist principles to Anglo-French relations did not fall completely into the void. In a fundamental memorandum, to Sir Alexander Cadogan, Permanent Under-secretary to the Foreign Office, on the 28 February 1939, Sir Orme Sargent complained that the British press gave little, or no space at all, to a passage in the speech given by Chamberlain on the 24 February, in which the Prime Minister stated that "we and France are determined to do what we can for security by the continuance of that complete identity of purpose and policy which now unites us and which will serve after the war" to establish that "authority and stability which are necessary for the security of Europe." Sargent also pointed out that "a permanent system of close co-operation with France is the contribution which we must be ready to make in the interests of a stable peace after the war."[97]

---

[95] CP, 22/6-7.

[96] *Ibidem.*

[97] FOP, FO371/24298, 134921, 184. On the Foreign Office's readiness, after Munich, to consider a closer union with France, see: D. Lammers, "From Whitehall after Munich: The Foreign Office and the Future Course of British

For "co-operation" Sargent did not mean a simple "political alliance, but the continuance and reinforcement of that unity of action and those special forms of joint executive machinery which have now been established for war purposes." In order to prevent the French from occupying Germany at the end of the war, the British had to offer an alternative to "count on such a system of close and permanent co-operation—political, military and economic—as will for all international purposes make of the two countries a single unit in post-war Europe." The Anglo-French Union could have represented an effective— possibly the only effective—counterbalance to a Germany of eighty million, at the centre of the Continent.[98]

British public opinion did not yet seem prepared to accept such a radical solution of the European question:

> the idea of the Federation of Europe can make its appeal to public sentiment so long as it appears only as a vague El Dorado, the details of which we need not bother our heads about at present. However, the application of this idea of Federation to the concrete case of Great Britain and France is quite another matter and it will need a considerable amount of education before the British public get accustomed to the notion of their having to make this unpalatable and unprecedented sacrifice on the altar of European peace.[99]

Since "the question of peace terms may at any moment become immediate and we must not be caught unprepared," Sargent suggested that the Foreign Office had to contribute to speed up the process of education for federalism. Now that the Prime Minister took the lead, it was the job of the Ministry of Information "to popularise the idea."[100]

The stand by Sargent immediately gained the support of Cadogan, Halifax, and Chamberlain. Writing to Chamberlain on the 13 February, Halifax noted: "I am more and more coming to feel that the answer to the Rhine claim is continuing complete unity of France and ourselves." On 1 March Chamberlain wrote at the foot: "I entirely agree with this

---

Policy," *Historical Journal*, 16, (1973): 831-56; Cadogan, *The Diaries*; Gaynor Johnson, *The Foreign Office and British Diplomacy in the Twentieth Century* (London: Routledge, 2005), 90.
[98] FOP, FO371/24298, 134921, 184-5.
[99] FOP, FO371/24298, 134921, 185-6.
[100] FOP, FO371/24298, 134921, 186.

memorandum and shall be glad if the Ministry of Information can do something to draw attention to the importance of the subject."[101]

On March 11, the Co-ordinating Committee of the Ministry of Information accepted in principle Sargent's ideas, and Perth charged Henry Hodson, editor of *The Round Table*, to comment on Sargent's memorandum, and suggest practical initiatives. In a memorandum of March 15, Hodson noted that Sargent's position was a "bold and striking lead for our propaganda at home and abroad," suggesting three lines of action to gain support from the public. First, it was the task of British and French "intellectual circles" to foster the study of the idea and its implications, using the press as a vehicle of persuasion.[102]

Second, it was necessary to promote the growth of "a sense of fellowship" and "common citizenship" among the two peoples. The British press and radio had to throw a "sympathetic and human light" on French people, and *vice versa*. In theatres, cinemas and public gatherings, the notes of "La Marseillaise" had to follow those of "God save the King". The French Tricolor had to appear side by side with the Union Jack. Those initiatives had only a symbolic character, but they could have "a tremendous effect in preparing the minds of the public at home and overseas for a permanent sacrifice of part of our national sovereignty on the altar of European peace."[103]

Third, the Ministry had "always taken for granted" in all official press releases and public events that the world could rely upon the Anglo-French Union as a permanent and fundamental factor in post-war Europe. Hodson concluded his memorandum by observing that it was better not to discuss the rationality of such an ambitious project, because it would have weakened its strength: "we are on safe political ground, since on the need for such post-war Anglo-French unity the government and opposition are as one."[104]

---

[101] CHP, NC 7/11/33/74; FOP, FO371/24299, C 4444/9/17; C. Self, *Neville Chamberlain: A Biography* (London: Ashgate Publishing, 2006), 421-2. On the perception by the Foreign Office of the crisis of the Third Republic, see: J. F. V. Keiger, "La perception de la puissance française par le Foreign Office," in *La puissance française à la 'belle époque': Mythe ou réalité?*, Pierre Milza and Raymond Poidevin eds. (Paris: Institute d'Histoire du Temps Présent, 1992); Michael Dockrill, "British Official Perceptions of France, 1936-1940," in Dockrill and Chassaigne, *Anglo-French Relations*, 94-106.

[102] FOP, FO371/24298, 134921, 166. For a representation of France by British public opinion, see John C. Cairns, "A Nation of Shopkeepers in Search of a Suitable France, 1919-40," *American Historical Review*, 79, 3, (1974).

[103] FOP, FO371/24298, 134921, 166.

[104] *Ibidem.*

Sargent did not just enunciate guiding ideas on which to build a closer Anglo-French Union, but also undertook to create an "experts' Committee...to examine the purely administrative implications" of the projected union. The Committee had to be chaired by a minister—Sargent suggested Lord Hankey, who had already volunteered himself—and be composed of representatives of the Army, the Treasury, the Ministry of Trade and the Foreign Office. At the beginning, the Committee had to be composed of British members only, and the French ought only to be brought in when they "had more or less cleared our minds and decided on the general outline of a scheme for which we would be prepared to work."[105]

Cadogan was in favour of Sargent's proposal, observing that it was "a good way to begin," and "if Lord Hankey would chair, there would already be a promise of success." Leeper however did not share Cadogan's optimism, and thought that the study would be carried out more effectively by Chatham House. In a memorandum of 19 March—requested by Halifax himself before taking a final decision—Leeper observed that the scholars who gravitated around Chatham House were better equipped than civil servants to point out "the broader aspects of the problem." The fundamental question was not just "co-operation between Governments," which however easy in war-time, could not endure in peace-time. It was necessary to start closer cultural relations between the two countries, and this could be favoured by the creation of a "Cultural Committee," possibly chaired by Lord Lloyd, and composed of Chatham House's members. This Committee could have backed up Hankey's political-administrative one. "Lord Lloyd and Lord Hankey would," Leeper concluded, "work well together."[106]

Halifax certainly did not want to exclude Chatham House from playing an active part in the study of the project of union and supported the proposal by Leeper. Sargent and Cadogan, however, who did not like the increasing interference of Chatham House in the Foreign Office, strongly resented it. A compromise was at last reached, with the creation of two committees which had to cooperate. "The only danger I foresee," Sargent wrote to Halifax on March 21, "is that there may be a certain overlapping between Chatham House and the Ministry of Information, who have been charged with publicising the idea of Anglo-French union." Writing to Chamberlain on the 25 March, Halifax suggested that the Ministry of

---

[105] FOP, FO371/24298, 134921, 179-80. On the role played by the BBC during the war, see Gerd Horten, *Radio Goes to War: The Cultural Politics of Propaganda during World War II* (Berckley, CA: University of California Press, 2002).
[106] FOP, FO371/24298, 134921, 181-2.

Information should be instructed to propagate the idea of a close Anglo-French collaboration after the war, that the two committees proposed by Sargent and Leeper be constituted as soon as possible, and that as a symbolic gesture that the teaching in both countries of the language, literature and history of the other be compulsory.[107]

Halifax, speaking on April 10 in London dealt directly with the question, remarking that the war was "part of the eternal struggle between right and wrong," and that French and British people were fighting not just for their own countries but for "all States that love liberty." In the realization of this historical task, France and Great Britain were "combining certain essential attributes of their individual sovereignty for the common good of both." The inspiring idea which animated the process under way was the federal one:

> I suggest to you that the conception behind all this movement is one which even the noted idealism of French statesmen has not yet been able to surpass. Many, many years ago, centuries ago, the grand design of Sully was indeed a design. M. Briand, I think, perhaps followed in late years the best plan for European Federation. We have neither a design nor a plan, but we have between our two nations a living union. Here, I think and trust, may be found the solid foundation built into the rock, and not built upon sand, from which may spring true collective security. I hope that others like-minded with France and with ourselves upon the fundamental elements of European life will be led to join what is becoming a close partnership for mutual benefit and mutual protection.[108]

Commenting on the Foreign Minister's pronouncement, Sargent wrote on April 14 to Oliver Harvey: "in fact it may be said that no minister opens his mouth now without making some allusion to the subject." The moment had come in which "a hint might be dropped to the French that a little bit of reciprocity might not come amiss," namely to cordially invite the French ministers to "mention this topic in their speeches." In Great Britain they were doing much to prepare the advent of the union:

---

[107] FOP, FO371/24298, 134921, 190-1. Writing to Lord Perth, on 14 March, when Halifax had not yet made up his mind about the possible involvement of Chatham House, partially evacuated to Balliol College, Oxford, Sargent commented: "Lord Halifax has thrown out the idea that the denizens of Balliol College…might be asked to undertake this task. I am not sure whether these are quite the right people for the job," *ibidem*, 177.

[108] Lord Halifax, *Speeches on Foreign Policy* (Oxford: Oxford University Press, 1940), 102.

a) by the Ministry of Information, with a view to educating the British
public and accustoming them to the idea of post-war Anglo-French union;
b) by the professors at Chatham House, who are studying the matter from
a loftier and broader angle and have already produced some very useful
suggestions; and c) by a small committee to be presided over by Lord
Hankey, which is going to examine the matter from the narrow but
eminently practical point of view of administration and procedure.[109]

Thus falling squarely on Hankey—who, as Lloyd George's Cabinet
Secretary in the course of the Paris Peace Conference of 1919 had
distinguished himself for manifest anti-French feelings—was the
responsibility to grasp or let go a historic opportunity that would never be
presented again on those terms!

However, in the space of a few months the federal option became
central to the debate on the conduct of war and the post-war order. The
objective that Kimber, Ransome and Rawnsley meant to achieve in a
couple of months when they created the Federal Union had been achieved
in little more than a year. The ascending popular consent for the federation
put the British Government in a condition to be able to choose between the
traditional policy of a defensive alliance, and a revolutionary policy of
pulling Anglo-French national sovereignty within the scheme of an ever
closer economic and political union.

VII. *The Hankey Committee*

On 30 April the "Inter-Departmental Committee for post-war Anglo-French
Collaboration" assembled under the chairmanship of Lord Hankey,
including Sargent—as the representative of the Foreign Office—T. K.
Bewley—as a substitute for S. D. Waley, the representative of the
Treasury—Clement Jones, H. L. Hopkinson—member of the Anglo-French
Liaison Section—and F. K. Roberts as Secretary. On the agenda there was
the discussion of the text of the "Act of Perpetual Association between
Great Britain and France," prepared by Zimmern, Toynbee and Leeper.
The document was however dismissed as too academic, and too alien from
the dry style of the official mind, with which ministerial civil servants
were acquainted. The "professors at Chatham House" had done a good
job, but being outside diplomatic practice they could not offer a
contribution which surmounted the limits of the abstract. Hankey was
pleased with the term "Association," but he did not like the fact that it was
open to other countries, which would certainly weaken it, even though at

---

[109] FOP, FO371/24298, 134921, 121.

the end of the war it should become the centre of gravity of European relations, based on the principle of alliances, and therefore on the old policy of the balance of power.[110]

Outlining the view of the Foreign Office, Sargent observed that at the end of the war France would claim territorial acquisitions, on the basis of her security particularly in Rhineland. If Great Britain "granted this French demand and then parted company with France as after the last war," Sargent observed, "there would inevitably be a German desire for revenge and a further war within a few years." It was necessary to offer the French people an alternative to the return to the old power politics and "the only possible alternative seemed to be a continuous association between Great Britain and France, which would set a bloc of 85 million people in Western Europe capable of withstanding German pressure and of acting as a single factor in post-war European politics." This solution of the German question would also have saved France from Communism, which was likely to spread at the end of the war.[111]

Hopkinson observed that the Dominions had been excluded by the proposed Association, and that their governments showed themselves to be "a little suspicious" about the links actually existing between Great Britain and France. It would be very difficult to "reconcile closer and permanent economic association with the Ottawa agreements," because the Anglo-French Union would have become even closer to that existing among the Commonwealth's countries. Hankey then observed that that Association was not so much based "upon feelings of sympathy between the two peoples," but upon the common fear of Germany, just as the Austro-Hungarian double monarchy was based upon the common fear of the Slavs. It was therefore necessary to produce a detailed study of the Austro-Hungarian and Swiss constitutional systems, and this task was finally given to the "professors of Chatham House."[112]

Entering into the context of the six articles of the Association, they saw as undesirable "a common foreign policy" because both countries had "a sovereign parliament which might be expected to resume a more active control of policy in peace conditions." It seemed necessary to have some kind of co-ordination of the foreign policies of the two countries, which in the last resort had to act freely. In peace time the Supreme War Council could have become a Supreme Council, and it would have dealt with the

---

[110] FOP, FO371/124299, 134921, 325-6. By Lord Hankey, see: *Diplomacy By Conference: Studies In Public Affairs 1920-1946* (London: Ernest Benn, 1946); id., *Politics Trials and Errors* (London: Henry Regnery, 1950).

[111] FOP, FO371/124299, 134921, 326-8.

[112] FOP, FO371/124299, 134921, 325-6.

co-ordination not only of foreign policy, but also of military, economic and financial policies, thus effectively performing the role of a "court of appeal" for all Anglo-French questions.[113]

It would not have been necessary to create—as the Act proposed—a common Foreign Office and Diplomatic Service, but the two ministries and the diplomatic staff of the two countries would have worked— although without explaining how—"in the closest harmony." Anglo-French co-operation would not limit itself to Europe, but should "necessarily cover the whole world." Regarding military policy, the co-operation would have continued on the basis of the discussion of common problems, which would have been presented to the two High Commands for decisions:

> in peace time there would not be the same need for quick decisions necessitating frequent personal meetings between the respective chiefs of staff, and the Allied Military Committee would be in a position to examine thoroughly the various military problems.[114]

Hankey then suggested the appointment of two sub-committees, "the first dealing with the questions of planning and intelligence and the second with questions of supply." Regarding monetary union, Bewley observed that lacking a "universally accepted gold standard," it was "infinitely" difficult to create a common currency, a fixed exchange rate between the pound and the franc and, in any case, it was the duty of the Bank of England and not of Chatham House to deal with the question. It was also premature to discuss the question of a custom union between the two countries, as the Board of Trade was already dealing with the question. It was therefore decided to adjourn the discussion to May 7, on the basis of more "in depth" documents.[115]

---

[113] *Ibidem.*

[114] *Ibidem.* On Anglo-French military collaboration in the 1930s, see: A. P. Adamthwaite, *France and the Coming of the Second World War, 1936-1939* (London: Routledge, 1977); Robert J. Young, "La Guerre de Longue Durée: Some Reflections on French Strategy and Diplomacy in the 1930s," in *General Staffs and Diplomacy before the Second World War* (London: Croom Helm, 1978); id., *In Command of France: French Foreign and Defence Policy, 1933-1940*, (Cambridge: Harvard University Press, 1978); A. Preston, *General Staffs and Diplomacy before the Second World War* (London: Croom Helm, 1978); Robert Boyce, *French Foreign and Defence Policy, 1918-1940: The Decline and Fall of a Great Power* (London: Routledge, 1998).

[115] FOP, FO371/124299, 134921, 328-30. On Anglo-French financial and monetary collaboration since Versailles, see: Arthur Turner, "Anglo-French Financial Relations in the 1920s", *European History Quarterly*, 26, 1, (1996): 31-55; Lars S. Skalnes, "Grand Strategy and Foreign Economic Policy: British Grand

The theme of custom union was dealt with in the memorandum "Implications of the Proposed 'Act of Association' between the United Kingdom and France with Particular Reference to a Custom Union" by Sir Arnold Overton, senior official at the Ministry of Trade. Written in the sober style of the civil servant, the memorandum presented the problems and implications of a full custom union between the two countries, which until then had followed independent as well as competitive policies of commercial expansion. The solutions proposed to the various questions studied were extremely interesting—such as the clause of the most favourite nation, which clearly had a more political than economic nature, meant to raise strategic considerations—and to show a sincere effort to marry pragmatism and idealism.[116]

The study of the Austro-Hungarian Compromise (*Ausgleich*) of 1867, which was the constitutional system that held the fate of the Double Monarchy until 1918, enabled Chatham House, and in particular the entourage of Zimmern, to deepen and strengthen the thesis espoused in the commentary to the "Act of Association." It is well-known that the compromise of 1867 was a consequence of the defeat by Prussia of Franz-Joseph's Austria, who was thus forced to acknowledge Hungary as a separate sovereignty. Two single governments were formed, responsible to two parliaments, united by some common bodies and by the loyalty to a common sovereign, at the same time King of Hungary and Emperor of Austria, commander-in-chief of the common army and navy. They had three common ministers—for foreign affairs, war and finance—responsible to the two delegations, which were parliamentary bodies composed of sixty members who represented the national parliaments. There was no common citizenship.[117]

Strategy in the 1930s," *World Politics*, 50, 4, (1998): 582-616; Kenneth Moure, *The Gold Standard Illusion: France, the Bank of France, and the International Gold Standard, 1914-1939* (New York: Oxford University Press, 2002).

[116] FOP, FO371/2300, 134992, 170-4.

[117] FOP, FO371/2300, 134992, 196-200. On the character and crisis of the Austro-Hungarian Empire, see: John W. Mason, *Dissolution of the Austro-Hungarian Empire, 1867-1918* (Harlow: Longman, 1986); Alan Sked, *The Decline and Fall of the Habsburg Empire, 1815-1918* (Harlow: Longman, 2001); Diarmuid Jeffreys, *The Austro-Hungarian Empire* (London: New Holland Publishers, 2007); Laurence Cole and Daniel L. Unowsky eds., *The Limits of Loyalty: Imperial Symbolism, Popular Allegiances and State Patriotism in the Late Habsburg Monarchy* (Oxford: Berghahn Books, 2007). On centrifugal forces represented by ethnic nationalism in the downfall of empires, see: Aviel Roshwald, *Ethnic Nationalism and the Fall of Empires: Central Europe, the Middle East and Russia, 1914-1923* (London: Routledge, 2000).

The indications which the Compromise of 1867 offered in relation to the Anglo-French collaboration were, according to the memorandum, primarily the necessity for continuous revisions of the original agreement to adapt it to the changed situations which it had to face and manage. The revisions had to be recurrent and compulsory, without the chance of a possible failure in reaching agreement. The difficulty in conducting negotiations between two independent States could be partially overcome by delegating negotiations on specific questions to competent bodies. Secondly, it appeared necessary to base the Anglo-French agreement "on the full responsibility of the joint ministers to some single authority, which could not be the head of either State and must presumably be of a representative character," namely a common Parliament.[118]

There was therefore the question of nationality, which indicated on one hand that it was possible for two States to reach a remarkable degree of co-operation without a common citizenship, and on the other that it was necessary to avoid, particularly concerning the question of British and French colonies, "those pitfalls of the compromise which made it impossible to regard questions of nationalities as stretching across the frontier between Austria and Hungary." The compromise of 1867 was, therefore, according to Chatham House, a missed federation, a political construction *sui generis*, a half-way house between a federation and a confederation, with a unique historical and ethnic character, which, while not hindering, could offer little help to the unification of two countries with great traditions and a great common destiny.[119]

The second meeting of the Hankey Committee took place on May 21, just at the vigil of the rout of Dunkirk—in the presence of Hankey himself, Sargent, Overton, Bewley, Jones, Hopkinson, and Roberts—and it was principally devoted to the discussion of the memorandum by Overton, showing a general opinion contrary to a full custom union between the two countries. In particular, it was noted that the principal difficulty in its realisation was the question of "financial sovereignty." The French seemed keener than the British to sacrifice their sovereignty in economic matters since they had always feared the competition of British industries, while as for agriculture, the view was just the opposite.[120]

---

[118] FOP, FO371/2300, 134992, 200-5.

[119] *Ibidem.* On trade relations within the Habsburg monarchy, see John Komlos, *The Habsburg Monarchy as a Customs Union: Economic Development in Austria-Hungary in the Nineteenth Century* (Princeton: Princeton University Press, 1983).

[120] FOP, FO371/2300, 134992, 207-8. On the Dunkirk's rout, see: Walter Lord, *Le miracle de Dunkerque, 4 juin 1940* (Paris: Robert Laffont, 1999); W. I. R. Gardner, *The Evacuation from Dunkirk: 'Operation Dynamo', 26 May-4 June*

According to Sargent the approach to the question should be gradual, even if it appeared much easier to adopt full custom union immediately, rather than wait and renegotiate the Ottawa agreements with the Dominions. British commercial policy had been always based on the principle that in order to "receive, in foreign countries, at least as favourable treatment as any other country...it was...essential to give reciprocity," except for the clause of Imperial preference. Great Britain had, in fact, been able to avoid participating in the general policy of the most favourite nation, and cut short the complaints regarding the Imperial preference, declaring that the Dominions were not foreign countries. If France was given preferential treatment, putting her in the same rank as the Dominions, the British feared they would have to denounce the existing commercial agreements and "risk the unfavourable consequences."[121]

In spite of the fact that two-thirds of British trade was carried out with non-European countries, France—Overton observed—had, by then, a privileged position compared with other foreign countries, a fact that had already raised protest from the United States. At the outbreak of war, Great Britain had, in fact, introduced restrictions on the import of luxury goods in order to preserve the exchange means, and this had particularly damaged France. With the monetary agreements of December it was finally agreed to abolish the exchange rate mechanism with France, and subsequently France was granted a return to the pre-war standard of exports towards Great Britain, while British exports towards France were strongly reduced by the tariffs imposed on imports.[122]

1940 (London: Routledge, 2000). On customs unions, see the study by James Meade, *The Theory of Customs Unions* (Westport, CT: Greenwood Press, 1980).

[121] FOP, FO371/2300, 134992, 207-8. On imperial preference, see: Alfred Gollin, *Balfour's Burden: Arthur Balfour & Imperial Preference* (Salt Lake City, UT: Garden City Press, 1965); Barry Eichengreen, *Golden Fetters: The Gold Standard and the Great Depression, 1919-1939* (New York: Oxford University Press, 1996); E. H. Carr, *The Twenty Years' Crisis 1919-1939: An Introduction to the Study of International Relations*, ed. Mike Cox (New York: Palgrave Macmillan, 2001); L. J. Butler, *Britain and Empire: Adjusting to a Post-Imperial World* (New York: I. B. Tauris, 2002); Robert Johnson, *British Imperialism* (New York: Palgrave Macmillan, 2003). On Anglo-French trade relations, see: Arvind Panagariya, *Regionalism in Trade Policy* (London: World Scientific Publishing, 1999); John V. C. Nye, *War, Wine, and Taxes: The Political Economy of Anglo-French Trade, 1689-1900* (Princeton: Princeton University Press, 2007). On the history of monetary unions, see John F. Chown, *A History of Monetary Unions* (London: Routledge, 2003).

[122] FOP, FO371/2300, 134992, 208-11.

This situation was however linked with the war emergency, and it should have returned to "normality" at the end of the war. However, it seemed impossible—the Committee convened—to realise a full custom union without creating a monetary union. This in turn would have shown the necessity of a common Government, since it would have requested a common policy of salaries, industry, and common measures regarding inflation and, therefore, a limitation of sovereignty. Hankey asserted to be "entirely opposed to giving up sovereignty to the French." The Committee should however be able—according to Hankey—to create a "machinery of Anglo-French co-ordination at least as close, and possibly closer, than that with the Dominions." Cutting off any discussion on the question of the "merging of sovereignty," Hankey declared that the British could go further in undertaking to "develop the closest possible economic and financial co-operation, and leave it to whatever common organ was set up to interpret these in practice."[123]

This was the last meeting of the Committee, not only because in June the war rendered "the whole question rather academic," but also because its inspirer, Sargent, was not happy about its outcomes, as by then it had become manifest that Hankey had no intention of engaging the Committee in the draft of a "full-fledged Anglo-French Constitution." The question of Anglo-French Union was not, according to Sargent, "merely to urge the necessity of the two peoples linking their fortunes during the war," because that was not enough. The Hankey Committee—Sargent avowed to Lord Perth on May 20—clearly failed to perform "what we had originally contemplated."[124]

Unless the Foreign Office was able to produce a cut-and-dried scheme of post-war unity, it was manifestly impossible to do all that was possible

---

[123] *Ibidem.*
[124] FOP, FO371/24298, 134921, 171-3. For a discussion of the military time-table which brought the downfall of France, see: Guy Chapman, *Why France Fell: The Defeat of the French Army in 1940* (New York: Holt, Rinehart and Winston, 1969); Michel Henri, *La Défaite de la France* (Paris: PUF, 1980); Robert A. Doughty, *The Breaking Point: Sedan and the Fall of France, 1940* (North Haven, CT: Archon Books, 1990); Nicole Jordan, *Strategy and Scapegotism: Reflections on French National Catastrophe, 1940*, in Blatt, *French Defeat of 1940*, 13-37; Stanley Hoffman, "The Trauma of 1940: A Disaster and its Traces," in Blatt, *French Defeat of 1940*, 354, 69; Ernest R. May, *Strange victory: Hitler's Conquest of France* (New York: Hill and Wang, 2000); Martin Marix Evans and Martin Marix Evans, *The Fall of France: Act with Daring: May-June 1940* (London: Osprey Publishing, 2000); Julian Jackson, *The Fall of France: The Nazi Invasion of 1940* (New York: Oxford University Press, 2004); Martin Thomas, *The French Empire at War, 1940-1945* (Manchester: Manchester University Press, 2007).

during the war to accustom public opinion here fully to the idea of Anglo-French post-war unity. The resistance of the Foreign Office to proceed on the constitutional path indicated by the professors of Chatham House, which had received country-wide popular support, blocked the whole process for a few weeks, during which Federal Union had reached the pinnacle of success, but by then the military time-table had come forcefully into operation, and it would just be a matter of time for the first attempt to create a European Union to be jeopardised.

A senior French official, Jean Monnet, nearly achieved the success missed by Chatham House, managing to deploy His Majesty's Government in support of an Act of Union between the two Allied countries. In order to be able to score so closely to the target, Monnet had to overcome the obstacle of the Foreign Office, acting on its own— without the assistance of Federal Union and other English federalists—and refer directly to Churchill, via Chamberlain.

Chatham House, however, had played an important role in linking the widespread debate on federalism to the future of Anglo-French relations. It was particularly due to the weight of Chatham House in support of that specific project that federalism was back in the political limelight in Great Britain after it had disappeared and reappeared, like a Karst river, several times in relation to the Irish and Imperial questions. The reason why it was on the agenda just for a season, is explained by considering that the geo-political content proposed—Anglo-French Union—although finding in Toynbee and Zimmern distinguished interpreters, was substantially extraneous to Chatham House's founders and explicitly opposed by Hankey.

The studies on the roles played by Lothian, Curtis, Astor and the other members of Milner's Kindergarten in the creation of Chatham House, have revealed the vital link between the federalist ideals and the historical process that led, in the long run, from the disintegration of the British Empire to the creation of the European Union, through the Atlantic Alliance policy. Inter-war Chatham House significantly contributed to offer the British political élite the cultural instruments to build what would become *Pax Atlantica,* on the basis of the experience of *Pax Britannica.* Chatham House managed to drive the transition from Imperial to post-Imperial Britain, introducing a new method of political action: the "education"—or more appropriately, as they called it, "moulding"—of public opinion avoiding any form of propaganda, and aiming for the application of "scientific methods of thought to international problems." This was the "political function" performed by Chatham House in the period between the wars, with an unprecedented success in that very peculiar British *milieu* where "small groups" can, if provided with the necessary instruments, come to exert a decisive influence on political power.[125]

---

[125] Andrea Bosco, "National Sovereignty and Peace: Lord Lothian's Federalist Thought," in *The Larger Idea*, 108-20; id., Introduction to Bosco and Navari, *Chatham House and British*, 1-12; id., "Chatham House and Federalism," in *ibidem*, 319-42; Christopher Thorne, "Chatham House, Whitehall, and Far Eastern Issues: 1941-1945," in *ibidem*, 261-97; Inderjeet Parmar, "Chatham House, the Foreign Policy Process and the Making of the Anglo-American Alliance," in *ibidem*, 299-317; Cornelia Navari, "Chatham House and the Broad Church View of British Foreign Policy," in *ibidem*, 345-72; Donald Watt, Foreword to Bosco and Navari, *Chatham House and British*, i-vii; Watt, *Personalities*, 1.

CHAPTER VI

FEDERAL UNION AND THE MAY CRISIS

In early May Federal Union's troops were organised in over two hundred sections; the movement was generally identified as the successor to the League of Nations Union; the national and local press gave a large space to its activities, and within the new Coalition Government the movement benefited from the backing of five ministers, including Churchill who, as President of the New Commonwealth Society, had already pronounced in favour of an Anglo-French "indissoluble union."[1]

Anthony Eden—Minister of War, Vice-president of the New Commonwealth Society, and President of the Federalist Parliamentary Intergroup in the House of Commons created by Coudenhove-Kalergi—had declared that Britain was not fighting to preserve the old order, but to "build a new one." Leo Amery—Minister for India—argued that although the European federation was "a distant goal," it was "feasible enough to be worth the effort." Sir Archibald Sinclair—Air Minister—had stated that the principle of the federation provided "an obvious approach" to the objective of the prevention of war. Clement Attlee—Leader of the Opposition and member of the War Cabinet—had declared that Europe "must federate or perish."[2]

---

[1] Sheila Lawlor, *Churchill and the Politics of War, 1940-1941* (Cambridge: Cambridge University Press, 1994). On Chamberlain's downfall and Churchill's appointment to Prime Minister, see: D. M. Roberts, "Clement Davies and the Fall of Neville Chamberlain, 1939-40," *Welsh History Review*, 8, 2, (1976); Graham Stewart, *Burying Caesar: The Churchill-Chamberlain Rivalry* (New York: Overlook, 2001); Olson, *Troublesome Young Men.* On the role played by Amery in Chamberlain's downfall, see William Roger Louis, *In the Name of God, Go!: Leo Amery and the British Empire in the Age of Churchill* (New York: W. W. Norton & Co, 1992). On the relations between Churchill and Chamberlain in 1940, see: David Dilks, "The Twilight War and the Fall of France: Chamberlain and Churchill in 1940," *Transactions of the Royal Historical Society*, 28, (1978): 61-86.

[2] On the relations between Sinclair and Churchill, see Ian Hunter ed., *Winston and Archie: The Letters of Sir Archibald Sinclair and Winston S. Churchill, 1915-1960*

I. *Federal Union and the recruitment of new forces*

The activities of the branches in the United Kingdom continued with renewed vigour despite military pressure absorbing, with conscription, the freshest energies. The Country had been divided into twelve regions, with two representatives each in the Council, favouring decentralization which was considered essential to effectively promote the growth of the movement. The regions were composed of groupings of branches for areas generally corresponding to the counties. New branches were offered the credit of a pound to buy the instruments of propaganda and federalist literature. The branches also had available a federalist itinerant library, and a list of official speakers, with freedom of choice.[3]

The vibrancy of the movement in one of the most difficult moments in British history is witnessed by *Federal Progress*, the monthly bulletin edited by Joad, which recorded the development of the movement. F. A. Campbell, Administrative Secretary, observed that the great success achieved by Federal Union's branches was the result of systematic personal contacts with those who seemed to have sympathy with the idea of the federation. Campbell encouraged the militants to obtain the support of the clergy, teachers and activists of local political organisations. Each branch should produce a list of at least two hundred names to approach, and it had to be a "systematic approach," differentiated on the basis of the degree of interest and possible involvement. To those who had already participated in a meeting, or required information, the militants had to send a "carefully formulated" invitation for a subsequent meeting with a personal letter. If unsuccessful, one or two members of the branch should pay a "personal visit." Each branch had to organise on a regular basis, weekly or monthly, a series of debates that were supposed to make every member feel "part of a large organisation."[4]

(London: Politico's Publishing, 2005). See also de Groot, *Liberal Crusader*. On Eden, see: V. Rothwell, *Anthony Eden: A Political Biography, 1931-1957* (Manchester: Manchester University Press, 1992); David Dutton, *Anthony Eden: A Life and Reputation* (New York: Hodder Arnold Publications, 1998).

[3] On the conscription issue, see Peter Dennis, *Decision by Default: Conscription and British Defence, 1919-1939* (Durham, NC: Duke University Press, 1972); Maurice Cowling, *The Impact of Hitler: British Politics and British Policy 1933-1940* (Cambridge: Cambridge University Press, 2005).

[4] *Federal Progress*, 1, (1940). The development of the movement took place in one of the most critical years of British history, see Malcolm Smith, *Britain and 1940: History, Myth and Popular Memory* (London: Routledge, 2001).

Towards those who did not show any interest, the militants should send a personal letter, enclosing instruments of propaganda, before they receive an invitation to attend a meeting, and a visit by members of the branch should follow. Ten members of the branch could write ten letters a week, which meant that in ten weeks it was possible to write five hundred short personal letters. The intention of the personal visit was not merely "to stand on the front steps," but to talk to the person they visited "for more than an hour, to cause their authentic reaction" to the federalist idea, and answer their questions. Only with "such a patient method" would their resistance be won at last. Although it appeared "tedious and difficult work," the results seemed to show that with an approach of this kind, based on a list compiled with care, "about fifty per cent of the people contacted are enrolled in the section."[5]

The monthly newsletter displayed records of the activities of the branches, by drawing the picture of a very lively movement. Among the speakers, in hundreds of public meetings across the country, there were the names of the Bishop of Chichester—Chairman of the Sussex "Local Committee"—Curry, Olaf Stapledon, Philip Edwards, Wootton, Robbins, Denis Saurat, Jennings, Mackay, Beveridge, Byron, Harold Nicolson, Lord Meston—President of the Liberal Party—the Labour MPs Sir Richard Acland, Sir Thomas Drummond Shiels, and John Strachey.[6]

In Mid Essex and South Wales the movement was under the leadership of three architects, W. W. Wood, Alwyn Lloyd and H. C. Lander. In Birmingham, at the instigation of Henry Usborne, members were

---

[5] *Federal Progress*, 1: 6.

[6] Lord James Scorgie Meston (1865-1943) was Governor of the United Provinces in India from 1912 to 1918; President of the Aberdeen University from 1928 to 1943; and President of the Liberal Party from 1936 to 1943. On Acland, founder of the movement of radical Left, Common Wealth, see: Randall Bennett Woods, *A Changing of the Guard: Anglo-American Relations, 1941-1946* (Chapel Hill, NC: University of North Carolina Press, 1990), 193-4; Mark Mazower, *Dark Continent: Europe's Twentieth Century* (New York: Vintage, 2000), 187-8; Arthur Marwick, *A History of the Modern British Isles, 1914-1999: Circumstances, Events and Outcomes* (Oxford: Wiley-Blackwell, 2000), 157-8; Frederick A. Hayek, *The Road to Serfdom* (London: Routledge, 2006), 217-8. On Drummond Shiels, Under-secretary for India, see: Woolf, *Downhill All the Way*, 233-4; Rory Miller, *Divided Against Zion: Anti-Zionist Opposition to the Creation of a Jewish State in Palestine, 1945-1948* (London: Routledge, 2000), 169-70; Roger Chickering and Stig Forster, *The Shadows of Total War: Europe, East Asia, and the United States, 1919-1939* (Cambridge: Cambridge University Press, 2003), 261-2. On Strachey see: Hugh Thomas, *John Strachey* (London: Methuen, 1973); Noel W. Thompson, *John Strachey* (New York: Palgrave Macmillan, 1993).

multiplying and, as a form of self-financing, the operetta Merrie England by Edward German was staged outdoors—thanks to the mercy of the weather and the Tatton Amateur Operetta Company. The secretaries of the forty-nine London branches were organising a "summer campaign" for the London area, which would be crowned with a "federalist week" from 17 to 23 July, aiming to double the number of militants.[7]

---

[7] At the beginning of June 1940 the number of branches was 225, subdivided in twelve regions and 39 areas. The region of Northern Ireland had a single branch in Belfast. In Scotland there were branches in Edinburgh, Aberdeen, Dumfries, Glasgow and Kilmarnock. In Wales there were 9 branches: Bangor, Cardiff, Carmarthen, Merthyr Tydfil, Penarth, Pontypridd, Prestatyn, Rhymney and Ystradgynlais. The Northern Counties were subdivided into three areas: Cumberland, with branches in Carlisle, Egremont, Frizington and Keswick; Durham with just a city branch; Northumberland with branches in Blyth and Newcastle. The North-western Counties were subdivided into four areas: Cheshire with branches in Bebington, Birkenhead, Bramhall-Cheadlehulme, Congleton, Heswall, Macclesfield and Wilmslow; Lancashire with branches in Ashton, Blackburn, Bolton, Burnley, Liverpool (3 city branches), Lostock, Manchester (2 city branches), Rochdale and Wigan; Westland with a branch in Grasmere; Yorkshire with branches in Bridington, Doncaster, Earby, Halifax, Huddersfield, Hull, Leeds, Sheffield, and Teesside. The Midlands were subdivided into 5 areas: Herefordshire with a branch in Pembridge; a branch in Shropshire; Staffordshire with branches in Lichfield, Newcastle, Stoke-on-Trent, Tettenhall, Walsall, Wednesbury and Wolverhampton; Warwickshire with branches in Birmingham, Barnt Green, Bourneville, Earlswood, Hallgreen, Harborne, Knowle, Langley Green, Selly Oak, Shirley, Small Heath, Warley Woods, Wylde Green, Coventry, Leamington, Rugby and Studley; Worcestershire with branches in Malvern, Stoke Prior and Worcester. The East Midlands were organised in 6 areas with a branch each in: Derbyshire, Lincolnshire (in Lincoln), Northamptonshire (in Kettering), Rutlandshire (in Rutland), Leicestershire and Nottinghamshire (in Nottingham). The Eastern Counties were subdivided into 5 areas: with just one branch in both Suffolk (in Felixstowe) and Huntingdonshire; and two branches in Cambridge and Bedfordshire (in Bedford and Dunstable). The South-west was organised in 5 areas: just one branch in Cornwall (in Launceston) and Gloucestershire (in Bristol); Devon branches in Exeter, Plymouth, Torbay and Totnes; Dorset branches in Beaminster, Marnhull and Milborne Port-Sherborne; and Somerset branches in Bath, Flax Bourton, Glastonbury, Taunton, Weston-super-Mare and Yeovil. The Southern Countries were subdivided into 4 areas: Berkshire with branches in Abingdon, Maidenhead, Reading and Windsor; Hampshire with branches in Bournemouth, Southsea and Winchester; Oxfordshire with branches in Bampton, Bletchington, Clanfield, Coombe, Oxford (a city and a University branch), Sibford and Shipton-under-Wychwood; and Wiltshire with a branch in Salisbury. The Home Counties were subdivided into 6 areas: Buckinghamshire with a branch in Speen; Essex with branches in Chelmsford, Colchester, Saffron Walden,

To criticisms of inefficiency that poured from time to time on the headquarters, Philip Edwards, Head of Recruitment, replied that the efficiency was "difficult to achieve by a youth movement" in constant growth, in which "we are all to some extent pioneers." To the remarks of those who claimed that Federal Union in more than a year had not yet become a "mass movement," Edwards replied that it was "undeniably extending its influence." As taught by Abraham Lincoln, they had to learn to wait for the "historic moment," catch it, and make history. "The time will come," Edward reassured the militants, "when we will be able to bring the country into the federation." In 1785 Hamilton, Madison and Jay started, without much clamour, the federalist movement in thirteen States, and in 1787 the United States of America were created. The federal goal "can be achieved," according to Edwards, "in the very near future."[8]

A tangible sign of the keen interest with which the national press looked to Federal Union is offered by *The Times Literary Supplement*, which on 25 May devoted two full pages to the federalist debate in the country. Taking up the slogan that Beveridge had launched when he urged the choice between "utopia and hell," *The Times* acknowledged that after the long and sinister doldrums of the first eight months of war, many authors, considered mostly as "very practical politicians and economists, began to develop constitutions for Utopia."

The opposition to the federalist project did not come from "reactionaries and patriots, but from Marxists." Pritt gave expression to that opposition, which instead of the organisation of the peace, favoured social revolution, the overthrow of capitalism, and the "abolition of the

---

Westcliff-on-Sea; Hertfordshire with branches in Bishop's Stortford, Hampstead, St Albans, Welwyn-Digswell and Welwyn Garden City; Kent with branches in Canterbury, Gillingham, Herne Bay, Longfield, Maidstone, Sevenoaks, and Tunbridge Wells; Surrey with branches in Dorking, Godalming, Haslemere, Oxted, Reigate-Redhill and Weybridge; Sussex with branches in Bexhill, Brighton-Howe, Chichester, Cuckfield, Ditchling, Horsham, Midhurst, Newhaven-Piddinghoe, St. Leonards-on-Sea and Seaford. Greater London was subdivided into 49 branches: Acton, Barnes, Beckenham, Bethnal Green, Bexley Heath, Chelsea, Chingford, Crouch End, Dulwich, Ealing, East Ham, Esher, Finchley, Forest Hill, Golders Green, Hammersmith, Hampstead, Highgate, Holborn, Hounslow, Kensington North, Kensington South, Kingstone, Loughton, Mill Hill, Moorgate, New Barnet, New Cross Gate, North Harrow, Norwood, Ockley, Old Coulsden, Peckham, Putney, Paddington, St. Marylebone, St. Pancras, Southgate, South Place Ethical Society, Streatham, Twickenham, Wallington, Westminster Abbey, Westminster-Dolphin Squ., Westminster-St. George, Wimbledon, Woodford Green and Wood Green.

[8] *Federal Progress*, 1: 3.

profit factor." The facts, however, had already demonstrated the groundlessness of the Marxist interpretation of the war, and proved, on the contrary, the soundness of the federalist approach, even though it was destined to remain valid for a long time only in theory, since the political conditions for federation still did not seem ripe. Any new international mechanism created at the end of the war, had to be "specifically structured to promote the growth of such loyalty," not simple political consent to a pact, but "a religious feeling of the same degree of intensity as national patriotism." The failure of the League of Nations was due to the fact that it did not require the loyalty of the common citizen who, at the time of trial, felt that his loyalty to his country lay "on a higher spiritual level rather than his obligations to the League." Curtis had expounded this theory in *Civitas Dei*, "the true source of the Federal Union movement," insisting that "political idealism" had to "become a religion."

The federalist debate received a major boost from the publication of *Union Now*, but the Streitian project had been "tacitly shelved by all the English federalists," committed to seek common elements not between States that were already natural allies, but among those States that threatened war or had actually caused it. The federalist project aimed essentially at restoring the unity of Christianity, which had been destroyed by the acceptance and the consolidation of the nation-State, which the federalists precisely wanted to abolish. The "supreme difficulty" in that enterprise lay exactly in this, because it meant "to overturn the fundamental course of political history" that had "developed with increasing force since the Reformation."

The old borders were "always there below the flood" and would re-surface as soon as the waters withdrew within "the old banks." The ideas of the federalists were essentially medieval, because medieval European society had many of the elements on which they relied. It did not virtually know the concept of sovereignty, and was instead based on that of fundamental law. It was permeated by the idea of various authorities: the lord, corporation, king, emperor, and Church, each entitled to demand the individual's obedience in certain aspects of life, but with no standing to demand absolute loyalty. The clergy had "international officials of all nationalities, formed by an educational system based on...a European University, that of Paris."[9]

---

[9] *The Times Literay Supplement*, 25 May, 1940.

II. *Federal Union in the face of internal difficulties*

On May 25, the same day that *The Times* exposed the federalist project to
the general public, the Executive Committee of Federal Union met in
Streatley-on-Thames; those present were Kimber, Ransome, McAllister,
Campbell, Edwards, Wootton, Joad, Jennings, Gray, Gillett, Fox, and
Curry. After a long discussion on the relationship between the movement
and the political parties, in which the thesis of autonomy prevailed, and on
the inter-party role of Federal Union, it was decided to intensify federalist
propaganda in the electoral constituencies, in order to secure the
designation, at any General Election before the peace conference, of a
parliamentary majority in favour of the federalist project. In particular, it
was decided to establish "informal contacts" with a number of prominent
ministers; to form a "Parliamentary Committee" made up of members of
both Houses; and to intensify propaganda towards trade unions and among
the armed forces.

As for the relationships of the movement with other organisations
interested in promoting a specific post-war order, such as the League of
Nations Union, Pan-Europa, and Political and Economic Planning, it was
decided that the best level of co-operation was at the local level, where the
branches were able to organise workshops and other activities aimed at
affirming the soundness of the federalist thesis. The branches would also
have to launch the recruitment of new militants, favouring the method of
"personal contacts" rather than that of public meetings and large-scale
propaganda. For the central office it seemed conversely "impossible to
make progress towards a common policy," because each organisation had
been formed "with different objectives." In particular, the New
Commonwealth Society should certainly have welcomed the opening to
Federal Union by Lord Davies, who had recently published *A Federated
Europe*, but they also had to severely oppose his willingness to accept
something that was not a true federation.[10]

Intervening in the newsletter, Kimber warned that Davies's volume
could "lead to a confusion of ideas among federalists." He considered
unfounded the Society's claim to label itself as "a federalist organisation"
for the simple fact that "its ultimate goal" was the federation. The
federalists could not consider as federalist a "design aimed to strengthen
the League of Nations with a Court of Justice." Recognising that the
League of Nations had been ineffective because it "was a league of

---

[10] *JP.* On Political and Economic Planning, see *Fifty Years of Political &
Economic Planning: Looking Forward, 1931-1981* (London: Heinemann, 1981).

governments and not a union of peoples," and that there was not "a common citizenship able to command the loyalty of the citizens," Davies suggested, as a remedy, the direct elections of the League's Assembly members, which would take control of foreign policy, an international police force, and "the right to collect taxes." Davies had, according to Kimber, got very much closer to Federal Union, but had not yet completed his conversion.

Controversially Kimber observed that "with his Court of Justice, which no one has ever understood," Davies already gave great headaches "to many jurists and politicians." Davies did not recognise the centrality of the Constitution and Parliament, which commanded the loyalty of the citizens, attributing it conversely to the courts and the police force. But it was a mistake to grant to the States the same treatment reserved to individuals within the State. The League's experience taught that the State could not be brought before a court of justice, and possibly punished with economic or military sanctions by a police force. The time to enforce the law towards the States, Kimber observed, was over. Law could be enforced only through war or economic sanctions. In both cases, the entire population of the State which violated the law was mobilised in support of its own government whether it agreed or disagreed with its policy, since national honour was at stake.[11]

Kimber advanced a reversal of perspective. It was no longer a question of the repression of the aggressors, but of conceiving "positive action by the federal Parliament," as an instrument to remove the causes of the conflict. Justice had certainly to be enforced by force, but if the federation was based "on the idea of repression," it would fail. In his book Davies also confused the concepts of federation and confederation, and did not take a firm position on the post-war order which the world needed. The federalists knew "what they wanted," and were not "willing to compromise" on the purposes for which they were fighting: "an international Government, accountable to the peoples of several countries, in the conduct of their common affairs and for relations with the rest of the world."

Examining the political project of Pan-Europa, Kimber was even more uncompromising. Judging it as a "new nationalism," based on the concept of the civilizing mission of the white race, and that of Europe as a "community of destiny and life," Kimber pointed out that such a project would certainly have resulted in "competition and hostility by other racial blocks." He also opposed Coudenhove-Kalergi's thesis according to which

---

[11] *Federal Union News*, 37.

it was not possible to achieve a "full federation at once," and concluded
that free peoples of the world were then "disunited and disheartened,"
since for many years they had lacked secure and daring leadership, were
losing faith in democracy, and thought that, after all, the totalitarian
system was "much more effective." "If we continue to patch up any
difficulties that emerge," Kimber argued, "without a large and comprehensive
project," it would be impossible to regain confidence in ourselves, and "a
centre of loyalty on which to base our European patriotism" would be
lost.[12]

Kimber proudly referred the readers to the fact that the newsletter had
long since crossed the seas, and had done much to bring about a movement
in South Africa for the union of democracies. It even reached Argentina,
where Easton Garrett—a retired engineer—in July 1939 had received from
a Scottish friend newspaper clippings of *Union Now,* and immediately
founded a branch. The French and Spanish translations of *The Ending of
Armageddon* by Lothian and *Union Now* had much contributed to the
spread of federalist ideas in Argentina, but it was only in January 1940 that
the movement had gained momentum, thanks mainly to the mission of
Marvin Sutton, a British militant in Buenos Aires.

A federalist movement supporting the Streitian project was even
established in Canada. However, as a Commonwealth member engaged in
the war against Nazi aggression, Canada profoundly differed from the
United States, which was still isolationist. The Atlantic idea was supported
there with a different spirit than in its place of origin, and the draft
Constitution proposed by Streit met strong criticism among federalists
themselves, as it gave the United States a hegemonic role within the
Union. The Canadians were still ready—L. W. Makovski observed in
Federal Union News on 13 May—to recognise the need for the federal
government for the world. In Australia the radio devoted a half-hour
weekly program to federalist debate in the United Kingdom.[13]

Despite the rapid growth, Federal Union did not enjoy a healthy
financial condition. The situation was serious because it seemed more and
more difficult to make the budget break even in the short term, without
progressive and drastic spending cuts. At the proposal of the Honorary
Secretary, Gillett, it was decided to close down the Department of Public
Relations, and therefore dismiss McAllister and his secretary Lumsden.
Gillett—who had been placed in that position by Kimber's opponents as a

---

[12] *Ibidem.*
[13] *Ibidem.* On Canada at war, see W. A. B. Douglas and Brereton Greenhouse, *Out
of the Shadows: Canada in the Second World War* (Toronto: Dundurn Press,
1995).

counterweight element—resigned too. This was a complete victory for Kimber—who saw his position within the Council significantly strengthened—but, as facts would soon prove, it was a short-lived victory, because in the two battles to defend his secretaryship Kimber had eroded his authority within the Council, particularly due to the inaccurate management of finance. The road had been virtually opened for Kimber's opponents to launch the last successful attack, a few weeks later. It was at that session of the Executive Committee that approval was given for the co-option within the Council and the Executive Committee of Ronald Mackay, Kimber's successor.[14]

The extraordinary deployment of forces had a price that the movement was not able to stand through self-financing. To cope with the severe financial crisis into which the movement had fallen, the Executive decided to make drastic cuts in personnel costs, and ask each member, for "the first time...in the history of the movement," for the contribution of one pound, which would have meant a potential income from twelve to fifteen thousand pounds. If in the past the leaders of the movement "used to spend the money much earlier", now they had to "find the money first" to have them.

From June 1 the newsletter changed format, by taking a more conventional look. The Executive Committee of 5 June was almost entirely devoted to the discussion on the future of the magazine, whose deficit also weighed heavily on the movement's finances. The idea of transforming it into a monthly and broader publication was shelved, and it was decided that it should remain an instrument of propaganda, at a dramatic moment, when the militants were called to the double pledge to defend their own country from a possible invasion, and propagate the federalist faith.[15]

---

[14] JP. Also N. Southern and T. C. Hart were admitted to the Council as representatives of Newcastle and Wales respectively, while Norman Bentwich was elected as a member of the Executive Committee.

[15] Subscribers to the newsletter numbered 1,200, guaranteeing an income of £14 per week. However the printed copies numbered 1,650 with expenditure totaling £16.50 per week. The deficit had been reduced since 26 May from £13 to £2.50 weekly, cutting down mainly on the salaries of the Editor and secretary, replaced by the same Kimber and F. A. Campbell. The costs of printing (£8.50) were equivalent to those for stationery and shipping (£8), *ibidem*.

III. *The Federal Union Research Institute*

After breaking up with Kimber, Curtis continued to help Ransome collect the necessary financial resources for the activities of the Federal Union Research Institute, which had in the meantime acquired a greater independence from the movement. Board members were Beveridge—who had made available the premises of University College, Oxford—Keeton—Director of the Institute of Research of the New Commonwealth—Kimber, Wootton, Jennings, Thomas Drummond Shiels, Harry Ross, and two distinguished scholars of the London School of Economics, von Hayek and Robbins.

Addressing the banker and Liberal MP Sir Georg Schuster on May 30, for financial help, Curtis recalled the efforts that Waldorf Astor was making through Chatham House to study the issue of the post-war order, which implied the fundamental question of whether it was possible or not to bring together sovereign States in "some form of federal union." The best way to study in advance the concrete possibility of creating a federalist world order was "for people like Beveridge, Ransome, and Ivor Jennings to continue to do their jobs," namely to produce constitutions. Curtis had direct experience of that, and then knew that the real difficulties appeared only when one dealt directly with these matters. The Federal Union Research Institute could prove to be "indispensable for researchers who are working under the supervision of Waldorf." Financial aid should however be made available only if the Institute became completely independent from the movement or Gillett—being a "member of an ancient bank of the City," and "the most valuable man of Federal Union"—succeeded in putting the movement on a "good standing." Curtis finally suggested to Schuster that he should discuss with Astor the possibility of letting the researchers of the Institute separate completely from Federal Union, to work as an auxiliary and specialised body of research under the direction of Schuster himself.[16]

Having received a negative answer from Schuster—engaged in those days in organising the evacuation from Dunkirk and the defence of the English coasts—Curtis turned for financial assistance on 6 June to "TJ", Tom Jones, former Private Secretary of Baldwin, and President of the Pilgrims Trust. "Thanks to my personal relationship with Halifax," Curtis revealed that "after this war will be considered the question of some form

---

[16] CP, 22/48-50. On the creation of the Institute and its activities, see Walter Lipgens, *Documents on the History of European Integration: Plans for European Union in Great Britain and in Exile, 1939-1949* (New York-Berlin: Walter de Gruyter, 1986), 26-155.

of federal union (which I hope will be in a very limited form) with our allies." The work to prepare a draft constitution in advance appeared therefore to Curtis "absolutely essential," and the Institute could have performed an invaluable role. Even this appeal went unheeded, and the Institute had thus to continue its activities without the injection of new funds, continuing to draw from Federal Union's precarious resources, with the consequence of a deterioration in the deficit, further weakening Kimber's position.[17]

The activities of the Institute—which was created in October 1939 as a Research Department of the movement and had become since March 1940 an independent body—had been very intense in the first eight months. It set up four Committees, dealing respectively with the economic, constitutional, colonial and psychological aspects of the federation. They met regularly at the rectory of University College, Oxford, and after June 1940 at 2 Stone Buildings, in the elegant Lincoln's Inn, London, just a few metres away from the London School of Economics. The two Committees of economists and constitutional experts had certainly produced the most interesting results, but an important contribution to the research was also offered by the Committee of colonial issues—consisting of Norman Bentwich, Sidney Caine, Curtis, Meyer Fortes, Arthur Lewis, Lucy Mair, Arnold Plant, Beveridge, Arthur Creech Jones, Drummond Shiels, Jennings, Lord Lugard, William Miller Macmillan and R. V. Vernon—with the publication of various studies, and by the "Psychological Committee" —composed of George Catlin, John Carl Flugel, de Madariaga, Ransome, Edmund Deuss, Kimber and Karl Mannheim—committed "to study the psychological motives which could be utilised to support the federal idea, and make recommendations, in the light of that study for the creation of a federal 'myth' or faith." For a brief period a Committee of study was also activated—composed of Beveridge, Hubert Ranfro Knickerbocker, James E. Meade, John Somerville, Deuss, Makay, A. Newell and Lloyd Steer—for the creation of an Anglo-American federation, but since the theme was very controversial within the

---

[17] CP, 22/124. On the evacuation from Dunkirk see Robert Jackson, *Dunkirk: The British Evacuation, 1940* (London: Rigel Publications, 2004). On Baldwin, see: Brian J. C. McKercher, *The Second Baldwin Government and the United States, 1924-1929: Attitudes and Diplomacy* (Cambridge: Cambridge University Press, 2003); Philip Williamson and Edward Baldwin ed., *Baldwin Papers: A Conservative Statesman, 1908-1947* (Cambridge: Cambridge University Press, 2004).

movement, the Institute decided not to publicise the proceedings of the
studies, which raised sharp divergences.[18]

---

[18] Federal Union Research Institute, *First Annual Report*, 9-11, published in
Ransome, *Towards the United States*, 49; Georg Schwarzenberger, *Federation and
the Colonial Problem,* in Channing-Pearce, *Federal Union. A Symposium*, 195,
206; Lord Lugard, "Federal Union and the Colonies," in Ransome, *Studies in
Federal Planning*; Norman Bentwich, "The Colonial Problem and the Federal
Solution," in *ibidem*. Sir Sydney Caine (1902-1991) was an official of the Colonial
Office and the Treasury, from 1926 to 1956; and Director of the London School of
Economics, from 1957 to 1967. Meyer Fortes (1906-1983) was Professor of Social
Anthropology at the London School of Economics, and at Oxford, from 1936 to
1950; and at Cambridge, from 1950 to 1978. Sir Arthur Lewis (1915-1991), was
Professor of Economics at the London School of Economics in 1938-1947; of
Political Economy at the University of Manchester, from 1948 to 1958; Vice-
Chancellor of the University of the West Indies, from 1959 to 1963; and Professor
of Public and International Affairs at Princeton, from 1963 to 1983. Lucy Mair
(1901-86), was Professor of Anthropology at the London School of Economics,
from 1927 to 1968. Sir Arnold Plant (1898-1978) was Professor of Economics at
the University of Cape Town, from 1924 to 1930, and at the London School of
Economics, from 1930 to 1965. Arthur Creech Jones (1891-1964) was the
Secretary of the TG Workers' Union, from 1919 to 1929; Secretary of the
Workers' Travel Association, from 1929 to 1939; Labour MP for Shipley 1935-
1950; for Wakefield, from 1954 to 1964; and Minister for the Colonies, from 1946
to 1950. Lord Frederick Lugard Dealtry (1858-1945) was High Commissioner and
Commander in Northern Nigeria, from 1900 to 1906; Governor and Commander-
in-chief of Hong Kong, from 1907 to 1912; Governor of Nigeria, from 1914 to
1919; and the British representative at the Permanent Mandates Commission of the
League of Nations, from 1922 to 1936. He was the author of the essay *Federal
Union and the Colonies* (London: Federal Union Publishing, 1941). William Miller
Macmillan (1885-1974) was Professor of African History at the University of
Witwatersrand 1917-1934; and Director of the Colonial Studies Department at the
University of St. Andrews, from 1947 to 1954. Sir George Edward Gordon Catlin
(1896-1979) was Professor of Politics at Cornell University, from 1924 to 1935; he
was active in the Fabian Society, in the English-Speaking Union, and in the
Atlantic Union Committee. John Carl Flugel (1884-1955) was Professor of
Psychology at University College, London, from 1929 to 1943. Karl Mannheim
(1893-1947) was Professor of Sociology at the University of Heidelberg, from
1926 to 1930; the University of Frankfurt, from 1930 to 1933; and the London
School of Economics, from 1933 to 1945. Hubert Renfro Knickerbodker (1898-
1949) was Berlin correspondent of the *New York Evening Post* and the
Philadelphia Public Ledger between 1928 and 1941. From 1933 he was a political
refugee in Britain. James Edward Meade (1907-1989) was Professor of Economics
at Oxford, from 1930 to 1937; an official of the Economic Department of the
League of Nations, from 1938 to 1940; Assistant and then Director of the
Economic Department of the Cabinet Office between 1940 and 1947; and

The Institute had established relations with the London School of Economics in Britain, with the Centre d'Etudes de Politique Étrangère in Paris, with the Institut Universitaire de Hautes Études Internationales in Geneva, and the Centre d'Economie Européenne in Brussels. But because of the war, "one by one...these bodies have been rendered inaccessible or have been forced, for the moment at any rate, to abandon their carefully considered plans."[19]
Ransome sadly commented:

> The descent of the Teutonic night has put out the lamps of intellectual speculation on the Continent and has made the pursuit of organised research even in Great Britain increasingly difficult...Reliance must therefore be placed in those individuals who might still be able to devote some part of their energies to a study of the future organisation of the great society of nations.[20]

The activities of the Constitutional Committee—composed of Beveridge, Curtis, Ransome, Arthur Lehman Goodhart, Joseph Perkins Chamberlain, F. Gahan, Ivor W. Jennings and Kenneth C. Wheare—developed in three conferences (11-12, 25-26 November, 1939, and 2-3 March, 1940), during which they discussed the text of a constitution prepared by Goodhart and Wheare, which then allowed Jennings to draft the Constitution of the Union. It is certainly a very valuable text, not only because it is the fruit of the work conducted jointly by some among the most prominent British constitutionalists and by Curtis himself, who had already worked on constitutional issues thirty years earlier in South Africa, but also because it aimed to be the British version of Streit's draft Constitution presented in *Union Now*, which had somehow facilitated the spread and success of the volume, but also attracted many criticisms, particularly from those who

---

Professor of Political Economy at Cambridge, from 1957 to 1968. He was awarded the Nobel Prize for economics in 1977.
[19] Ransome, *Towards*, 50. Since the 1930s, Chatham House had already established relations with the Centre d'Études de Politique Étrangère of Paris. On this regard, see Tony Chafer and Amanda Sackur, *Promoting the Colonial Idea: Propaganda and Visions of Empire in France* (New York: Palgrave Macmillan, 2002), 178-9. On the Istitut Universitaire de Hautes Études Internationales, see Paul Mantoux and Guglielmo Ferrero, *La Crise Mondiale par les Professeurs de l'Institut Universitaire de Hautes Études Internationales* (Zurig: Editions Polygraphiques, 1937); Frederick A. Hayek, *Good Money: The Standard*, ed. Stephen Kresge (Chicago, IL: University of Chicago Press, 1999), 39-40; Carlos Fuentes, *This I Believe: An A to Z of a Life* (New York: Random House, 2005), 268-9.
[20] Ransome, *Towards*, 50.

did not know or appreciate the American Constitution on which it was largely based. Jennings's draft certainly represents the most mature fruit of the British federalist culture at the constitutional level and, even today, appears to be a standard architectural construction. In its essentials, Jennings's draft expressed a federal system (including Germany, France, Britain, Ireland, Belgium, Holland, Denmark, Finland, Norway, Switzerland, Sweden, Luxembourg, the Dominions and the colonies) with a Chamber of citizens elected by universal suffrage—on a ratio of one deputy for every five hundred thousand voters—and a Chamber of the States elected by national parliaments; a President elected by the Federal Parliament as guarantor of the federation, being the head of the diplomatic service and the armed forces; and a Prime Minister responsible before the Federal Parliament. The competencies of the Federal Parliament were limited to the areas of military, foreign, commercial, financial, industrial, and communications policies.[21]

The debate on Jennings's draft was held in Oxford on 2-3 March, in the presence of Jennings, Beveridge, J. Chamberlain, Curtis, A. L.

---

[21] Jennings, *A Federation for*, 160-83. Arthur Lehman Goodhart (1891-1978) was Law Professor at Cambridge, from 1919 to 1931; at Oxford, from 1931 to 1951; and then Rector of University College, Oxford, between 1951 and 1963. Among his works, see: *International Law and the Causes of War* (London: Grotius Society, 1943); id, *English Law and Moral Law* (London: Stevens & Sons, 1953); id, *Poland and the Minority Races* (London: Ayer Publications, 1970). Joseph Perkins Chamberlain (1873-1951) was Professor of Public Law at Columbia University, from 1923 to 1950. He was active in refugee organisations. Among his works, see: *The Fate of Refugees and Displaced Persons* (New York: Columbia University Press, 1947); id, *Legislative Processes: National and State* (Westport, CT: Greenwood Press, 1969). Kenneth Clinton Wheare (1907-79) was Warden of University College, Oxford, from 1942 to 1945; Gladstone Professor at Oxford, from 1944 to 1957; and Vice-Chancellor of Oxford University, from 1964 to 1966: He was the author of the essay *What Federal Government is* (London: Federal Union Publishing, 1941), the classic *Federal Government* (Oxford: Oxford University Press, 1946), and *The Constitutional Structure of the Commonwealth* (Westport, CT: Greenwood Press, 1982). For a panorama of the cultural climate of the period, and the contribution of the Committee to the constitutional debate, see: Frederick Madden ed., *Oxford and the Idea of Commonwealth* (London: Routledge, 1983); Frederick Madden and Kenneth Robinson eds., *Essays in Imperial Government* (Westport, CT: Greenwood Press, 1984); R. C. Van Caenegem, *Judges, Legislators and Professors: Chapters in European Legal History* (Cambridge: Cambridge University Press, 1992); id., *An Historical Introduction to Western Constitutional Law* (Cambridge: Cambridge University Press, 1995); id., *Legal History: A European Perspective* (London: Hambledon & London, 2004).

Goodhart, and Ransome, and had been very lively. Doubts had been expressed about the proposal to grant the Dominions only the right to secession, as this would help to perpetuate their "parasitic state of mind…produced by power without responsibility." They "should be admitted on equal terms or not at all." This "state of mind and the rejection of Imperial Federalism" were the result of "the certainty of defence by Great Britain," which would have brought many Dominions to become members of the federation. The right of secession limited to ten years should rather be granted to the Dominions, as "bait to induce the Dominions to join the Federation," and "eventually some of them might wish to join other Federations geographically more suitable." To European States this right would not have been granted, for fear that "it might be used…as an instrument of blackmail in federal politics."[22]

Criticism was also raised on Article III, which sanctioned the commitment by the Federal Government "to protect the democratic system in every… State" and "to assist each federated State in the maintenance of public order within the State." The Committee, while acknowledging that the Constitution should include guarantees at a minimum level for civil rights within member-States, believed that the Federal Government could not exercise direct control over the internal life of the States, and that this function as in the United States, was rather up to the Supreme Court. Regarding the power of taxation, Curtis criticised the direct system provided by Jennings, remembering—manifestly contradicting himself— that when with Milner he was working out an Imperial federation scheme, the indirect method had appeared the best in order to ensure common defence, and to prevent interference by the Federal Government in the social systems of the States. The Committee, while considering the indirect system suggested by Curtis "incompatible with the wide economic powers recommended by the economists," and "a great psychological advantage for Federal taxation to be levied direct from the peoples rather than contributed by the governments," asked Jennings to define more clearly the powers of taxation at the federal level.[23]

The Committee also questioned the General Welfare Clause—Section II of Article XI—for "further extending the powers of the Federation," allowing the Federal Government "to exercise wider powers than appeared

---

[22] *Report on the Third Conference of the Constitutional Committee*, in Ransome, *Towards*, 158-9. By Jennings see also: *The British Constitution* (London: The University Press, 1942); id., *Cabinet Government* (Cambridge: Cambridge University Press, 1969).
[23] *Report on the Third Conference of the Constitutional Committee*, in Ransome, *Towards*, 159-63.

in the Constitution," which would have raised controversies in the future. As it seemed very unlikely that a State would be willing to give other member-States financial contributions without a counterpart, the Committee considered General Welfare as necessary, because the "particular advantage of conditional grants-in-aid" would allow the Federation to control colonial policy and ensure "a liberal policy throughout the Federation."[24]

Finally, the Committee raised a criticism of Section 2 of Article XII, that the President had the power "to disallow any law of a federated State which, in the opinion of the Council of Ministers a) tends to interfere with the freedom of elections to the People's House," observing that in certain cases the power "of disallowance" by the Federation "might not be enough to guarantee the rights of the man." Some members of the Committee also supported the extension of and assignment to the Federal Parliament of the "power of disallowance," in order to prevent member-States "from prohibiting the formation of political parties" in contrast with "Federal objects." It was finally decided to attach a Bill of Rights to Section 2 of Article XII, precisely to safeguard the respect of civil rights.[25]

IV. *Federal Union and the constitutional debate*

The constitutional debate did not remain confined to a few authoritative experts, within the walls of one of the most prestigious Oxonian colleges, but spread through the newsletter to all the militants. And from this came a contribution of no small account to outline the shape of the desired European Constitution. The debate was opened on April 6 by a letter from S. J. Beck, of the branch of Gillingham, in which it was argued that Federal Union should "teach the basic principles of democratic thought." The greatest danger that the movement was running was to be "merely a wartime movement," as Federal Union had risen "to a large extent" as "a reaction to the war." It seemed necessary to "stir the most durable impulses," which would undoubtedly spring from the teachings of democratic principles, of which federalism was a "logical development." In all democratic countries, there was a "growing need" for teaching the rights and duties of the citizen, which had once been the task of the Church but, following the decline of its moral authority, had not been replaced by any other power. If Federal Union had assumed this task, for

---

[24] *Ibidem*, 163.
[25] *Ibidem*, 145, 164.

which it was fully legitimated, the movement would in fact have taught the "rights and duties of the citizens of the federation."[26]

The magazine accepted Beck's suggestion and opened the debate on 13 April with the article *Federal Union and Parliament*, whose author, John H. Humphreys, called for the reform of the British electoral system on the basis of proportional representation, thus allowing the "supporters of a new world order" to be "adequately represented, and with capacity" in the Parliament which would result from the elections at the end of the war. Recalling the far-reaching consequences of the notorious telegram to Lloyd George from 377 MPs on the conclusions of the Paris Peace Conference of 1919, Humphreys observed that "the fate of the federation will probably be decided by this Parliament," therefore by a specific electoral system. Reform according to proportional lines would reduce the constituencies in Great Britain from six hundred to one hundred and twenty, and federalists could therefore nominate their candidates, "ensuring during the election campaign a continuous discussion of the proposals for peace." The instrument of preference would also give voters the power to decide which of the candidates presented by the parties should be elected. Parliament would become a "place where the discussion is free and the decisions are taken by the entire population."[27]

Intervening again on May 4, Beck noted that the proportional system did not overcome the two main limitations of the representative system, namely the choice of candidates to be elected, and their control once elected. In both cases it was the "party machine," and not the electorate, who exercised control. The only way it was possible to bridge the gap between the electorate and their representatives was not through electoral reform, but through "an expression of public opinion organised from all points of views, and more effective." In a Federal State the gap between the electorate and its representatives was even wider, Beck observed. A possible solution would consist of the creation, "in every social community of the federation," of "well-organised groups of individuals, motivated by the concern to promote social progress," assembled in all the cities in "mini Federal Parliaments." The City Hall would thus become the true centre of the local political and social life "for which it was created." "The educational value of these Parliaments," Beck concluded, was "that they would have a decisive role in the election of the delegates."[28]

Beck dealt with an aspect of federalism almost entirely neglected by the political culture expressed by the Federal Union. It was an aspect of

---

[26] *Federal Union News*, 29.
[27] *Ibidem.*
[28] *Ibidem*, 30.

federalism—namely the material and social conditions that make possible a federalist organisation of human society, from the municipal level up to the world stage—that will be highlighted by Mario Albertini in the 1960s. Beck had sensed the great potentiality of federalism in the development of democracy as a form of expression of public will, but his intuition found no hearing in the group of intellectuals who gravitated around the Research Institute of the movement.[29]

Nor was it understood by Humphreys in his reply to Beck in May 18, reaffirming that what most mattered was not the quality of the electoral debate, but the way in which the votes were counted. That was the decisive factor in determining the composition of parliaments, and thus the historic course itself. Federal Union should certainly stimulate a wider pre-electoral debate, choose candidates who would fight for the federation and, above all, give them the material possibility of being elected through the proportional system.[30]

There were, however, those who had literally taken up Beck's suggestion, and in West Bromwich they organised a "local parliament" for those under thirty years old, open to anyone who wanted to offer young people of the county experience of the functioning of the democratic system, in order to discuss their various problems, and thus promote a better mutual understanding. The experiment had a following, on the initiative of a number of Federal Union's militants, also in Birmingham and London. Young people would, however, find themselves a little later defending the freedom of their own land, by embracing the rifle, without being able to express their vision of the new Europe.[31]

V. *The federalist debate and the Spectator*

In spring 1940 the *Spectator* intervened in the federalist debate, which had been going on in the British press since the outbreak of the war, with a series of six articles titled "Federal Union Examined," four of which were by Lionel Robbins, and two by the editor, Wilson Harris.

Robbins's federal views had been outlined in the volume *The Economic Causes of War*, published in November 1939, which followed two years on from *Economic Planning and International Order*. Both volumes were based on a series of conferences held, on the invitation of William Rappard, at the Institut Universitaire de Hautes Etudes Internationales

---

[29] Mario Albertini, *Una rivoluzione pacifica* (Bologna: Il Mulino, 1999).

[30] *Federal Union News*, 32.

[31] *Ibidem,* 34.

of Geneva. In *The Economic Causes of War*, Robbins refuted the Marxist-Leninist interpretation of war, identifying in "independent national sovereignty" the fundamental cause of international conflicts:

> The pacifists would say that it was due to lack of virtue. The biologists would say it was an aspect of the inevitable struggle for existence. The psychologists would say it was a manifestation of the death instinct which it would take a thousand years to learn to sublimate. The Marxists would say it was all due to the capitalist system. And the historians would hint that it was the result of dark subtle forces of which only they understood the mystery. But, in fact, it would be due to the existence of independent sovereign States.[32]

The remedy was simple, according to Robbins: "Independent sovereignty must be limited." The architects of the League had rightly understood the necessity of a "supernational authority," without realising however that its effectiveness was "incompatible with independent national sovereignty." "Today we know this," Robbins remarked, "that unless we destroy the sovereign State, the sovereign State will destroy us." It was neither desirable nor possible to create "a unitary world State," and it was utopian to imagine the creation of "a federation of world dimensions" in the space of a generation which, according to Robbins, had to be considered "the divine event towards which all that is good in the heritage of the diverse civilizations of the world invites us to thrive." However, it was not utopian to work for the creation of a European federation:

> No one with any sense of history and art will deny the existence of a real German problem in Europe: the incapacity for self-government, the tendency to brutality and sadism, the fascination with the death motive, the moral clumsiness, the deep sense of spiritual insecurity, which again and again, since the rise of Prussia, have been a menace to the peace and liberties of Europe. But for all that, Germans are Europeans. They are part of our civilization; and Europe can never be completely healthy till Germany is healthy too. Somehow or other we must create a framework in which German *Geist* can give its best, not its worst, to Europe. A draconian peace will do nothing. The Nazis must be extirpated: but we have neither the strength nor the will to keep Germans in subjection for ever. What more appropriate outcome of our present agonies, therefore, what more fitting consecration of the blood which is being shed, than a

---

[32] Robbins, *The Economic Causes*, 125-6; id., *Economic Planning*, see particularly Chs. 9-11.

peace in which this great people, purged of its devils, shall be coerced into free and equal citizenship of the United States of Europe?[33]

On 29th March 1940, the day after the "solemn declaration," Robbins wrote that since he did not believe in Streit's plan of the union of the democracies, and in the vague idea of a world federation, the question of federalism was mainly "a European problem." If outside Europe the maintenance of peace depended "on the goodwill and the power of the more strongly organised States," Europe was going through "one of those historical crises in which extensive change is ultimately the sole alternative to chaos."[34]

European civilization could not survive in the conditions which had dominated European political life "since the rise of the Bismarckian Empire." During the intervals between the wars which Europe had experienced throughout the last seventy years, "the expense and dislocation of preparing for war" negated the benefits created by science and technology, and generated periods of "retrogression and decay." The experience of the League of Nations showed that it was misleading to place the maintenance of peace upon the "knowledge and goodwill" of nations, because in a system of sovereign States the strategic considerations—namely the defence of national territory in the event of war—overwhelmed the moral ones:

> If we could assume knowledge and goodwill everywhere, then we should not need to worry about institutions; any institution would be as good as another...Neither within States nor between States can the rule of law rest upon a wholly voluntary basis.[35]

Analysing the economic aspects of the European question, Robbins observed that it is "the conclusion of everyone who has given serious attention to the subject," that the existence of barriers to trade and migration "is a cause of grave economic dislocation and a perpetual irritant in international relations." In the absence of "central control within a national area, there would be no reason to expect that the towns and counties would not resort to anti-social economic policies," such as local restrictions on the movement of people, capital and goods, "as they did in the Middle Ages." Similarly,

[33] Robbins, *The Economic*, 99-109.
[34] Lionel Robbins, "Federal Union Examined," *The Spectator*, 29 March 1940: 404-5.
[35] *Ibidem*, 441.

in the absence of an international authority with overriding powers, there is no reason to suppose that sovereign States will not resort to parallel practices. The idea that there can be a satisfactory economic reconstruction in Europe without an antecedent political reconstruction runs counter, not merely to all reasonable supposition, but also to the lessons of all recent experience. The economic problem is essentially political.[36]

The defence of European civilization demanded that its peoples come together to form a "union more permanent and more far-reaching in its powers than the confederate system of the League of Nations." European nations had to renounce "their right to make war and peace," and also "the right to pursue economic policies which embarrass and impoverish their neighbours." The fundamental condition to create a European federation was "the surrender to a central authority...those powers whose independent exercise is inimical to stability and justice," and that did not just mean the existence of a common culture, but institutions and behaviours, "more or less similar."[37]

The federation should include all Europe except Russia, because "a smaller Federation, limited to the western powers," would "run the risk of raising up rivals," and the elections of the federal Parliament should be direct. Such a political construction could not be built immediately, or during an entire generation. It was plausible to hope that it could be built only if in the post-war period "a solid nucleus of stability and power in the West" could be consolidated.[38]

In the short term it could be realised only where existed "the main conditions necessary for a permanent federal union," namely between Great Britain and France:

Unless there is a permanent association between our two peoples—permanent pooling of military and economic resources and continued identity of foreign policy—there is no hope of even the beginnings of a successful peace settlement. Why should we not proceed immediately to construct it, not only as a consolidation of defensive power but also as the foundation-stone of an eventual United States of Europe?[39]

Intervening again in the *Spectator* on 12th April, Robbins criticised the view expressed by Wilson Harris who thought it was possible to achieve an "economic disarmament...without a political framework." It was not

---

[36] *Ibidem.*
[37] *Ibidem.*
[38] *Ibidem,* 442.
[39] *Ibidem.*

plausible to expect, Robbins argued, on the basis of reason and experience, that independent, neighbouring States could live in harmony on the basis of wisdom and good will. The fundamental question was "the surrender of the liberty to make war and liberty to limit the economic opportunities of one's neighbours":

> I am sure that...his hesitations are due to the fact that he believes...that the nations of Europe can retain an ultimate liberty and yet be restrained from abusing it; that they can enjoy at once the prestige of independence and the benefits of indissoluble union; that there can accrue from the voluntary association of central government what he would never expect to accrue from the voluntary associations of lesser governmental authorities. If I could persuade him that this is only likely, in any circumstances, as the result of an accidental equilibrium of inherently unstable forces, and that, in the present state of Europe, it is in the highest degree improbable, I do not think he would shirk the task of attempting a more solid construction.[40]

Answering Robbins on 19th April, Harris conceded that he did not "reject federal union as an ultimate objective," but emphasised "the words 'gradually' and 'naturally', particularly the second":

> An artificial union, if ever ingenious framers of paper Constitutions could persuade the peoples of Europe in a moment of enthusiasm or exhaustion to adopt it as a part of the peace settlement, would lead inevitably to early and complete disaster. There can be no legislative union where there is no union of hearts and no spiritual allegiance.[41]

It was not possible to "reverse natural processes or skip stages":

> Co-operation had to precede fusion. And till the one has been effected it is futile to press for the other. On the other hand, fusion may well emerge as the natural goal of co-operation. Nations that will not dream of divesting themselves of their sovereignty once and for all by a single act may well divest themselves of it bit by bit, as their co-operation breeds confidence, through political, economic and disarmament agreements, by all of which they sacrifice some part of their full freedom of action.[42]

---

[40] Lionel Robbins, "Federal Union Examined," *The Spectator*, 12 Apr. 1940: 517-8.
[41] Wilson Harris, "Federal Union Examined," *The Spectator*, 19 April 1940: 549. Henry Wilson Harris (1883-1955) debuted as journalist at the *Daily News*, and was Editor of the *Spectator* from 1932 to 1953. He was Independent MP for the University of Cambridge from 1945 to 1950. On the *Spectator*, see Joseph Addison and Richard Steele, *The Spectator* (London: IndyPublish, 2004).
[42] Harris, "Federal Union", 550.

Harris envisaged the creation of a "European Council within the League," able to "gradually generate that sense of Europeanism which is lacking today and without which any European union would be built on sand, or, worse still, on friable parchment." Within Europe "groups of like-minded and contiguous nations may be able to put Federal Union to the proof on a small scale and so provide a working model for the whole Continent."[43]

VI. *Federal Union and the May crisis*

The repercussions of the May military crisis, following Hitler's offensive of the 10th, were soon felt in daily life, and the newsletter suddenly became "the only real instrument of contact which keeps the movement together." Even for Federal Union had come—according to the Executive Committee—"the moment of trial," since general attention had suddenly turned to the battlefield, which was gradually absorbing all the vital energies of the country, and it appeared necessary to persuade the public that the federalist project was "the answer of the free man to *Mein Kampf*, and an essential part of the struggle to overthrow Nazism." It was also necessary to remember that it was not enough to defeat the German army. It was essential to also achieve "a victory on Nazi ideas" and, therefore, mobilise "the Democrats of all States" in support of the federalist project. Federalist propaganda was not to be limited to Allied countries, but should reach the neutrals and even "cross the Siegfried Line, where Christians and Democrats expect the defeat of Nazism means a new order based on justice and the rule of law, democratically expressed and legitimately enforced."

There were, however, few available means for the movement because of the shortage of paper, and the gatherings were more and more difficult to organise. It was therefore necessary to focus the efforts of the militants on personal contacts and private meetings. Reminding militants that peace depended on their "perseverance," the Executive Committee pleaded with the militants not to expect that anybody else would carry out their job. "Whatever happens," the newsletter urged, "you keep talking about Federal Union to everyone you meet, patiently explaining its meaning and its aims." The London headquarters urgently needed financial aid, and with the total commitment of the thirteen thousand militants "the demand for the federation will spread, overcoming every barrier," and the

---

[43] *Ibidem.*

federation will become the "reason and the purpose for which the free peoples are fighting."[44]

During the first fifteen months of its life, Federal Union had overcome the narrow room of the ideal debate, and authoritatively participated in the debate on the future of Anglo-French relations. The fact that the Foreign Office had been interested, for the first time in the history of the Empire, in federalism in order to draw up a new structure of relations with France, was undoubtedly to the merit of Chatham House, but this could not have happened without the broad popular support that the movement had meanwhile gained within British civil society at large. If the British waited too long before taking the extreme measures which could save the bonds of the Alliance, and lay the foundations of a new world order, this was probably due to the failure of pre-war federalists—such as Lothian and Curtis—who had identified not in a European federation, but in an Atlantic one, the first stage in the transition towards world federation. Their story reminds us "how difficult," John Pinder remarked, "the British then found it to choose an attachment with the European Continent, against the pull from the Commonwealth and the USA."[45]

It was not easy for the British people to overcome their phobia of federalism as it was associated with a historical process of disintegration, not only of the Empire, but of the British Isles themselves. The role played by the Federal Union in producing literature of high quality, and in

---

[44] *Ibidem,* 35. On the transformation of the war from "'phoney'" into real, see: Gordon Wright, *The Ordeal of Total War: 1939-1945* (Long Grove, IL: Waveland Press, 1997); John Lukacs, *The Last European War: September 1939-December 1941* (New Haven: Yale University Press, 2001); Graham Darby, *Europe at War, 1939-1945* (New York: Hodder Arnold, 2003); Norman Davies, *No Simple Victory: World War II in Europe, 1939-1945* (London: Viking, 2007); Edward Hooton, *Blitzkrieg in the West 1939-1940* (Milbank, SD: Midland Publishing, 2007). For a picture of those dramatic days, see: Clive Ponting, *1940: Myth and Reality* (London: Ivan Dee Publisher, 1993); John Lukacs, *Five Days in London, May 1940* (New Haven: Yale University Press, 2001).
[45] John Pinder, "Prophet not Without Honour: Lothian and the Federal Idea," in Turner, *The Larger Idea,* 148. On the creation of the special relationship see: James R. Leutze, *Bargaining for Supremacy. Anglo-American Naval Collaboration, 1937-1941* (Chapel Hill: University of North Carolina Press, 1977); John Charmley, *Churchill's Grand Alliance: The Anglo-American Special Relationship, 1940-57* (San Diego, CA: Harcourt Brace Jovanovich, 1995); Mark A. Stoler, *Allies in War: Britain and America against the Axis Powers, 1940-1945* (New York: Hodder Arnold, 2005); S. Marsh and J. Baylis, "The Anglo-American 'Special Relationship': The Lazarus of International Relations," in *Diplomacy and Statecraft,* 7, (2006).

generating a wide debate in the press was fundamental, but the space of time available to "convert" the majority of public opinion to federalism was however too short. In the late spring of 1940 the British, even though forced to do so by necessity, were ready to accept the beginnings of a European federation with France and, possibly, with the other European governments in exile in London: Poland, Holland, Belgium, Czechoslovakia, Norway, Sweden, and Denmark.

The fact that it was just a high French official, Jean Monnet, who acted as a catalyst of that policy—even if he had remained until then a stranger to the federalist perspective, and had no connection with the Federal Union in London and the federalists in France—makes even more evident the limits of the pre-war federalists, who understood too late—Curtis in late April, and Amery in early June—the importance of starting with France. They were in fact the only ones—unless you consider Toynbee and Zimmern within Chatham House—who could, with a resolute intervention on the Government, overcome the stagnation into which the Hankey Committee had fallen, and bring in mid-May, shortly after the start of the German offensive, before the Government an organic project of union with France, when the spirit of capitulation had not yet permeated the French Government. As British Ambassador to Washington, and for the special role that he played in Halifax's appointment as head of the Foreign Office, Lothian could take such an extreme initiative—as suggested by Kimber himself—but he did not. He had in mind another future for the fate of Western civilization.

Federal Union was essentially a movement of young men, and it expressed the revolt of the younger generation against the policy which brought the war. It could work in depth, organising the consent of public opinion to the federalist project, while leaving to federalists of more seasoned militancy the task of overcoming the resistance of the senior officials and politicians. The ideological—but also generational—gap between "young" and "experienced" federalists weakened the strike force of the movement which, at the crucial moment, during the May crisis, was unable to intervene decisively in the course of events.

The leadership of the movement was in those days still under Kimber's control, but it had been strongly weakened, because the financial situation of the movement was very critical, and Kimber had become a target of attacks being a conscientious objector. Federal Union—which had by then become a first-rate political reality, with 12,000 members and 300 branches all over the country, and bridge-heads in Paris and Geneva—required a more "political" rather than "moral" leadership. Kimber resigned, continuing to serve the movement from a detached position, and allowed a Socialist Australian lawyer, Ronald Gordon Mackay, author of *Federal Europe*, to take over.

The changing of the guard happened during the Battle of Britain, without generating the conflicts which had characterised previous attacks on the Secretaryship, because the 'Atlanticists' had by then deserted the movement. Mackay's task was not easy, however, because besides facing a very critical financial situation, he also had to elaborate a political action according to the new strategic situation of the war.[46]

Just when the 'Europeanists' won all along the line against the 'Atlanticists', the material conditions for the creation of a European federation in the short term did not exist any longer. It was this contradiction—together with the fact that the resistance to Hitler to the bitter end was mobilising all available forces—that marked the rapid decline of Federal Union, whose membership fell, at the end of 1940 to little more than 2,000. The movement was clearly not ready to face a 'long march' through the desert which, by selecting the forces during the war, could enable a fresh start for the federalist initiative in Great Britain at the end of the war. It was, on the contrary in Italy, that these forces organised themselves into a movement modelled on the Federal Union, while Federal Union literature became the source of formation for militants.

The birth, in 1943, in Milan, of the European Federalist Movement continued, not without producing a breakthrough, the battle of Federal Union, bringing it from the periphery to the heart of Europe. The most influential and dynamic starting-point of federalist Resistance had definitely been the island of Ventotene, off the coast of Naples, where Altiero Spinelli and Ernesto Rossi were confined as anti-Fascist militants. At the beginning of 1939, Luigi Einaudi—later to become President of the Italian Republic, who was then Professor of Economics at the University of Turin, and one of the very few liberal intellectuals to whom the Fascists accorded a certain freedom of action—sent Rossi some books by British federalists, which he had received from the Federal Union. Spinelli recollects:

> There we found, among his articles of 1918, some dedicated to criticism of the idea of the League of Nations and in defence of the idea of a European

---

[46] On the Battle of England, see: Tim Clayton and Phil Craig, *The Finest Hour. The Battle of Britain* (New York: Simon & Schuster, 2000); Matthew Parker, *The Battle of Britain June-October 1940* (London: Headline, 2001); Walter Schellenberg, *Invasion 1940: The Nazi Invasion Plan for Britain by SS General Walter Schellenberg* (Toronto: Brown Book, 2001); Martin Marix Evans, *Invasion!: Operation Sea Lion, 1940* (Harlow: Longman, 2004).

federalism. Ernesto Rossi then asked Einaudi if he could send us some study on this subject and Einaudi sent him several essays of British federalists.[47]

The drafting of the *Manifesto of Ventotene*, the most lucid document of European Resistance of federalist inspiration, and a manifesto of militant federalism, owed much to those readings. "Their analysis of the political and economic perversion to which nationalism leads," Spinelli recollected, "and their reasoned presentation of the federal alternative, have remained to this day in my memory like a revelation." Since Spinelli "was seeking clarity and precision of thought," his attention

> was not attracted by the nebulous, contorted and hardly coherent ideological federalism of the Proudhonian or Mazzinian type, which thrived in France and Italy, but by the polished, precise and antidoctrinaire thought of the English federalists...who proposed to transplant to Europe the great American political experience.[48]

The literature produced and disseminated by Federal Union—and in particular Lothian and Robbins's writings, which were given substance and strength by Kimber, Rawnsley, and Ransome, embodying all that was thought "clean" and "precise" in a political movement with a broad popular base—propitiated the revival of federalism on the Continent, during and after the war, just at the moment when, after the collapse of

[47] Altiero Spinelli and Ernesto Rossi, *Il manifesto di Ventotene* (Naples: Guida, 1982), 173; Lucio Levi and Sergio Pistone eds., *Trent'anni di vita del Movimento Federalista Europeo* (Milan: Angeli, 1973); Walter Lipgens ed., *Documents on the History of European Integration: Continental Plans for European Union, 1939-1945* (New York-Berlin: Walter De Gruyter, 1984); id., *Documents on the History of European Integration: The Struggle for European Union by Political Parties and Pressure Groups in Western European Countries, 1939-1945* (New York-Berlin: Walter De Gruyter, 1988); id., *Documents on the History of European Integration: Transnational Organizations of Political Parties and Pressure Groups in the Struggle for European Federation* (New York-Berlin: Walter De Gruyter, 1991); Sergio Pistone ed., *I movimenti per l'unità europea, 1945-1954* (Milan: Jaca, 1992); Michael Smith and Peter Stirk, *Making the New Europe: European Unity and the Second World War* (London: Pinter, 1993); Thierry Grosbois, *L'idée Européenne en temps de guerre: 1940-1944* (Louvain-la-Neuve: Academia, 1994); Christophe Réveillard, *Les premières tentatives de construction d'une Europe fédérale. Des projets de la Résistance au Traité CED: 1940-1954* (Paris: Editions Xavier Guibert, 2001).
[48] Altiero Spinelli, *Il lungo monologo* (Rome: Edizioni dell'Ateneo, 1968), 135; id., *Come ho tentato di diventare saggio: Io, Ulisse* (Bologna: Il Mulino, 1984), 307.

France, the decline of Federal Union also started. If it is true that Federal Union's publications reached Spinelli through the Swiss branch of the movement, this was then the conjunction between insular and Continental federalism on the one hand, and the starting point of the experience of Continental militant federalism on the other.[49]

[49] Altiero Spinelli, *Diario europeo*, ed. Edmondo Paolini (Bologna: Il Mulino, 1989-1992); Luigi Einaudi, *La guerra and l'unità europea* (Bologna: Il Mulino, 1986). See also: Umberto Morelli, "Federalismo sovrannazionale and federalismo infranazionale in Luigi Einaudi", Preda and Rognoni, *Storia e percorsi*, 749-75; Sergio Pistone, *Altiero Spinelli e Mario Albertini: la Costituente europea*, in *ibidem*, 893-915; Antonella Braga, *Un federalista giacobino. Ernesto Rossi pioniere degli Stati Uniti d'Europa* (Bologna: Il Mulino, 2007), 166-90. On the relations between Spinelli and Monnet see Mariagrazia Melchionni, "The Spinelli-Monnet Correspondence. For a Biographical Archive of the Protagonists of the Movement for European Union," *Annals of the Lothian Foundation*, 4, (1994): 345-69.

CHAPTER VII

JEAN MONNET, CHURCHILL'S PROPOSAL AND THE DOWNFALL OF FRANCE

At 4.30 pm on Sunday 16 June, 1940 de Gaulle telephoned Reynaud with the following declaration of the British government:

> At the most fateful moment in the history of the modern world, the Governments of the United Kingdom and of the French Republic desire to make this declaration of indissoluble union and unyielding resolution in defence of liberty and freedom against subjection to a system which reduces mankind to a life of robots and slaves. The two Governments declare that France and Great Britain shall no longer be two nations but one. There will thus be created a Franco-British Union. Every citizen of France will enjoy immediately citizenship of Great Britain; every British subject will become a citizen of France. The devastation of war, wherever it occurs, shall be the common responsibility of both countries and the resources of both shall be equally, and as one, applied to its restoration. All customs are abolished between Britain and France. There shall not be two currencies, but one. During the war there shall be one single War Cabinet. It will govern from wherever it best can. The two Parliaments will unite. A constitution of the Union will be written providing for joint organs of defence and economic policies. Britain is raising at once a new army of several million men, and the Union appeals to the United States to mobilise their industrial power to assist the prompt equipment of this new army. All the forces of Britain and France, whether on land, sea or in the air, are placed under a supreme command. This unity, this union, will concentrate the whole of its strength against the concentrated strength of the enemy, no matter where the battle may be. And thus we shall conquer.[1]

---

[1] Jean Monnet, *Cittadino d'Europa* (Milan: Rusconi, 1978), 19-20. For a background discussion, see: Eleanor M. Gates, *The End of the Affair: The Collapse of the Anglo-French Alliance, 1939-1940* (London: Routledge, 1981); Robert Leckie, *Delivered from Evil: The Saga of World War II* (London: Harper Perennial, 1988), 174-6; Spencer Tucker, *The Second World War* (New York: Palgrave Macmillan, 2003), 60-1. On de Gaulle, see Charles Williams, *The Last Great Frenchman: A Life of General de Gaulle* (Oxford: Wiley, 1997).

Sir Ronald Campbell and Sir Edward Spears told later how the face of
Reynaud became radiant while the dictation by de Gaulle proceeded.
Spears remembers:

> the telephone rang. Reynaud took up the receiver. The next moment his
> eyebrows went up so far they became indistinguishable from his neatly
> brushed hair: one eyebrow to either side of the parting. 'One moment' he
> said, 'I must take it down', and grasping a sheet of foolscap on the slippery
> table, he began to write...Reynaud was taking down in French, from de
> Gaulle's dictation in London, the text of the Declaration of Union
> proposed by the British Government. On he wrote in a frightful scrawl,
> getting more excited as the message unfolded. The paper skidded on the
> smooth surface of the table. I held it. As each sheet was covered I handed
> him a fresh one. His pencil gave out; I handed him mine. Finally he
> stopped and said into the telephone: 'Does he agree to this? Did Churchill
> give you this personally?' There was a moment's pause and now he was
> speaking in English. It was evident that de Gaulle had handed the receiver
> to Churchill, who was assuring him that the document was a decision of
> the Cabinet. If there were alterations, they would be merely verbal.
> Reynaud put the receiver down. He was transfigured with joy.[2]

I. *Jean Monnet and the Anglo-French Co-ordinating Committee*

The principal architect of Churchill's proposal had been Jean Monnet,
Chairman of the Anglo-French Co-ordinating Committee. The origins of
the Committee are well known. Monnet recollects in his memoirs that in
late August 1939, the French Government asked him to go to the United

---

[2] Edward Spears, *Assignment to Catastrophe. The Fall of France. June 1940*, 2,
(London: William Heinemann, 1954), 291; M. Egremont, *Under Two Flags: The
Life of Major-General Sir Edward Spears* (London: Weidenfeld, 1997). On the
role played by Campbell, Spears and de Gaulle at Bordeaux in those days, see:
Jean Lacouture, *De Gaulle: The Rebel 1890-1944* (New York: W. W. Norton &
Company, 1993), 195-200; Charles Williams, *The Last Great Frenchman: A Life
of General de Gaulle* (Oxford: Wiley, 1997); Charles de Gaulle, *The Complete
War Memoirs of Charles de Gaulle* (London: Carroll & Graf Publishers, 1998), 72-
80; Daniel J. Mahoney, *De Gaulle: Statesmanship, Grandeur, and Modern
Democracy* (Piscataway, NJ: Transaction Publishers, 2000); John Lukacs, *The
Duel: The Eighty-Day Struggle Between Churchill and Hitler* (New Haven: Yale
University Press, 2001), 125-30; M. R. D. Foot, *SOE in France: An Account of the
Work of the British Special Operations Executive in France*, 1940-1944 (London:
Routledge, 2004), 119-20.

States to negotiate the purchase of three thousand aeroplanes and ten thousand engines:

> A new aspect of the situation which from now on, I thought, was going to dominate all others. It was no longer a question of French needs and French orders: what mattered now was the Allies' common effort.[3]

Monnet aimed to triple the United States's production of aeroplanes. That would be possible only by creating a "Franco-British Aviation Council...whose staff would maintain a continuing balance-sheet of French and British air strength, and then supervise the necessary purchases."[4]

In order to persuade Daladier, Monnet went back to the experience of the First World War, during which he suggested to Prime Minister René Viviani the creation of an Allied body for the co-ordination of supplies to the armed forces:

> It is no exaggeration to say that supplies for the armies and the civil population in 1917 and 1918 could be ensured only by a system with almost dictatorial powers, whose strength lay in France's and Britain's agreement to pool their resources and act together in carrying out decisions.[5]

---

[3] Jean Monnet, *Memoirs* (New York: Doubleday& Co, 1978), 125.

[4] Monnet, *Cittadino*, 14. On the role played by Monnet in the United States, see John McVickar Haight, "Les négociations relatives aux achats d'avions américains par la France pendant la période qui précéda immédiatement la guerre", *Revue d'Histoire de la Deuxième Guerre Mondiale*, 58, (1965): 1-34; id., "Jean Monnet and the American Arsenal after the beginning of the War", in *French Society and Culture since the Old Regime*, eds. E. M. Acomb and M. C. Brown (New York: Holt Rinehart and Winston, 1966); id., *American Aid to France 1938-1940* (New York: Atheneum, 1970); Irwin Wall, "Jean Monnet, les Etats-Unis et le plan français", *Vingtième Siècle*, 30, (1991): 3-15. On the conditions of the French air force, see: Charles Christienne and Pierre Lissarague, *Histoire de l'aviation militaire: L'armée de l'Air, 1928-1981* (Paris: 1981); Emmanuel Chadeau, *L'industrie aéronautique en France, 1900-1950: de Blériot à Dassaul* (Paris: 1987); H. Chapman, *State Capitalism and Working-Class Radicalism in the French Aircraft Industry* (Berkeley: Berkeley University Press, 1991), 101-74; Philippe Garraud, "Les contraintes industrielles dans la préparation de la guerre de 1939-1940: La modernisation inachevée de l'aviation française," *Guerres Mondiales et conflits contemporains*, 207, (2002): 37-59.

[5] Monnet, *Cittadino*, 14-5; Elisabeth du Réau, "Edouard Daladier: The Conduct of the War and the Beginnings of Defeat," in Blatt, *The French Defeat*, 171-81. On Anglo-French air rearmament, see: J. Truelle, "La production aéronautique

On the 20 September 1939, Daladier urged Chamberlain to re-create the Allied body of 1917-18, which made "possible the arrival of American troops in France." On 26 September 1939 Monnet was in London, where Sir Edward Bridges, Secretary of the British War Cabinet, "opened all doors," trying to convince his interlocutors of the necessity to share the global deficit of the supplies "which were national no longer, and became common" between the two countries.[6]

The success of Monnet's mission to London brought, on 18 October, to the Daladier-Chamberlain agreement, and the creation of five permanent Executive co-ordinating Committees (supplies, armament and raw materials, oil, aeronautic and transport), which had to decide a single programme of supplies, an inventory of the available resources, and purchasing priorities, guaranteeing the most rational utilisation of the resources in the common interest, and the equitable repartition of expenditures. These Executive Committees were put under the authority of an Anglo-French Co-ordinating Committee, under the ministerial supervision of a "Franco-British Executive." Asking Monnet to assume the presidency of the Committee, Chamberlain and Daladier reminded him that his duty was to reach decisions from the point of view of the Allies:

> You will note…that the Chairman of the Co-ordinating Committee is to be
> an Allied official; and while in no way an arbiter, you must use your best

---

militaire française jusqu'en juin 1940," *Revue d' histoire de la Deuxième Guerre mondiale*, 73, (1969); J. Lecuir and P. Fridenson, "L'organisation de la coopération aérienne franco-britannique, 1935-mai 1940", *Revue d'histoire de la Deuxième Guerre mondiale*, 73, (1969); Patrick Fridenson, *La France et la Grande-Bretagne face aux problèmes aériens, 1935-mai 1940* (Vincennes: 1976); A. D. Harvey, "The French Armée de l'Air in May-June 1940: A Failure of Conception," *Journal of Contemporary History*, 25, (1990): 447-65; T. Vivier, *La politique aéronautique militaire de la France. Janvier 1933-septembre 1939* (Paris: L'Harmattan, 1997); Philippe Garraud, "Le cas de l'armée de l'Air," *Guerres Mondiales et conflits contemporains*, 194, (1999).

[6] Regarding the appointment of Monnet as Chairman of the Committee, E. E. Bridges said at an inter-departmental meeting at the Treasurer on 24 November 1939, that "there were sound reasons for appointing a British chairman on all the committees," however, "it was necessary to decide in which cases the least harm would be done by entrusting the chairmanship to a Frenchman," Cab 21/746-749. On the state of Anglo-French military relations, see Martin S. Alexander and William J. Philpott, *Anglo-French Defence Relations Between the Wars* (New York: Palgrave Macmillan, 2003).

efforts to smooth out differences and bring about joint decisions by adopting an Allied rather than a national point of view.[7]

"This was certainly an innovation," Monnet remarks in his memoires, "at least as regards traditional civil administration, and I hoped that it would set a precedent." If for "Allied" one reads "Community," there would be "no better definition of the role to be played later by the President of the European Coal and Steel Community's High Authority" which, Monnet observes, "is doubtless no coincidence."[8]

Monnet's first task was to elaborate an enquiry of the essential needs and resources available to the Allies. The fundamental problem, Monnet recollects, was that of producing accurate balance sheets, on which political decisions were taken. On the basis of the balance sheet thus elaborated, action resulted "spontaneously," because it followed the logic of necessity. Absolute priority went to the supply of aeroplanes which, according to Monnet, would decide the fate of the war, and the task was certainly made easier after the abrogation, on 4 November, of the Neutrality Act, with which the United States put an embargo on the consignment of war materials to belligerent countries.[9]

Once Chamberlain's resistance had been won—he had thought Britain could rely on the Commonwealth industries and save gold reserves—, the Supreme War Council of 5 February adopted the recommendations of the Pleven mission, which contemplated the acquisition in the United States of 8,000 aeroplanes, quadrupling the normal production of the American engineering industry. Monnet observed:

> That gave the necessary boost to production, which now began in earnest and took on gigantic proportions once the United States had abandoned isolationism and come into the front line. When the German offensive began, in May 1940, the results of so much effort on our part no doubt seemed tardy and inadequate. Only a few hundred American aircraft faced the Germans in the Battle of France. A larger number took part in the Battle of Britain, and helped decide the war on the Western Front. Most of

---

[7] Monnet, *Memoirs*, 128.

[8] *Ibidem.*

[9] Monnet, *Cittadino*, 96-7. On the role played by Canada in the rearmament of the British Empire, see Hector Mackenzie, "'Arsenal of The British Empire'? British Orders for Munitions Production in Canada, 1936-39," *Journal of Imperial and Commonwealth History* , 31, 3, (2003): 46-73.

them were lost, with their crews, in these heroic struggles; but others at
once arrived to take their place.[10]

It was however only at the beginning of June that Monnet understood
the necessity of "a bold stroke that would fire the imagination of the two
peoples on the edge of despair," a "total union, an immediate merger, that
seemed necessary if we were to face together the choice between tyranny
and freedom that was now being thrust upon us." France and Great Britain
had to "join forces, in war and for the future." Persuaded that they should
begin from a merger of the two air forces, Monnet appealed to Churchill
on the 6 June:

> If the forces of our two countries are not treated as one, we shall see the
> Nazis gain mastery of the air in France, overpowering her, and then
> concentrating all their strength against the United Kingdom. The Allied
> aircraft now operating in France are outnumbered by several to one. But if
> we combine the two countries' air forces, the ratio becomes about one to
> one-and-a-half; and with our proven superiority when evenly matched we
> should then have a chance of winning. In a word, victory or defeat may be
> determined by an immediate decision to use our respective aircraft and
> pilots in the present battle as a single force. If that in turn requires a
> unified command for our two air forces, then this problem should in my
> opinion be studied, and studied now.[11]

In fact the French army was retreating, and the British troops escaped
massacre on the shores of Dunkirk by a miracle. It was too late to re-
organise the resistance, or to think in terms of traditional strategy. Thus
Monnet recollects those dramatic days:

> Paradoxically, as we lost the opportunity to take the most logical decisions
> and co-operate in the simplest ways, we were led to raise our sights and try
> to recover on the political level the control of events that was escaping us
> in the field. When there was no longer any hope of achieving a unified
> command, a merger of sovereignty became conceivable. With the

---

[10] Monnet, *Cittadino*, 140. On the Pleven mission, and economic and military
American aid to France, see: John McVickar Haight, *American Aid to France,
1938-1940* (New York: Atheneum, 1970); Gerard Bossuat, *Les Aides Américaines
Economiques et Militaires a la France 1938-1960: Une Nouvelle Image des
Rapports de Puissance* (Paris: Comite pour l'Histoire Economique et Financière de
la France, 2001). On the Battle of France, see: Robert Jackson, *Air War over
France, May-June 1940* (Paris: Allan, 1974); R. J. Overy, *The Air War, 1939-1945*
(London: Europa Publications, 1980). On the German offensive on the Western
front, see Woodward, *British Foreign Policy*, 1, 174-77.
[11] Monnet, *Memoirs*, 20.

Germans threatening Paris, we had to think of saving London, still untouched as a centre of the Alliance. France might be invaded, but not the French Empire. Yet in whose name could unity on this basis be maintained? And would men go on fighting when it looked as if they had lost the war? Arthur Salter and I decided to use every means in our power to put into effect the bold plan that events had made both reasonable and essential.[12]

II. *Monnet, de Gaulle and Churchill*

On 13 June, while Nazi troops entered Paris, Monnet and Salter drafted a note to be issued by the two governments on a total union between the two countries, for which resistance to the bitter end acquired a completely different meaning: the Allies were fighting not just to save France and Great Britain from totalitarian domination, and to restore national sovereignty of the two countries, but also to liberate Europe from the "demonic consequences of national sovereignty," which, in that particular context, meant Nazi-Fascism. The creation of an Anglo-French federal nucleus would have implied "the pooling of the sovereignties" between the two eldest European democracies. On that basis it would have facilitated American intervention, without which, it was by then clear that Hitler could not have been defeated, and the roots of Nazism uprooted:

> Paris has fallen—warned the document—and the maintenance of a continuous line of resistance could prove impractical. France could immediately be faced with the choice between the surrender of her army, her fleet, and part of her territories, or the continuation of a struggle in which she has little hope of succeeding to keep any line behind Paris, and has the certainty that the Germans will kill and destroy mercilessly…Even if the French forces are thrown back further and further, even if no front can be held, even if the struggle has to be continued in pockets of desperate resistance, France can, with Britain, continue the war. Even if the worst happens and the Germans conquer the whole of France, at least her fleet and her air force will be able to go on fighting alongside Britain, and a large part of the French army and its equipment will be able to embark and join forces with the British troops. In this case the two countries will be able to continue the battle until at last the infinitely

---

[12] *Ibidem*, 21. For a background analysis, see: Walter Lord, *The Miracle of Dunkirk* (New York: Combined Publishing, 1998); Thompson, *Churchill and Morton*; Winston Churchill, *The Second World War*, 2 (London: Cassell, 1949); Martin Gilbert, *Finest Hour. Winston S. Churchill, 1939-1941* (London: 1983); Lord Moran, *Churchill at War 1940-1945* (London: Constable & Robinson, 2002).

superior resources of the Allied Empires and the United States bring them victory.[13]

This scenario, the only one able to give the two countries "a chance of a tolerable future," could only have been realised if the two countries had acted "like a single country," and the two peoples felt as a "single people." The spirit of Anglo-French unity, more than any other factor, would "appeal both to American idealism, which wants the survival of the two democracies, and to realism, according to which, if America has to undertake a crusade, it should not be a vain hope." To this regard, the document suggested that

> There should be a dramatic declaration by the two Governments on the solidarity of the two countries' interests, and on their mutual commitment to restore the devastated areas, making clear also that the two Governments are to merge and form a single Cabinet and to unite the two Parliaments.[14]

Monnet thought that it was necessary to draw up prospects "for a common destiny." "In exceptional times," Monnet commented, "anything is possible—so long as one is prepared and has a clear plan to put forward when all else is confusion."[15]

Monnet had to declare, in retrospect, in an interview with the Canadian historian John Cairns, that he had been influenced, in the formation of this strategic plan, by reading various British newspaper articles, and in particular editorials of *The Times* which, as has been discussed, repeatedly supported, from the beginning of hostilities, the need for a comprehensive Anglo-French economic and political union. Monnet remembers discussing it with Chamberlain himself, when he was still Prime Minister:

---

[13] Monnet, *Memoirs*, 21. PJM, AME 8/1/1. On the collapse of the Third Republic, see: Andre Geraud, *The Gravediggers of France: Gamelin, Daladier, Reynaud, Petain, and Laval: Military Defeat, Armistice, Counter-Revolution* (New York: Doubleday Doran, 1944); William L. Shirer, *The Collapse of the Third Republic: An Inquiry into the Fall of France in 1940* (Cambridge, MA: Da Capo Press, 1994); Noel Barber, *The Week France Fell, June 10-16, 1940* (New York: Cooper Square Press, 2000); J. Jackson, *The Fall of France: The Nazi invasion of 1940* (New York: Oxford University Press, 2003).

[14] Monnet, *Memoirs*, 22. PJM, AME 8/1/1. On the question of the possible fall of the French fleet into the hands of Hitler, see Woodward, *British Foreign Policy*, 1: 223-4.

[15] Monnet, *Cittadino*, 13, 107. Salter was Deputy Chairman of the Coordinating Committee and assisted Monnet in drafting the declaration, see Arthur Salter, *Memoirs of a Public Servant* (London: Faber & Faber, 1961), 266-7.

I discussed with him many times on the question about the possibility of a union between France and England. I have always been persuaded that some form of union had to be created—I did not know exactly which kind —and that we lived in a world in which union is necessary.[16]

Monnet remembers that at the beginning of the war its aims were not clear, and in front of the "fundamental question," namely "the hegemonic attempt by Hitler," France and Great Britain should have launched the unequivocal message that they "did not join as mere allies, but in closer forms."[17]

Monnet also denied that he had been influenced by the reading of *Union Now*, contradicting what Streit himself wrote in 1941 in *Union Now with Britain*. Thus he declared, marking with a smile his disentanglement from Streit:

The volume proposed an Atlantic union, not an Anglo-French one. There is a fundamental difference...I did not think an Atlantic union was attainable before Europe had been made. But at that time I did not think of making Europe the way we are making it today...At that time I did not think...to an Atlantic union, this idea had never crossed my mind. The situation was becoming most critical, I thought it was essential to give to the world and to ourselves, or, if you prefer, to ourselves and to the world, a real reason for fighting.

Even distancing himself from Streit, Monnet however pointed out that the American journalist was in any case doing excellent preparatory work in front of American public opinion, which would prove "very useful" when the time came.[18]

---

[16] PJM, AME 8/3/1, 5. See John C. Cairns, "Great Britain and the Fall of France: A Study in Allied Disunity," *Journal of Modern History*, 27, 4, (1955); id., "Some Recent Historians and the Strange Defeat of 1940," *Journal of Modern History*, 46, 1, (1974).

[17] PJM, AME 8/3/1, 5.

[18] PJM, AME 8/3/1, 6; Clarence Streit, *Union Now with Britain* (London: Jonathan Cape, 1941). Historiography reinforced Streit's version, and even identified in Emmanuel Monik, financial attaché at the French Embassy in London, the real inspirator behind the proposal. According to Jacques Freymond "it was Monik, struck by the ideas put forward by Clarence Streit and by the Atlantic union proposals, to see in a union of France with England the first step towards an Atlantic union. He discussed it with the French Ambassador Charles Corbin, and Jean Monnet," Jacques Freymond, *Western Europe since the War* (London: Pall Mall Press, 1964), 8, 7, 26. See also: Léon Noël, "Le projet d'union franco-britannique de juin 1940," *Revue d'histoire de la deuxième guerre mondiale*, 21, (1956): 34-5; Eric Roussel, *Jean Monnet, 1888-1979* (Paris: Fayard,

Deepening the role played by Chamberlain, Monnet noted how the former Prime Minister was "in favour of the proposal of union before Churchill was." Despite repeated attempts by Monnet to interest Churchill directly, or indirectly, by means of his entourage, he did not seem to take Monnet seriously, since he did not hold governmental responsibilities, and therefore was considered incapable of effectively influencing the French Government. Only when the situation had become desperate, on June 13, on the suggestion of Desmond Morton, Churchill's Private Secretary, Monnet decided to act. He then interested Chamberlain in the project, through his friend Horace Wilson, head of the former Prime Minister's Office, in order to persuade Churchill to take the initiative, and the bold proposal began quickly to follow its process, arriving on the Cabinet's table. But it was too late. As Monnet pointed out, "if Churchill had presented it just ten days before the French Government had become so defeatist, France would have accepted it."[19]

It was in fact just the question of the time-table which decided the fate of that daring enterprise. The German army was advancing, and Churchill was greatly worried about the future of the French fleet, which could fall into Hitler's hands, since it had been offered to the Germans as compensation for less severe armistice terms. On a suggestion by Chamberlain, Churchill decided to despatch on 13 June a message to Reynaud, who knew he could count on Churchill, exhorting the French Premier to resistance: "We see before us a definite plan of campaign and the light which you spoke of shines at the end of the tunnel." Moreover, addressing the French Government on the same day, Churchill went so far as to speak, for the first time, of an "indissoluble union": "We take this opportunity of proclaiming the indissoluble union of our two peoples and

---

1996), 226; Emmanuel Monick and Michel Debré, *Demain la paix. Esquisse d'un ordre international* (Paris: Plon, 1945).

[19] PJM, AME 8/3/1, 7. For an analysis, see: Robert Blake, *Churchill: A Major New Assessment of His Life in Peace and War* (New York: W. W. Norton & Company, 1993), 245-7; Clifford P. Hackett, *Monnet and the Americans: The Father of a United Europe and His U.S. Supporters* (Washington, DC: Jean Monnet Council, 1995), 13; John Ramsden, *Man of the Century: Winston Churchill and His Legend Since 1945* (New York: Columbia University Press, 2003), 274-5. On the relations between Morton and Churchill, see: Reginald William Thompson, *Churchill and Morton* (London: Hodder & Stoughton, 1976); Gill Bennett, *Churchill's Man of Mystery: Desmond Morton and the World of Intelligence* (London: Routledge, 2006).

of our two Empires...the ordeal by fire will only fuse them together into an unconquerable whole."[20]

The British Government—which on the evening of June 15 was awaiting the arrival in London of de Gaulle, recently appointed Under-secretary of State for War by Reynaud, and sent to London to secretly arrange the transportation of the French Government to North Africa—let twenty-four hours lapse before giving concreteness to the project of union which, as will be discussed, turned out to be fatal. Only on 15 June, did the Cabinet appoint Monnet, Sir Robert Vansittart—Permanent Under-secretary to the Foreign Office—Salter, Morton and René Pleven to draft the text of the declaration of union, which was immediately submitted to Churchill.[21]

Thus Monnet recollects Churchill's reaction:

> Churchill, who had come to power to defend the very existence of the British Empire, was startled when he read our words. They called upon Britain to embark on a new course, turning her back on the past and on her island history. He raised objections: he refused to be convinced. But his sense of duty was more powerful, and because he saw in our plan a chance to change the course of events he put the text to the War Cabinet that afternoon. There, to his great surprise, statesmen whom he respected, from all parties, welcomed the project warmly, and quickly turned to studying its practical consequences. Apparently, the romantic in Churchill was troubled by this enthusiasm—but won over by its generosity. He decided

---

[20] Churchill, *The Second World*, 2: 162-5. For a background discussion, see: Gilbert, *Finest Hour. Winston S. Churchill;* Moran, *Churchill at War.* On Anglo-French relations and the Mers-el-Kébir's crisis, see: A. J. Marder, *From the Dardanelles to Oran* (Oxford: Oxford University Press, 1974), 179-288; Peter M. H. Bell, *A Certain Eventuality: Britain and the Fall of France* (Farnborough: Saxon House, 1974), 137-64; Warren Tute, *The Deadly Stroke: The Tragic Story of the British Destruction of the French Fleet in Oran* (Coward: McCann & Geoghegan, 1973); H. Coutau-Bégarie and C. Huan, *Mers-el-Kébir, 1940: La Rupture Franco-Britannique* (Paris: Economica, 1994); David Brown, *The Road to Oran: Anglo-French Naval Relations, September 1939-July 1940* (London: Routledge, 2004); David Wragg, *'Sink the French': At War with an Ally, 1940* (London: Pen and Sword, 2007).
[21] On de Gaulle's appointment and Reynaud's determination to continue to fight from North Africa, see Martin Gilbert, *Churchill: A Life* (New York: Holt Paperbacks, 1992), 658; I. C. B. Dear and M. R. D. Foot eds., *The Oxford Companion to World War II* (New York: Oxford University Press, 2002), 328; Peter Mangold, *The Almost Impossible Ally: Harold Macmillan and Charles de Gaulle* (New York: I. B. Tauris, 2006), 25.

to support the proposal, which was to be put formally to a further meeting of the Cabinet on the next day.[22]

Churchill, in his memoirs, confirms Monnet's judgement:

My first reaction was unfavourable. I asked a number of questions of a critical character, and was by no means convinced. However, at the end of our long Cabinet that afternoon the subject was raised. I was somewhat surprised to see the staid, solid, experienced politicians of all parties engage themselves so passionately in an immense design whose implications and consequences were not in any way thought out. I did not resist, but yielded easily to these generous surges which carried out resolves to a very high level of unselfish and undaunted action.[23]

---

[22] Monnet, *Memoirs*, 24. On the relations between Churchill and de Gaulle, and Churchill's alleged gallomania, see: D. W. J. Johnson, "Britain and France in 1940", *Transactions of the Royal Historical Society*, 22, (1972): 141-57; François Kersaudy, *Churchill and de Gaulle* (London: Collins, 1981); D. W. J. Johnson, "Churchill and France", in *Churchill*, eds. Robert Blake and William R. Louis (Oxford: Oxford University Press, 1996); Yves Rochas, *1940: Churchill et les Français: Un Eté Fertile en Légendes* (Paris: Nouvelles Éditions Latines, 1998); François Bédarida, *Churchill* (Paris: Fayard, 1999); id, "Winston Churchill's Image of France and the French", in Dockrill and Chassaigne, *Anglo-French Relations*, 125-38; François Kersaudy, *De Gaulle et Churchill* (Paris: Perrin, 2003), 70-2. On Vansittart's role at the Foreign Office, see: Ian Colvin, *Vansittart in Office: An Historical Survey of the Origins of the Second World War Based on the Papers of Sir Robert Vansittart* (London: Victor Gollancz, 1965); Norman Rose, *Vansittart: Study of a Diplomat* (London: William Heinemann, 1978). On the relations between de Gaulle and Monnet, see: Jean Baptiste Duroselle, *Deux types de grands hommes: Le général de Gaulle et Jean Monnet* (Geneve: Institut Universitaire des Hautes Études Internationales, 1977); Michèle Cointet, *La France a Londres: Renaissance d'un Etat, 1940-1943* (Paris: Editions Complexe, 1990); Antony Beevor and Artemis Cooper, *Paris After the Liberation 1944-1949* (London: Penguin, 2004), 24-5.

[23] Winston Churchill, *The Second World War*, 2 (London: 1948), 180-1. Douglas Brinkley and Clifford Hackett, *Jean Monnet. The Path to European Unity* (New York: St. Martin's Press, 1991), 69-74. The purpose of the declaration was, according to Churchill "apart from its general merits, of giving M. Reynaud some new fact of a vivid and stimulating nature which would carry a majority of his Cabinet into the move to Africa and the continuance of the war", Winston Churchill, *The Second World War*, 2 (London: 1965), 180. In September 1939 the French Government sent René Pleven to the United States in order to define with the Roosevelt Administration the conditions of a contract for the purchase of fighter and bomber aircrafts. On Churchill as strategist and historian, see David Reynolds, *In Command of History: Churchill's Fighting and Writing of the Second*

Also de Gaulle was initially not in favour of such an extreme step, but understanding that it could change the course of events, acted loyally to guarantee its success. To the exclamation by Churchill, "But it is an enormous mouthful," de Gaulle replied: "Yes, that means that its realisation would involve a great deal of time. But the gesture must be immediate."[24]

Monnet's action was not, however, developing on completely virgin soil, because just on the morning of the 15th, the War Cabinet discussed and approved in principle a document prepared by Salter and Amery—Minister for the Colonies—which called for the immediate creation of an organic union with France. Reservations on matters of detail had come from Chamberlain—who did not seem favourable to the formula of a common Parliament and Executive—and from other ministers who, at that stage in the debate considered frequent meetings of the Supreme War Council to be sufficient.[25]

On the morning of 16 June, at 12.30, de Gaulle telephoned Reynaud and, without revealing the content of the declaration, asked him not to take important decisions before knowing the terms of Churchill's offer:

> De Gaulle: I just met Churchill. Something stupendous is in preparation affecting the entity of the two countries. Churchill proposes the establishment of a single Franco-British Government, with you, perhaps, M. le President, as head of a Franco-British War Cabinet...Paul Reynaud:

World War (London: Basic Books, 2004). On the reactions of the members of War Cabinet, see Roy Jenkins, *Churchill: A Biography* (New York: Farrar, Straus & Giroux, 2001), 627-8.

[24] Charles de Gaulle, *War Memoirs,* 1 (London: Collins, 1955), 82-3; Churchill, *The Second World War*, 2: 182. On the reasons which brought the two statesmen to endorse the declaration, see: William L. Langer, *Our Vichy Gamble* (New York: Alfred A. Knopf, 1947), 38; Adrienne Doris Hytier, *Two Years of French Foreign Policy: Vichy 1940-1942* (Paris: Minard, 1958): 24; Charles Cogan, *French Negotiating Behaviour: Dealing with la 'Grande Nation'* (Washington, DC: United States Institute of Peace Press, 2004), 79-80; Mangold, *The Almost Impossible*, 21-6; K. Munholland, *Rock of Contention* (Oxford: Berghahn Books, 2007), 8-10.

[25] CaP, WM (40) 167.6; Alexander Cadogan, *The Diaries of Sir Alexander Cadogan*, ed. David Dilks (London: Cassell, 1971), 299; Norman Moss, *19 Weeks: America, Britain, and the Fateful Summer of 1940* (London: Houghton Mifflin, 2003), 178-9.

it is the only possible solution for the future. But it must be done quickly. It is a question of minutes. I give you half an hour. It would be splendid.[26]

After the telephone call, Monnet, de Gaulle, Pleven and Vansittart revised the text, whose main features had been approved by the War Cabinet the previous day, trying to give it "the form of a proclamation." It was a Sunday morning, and the Foreign Office was closed; they needed to find a "red binding," the red folder in which documents had to be presented in order to be discussed. "After long research," Monnet remembered, "we found a red binding which could be used, even if it was white."[27]

While de Gaulle lunched with Churchill at the Carlton Club, he showed him the text of the message written by Monnet and Vansittart. Halifax, Morton and Charles Corbin were also present. Monnet was desperately trying, with the assistance of Sir Ronald Campbell—British Ambassador to Bordeaux—to thwart a gross manoeuvre by the British War Cabinet on the question of the separate peace. In a telegram sent in the late morning to Reynaud—requested by the French Government after the oral authorisation given by Churchill to Reynaud to negotiate with Hitler—the British Government in fact gave the French Government a free hand in negotiating a separate peace, on the condition that the French fleet would be brought "out of reach of the enemy."[28]

The contradiction was apparent. The telegram which authorised the request for a separate armistice negated the offer of union which should officially reach the French Government at 5 pm. Or rather, the British Government freed the French Government of the constraints of the Alliance, and put the French Cabinet in front of its own responsibilities in a historical hour: to choose between union with the British people or accept Hitler's conditions. A desolate Monnet commented, in retrospect: "British empiricism, which has its limits, could not explain such contradictory steps, and certainly these were the consequences of the disorder that reigned in the minds." In the afternoon, Reynaud would have in hand, "two English documents of opposite content, among which...he

---

[26] Paul Reynaud, *In the Thick of the Fight* (London: Cassell, 1955), 539-40; De Gaulle, *The Complete War Memoirs*, 76-7; Kenneth S. Davis, *FDR: Into the Storm 1937-1940* (New York: Random House, 1995), 559-60.

[27] Monnet, *Memoirs*, 26-7. See also Alan J. P. Taylor, *English History 1914-1945* (New York: Oxford University Press, 2001), 486-7.

[28] Monnet, *Memoirs*, 27. For an analysis of this episode, see: A. Krammer, *La Vérité sur l'Armistice* (Paris: 1945), 80; Davis, *FDR: Into*, 559-60; Stanley Henig, *The Uniting of Europe: From Discord to Concord* (London: Routledge, 1997), 58-9; Moss, *19 Weeks*, 179-80.

could have chosen to his talent." "It was poker that was too risky," Monnet concluded.[29]

Monnet then solicited Campbell to immediately see Reynaud, asking the French Premier to postpone the reading of the telegram authorising the separate peace, and with Vansittart and Pleven reached Morton's Office, at 10 Downing Street, where at 3 pm the War Cabinet was going to meet, and ratify the final text of the declaration. So Monnet recollects those moments of an anxious wait:

> Morton's office was next to the Cabinet Room, and various Ministers came and went, proposing changes in the text. These did not affect its contents, and although they made it less precise it remained nonetheless imposing. Churchill had behaved very fairly. Although he did not conceal his own objections, he encouraged his colleagues to make the gesture that could have so profound an effect.

"At a time as grave as this," he said to me, "it shall not be said that we lack imagination." I can see him now as he came out of the Cabinet Room to talk to us, in a grey suit with pink stripes, a cigar in his mouth, treating it all with a careless air. It was his way of rising above events.[30]

III. *The British Government approves the text of the Union*

The War Cabinet met in the presence of Churchill, Chamberlain, Halifax, Attlee, A. Greenwood, Eden, Lord Caldecote, Sir Dudley Pound, Sir Archibald Sinclair, Sir Cyril L. N. Newall, and Sir John Dill. The text drafted by Monnet, Salter and Vansittart was approved with some significant amendments. The abolition of customs and excise would have raised "extremely difficult" problems, such as the revision of the Ottawa agreements, and other commercial treaties, since the tariffs policy was "a fundamental part of the economy of several Dominions."

Full monetary union seemed unrealisable, and the Cabinet agreed that the same objective could be attained "by a stabilisation of the rate of exchange," concurring that it would be better "to delete any specific reference to these matters in the proclamation."[31]

---

[29] Monnet, *Memoirs*, 27. On the question of the negotiated armistice, see Woodward, *British Foreign Policy*, 1: 209-12.

[30] Monnet, *Memoirs*, 28.

[31] CaP, Cab, 65/7, 134992. See also Brown, *The Road to Oran*, 36. On the discussion within the War Cabinet on France's downfall, see: Hill, *Cabinet Decisions*, 146-86; Paul de Villelume, *Journal d'une défaite, 23 août 1939-16 juin 1940* (Paris: 1976), 238.

It was agreed not to modify the text regarding the creation of a single War Cabinet. However, in fact it was "necessary to maintain the two existing Cabinets with a 'super Cabinet' in addition." "The result would be something very similar to our present arrangements," the minutes maintained, "but the use of the phrase 'War Cabinet' instead of 'Supreme War Council' would emphasise the closeness of the union." The two parliaments could not legislate as a single body, but it was possible to study "some arrangement for occasional joint Sessions." Finally, regarding the institutional question, "a written Constitution of the Union providing for joint organs of defence and economic policies could no doubt be drafted, and, provided it was kept on very broad lines, would seem to present no insuperable objection."[32]

Sir Archibald Sinclair—Air Minister and member of the Federal Union—expressed his "warm support" for the proposal as a whole, and welcomed "any means of tightening the union between the two nations." Greenwood—Minister without portfolio—"stressed the need of keeping the proclamation in as simple terms as possible, and making it clear that the Union included the whole British Commonwealth of Nations and the French Empire." Lord Caldecote—formerly Sir Thomas Inskip, Defence Minister in the Chamberlain Administration and at the time Dominion Minister—observed that the scheme involved post-war settlement, and "it raised issues which were too stupendous to give any opinion upon at such short notice." The institutional difficulties would have been too complex, as for instance the role of the monarchy, "and would take a generation to adjust." He feared that the proposal would provoke "very grave criticism in the country."[33]

Halifax declared that some risks had to be taken, and the only sentence of the document which would raise "really fundamental issues" was that "France and Great Britain shall no longer be two nations but one." Churchill, closing the debate, noted: "in this grave crisis we must not let ourselves be accused of a lack of imagination. Some dramatic announcement was clearly necessary to keep the French going."[34]

Sir John Colville—Private Secretary to Churchill—thus recollected that Sunday afternoon in his diaries, *The Fingers of Power*:

---

[32] CaP, Cab, 65/7, 134992. On the spirit of Churchill's Coalition, see J. M. Lee, *The Churchill Coalition, 1940-1945* (North Haven, CT: Archon, 1980), 37-58.

[33] CaP, Cab, 65/7, 134992. De Groot, *Liberal Crusader*; Hill, *Cabinet Decisions*, 170; P. M. H. Bell, *A Certain Eventuality. Britain and the Fall of France* (London: 1974).

[34] CaP, Cab, 65/7, 134992.

I ushered Corbin and de Gaulle into Desmond Morton's room to wait until they were summoned. Shortly afterward I saw Morton who told me what the meeting was for and why the stern telegrams sent off this morning, refusing to release France from her 'no separate peace' pledge, but in reality agreeing to an armistice, were being held up. Apparently there is a stupendous idea of declaring the political unity of England and France and Reynaud has said that, in these circumstances, France would fight on, having seen 'the ray of light at the end of the tunnel'. I am not clear about the details of this epoch-making idea; but apparently Chamberlain is 'in on it' with Salter, Amery, Lloyd and Vansittart, and de Gaulle is one of its most ardent supporters. 'De Gaulle is a magnificent crook' said Morton, 'another Max Beaverbrook, just what we want!' Bridges came out of the Cabinet and dictated the Declaration of Union to Mrs Hill in my room. It sounded inspiring, something which will revive the flagging energies of the French and invigorate our own people. It is an historic document and its effects will be more far-reaching than anything that has occurred this century...There would have been great difficulties to surmount but we had before us the bridge to a new world, the first elements of European or even World Federation.[35]

Sir John Colville saw it rightly. The offer to France certainly represented a last ditch attempt by the British Government to keep France in the war, to avoid the French fleet falling into German hands, and to promote resistance to the dictatorships on the Continent. If it came in time, and the French Government accepted it, not only would the course of the war have been different—the United States would have entered the war as an equal partner of the European democracies united with federal bonds—but also the post-war settlement would have been very different. It would have been based on the Anglo-French Union as the nucleus of the European federation and, in perspective, on a tri-polar world order. If the proposal had been accepted—as Coudenhove-Kalergi rightly commented—it would have immediately been extended to the exiled governments in London of Poland, Czechoslovakia, Belgium, Holland, Luxembourg and Norway, with the creation of the United States of Europe.[36]

The British proposal was not, however, taken seriously and considered by the French Government. The spirit of capitulation, embodied by War Minister Maxime Weygand—who had intercepted the telephone call by de Gaulle to Reynaud, and had therefore "hastened his offensive"—and Pétain prevailed, and France submitted herself to the German will for the second time in seventy years. The announcement of the capitulation

---

[35] Colville, *The Fringes of Power*, 159-61. See also id., *Winston Churchill and His Inner Circle* (London: Simon & Schuster, 1981).
[36] Coudenhove-Kalergi, *An Idea Conquers*, 226.

reached Churchill at Victoria Station, at 6.30 pm, when he had already taken his seat on the train that was to take him to Southampton, and then, joined by a Delegation of the British Government, was meant to meet Reynaud and the French Government on board a destroyer at Concarneau, on the French coast, to sign the Act of Union. Churchill got out from the train "with a heavy heart." Clement Attlee—a member of the delegation formed by representatives of the three parties and civil and army experts— remembered that moment: "We knew then it was all over and Reynaud had lost. We got out of the train and drove back to Downing Street and went back to work." Great Britain was alone to face the enemy.[37]

IV. *The Reactions of the French Government*

On 16 June, a Sunday afternoon, the French Government was faced with a dramatic choice: to continue the war on the side of Great Britain, conducting operations from Algiers, or surrender.

The message from Churchill, "acted like a tonic on M. Reynaud," Campbell recollected, "who said that for a document like that he would fight to the last...M. Reynaud then left with a light step to read the document to the President of the Republic." When Reynaud reached Lebrun, and with visible emotion read him the document, he found him with Paul Baudouin and Yves Bouthilier, who immediately expressed deep concerns to the Prime Minister:

---

[37] Francis Williams, *A Prime Minister Remembers: The War and Post-War Memoirs of the Rt. Hon. Earl Attlee* (London: Heinemann, 1951): 43-4; Francis Beckett, *Clem Attlee: A Biography* (London: Politico's Publishing, 2000): 95-6; Kenneth Harris, *Attlee* (London: Weidenfeld & Nicolson, 1995). For an analysis of the revision of British war strategy in the perspective of France's downfall, see: Ashley Jackson, *The British Empire and the Second World War* (London: Hambledon, 2007); Martin Gilbert, *Churchill: A Life* (London: Pimlico, 2000); Winston Churchill and Martin Gilbert eds., *The Churchill War Papers: Never Surrender. May 1940-December 1940* (New York: W.W. Norton, 1995); Basil Henry and Liddell Hart, *History of the Second World War* (Cambridge, MA: Da Capo, 1999). On Churchill's determination at the end of May to fight to the bitter end, as opposed to the supporters, headed by Halifax within the War Cabinet, to negotiate peace conditions with Hitler, see: David Reynolds, *Churchill and the British Decision to Fight on in 1940: Right Policy, Wrong Reasons*, in Langhorne, *Diplomacy and Intelligence*, 147-67; William Manchester, *The Last Lion: Winston Spencer Churchill, Alone 1932-1940* (London: Little, Brown & Co, 1988); Ian Kershaw, *Fateful Choices: Ten Decisions That Changed the Wold, 1940-1941* (London: The Penguin Press, 2007).

A proposition so fraught with consequences and with such promise for the future, could not be examined, then accepted or rejected by a mere Council of Ministers. Moreover, it would do nothing to unravel the knot that was choking the country. This evening the Council of Ministers ought to discuss one problem, and one problem only, was it or was it not necessary to try to stop the war?[38]

The proposal seemed irrelevant compared with the gravity of the hour, for the real question was whether to come to terms with the Germans, or resistance.

The session of the Council of Ministers began at 5.00 pm, and Reynaud, after having communicated—lying to his ministers—the British refusal to free France from the ties of the Alliance, read Churchill's offer twice, declaring that he had already accepted it in principle, and that the following day he would go to Concarneau to discuss secondary matters with Churchill. The reaction by the ministers was generally very hostile. Camille Chautemps and Jean Ybarnégaray declared that the proposal would relegate France to the status of a British Dominion, while others considered it as a "last minute plan," a "surprise," and a "scheme to put France in tutelage and to carry off her colonial Empire."[39]

Pétain, persuaded of the imminence of the defeat of Great Britain, dismissed the offer as a "fusion with a corpse," and Ybarnégaray—who according to Churchill himself had been so "brave" during the First World War—declared: "Better be a Nazi province. At least we know what it means." Some ministers even thought that it was a "trap," or a "takeover bid." The extreme weakness of France would put that union, according to Weygand, on a vassalage basis. Reynaud recollected that bitter epilogue of the Third Republic:

My exposure produced no reaction. No one within the Council took the floor to support me. Neither Campinchi, nor Mandel, nor Louis Marin! I was completely alone in supporting the unexpected offer of incredible generosity by Churchill…Such was the cavalier fashion with which the proposal that Britain should unite with France to create the core of a new

---

[38] Baudouin, *The Private Diaries,* 116-7; Yves Bouthillier, *Le Drame de Vichy. Face à l'ennemi,* 1 (Paris: Plon, 1950), 86-7.
[39] Camille Chautemps, *Cahiers Secrets de l'Armistice 1939-1940* (Paris: Plon, 1963), 161; François Charles-Roux, *Cinq Mois tragiques aux Affaires étrangères* (Paris: Plon, 1949), 46-7; Maxime Weygand, *Recalled to Service* (London: William Heinemann, 1952), 175; Albert Lebrun, *Témoignage* (Paris: Plon, 1945), 83; FOP, FO371/ C7294/65/17; Reynaud, *In the Thick,* 541. On Mandel, see: Georges Wormser, *Georges Mandel, l'homme politique* (Paris: Plon, 1967); Jean-Noël Jeanneney, *Georges Mandel* (Paris: Seuil, 1991).

Europe was treated...Those who rose in indignation at the idea of union with our ally were the same individuals who were getting ready to bow and scrape to Hitler.[40]

Yet Reynaud knew he could at least count on Mandel, Louis Marin, and also the President of the Republic, Albert Lebrun who, commenting on the low consideration in which it was held—it was not even put to a vote—observed: "it slumped by itself in a sort of indifference." Reynaud, convinced that he had lost the support of the majority of his ministers, rather than put his own weight in support of the request by Mandel—the chief advocate of resistance to the bitter end—put to a vote the renewed proposal by Chautemps of an armistice, preferring to gain more time and consult Lebrun in the meantime, adjourning the meeting 10.00 pm. When the ministers assembled at the fixed time, they learned that the Government had resigned. The Third Republic thus ended.[41]

The proposal of union came, in fact, at the worst moment, when the spirit of capitulation was conquering everyone's mind, and it was therefore very difficult to recognise the meaning and the revolutionary implications of that offer. Moreover, the fact that Weygand intercepted the first message by de Gaulle—which anticipated the contents of Churchill's proposal without entering into details—offered him the chance to exploit the interval between 12.30 and 5.00 pm to provoke a hostile reaction from the ministers whom he met. Weygand's action removed the surprise element from Churchill's proposal which, if it had been well exploited in a moment when emotions were overwhelming reason, could have produced the hoped effect.

There was also the question of leadership—of fundamental importance at crucial moments—and Reynaud, after the initial enthusiasm witnessed by Campbell's telephone call, did not appear to be able to command a situation which required resolute action. As Mandel told Spears, "it was like pressing the trigger and the cartridge not going off." Reynaud presented the proposal to his colleagues "without heat or fire," and, according to Spears, always behaved "like a lawyer defending a cause he

---

[40] Paul Reynaud, *Mémoires,* 2 (Paris: Flammarion, 1963), 428-30. For an analysis of the role played by Reynaud in the collapse of the Third Republic, see: Stefan Gruner, *Paul Reynaud, 1878-1966* (Frankfurt: Oldenbourg, 2001); Marcel Lesbros, *Paul Reynaud: alpin, européen, contemporaine* (Paris: Ophrys, 1993); Raymond Krakovitch, *Paul Reynaud: Dans la tragédie de l'histoire* (Paris: Tallandier, 1998).
[41] Lebrun, *Témoignages,* 82-5. On the collapse of the Third Republic, see Jean-Baptiste Duroselle, "1940: la France sans stratégie", in *L'Histoire. Études sur la France de 1939 à nos jours,* ed. Jean Baptiste Duroselle (Paris: Le Seuil, 1985).

did not believe in, and for which he had been promised an inadequate fee."[42]

Moreover, the proposal fell into an atmosphere not only of defeatism, but, as de Gaulle recorded, one which was also dominated by "an extremely acute anglophobe feeling." After Dunkirk the French felt, if not betrayed, then certainly abandoned to their own destiny. Norway, for example, which, if defended, would certainly have relieved the pressure on France, seemed to prove the unreliability of an ally who, the majority of the French ministers thought, would have done nothing against its own interests for the sake of a moral principle. "The worst defeat which we could suffer," Pierre Laval declared at Bordeaux, "would be that negotiations would take place between Britain and the Reich for the conclusion of peace. France would then have to pay all the expenses of the war."[43]

Charles Roux, General Secretary at the *Quai d'Orsay*, and former Ambassador to the Vatican, noted:

> At the moment when it was produced it was not an advantage for it to have as an end, and as an effect, the welding more solidly of our country to her British ally, because this end and this effect were not likely to appeal to the opponents of M. Paul Reynaud. It assumed a faith in the final victory of the English, and this faith, abandoned by some of the ministers, vacillated in the hearts of some others.[44]

---

[42] Reynaud, *In the Thick*, 539-41; Spears, *Assigment to Catastrophe*, 2: 293, 300, 315.

[43] J. R. Tournoux, *Secrets d'Etats*, 2: 430. On Laval's statement, see the evidence by Colonel A. Goutard in *Le Monde* of 26 June 1970. For a discussion of Laval's attitude, see: Renè de Chambrun, *Pierre Laval: Traitor or patriot?* (Cambridge, MA: Scribner, 1984); Jean-Paul Cointet, *Pierre Laval* (Paris: Fayard, 1993); Yves-Frederic Jaffre, *Il y a cinquante ans, Pierre Laval: Le procès qui n'a pas eu lieu* (Paris: A. Michel, 1995); Henry Torres, *Pierre Laval* (Whitefish, MT: Kessinger Publishing, 2007). On Allied policy towards Norwey, see: Woodward, *British Foreign Policy*, 1: 118-29; Richard Petrow, *The Bitter Years. The Invasion and Occupation of Denmark and Norway, April 1940-May 1945* (New York: William Morrow, 1974); François Kersaudy, *Stratèges et Norvège, 1940* (Paris: Hachette, 1977); Peter Ludlow, "Britain and Northern Europe, 1940-1945", *Revue Internationale d'Histoire Militaire*, 53, (1982): 149-180; Doug Dildy, *Denmark and Norway 1940: Hitler's Boldest Operation* (London: Osprey Publishing, 2007).

[44] Charles-Roux, *Cinq Mois Tragiques*, 46. See also: Winston S. Churchill, *Memoirs of the Second World War* (London: Mariner Books, 1991), 323; Julian Jackson, *France: The Dark Years, 1940-1944* (New York: Oxford University Press, 2003).

The British proposal appeared irrelevant for the gravity of the hour, and came too late to be taken into serious consideration, because the French Government had to take a decision long postponed, and which could no longer be deferred: resistance or surrender. According to Marin and Lebrun, if it had come only three days earlier, it would almost certainly have been accepted, because Weygand and Pétain could not then have built the consent within the Cabinet to reject it. "The ministers," Bouthilier observed, "were emotionally little inclined to accept an indissoluble union with a nation, however noble and loyal, which on the battlefield could not furnish the effective aid that was needed." "When a man," Chautemps declared, "has a dagger to the throat and calls for help, he asks someone to arrest the killer's arm, and nothing else can satisfy him."[45]

It was just in the forty-eight hours between 14 and 16 June, that the gap opened up, through which Pétain and Weygand managed to turn in their favour the balance of power within the French Government. This fatal uncertainty reveals to us what difficulties the British had to face in order to choose union with the European Continent, against the attraction which they felt for the Commonwealth and the United States. From summer 1940 the British, determined to resist to the bitter end, turned permanently to the United States and the English-speaking peoples in the implementation of that "special relationship" which such a vital role had in deciding the fate of the war itself, and the question of the post-war order.

The proposal of union fell in the interlude between Dunkirk and the Battle of Britain, at the moment in which the German combination of

[45] Louis Marin, "Contributions à l'Etude des Prodromes de l'Armistice", *Revue d'Histoire de la Deuxième Guerre Mondiale*, 2, (1951): 17; Lebrun, *Témoignages*, 84; Bouthilier, *Le Drame de Vichy*, 1: 86; Chautemps, *Cahiers Secrets*, 161. On Marin's view of "Great France", see Herman Lebovics, *True France: The Wars over Cultural Identity, 1900-1945* (Ithaca, NY: Cornell University Press, 1994), 49-51. On Petain and Weygand, see: Philip Bankwitz, "Maxime Weygand and the Fall of France: A Study in Civil-Military Relations", *Journal of Modern History*, 31, 1, (1959): 225-39; Georges Blond, *Petain, 1856-1951* (Paris: Presses de la Citè, 1966); Philip Charles and Farwell Bankwitz, *Maxime Weygand and Civil-Military Relations in Modern France* (Boston, MA: Harvard University Press, 1967); Bernard Destremau, *Weygand* (Paris: Perrin, 1989); Richard Griffiths, *Marshal Petain* (Philadelphia, PA: Trans-Atlantic Publications, 1994); Nicholas Atkin, *Petain* (Boston, MA: Addison Wesley Publishing, 1997); Bernard Destremau, *Weygand* (Paris: Perrin, 2001); Charles Williams, *Petain: How the Hero of France Became a Convicted Traitor and Changed the Course of History* (New York: Palgrave Macmillan, 2005); Robert B. Bruce, *Petain: From Verdun to Vichy* (Dulles, VA: Potomac Books, 2007).

military and air power conquered most of Continental Europe, before clashing with the British combination of naval and air power. The success of the German war machine appeared invincible to the French Government, and therefore, the fall of Great Britain herself seemed imminent. Since resistance appeared unmanageable, and the French Cabinet was unwilling to accept the offer of union on a basis of subservience, they opted for the breaking-up of the Alliance, confiding in the clemency of the winner, rather than binding their destiny "indissolubly" to that of the British Empire.[46]

In spite of the fact that with the offer of union Great Britain impressed a dramatic change on her tradition of foreign policy, it came however too late and unexpectedly. Daladier and Léger—the main architects of the Anglo-French process of unification on the French side—had been removed from the inner circle of decision making, and Reynaud seemed not to have the strength, or the will power to bring that process to its extreme consequences. The British attitude of disengagement following Hitler's attack on Norway, strained Anglo-French relations showing the artificiality of the "solemn" declaration of 28 March.[47]

V. The state of Anglo-French relations

It appears, then, necessary to consider more closely the question of the military time-table, and the state of Anglo-French relations.

---

[46] On the Battle of England, see: Stephen Bungay, *The Most Dangerous Enemy: A History of the Battle of Britain* (London: Aurum Press, 2001); John Lukacs, *The Duel: The Eighty-Day Struggle Between Churchill and Hitler* (New Haven: Yale University Press, 2001); Phil Craig and Tim Clayton, *Finest Hour: The Battle of Britain* (London: Simon & Schuster, 2002); Andrew Roberts *Hitler and Churchill: Secrets of Leadership* (London: Orion Publishing, 2004); Norman Moss, *19 Weeks: America, Britain, and the Fateful Summer of 1940* (London: Houghton Mifflin, 2003).

[47] For a background discussion, see: Nichol Mansergh, *Survey of British Commonwealth Affairs: Problems of Wartime Cooperation and Post-War Change 1939-1952* (London: Routledge, 1968), 39-40; René and Janine Bourdin ed., *Edouard Daladier. Chief de Gouvernement, avril 1938-septembre 1939* (Paris: Presses de la Fondation Nationale des Sciences Politiques, 1977), 187-9; Frank W. Thackeray and John E. Findling, *Statesmen Who Changed the World: A Bio-Bibliographical Dictionary of Diplomacy* (Westport, CT: Greenwood Press, 1993), 356-7; Du Réau, *Edouard Daladier*, 305-9; Leeds, *These Rule France*, 224-6; Kershaw, *Fateful Choices*, 14-15. On French plans to defend the Scandinavian countries, and the sixth meeting of the Supreme War Council, see: Woodward, *British Foreign Policy*, 1: 100-4, 138-45.

During the early months of the war the British strategy was entirely defensive, because the British also did not rely on the capacity of resistance of France. Appeasement had in fact largely been a rationalisation of the military and economic weakness of Great Britain, and the decline of French power. The "unwinding" of appeasement had, conversely, strengthened the belief in the Foreign Office—supported by Halifax and Chamberlain—that after the war it was essential to establish a deeper Anglo-French co-operation, not necessarily as extreme as a federal union, but based on strong cohesion in the field of foreign policy and defence. Anglo-French relations however were, in those crucial months, undermined by a mutual lack of trust: the French felt neglected by the ally across the Channel—believing that the British were only committed to maintaining their naval supremacy over Germany, and unwilling to sacrifice men and means in the defence of France—while the British feared being abandoned as a serious crisis approached.[48]

The German offensive of 10 May swept away, in the space of four weeks, the resistance, and also the solidity of the French army. General Weygand—Commander-in-Chief of the Armed Forces—declared on 11 June, during the Supreme War Council of Briare, that the army was fighting on the last line of defence—a line which Germany had already broken in several points—and that no reserves were available to line up in the fields.[49]

---

[48] For a background discussion, see: Davis, *Anglo-French Relations*; Martin Thomas, *Britain, France and Appeasement: Anglo-French Popular Front Era* (London: Berg, 1997); Phillipe Chassaigne and Michael Dockrill, *Anglo-French Relations 1898-1998* (New York: Palgrave Macmillan, 2002). On the solidity of French armed forces, see: Jeffery A. Gunsburg, *Divided and Conquered: The French High Command and the Defeat of the West, 1940* (Westport, CT: Greenwood Press, 1979); Robert A. Doughty, *The Seeds of Disaster: The Development of French Army Doctrine, 1919-1939* (North Haven, CT: Archon Books, 1986); Robert A. Doughty, "The French Armed Forces, 1918-40", in *Military Effectiveness: The Interwar Period,* eds. Allan R. Millett and Murray Williamson Jeffery (London: Unwin Hyman, 1988); Martin Alexander, *The Republic in Danger: General Maurice Gamelin and the Politics of French Defence, 1933-1940* (Cambridge: Cambridge University Press, 2003).

[49] Paul Reynaud, *La France a Sauvé l'Europe*, 2 (Paris: Flammarion, 1947), 297-301, 304-11; Churchill, *The Second World War*, 2: 136-8; Anthony Eden, *The Memoirs of Sir Anthony Eden*, 2 (London: Cassell, 1965), 115-6; Spears, *Assignment to Catastrophe,* 2: 139-59. For a background discussion, see: Guy Rossi-Landi, *La Drôle de guerre. La vie politique en France: 2 septembre 1939-10 mai 1940* (Paris: A. Colin, 1971), 47-64; Don W. Alexander, "Repercussions of the Breda Variant", *French Historical Studies,* 8, (1974), 459-488; Robert A. Doughty,

To Churchill's suggestion of defending Paris, Pétain replied that "making Paris into a ruin" would not alter the "final result." Furthermore, Churchill's suggestion of a "war of columns" had been rejected by Weygand with the comment that it would have meant the destruction of the country. The idea of the armistice, openly put forward by Weygand, and set aside for the time being by Reynaud, raised a reaction from Churchill which could be interpreted as a concession to a separate peace: "If it is thought best for France in her agony that her army should capitulate, let there be no hesitation on our account because whatever you may do, we shall fight on for ever and ever and ever."[50]

During the Council of Ministers' meeting on 12 June, Weygand, for the first time, posed openly the question of a separate peace, but his suggestion only found the support of Pétain, since all the other ministers lined up with Reynaud, who was a strong supporter of the Alliance with Great Britain, and the continuation of the war, if necessary, from the French colonies in North Africa. The split within the Council between the leaders of the civilian and armed forces was, by then, clearly defined, and only the replacement of Weygand and Pétain with generals willing to conduct the resistance to the bitter end would settle the divergence of strategies. Since Reynaud was unable to take such an extreme decision, he accepted Chautemps's suggestion not to take any decision before knowing the intentions of the British Government, and to ask Churchill himself to expound them the following day at Tours, during a meeting of the Supreme War Council. Reynaud, however, acting against the Council's decisions, preferred to lie to his ministers, telling them that Churchill did not wish to meet them, and so raised their resentment. He met Churchill privately in order to extend the negotiations on other issues, and to gain a stronger hold on events.[51]

The Breaking Point: Sedan and the Fall of France, 1940 (North Haven, CT: Archon Books, 1990); Pierre Le Goyet, *La defaite, 10 mai-25 juin 1940* (Paris: Economica, 1990). On the state of Anglo-French relations in April 1940, see the correspondence of Colonel Redman, officer at the British Embassy in Paris, in CaP, Cab. 21. On the French High Command, see Gunsburg, *Divided and Conquered.*

[50] Weygand, *Recalled to Service*, 148-53; Franca Avantaggiato Puppo, *Gli armistizi francesi del 1940* (Milan: 1963), 98-100. For an analysis of the downfall of France, see: Alan Shepperd, *France 1940: Blitzkrieg in the West* (Oxford: Osprey Publishing, 1990); Gilbert Martin, *The Second World War. A Complete History* (New York: Henry Holt, 2004), ch. 1, 2.

[51] For a discussion, see François Bédarida, "La rupture Franco-Britannique de 1940: le Conseil Suprême Interallié de l'invasion à la défaite de la France",

Faced with a situation in which Reynaud arbitrarily inserted the consent of his ministers to a separate peace if the worst happened, Churchill replied—according to Reynaud himself—that

> in no case would Britain waste time and energy in reproaches and recriminations, that did not mean that she would consent to action contrary to the recent agreement. The first step ought to be M. Reynaud's further message putting the present situation squarely to President Roosevelt. Let them await the answer before considering anything else. If England won the war, France would be restored in her dignity and her greatness.[52]

After meeting Churchill at Tours, Reynaud went to the castle of Cangé to meet his ministers, to whom he said that he had told Churchill that the French Government was determined to continue the resistance to the bitter end. The strong protests over his arbitrary conduct of the negotiations with Churchill much weakened Reynaud's position, and at the same time offered Pétain the chance to emerge as leader of the group favouring the armistice, supporting its inevitability, and warning his colleagues that if the Government escaped to North Africa, it would have "killed the soil of France."[53]

Vingtième siècle, 25, (1990): 37-48. On the meeting at Tours on 13 June of the Supreme War Council, see Woodward, *British Foreign Policy*, 1: 255-8.

[52] Just before the Council of Ministers of 12 June, Weygand warned Reynaud: "the country will never forgive you if, in order to remain faithful to the English, you refused a possibility of peace", Reynaud, *La France a Sauvé*, 303. For an account of the Council of Ministers, see *ibidem*, 313-6; Weygand, *Recall to Service*, 157-9; Camille Chautemps, *Cahiers Secretes de l'Armistice* (Paris: Plon, 1963), 118-34; Yves Bouthillier, *Le Drame*, 2: 54-9; Baudouin, *The Private Diaries*, 97-100, 106-7; Lebrun, *Témoignages*, 75-7; Marin, *Contributions à l'Etude*, 158-61. On the meeting between Churchill and Reynaud, see: Paul Reynaud, *Au Cœur de la Mêlée* (Paris: Flammarion, 1951), 770-4; House of Commons Debates, 25 June 1940, *Hansard*, 5th series, 362, col. 302-3; CaP, WM (40) 165. On the resentment by French ministers, and Churchill's intentions, see Churchill, *The Second World War*, 160; Spears, *Assignment to Catastrophe*, 225-6; Reynaud, *La France à Sauvé*, 316, 322-3; John C. Cairns, "Great Britain and the Fall of France: A Study in Allied Disunity", *Journal of Modern History*, (1955): 390. On the French illusion of an American intervention, see William R. Keylor, "France and the Illusion of American Support, 1919-1940", in Blatt, *The French Defeat*, 204-42. On Reynaud's messages to Roosevelt, see Woodward, *British Foreign Policy*, 1: 259-69.

[53] Reynaud, *La France a Sauvé*, 322-7; Weygand, *Recalled to Service*, 160-3; Chautemps, *Cahiers Secrets*, 134-6; Bouthilier, *Le Drame de Vichy*, 1: 66-71; Baudoin, *The Private Diaries*, 106-9; Lebrun, *Témoignages*, 77-9; Marin,

Anything might have happened. Pétain might have remained in France, in which case it was understood that he would have assumed power in accordance with Hitler. The following day, while the Germans entered Paris, Reynaud sent a second message to Roosevelt—who had not replied to his first, sent on 10 June—in which he declared that the continuation of the war on the side of Great Britain depended on the United States' entry into the war. "We can only choose," Reynaud declared, "resistance if the chance of victory appears on the horizon, if the light shines at the end of the tunnel."[54]

Roosevelt's answer to the second message from Reynaud came on 15 June, and it did not leave any doubts regarding the position of the United States, morally on the side of the Allies, but resolutely neutral. It arrived just after the end of a meeting of the Council of Ministers which recorded a deadlock between the two rival groups. Approval was given, with a majority of 13 to 6, to a compromise proposal by Chautemps— Vice-President of the Council—authorising the Government to start secret contact, through a third party, with the Germans, so as to discover the conditions of an armistice. If they were moderate, then the French Government would ask the British Cabinet to dissolve the Alliance. Albert Lebrun, President of the Republic, barely persuaded Reynaud not to resign, and he succeeded in making his opponents agree to ask the British Government for authorisation to establish the first contact with the Germans, hoping that the British colleagues would refuse it.[55]

Contributions à l'Etude, 8-10; Edouard Herriot, *Épisodes 1940-1944* (Paris: Flammarion, 1950), 63.

[54] On Reynaud's second message to Roosevelt, see: Reynaud *La France a Sauvé*, 330-1. On Franco-American relations, see: Gordon Wright, "Ambassador Bullitt and the Fall of France", *World Politics*, 10, 1, (1957): 63-90; Ann Ratcliff, "Les relations diplomatiques entre la France et les Etats-Unis (du 29 Septembre 1938 au 16 Juin 1940)", *Revue d'Histoire de la Deuxieme Guerre Mondiale*, 19, (1969): 1-40; Henry Blumenthal, *Illusion and Reality in Franco-American Diplomacy* (Baton Rouge, LA: Louisiana State University Press, 1986); Sally Marks, "The World According To Washington", *Diplomatic History*, 11, 3, (1987): 265-282; Mario Rossi, *Roosevelt and the French* (Westport, CT: Praeger, 1993); Andre Kaspi, "Franco-American Relations, 1918-1941", *Amerikastudien-American Studies*, 39, 1, (1994): 67-72.

[55] Reynaud, *La France a Savée*, 2: 338-42; Weygand, *Recalled to Service*, 169-70; Chautemps, *Cahiers Secrets*, 145-57; Bouthilier, *Le Drame de Vichy*, 1: 75-8; Baudouin, *The Private Diaries*, 112-4; Lebrun, *Témoignages*, 80-2; Marin, *Contributions à l'Etude*, 12-4; Herriot, *Episodes,* 67-9. On the rout of the French Army, see: André Beaufre, *Le Drame de 1940* (Paris: Plon, 1965); Mysyrowicz Ladislas, *Autopsie d'une défaite, origines de l'effondrement français de 1940*

Following the entry of German troops into Paris, the Government moved from Cangé to Bordeaux, where on 16 June, at 11.00 am they had a meeting, requested by Reynaud, of the Council of Ministers, together with Edouard Herriot and Julies Jeanneney, Presidents of the Chamber and the Senate. During the meeting, Pétain read his own resignation letter as a protest for the delay in the negotiations for an armistice. With that frontal and direct attack—since Reynaud still had the strength to control the majority of his ministers—the struggle between the two groups entered its final phase. As the supporters for the armistice were convinced that they had the majority of the ministers on their side, thanks to the pressure of events and the indecision of the opponents, they suggested to the Council, for the first time, the possibility of a coup by the military leaders. In view of this new fact, the Government preferred to delay—once again—the crucial choice until they had received an answer from London.[56]

Reynaud was faced with five possibilities: military capitulation and the maintenance of the Alliance with Great Britain; military resistance—the so-called scheme for a "Breton redoubt"—which would concentrate the remaining forces in a region of France; the continuation of the war from North Africa; persuading the British to free France from the agreements of

---

(Lausanne: L'Age d'homme, 1973); Pierre Le Goyet, *Le Mystère Gamelin* (Paris: Presses de la Cité, 1976); Guy Devautour and Eric Lefevre, *Mai-Juin 1940, les combattants de l'honneur* (Paris: Copernic, 1980); Stanley Hoffmann, "Le désastre de 1940", in *Études sur la France de 1939 à nos jours,* eds. Jean-Pierre Azéma and Jean-Baptiste Duroselle (Paris: Seuil, 1985); P. Le Goyet, *La défaite. 10 mai- 25 juin 1940* (Paris: Economica, 1990); Brian Bond, "Maurice Gamelin, and the Defeat of France, 1939-1940", in *Fallen Stars. Eleven Studies of Twentieth Century Military Disasters*, ed. Brian Bond (London: Brasseys', 1991), 107-40; Martin S. Alexander, "Les hommes, les munitions et la mobilisation de 1939", in *Histoire de l'armement en France de 1914 à 1962* (Paris: Editions Addim, 1994); P. Facon, *L'armée de l'Air dans la tourmente. La bataille de France, 1939-1940* (Paris: Economica, 1997); H. de Wailly, *1940, l'effondrement* (Paris: Perrin, 2000); C. Levisse-Touzé ed., *La campagne de 1940* (Paris: Tallandier, 2001); Philippe Garraud, "Le rôle de la doctrine défensive dans la défaite de 1940: une explication trop simple et partielle", *Guerres mondiales et conflits contemporains*, 214, (2004); id, "La politique française de réarmement de 1936 à 1940: priorités et contraintes", *ibidem*, 219 (2005): 87-102; id, "La politique française de réarmement de 1936 à 1940: Une production tardive mais massive", *ibidem*, 220, (2005): 97-113.
[56] Reynaud, *La France a Sauvé*, 2: 342-3; Chautemps, *Cahiers Secrets*, 157-9; Bouthilier, *Le Drame de Vichy*, 1: 81-3; Braudoin, *The Private Diaries*, 114-5. On the transfer of the French Government to Bordeaux, and its last phase, see Woodward, *British Foreign Policy*, 1: 259-82.

28 March, and to explore the possibilities of an armistice; or, finally, to resign, which meant an unconditional surrender.[57]

During the two weeks after Dunkirk, Reynaud was at the centre of contrasting forces. On one side there were the defeatists led by Weygand, and on the other the advocates of resistance to the bitter end, who had in Mandel, Herriot, Jeanneney and de Gaulle the strongest supporters. However, he was unable to make a choice. This indecision was fatal to the Alliance with Great Britain, and also to the military and moral resistance to the Germans. In moments of crisis, when a stable situation becomes fluid, the factor of leadership always plays a decisive role. France was at a crossroads, one of the most dramatic during her history. The brave and revolutionary act suggested by Monnet and de Gaulle—which was accepted with enthusiasm in Great Britain where there was a resolute leadership and a strong popular movement in support of it—was not enough to act as a catalyst for resistance, since France was lacking at that time both a resolute leadership and public support to a revolutionary line of resistance.

History shows that new ideas and innovative schemes need firm leadership in order to be realised, together with a general popular consent. That background existed in Great Britain, and belonged to the British political tradition, whereas in France, historical seat of the birth and consolidation of the nation-State, the widespread cult of national ideology prevented the growth of a federalist movement on the model of Federal Union.

In the last resort, it was the different degrees of maturity of the cultural and political forces which made the difference in the two countries. If in Great Britain there existed a well organised and influential popular movement, in France only enlightened individuals supported the federalist alternative.

To get an idea of the climate at Bordeaux this is revealed in the testimony by Emmanuel Monick on a visit that Jean Monnet, René Pleven and Robert Marjolin made in the late afternoon of June 19 to Edouard Herriot:

> The house where the President of the Chamber was staying was an astonishing sight. A large stone staircase led to the first floor. On it, as on a grand staircase at Versailles, in the time of Louis XIV, there was a crowd of courtiers—in this case, Members of Parliament waiting for news. Not

---

[57] On the possibility of continuing to fight, see A. Merglen, "La France pouvait continuer la guerre en Afrique française du Nord en juin 1940", *Guerres mondiale set conflits contemporains*, 168, (1992).

knowing what to do, they spent the whole day there standing or sitting on the steps. Asking each other questions, they passed on the most unlikely rumours, and smoked countless cigarettes. Everywhere one trod on cigarette ends. After fighting one's way through this smoke-filled throng, one reached the large first-floor antechamber. There, more important people were admitted—senior members of Parliament, former Ministers. It was like the Salon de l'Œil-de-Boeuf, reserved for the King's favourites. They speculated among themselves, sad and weary. Finally, we were ushered into the dining-room. It was lunchtime. Alone at the huge table, his napkin tucked into his waistcoat, Herriot, like the King, was eating in public. It was a *carré d'agneau à l'oseille*. Seated on chairs around the room, but not around the table, were the dignitaries of the realm: the President of the Senate, former Prime Ministers, and former Ministers. They were watching the old lion at feeding time.[58]

VI. *The reactions of the press*

The comments of the British press on Churchill's offer did not come for a few days. The text of the proposal had been published by *The Times* on 18 June—the day of the celebrated de Gaulle's appeal for the resistance to the bitter end—and its first appearance in the French press waited until 22 June in the *Petite Gironde*. According to the *Spectator* of 21 June, it was a "heroic gesture, designed to convince every Frenchman irresistibly of our resolve to stand by his country to the end."[59]

---

[58] Quoted in Monnet, *Memoirs*, 33.

[59] For a discussion on the reactions in France and Great Britain to France's downfall, see: François Seydoux, "Un certain 18 Juin", *Nouvelle Revue des Deux Mondes*, 7, (1980): 37-51; Michele Cointet, *La France a Londres: Renaissance d'un Etat, 1940-1943* (Paris: Editions Complete, 1990); Jean-Louis Crémieux-Brilhac, *La France Libre: De l'Appel du 18 Juin à la Libération* (Paris: Gallimard, 1996); Nicholas Atkin, *The Forgotten French: Exiles in the British Isles, 1940-44* (Manchester: Manchester University Press, 2003). On the controversial relations between de Gaulle and the Biritsh Government during WWII, see: Jean-Paul Cointet, "Les relations entre de Gaulle et le gouvernement britannique durant la seconde guerre mondiale", *Revue Historique*, 268, (1982): 431-451; G. E. Maguire, *Anglo-American Policy Towards the Free French* (New York: Palgrave Macmillan, 1995); David Dilks, *De Gaulle and the British*, in *Digital Convergence: Libraries of the Future*, eds. Rae A. Earnshaw and John A. Vince (Berlin: Springer, 2007), 359-79. According to John Cairns the negative attitude of de Gaulle towards British governments in the post-war years was solely related to the experience of those months in London: John C. Cairns, "De Gaulle Confronts the British: The Legacy of 1940", *International Journal*, 23, 2, (1968): 187-210. On de Gaulle's involvement in the creation, during WWII, of a policy of Atlantic

If the *Economist* of 22 June assessed it as "a milestone in the slow journey away from frenzied and stultifying nationalism," the *New Statesman and Nation* of the same day presented the idea as innovative, giving "to our struggle for European freedom a dynamic meaning":

> Continental unity must come out of this war. Shall it be on this basis of federal democracy or must it be the hegemony of a German master-race over herds of helots? What Mr Churchill by this brilliant inspiration offered to the French will presumably be open, *mutatis mutandis*, to our other allies.

The *Spectator* returned to the matter on 28 June:

> if such a Union had existed, Germany would not have been able to profit from the divisions of our foreign policies to make this war;...if we are now victorious, the absence of Union will again be our enemies' opportunity;...those who look for a wider European federation must find in the union of England and France the only practical nucleus of their dream;...a pooling of Anglo-French resources offers the only possibility of saving post-war Europe from economic chaos.[60]

Many of those who had been recently converted to the idea of co-operation and understanding with France and the Continent were disenchanted. The British people, having just achieved a European identity, psychologically broke off with Europe. "The marriage so carefully contrived by the French and their friends in London," Ludlow commented, "was never consummated, not because the British were unwilling, but because by the time they plighted their troth, the French themselves were no longer able to see it through."[61]

One should therefore not be surprised at the negative response by Eden to Guy Mollet, when the French Prime Minister asked his colleague across

---

union, see Andrew Williams, "France and the New World Order, 1940-1947", *Modern and Contemporary France*, 8, 2, (2000): 191-202.

[60] "And Now Britain", *Spectator*, 21 June 1940; "The Fate of France", *The Economist*, 22 June 1940; "If Necessary Alone", *New Statesman and Nation*, 22 June 1940; Charles Morgan, "The United Powers", *Spectator*, 28 June 1940.

[61] Peter Ludlow, "Français et Britannique dans la Drôle de Guerre", in *Actes du Colloque franco-britannique tenu à Paris du 8 au 12 décembre 1975*, ed. Peter Ludlow (Paris: 1979); id, "The Unwinding of Appeasement", in *Das 'Andere Deutschland' im Zweiten Weltkrieg*, ed. L. Kettenacker (Stuttgart: 1978), 46.

the Channel, in the middle of the Suez crisis, if the British Government was ready to renew the offer of common citizenship made in 1940.[62]

The summer of 1940 was certainly of fundamental importance to British attitudes to European integration. Before May, a closer relationship with France was the main object of British policy. After June, the British were forced to rely on their 'kin' across the Atlantic. Britain was still, genuinely at that stage, a world power—albeit in rapid decline—with global interests in the Middle East, Africa and Asia. Given the legacy of the summer of 1940—gratitude to the United States and the Commonwealth, and bitterness towards the French and the Low Countries for "letting us down", as they saw it—Great Britain took a negative attitude to the process of European integration during the post-war years. In those crucial months of 1940, deep currents and attitudes were formed and reformed in Great Britain, and a new sense of community with the United States rendered the North Atlantic an Anglo-Saxon lake around which free institutions flourished after the war.

---

[62] CaP, Cab 128/30. On the strengthening of British Atlantic policy, see: Eleanor M. Gates, *The End of the Affair: The Collapse of the Anglo-French Alliance 1939-1940* (Berkeley, CA: University of California Press, 1981); David Reynolds, "1940: Fulcrum of the Twentieth Century?", *International Affairs*, 56, 2, (1990). On the consequences of summer 1940 on British foreign policy, see Peter Calvocoressi, *Fall Out. World War II and the Shaping of Postwar Europe* (Harlow: Longman, 1997).

CONCLUSION

The fall of France was followed by the Battle of Britain, and with it began a new phase of the war: the overwhelming force of the strategy of the *blitzkrieg* was exhausted, and a "war of positions" began.[1]

The success of the combination of land and air forces allowed Hitler to break any resistance, and become, in the space of only ten months, the master of Central and Western Europe. The Channel however stopped the spread of German tanks, confining Hitler to the West, but before turning to the East and South, he continued the fight at sea, after losing the battle in the English skies. The German fleet, and in particular the submarines, inflicted serious losses on the British fleet, which was engaged in defending not only the coasts of the British Isles, but also those of the Mediterranean, the North Sea, the North Atlantic, and the Indian and Pacific Oceans. Hitler's first failure coincided with Britain's determination to resist to the bitter end. Meanwhile in the United States, a complex psychological and material process began, which brought the Americans from neutrality to intervention.[2]

It took the British naval crisis to awaken the Americans, who even though alarmed by the downfall of France, thought that Great Britain would be able to resist German attacks, with the help of the Commonwealth. While Great Britain was getting ready for resistance to the bitter end, Federal Union—having just failed to achieve an astonishing success—saw the militants leave for the front and the branches close down.

---

[1] On the *Blitzkrieg* strategy, see: Ward Rutherford, *Blitzkrieg 1940* (London: G.P. Putnam's Sons, 1980); Victor Bingham, *Blitzkrieg: The Battle of France, May-June 1940* (Alexandria, VA: Phalanx Publications, 1990); E. and H. W. Kaufmann, *Hitler's Blitzkrieg Campaigns: The Invasion and Defense of Western Europe, 1939-1940* (New York: Combined Publishing, 1993); Karl-Heinz Frieser and John T. Greenwood, *The Blitzkrieg Legend: The 1940 Campaign in the West* (Annapolis, MD: US Naval Institute Press, 2005).

[2] For a background discussion, see: Waldo Heinrichs, *Threshold of War: Franklin D. Roosevelt and American Entry Into World War II* (New York: Oxford University Press, 1990); Dallek, *Franklin D. Roosevelt*; T. R. Fehrenbach, *F.D.R.'s Undeclared War, 1939 to 1941* (New York: David McKay, 2000); Reynolds, *From Munich to.*

At that moment the role of Lothian in Washington suddenly increased in importance. It was up to Lothian to convince the Americans that their lack of confidence in the capacity of resistance of the British people was groundless, and that Great Britain was the outer ring of the United States's defence. It was also up to Lothian to persuade an initially reluctant Roosevelt to accept Churchill's official request of 15 May 1940 for fifty old American destroyers, to replace, at least partially, the losses inflicted on the British fleet by the German submarines.[3]

During the fifteen months of his diplomatic mission as British Ambassador—Lothian died in Washington on 13th December 1940—Lothian drove Roosevelt to recognise the gravity of the overall strategic situation of Great Britain, and to take immediate action. In so doing, Roosevelt could shape American foreign policy while it was still fluid. Not only had Lothian been the architect of the Destroyers-for-Bases deal, but also the inspirer of Roosevelt's "lend-lease" policy.

On 17th December, the day after his return to Washington from the Caribbean, Roosevelt announced to a very crowded press conference that it was essential to help Great Britain in all possible ways: "Suppose my neighbour's home catches fire, and I have a length of garden hose four or five hundred feet away. If he can take my garden hose and connect it up with his hydrant, I may help him to put out his fire." With this announcement, there began the period of the so-called "phoney war" in the United States, culminating with the Japanese attack on Pearl Harbour, and Hitler's declaration of war on the United States. These are two events which would probably never have happened, had Roosevelt not courageously and decisively sided with Great Britain from the summer of 1940 onwards.[4]

The thesis that the United States actually entered the war on 10 March 1941, once Congress gave its approval to the "lend-lease" programme,

---

[3] Bosco, *Lord Lothian*, 317-23. On the Destroyers-Bases Deal, see: Philip Goodhart, *Fifty Ships That Saved the World. The Foundations of the Anglo-American Alliance* (London: Heinemann, 1965); Robert Shogan, *Hard Bargain: How FDR Twisted Churchill's Arm, Evaded the Law, and Changed the Role of the American Presidency* (Boulder, CO: Westview Press, 1999). On Roosevelt's support of intervention, see: Wayne S. Cole, *America First: The Battle Against Intervention, 1940-1941* (Madison: University of Wisconsin Press, 1953); id, *Roosevelt and the Isolationists, 1932-1945* (Lincoln, NE: University of Nebraska Press, 1983); James MacGregor Burns, *Roosevelt: The Lion and the Fox 1882-1940* (San Diego, CA: Harvest/HBJ Book, 2002); id, *Roosevelt: Soldier of Freedom 1940-1945* (San Diego, CA: Harvest/HBJ Book, 2002).

[4] Bosco, *Lord Lothian*, 327-331.

does seem valid, and therefore Roosevelt's crucial decision was to appear before Congress with a clearly defined policy and the determination to win. This was just what Lothian had planned. Recourse to Congress for the Destroyers-for-Bases deal which Lothian and Roosevelt conspired to avoid, would almost certainly have been fatal, as the American public was still not ready to weigh up the political and psychological—let alone military—consequences. Lothian was not simply seeking an increase of American aid to Great Britain in order to cope with contingencies, but rather to gain political support from the American public, and hence Congress, for an organic policy of military aid, such as semi-belligerence.[5]

If during the 1930s Lothian was a pioneer, having to convince his countrymen that with the decline of British power, a historic era—that of the *Pax Britannica*—had come to an end, it was during his diplomatic mission that he became a strategist, having not only to give his own country the means to better organise resistance to Nazism, but also to give a definite shape to British foreign policy.[6]

Moreover, in the history of British federalism, Lothian and the Round Table had been the link between Imperial and international federalism. Lothian began his public life as a Milnerite imperialist. Until the Great War his political background had been the Round Table, which was the heir of the Imperial Federation League. After the First World War, he was primarily involved with the Rhodes Trust and the Royal Institute of International Affairs. He ended his public life in London by taking a leading part in shaping the Federal Union, and in Washington as the architect of closer Anglo-American cooperation during war and peace.

Lothian produced a political doctrine to show that only with a federal system could cooperation be stable and lasting. At that time he regarded federalism as a mould to be filled by historical content: the Atlantic

[5] For a general discussion see: Warren Kimball, *The Most Unsordid Act: Lend Lease, 1939-1941* (Baltimore, VI: The Johns Hopkins University Press 1969); Alan P. Dobson, *US Wartime Aid to Britain, 1940-1946* (New York: Palgrave Macmillan, 1986); Dallek, *Franklin D. Roosevelt*; Phil Butler, *Air Arsenal North America: Purchases and Lend-Lease, Aircraft for the Allies 1938-1945* (Milbank, SD: Midland, 2005).
[6] On the role which the United States played in the process of formation of the policy of Atlantic union, see: Donald C. Watt, *Succeeding John Bull: America in Britain's Place, 1900-1975* (Cambridge: Cambridge University Press, 1984); David Dimbleby and David Reynolds, *An Ocean Apart: The Relationship Between Britain and America in the Twentieth Century* (London: Trafalgar Square Press, 1988); Brian J. C. McKercher, *Transition of Power: Britain's Loss of Global Pre-eminence to the United States, 1930-45* (Cambridge: Cambridge University Press, 1999).

democracies. The Round Table enabled Lothian to grasp the meaning of
the experience of the Imperial Federation League, to adapt it to the
changing political conditions of the British Empire in the twentieth
century, and to bring it to its logical (albeit extreme) conclusion: the
political unity of the English-speaking peoples as the nucleus of world
federation. Federal Union was, then, regarded by Lothian—but not by its
three founders—as the heir to the Round Table, in a direct line of
succession from the Imperial Federation League.

In spite of the obvious dislike for federalism in Great Britain, there is a
strong federalist trend in British political culture. In three very different
historical contexts, federalism inspired an important section of British
political life. The rise of political movements such as the Imperial
Federation League, the Round Table and Federal Union, resulted from the
pressure of events connected in each case with the future of the Empire.
Federalism was regarded as the solution to problems arising from the first
signs of crisis, the disintegration and the possible collapse of Great Britain
and its Empire.

Yet political conditions did not favour the success of these solutions.
The British unitary tradition and the very fact that federalism was linked to
a sense of decline, militated against widespread enthusiasm for such
causes. The lives of those movements were relatively short, and as a result
of their political failure, they became educational organisations: the
Imperial Institute, the Royal Institute of International Affairs, and the
Federal Trust for Education and Research. The leaders of these movements
were—with some exceptions such as Kimber and Rawnsley—more men
of thought than of action. Their influence was generally limited to
intellectual circles with some weight in the press, but with little impact on
politics.

With the descent of the Teutonic night—and the consequent shifting of
the centre of gravity of world power from the Channel to the North
Atlantic—the only lights which allowed Europeans to comprehend the
deep meaning of the tragedy which was all-consuming, and to imagine
which way they could, one day, follow in order to return to the centre of
great history, were those fed by federalist ideals. From the eclipse of
Federal Union immediately followed the rise of the European Federalist
Movement, a political organisation that, under the leadership of Spinelli
and Mario Albertini, marked the path of the European rescue. It is not a
coincidence that this long march, from division to unity, has been initiated
definitely from Resistance to Nazi-Fascism. Without the federalist
perspective, the re-conquest of freedom would have been thwarted in the
archaic forms of national sovereignty. National restoration, followed by

the starting of the Cold War, has however been unable to stop the process of transferring portions of sovereignty by national States to the first supranational formation of contemporary history, the European Union.

In the history of organised federalism, Federal Union represents a quantum leap, compared to previous experiences. According to a widely accepted definition, the mature form of organised federalism must have three basic characteristics. First of all, being designed to unify all the supporters of the federation, irrespective of their political beliefs and social affiliations, a federalist organisation should not be constituted as a political party, aimed at the conquest of national power, and antagonistic, within the society, to political organisations. The struggle for national political power is, in fact, in sharp contradiction to the transfer to supranational institutions of substantial portions of national sovereignty. Secondly, they should be movements aimed at uniting all supporters of the federation, beyond their national loyalty, and directed to strengthen a supranational loyalty able to generate a political action on a supranational level. Finally, such action should aim to directly influence public opinion, regardless of national electoral campaigns, in order to influence the process of formation of a supranational political will.

However, the existence of movements with these characteristics represents only the subjective condition for effective action. There must also be objective conditions, produced by periodic crises of national political systems. In periods of relative stability, when national governments seem able to successfully settle economic, political and social problems, the movements for European federation are not able to exercise effective influence on national governments, because public opinion tends to support governmental policies. Only at times of acute crisis, when governments are not able to cope with the pressure of events, public opinion appears willing to support a supranational solution. During these crises, the movements are able—if they are well organised and influential—to mobilise the support for such solutions, and to induce governments to adopt them.

In the course of such a crisis, the moderate school has adopted in Europe a functionalist approach, while the radical school has fought to initiate a democratic constitutional process, in which the ultimate responsibility to define the nature of the new supranational institutions falls into the hands of the representatives of the European people, on the model of the Philadelphia Convention of 1787, and the successive passage of national ratifications.

The existence of these three fundamental characteristics manifested itself for the first time in the history of organised federalism specifically with the Federal Union. The preceding movements had had the key feature of gravitating around the figure of the founder, who played a guiding role within them—such as Coudenhove-Kalergi in the case of Pan Europe—or to constituting themselves as leagues, in order to achieve a specific political goal, and then dissolving themselves after attaining the aim for which they had been created, or as a consequence of the failure in achieving it, as in the case of the Imperial Federation League and the Round Table.

The movements which followed Federal Union were certainly occasionally influenced by charismatic leaders—it suffices here to mention Spinelli, Albertini, Alexandre Marc, Henri Brugmans, and Denis de Rougemont—but they continued to exist even after the disappearance of their charismatic leaders. Moreover, they identified from the very beginning the temporal dimension of their existence with the historical course itself, since the battle for the European federation is just a stage—and certainly not the most critical—in the fight for the realisation of the rule of law in the world as a whole. Their fundamental *raison d'etre* lies in fact in the affirmation of an absolute value—therefore with a metahistorical character—that of universal peace.

If it is true that Federal Union marks the watershed between an archaic and a mature form of organised federalism, it appears plausible to identify the year zero of militant federalism with the birth of Federal Union. Since it is not possible to prescind from Federal Union in order to assess the significance of the first supranational political action in modern history—it is not possible, in fact, to consider as such the attempts to reform on federal lines the British Empire, or that by Briand to create a European confederation—it is also not possible to prescind from Federal Union in order to assess the significance of the emergence in history of a new political behaviour, according to which the end of the political struggle is no longer the conquest of national power, but the construction of a supranational institution.

Federal Union also represented a paradigmatic experience as regards the manifestation of this new political behaviour in two schools: the moderate and the radical one. Federal Union was primarily the expression of the radical school—defined constitutional by Spinelli —but, as we have seen, stances by the functionalist school coexisted, either within the movement itself, or within the broad debate generated by the movement.[7]

---

[7] On the dialectics between functionalism and federalism, see Cornelia Navari, "The Dialectics of Functionalism and Federalism," in *Annals of the Lothian Foundation*, 4, (1994): 371-298.

Following June's failure, it was precisely Monnet who, inspired by Mitrany, became the champion of that functionalism which has marked the history of the European post-war construction. The battle which the three young founders of Federal Union thought they could win in the space of a few months has developed over more than half a century, involving more than a generation. At its most critical period, the European Union owes much to those intrepid young men who, in the autumn of 1938, devoted themselves to the impossible, proving to the world that that venture was considered as such only for having never been attempted.

BIBLIOGRAPHY

Primary Sources

Papiers de l'Association Suisse pour la Société des Nations (ASSN), Library of the Société des Nations, Geneva.
Beveridge Papers (BP), Library of the London School of Economics, Manuscript Division.
Cabinet Papers (CaP), National Archives, Kew.
Chatham House Papers (CHP), Archive of the Royal Institute of International Affairs, London.
Coudenhove-Kalergi Papers (CKP), Fondation Archives Européennes, Geneve.
Lionel Curtis Papers (CP), Bodleian Library, Oxford.
Clarence Streit Papers (CSP), Library of the Congress, Manuscripts Division, Washington DC.
Foreign Office Papers (FOP), National Archives, Kew.
Josephy Papers (JP), Library of the London School of Economics, Manuscript Division.
Lothian Papers (LP), National Archives of Scotland, Edinburgh.
Papiers Jean Monnet (PJM), Fondation Jean Monnet pour l'Europe, Lausanne.
Papiers 1940. Bureau d'études Chauvel (P40), Archive of the Ministère des Affaires Étrangères, Paris.
Rappard Papers (RP), Archives Fédérales, Bern.
Stokes Papers (SP), Bodleian Library, Oxford.

Secondary Sources

Aarons, Mark, and Loftus, John. *Unholy Trinity: The Vatican, The Nazis, and The Swiss Banks*. New York: St. Martin's Griffin, 1998.
Adamthwaite, Anthony. *France and the Coming of the Second World War, 1936-1939*. London: Routledge, 1977.
—— *Grandeur and Misery: France's Bid for Power in Europe, 1914-1940*. London: E. Arnold, 1995.

Addison, Paul. "Lloyd George and Compromise Peace in the Second World War", in *Lloyd George: Twelve Essays*. Edited by A. J. P. Taylor. London: Atheneum, 1971.

Agnelli, Giovanni and Cabiati, Andrea. *Federazione europea o Società delle Nazioni*. Turin: 1919.

Albertini, Mario. *Proudhon*. Milan: Giuffrè, 1974.

— *Il federalismo. Antologia e definizione*. Bologna: Il Mulino, 1979.

— *Una rivoluzione pacifica*. Bologna: Il Mulino, 1999.

— *Tutti gli scritti*, 9 vols. Bologna: Il Mulino, 2006-10.

Alexander, Don W. "Repercussions of the Breda Variant", *French Historical Studies,* 8, (1974).

Alexander, Martin S. *The Republic in Danger: General Maurice Gamelin and the Politics of French Defence, 1933-1940*. Cambridge: Cambridge University Press, 1992.

— "Les hommes, les munitions et la mobilisation de 1939", in *Histoire de l'armement en France de 1914 à 1962*. Paris: Editions Addim, 1994.

— "'Fighting to the Last Frenchman?' Reflection on the BEF Deployment to France and the Strains in the Franco-British Alliance, 1939-1940", in *The French Defeat of 1940. Reassessments*. Edited by Joel Blatt. Oxford: Berghahn, 1997.

— *The Republic at War: Franco-British Strategy, Politics and Defeat, 1939-1940*. Cambridge: Cambridge University Press, 1998.

— and Graham, Helen. *The French and Spanish Popular Fronts: Comparative Perspectives*. Cambridge: Cambridge University Press, 2002.

— and Philpott, William J. *Anglo-French Defence Relations Between the Wars*. New York: Palgrave Macmillan, 2003.

Alexandroff, Alan and Rosecrance, Richard. "Deterrence in 1939", *World Politics*, 29, 3, (1977).

Alonso, Harriet Hyman. *Peace as a Women's Issue: A History of the U.S. Movement for World Peace and Women's Rights*. Syracuse: Syracuse University Press, 1993.

— *The Women's Peace Union and the Outlawry of War, 1921-1942*. Knoxville, TN: University of Tennessee Press, 1997.

Ambrosius, Lloyd E. *Wilsonianism: Woodrow Wilson and His Legacy in American Foreign Relations*. New York: Palgrave Macmillan, 2002.

Anderson, David G. "British Rearmament and the 'Merchants of Death': 1935-1936", *Journal of Contemporary History*, 29, 1, (1994).

Angell, Norman. *The Great Illusion*. London: William Heinemann, 1909.

— *For What Do We Fight?* London: 1939.

330 Bibliography

Arnal, Oscar L. *Ambivalent Alliance: The Catholic Church and Action Française 1899-1939*. Pittsburgh: University of Pittsburgh Press, 1985.
Aron, Raymond and Marc, Alexandre. *Principes du fédéralisme*. Paris: Le Portulan, 1948.
— *Paix et guerre entre les nations*. Paris: Calmann-Lévy, 2004.
Ashworth, Lucian M. and Long, David. *New Perspectives on International Functionalism*. New York: Palgrave Macmillan, 1998.
Astor, Nancy. *Nancy Astor's Canadian Correspondence, 1912-1962*. Edited by Martin Thornton. Lewiston: Edwin Mellen Press, 1997.
Atkin, Nicholas. *The Forgotten French: Exiles in the British Isles, 1940-44*. Manchester: Manchester University Press, 2003.
Attlee, Clement. *Labour's Peace Aims*. London: Labour Party, 1940.
Auvray, Michel. *Objecteurs, insoumis, déserteurs: Histoire des réfractaires en France*. Paris: Stock 2, 1983.
Avril, Michel. *Raoul Dautry: la passion de servir, 1880-1951*. Paris: France-Empire, 1993.
Ayerst, David. *Garvin of the Observer: A Life*. London: Croom Helm, 1984.
Bailey, Gerald. *The Politics of Peace*. Earlham: Earlham College Press, 1963.
— *Problems of Peace*. London: Ginn, 1970.
Baker, Andrew. "Anglo-Irish Relations, 1939-1941: A Study in Multilateral Diplomacy and Military Restraint", *Twentieth Century British History*, 15, 4, (2005).
Baker, J. R. *Julian Huxley, Scientist and World Citizen, 1887-1975*. London: Unipub, 1978.
Ball, Stuart. *Parliament and Politics in the Age of Churchill and Attlee: The Headlam Diaries 1935-1951*. Cambridge: Cambridge University Press, 2000.
Bán, András D. *Pax Britannica*. New York: Columbia University Press, 1997.
Bankwitz, Philip. "Maxime Weygand and the Fall of France: A Study in Civil-Military Relations", *Journal of Modern History*, 31, 1, (1959).
Bankwitz, Philip, and Farwell, Charles. *Maxime Weygand and Civil-Military Relations in Modern France*. Boston, MA: Harvard University Press, 1967.
Baratta, Joseph Preston "Clarence Streit e l'idea dell'unione delle democrazie", *Il Federalista*, 30, 2, (1988).
— "Henry Usborne and the Creation of the World Movement for World Federal Government", in *The Federal Idea: The History of Federalism*

from the Enlightenment to 1945. Edited by Andrea Bosco. London: Lothian Foundation Press, 1991.

Barber, Noel. *The Week France Fell, June 10-16, 1940*. New York: Cooper Square Press, 2000.

Barbier, J. B. *Le Pacifisme dans l'histoire de France*. Paris: La librairie française, 1966.

Barnes, John and Nicholson, David eds. *The Empire at Bay. The Leo Amery Diaries, 1929-1945*. London: Hutchinson, 1988.

Batowski, Henryk. "Les relations diplomatiques franco-polonaises pendant la 'drôle de guerre'", *Guerres Mondiales et Conflits Contemporains*, 42, (1992).

Bauden, P. "Finances publiques et Économie pendant la drôle de guerre", *Revue Historique*, 561, (1987).

Baudoui, Remi. *Raoul Dautry, 1880-1951: le technocrate de la République*. Paris: Balland, 1992.

Baudouin, Paul. *The Private Diaries (March 1940 to January 1941) of Paul Baudouin*. London: Eyrie & Spottiswoode, 1948.

Bauer, Hans. *Le 50 ans de l'Union européenne de Suisse, 1934-1984*. Bern: Europa Union, 1984.

Beaufre, André. *Le Drame de 1940*. Paris: Plon, 1965.

Becker, Jean-Jacques. "L'Europe dans la 'drôle de guerre'", *Histoire*, 129, (1990).

Beckett, Francis. *Clem Attlee: A Biography*. London: Politico's Publishing, 2000.

Bédarida François. *La stratégie secrète de la drôle de guerre: la Conseil Suprême Interallié, septembre 1939-avril 1940*. Paris: Presses de la Fondation Nationale des Sciences Politiques, 1979.

— "La rupture Franco-Britannique de 1940: le Conseil Suprême Interallié de l'invasion à la défaite de la France", *Vingtième siècle*, 25, (1990).

— and Peschanski, Denis eds. "Marc Bloch à Etienne Bloch: Lettres de la drôle de guerre", *Cahiers de l'Institut d'Histoire du Temps Présent*, 19, (1991).

— *Churchill*. Paris: Fayard, 1999.

— "Winston Churchill's Image of France and the French", in *Anglo-French Relations, 1898-1998: From Fashoda to Jospin*. Edited by Michael Dockrill and Philippe Chassaigne. New York: Palgrave Macmillan, 2002.

Beevor, Antony and Cooper, Artemis. *Paris After the Liberation 1944-1949*. London: Penguin, 2004.

Bell, B. G. *Route to Potsdam: The Story of the Peace Aims, 1939-1945*. London: Allan Wingate, 1945.

Bell, Peter M. H. *A Certain Eventuality: Britain and the Fall of France.* Farnborough: Saxon House, 1974.
— *The Origins of the Second World War in Europe.* Harlow: Longman, 1986.
— *France and Britain, 1900-40: Entente and Estrangement.* Harlow: Longman, 1996.
"Uncle Sam Prepares: The Presentation of the United States in British Newsreels before the Second World War", *Film & History*, 30, 2, (2000).
Beloff, Max. "The Anglo-French Union Project of June 1940", in *The Intellectual in Politics and Other Essays.* Edited by Max Beloff. London: The Library Press, 1970.
— "Leo Amery: The Last Imperialist", *History Today*, 39, 1, (1989).
Bennett, Gill. *Churchill's Man of Mystery: Desmond Morton and the World of Intelligence.* London: Routledge, 2006.
Bennett, Todd. "The Celluloid War: State and Studio in Anglo-American Propaganda Film-Making, 1939-1941", *International History Review*, 24, 1, (2002).
Bentwich, Norman. "The Colonial Problem and the Federal Solution", in *Studies in Federal Planning.* Edited by Patrick Ransome. London: Lothian Foundation Press, 1990.
Berlia, Georges. *Problèmes de sécurité internationale et de défense.* Paris: Les Cours de droit, 1975.
— *Le maintien de la paix: Doctrines et problèmes: 1919-1976.* Paris: Les Cours de droit, 1976.
Bernard, Philippe and Dubief, Henri. *The Decline of the Third Republic, 1914-1938.* Cambridge: Cambridge University Press, 1988.
Berstein, Serge. *La France des années 30.* Paris: 1993.
Beveridge, William. "Peace by Federation?", in *World Order Papers.* Oxford: Oxford University Press, 1940.
— *Power and Influence.* London: Hodder & Stoughton, 1953.
Bialer, Uri. "Elite Opinion and Defence Policy: Air Power Advocacy and British Rearmament During the 1930s", *British Journal of International Studies*, 6, 1, (1980).
Bidault, Georges. *Resistance: The Political Autobiography of Georges Bidault.* Westport, CT: Praeger, 1967.
Bilis, Michel. *Socialistes et pacifists 1933-1939: Ou l'intenable dilemma des socialistes français.* Paris: Editions Syndicalistes, 1979.
Billington, David P. *Lothian: Philip Kerr and the Quest for World Order.* Westport, CT: Praeger, 2006.

Bingham, Victor. *Blitzkrieg: The Battle of France, May-June 1940*. Alexandria, VA: Phalanx Publications, 1990.

Birkenhead, Frederick Winston. *Halifax: The Life of Lord Halifax*. London: Houghton Mifflin, 1966.

Birkett, Jennifer and Briganti, Chiara eds. *Margaret Storm Jameson: Writing in Dialogue*. Cambridge: Cambridge Scholars Publishing, 2007.

Birn, Donald S. *League of Nations Union, 1918-1945*. Oxford: Oxford University Press, 1981.

Blackwell, Joyce. *No Peace Without Freedom: Race and the Women's International League for Peace and Freedom, 1915-1975*. Carbondale, IL: Southern Illinois University Press, 2004.

Blake, Robert. *Churchill: A Major New Assessment of His Life in Peace and War*. New York: W. W. Norton & Company, 1993.

Blet, Pierre. *Pius XII and the Second World War: According to the Archives of the Vatican*. New York: Paulist Press, 1999.

Bloch, Marc. *L'étrange défaite*. Paris: Gallimard, 1990.

Blond, Georges. *Petain, 1856-1951*. Paris: Presses de la Citè, 1966.

Bloom, Harold. *H. G. Wells*. London: Chelsea House Publications, 2005.

Blumenthal, Henry. *Illusion and Reality in Franco-American Diplomacy*. Baton Rouge, LA: Louisiana State University Press, 1986.

Boadle, Donald Graeme. "The Formation of the Foreign Office Economic Relations Section, 1930-1937", *Historical Journal*, 20, 4, (1977).

Boemeke, Manfred F. *et al. The Treaty of Versailles: A Reassessment after 75 Years*. Cambridge: Cambridge University Press, 1998.

Boettke, Peter J. *The Legacy of Friedrick von Hayek*. London: Edward Elgar Publications, 2000.

Bond, Brian J. *British Military Policy between the Two World Wars*. Oxford: Clarendon Press, 1980.

— "The Calm Before the Storm: Britain and the Phoney War, 1939-1940", *Journal of the United Service Institution*, 135, 1, (1990).

— "Maurice Gamelin and the Defeat of France, 1939-1940", in *Fallen Stars. Eleven Studies of Twentieth Century Military Disasters*. Edited by Brian Bond. London: Brasseys', 1991.

Bosco, Andrea. "L'eredità kantiana e Lord Lothian", in *Coscienza civile ed esperienza religiosa nell'Europa moderna*. Edited by Romeo Crippa. Brescia: Morcelliana, 1983.

— "Lord Lothian e la nascita di Federal Union: 1939-40", *Il Politico*, 48, 2, (1983).

— "La dottrina politica di Lord Lothian", *Annali della Fondazione Luigi Einaudi*, 18, (1985).

— "Lord Lothian e la grande illusione: 1928-30", *Critica Storica*, 21, 4, (1985).

— "National Sovereignty and Peace: Lord Lothian's Federalist Thought", in *The Larger Idea: Lord Lothian and the Problem of National Sovereignty*. Edited by John Turner. London: The Historians' Press, 1988.

— *Lord Lothian. Un pioniere del federalismo, 1882-1940*. Milan: Jaca, 1989.

— Introduction to *Towards the United States of Europe. Studies in the Making of the European Constitution*. Edited by Patrick Ransome. London: Lothian Foundation Press, 1991.

— ed., *The Federal Idea. The History of Federalism from the Enlightenment to 1945*. London: Lothian Foundation Press, 1991.

— "Lord Lothian, Lionel Curtis and the Making of the Indian Federation", *Annals of the Lothian Foundation*, 1, (1991).

— ed., *The Federal Idea. The History of Federalism since 1945*. London: Lothian Foundation Press, 1991.

— and Navari, Cornelia eds. *Chatham House and British Foreign Policy. The Royal Institute of International Affairs During the Inter-War Period 1919-1945*. London: Lothian Foundation Press, 1994.

— "Lord Lothian's Political Doctrine", *Annals of the Lothian Foundation*, 4, (1994).

— and May, Alex eds. *The Round Table Movement, the Empire/ Commonwealth and British Foreign Policy*. London: Lothian Foundation Press, 1997.

— ed., *Two Musketeers for the Empire. The Lionel Curtis-Philip Kerr (Lord Lothian) Correspondence 1909-1940*. London: Lothian Foundation Press, 1997.

— "The British Foreign Office and the Briand Plan", in *Le Plan Briand d'Union fédérale européenne*. Edited by Antoine Fleury and Lubor Jilek. Geneva: Peter Lang, 1997.

— *Federal Union e l'unione franco-britannica. Il dibattito federalista nel Regno Unito dal Patto di Monaco al crollo della Francia. 1938-1940*. Bologna: Il Mulino, 2009.

— *From Empire to Atlantic Order. The Round Table Movement and the Unwinding of the British Empire, 1909-1919*. Cambridge, Cambridge Scholars Publishing, 2016.

Bossuat, Gerard. *Les Aides Américaines Economiques et Militaires a la France 1938-1960: Une Nouvelle Image des Rapports de Puissance*. Paris: Comite pour l'Histoire Economique et Financière de la France, 2001.

Bourdé, Guy. *La Défaite du Front Populaire*. Paris: La Découverte, 1977.

Bourdin, René and Janine eds. *Edouard Daladier. Chief de Gouvernement, avril 1938-septembre 1939*. Paris: Presses de la Fondation Nationale des Sciences Politiques, 1977.

Bourgeois, Daniel. "Entre l'engagement et le réalisme: William E. Rappard et l'Association suisse pour la SdN face à la crise de 1940", in *L'historien et les relations internationales*. Geneve: Institut Universitaire de Hautes Études Internationales, 1981.

Bouthillier, Yves. *Le Drame de Vichy. Face à l'ennemi, 1.* Paris: Plon, 1950.

Bouvier, René. *Quels sont les buts de guerre franco-anglais?* Paris: La vie, 1940.

Boyce, George. "From War to Neutrality: Anglo-Irish Relations, 1921-1950", *British Journal of International Studies*, 5, 5, (1979).

— *French Foreign and Defence Policy, 1918-1940: The Decline and Fall of a Great Power*. London: Routledge, 1998.

— *Decolonisation and the British Empire, 1775-1997*. New York: Palgrave Macmillan, 1999.

— "'Breaking the Banque': The Great Crisis in Franco-British Central Bank Relations between the Wars", in *Anglo-French Relations, 1898-1998: From Fashoda to Jospin*. Edited by Michael Dockrill and Philippe Chassaigne. New York: Palgrave Macmillan, 2002.

— *The Origins of World War Two: The Debate Continues*. New York: Palgrave Macmillan, 2003.

Boyd Orr, John and Cole, G. D. H. *Welfare and Peace*. London: National Peace Council, 1945.

Boyer, Alain Canguilhem, *et al. Raymond Aron, la philosophie de l'histoire et les sciences sociales*. Paris: Rue d'Ulm, 2005.

Boyle, Francis Anthony. *Foundations of World Order: The Legalist Approach to International Relations, 1898-1922*. Durham, NC: Duke University Press, 1999.

Bradford, A. Lee. "Strategy, Arms and the Collapse of France, 1930-1940", in *Diplomacy and Intelligence During the Second World War: Essays in Honour of F. H. Hinsley*. Edited by Richard Langhorne. Cambridge: Cambridge University Press, 2004.

Braga, Antonella. *Un federalista giacobino. Ernesto Rossi pioniere degli Stati Uniti d'Europa*. Bologna: Il Mulino, 2007.

Brailsford, Henry Noel. *Our Settlement with Germany*. New York: The John Day Company, 1945.

— *The Levellers and the English Revolution*. Standford, CA: Standford University Press, 1961.

Brewer, Susan A. *To Win the Peace: British Propaganda in the United States during World War II*. Ithaca, NY: Cornell University Press, 1997.

Brewin, Christopher. "Research in a Global Context: A Discussion of Toynbee's Legacy", *Review of International Studies*, 18, 2, (1992).

Brinkley, Douglas and Hackett, Clifford. *Jean Monnet. The Path to European Unity*. New York: St. Martin's Press, 1991.

Brocker, Mark S. *Dietrich Bonhoeffer: Conspiracy and Imprisonment, 1940-1945*. Minneapolis: Fortress Press, 2006.

Brodie, Frawn McKay. *Peace Aims and Post-war Planning: A Bibliography*. Boston, MA: World Peace Foundation, 1942.

Brown, David. *The Road to Oran: Anglo-French Naval Relations, September 1939-July 1940*. London: Routledge, 2004.

Bruce, Robert B. *Petain: From Verdun to Vichy*. Dulles, VA: Potomac Books, 2007.

Brugmans, Henri. *L'idée Européenne 1918-1965*. Bruges: De Tempel, 1965.

— *La pensée politique du fédéralisme*. Leyden: A. W. Sijthoff, 1969.

Buffotot, P. *Le socialisme français et la guerre. Du soldat citoyen à l'armée professionnelle. 1871-1998*. Paris: Bruylant, 1998.

Bullock, Alan and Brivati, Brian. *Ernest Bevin: A Biography*. London: Politico's Publishing, 2002.

Bungay, Stephen. *The Most Dangerous Enemy: A History of the Battle of Britain*. London: Aurum Press, 2001.

Burgess, Michael. "Imperial Federation: Continuity and Change in British Imperial Ideas, 1869-1871," *The New Zealand Journal of History* 17, 2, (1983).

— "'Forgotten Centenary': The Formation of the Imperial Federation in the UK," *The Round Table* 289, (1984).

— "The Federal Plan of the Imperial Federation League 1892: Milestone or Tombstone?" in *The Federal Idea. The History of Federalism from the Enlightenment to 1945*. Edited by Andrea Bosco. London: Lothian Foundation Press, 1991.

— *The British Tradition of Federalism*. Leicester: Leicester University Press, 1995.

Burns, James MacGregor. *Roosevelt: The Lion and the Fox 1882-1940*. San Diego, CA: Harvest/HBJ Book, 2002.

— *Roosevelt: Soldier of Freedom 1940-1945*. San Diego, CA: Harvest/HBJ Book, 2002.

Butler, James R. M. *Lord Lothian (Philip Kerr) 1882-1940*. London: Macmillan, 1960.

Butler, L. J. *Britain and Empire: Adjusting to a Post-Imperial World*. New York: I. B. Tauris, 2002.

Butler, Phil. *Air Arsenal North America: Purchases and Lend-Lease, Aircraft for the Allies 1938-1945*. Milbank, SD: Midland, 2005.

Buzan, Barry and Little, Richard. *International Systems in World History: Remaking the Study of International Relations*. New York: Oxford University Press, 2000.

Byron, Robert. "Le Mouvement de l'Union Fédérale en Grand Bretagne", *Nouveaux Cahiers*, 54, (1940).

— *The Road to Oxiana*. New York: Oxford University Press, 2007.

Cadogan, Alexander. *The Diaries of Sir Alexander Cadogan*. Edited by David Dilks. London: Cassell, 1971.

Caedel, Martin. *Pacifism in Britain, 1914-45: The Defining of a Faith*. Oxford: Oxford University Press, 1980.

— *Thinking About Peace and War*. Oxford: Oxford University Press, 1987.

— "Supranationalism in the British Peace Movement During the Early Twentieth Century", in *The Federal Idea. The History of Federalism from the Enlightenment to 1945*. Edited by Andrea Bosco. London: Lothian Foundation Press, 1991.

Cairns, John C. "Great Britain and the Fall of France: A Study in Allied Disunity", *Journal of Modern History*, 27, 4, (1955).

— "De Gaulle Confronts the British: The Legacy of 1940", *International Journal*, 23, 2, (1968).

— "A Nation of Shopkeepers in Search of a Suitable France, 1919-40", *American Historical Review*, 79, 3, (1974).

— "Some Recent Historians and the Strange Defeat of 1940", *Journal of Modern History*, 46, 1, (1974).

Calvocoressi, Peter. *Fall Out. World War II and the Shaping of Post-war Europe*. Harlow: Longman, 1997.

Campbell Johnson, Alan. *Anthony Eden: A Biography*. Whitefish, MT: Kessinger Publishing, 2007.

Caraffini, Paolo. *Costruire l'Europa dal basso. Il ruolo del Consiglio italiano del movimento europeo, 1948-1985*. Bologna: Il Mulino, 2005.

Carley, Michael Jabara. *1939. The Alliance That Never Was and the Coming of the Second World War*. Chicago: Ivan R. Dee, 1999.

— "Prelude to Defeat: Franco-Soviet Relations, 1919-1939", in *The French Defeat of 1940: Reassessments*. Edited by Joel Blatt. Oxford: Berghahn Books, 2000.

Carlton, David. *Anthony Eden: A Biography*. New York: Harper Collins, 1986.

Carr, E. H. *The Twenty Years' Crisis 1919-1939: An Introduction to the Study of International Relations*. Edited by Mike Cox. New York: Palgrave Macmillan, 2001.

Carter, April. *Political Theory of Global Citizenship*. London: Routledge, 2001.

Carter, Horsfall. "Vers l'Europe de Demain", *Nouveaux Cahiers*, 54, (1940).

Casey, Steven. *Cautious Crusade: Franklin D. Roosevelt, American Public Opinion, and the War against Nazi Germany*. New York: Oxford University Press, 2001.

Cecil, Robert. *A Great Experiment. An Autobiography by Viscount Cecil*. Oxford: Oxford University Press, 1941.

— *Letters from Sir Robert Cecil to Sir George Carew*. Edited by John Maclean. Whitefish, MT: Kessinger Publishing, 2007.

Chadeau, Emmanuel. *L'industrie aéronautique en France, 1900-1950: de Blériot à Dassaul*. Paris: 1987.

Chadwick, Owen. *Gran Bretagna e Vaticano durante la Seconda guerra mondiale*. Rome: San Paolo Edizioni, 2007.

Chafer, Tony and Sackur, Amanda. *Promoting the Colonial Idea: Propaganda and Visions of Empire in France*. New York: Palgrave Macmillan, 2002.

Chamberlain, Joseph Perkins. *The Fate of Refugees and Displaced Persons*. New York: Columbia University Press, 1947.

— *Legislative Processes: National and State*. Westport, CT: Greenwood Press, 1969.

Chamberlain, Neville. *Britain's Peace Aims*. London: His Majesty's Stationery Office, 1940.

— *The Neville Chamberlain Diary Letters: The Downing Street Years, 1934-1940*. Edited by Robert Self. London: Ashgate Publishing, 2005.

Channing-Pearce, Melville ed. *Federal Union. A Symposium*. London: Jonathan Cape, 1940.

Chapman, Guy. *Why France Fell: The Defeat of the French Army in 1940*. New York: Holt, Rinehart and Winston, 1969.

Chapman, H. *State Capitalism and Working-Class Radicalism in the French Aircraft Industry*. Berkeley, CA: Berkeley University Press, 1991.

Chapman, James. *The British at War: Cinema, State and Propaganda, 1939-1945*. New York: Tauris Academic Studies, 1998.

Charles-Roux, François. *Cinq Mois tragiques aux Affaires étrangères*. Paris: Plon, 1949.

Charmley, John. *Duff Cooper: The Authorised Biography*. London: Orion Publishing, 1987.

— *Chamberlain and the Lost Peace*. London: Hodder & Stoughton, 1989.

— *Churchill's Grand Alliance: The Anglo-American Special Relationship, 1940-57*. San Diego, CA: Harcourt Brace Jovanovich, 1995.

Charteris, A. H. "An Australian Comment on Streit's 'Union Now'", *New Commonwealth Quarterly*, 5, (1939).

Chassaigne, Phillipe and Dockrill, Michael eds. *Anglo-French Relations 1898-1998: From Fashoda to Jospin*. New York: Palgrave Macmillan, 2002.

Chatfield, Twayne. *The American Peace Movement: Ideals and Activism*. Boston, MA: Twayne Publications, 1992.

Chautemps, Camille. *Cahiers Secrets de l'Armistice 1939-1940*. Paris: Plon, 1963.

Chickering, Roger and Forster, Stig. *The Shadows of Total War: Europe, East Asia, and the United States, 1919-1939*. Cambridge: Cambridge University Press, 2003.

Chown, John F. *A History of Monetary Unions*. London: Routledge, 2003.

Christienne, Charles and Lissarague, Pierre. *Histoire de l'aviation militaire: L'armée de l'Air, 1928-1981*. Paris: 1981.

Churchill, Winston. *The Second World War*, 2. London: 1948.

— *Memoirs of the Second World War*. London: Mariner Books, 1991.

— *Blood, Toil, Tears and Sweat: The Great Speeches*. Edited by David Cannadine. London: Penguin Classics, 2007.

Clayton, Tim and Craig, Phil. *The Finest Hour. The Battle of Britain*. New York: Simon & Schuster, 2000.

Clogg, Richard. *Politics and the Academy: Arnold Toynbee and the Koraes Chair*. London: Routledge, 1986.

Cockett, Richard. *David Astor and the Observer*. London: Andre Deutsch, 1992.

Cogan, Charles. *French Negotiating Behaviour: Dealing with la 'Grande Nation'*. Washington, DC: United States Institute of Peace Press, 2004.

Cohen, Gidon. *The Failure of a Dream: The Independent Labour Party from Disaffiliation to World War II*. New York: Tauris Academic Studies, 2007.

Cohrs, Patrick O. *The Unfinished Peace after World War I: America, Britain and the Stabilisation of Europe, 1919-1932*. Cambridge: Cambridge University Press, 2006.

Cointet, Jean-Paul. "Les relations entre de Gaulle et le gouvernement britannique durant la seconde guerre mondiale", *Revue Historique*, 268, (1982).

— *Pierre Laval*. Paris: Fayard, 1993.

Cointet, Michèle. *La France a Londres: Renaissance d'un Etat, 1940-1943*. Paris: Editions Complexe, 1990.

Cole, G. D. H. *War Aims*. London: The New Statesman and Nation, 1939.

— *When the Fighting Stops*. London: National Peace Council, 1943.

— *Great Britain in the Post War World*. London: Victor Gollancz, 1945.

— *Communism and Social Democracy, 1914-1931*. London: Macmillan, 1958.

— *Socialism and Fascism, 1931-1939*. New York: St. Martin's Press, 1960.

— *Fabian Socialism*. London: Routledge, 1971.

Cole, Laurence and Unowsky Daniel L. eds. *The Limits of Loyalty: Imperial Symbolism, Popular Allegiances and State Patriotism in the Late Habsburg Monarchy*. Oxford: Berghahn Books, 2007.

Cole, Wayne S. *America First: The Battle Against Intervention, 1940-1941*. Madison: University of Wisconsin Press, 1953.

— *Roosevelt and the Isolationists, 1932-1945*. Lincoln, NE: University of Nebraska Press, 1983.

Colton, Joel. *Léon Blum: Humanist in Politics*. Durham, NC: Duke University Press, 1987.

Colville, John. *Winston Churchill and His Inner Circle*. London: Simon & Schuster, 1981.

— *The Fringes of Power*. London: Hodder and Stoughton, 1985.

Colvin, Ian. *Vansittart in Office: An Historical Survey of the Origins of the Second World War Based on the Papers of Sir Robert Vansittart*. London: Victor Gollancz, 1965.

Conze, Vanessa. *Richard Coudenhove-Kalergi*. Zurig: Muster-Schmidt Verlag, 1998.

Cooper, Duff. *The Second World War*. London: 1949

Corbett, Percy Ellwood. *War Aims and Post-War Plans*. New York: American Committee of International Studies, 1941.

Cornick, Martin. *French Intellectuals and History: The 'Nouvelle Revue Française' under Jean Paulhan, 1925-1940*. Amsterdam: Rodopi Bv Editions, 1995.

Cornwell, John. *Hitler's Pope: The Secret History of Pius XII*. London: Penguin, 2000.

Côt, Pierre. *Triumph of Treason: Contre Nous de la tyrannie*. London: Ziff-Davis, 1944.

Coudenhove-Kalergi, Richard. *Pan Europe*. New York: A. A. Knopf, 1926.

— *Europe Must Unite*. Plymouth: Mayflower Press, 1938.

— *Crusade for Pan-Europa*. New York: A. A. Knopf, 1943.

— *Europe Seeks Unity*. New York: A. A. Knopf, 1948.

— *An Idea Conquers the World*. London: Hutchinson, 1953.

Courtin, Emilie. *Droit et politique dans l'ouvre d'Alexandre Marc: L'inventeur du fédéralisme intégral*. Paris: L'Harmattan, 2007.

Courtois, Stéphane. *Le PCF dans la guerre*. Paris: 1980.

Coutau-Bégarie H. and Huan, C. *Mers-el-Kébir, 1940: La Rupture Franco-Britannique*. Paris: Economica, 1994.

Cowles, Virginia. *The Astors: The Story of a Transatlantic Family*. London: Weidenfeld & Nicolson, 1979.

Cowling, Maurice. *The Impact of Hitler: British Politics and British Policy 1933-1940*. Cambridge: Cambridge University Press, 2005.

Craig, Phil and Clayto, Tim. *Finest Hour: The Battle of Britain*. London: Simon & Schuster, 2002.

Crankshaw, Edward. *The Forsaken Idea: A Study of Viscount Milner*. Westport, CT: Greenwood Press, 1974.

Crawford, John. *Kia Kaka: New Zealand in the Second World War*. New York: Oxford University Press, 2002.

Crémieux-Brilhac, Jean-Louis. *Les Français de l'an 40. La Guerre, Oui ou Non?*, 1. Paris: Gallimard, 1990.

— *La France Libre: De l'Appel du 18 Juin à la Libération*. Paris: Gallimard, 1996.

Crowson, N. J. "Conservative Parliamentary Dissent Over Foreign Policy During the Premiership of Neville Chamberlain: Myth or Reality?", *Parliamentary History*, 14, 3, (1995).

Crozier, Andrew J. *The Causes of the Second World War*. Oxford: Blackwell, 1997.

Cubitt, C. E. *A Life of Friedrick August von Hayek*. Gamlingay: Authors onLine, 2006.

Cuisenier, André. *Jules Romains, l'onanisme et les hommes de bonne*. Paris: Flammarion, 1992.

Cull, John. *Selling War: The British Propaganda Campaign against American 'Neutrality' in World War*. New York: Oxford University Press, 1996.

— "Selling Peace: The Origins, Promotion and Fate of the Anglo-American New Order During the Second World War", *Diplomacy & Statecraft*, 7, 1, (1996).

— "Overture to an Alliance: British Propaganda at the New York World's Fair, 1939-1940", *Journal of British Studies*, 36, 3, (1997).

— "The Munich Crisis and British Propaganda Policy in The United States", *Diplomacy & Statecraft*, 10, 3, (1999).

Curry, William. *The Case for Federal Union*. London: Penguin, 1940.

Curtis, Lionel. *Civitas Dei. The Commonwealth of God*. London: Macmillan, 1939.

— *World War. Its Cause and Cure*. Oxford: Oxford University Press, 1945.

— *World Revolution in the Cause of Peace*. Oxford: Basil Blackwell, 1947.

Daddow, Oliver. *Harold Wilson and European Integration: Britain's Second Application to Join the EEC*. London: Routledge, 2002.

Dallek, Robert. *Franklin D. Roosevelt and American Foreign Policy, 1932-1945*. New York: Oxford University Press, 1995.

Daniel Gorman. "Lionel Curtis, Imperial Citizenship, and Quest for Unity", *The Historian*, 68, (2005).

Darby, Graham. *Europe at War, 1939-1945*. New York: Hodder Arnold, 2003.

Dard, Olivier. *Bertrand de Jouvenel*. Paris: Librairie Académique Perrin, 2008.

Davies, David. *The Way to Peace: A Brief Exposition of the New Commonwealth Programme*. London: New Commonwealth Press, 1937.

— *A Federated Europe*. London: Victor Gollancz, 1940.

— *The Way to Peace*. London: Oxford University Press, 1944.

Davies, Norman. *No Simple Victory: World War II in Europe, 1939-1945*. London: Viking, 2007.

Davis, Kenneth S. *FDR: Into the Storm 1937-1940*. New York: Random House, 1995.

Davis, Richard. *Anglo-French Relations before the Second World War: Appeasement and Crisis*. New York: Palgrave Macmillan, 2001.

Dazet-Brun, Frank. *Champetier de Ribes 1882-1947*. Paris: Seguier, 2008.

de Chambrun, Renè. *Pierre Laval: Traitor or patriot?* Cambridge, MA: Scribner, 1984.

de Gaulle, Charles. *War Memoirs, 1*. London: Collins, 1955.

— *The Complete War Memoirs of Charles de Gaulle*. London: Carroll & Graf Publishers, 1998.

de Groot, Gerard. *Liberal Crusader: The Life of Sir Archibald Sinclair*. New York: New York University Press, 1993.

de Jouvenel, Bertrand. *Vers les Etats-Unis d'Europe*. Paris: 1930.

de Lanux, Pierre. *Young France and New America*. London: Macmillan, 1917.

— *European Manifesto*. London: Creative Age Press, 1945.

de Sainte-Suzanne, Raymond. *Une politique étrangère: Le Quai d'Orsay et Saint-John Perse à l'épreuve d'un regard Novembre 1938-Juin 1940*. Paris: Viviane Hamy, 2000.

de Villelume, Paul. *Journal d'une défaite, 23 août 1939-16 juin 1940*. Paris: 1976.

de Wailly, H. *1940, l'effondrement*. Paris: Perrin, 2000.

Dean, Kenda Creasy. *Practicing Passion: Youth and the Quest for a Passionate Church*. New York: Harper Collins, 2006.

DeBenedetti, Charles. *Origins of the Modern American Peace Movement, 1915-1929*. New York: Kto Press, 1978.

Dehio, Ludwig. *The Precarious Balance. The Politics of Power in Europe, 1495-1945*. London: Chatto & Windus, 1965.

Delos, J. T. "L'Union Franco-Britannique", *New Commonwealth Quarterly,* 5, (1939).

Delporte, Christian. *La troisième République, 1919-1940. De Poincaré à Paul Reynaud*. Paris: Pygmalion, 1998.

Demory, Jean-Claude. *Georges Bidault, 1899-1983: Biographie*. Paris: Julliard, 1995.

Dennis, Peter. *Decision by Default: Conscription and British Defence, 1919-1939*. Durham, NC: Duke University Press, 1972.

— *The Territorial Army, 1906-1940*. Woodbridge: Royal Historical Society, 1987.

Destremau, Bernard. *Weygand*. Paris: Perrin, 1989.

Devautour, Guy and Lefevre, Eric. *Mai-Juin 1940, les combattants de l'honneur*. Paris: Copernic, 1980.

Dezsy, John. *Gentleman Europas. Erinnerungen an Richard Coudenhove-Kalergi*. Wien: Czerning Verlag, 2001.

Dildy, Doug. *Denmark and Norway 1940: Hitler's Boldest Operation*. London: Osprey Publishing, 2007.

Dilks, David. "The Twilight War and the Fall of France: Chamberlain and Churchill in 1940", *Transactions of the Royal Historical Society*, 28, (1978).

— "Great Britain and Scandinavia in the Phoney War", *Scandinavian Journal of History*, 2, 1-2, (1987).

— *Neville Chamberlain*. Cambridge: Cambridge University Press, 2002.

— "De Gaulle and the British", in *Digital Convergence: Libraries of the Future*. Edited by Rae A. Earnshaw and John A. Vince. Berlin: Springer, 2007.

Dimbleby, David and Reynolds, David. *An Ocean Apart: The Relationship Between Britain and America in the Twentieth Century*. London: Trafalgar Square Press, 1988.

Dobson, Alan P. *U.S. Wartime Aid to Britain, 1940-1946*. New York: Palgrave Macmillan, 1986.

Dockrill Michael and Goold, Douglas. *Peace Without Promise: The Peace Conferences 1919-23*. London: Batsford, 1981.

— "Philip Kerr at 10 Downing Street", 1916-1921, in *The Larger Idea. Lord Lothian and the Problem of National Sovereignty*. Edited by John Turner. London: The Historians' Press, 1988.

— "The Foreign Office and France During the Phoney War, September 1939-May 1940", in *Diplomacy and World Power: Studies in British Foreign Policy, 1890-1950*. Edited by Michael Dockrill and B. J. C. Mckercher. Cambridge: Cambridge University Press, 1996.

— and Mckercher, B. J. C. eds. *Diplomacy and World Power: Studies in British Foreign Policy, 1890-1950*. Cambridge: Cambridge University Press, 1996.

— and Fisher, John eds. *The Paris Peace Conference, 1919: Peace Without Victory?* New York: Palgrave Macmillan, 2001.

— "British Official Perceptions of France, 1936-1940", in *Anglo-French Relations, 1898-1998: From Fashoda to Jospin*. Edited by Michael Dockrill and Philippe Chassaigne. New York: Palgrave Macmillan, 2002.

— and Chassaigne, Philippe eds. *Anglo-French Relations, 1898-1998: From Fashoda to Jospin*. New York: Palgrave Macmillan, 2002.

Doenecke, Justus D. "U.S. Historiography and the European War, 1939-1941", *Diplomatic History*, 19, (1995).

Donelly, M. S. "J. W. Dafoe and Lionel Curtis: Two Concepts of Commonwealth", *Political Studies*, 7, 2, (1960).

Douds, Gerard. *Lothian and the Indian Federation*, in *The Larger Idea*: *Lord Lothian and the Problem of National Sovereignty*. Edited by John Turner. London: The Historians' Press, 1988.

Doughty, Robert A. *The Seeds of Disaster: The Development of French Army Doctrine, 1919-1939*. North Haven, CT: Archon Books, 1986.

— "The French Armed Forces, 1918-40", in *Military Effectiveness: The Interwar Period*. Edited by Allan R. Millett and Murray Williamson Jeffery. London: Unwin Hyman, 1988.

— *The Breaking Point: Sedan and the Fall of France, 1940*. North Haven, CT: Archon Books, 1990.

Douglas, W. A. B. and Greenhouse, Brereton. *Out of the Shadows: Canada in the Second World War*. Toronto: Dundurn Press, 1995.

Douglas-Home, Alec. *Our European Destiny*. London: Conservative Group for Europe, 1971.

— *The Way the Wind Blows: An Autobiography*. London: Times Book, 1977.

Dreyfus, Michel. "Le Parti communiste français et la lutte pour la paix du Front populaire à la Seconde Guerre Mondiale", *Communisme*, 18-9, (1988).

Drinkwater, Derek. *Sir Harold Nicolson and International Relations: The Practitioner as Theorist*. New York: Oxford University Press, 2005.

du Réau, Elisabeth. *Edouard Daladier, 1884-1970*. Paris: Fayard, 1993.

— "Edouard Daladier: The Conduct of the War and the Beginnings of Defeat", in *The French Defeat of 1940. Reassessments*. Edited by Joel Blatt. Oxford: Berghahn, 1997.

— *L'idée d'Europe au XXe siècle. Des mythes aux réalités*. Paris: Complexe, 2001.

Dunbabin, John. "British Rearmament in the 1930s: A Chronology and Review", *Historical Journal*, 18, 3, (1975).

Dunn, David J. *The First Fifty Years of Peace Research. A Survey and Interpretation*. London: Ashgate Publishing, 2005.

Duroselle, Jean Baptiste. *Deux types de grands hommes: Le général de Gaulle et Jean Monnet*. Geneva: Institut Universitaire des Hautes Études Internationales, 1977.

— "1940: la France sans stratégie", in *L'Histoire. Études sur la France de 1939 à nos jours*. Edited by Jean Baptiste Duroselle. Paris: Le Seuil, 1985.

— ed. *L'Histoire. Études sur la France de 1939 à nos jours*. Paris: Le Seuil, 1985.

Dutton, David. *Anthony Eden. A Life and Reputation*. New York: Hodder Arnold, 1998.

— *Douglas Home*. London: Haus Publishers, 2006.

Eastby, John. *Functionalism and Interdependence*. Washington, DC: University Press of America, 1985.

Eden, Anthony. *The Memoirs of Sir Anthony Eden*, 2. London: Cassell, 1965.

Egerton, George W. *Great Britain and the Creation of the League of Nations: Strategy, Policy and International Organisation, 1914-1919*. Chapel Hill, NC: University of North Carolina Press, 1978.

— "Collective Security as Political Myth: Liberal Internationalism and the League of Nations in Politics and History", *International History Review*, 5, (1983).

Egremont, M. *Under Two Flags: The Life of Major-General Sir Edward Spears*. London: Weidenfeld, 1997.

Eichelberger, Clark M. *Organizing for Peace: A Personal History of the Founding of the United Nations.* New York: Harper & Row, 1977.

Eichengreen, Barry. *Golden Fetters: The Gold Standard and the Great Depression, 1919-1939.* New York: Oxford University Press, 1996.

Eikemeier, Peter. *Sammlung Fritz Thyssen: Ausgewählte Meisterwerke.* Munich: Hirmer Verlag, 1986.

Einaudi, Luigi. *La guerra e l'unità europea.* Bologna: Il Mulino, 1986.

Elisha, Achille. *Aristide Briand: La paix mondiale et l'union européenne.* Louvain-la Neuve: Bruylant, 2000.

Ellinwood, Dewitt Clinton. "The Round Table Movement in India", *Journal of Commonwealth Political Studies*, 9, 1, (1971).

Evans, Martin Marix. *The Fall of France: Act with Daring: May-June 1940.* London: Osprey Publishing, 2000.

— *Invasion!: Operation Sea Lion, 1940.* Harlow: Longman, 2004.

Faber, David. *Speaking for England: Leo, Julian and John Amery, the Tragedy of a Political Family.* Washington, DC: Free Press, 2005.

Facon, P. *L' armée de l'Air dans la tourmente. La bataille de France, 1939-1940.* Paris: Economica, 1997.

Fagley, Richard Martin. *The Study of Peace Aims in the Local Church: Why? What? How? Suggestions for Groups Concerned with Principles of World Order.* London: Church Peace Union, 1941.

Fairbank, John K. "William Holland and the IPR in Historical Perspective", *Pacific Affairs*, 52, 4, (1979).

Faucier, Nicolas. *Pacifisme et antimilitarisme dans l'entre-deux-guerres.* Paris: Editions Syndicalistes, 1983.

Fear, Jeffrey. *Organizing Control: August Thyssen and the Construction of German Corporate Management.* Boston, MA: Harvard University Press, 2005.

Fehrenbach, T. R. *F.D.R.'s Undeclared War, 1939 to 1941.* New York: David McKay, 2000.

Feiling, Keith. *Life of Neville Chamberlain.* London: Macmillan, 1947.

Feldkamp, Michael F. *Pius XII und Deutschland.* Göttingen: Vandenhoeck & Ruprecht, 2000.

Fernand-Laurent, Jean. *Un Peuple Ressuscite.* New York: Brentano's, 1943.

— *Gallic Charter: Foundations of Tomorrow's France.* London: Little, Brown & Co., 1944.

— *Activities for the Advancement of Women: Equality, Development, and Peace.* New York: United Nations Publications, 1986.

Fimmen, Edo. *Labour's Alternative: The United States of Europe or Europe Limited.* London: 1924.

Fink, Carole. *Marc Bloch: A Life in History*. Cambridge: Cambridge University Press, 1989.

— "Marc Bloch and the drôle de guerre: Prelude to the Strange Defeat", in *The French Defeat of 1940: Reassessments*. Edited by Joel Blatt. Oxford: Berghahn Books, 2000.

Fitch, Noel Riley. *Sylvia Beach and the Lost Generation: A History of the Literary Paris in the Twenties and Thirties*. New York: W. W. Norton & Company, 1985.

Fleishman, Joel. *The Foundation: A Great American Secret. How Private Wealth Is Changing the World*. New York: Public Affairs, 2007.

Fleury, Antoine and Jilek, Lubor eds. *The Briand Plan of a European Federal Union*. Oxford: Peter Lang Publishing, 1998.

Fonvieille-Alquier, François. *The French and the Phoney War, 1939-40*. London: T. Stacey, 1973.

Forbes, Neil. *Doing Business with the Nazis: Britain's Economic and Financial Relations with Germany, 1931-1939*. London: Frank Cass, 2000.

Fosdick, Raymond D. *The Story of the Rockefeller Foundation*. Piscataway, NJ: Transaction Publishers, 1988.

Foster, Catherine. *Women for All Seasons: The Story of the Women's International League for Peace and Freedom*. Athens, GA: University of Georgia Press, 1989.

Foster, Leonie. *The Men and Motives of the Australian Round Table*. Melbourne: Melbourne University Press, 1986.

Frank, Joseph. "French Intellectuals Between Wars", *Dissent* 31, 1, (1984).

Frank, R. *La Hantise du déclin. La France, 1920-60: finances, défense et identité nationale*. Paris: 1994.

Fridenson, Patrick. *La France et la Grande-Bretagne face aux problèmes aériens, 1935-mai 1940*. Vincennes: 1976.

Frieser, Karl-Heinz and Greenwood, John T. *The Blitzkrieg Legend: The 1940 Campaign in the West*. Annapolis, MD: US Naval Institute Press, 2005.

Fritzinger, Linda. *Diplomat without Portfolio: Valentine Chirol, His Life and 'The Times'*. New York: I. B. Tauris, 2006.

Fuchser, Larry W. *Neville Chamberlain and Appeasement: A Study in Political History*. New York: W. W. Norton, 1982.

Fuentes, Carlos. *This I Believe: An A to Z of a Life*. New York: Random House, 2005.

Gaillard, Jean-Michel. *Les 40 jours de Blum*. Paris: Perrin, 2001.

Gardner, W. I. R. *The Evacuation from Dunkirk: 'Operation Dynamo', 26 May-4 June 1940*. London: Routledge, 2000.

Garraud, Philippe. "Les contraintes industrielles dans la préparation de la guerre de 1939-1940: La modernisation inachevée de l'aviation française", *Guerres Mondiales et conflits contemporains*, 207, (2002).

— "Le rôle de la doctrine défensive dans la défaite de 1940: une explication trop simple et partielle", *Guerres mondiales et conflits contemporains*, 214, (2004).

— "La politique française de réarmement de 1936 à 1940: priorités et contraintes", *Guerres mondiales et conflits contemporains*, 219, (2005).

— "La politique française de réarmement de 1936 à 1940: Une production tardive mais massive", *Guerres mondiales et conflits contemporains*, 220, (2005).

Garrett, Garet. *Defend America First: The Anti-war Editorials of the Saturday Evening Post, 1939-1942*. London: Caxton Press, 2003.

Gates, E. *Race and U.S. Foreign Policy During the Cold War*. London: Routledge, 1998.

Gates, Eleanor M. *The End of the Affair: The Collapse of the Anglo-French Alliance, 1939-1940*. London: Routledge, 1981.

Gathorne-Hardy, Geoffrey. *A Short History of International Affairs, 1920 to 1934*. Oxford: Oxford University Press, 1934.

Gennaro Lerda, Valeria ed. *Which 'Global Village'?: Societies, Cultures, and Political-Economic Systems in a Euro-Atlantic Perspective*. Westport, CT: Praeger, 2002.

Geraud, André. *The Gravediggers of France: Gamelin, Daladier, Reynaud, Petain, and Laval: Military Defeat, Armistice, Counter-Revolution*. New York: Doubleday Doran, 1944.

Germaine, Willard. *La drôle de guerre et la trahison de Vichy*. Paris: Editions Sociales, 1960.

— *De Munich à Vichy: La drôle de guerre*. Paris: Editions Sociales, 1975.

Geyer, Michael and Boyer, John W. *Resistance Against the Third Reich: 1933-1945*. Chicago, IL: University of Chicago Press, 1995.

Gilbert, Martin. *Finest Hour. Winston S. Churchill, 1939-1941*. London: 1983.

— *Churchill: A Life*. New York: Holt Paperbacks, 1992.

— ed. *The Churchill War Papers: Never Surrender. May 1940-December 1940*. New York: W. W. Norton, 1995.

— *Churchill: A Life*. London: Pimlico, 2000.

— *Winston Churchill's War Leadership*. London: Vintage, 2004.

Goda, Norman J. W. *Tales from Spandau: Nazi Criminals and the Cold War*. Cambridge: Cambridge University Press, 2006.

Goldstein, Erik. *Winning the Peace: British Diplomatic Strategy, Peace Planning, and the Paris Peace Conference, 1916-1920*. New York: Oxford University Press, 1991.

Gollancz, O. "Practical Steps Towards Anglo-French Union", *New Commonwealth Quarterly*, 5, (1939).

Gollin, Alfred M. *The Observer and J. L. Garvin, 1908-1914: A Study in a Great Editorship*. Oxford: Oxford University Press, 1960.

— *Balfour's Burden: Arthur Balfour & Imperial Preference*. Salt Lake City, UT: Garden City Press, 1965.

Gombin, Richard. "Socialisme et pacifisme", in *La France et les Français en 1938-1939*. Edited by René Rémond and Janine Bourdin. Paris: Les Presses de Sciences Po, 1978.

Goodhart, Philip. *Fifty Ships That Saved the World. The Foundations of the Anglo-American Alliance*. London: Heinemann, 1965.

Gorman, Daniel. *Imperial Citizenship: Empire and the Question of Belonging*. Manchester: Manchester University Press, 2007.

Gottfried, Ted. *The Fight for Peace: A History of Anti-War Movements in America*. New York: 21st Century, 2004.

Gouzy, Jean-Pierre. *Les pionniers de l'Europe communautaire*. Lausanne: Centre de Recherches Européennes, 1968.

Gowing, M. "Anglo-French Economic Collaboration Up to the Outbreak of the Second World War", in *Les relations franco-britanniques de 1935 à 1939*. Paris: Editions du CNRS, 1975.

Graham, B. D. *Choice and Democratic Order: The French Socialist Party, 1937-1950*. Cambridge: Cambridge University Press, 1994.

Grayson, Richard S. *Liberals, International Relations, and Appeasement: The Liberal Party, 1919-1939*. London: Frank Cass, 2001.

Greilsamer, Alain. *Blum*. Paris: Flammarion, 1996.

Griffin, William V. *Sir Evelyn Wrench and His Continuing Vision of International Relations During 40 Years*. Whitefish, MT: Kessinger, 2006.

Griffiths, Richard. *Marshal Petain*. Philadelphia, PA: Trans-Atlantic Publications, 1994.

Grigg, John. *Nancy Astor: A Lady Unshamed*. London: Little, Brown & Co., 1983.

— *Lloyd George: War Leader, 1916-1918*. London: Penguin Books, 2003.

Grosbois, Thierry. *L'idée Européenne en temps de guerre: 1940-1944*. Louvain-la-Neuve: Academia, 1994.

Grose, Peter. *Continuing the Inquiry: The Council on Foreign Relations from 1921 to 1996*. New York: Council on Foreign Relations Press, 1996.

Gruner, Stefan. *Paul Reynaud. 1878-1966*. Frankfurt: Oldenbourg, 2001.

Guderzo, Giulio ed. *Lord Lothian. Una vita per la pace. Atti del Lothian Colloquium. Londra, 23 novembre 1982*. Florence: La Nuova Italia, 1985.

Gunsburg, A. *Divided and Conquered: The French High Command and the Defeat of the West, 1940*. Westport, CT: Greenwood Press, 1979.

Haas, Ernst B. *Beyond the Nation-State Functionalism and International Organization*. Standford, CA: Stanford University Press, 1968.

Hackett, Clifford P. *Monnet and the Americans: The Father of a United Europe and His U.S. Supporters*. Washington, DC: Jean Monnet Council, 1995.

Halifax, Edward. *Speeches on Foreign Policy*. Oxford: Oxford University Press, 1940.

Hallet, Edward. *The Future of International Government*. London: National Peace Council, 1941.

Halperin, Vladimir. *Raoul Dautry: Du rail a l'atome: L'aventure sociale et technologique de la France dans la première moitié du XXe siècle*. Paris: Fayard, 1997.

Hammarlund, A. *Liberal Internationalism and the Decline of the State: The Thought of Richard Cobden, David Mitrany, and Kenichi Ohmae*. New York: Palgrave Macmillan, 2005.

Hankey, Maurice. *Diplomacy By Conference: Studies In Public Affairs 1920-1946*. London: Ernest Benn, 1946.

— *Politics Trials and Errors*. London: Henry Regnery, 1950.

Hansen, Harold Albert. *Issues and Aims of the War*. Pasadena, CA: Pasadena Junion College Press, 1943.

Harris, J. P. "British Armour and Rearmament in the 1939s", *Journal of Strategic Studies*, 11, 2, (1988).

Harris, Jose. *William Beveridge: A Biography*. New York: Oxford University Press, 1997.

Harris, Kenneth. *Attlee*. London: Weidenfeld & Nicolson, 1995.

Harvey, A. D. "The French Armée de l'Air in May-June 1940: A Failure of Conception", *Journal of Contemporary History*, 25, (1990).

Hayek, Frederick A. *Good Money: The Standard*. Edited by Stephen Kresge. Chicago, IL: University of Chicago Press, 1999.

— *The Road to Serfdom*. London: Routledge, 2006.

Hazlehurst, Cameron and Woodland, Christine. *A Guide to the Papers of British Cabinet Ministers 1900-1964.* Cambridge: Cambridge University Press, 1997.

Heath, Carl. *The Present Crisis and the Spirit of Man.* London: National Peace Council, 1941.

Heinrichs, Waldo. *Threshold of War: Franklin D. Roosevelt and American Entry Into World War II.* New York: Oxford University Press, 1990.

Henig, Stanley. *The Uniting of Europe: From Discord to Concord.* London: Routledge, 1997.

Henri, Michel. *La Défaite de la France.* Paris: PUF, 1980.

Henry, Basil and Hart, Liddell. *History of the Second World War.* Cambridge, MA: Da Capo, 1999.

Herbstritt, Georg. *Ein Weg der Verständigung?: Die umstrittene Deutschland und Ostpolitik des Reichskanzlers a. D. Dr. Joseph Wirth in der Zeit des Kalten Krieges.* Frankfurt am Main: Peter Lang, 1993.

Herman, John. *The Paris Embassy of Sir Eric Phipps: Anglo-French Relations and the Foreign Office, 1937-1939.* Eastbourne: Sussex Academic Press, 1998.

Herrera, Carlos-Miguel. *Théorie juridique et politique chez Hans Kelsen.* Paris: Kime, 1997.

Herriot, Edouard. *Épisodes 1940-1944.* Paris: Flammarion, 1950.

Hertslet, Edward. *Recollections of the Old Foreign Office.* London: Adamant Media Corporation, 2002.

Hewes, Amy. *Labour's Aim in War and Peace.* London: Commission to Study the Organisation of Peace, 1944.

Hill, Christopher. *Two Worlds of International Relations.* London: Routledge, 1994.

— *Cabinet Decisions on Foreign Policy: The British Experience, October 1938-June 1941.* Cambridge: Cambridge University Press, 2002.

Hills, John Ditch and Glennester, Howard. *Beveridge and Social Security: An International Retrospective.* New York: Oxford University Press, 1994.

Hinden, Rita. *Freedom for Colonial People.* London: National Peace Council, 1942.

Hinton, James. *Protests and Visions: Peace Politics in Twentieth Century Britain.* Oxford: Oxford University Press, 1989.

Hirst, Paul Q. *The Pluralist Theory of the State: Selected Writings of G. D. H. Cole, J. N. Figgis and H. J. Laski.* London: Taylor & Francis, 2007.

Hodge, Carl C. *NATO for a New Century: Atlanticism and European Security.* Westport, CT: Praeger, 2002.

Hodson, Henry. "The Round Table: Until the Early 1930s", *The Round Table*, 352, (1999).

Hoffmann, Stanley. "Le désastre de 1940", in *Études sur la France de 1939 à nos jours*. Paris: Seuil, 1985.

— "The Trauma of 1940: A Disaster and its Traces", in *The French Defeat of 1940: Reassessments*. Edited by Joel Blatt. Oxford: Berghahn Books, 2000.

Hogan, Michael J. *Woodrow Wilson's Western Tour: Rhetoric, Public Opinion and the League of Nations*. Tamu, TX: Texas A&M University Press, 2006.

Holland, William L. "Source Materials on the Institute of Pacific Relations", *Pacific Affairs*, 58, 1, (1985).

Hooper, Paul. "The Institute of Pacific Relations and the Origins of Asian and Pacific Studies", *Pacific Affairs*, 61, 1, (1988).

Hooton, Edward. *Blitzkrieg in the West 1939-1940*. Milbank, SD: Midland Publishing, 2007.

Hoover, A. J. *God, Britain and Hitler in World War II: The View of the British Clergy, 1939-1945*. Westport, CT: Praeger, 1999.

Horster-Philipps, Ulrike. *Joseph Wirth 1879-1956: Eine politische Biographie*. Paderborn: F. Schoningh, 1998.

Horten, Gerd. *Radio Goes to War: The Cultural Politics of Propaganda during World War II*. Berckley, CA: University of California Press, 2002.

Hostie, Jan. "Conceptions Fédératives", *La Société des Nations*, 18, 4, (1940).

Houseman, Gerald L. *G. D. H. Cole*. London: Twayne Publications, 1979.

Howard, Michael S. *Jonathan Cape, Publisher*. London: Penguin, 1977.

— *War and the Liberal Conscience*. London: Maurice Temple Smith, 1981.

Howell, David. *Attlee*. London: Haus Publishers, 2006.

Howlett, Charles F. *The American Peace Movement: History and Historiography*. Washington, DC: American Historical Association, 1985.

— *History of the American Peace Movement 1890-2000: The Emergence of a New Scholarly Discipline*. Lewiston: Edwin Mellen Press, 2005.

Hughes, Michael. *British Foreign Secretaries in an Uncertain World, 1919-1939*. London: Routledge, 2005.

Hunter, Ian ed. *Winston and Archie: The Letters of Sir Archibald Sinclair and Winston S. Churchill, 1915-1960*. London: Politico's Publishing, 2005.

Huxley, Julian. *Religion Without Revelation*. London: Harper & Brothers Publishers, 1957.
— *Evolutionary Humanism*. London: Prometheus Books, 1992.
Hyam, Ronald. *Britain's Declining Empire: The Road to Decolonisation, 1918-1968*. Cambridge: Cambridge University Press, 2007.
Hytier, Adrienne Doris. *Two Years of French Foreign Policy: Vichy 1940-1942*. Paris: Minard, 1958.
Imlay, Talbot. "From Villain to Partner: British Labour Party Leaders, France and International Policy during the Phoney War, 1939-40", *Journal of Contemporary History*, 38, 4, (2003).
Ingham, Kenneth. "Philip Kerr and the Unification of South Africa", in *The Larger Idea: Lord Lothian and the Problem of National Sovereignty*. Edited by John Turner. London: The Historians' Press, 1988.
Ingram, Norman. "Romain Rolland, Interwar Pacifism and the Problem of Peace", in *Peace Movements and Political Cultures*. Edited by Charles Chatfield and Peter van den Dungen. Knoxville: University of Tennessee Press, 1988.
— *The Politics of Dissent*. Oxford: Oxford University Press, 1991.
Irvine, William D. "Domestic Politics and the Fall of France in 1940" in *The French Defeat of 1940. Reassessments*. Edited by Joel Blatt. Oxford: Berghahn, 1997.
Isaacson, Walter and Thomas, Evan. *The Wise Men: Six Friends and the World They Made*. New York: Simon & Schuster, 1997.
Jackson, Ashley. *The British Empire and the Second World War*. London: Hambledon, 2007.
Jackson, J. *The Fall of France: The Nazi Invasion of 1940*. New York: Oxford University Press, 2003.
Jackson, Julian. *France: The Dark Years, 1940-1944*. New York: Oxford University Press, 2003.
— *The Fall of France: The Nazi Invasion of 1940*. New York: Oxford University Press, 2004.
Jackson, P. *France and the German Menace, 1933-1939*. Oxford: Oxford University Press, 2000.
Jackson, Robert. *Air War over France, May-June 1940*. Paris: Allan, 1974.
— *Dunkirk: The British Evacuation, 1940*. London: Rigel Publications, 2004.
Jaffre, Yves-Frederic. *Il y a cinquante ans, Pierre Laval: Le procès qui n'a pas eu lieu*. Paris: A. Michel, 1995.
Jakab, Elisabeth. "The Council on Foreign Relations", *Book Forum*, 4, 3, (1978).

James, Robert Rhodes. *Victor Cazalet: A Portrait.* London: Hamilton, 1976.

Jansen, Sabine. *Pierre Côt: Les pièges de l'antifascisme, 1895-1977.* Paris: Fayard, 2002.

Jeanneney, Jean-Noël. *Georges Mandel.* Paris: Seuil, 1991.

Jeffreys, Diarmuid. *The Austro-Hungarian Empire.* London: New Holland Publishers, 2007.

Jeffreys-Jones, Rhodri. "The Inestimable Advantage of Not Being English: Lord Lothian's American Ambassadorship, 1939-1940", *Scottish Historical Review*, 63, 1, (1984).

— "Lord Lothian and American Democracy: An Illusion in Pursuit of an Illusion", *Canadian Review of American Studies*, 17, 4, (1986).

— "Lord Lothian: Ambassador 'To a People', in *The Larger Idea: Lord Lothian and the Problem of National Sovereignty.* Edited by John Turner. London: The Historians' Press, 1988.

Jenkins, Brian. *France in the Era of Fascism: Essays on the French Authoritarian Right.* Oxford: Berghahn Books, 2007.

Jenkins, Roy. *Churchill: A Biography.* New York: Farrar, Straus & Giroux, 2001.

Jenks, John. *British Propaganda and News Media in the Cold War*, Edinburgh: Edinburgh University Press, 2006.

Jennings, Ivor. *A Federation for Western Europe.* Cambridge: Cambridge University Press, 1940.

— *The British Constitution.* London: The University Press, 1942.

— *International Law and the Causes of War.* London: Grotius Society, 1943.

— *English Law and Moral Law.* London: Stevens & Sons, 1953.

— *Cabinet Government.* Cambridge: Cambridge University Press, 1969.

— *Poland and the Minority Races.* London: Ayer Publications, 1970.

Jilek, Lubor. *L'esprit européen en Suisse da 1860 à 1940.* Geneva: Cahiers d'Histoire Contemporaine, 1990.

— "L'Union européenne à Bâle entre 1938 et 1946: pôle helvétique et versant mondial dans les projets d'une association européaniste", in *Plans des temps de guerre pour l'Europe d'après-guerre, 1940-1947.* Bruxelles: Bruylant, 1995.

Joad, Cyril E. M. *The Story of Civilization.* London: A. & C. Black, 1931.

— *Manifesto: Being the Book of the Federation of Progressive Societies and Individuals.* London: George Allen & Unwin, 1934.

— *Why War?* London: Penguin Book, 1939.

— *The Philosophy of Federal Union.* London: Macmillan, 1942.

— *Philosophy for Our Times.* Pomona, CA: Pomona Press, 2007.

John, Angela V. *War, Journalism and the Shaping of the Twentieth Century: The Life and Times of Henry W. Nevinson*. New York: I. B. Tauris, 2006.

Johnsen, Julia E. *The Eight Points of Post War World Reorganization*. New York: The H. W. Wilson Company, 1942.

Johnson, D. W. J. "Britain and France in 1940", *Transactions of the Royal Historical Society*, 22, (1972).

— "Churchill and France", in *Churchill*. Edited by Robert Blake and William R. Louis. Oxford: Oxford University Press, 1996.

Johnson, Gaynor. *The Foreign Office and British Diplomacy in the Twentieth Century*. London: Routledge, 2005.

Johnson, Robert. *British Imperialism*. New York: Palgrave Macmillan, 2003.

Johnson, Robert David. *The Peace Progressives and American Foreign Relations*. Boston, MA: Harvard University Press, 1995.

Johnson, Walter. *The Battle Against Isolation. FDR and the Era of the New Deal*. Cambridge, MA: Da Capo, 1973.

Johnstone, Andrew. "Private Interest Groups and the Lend-Lease Debate, 1940-1942", *49th Parallel. An interdisciplinary Journal of North American Studies*, 7, (2001).

Johnston-Liik, E. M. *Managing an Inheritance: Colonel J. C. Wedgwood, the History of Parliament and the Lost History of the Irish Parliament*. Dublin: Royal Irish Academy, 1989.

Jones, Charles. *E. H. Carr and International Relations: A Duty to Lie*. Cambridge: Cambridge University Press, 1998.

Jones, G. W. and Donoughue, Bernard. *Herbert Morrison: Portrait of a Politician*. Prai: Phoenix Press, 2001.

Jordan, Nicole. *The Popular Front and Central Europe: The Dilemmas of Impotence, 1918-1940*. Cambridge: Cambridge University Press, 1992.

— "Strategy and Scapegotosm: Reflections on French National Catastrophe, 1940", in *The French Defeat of 1940: Reassessments*. Edited by Joel Blatt. Oxford: Berghahn Books, 2000.

Judt, Tony. *The Burden of Responsibility: Blum, Camus, Aron, and the French Twentieth Century*. Chicago, IL: University of Chicago Press, 1998.

Kadish, Alon. *Apostle Arnold: The Life and Death of Arnold Toynbee, 1852-1883*. Durham, NC: Duke University Press, 1986.

Kaiser, David E. *Economic Diplomacy and the Origins of the Second World War: Germany, Britain, France and Eastern Europe, 1930-1939*. New Haven: Yale University Press, 1980.

Kaiser, Volfram. *Political Catholicism in Europe, 1918-1945.* London: Routledge, 2004.

Kaspi, André. "Franco-American Relations, 1918-1941", *Amerikastudien-American Studies*, 39, 1, (1994).

Kaufmann, E. and Kaufmann, H. W. *Hitler's Blitzkrieg Campaigns: The Invasion and Defence of Western Europe, 1939-1940.* New York: Combined Publishing, 1993.

Kedourie, Elie. "Arnold Toynbee", *New Criterion*, 7, 7, (1990).

— *The Chatham House Version and Other Middle Eastern Studies.* London: Ivan Dee, 2004.

Keeton, George William. *National Sovereignty and International Order: An Essay upon the International Community and International Order.* London: Peace Book Company, 1939.

— "Anglo-French Union. A Suggestion", *New Commonwealth Quarterly*, 5, 3, (1939).

Kefauver, Estes. *Atlantic Union: The Way to Peace.* Washington, DC: United States Press, 1953.

Keiger, J. F. V. "La perception de la puissance française par le Foreign Office", in *La puissance française à la 'belle époque': Mythe ou réalité?* Edited by Pierre Milza and Raymond Poidevin. Paris: Institute d'Histoire du Temps Présent, 1992.

Keith, A. B. "Constitutional Aspects of Anglo-French Union", *New Commonwealth Quarterly,* 5, (1939).

Kelsen, Hans. *The Legal Process and International Order.* London: New Commonwealth Institute, 1934.

Kendle, John. *The Round Table Movement and Imperial Union.* Toronto: University of Toronto Press, 1975.

— *Federal Britain: A History.* London: Routledge, 1997.

Kennedy, Greg. "Neville Chamberlain and Strategic Relations with the U.S. During His Chancellorship", *Diplomacy & Statecraft*, 13, 1, (2002).

— *Anglo-American Strategic Relations and the Far East, 1933-1939: Imperial Crossroads.* London: Routledge, 2002.

Kennedy, Paul. "The Study of Appeasement: Methodological Crossroads or Meeting-Place?", *British Journal of International Studies*, 6, 3, (1980).

Kent, John. "Anglo-French Colonial Co-operation, 1939-49", *Journal of Imperial and Commonwealth History*, 17, 1, (1988).

Kercher, B. J. C. "'The Deep and Latent Distrust': The British Official Mind and the United States, 1919-1929," in *Anglo-American Relations in the 1920s: The Struggle for Supremacy.* Edited by B. J. C. Kercher. London: 1991.

Kergoat, Jacques. *La France du Front Populaire.* Paris: La Découverte, 2003.

Kersaudy, François. *Stratèges et Norvège, 1940.* Paris: Hachette, 1977.

— *Churchill and de Gaulle.* London: Collins, 1981.

Kershaw, Ian. *Hitler: 1936-1945: Nemesis.* New York: W. W. Norton & Company, 2001.

— *Making Friends with Hitler: Lord Londonderry, the Nazis, and the Road to War.* London: Penguin Press, 2004.

— *Fateful Choices: Ten Decisions That Changed the Wold, 1940-1941.* London: The Penguin Press, 2007.

Keylor, William R. "France and the Illusion of American Support, 1919-1940", in *The French Defeat of 1940. Reassessments.* Edited by Joel Blatt. Oxford: Berghahn, 1997.

Keyserlingk, Robert H. "Arnold Toynbee's Foreign Research and Press Service and Its Post-war Plans for South-East Europe 1939-1945", *Journal of Contemporary History*, 21, (1986).

Kimball, Warren. *The Most Unsordid Act: Lend Lease, 1939-1941.* Baltimore, VI: The Johns Hopkins University Press 1969.

Kimber, Charles. "Federal Union", in *Lord Lothian. Una vita per la pace. Atti del Lothian Colloquium. Londra, 23 novembre 1982.* Edited by Giulio Guderzo. Florence: La Nuova Italia, 1985.

— Introduction to *Studies in Federal Planning.* Edited by Patrick Ransome. London: Lothian Foundation Press, 1990.

King-Hall, Stephen. *Chatham House: A Brief Account of the Origins, Purposes and Methods of the Royal Institute of International Affairs.* Oxford: Oxford University Press, 1937.

Kinsky, Ferdinand. *Fédéralisme et personalisme.* Paris: Presses d'Europe, 1976.

Kitching, Carolyn. "The Search for Disarmament: Anglo-French Relations, 1935-1939", in *Anglo-French Relations, 1898-1998: From Fashoda to Jospin.* Edited by Michael Dockrill and Philippe Chassaigne. New York: Palgrave Macmillan, 2002.

— *Britain and the Geneva Disarmament Conference: A Study in International History.* New York: Palgrave Macmillan, 2003.

Klejment, Anne and Roberts, Nancy L. *American Catholic Pacifism: The Influence of Dorothy Day and the Catholic Worker Movement.* Westport, CT: Praeger, 1996.

Knapp, Wilfrid. "Fifty Years of Chatham House Books", *International Affairs*, 46, 5, (1970).

Knock, Thomas J. *To End All Wars: Woodrow Wilson and the Quest for a New World Order*. Princeton, NJ: Princeton University Press, 1995.

Knox, James. *Robert Byron*. London: John Murray, 2004.

Komlos, John. *The Habsburg Monarchy as a Customs Union: Economic Development in Austria-Hungary in the Nineteenth Century*. Princeton: Princeton University Press, 1983.

Koskenniemi, Marti. *From Apology to Utopia: The Structure of International Legal Argument*. Cambridge: Cambridge University Press, 2006.

Krakovitch, Raymond. *Paul Reynaud: Dans la tragédie de l'histoire*. Paris: Tallandier, 1998.

Kranold, Herman. *Vereinigte Stäten von Europa*. Munich: 1924.

Krull, Catherine and McKercher, B. J. C. "The Press, Public Opinion, Arms Limitation, and Government Policy in Britain, 1932-34: Some Preliminary Observations", *Diplomacy & Statecraft*, 13, 3, (2002).

Kurth, Peter. *American Cassandra: The Life of Dorothy Thompson*. London: Little, Brown & Co., 1991.

Lacouture, Jean. *Léon Blum*. Paris: Seuil, 1979.

— De G*aulle: The Rebel 1890-1944*. New York: W. W. Norton & Company, (1993).

Ladislas, Mysyrowicz. *Autopsie d'une défaite, origines de l'effondrement français de 1940*. Lausanne: L'Age d'homme, 1973.

Lafay, Arlette. *La sagesse de Georges Duhamel*. Paris: Minard, 1984.

Laforest, Christophe. "La stratégie française et la Pologne, 1919-1939. Aspects économiques et implications politiques", *Histoire, Economie et Société*, 22, 3, (2003).

Lammers, D. "From Whitehall after Munich: The Foreign Office and the Future Course of British Policy", *Historical Journal*, 16, (1973).

Landuyt, Ariane and Preda, Daniela eds. *I movimenti per l'unità europea, 1970-1986*. Bologna: Il Mulino, 2000.

Langer, William L. *Our Vichy Gamble*. New York: Alfred A. Knopf, 1947.

Laqua, Daniel. *Internationalism Reconfigured: Transnational Ideas and Movements Between the World Wars*. New York: I.B. Tauris, 2011.

Larcan, Alain. *Richard Coudenhove-Kalergi et Charles de Gaulle*. Paris: Fondation Charles de Gaulle, 1999.

Large, David Clay. *Contending with Hitler: Varieties of German Resistance in the Third Reich*. Cambridge: Cambridge University Press, 1994.

Lash, Joseph P. *Roosevelt and Churchill, 1939-1940. The Partnership That Saved the West*. London: André Deutsch, 1976.

Laski, Harold Joseph. *Studies in the Problem of Sovereignty*. New Heaven:
Yale University Press, 1917.
— *The Foundation of Sovereignty and Other Essays*. London: Allen &
Unwin, 1922.
— *A Grammar of Politics*. London: Allen & Unwin, 1925.
— *Nationalism and the Future of Civilization*. London: Watts, 1932.
— *The Economic Revolution*. London: Stanhope Press, 1941.
Launay, Morinosuke and de Kajima, Jacques. *Coudenhove-Kalergi: Le
pionnier de l'Europe unie*. Lausanne: Fondation Jean Monnet, 1971.
Lavin, Deborah. "Lionel Curtis and Indian Dyarchy", in *The Federal Idea.
The History of Federalism from the Enlightenment to 1945*. Edited by
Andrea Bosco. London: Lothian Foundation Press, 1991.
— *From Empire to International Commonwealth: A Biography of Lionel
Curtis*. Oxford: Clarendon, 1995.
Lawlor, Sheila. *Churchill and the Politics of War, 1940-1941*. Cambridge:
Cambridge University Press, 1994.
Le Goyet, Pierre. *Le Mystère Gamelin*. Paris: Presses de la Cité, 1976.
— *La defaite, 10 mai-25 juin 1940*. Paris: Economica, 1990.
Lebovics, Herman. *True France: The Wars over Cultural Identity, 1900-
1945*. Ithaca, NY: Cornell University Press, 1994.
Lebrun, Albert. *Témoignage*. Paris: Plon, 1945.
Leckie, Robert. *Delivered from Evil: The Saga of World War II*. London:
Harper Perennial, 1988.
Lecuir, J. and Fridenson, P. "L'organisation de la coopération aérienne
franco-britannique, 1935-mai 19402, *Revue d' histoire de la Deuxième
Guerre mondiale*, 73, (1969).
Ledermann, Laszlo. *Official Statements of War and Peace Aims. European
Belligerents, September 1, 1939 to August 31, 1940*. Geneva: Geneva
Research Center, 1940.
Lee, J. M. *The Churchill Coalition, 1940-1945*. North Haven, CT: Archon,
1980.
Leeds, Stanton B. *These Rule France: The Story of Edouard Daladier and
the Men Around Daladier*. Whitefish, MT: Kessinger Publishing 2007.
Lefranc, Georges. *Le Mouvement socialiste sous la Troisième République*.
Paris: 1963.
Leitz, Christian. *Nazi Foreign Policy 1933-1941. The Road to Global
War*. London: Routledge, 2003.
Lentin, Antony. *Lloyd George and the Lost Peace: From Versailles to
Hitler, 1919-1940*. New York: Palgrave Macmillan, 2001.
Lesbros, Marcel. *Paul Reynaud: alpin, européen, contemporaine*. Paris:
Ophrys, 1993.

Leslie, Edgworth. "Die bündische Idee: der Wegweiser zu einem dauernden Frieden", *La Société des Nations*, 1, 20, (1940).

Leutze, James R. *Bargaining for Supremacy. Anglo-American Naval Collaboration, 1937-1941*. Chapel Hill, NC: University of North Carolina Press, 1977.

Leventhal, F. M. *The Last Dissenter: H. N. Brailsford and His World*. Oxford: Oxford University Press, 2000.

Leveque, François. "Des diplomaties dans l'impasse: Les relations franco-soviétiques de Septembre 1939 à juin 1941", *Guerres Mondiales et Conflits Contemporains*, 43, (1993).

— "Les relations franco-soviétiques pendant la seconde guerre mondiale: De la défaite à l'alliance, 1939-1945", *Revue des Etudes Slaves*, 69, 3, (1997).

Levi, Lucio and Pistone, Sergio eds. *Trent'anni di vita del Movimento Federalista Europeo*. Milan: Angeli, 1973.

Levisse-Touzé C. ed. *La campagne de 1940*. Paris: Tallandier, 2001.

Lewis, Jeremy. *David Astor*. London: Vintage, 2016.

Lewis, Julian. *Changing Direction: British Military Planning for Post-war Strategic Defence, 1942-1947*. London: Routledge, 2002.

Liddell, Hart Basil Henry. *History of the Second World War*. Cambridge, MA: Da Capo Press, 1999.

Lind, Michael. "Pax Atlantica: The Case for Euramerica", *World Policy Journal*, 13, 1, (1996).

Lipgens, Walter. *A History of European Integration, 1945-1947. The Formation of the European Unity Movement*. Oxford: Clarendon Press, 1982.

— ed. *Documents on the History of European Integration: Continental Plans for European Union, 1939-1945*. New York-Berlin: Walter De Gruyter, 1984.

— "Swiss Plans for the Post-war Order in Europe", in *Documents on the History of European Integration*, 1. Edited by Walter Lipgens. Berlin-New York: Walter De Gruyter, 1985.

— ed. *Documents on the History of European Integration: Plans for European Union in Great Britain and in Exile, 1939-1949*. New York-Berlin: Walter de Gruyter, 1986.

— ed. *Documents on the History of European Integration: The Struggle for European Union by Political Parties and Pressure Groups in Western European Countries, 1939-1945*. New York-Berlin: Walter De Gruyter, 1988.

— ed. *Documents on the History of European Integration: Transnational Organizations of Political Parties and Pressure Groups in the Struggle for European Federation*. New York-Berlin: Walter De Gruyter, 1991.

Lippmann, Walter. *U.S. War Aims*. London: Hamish Hamilton, 1944.

Lord, Walter. *Le miracle de Dunkerque, 4 juin 1940*. Paris: Robert Laffont, 1999.

Lormier, Dominique. *La drôle de guerre*. Paris: Les Chemins de la Mémoire, 1999.

Loth, Wilfred. *Der Weg nach Europa: Geschichte der europäischen Integration 1939-1957*. Göttingen: Vandenhoech & Ruprecht, 1990.

Lothian, Lord (Philip Kerr). "The Demonic Influence of National Sovereignty", in *The Universal Church and the World of Nations*. London: Jonathan Cape, 1938.

— *The Ending of Armageddon*. London: Federal Union Publishing, 1939.

— *The American Speeches of Lord Lothian*. London: Oxford University Press, 1941.

— *Pacifism is not Enough. Collected Lectures and Speeches of Lord Lothian (Philip Kerr)*. Edited by Andrea Bosco and John Pinder. London: Lothian Foundation Press, 1990.

Lottman, Herbert R. *The Left Bank Writers, Artists and Politics from the Popular Front to the Cold War*. Chicago, IL: Chicago University Press, 1988.

Louis, William Roger. "'In the Name of God, Go!': Leo Amery and the British Empire in the Age of Churchill", *Neue Politische Literatur*, 37, 3, (1992).

— *In the Name of God, Go!: Leo Amery and the British Empire in the Age of Churchill*. New York: W. W. Norton & Co, 1992.

Ludlow, Peter. "Papst Pius XII, die britische Regierung und die deutsche Opposition im Winter 1939/40", *Vierteljahrs Hefte für Zeitgeschichte*, 22, (1974).

— "The Unwinding of Appeasement", in *Das 'Andere Deutschland' im Zweiten Weltkrieg*. Stuttgard: Klett, 1977.

— ed. *Français et Britannique dans la Drôle de Guerre: Actes du Colloque franco-britannique tenu à Paris du 8 au 12 décembre 1975*. Paris: Editions du Centre Nationale de la Recherche Scientifique, 1979.

— "Le débat sur le buts de paix", in *Français et Britanniques dans la drôle de guerre: Actes du Colloque franco-britannique tenu à Paris du 8 au 12 décembre 1975*. Edited by Peter Ludlow. Paris: Editions du Centre Nationale de la Recherche Scientifique, 1979.

— "Britain and Northern Europe, 1940-1945", *Revue Internationale d'Histoire Militaire*, 53, (1982).

Luetzens, G. O. G. *A New Order for Germany*. London: National Peace Council, 1941.

Lukacs, John. *Five Days in London, May 1940*. New Haven: Yale University Press, 2001.

— *The Duel: The Eighty-Day Struggle Between Churchill and Hitler*. New Haven: Yale University Press, 2001.

— *The Last European War, September 1939-December 1941*. New Haven: Yale University Press, 2001.

Lukaszewski, Jerzy. *Coudenhove-Kalergi*. Lausanne: 1977.

Lynch, Cecelia. *Beyond Appeasement: Interpreting Interwar Peace Movements in World Politics*. Ithaca, NY: Cornell University Press, 1999.

MacDonald, C. A. *The United States, Britain and Appeasement, 1936-1939*. London: Macmillan, 1981.

Mackay, Ronald Gordon. *Federal Europe*. London: Michael Joseph, 1940.

— *Peace Aims and the New Order: Being a Revised and Popular Edition of 'Federal Europe', Outlining the Case for European Federation, Together with a Draft Constitution of a United States of Europe*. London: M. Joseph, 1941.

— *Towards a United States of Europe: An Analysis of Britain's Role in a European Union*. Westport, CT: Greenwood Press, 1976.

Mackenzie, Hector. "'Arsenal of The British Empire'? British Orders for Munitions Production in Canada, 1936-39", *Journal of Imperial and Commonwealth History*, 31, 3, (2003).

Macklin, Graham. *Chamberlain*. London: Haus Publisher, 2006.

Macmillan, Margaret. *Paris 1919: Six Months That Changed the World*. New York: Random House, 2003.

MacMurray, John. *The Foundations of Economic Reconstruction*. London: National Peace Council, 1942.

MacShane, Denis. "Britain, Switzerland and the Second World War", *International Affairs*, 82, 3, (2006).

Madden Frederick ed. *Oxford and the Idea of Commonwealth*. London: Croom Helm, 1983.

Maguire, G. E. *Anglo-American Policy Towards the Free French*. New York: Palgrave Macmillan, 1995.

Mahoney, Daniel J. *De Gaulle: Statesmanship, Grandeur, and Modern Democracy*. Piscataway, NJ: Transaction Publishers, 2000.

Majocchi, Luigi Vittorio. *La difficile costruzione dell'unità europea*. Milan: Jaca Book, 1996.

Manchester, William. *The Last Lion: Winston Spencer Churchill, Alone 1932-1940*. London: Little, Brown & Co., 1988.

Mangold, Peter. *The Almost Impossible Ally: Harold Macmillan and Charles de Gaulle*. New York: I. B. Tauris, 2006.

Mansergh, Nichol. *Survey of British Commonwealth Affairs: Problems of Wartime Cooperation and Post-War Change 1939-1952*. London: Routledge, 1968.

Mantoux, Paul and Ferrero, Guglielmo. *La Crise Mondiale par les Professeurs de l'Institut Universitaire de Hautes Études Internationales*. Zurig: Editions Polygraphiques, 1937.

Manuel, Roger. *L'union européenne*. Paris: 1932.

Marabell, George Peter. *Frederick Libby and the American Peace Movement, 1921-1941*. New York: Arno Press, 1982.

Marc, Alexandre. *Proudhon*. Paris: Egloff, 1945.

— *L'Europe pour quoi faire?* Paris: Presses d'Europe, 1962.

— "Histoires des mouvements fédéralistes depuis la première guerre mondiale", in *Le Fédéralisme*. Nice: Presses d'Europe, 1964.

— *L'Europe dans le monde*. Paris: Presses d'Europe, 1965.

— *La révolution fédéraliste*. Paris: Presses d'Europe, 1969.

— *De la méthodologie à la dialectique*. Paris: Presses d'Europe, 1970.

Marder, A. J. *From the Dardanelles to Oran*. Oxford: Oxford University Press, 1974.

Marin, Louis. "Contributions à l'Etude des Prodromes de l'Armistice", *Revue d'Histoire de la Deuxième Guerre Mondiale*, 2, (1951).

Marks, Sally. "The World According To Washington", *Diplomatic History*, 11, 3, (1987).

Markwell, D. J. "Sir Alfred Zimmern Revisited", *Review of International Studies*, 12, 4, (1986).

Markwell, Donald John. *John Maynard Keynes and International Relations: Economic Paths to War and Peace*. New York: Oxford University Press, 2006.

Marlowe, John. *Milner, Apostle of Empire*. London: Hamish Hamilton Press, 1976.

Marsh, S. and Baylis, J. "The Anglo-American 'Special Relationship': The Lazarus of International Relations", *Diplomacy and Statecraft*, 17, (2006).

Martel, Gordon. *The Origins of the Second World War Reconsidered: A. J. P. Taylor and the Historians*. London: Routledge, 1999.

Martin, Benjamin F. *France in 1938*. Baton Rouge, LA: Louisiana State University Press, 2006.

Marwick, Arthur. *A History of the Modern British Isles, 1914-1999: Circumstances, Events and Outcomes*. Oxford: Wiley-Blackwell, 2000.

Mason, John W. *Dissolution of the Austro-Hungarian Empire, 1867-1918*. Harlow: Longman, 1986.

Mattelart, Armand. *Histoire de l'utopie planétaire*. Geneva: La Decouvérte, 2000.

Mauriac, François. *Le croyant et l'humaniste inquiet: Correspondance, François Mauriac-Georges Duhamel. 1919-1966*. Paris: Klincksieck, 1997.

May, Ernest R. *Strange victory: Hitler's Conquest of France*. New York: Hill and Wang, 2000.

Mazower, Mark. *Dark Continent: Europe's Twentieth Century*. New York: Vintage, 2000.

McAllister Linn, Brian. *Guardians of Empire: The U.S. Army and the Pacific, 1902-1940*. Chapel Hill, NC: University of North Carolina Press, 1999.

McGibbon, Ian. *New Zealand and the Second World War: The People, the Battles and the Legacy*. Auckland: Hodder Moa Beckett, 2004.

McKercher, Brian J. C. "'Our Most Dangerous Enemy': Great Britain Pre-Eminent in the 1930s", *International History Review*, 13, 4, (1991).

— "No Eternal Friends or Enemies: British Defence Policy and the Problem of the United States, 1919-1939", *Canadian Journal of History*, 28, 2, (1993).

— *Transition of Power: Britain's Loss of Global Pre-eminence to the United States, 1930-45*. Cambridge: Cambridge University Press, 1999.

— *The Second Baldwin Government and the United States, 1924-1929: Attitudes and Diplomacy*. Cambridge: Cambridge University Press, 2003.

McKernan, Michael. *The Strength of a Nation: Six Years of Australians Fighting For the Nation and Defending the Home-front in World War II*. London: Allen & Unwin, 2007.

McLachlan, Donald. *In the Chair: Barrington-Ward of 'The Times', 1927-1948*. London: Weidenfeld and Nicolson, 1971.

McNeal, Patricia F. *The American Catholic Peace Movement, 1928-1972*. Boston, MA: Ayer Publications, 1980.

McNeill, William H. *Arnold J. Toynbee: A Life*. New York: Oxford University Press, 1990.

McVickar Haight, John. "Les négociations relatives aux achats d'avions américains par la France pendant la période qui précéda immédiatement la guerre", *Revue d'Histoire de la Deuxième Guerre Mondiale*, 58, (1965).

— "Jean Monnet and the American Arsenal after the beginning of the War", in *French Society and Culture since the Old Regime*. Edited by E. M. Acomb and M. C. Brown. New York: Holt Rinehart and Winston, 1966.

— *American Aid to France 1938-1940*. New York: Atheneum, 1970.

Meade, James. *The Theory of Customs Unions*. Westport, CT: Greenwood Press, 1980.

Melchionni, Mariagrazia. "The Spinelli-Monnet Correspondence. For a Biographical Archive of the Protagonists of the Movement for European Union", *Annals of the Lothian Foundation*, 4, (1994).

Memmi, Dominique. *Jules Romains ou la passion de parvenir*. Paris: La Dispute, 1998.

Meredith, Charles M. *Peace? A Critical Study of America's Peace Aims*. Washington, DC: The Universal Press, 1944.

Meredith, David. "Lionel Curtis, the Round Table Movement and the Montagu-Chelmsford Reforms, (1919)", in *The Round Table Movement, the Empire/Commonwealth and British Foreign Policy*. Edited by Andrea Bosco and Alex May. London: Lothian Foundation Press, 1997.

Merglen, A. "La France pouvait continuer la guerre en Afrique française du Nord en juin 1940", *Guerres mondiale set conflits contemporains*, 168, (1992).

Micaud, Charles A. *The French Right and Nazi Germany, 1933-1943: A Study of Public Opinion*. London: Octagon Books, 1964.

Middleton, Murray J. *The Third Challenge*. London: National Peace Council, 1945.

Miller, Rory. *Divided Against Zion: Anti-Zionist Opposition to the Creation of a Jewish State in Palestine, 1945-1948*. London: Routledge, 2000.

Milne, James Lee. *Harold Nicolson: A Biography, 1886-1929*. London: Trafalgar Square Publishing, 1988.

Minion, Mark. "Left, Right or European? Labour and Europe in the 1940s: The Case of the Socialist Vanguard Group", *European Review of History*, 7, 2, (2000).

Mitrany, David. *Progress of International Government*. London: Elliots Books, 1933.

— *American Interpretations. Four Political Essays*. London: Contact Publications, 1946.

— *World Unity and the Nations*. London: National Peace Council, 1950.

— *Marx Against the Peasant: A Study in Social Dogmatism.* London: George Weidenfeld & Nicolson, 1952.

— *A Working Peace System.* London: Quadrangle Books, 1966.

— *The Functional Theory of Politics.* London: M. Robertson, 1975.

Mollin, Marian. *Radical Pacifism in Modern America: Egalitarianism and Protest.* Philadelphia, PA: University of Pensylvania Press, 2006.

Monick, Emmanuel and Debré, Michel. *Demain la paix. Esquisse d'un ordre international.* Paris: Plon, 1945.

Monnet, Jean. *Memoirs.* New York: Doubleday& Co, 1978.

Monnier, Victor. *William E. Rappard: Défenseur des libertés, serviteurs de son pays et de la communauté internationale.* Basel: Helbing et Lichtenhahn, 1995.

Morelli, Umberto. *Contro il mito dello Stato sovrano: Luigi Einaudi e l'unità europea,* Milan: Angeli, 1990.

Morgan, Austen. *Harold Wilson: A Life.* London: LPC Group, 1992.

Morgan, Roger. "'To Advance the Study of Political Sciences...': Chatham House's Early Research", in *Chatham House and British Foreign Policy. The Royal Institute of International Affairs During the Inter-War Period 1919-1945.* Edited by Andrea Bosco and Cornelia Navari. London: Lothian Foundation Press, 1994.

Moritzen, Julius. *The Peace Movement of America.* Whitefish, MT: Kessinger Publishing, 2007.

Morris, Jan. *Pax Britannica: Climax of an Empire.* Fort Washington, PA: Harvest Books, 2002.

Moss, Norman. *19 Weeks: America, Britain, and the Fateful Summer of 1940.* London: Houghton Mifflin, 2003.

Moure, Kenneth. *The Gold Standard Illusion: France, the Bank of France, and the International Gold Standard, 1914-1939.* New York: Oxford University Press, 2002.

Munch-Petersen, Thomas. *The Strategy of Phoney War, Britain Sweden and the Iron Ore Question, 1939-1940.* Stockholm: Militarhistoriska Forlaget, 1981.

Munholland, K. *Rock of Contention.* Oxford: Berghahn Books, 2007.

Murray, Williamson. *The Change in the European Balance of Power, 1938-1939: The Path to Ruin.* New Haven: Princeton University Press, 1984.

Musolf, Karen J. *From Plymouth To Parliament: A Rhetorical History of Nancy Astor's 1919 Campaign.* New York: Palgrave Macmillan, 1998.

Namikas, Lise. "The Committee to Defend America and the Debate between Internationalists and Interventionists, 1939-1941", *The Historian,* 61, 4, (1999).

Naquet, Emmanuel. "Eléments l'étude d'une génération pacifiste dans l'entre-deux-guerres. La laures et le rapprochement franco-allemand, 1924-1933", in *Matériaux pour l'Histoire de Notre Temps*, 18, (1990).

Navari, Cornelia. "Chatham House and the Broad Church View of British Foreign Policy", in *Chatham House and British Foreign Policy. The Royal Institute of International Affairs During the Inter-War Period 1919-1945*. Edited by Andrea Bosco and Cornelia Navari. London: Lothian Foundation Press, 1994.

— "David Mitrany and International Functionalism", in *Thinkers of the Twenty Year's Crisis*. Edited by David Long and Peter Wilson. Oxford: Clarendon Press, 1995.

Neave Hill, W. B. R. "Franco-British Strategic Policy, 1939", in *Relations franco-britanniques, 1935-1939*. Paris: CNRS, 1975.

Neilson, Keith. *Britain, Soviet Russia and the Collapse of the Versailles Order, 1919-1939*. Cambridge: Cambridge University Press, 2006.

— *Hitler and Appeasement: The British Attempt to Prevent the Second World War*. London: Hambledon Continuum, 2006.

— "Perception and Posture in Anglo-American Relations: The Legacy of the Simon-Stimson Affair, 1932-41", *International History Review*, 29, (2007).

Neville, Peter. *Appeasing Hitler: The Diplomacy of Sir Neville Henderson, 1937-9*. London: Macmillan, 1999.

— "Sir Alexander Cadogan and Lord Halifax's 'Damascus Road' Conversion Over the Godesberg Terms 1938", *Diplomacy & Statecraft*, 11, 3, (2000).

— "The Foreign Office and Britain's Ambassadors to Berlin, 1933-39", *Contemporary British History*, 18, 3, (2004).

Newman, Michael. "British Socialists and the Question of European Unity, 1939-45", *European Studies Review*, 10, (1980).

Newton, Scott. *Profits of Peace: The Political Economy of Anglo-German Appeasement*. New York: Oxford University Press, 1996.

Nichols, Ray L. *Treason, Tradition and the Intellectual: Julien Benda*. Lawrence, KS: University Press of Kansas, 1979.

Nicolson, Harold. "Divergence possible entre les buts de guerre de la France et de l'Angleterre", *Nouveaux Cahiers*, 54, (1940).

Nicolson, Nigel ed. *The Harold Nicolson Diaries, 1907-1963*. London: Orion Publishing, 2005.

Nimocks, Walter. *Milner's Young Men: The Kindergarten in Edwardian Imperial Affairs*. London: Hodder & Stoughton, 1970.

Nobécourt, Jacques. *Le colonel de La Rocque, 1885-1946: Ou Les pièges du nationalisme chrétien*. Paris: Fayard, 1996.

Noël, Léon. "Le projet d'union franco-britannique de juin 1940", *Revue d'histoire de la deuxième guerre mondiale*, 21, (1956).

Norwich, John Julius. *The Duff Cooper Diaries*. London: Orion Publishing, 2007.

Nye, John V. C. *War, Wine, and Taxes: The Political Economy of Anglo-French Trade, 1689-1900*. Princeton: Princeton University Press, 2007.

O'Brien, Denis Patrick. *Lionel Robbins*. New York: Palgrave Macmillan, 1988.

— *Lionel Robbins and the Austrian Connection*. Durham, NC: Duke University Press, 1989.

O'Brien, Terence Henry. *Milner: Viscount Milner of St. James's and Cape Town, 1854-1925*. London: Constable & Robinson, 1979.

Oliver, Frederick. *Federalism and Home Rule*. London: John Murray, 1910.

— *The Alternatives to Civil War*. London: John Murray, 1913.

— *What Federalism Is not*. London: John Murray, 1914.

Olson, Linne. *Troublesome Young Men: The Rebels Who Brought Churchill to Power and Helped Save England*. New York: Farrar, Straus & Giroux, 2007.

Ovendale, Ritchie. *'Appeasement' and the English-Speaking World: Britain, the United States, the Dominions, and the Policy of Appeasement, 1937-1939*. Cardiff: University of Wales Press, 1975.

Overy, Richard J. *The Air War, 1939-1945*. London: Europa Publications, 1980.

— *The Origins of the Second World War*. Harlow: Longman, 1998.

Palmer, William. *The Selborne Memorandum*. London: Humphrey Milford, 1925.

Panagariya, Arvind. *Regionalism in Trade Policy*. London: World Scientific Publishing, 1999.

Parker, Matthew. *The Battle of Britain June-October 1940*. London: Headline, 2001.

Parker, R. A. C. "The Anglo-French Conversations April and September 1938", in *Les relations franco-allemandes, 1933-1939*. Paris: 1976.

— "British Rearmament 1936-1939: Treasury, Trade Unions and Skilled Labour", *English Historical Review*, 96, (1981).

— *Chamberlain and Appeasement: British Policy and the Coming of the Second World War*. New York: Palgrave Macmillan, 1993.

— *Churchill and Appeasement*. London: Macmillan, 2000.

Parmar, Inderjeet "Chatham House and the Anglo-American Alliance", *Diplomacy & Statecraft*, 3, 1, (1992).

— "Chatham House, the Foreign Policy Process and the Making of the Anglo-American Alliance", in *Chatham House and British Foreign Policy. The Royal Institute of International Affairs During the Inter-War Period 1919-1945*. Edited by Andrea Bosco and Cornelia Navari. London: Lothian Foundation Press, 1994.

— *Special Interests, the State and the Anglo-American Alliance, 1939-1945*. London: Routledge, 1995.

— "The Issue of State Power: The Council on Foreign Relations as a Case Study", *Journal of American Studies*, 29, 1, (1995).

— "Anglo-American Elites in the Interwar Years: Idealism and Power in the Intellectual Roots of Chatham House and the Council on Foreign Relations", *International Relations*, 16, (2002).

— *Think Tanks and Power in Foreign Policy: A Comparative Study of the Role and Influence of the Council on Foreign Relations and the Royal Institute of International Affairs, 1939-1945*. New York: Palgrave Macmillan, 2004.

Parr, Helen. *British Policy Towards the European Community: Harold Wilson and Britain's World Role, 1964-1967*. London: Routledge, 2005.

Partington, John S. *H. G. Wells's Fin-de-Siecle: Twenty-first Century Reflections on the Early H. G. Wells*. Oxford: Peter Lang, 2007.

Pearce, Robert D. *Attlee*. London: Addison Wesley, 1997.

Peden, G. C. *British Rearmament and the Treasury, 1932-1939*. Edinburgh: Scottish Academic Press, 1979.

— "Sir Warren Fisher and British Rearmament Against Germany", *English Historical Review*, 94, (1979).

Perloff, James. *The Shadows of Power: The Council on Foreign Relations and the American Decline*. Appleton, WI: Western Islands, 1988.

Perry, Marvin. *Arnold Toynbee and the Crisis of the West*. Washington, DC: University Press of America, 1982.

— *Arnold Toynbee and the Western Tradition*. London: Grove/Atlantic, 1996.

Peter, Ania. *William E. Rappard und der Völkerbund: Ein Schweizer Pionier der internationalen Verständigung*. Frankfurt am Main: Peter Lang, 1973.

Peters, A. R. *Anthony Eden at the Foreign Office, 1931-38*. New York: Dartmouth Publishing, 1986.

Petit, Hugues. *L'église, le Sillon et l'Action Française*. Paris: Nouvelles Editions Latines, 1998.

Petrow, Richard. *The Bitter Years. The Invasion and Occupation of Denmark and Norway, April 1940-May 1945*. New York: William Morrow, 1974.

Philippe, Garraud. "Le cas de l'armée de l'Air", *Guerres Mondiales et conflits contemporains*, 194, (1999).

Philpott, William. "The Supreme War Council and the Allied War Effort, 1939-1940", in *Anglo-French Relations, 1898-1998: From Fashoda to Jospin*. Edited by Michael Dockrill and Philippe Chassaigne. New York: Palgrave Macmillan, 2002.

Picknett, Lynn *et al. Double Standards: The Rudolf Hess Cover-Up*. London: Little, Brown & Co., 2002.

Pimlott, Ben. *Harold Wilson*. London: Harper Collins Publishers, 1993.

Pinder, John. "Prophet not without Honour: Lothian and the Federal Idea", in *The Larger Idea: Lord Lothian and the Problem of National Sovereignty*. Edited by John Turner. London: The Historians' Press, 1988.

— and Maine, Richard. *Federal Union. The Pioneers*. London: Macmillan, 1990.

Pine, Melissa. *Harold Wilson and Europe: Pursuing Britain's Membership of the European Community*. New York: Tauris Academic Studies, 2007.

Pistone, Sergio ed., *I movimenti per l'unità europea, 1945-1954*. Milan: Jaca, 1992.

— *I movimenti per l'unità europea, 1954-1969*. Pavia: Pime, 1996.

Post, Gaines. "Mad Dogs and Englishmen: British Rearmament, Deterrence and Appeasement, 1934-35", *Armed Forces*, 14, 3, (1988).

Potter, Simon J. *News and the British World: The Emergence of an Imperial Press System 1876-1922*. New York: Oxford University Press, 2003.

Powaski, Ronald E. *Towards an Entangling Alliance: American Isolationism, Internationalism and Europe, 1901-1950*. Westport: CT: Greenwood Press, 1991.

Pozzoli, Francesca. "Svizzera e federalismo europeo durante la seconda guerra mondiale", in *Storia e percorsi del federalismo. L'eredità di Carlo Cattaneo*. Edited by Daniela Preda and Cinzia Rognoni Vercelli. Bologna: Il Mulino, 2005.

Pragier, Adam. *Polish Peace Aims*. London: Maxlove, 1944.

Prazmowska, Anita J. *Britain and Poland 1939-1943: The Betrayed Ally*. Cambridge: Cambridge University Press, 1995.

Pressnell, L. S. "Les finances de guerre britannique et la coopération économique franco-britannique en 1939 et en 1940", in *Français et*

Britanniques dans la drôle de guerre: Actes du colloque franco-britannique tenu à Paris du 8 au 12 décembre 1975. Edited by Peter Ludlow. Paris: Editions du Centre Nationale de la Recherche Scientifique, 1979.

Preston, A. *General Staffs and Diplomacy before the Second World War.* London: Croom Helm, 1978.

Pritt, Denis Nowell. *Federal illusion?* London: Muller, 1940.

Proudhon, Pierre-Joseph. "Du principe Fédératif", in *Ouvres complètes.* Paris: Romillat, 2004.

Pugh, M. *Liberal Internationalism: The Interwar Movement for Peace in Britain.* New York: Palgrave Macmillan, 2012.

Purcell, Hugh. *Lloyd George.* London: Haus Publishers, 2006.

Purdue, A. W. *The Second World War.* London: Macmillan, 1999.

Ragsdale, Hugh. *The Soviets, the Munich Crisis, and the Coming of World War II.* Cambridge: Cambridge University Press, 2004.

Ramsden, John. *Man of the Century: Winston Churchill and His Legend Since 1945.* New York: Columbia University Press, 2003.

Rappard, William. *The Geneva Experiment.* Oxford: Oxford University Press, 1931.

— *Pacifism is not Enough. Lectures Delivered at the Geneva Institute of International Relations, August 1934.* London: Allen & Unwin, 1935.

— *The Crisis of Democracy.* Chicago, IL: University of Chicago Press, 1938.

— *The Quest for Peace since the World War.* Boston, MA: Harvard University Press, 1940.

Ratcliff, Ann. "Les relations diplomatiques entre la France et les Etats-Unis. du 29 Septembre 1938 au 16 Juin 1940)", *Revue d'Histoire de la Deuxième Guerre Mondiale*, 19, (1969).

Raushning, Hermann. *The Revolution of Nihilism.* London: Alliance Book Corporation, 1940.

Raymond, Krakovitch. *Paul Reynaud.* Paris: Tallandier, 2002.

Raymond, Raymond J. "Irish Neutrality and Anglo-Irish Relations: 1921-1941", *International History Review*, 9, 3, (1987).

Rémy, Jean-Pierre. *Diplomates en guerre: La Seconde Guerre mondiale racontée à travers les archives du Quai d'Orsay.* Paris: Jean-Claude Lattès, 2007.

Renoult, Maurice *La Fédération et la paix.* Paris: 1930.

Revah, Louis Albert. *Julien Benda: Un misanthrope juif dans la France de Maurras.* Paris: Plon, 1991.

Réveillard, Christophe. *Les premières tentatives de construction d'une Europe fédérale. Des projets de la Résistance au Traité CED: 1940-1954*. Paris: Editions Xavier Guibert, 2001.

Reynaud, Paul. *La France a Sauvé l'Europe*, 2. Paris: Flammarion, 1947.

— *Au Cœur de la Mêlée*. Paris: Flammarion, 1951.

— *In the Thick of the Fight*. London: Cassell, 1955.

— *Mémoires*, 2. Paris: Flammarion, 1963.

Reynolds, David. "Competitive Co-Operation: Anglo-American Relations in World War Two", *Historical Journal*, 23, 1, (1980).

— *The Creation of the Anglo-American Alliance, 1937-41: A Study in Competitive Co-operation*. London: Europa Publishing, 1981.

— "Lord Lothian and Anglo-American Relations, 1939-40", *The American Philosophical Society*, 93, (1983).

— "Lothian, Roosevelt, Churchill and the Origins of Lend-Lease", in *The Larger Idea: Lord Lothian and the Problem of National Sovereignty*. Edited by John Turner. London: The Historians' Press, 1988.

— "1940: Fulcrum of the Twentieth Century?", *International Affairs*, 56, 2, (1990).

— "The Origins of the Two 'World Wars': Historical Discourse and International Politics", *Journal of Contemporary History*, 38, 1, (2003).

— "Churchill and the British Decision to Fight on in 1940: Right Policy, Wrong Reasons", in *Diplomacy and Intelligence During the Second World War: Essays in Honour of F. H. Hinsley*. Edited by Richard Langhorne. Cambridge: Cambridge University Press, 2004.

— *In Command of History: Churchill's Fighting and Writing of the Second World War*. London: Basic Books, 2004.

— *From World War to Cold War: Churchill, Roosevelt and the International History of the 1940s*. Oxford: Oxford University Press, 2006.

— *From World War to Cold War: Churchill, Roosevelt, and the International History of the 1940s*. New York: Oxford University Press, 2006.

Rhodes, Benjamin D. *United States Foreign Policy in the Interwar Period, 1918-1941: The Golden Age of American Diplomatic and Military Complacency*. Westport, CT: Praeger Publishers, 2001.

Rhodes, James. *Anthony Eden*. New York: McGraw-Hill, 1986.

Rich, Norman. *Hitler's War Aims: Ideology, the Nazi State, and the Course of Expansion*. New York: W. W. Norton & Company, 1973.

Robbins, Lionel. *Economic Planning and International Order*. London: Macmillan, 1937.

— *The Economic Basis of Class Conflict and Other Essays of Political Economy*. London: Macmillan, 1939.

— *Economic Aspects of Federation*. London: Federal Union Publishing, 1941.

— *Autobiography of an Economist*. London: Macmillam, 1971.

Robbins, K. G. "Free Churchmen and the Twenty Years' Crisis", *Baptist Quarterly*, 27, 8, (1978).

Roberts, Andrew. *The Holy Fox. A Biography of Lord Halifax*. London: Weidenfeld & Nicolson, 1991.

— *Hitler and Churchill: Secrets of Leadership*. London: Orion Publishing, 2004.

Roberts, D. M. "Clement Davies and the Fall of Neville Chamberlain, 1939-40", *Welsh History Review*, 8, 2, (1976).

Roberts, John C. *World Citizenship and Mundialism: A Guide to the Building of a World Community*. Westport, CT: Praeger, 1999.

Roberts, Owen J. *Background for Atlantic Union. A Study of International Federalism: Its Implications and Possibilities in Our Times*. Washington, DC: American Association of G.P.O, 1950.

Roberts, Priscilla. "Lord Lothian and the Atlantic World", *The Historian*, 67, (2004).

Robertson, A. J. "British Rearmament and Industrial Growth, 1935-1939", *Research in Economic History*, 8, (1982).

Rochas, Yves. *1940: Churchill et les Français: Un Eté Fertile en Légendes*. Paris: Nouvelles Éditions Latines, 1998.

Rock, William R. *Chamberlain and Roosevelt: British Foreign Policy and the United States, 1937-1940*. Columbus, OH: Ohio State University Press, 1988.

Rocolle, Pierre. *La Guerre de 1940*. Paris: Armand Colin, 1990.

Rose, Inbal. *Conservatism and Foreign Policy During the Lloyd George Coalition 1918-1922*. London: Routledge, 1999.

Rose, Norman. *Vansittart: Study of a Diplomat*. London: William Heinemann, 1978.

— *The Cliveden Set: Portrait of an Exclusive Fraternity*. New York: Random House, 2000.

— *Harold Nicolson*. New York: Random House, 2006.

Rosencrance, R. and Steiner, Zara. "British Grand Strategy and the Origins of World War II", in *The Domestic Bases of Grand Strategy*. Edited by R. Rosencrance and A. A. Stein. Ithaca, NY: Cornell University Press, 1993.

Roshwald, Aviel. *Ethnic Nationalism and the Fall of Empires: Central Europe, the Middle East and Russia, 1914-1923*. London: Routledge, 2000.

Ross, Graham. *The Great Powers and the Decline of the European States System, 1914-1945*. Harlow: Longman, 1983.

Rossi, Mario. *Roosevelt and the French*. Westport, CT: Praeger, 1993.

Rossi-Landi, Guy. *La Drôle de guerre. La vie politique en France: 2 septembre 1939-10 mai 1940*. Paris: A. Colin, 1971.

— "Le pacifisme en France, 1930-1940", in *Français et Britanniques dans la drôle de guerre: Actes du colloque franco-britannique tenu à Paris du 8 au 12 décembre 1975*. Paris: Editions du Centre Nationale de la Recherche Scientifique, 1979.

Rossini, Daniela. *From Theodore Roosevelt to FDR: Internationalism and Isolationism in American Foreign Policy*. Keele: Keele University Press, 1995.

Rostow, Nicholas. *Anglo-French Relations, 1934-1936*. New York: St. Martin's Press, 1984.

Rothwell, V. *Anthony Eden: A Political Biography, 1931-1957*. Manchester: Manchester University Press, 1992.

Roussel, Eric. *Jean Monnet, 1888-1979*. Paris: Fayard, 1996.

Rowntree, John S. *The Society of Friends: Its Faith and Practice*. Whitefish, MT: Kessinger Publishing, 2006.

Roz, Firmin. *La Lumière de Paris*. Paris: La Renaissance du Livre, 1933.

Russell, Bertrand. *Freedom and Organisation, 1814-1914*. London: Allen & Unwin, 1934.

Rutherford, Ward. *Blitzkrieg 1940*. London: G. P. Putnam's Sons, 1980.

Sabine, B. E. V. "The Six Budgets of Neville Chamberlain, 1932-1937", *British Tax Review*, 4, (1981).

Salter, Arthur. *Memoirs of a Public Servant*. London: Faber & Faber, 1961.

Sanders, Marion K. *Dorothy Thompson: A Legend in Her Time*. New York: Avon Books, 1974.

Sandu, Traian. "La présence française en Europe centrale dans entre-deux-guerres", *Revue d'Europe Centrale*, 3, 2, (1995).

Schellenberg, Walter. *Invasion 1940: The Nazi Invasion Plan for Britain by SS General Walter Schellenberg*. Toronto: Brown Book, 2001.

Schlabach, Theron F. and Hughes, Richard T. *Proclaim Peace: Christian Pacifism from Unexpected Quarters*. Champaign, IL: University of Illinois Press, 1997.

Schlesinger, Arthur. *Federalism in Central and Eastern Europe*. New York: K. Paul, 1945.

Schneider, James C. *Should America Go To War? The Debate over Foreign Policy in Chicago, 1939-1941*. Chapel Hill, NC: University of North Carolina Press, 1989.

Schreiner, Reinhard. *Bidault, der MRP und die französische Deutschlandpolitik 1944-1948*. Frankfurt am Main: Peter Lang, 1945.

Schuker, Stephen A. *The End of French Predominance in Europe*. Chapel Hill, NC: North Carolina University Press, 1989.

Schulzinger, Robert D. *The Wise Men of Foreign Affairs*. New York: Columbia University Press, 1984.

Schwartz, Joseph. *Atlantic Federal Union*. Milwaukee: Marquette University Press, 1950.

Schwarzenberger, Georg. *William Ladd: An Examination of an American Proposal for an International Equity Tribunal*. London: Constable & Robinson, 1935.

— "Federation and the Colonial Problem", in *Federal Union. A Symposium*. Edited by Melville Channing-Pearce. London: Jonathan Cape, 1940.

— *Atlantic Union: A Practical Utopia?* Washington, DC: Federal Educational and Research Trust, 1957.

Scott, R. B. Y. and Vlastos, Gregory. *Towards the Christian Revolution*. Whitefish, MT: Kessinger Publishing, 2006.

Seager, Fréderic. "Les buts de guerre allies devant l'opinion, 1939-1940", *Revue d' histoire moderne et contemporaine*, 32, (1985).

Self, Robert. *Britain, America and the War Debt Controversy: The Economic Diplomacy of an Unspecial Relationship, 1917-1941*. London: Routledge, 2006.

— *Neville Chamberlain: A Biography*. London: Ashgate Publishing, 2006.

— "Perception and Posture in Anglo-American Relations: The War Debt Controversy in the 'Official Mind', 1919-1940", *International History Review*, 29, (2007).

Serfaty, Simon. *Visions of the Atlantic Alliance: The United States, the European Union, and NATO*. Washington, DC: Center for Strategic & International Studies, 2005.

Seydoux, François. "Un certain 18 Juin", *Nouvelle Revue des Deux Mondes*, 7, (1980).

Shamir, Haim. "The 'drôle de guerre' and French Public Opinion", *Journal of Contemporary History*, 11, 1, (1976).

Shaplen, Robert. *Towards the Well-Being of the Mankind: Fifty Years of the Rockefeller Foundation*. New York: Doubleday & Co., 1964.

Sharp, Alan. *Anglo-French Relations in the Twentieth Century*. London: Routledge, 2000.

Shaw, Louise. *The British Political Elite and the Soviet Union, 1937-1939.* London: Frank Cass, 2003.

Shen, Peijian. *The Age of Appeasement. The Evolution of British Foreign Policy in the 1930s.* Stroud: Sutton Publishing, 1999.

Shepperd, Alan. *France 1940: Blitzkrieg in the West.* Oxford: Osprey Publishing, 1990.

Shiozaki, Hiroaki. *Seeking International Order: The Lineage of the RIIA, CFR, and the IPR and their Interconnections to the Two World Wars.* Fukuoka: 1998.

Shirer, William L. *The Collapse of the Third Republic: An Inquiry into the Fall of France in 1940.* Cambridge, MA: Da Capo Press, 1994.

Shlaim, Avi. "Prelude to Downfall: The British Offer of Union to France, June 1940", *Journal of Contemporary History*, 9, 3, (1974).

Shogan, Robert. *Hard Bargain: How FDR Twisted Churchill's Arm, Evaded the Law, and Changed the Role of the American Presidency.* Boulder, CO: Westview Press, 1999.

Shook, John R. and Backe, Andrew. *The Chicago School of Functionalism.* Bristol: Thoemmes Continuum, 2000.

Short, K. R. M. "The White Cliffs of Dover: Promoting the Anglo-American Alliance in World War II", *Historical Journal of Film, Radio and Television*, 2, 1, (1982).

Shoup, Laurence H. "Shaping the Post-war World: The Council on Foreign Relations and the United States War Aims During World War Two", *Insurgent Sociologist*, 5, 3, (1975).

— and Minter, William. *Imperial Brain Trust: The Council on Foreign Relations and United States Foreign Policy.* New York: Authors Choice Press, 2004.

Siegel, Mona L. *The Moral Disarmament of France: Education, Pacifism, and Patriotism, 1914-1940.* Cambridge: Cambridge University Press, 2005.

Sifton, Elisabeth. *The Serenity Prayer: Faith and Politics in Times of Peace and War.* New York: W. W. Norton & Company, 2003.

Skalnes, Lars S. "Grand Strategy and Foreign Economic Policy: British Grand Strategy in the 1930s", *World Politics*, 50, 4, (1998).

Sked, Alan. *The Decline and Fall of the Habsburg Empire, 1815-1918.* Harlow: Longman, 2001.

Smart, Nick. *British Strategy and Politics During the Phony War: Before the Balloon Went Up.* Westport, CT: Praeger Publishers, 2003.

Smirnov, V. P. "Le Komintern et le Parti Communiste français pendant la 'drole de guerre'", *Revue des Études Slaves*, 65, 4, (1993).

Smith, Michael and Stirk, Peter. *Making the New Europe: European Unity and the Second World War*. London: Pinter, 1993.

Smith, Alison. *Margery Perham and British Rule in Africa*. London: Routledge, 1992.

Smith, David C. *H. G. Wells: Desperately Mortal: A Biography*. New Haven: Yale University Press, 1988.

Smith, Malcolm. *Britain and 1940: History, Myth and Popular Memory*. London: Routledge, 2001.

Smith, Rennie. *General Disarmament or War?* London: George Allen & Unwin, 1927.

Smith, Timothy E. *Opposition Beyond the Water's Edge: Liberal Internationalists, Pacifists and Containment, 1945-1953*. Westport, CT: Greenwood Press, 1999.

Soucy, Robert. *Le Fascisme français 1924-1933*. Paris: Presses Universitaires de France, 1989.

Spears, Edward. *Assignment to Catastrophe. The Fall of France. June 1940*, 2. London: William Heinemann, 1954.

Spinelli, Altiero. *Il lungo monologo*. Rome: Edizioni dell'Ateneo, 1968.

— and Rossi, Ernesto. *Il manifesto di Ventotene*. Naples: Guida, 1982.

— *Come ho tentato di diventare saggio: Io, Ulisse*. Bologna: Il Mulino, 1984.

— *Diario europeo*. Edited by Edmondo Paolini. Bologna: Il Mulino, 1989-1992.

Spring, Powell. *The Peace Aims of Humanity*. London: Orange Press, 1944.

Staffelbach, Thomas. "Die Europa-Union 1945 bis 1949", *Studi e fonti*, 18, (1992).

Steed, Wickham. *Vital Peace: A Story of Risks*. London: Macmillan, 1936.

— *The Press*. London: Penguin Books, 1938.

— *Our War Aims*. London: Secker & Warburg, 1939.

— "Foreground and Background", *Fortnightly Review*, 146, (1939).

Steele, Richard W. *Propaganda in an Open Society: The Roosevelt Administration and the Media*. Westport, CT: Greenwood Press, 1985.

Stella, Tiziana. "Euro-Atlantismo. L'eredità del federalismo americano nel secondo conflitto mondiale", in *Storie e percorsi del federalismo. L'eredità di Carlo Cattaneo*. Edited by Daniela Preda and Cinzia Rognoni Vercelli. Bologna: Il Mulino, 2005.

Stephens, Mark. *Ernest Bevin: Unskilled Labourer and World Statesman 1881-1951*. London: Spa Books, 1989.

Stevenson, David. *French War Aims and Peace Planning*. Berkeley, CA: University of California Press, 1994.

Stewart, Graham. *Burying Caesar: The Churchill-Chamberlain Rivalry.* New York: Overlook, 2001.

Stokes, Richard L. *Léon Blum: From Poet to Premier.* Whitefish, MT: Kessinger Publishing, 2007.

Stoler, Mark A. *Allies in War: Britain and America against the Axis Powers, 1940-1945.* New York: Hodder Arnold, 2005.

Stone, Glyn. "Yvon Delbos and Anthony Eden: Anglo-French Cooperation, 1936-1938", *Diplomacy & Statecraft*, 17, 4, (2006).

Storm, Margaret Jameson. *The Decline of Merry England.* London: Jameson Press, 2007.

Straus, Ira. "Lothian and the Anglo-American Problematic", in *The Larger Idea: Lord Lothian and the Problem of National Sovereignty.* Edited by John Turner. London: The Historians' Press, 1988.

Streit, Clarence. *Union Now. A Proposal for a Federal Union of the Democracies of the North Atlantic.* London: Jonathan Cape, 1939.

— *Union Now with Britain.* London: Jonathan Cape, 1941.

— "Lionel Curtis: The Federalist", *Freedom and Union*, 9, 4, (1949).

— "Lionel Curtis: Prophet of Federal Union", *Freedom and Union*, 16, 1, (1956).

Stromberg, Roland N. *Arnold J. Toynbee: Historian for an Age in Crisis.* Carbondale, IL: Southern Illinois University Press, 1972.

Strupp, Karl. *Legal Machinery for Peaceful Change.* London: Constable & Robinson, 1937.

Studdert-Kennedy, Gerard. *Dog-Collar Democracy: The Industrial Christian Fellowship, 1919-1929.* New York: Palgrave Macmillan, 1982.

— "Political Science and Political Theology: Lionel Curtis, Round Tablers and India", in *Annals of the Lothian Foundation*, 4, (1994).

— "Christianity, Statecraft and Chatham House: Lionel Curtis and Word Order", *Diplomacy and Statecraft*, 6, 2, (1995).

— "Lionel Curtis: Federalism and India", *Journal of Imperial and Commonwealth History*, 24, 2, (1996).

— "Curtis, Lionel George: Intense Beliefs of", in *The Round Table Movement, the Empire/Commonwealth and British Foreign Policy.* Edited by Andrea Bosco and Alex May. London: Lothian Foundation Press, 1997.

Swift, John. *Labour in Crisis: Clement Attlee and the Labour Party Opposition, 1931-1940.* New York: Palgrave Macmillan, 2001.

Szent-Miklosy, Istvan. *The Atlantic Union Movement, Its Significance in World Politics.* Southlake, TX: Fountainhead Press, 1965.

Taylor, Alan J. P. *English History 1914-1945*. New York: Oxford University Press, 2001.

Taylor, Gary. *G. D. H. Cole and the National Guilds League*. London: Ihs Press, 2004.

Taylor, Philip M. *British Propaganda in the Twentieth Century*. Edinburgh: Edinburgh University Press, 2001.

— *The Projection of Britain: British Overseas Publicity and Propaganda 1919-1939*. Cambridge: Cambridge University Press, 2007.

Teeling, William. *After the War: A Symposium of Peace Aims*. London: Sidgwick & Jackson, 1940.

Tellier, Thibault. *Paul Reynaud. 1878-1966. Un indépendant en politique*. Paris: Fayard, 2005.

Teroni, Sandra. *La passione della democrazia: Julien Benda*. Rome: Bulzoni, 1993.

Thomas, Hugh. *John Strachey*. London: Methuen, 1973.

Thomas, Martin. *Britain, France and Appeasement: Anglo-French Relations in the Popular Front Era*. Oxford: Clarendon Press, 1996.

— *The French Empire at War, 1940-1945*. Manchester: Manchester University Press, 2007.

Thompson, Andrew. *Imperial Britain: The Politics, Economics, and Ideology of Empire, 1880-1932*. Harlow: Longman, 2000.

Thompson, J. Lee. *A Wider Patriotism: Alfred Milner and the British Empire*. London: Pickering & Chatto Publishers, 2007.

Thompson, Kenneth W. *Ethics, Functionalism, and Power in International Politics: The Crisis in Values*. Baton Rouge, LA: Louisiana State University Press, 1979.

Thompson, Neville. *The Anti-Appeasers: Conservative Opposition to Appeasement in the 30s*. Oxford: Clarendon Press, 1971.

Thompson, Reginald William. *Churchill and Morton*. London: Hodder & Stoughton, 1976.

Thorne, Christopher. "Chatham House, Whitehall, and Far Eastern Issues: 1941-1945", in *Chatham House and British Foreign Policy. The Royal Institute of International Affairs During the Inter-War Period 1919-1945*. Edited by Andrea Bosco and Cornelia Navari. London: Lothian Foundation Press, 1994.

Thorpe, D. R. *Eden: The Life and Times of Anthony Eden, First Earl of Avon, 1897-1977*. New York: Random House, 2004.

Thorpe, Richard. *Alec Douglas-Home*. London: Sinclair-Stevenson, 1996.

Tillich, Paul. *War Aims. The Real Meaning of this War. Who Can, and Who Can't Carry Out these War Aims*. New York: Protestant Press, 1942.

Tomoko, Akami. *Internationalizing the Pacific: The United States, Japan and the Institute of Pacific Relations in War and Peace, 1919-1945*. London: Routledge, 2001.

Toomey, Jane. *Harold Wilson's Second EEC Application*. Dublin: University College Dublin Press, 2007.

Torres, Henry. *Pierre Laval*. Whitefish, MT: Kessinger Publishing, 2007.

Toynbee, Arnold. *Civilization on Trial*. Oxford: Oxford University Press, 1948.

Truelle, J. "La production aéronautique militaire française jusqu'en juin 1940", *Revue d' histoire de la Deuxième Guerre mondiale*, 73, (1969).

Tucker, Spencer. *The Second World War*. New York: Palgrave Macmillan, 2003.

Turner, Arthur. "Anglo-French Financial Relations in the 1920s", *European History Quarterly*, 26, 1, (1996).

Turner, John. *Lloyd George Secretariat*. Cambridge: Cambridge University Press, 1980.

— ed. *The Larger Idea: Lord Lothian and the Problem of National Sovereignty*. London: The Historians' Press, 1988.

Tute, Warren. *The Deadly Stroke: The Tragic Story of the British Destruction of the French Fleet in Oran*. Coward: McCann & Geoghegan, 1973.

Tyler, J. E. "Military Aspects of Anglo-French Union", *New Commonwealth Quarterly*, 6, (1940).

Usborne, Henry Charles. *A Warning and a Way Round: The Case for a Minimal Federation of Nations*. Birmingham: Minifed Publications, 1980.

— "A History of the British Parliamentary Group for World Government", in *The Federal Idea: The History of Federalism since 1945*. Edited by Andrea Bosco. London: Lothian Foundation Press, 1991.

Van Caenegem, R. C. *Judges, Legislators and Professors: Chapters in European Legal History*. Cambridge: Cambridge University Press, 1992.

— *An Historical Introduction to Western Constitutional Law*. Cambridge: Cambridge University Press, 1995.

— *Legal History: A European Perspective*. London: Hambledon & London, 2004.

Vereechten, Frank. *La lutte pour les Etats-Unis d'Europe. Richard Coudenhove-Kalergi en exil, 1938-1947*. London: Lothian Foundation Press, 1996.

Vessey, Ben. "Anglo-German Relations 1918-1939", *Modern History Review*, 15, 2, (2003).

Vidal, Georges. "Le PCF et la défense nationale à l'époque du Front Populaire, 1934-1939", *Guerres Mondiales at conflits contemporains*, 215, (2004).

Vinx, Lars. *Hans Kelsen's Pure Theory of Law: Legality and Legitimacy.* New York: Oxford University Press, 2007.

Vivier, T. *La politique aéronautique militaire de la France. Janvier 1933-septembre 1939*. Paris: L'Harmattan, 1997.

Voyenne, Bernard. *Histoire de l'idée européenne*. Paris: Payot Saint-Amand, 1964.

— *Le Fédéralisme de Pierre-Joseph Proudhon*. Paris: Presses d'Europe, 1973.

— *Histoire de l'idée fédéraliste*. Nice: Presses d'Europe, 1981.

Waechter, Max. *How to Abolish War: The United States of Europe.* London: 1924.

Walker, Stephen. "Solving the Appeasement Puzzle: Contending Historical Interpretations of British Diplomacy During the 1930s", *British Journal of International Studies*, 6, 3, (1980).

Wall, Irwin. "Jean Monnet, les Etats-Unis et le plan français", *Vingtième Siècle*, 30, (1991).

Wandycz, Piotr S. *The Twilight of French Eastern Alliances, 1926-1936.* Princeton: Princeton University Press, 1988.

Wank, Solomon. *Doves and Diplomats: Foreign Offices and Peace Movements in Europe and America in the Twentieth Century.* Westport, CT: Greenwood Press, 1978.

Ward, Barbara. *Britain's Interest in Atlantic Union*. Washington, DC: Friends of Atlantic Union, 1954.

Waters, Kenneth C. and Van Helden, Albert. *Julian Huxley: Biologist and Statesman of Science: Proceedings of a Conference Held at Rice University 25-27 September 1987*. Houston, TX: Rice Univesity Press, 1992.

Watt, Donald Cameron. *Personalities and Policies. Studies in the Formulation of British Foreign Policy in the Twentieth Century.* Harlow: Longmans, 1965.

— "Roosevelt and Neville Chamberlain: Two Appeasers", *International Journal*, 28, 2, (1973).

— *Succeeding John Bull: America in Britain's Place, 1900-1975.* Cambridge: Cambridge University Press, 1984.

— *How War Came: The Immediate Origins of the Second World War.* London: Pantheon, 1989.

— Foreword to *Chatham House and British Foreign Policy. The Royal Institute of International Affairs During the Inter-War Period*

1919-1945. Edited by Andrea Bosco and Cornelia Navari. London: Lothian Foundation Press, 1994.

Wearing, J. P. ed. *Bernard Shaw and Nancy Astor*. Toronto: University of Toronto Press, 2005.

Weber, Eugen. *L'Action Française*. Paris: Hachette, 1990.

Wehberg, Hans. *The Outlawry of War*. New York: Carnegie Endowment for International Peace, 1931.

— *Civil War and International Law*. Harlow: Longman, 1938.

Weiler, Peter. *Ernest Bevin*. Manchester: Manchester University Press, 1993.

Weisbrode, Kenneth. *The Atlantic Century. Four Generations of Extraordinary Diplomats Who Forged America's Vital Alliance with Europe*. Philadelphia, PA: Da Capo Press, 2009.

Welles, Benjamin. *Sumner Welles: FDR's Global Strategist. A Biography*. New York: Palgrave Macmillan, 1997.

Wells, Herbert George. *The Outline of History*. London: Garden City Publisher, 1925.

— *The Open Conspiracy*. New York: Doubleday, 1928.

— *The Shape of Things to Come*. London: Hutchinson, 1933.

— *A Modern Utopia*. New York: 1st World Library, 2007.

— *The New World Order*. London: FQ Classics, 2007.

Werth, Alexander. *France and Munich Before and After the Surrender*. London: Brousson Press, 2007.

West, Anthony. *H. G. Wells: Aspects of a Life*. New York: Random House, 1984.

Weygand, Maxime. *Recalled to Service*. London: William Heinemann, 1952.

Wheare, Kenneth Clinton. *What Federal Government is*. London: Federal Union Publishing, 1941.

— *Federal Government*. London: Oxford University Press, 1946.

— *The Constitutional Structure of the Commonwealth*. Westport, CT: Greenwood Press, 1982.

White, Ellen Gould Harmon. *Atlantic Union Gleaner Articles*. Payson, AZ: Leaves-of-Autumn Press, 1981.

Whiting, William. *The Society of Friends and What It Stands For*. Whitefish, MT: Kessinger Publishing, 2005.

Wildford, R. A. "The Federal Union Campaign", *European Studies Review*, 10, (1980).

Williams, Andrew. "France and the New World Order, 1940-1947", *Modern and Contemporary France*, 8, 2, (2000).

— "Before the Special Relationship: The Council on Foreign Relations, The Carnegie Foundation and the Rumour of an Anglo-American War", *Journal of Transatlantic Studies*, 1, 2, (2003).

— *Liberalism and War: The Victors and the Vanquished.* London: Routledge, 2006.

Williams, Charles. *The Last Great Frenchman: A Life of General de Gaulle.* Oxford: Wiley, 1997.

— *Petain: How the Hero of France Became a Convicted Traitor and Changed the Course of History.* New York: Palgrave Macmillan, 2005.

Williams, Francis. *A Prime Minister Remembers: The War and Post-War Memoirs of the Rt. Hon. Earl Attlee.* London: Heinemann, 1951.

— *Twilight of Empire: Memoirs of Prime Minister Clement Attlee.* Westport, CT: Greenwood Press, 1978.

Williams, Paul. "A Commonwealth of Knowledge: Empire, Intellectuals and the Chatham House Project, 1919-1939", *International Relations*, 17, 1, (2003).

Williamson, Philip and Baldwin, Edward eds. *Baldwin Papers: A Conservative Statesman, 1908-1947.* Cambridge: Cambridge University Press, 2004.

Williamson, Murray. "The Strategy of the Phoney War: A Re-evaluation", *Military Affairs*, 4, 1, (1981).

Wilson, Derek. *The Astors: 1763-1992: Landscape with Millionaires.* London: St. Martin's Press, 1993.

Winetrout, Kenneth. *After One Is Dead: Arnold Toynbee as Prophet.* London: Hillside Press, 1989.

Winkler, Henry R. *The League of Nations Movement in Great Britain.* New Brunswich, NJ: Rutgers University Press, 1952.

— *Paths Not Taken: British Labour and International Policy in the 1920s.* Chapel Hill: University of North Carolina Press, 1994.

Wolffe, John. *God and Greater Britain: Religion and National Life in Britian and Ireland 1843-1945.* Harlow: Longman, 2007.

Wood, Herbert George. *The Spiritual Basis of Peace.* London: National Peace Council, 1941.

Wood, John. *Friedrick von Hayek.* London: Routledge, 2004.

Woods, Randall Bennett. *A Changing of the Guard: Anglo-American Relations, 1941-1946.* Chapel Hill, NC: University of North Carolina Press, 1990.

Wootton, Barbara. *Socialism and Federation.* London: Federal Union Publishing, 1940.

Wormser, Georges. *Georges Mandel, l'homme politique.* Paris: Plon, 1967.

Wragg, David. *'Sink the French': At War with an Ally, 1940*. London: Pen and Sword, 2007.

Wrench, Evelyn. *Geoffrey Dawson and Our Times*. London: Hutchinson, 1955.

Wright, A. W. *G. D. H. Cole and Socialist Democracy*. Oxford: Oxford University Press, 1979.

Wright, Gordon. "Ambassador Bullitt and the Fall of France", *World Politics*, 10, 1, (1957).

Wright, Julian. *The Regionalist Movement in France 1890-1914: Jean-Charles Brun and French Political Thought*. New York: Oxford University Press, 2003.

Wylie, Neville. "'Keeping The Swiss Sweet': Intelligence as a Factor in British Policy Towards Switzerland During the Second World War", *Intelligence and National Security*, 11, 3, (1996).

— *European Neutrals and Non-Belligerents during the Second World War*. Cambridge: Cambridge, University Press, 2002.

— *Britain, Switzerland, and the Second World War*. New York: Oxford University Press, 2004.

Young, R. J. "The Aftermath of Munich: The Course of French Diplomacy, October 1938 to March 1939", *French Historical Studies*, 8, (1973).

Young, Robert. *France and the Origins of the Second World War*. London: Macmillan, 1996.

Young, Robert J. *In Command of France: French Foreign and Defence Policy, 1933-1940*. Cambridge, MA: Harvard University Press, 1978.

— "La Guerre de Longue Durée: Some Reflections on French Strategy and Diplomacy in the 1930s", in *General Staffs and Diplomacy before the Second World War*. Edited by Antony Preston. London: Croom Helm, 1978.

— *Post-colonialism: An Historical Introduction*. Oxford: Wiley, 2001.

Zahniser, Marvin R. *Then Came Disaster: France and the United States, 1918-1940*. Westport, CT: Praeger, 2002.

Zimmern, Alfred. *Nationality & Government*. London: Chatto & Windus, 1919.

— *The Prospects of Democracy and Other Essays*. London: Chatto & Windus, 1929.

— *Spiritual Values and World Affairs*. Oxford: Oxford University Press, 1938.

— *Modern Political Doctrines*. Oxford: Oxford University Press, 1939.

— *The League of Nations and the Rule of Law, 1918-1935*. London: Macmillan, 1939.

INDEX

A

Abraham, E.; 22; 44.
Acland, Sir Richard; 102; 262.
Acworth, E.; 102.
Adams, David; 227.
Albertini, Mario; 4; 14; 123; 278; 288; 324; 326; 329.
Amery, Loepold; 4-5; 11; 188-9; 211-2; 216-8; 220; 223; 233; 260; 284-5; 301; 305.
Angell, Norman; 3; 11; 143-4; 167-8; 227; 329.
Aron, Raymond; 123-4.
Artmann, Robert; 123.
Astor, David; 14; 227.
Astor, Waldorf; 5; 11; 59; 75; 83; 209; 220; 227-31; 233-5; 258; 270.
Attlee, Clement; 2; 4; 92; 124; 130; 136; 176-7; 191; 227; 260; 303; 306; 330-1; 351-2; 369; 379; 383.
Aubert, L. F.; 237.
Aydelotte, Frank; 23.

B

Bailey, Gerald; 34; 50; 53; 167; 208.
Bailly, Léon; 130.
Baldwin, Stanley; 169; 270-71; 365; 383.
Balfour, J.; 182; 256; 349.
Barker, Ernest; 151-2; 168.
Barrington-Ward, Robert; 17; 46; 178; 365.

Barry, Gerard; 208; 227; 256; 337; 346.
Baudouin, Paul; 196; 306-7; 314-5; 331.
Bauer, Hans; 111-2; 133; 189; 331.
Bavetta, Julian; 14.
Beck, S. J.; 276-8.
Benda, Julien; 13.
Bentwich, Norman; 3; 75; 95-6; 102; 269; 271-2; 332.
Berlia, Georges; 189; 190; 332.
Bernus, Pierre; 130.
Beveridge, Sir William; 2-4; 50; 70-1; 78; 82-3; 91-8; 102; 117; 119; 121; 161-3; 226-7; 229; 231; 233; 239; 244; 262; 264; 270-1; 273-4.
Bevin, Ernest; 2; 4; 47; 59-60; 75; 226.
Bewley, T. K.; 251; 253; 255.
Bidault, Georges; 129.
Blum, Léon; 124; 130-31; 200; 340; 348-9; 356; 358; 378.
Boissier, Leopold; 106; 109.
Borel, Emile; 106; 110; 201.
Bouthilier, Yves; 306; 310; 314-6.
Bouverie, John; 143.
Bradish, Margaret; 100.
Brailsford, Henry Noel; 3; 95-8; 119; 120-1; 154; 233; 335; 360.
Brand, Robert; 5.
Brewer, Herbert; 64-65; 68; 71; 175; 336.
Briand, Aristide; 12; 26; 126-7; 131; 133; 148; 215-7; 219; 221; 223; 232; 250; 326; 334; 346-7.
Brice, James; 79.
Bridges, Sir Edward; 292; 305.

Brugmans, Henry; 11; 123-4; 326; 336.
Brun, Jean-Charles; 110; 117; 122; 124-5; 342; 384.
Burgess, Michael; 3.
Burns, Raymond; 101; 322; 336.
Butler, Harold; 35; 39; 226.
Butler, R. A.; 7; 37-8; 42; 57; 59; 60; 67; 119; 175; 182; 188; 238-9; 256; 323; 336-7.
Byron, Robert; 70; 72; 75; 80; 93; 96; 102; 132-3; 262; 337; 358.

C

Cadogan, Sir Alexander; 178; 196; 212; 241-2; 246-7; 249; 301; 337; 367.
Caine, Sidney; 271-2.
Cairns, D. S.; 76.
Cairns, John; 296.
Caldecote, Lord; 303-4.
Campbell, F. A.; 51; 96; 98; 102-3; 117; 188; 261; 266; 269; 290; 337.
Campbell, Sir Ronald; 117; 290; 302-3; 306; 308.
Campinchi, César; 196; 307.
Cape, Jonathan; 4-5; 15; 22; 29; 35; 43; 59; 70; 82; 94; 272; 297; 338; 352; 357; 368; 375; 378.
Carter, Vivian; 39-40; 71; 338.
Castier, Jules; 131.
Catlin, Geroge; 59; 153; 271-2.
Cazalet, Victor; 218; 354.
Cecil, Lord Robert; 18; 20; 91-2; 98; 169-170; 338.
Chamberlain, Neville; 4- 5; 29; 31-2; 37; 58; 66-7; 129; 131; 135; 177; 188; 192-8; 229; 231; 241; 246-9; 258; 260; 274; 292-3; 296; 298; 301; 303-5; 312; 338-9; 341; 343; 346; 348; 357; 362; 369; 373-5; 378; 382.
Chamberlain, Joseph; 152.
Chamberlain, Joseph Perkins; 273.

Channing-Pearce, Melville; 59; 68-9; 71-4; 80-4; 91-6; 120; 272; 338; 375.
Chautemps, Camille; 307-8; 310; 313-6; 339.
Chauvigne, Jean; 123.
Churchill, Sir Winston; 1-2; 4; 7; 12; 18; 92; 136; 177-8; 191; 196; 199; 211-2; 226-7; 233; 235; 240; 242; 258; 260; 284; 289-90; 294-5; 298-309; 311-4; 318-9; 322; 330-3; 339-340; 343; 348-9; 353-5; 357; 359; 360-3; 368-9; 371-3; 376; 378-379.
Clark, Sir George; 53; 147; 218; 232; 346.
Cleeve, Margaret; 216; 229; 232.
Cole, George D. Howard; 3; 53; 137; 157-8; 254; 322; 335; 340; 352; 379; 384.
Colville, Sir John; 2; 304-5; 340.
Comert, Pierre; 189.
Corbin, Charles; 196; 297; 302; 305.
Corniere, Louis; 123.
Côt, Pierre; 189.
Coudenhove-Kalergi, Richard; 12-3; 109; 124; 127; 133; 146; 161; 188; 210-223; 260; 267; 305; 326; 328; 340-1; 359; 362; 381.
Cranbourne, Lord Robert; 47.
Creech Jones, Athur; 271-2.
Curry, William; 3-4; 79; 95-8; 102; 119; 153; 166; 262; 266; 342.
Curtis, Lionel; 3-6; 8-10; 12; 13-22; 25; 26; 31; 34-5; 38-9; 41-2; 46-9; 51-4; 59-70; 72-4; 77; 79-86; 93-5; 105; 109; 118-20; 127; 170-1; 179; 202-9; 220; 223-35; 242-6; 258; 265; 270-1; 273-5; 284-5; 328; 334; 342-4; 359; 365; 378; 379.

D

D'Ormesson, Vladimir; 130; 199-200.

Daladier, Edouard; 171; 192; 195-6;
     229; 231; 245; 291-2; 296; 311;
     335; 345; 348; 360.
Dandieu, Arnaud; 123.
Daniell, Raymond; 160.
Darlan, Francois; 196.
Darvall, Frank; 26.
Dautry, Raoul; 129; 330-1; 350.
Davies, Lord David; 11-12; 18; 42;
     44; 60; 109; 146; 148; 189-190;
     227; 260; 266-7; 284; 342; 373.
Dawson, Geoffrey; 5; 11; 98; 158;
     384.
de Gaulle, Charles; 2; 211; 289-90;
     295; 299; 300-2; 305; 308-9;
     317-8; 340; 342; 344-45; 357;
     359; 363; 383.
De Kerillis, Henri; 200.
de La Rocque, François; 117; 122;
     368.
de Lanux, Pierre Combret; 132; 343.
de Madariaga, Salvador; 11-12; 39-
     42; 98; 131; 271.
de Monzie, Anatole; 121.
de Pange, Jean; 125; 126.
de Ribes, Champetier; 116-7; 122;
     342.
de Rougemont, Denis; 123; 326.
de Souches, Jean; 117.
Debu, G.; 201.
Detoeuf, André; 117; 122.
Deuss, Edmund; 271.
Dill, Sir John; 303.
Douglas Home, Alec; 79-80; 345.
Dove, John; 5; 206.
Duff Cooper, Alfred; 218-20; 339;
     368.
Duhamel, Georges; 122; 130; 359;
     364.
Dunford, D.; 68; 87; 97-98.
Durbin, E. F. M.; 59; 75; 78; 102.
Duval, Raymond; 201.

E

Eden, Anthony; 4; 12; 18; 47; 51;
     187-8; 212; 219; 260-1; 303;
     312; 319; 337; 345; 370; 373-4;
     378; 380.
Edwards, A. Cecil; 97-8; 147; 154.
Edwards, Philip; 262; 264; 266.
Elton, Lord; 120-121.
Eynac, Laurent; 196.

F

Fawcett, C. B.; 155.
Fernand-Laurent, Jean; 199; 346.
Fischer-Williams, Sir John; 75; 119;
     192; 225; 231.
Fisher, H. A. L.; 66; 120; 206; 233;
     344; 370.
Fleming, C. J. N.; 59; 78.
Flugel, John Carl; 153; 271-2.
Forrester, Lord James; 20; 97; 98.
Fortes, Meyer; 271-2.
Fox, Howard; 68; 87; 97-8; 102;
     147; 182; 184; 245; 266; 322;
     336; 373.
Fox, Stephenson; 89.
Fyfe, Hamilton; 47; 59; 72; 75; 92;
     153.

G

Gamelin, Maurice; 196; 198; 296;
     312; 316; 329; 333; 348; 360.
Garrett, Easton; 175; 268; 348.
Gathorne-Hardy, Geoffrey; 215;
     225; 231-2; 348.
Geikie-Cobb. W. F.; 173.
Gillet, R. B.; 26; 89; 97; 103.
Gillett, J. H.; 82; 98; 102-3; 266;
     268-70.
Giraudoux, Jean; 237.
Gladstone, William; 7.
Gladwyn, Lord; 238.
Golay, H.; 110.
Goodhart, Athur Lehman; 273-5;
     322; 349.

Gray, L. T. M.; 97-; 98; 102; 266.
Greenwood, A.; 5; 24; 30; 60; 142;
148; 181; 191; 208; 256; 274;
303-4; 311-2; 321; 338; 341;
347; 350; 362; 365; 371; 377-8;
381; 383.
Gregory, Richard; 14; 47; 59; 75;
79; 148; 375.
Grieg, Sir Robert; 76; 102.
Grierson, Sir Herbert; 76.
Grigg, Sir Edward, ; 5.
Guderzo, Giulio; 13.

H

Haden Guest, Leslie; 218.
Halasz, Nicolas; 132.
Halifax, Edward; 4; 34; 57; 111;
117; 127; 164; 177; 182; 184;
186-7; 190-1; 196-7; 229; 235;
238; 241-2; 245; 247; 249-50;
263; 270; 285; 302-4; 306; 312;
333; 350; 367; 373.
Hamilton, Alexander; 5; 47; 59; 72;
75; 79; 92; 138; 158; 218; 264;
354; 361; 364.
Hammond, J. L.; 75; 121.
Hancock, W. K.; 34.
Hankey, Sir Maurice; 5; 13; 241;
245; 249; 251-3; 255; 257-8;
285; 350.
Harlow, Vincent; 23; 28; 35; 190;
203; 206; 213; 240; 254; 286;
320; 332; 337; 346; 364; 369;
374; 377; 379; 382; 384.
Harris, Henry; 50; 67; 68; 98; 120;
233; 281-2; 306; 350; 351.
Harris, Wilson; 278; 282.
Harrod, R. F.; 78.
Hart, Liddell; 75; 121; 196; 269;
306; 351; 361.
Harvey, H. J.; 227.
Harvey, Oliver; 128; 232; 250; 292.
Hastilow, D. M.; 97; 100.
Havelock, Sydney; 146.

Hayek, von Friedrich; 50; 78; 117;
270.
Healey, Lord Denis; 225.
Henderson, Arthur; 18; 136; 148;
367.
Hennessy, Jean; 124.
Heppenstall, F.; 97; 102.
Herriot, Edouard; 12; 245; 315-7;
318; 351.
Hichens, Lionel; 5.
Hitler, Adolf; 15; 26; 28; 30; 37; 52;
56; 58; 66; 76; 96; 99; 135-6;
147; 157; 169; 171-3; 197-9;
207; 225; 241; 246; 257; 261;
283; 286; 290; 295-8; 302; 306;
308-9; 311; 315; 321-2; 340-41;
343; 352; 356-7; 359; 360; 362;
364; 367; 373.
Hodson, Henry; 23; 248; 352.
Hogben, Lancelot; 39; 70-2; 74-5;
80; 93; 139-40; 148.
Holland-Martin, Robert; 39; 41.
Honnart, Vincent; 237.
Hope-Simpson, R. E.; 77.
Hopkinson, H. L.; 251-2; 255.
Horsfall Carter, W.; 26; 131-3.
Hostie, Jean; 113; 352.
Hugo, Victor; 98; 151; 173.
Hulton, Edward; 83; 227.
Humphreys, John H.; 98; 277-8.
Hutton, J. A.; 227.
Huxley, Julian; 3; 72; 75; 140-1;
155; 160; 164-6; 330; 353; 381.

I

Ironside, Sir Edmund; 196.

J

Jacks, L. P.; 194.
Jameson, J. G.; 76.
Jay, John; 79; 264.
Jeanneney, Julies; 307; 316-7; 354.

Jennings, Ivor; 3-4; 97-8; 102; 244; 262; 266; 270-1; 273-5; 354.

Jeze, Gaston; 126.

Jilek, Lubor; 14; 26; 112; 127; 334; 347; 354.

Joad, Cyril Edwin; 3; 26; 34; 39; 55; 59; 61; 70; 72; 74-5; 77; 89-90; 93; 95; 96-8; 101-3; 141-2; 167; 261; 266; 355.

Jones, Caradog; 39.

Jones, Clement; 251.

Jones, Greg; 14.

Jones, Tom; 226; 270.

K

Kahane, E.; 117.

Kant, Immanuel; 133.

Keeton, George; 12; 43; 45; 71; 79; 94; 167; 270; 356.

Kelsen, Hans; 42; 125; 189-90; 351; 356; 381.

Kendle, John; 3.

Keynes, Maynard; 48; 364.

Kimber, Sir Charles; 2; 12; 14; 30-6; 38-9; 41-4; 46-7; 49; 53-7; 63-70; 72-4; 77; 79-86; 88-97; 100-3; 105; 133-4; 142; 168; 173; 251; 266-7; 268-9; 270-1; 285; 287; 324; 358.

King-Hall, Stephen; 19; 218; 358.

Kirkpatrick, I.; 107; 178.

Knickerbocker, Hubert Ranfro; 271.

Koeltz, Louis; 196.

L

Lafage, Achille; 123.

Lander, H. C.; 262.

Laski, Harold; 11; 33; 97-98; 137; 157; 352; 359.

Lauterpacht, H.; 32-33; 97-8.

Laval, Pierre; 296; 309; 340; 342; 348; 354; 380.

Lavergne, Bernard; 126; 201.

Law, Richard; 33; 40; 43; 59; 72; 75; 82; 93; 98; 105; 109; 121; 190; 267; 274; 322; 354; 376; 381; 382; 385.

Lawrence, Sir Henry; 16; 77; 82; 121; 130; 144; 147; 368.

Layton, Sir Walter; 148-9; 218; 227; 237.

Leach, D.; 59; 188.

Lebrun, Albert; 306-8; 310; 314-5; 360.

Leeper, Rex; 118-9; 234; 240; 245; 249; 250-1-

Leger, Alexis; 18; 196.

Leslie, Edgeworth; 98; 106; 108-9; 112-6; 153; 360.

Lewis, Arthur; 148; 227; 234; 271-2; 361.

Lincoln, Abraham; 10; 22; 53; 263; 264; 271; 322; 340.

Lippmann, Walter; 9; 117; 138; 361.

List, Friedrick; 222.

Livingston, H. B.; 105; 107.

Lloyd George, David; 207; 251; 277.

Lloyd, Alwyn; 262.

Lloyd, Lord; 7; 20; 49; 68; 77; 135-6; 207; 249; 305; 329; 350; 360; 371; 374; 380.

Lothian, 11th Marquess of (Philip Kerr); 3-8; 10; 12-5; 17; 22-32; 34-9; 41-57; 60; 64-5; 67; 109; 127; 138; 151; 159; 164; 174-87; 202-3; 205-8; 209; 212; 220; 258-9; 268; 284-5; 287-8; 322-4; 326; 328;

Lowe, Drury; 59; 68.

Lowell, Lawrence; 16.

Lugard, Lord F. Dealtry; 3; 271; 272.

Lumsden, Quentin; 102; 155-6; 268.

Lytton, Lord Victor Alexander; 20; 91; 97-98.

M

Mack, W.; 121.
Mackay, Ronald Gordon; 3-4; 98; 141-2; 262; 269; 286; 362.
Macmillan, William Miller; 271.
Madison, James; 79; 145; 264; 322.
Mahan, Alfred; 224.
Mair, Lucy; 271-2.
Majocchi, Luigi Vittorio; 14.
Makins, R. M.; 186.
Makovski, L. W.; 268.
Mandel, Ernest; 171; 307-8; 317.
Mander, Geoffrey; 188; 189; 218.
Mannheim, Karl; 94; 271; 272.
Marc, Alexandre; 11; 123-124; 186; 326.
Marin, Louis; 307-8; 310; 314-5; 363.
Marjolin, Robert; 317.
Markins, R. M.; 121.
Marlio, Louis; 116; 117.
Marris, William; 5.
Matthews, Walter; 21; 22.
May, Alex; 5.
Mazzini, Giuseppe; 222.
McAllister, Gilbert; 30; 93; 97-98; 103; 266; 268; 364.
McLellan, J.; 140.
McLeod, Alexander; 21.
Meade, James; 3; 256; 271-2; 365-
Mears, Dorothy; 79.
Mercier, Claude; 116.
Meston, Lord; 232; 262.
Meyhoffer, Paul; 111.
Milne, A. A.; 132-3; 148; 191.
Milner, Alfred; 5; 17; 38; 158; 211; 220; 258; 275.
Mitrany, David; 164-5; 327; 350; 366-7.
Mollet, Guy; 319.
Monick, Emmanuel; 298; 317.
Monnet, Jean; 2-5; 211; 258; 285; 288-303; 317-8; 327-8.
Morrison, Herbert; 18; 47.
Morton, Beatrice E.; 154.

Morton, Desmond; 295; 298-9; 302-3; 305.
Mougin, Jacques; 123.
Muir, Ramsay; 59; 75; 168.
Murray, Gilbert; 8; 19-20; 41; 54; 81; 91-92; 94; 98; 133; 137; 206; 233; 312.
Mussolini, Benito; 26; 52; 56; 106.

N

Namier, Lewis; 234.
Newall, Sir Cyril; 196; 303.
Newell, A.; 271.
Neylan, D.; 68; 71; 97.
Nicholson, E. M.; 18; 211; 227; 331.
Nicolson, Harold; 18; 46; 131-2; 161; 164; 182; 191; 209; 212; 218; 223; 225; 262; 306.
Nicolson, Max; 164.
Noel-Baker, Philip; 188.
Norrah, Dermot; 158.

O

O'Malley, Raymond; 146.
Ohlin, Bertil G.; 117.
Oldham, J. H.; 94; 131; 233.
Oliver, Frederick; 5; 8; 78.
Orr, John; 59; 72; 75; 92; 137; 148.
Overton, Sir Arnold; 254; 255; 256.

P

Pakenham, Frank; 25.
Paterson, G. M.; 59.
Perowne, J. V.; 182; 186.
Pétain, Henri Philippe; 2; 305; 307; 310; 313-6.
Pinder, John; 3; 14.
Plant, Arnold; 98; 271-2.
Pleven, René; 293-4; 299-300; 302-3; 317.
Ponthiere, Maurice; 123.
Pound, Sir Dudley; 196; 303.
Price, J. F.; 148; 155.

Priestley, John B.; 3; 75; 120-1.
Proudhon, Pierre-Joseph; 123-4;
146; 329.

R

Ransome, Patrick; 2-3; 30; 32-4; 36-
9; 41-2; 44; 46-7; 49; 52; 64; 69-
70; 72; 74; 78; 82; 85-6; 90-1;
93; 95-7; 102; 117; 231; 251;
266; 270-3; 275; 287; 332; 334;
358.
Rappard, William; 12; 105; 108-9;
111; 189; 278; 328.
Raushning, Hermann; 189; 190.
Raven, C. E.; 47; 59; 75; 94.
Rawnsley, Derek; 2; 30-6; 38-9; 41-
2; 44; 46-7; 49-50; 64; 69; 72;
74; 85-86; 89; 91; 93; 97; 102-
11; 114-8; 121-3; 127; 251; 287;
324.
Rendel, S. G.; 106.
Revilliod, Henri; 109; 110-111.
Reynaud, Paul; 2; 171; 189; 196-7;
241; 289-90; 296; 298-303; 305-
309; 311-7.
Rhondda, Lady; 59; 75
Robbins, Lionel; 3; 4; 10-1; 48-50;
75; 78-9; 95; 97-8; 102; 117;
121; 153; 174; 233; 262; 270;
278-9; 280; 281; 282; 287.
Roberts, F. K.; 15; 25; 29; 71; 107;
154; 182; 184; 245; 251; 255;
260; 311.
Robinson, Sir Christopher; 5; 43;
98; 133; 274; 295.
Robinson, Vandeleur; 217.
Rollin, Henry; 18.
Romains, Jules; 122; 341; 365.
Roosevelt, Franklin D.; 7; 24-5; 30;
32; 53; 140; 177-8; 181; 227;
233; 300; 314-5; 321-3; 336;
338; 340; 342; 351; 359; 372-4;
378.
Ross, Harry; 98; 206; 270.

Rossi, Ernesto; 122; 286-8; 312;
315.
Roux, Charles; 307; 309.
Rowse, Alfred Leslie; 3; 152; 153.
Royden, Maude; 98; 146.
Roz, Firmin; 131; 132.
Russell; 11; 148.
Ryle, W.; 96.

S

Salter, Sir Arthur; 2; 18; 25; 44; 82;
218; 226; 295-6; 299; 301; 303;
305.
Sanders, Douglas; 71; 97; 103; 181.
Sargent, Orme; 128; 190; 240-1;
246-52; 255-7.
Saurat, Denis; 262.
Scelle, Georges; 12; 125; 132; 189.
Schiotz, John; 188.
Schuster, Sir Georg; 25; 270; 286;
305; 311.
Scott Lidgett, John; 47; 59; 75.
Seebohm Rowntree, B.; 59; 75.
Sforza, Carlo; 18.
Shiels, Sir Drummond; 47; 52; 59;
75; 96-7; 102; 262; 270; 271.
Siegfried, André; 105.
Sinclair, Sir Archibald; 2; 4; 47; 80;
92; 121; 219; 260; 303; 304.
Smith, Rennie; 138; 142; 146-7;
208; 215; 218; 234; 261; 287.
Somerville, John; 271.
Sorensen, Reginald; 60.
Spears, Sir Edward; 290; 308-9;
312; 314.
Spencer Churchill, Lord Ivor; 227.
Spinasse, Charles; 116; 122.
Spinelli, Altiero; 3; 286-8; 324; 326.
Spühler, E.; 108-9.
Stainley, Oliver; 196.
Stapledon, Olaf; 3; 39-40; 68; 77;
94-95; 97; 144; 262.
Steed, Wickham Henry; 3; 18; 20;
25; 47; 59; 61; 70; 72; 74-5; 77;
82; 93-4; 121; 144-6; 209; 377.

Steer, Lloyd; 271.
Stokes, Richard; 131; 226.
Storm Jameson, Margaret; 3; 75; 94; 163-4; 333; 354.
Strachey, John; 27; 262.
Straus, Ira; 14.
Streit, Clarence; 15-8; 20-4; 26-9; 35-7; 39; 42-3; 45-9; 51-5; 58; 60; 63-5; 67-8; 71; 73-5; 85; 87; 109; 111; 119; 122-3; 127; 151; 154; 158; 161-2; 171; 217; 223-5; 228; 244; 268; 273; 280; 297; 328; 330.
Stresemann, Gustav; 12.
Summerskill, Edith; 59.
Swinton, Sir Ernest; 47; 59; 75.

T

Temperley, Harold; 43.
Temple, William; 47; 138; 172-4-
Tennyson, Alfred; 45; 60.
Thudichum, Georges; 109; 110-1.
Thyssen, Fritz; 189-90.
Tillyard, Eustace M. W.; 59; 68; 71; 77; 94-95; 97-8.
Titulescu, Nicolae; 18.
Torr, C. J. W.; 105-7.
Toynbee, Arnold; 3; 5; 11; 13; 20; 59; 75; 121; 210; 225-6; 228-9; 233-42; 245-6; 251; 258; 285.
Truptil, Roger J.; 117.

U

Urie, R. W.; 166; 167.
Usborne, Henry; 68; 71-2; 74-5; 77; 82; 88; 92-3; 97-8; 262.
Usborne, John; 102.
Usborne, T. G.; 71; 77; 90.

V

Valentine, G. B.; 68; 144; 210.
Van Zeeland, Paul; 18.

Vansittart, Sir Robert; 2; 212; 299-300; 302-3; 305; 340.
Vernon, R. V.; 98; 271.
Vickers, C. G.; 225; 233.
Vincent, Simon; 35; 123.
Viviani, René; 291.
Vuillemin, Joseph; 196.

W

Waddy, Lawrence; 77.
Waley, S. D.; 251.
Warner, Sir Christopher; 127; 245.
Warr, Charles; 76; 116; 118; 119; 121.
Watt, Donald Cameron; 32; 203; 259; 323.
Webster, C. K.; 20; 232; 233
Wedgwood, Josiah C,; 188-9.
Wehberg, Hans; 189; 190.
Wells, Herbert George; 11; 34; 39-40; 60; 79; 92; 94-5; 97-8; 131; 141-3; 153; 156; 160; 167; 264.
Wessel, Richard; 79.
Weygand, Maxime; 2; 305; 307-8; 310; 312-5; 317.
Wheare, Kenneth; 3; 4; 273-4.
Wilson, Harold; 106; 120.
Wilson, Woodrow; 183.
Wood, Sir Kingsley; 50; 77; 97; 137; 148; 196; 264; 384.
Wood, W. W.; 262.
Wootton, Barbara; 3-4; 39; 47; 55; 59; 61; 70; 72; 74-75; 78; 80; 93; 95; 96-8; 101-3; 153; 156; 167; 262; 266; 270.
Wrench, Sir Evelyn; 158; 218.
Wright, B. F.; 117; 124; 125; 157; 284; 315.
Wyndham, Hugh; 225.

Y

Ybarnégaray, Jean; 307.

Z

Zilliacus, Konni; 3; 57-8.

Zimmern; 5; 11; 13; 75; 109; 225; 232-33; 237-8; 239; 241-2; 246; 251; 254; 258; 285.